Keys to Educational Success

Teaching Students with Visual Impairments and Multiple Disabilities

Sharon Z. Sacks and Mary C. Zatta
Editors

AFBPress

American Foundation for the Blind

Published in conjunction with:

Perkins SCHOOL FOR THE BLIND

Printed in the United States of America

Library of Congress Cataloging-in-Publication Data

Names: Sacks, Sharon, editor.
Title: Keys to educational success : teaching students with visual impairments and multiple
   disabilities / Sharon Z. Sacks and Mary C. Zatta, editors.
Description: New York, NY : AFB Press, 2016. | "Published in conjunction with the Perkins
   School for the Blind." | Includes bibliographical references and index.
Identifiers: LCCN 2016018001 (print) | LCCN 2016018290 (ebook) | ISBN 9780891285519
   (pbk. : alk. paper) | ISBN 9780891287629 (online subscription) | ISBN 9780891287636
   (epub) | ISBN 9780891287643 (mobi) | ISBN 9780891287636 (ePub)
Subjects: LCSH: Children with visual disabilities—Education. | Children with disabilities—
   Education.
Classification: LCC HV1631 .K49 2016 (print) | LCC HV1631 (ebook) | DDC 371.9—dc23
LC record available at https://lccn.loc.gov/2016018001

The American Foundation for the Blind removes barriers, creates solutions, and expands possibilities so people with vision loss can achieve their full potential.

It is the policy of the American Foundation for the Blind to use in the first printing of its books acid-free paper that meets the ANSI Z39.48 Standard. The infinity symbol that appears above indicates that the paper in this printing meets that standard.

To our mentors, Michael Collins, Robert Gaylord-Ross, Philip Hatlen, and Barbara McLetchie, who taught us to respect and have high expectations for students with visual impairments and multiple disabilities.

Contents

Part 4

Essential Areas of Instruction

Part 5

Preparing for Life Before and After School

Foreword

The number of students with visual impairments and multiple disabilities has continued to increase dramatically in recent decades, resulting in the changing role of professionals who are responsible for educating this diverse and challenging population. Despite the tremendous need for practical information to address the unique needs of these students, the last major published text in this area was a collaborative endeavor by my friend and colleague, Sharon Sacks and myself, *Educating Students Who Have Visual Impairments with Other Disabilities,* almost 20 years ago.

I am thrilled that Sharon has joined forces with Mary Zatta, another highly regarded professional in the field, to provide a new, up-to-date text. *Keys to Educational Success: Teaching Students with Visual Impairments and Multiple Disabilities* will be a practical resource for faculty in teacher preparation programs in colleges and universities and for graduate and undergraduate teacher candidates in the field of blindness and visual impairment. In addition, the text will be valuable for new and experienced practitioners who are responsible for providing direct services in specialized or inclusive settings; it also will benefit consultants from a variety of disciplines who work with students with visual impairments and multiple disabilities. Professionals who will consider *Keys to Educational Success* a must read include teachers of students who are blind or visually impaired; orientation and mobility specialists; other special educators, including those in the area of severe disabilities; general educators; physical and occupational therapists; speech-language pathologists; paraeducators; and families of children in this low-incidence population.

While Sharon and Mary have written several excellent chapters in the text, they should be commended for recruiting other highly regarded authors to present content specific to each of their areas of expertise. *Keys to Educational Success* is a practical resource with a myriad of up-to-date strategies and interventions that can be used to support diverse students with visual impairments and multiple disabilities, particularly those with deafblindness, in any type of service delivery model. A particular strength of this high-quality text is its emphasis on providing effective assessment and practical interventions, real-life examples, and methods founded on evidence-based research and practice. The book presents numerous strategies for infusing the expanded core curriculum into the education of students with visual impairments and multiple disabilities. Furthermore, the innovative and practical suggestions provided in *Keys to Educational Success* are applicable to children and youths with visual impairments and multiple disabilities from infancy through transition age.

My challenge to our field is to implement the innovative practices presented in *Keys to Educational Success* to enhance the quality of educational services provided to the broad array of diverse students with visual impairments and multiple disabilities. Thank you, Sharon and Mary, for writing and coordinating the contributions of several authors with a much-needed publication on this crucial topic! You are continuing my more than half a century career of commitment and passion. You deserve our highest accolades!

Rosanne K. Silberman, Ed.D.
Professor and Coordinator
Programs in Blindness and Visual Impairment
and Severe Disabilities including
Deafblindness
Hunter College
City University of New York

Acknowledgments

· ·

We are most appreciative of those who helped and supported us in the development and production of this book. This endeavor would not have been possible without the support of our families and colleagues. We wish to thank our husbands who provided us with time to write and edit. We are grateful to our colleagues at California School for Blind and Perkins School for the Blind who shared their resources and encouragement throughout. We especially want to thank Dr. Stuart Wittenstein, Superintendent Emeritus (CSB), and David Powers, President and CEO of Perkins, for their generous support.

The AFB Press staff provided us with continuous support and guidance throughout the development, writing, editing, and production of this book. We especially wish to thank Natalie Hilzen, who worked tirelessly with us in the beginning stages of the writing process. She assisted us with the structure and development of the book and gave us thoughtful feedback as we completed initial chapter drafts. Also, we wish to acknowledge Ellen Bilofsky for her outstanding editing skills. She kept us on schedule and was ready to assist when we needed her expertise. The leadership at the American Foundation for the Blind, Carl Augusto, President, and George Abbott, Director of AFB Press and Professional Development, recognized the need for this book, and provided us with the personnel and funding to accomplish our goal.

The vast amount of information and the expertise needed to complete this textbook would not have been possible without the extraordinary skills of our chapter authors. We wish to thank Tanni Anthony, Susan Bruce, Christopher Brum, Jennifer Cmar, Charlotte Cushman, Laurie Denno, Jane Erin, Diane Fazzi, Elizabeth Hartmann, Robyn Herrera, Stacy Kelly, Frances Liefert, Angela Martyn, Betsy McGinnity, Terry Rafalowski Welch, and Derrick Smith. They have done an amazing job.

Finally, we wish to thank all of the students and their families who have touched our lives and given us the opportunity to learn from them. They have helped us to understand the essential skills needed to effectively teach students with visual impairment and multiple disabilities in a systematic and comprehensive manner.

About the Contributors

Editors

Sharon Z. Sacks, Ph.D., is Superintendent of the California School for the Blind in Fremont, with over 40 years' experience in the field of education and rehabilitation of people who are blind or visually impaired. She is co-editor of *Teaching Social Skills to Students with Visual Impairments: From Theory to Practice; The Development of Social Skills by Blind and Visually Impaired Students: Exploratory Studies and Strategies; Educating Students Who Have Visual Impairments with Other Disabilities;* and the *Focused on ... Social Skills* series of videos and study guides. Dr. Sacks has presented and published widely throughout the United States and abroad on the topics of social skills instruction for students with visual impairments, transition programming for students with visual impairments and multiple disabilities, psychosocial implications of low vision, and issues related to braille literacy. She previously served as executive editor of the journal *RE:view* and was the research team leader on the ABC Braille Study. Dr. Sacks is a recipient of the Outstanding Educator and Women of Vision Awards from the Blind Babies Foundation, where she also served on the Board of Directors. She is also past president of the Association for Education and Rehabilitation of the Blind and Visually Impaired (AER) and recipient of its Mary K. Bauman Award for outstanding contribution to the education of students with visual impairments.

Mary C. Zatta, Ph.D., is Directr of Professional Development, Training and Educational Resources Program at Perkins School for the Blind in Watertown, Massachusetts, where she previously served as Assistant Education Director of the Deafblind Program. She is co-author of *School-to-Work: Developing Transition Portfolios for Students with Significant Disabilities* and *Total Life Learning: Preparing for Transition: A Curriculum for ALL Students with Sensory Impairments,* and is a contributing author to *Deafblindness: Educational Service Guidelines.* Dr. Zatta has written about and given presentations nationally and internationally on various topics related to instruction of young adults with visual impairments and multiple disabilities.

Chapter Authors

Tanni L. Anthony, Ph.D., is Director of the Access, Learning, and Literacy Team in the Exceptional Student Services Unit of the Colorado Department of Education in Denver, and serves as an adjust instructor at the University of Denver and Florida State University in Tallahassee. She is co-editor of *Developmentally Appropriate Orientation and Mobility* and has presented and published extensively on the topics of early childhood development, orientation and mobility for young children who are blind or visually impaired, motor development and movement, sensory and developmental assessment, literacy, and early intervention. Dr. Anthony is a recipient of the Distinguished Service Award from the National Federation of the Blind of Colorado and the Exemplary Advocate Award from the Council for Exceptional Children Division on Visual Impairments and Deafblindness.

Susan Bruce, Ph.D., is Professor and Chair, Teacher Education, Special Education, Curriculum and Instruction Department at the Lynch School of Education at Boston College in Boston, Massachusetts. She is co-author of *Action Research in Special Education: An Inquiry Approach for Effective Teaching and Learning* and has published numerous articles and presented nationally and internationally on the topics of communication development, evidence-based practices, assessment, and symbolic understanding and expression in children who are blind, visually impaired, or have multiple disabilities, especially those who are congenitally deafblind. Dr. Bruce is a recipient of the Virginia M. Sowell Award from AER.

Chris Brum, M.Ed., is a doctoral candidate and an adjunct faculty member and research scientist at San Diego State University in California. He has also served in various teaching positions at Boston College and Boston Public Schools and was a fellow of the National Leadership Consortium on Sensory Disabilities. Dr. Brum is a team member of a research project from the Center on Secondary Education for Students with Autism Spectrum Disorders.

Jennifer Cmar, Ph.D., is Assistant Research Professor at the National Research and Training Center on Blindness and Low Vision at Mississippi State University. She previously served as adjunct lecturer at California State University, Los Angeles, as an orientation and mobility specialist at the Department of Veterans Affairs and the Society for the Blind, and was a fellow of the National Leadership Consortium in Sensory Disabilities.

Charlotte Cushman, M.Ed., MLS, is Educational Resources Manager, Training and Educational Resources Program at Perkins School for the Blind in Watertown, Massachusetts. She is one of the principal authors of the *Perkins Activity and Resource Guide: A Handbook for Teachers and Parents of Students with Visual and Multiple Disabilities* and the editor of *Learning through Doing: A Manual for Parents and Caregivers of Children Who Are Visually Impaired with Additional Disabilities.* Ms. Cushman has been a classroom teacher and an international educational consultant for Perkins, and served as a Peace Corps volunteer in Africa. A librarian and archivist, she now manages Paths to Literacy and other educational websites for Perkins.

Laurie Denno, Ph.D., is an affiliate professor at Antioch University New England in Keene, New Hampshire, and a board certified behavior analyst and licensed mental health counselor working as a consultant in Westford, Massachusetts, with residential programs, day programs, and educational programs as well as organizations such as Perkins School for the Blind, where she worked for over 25 years. She specializes in dual sensory impairment, deafblind education and behavior treatment, CHARGE syndrome, intellectual disabilities, and mental health issues and has taught courses in applied behavior analysis, group behavioral contingencies, behavior contracting, and research design. She has published articles on the effects of CHARGE syndrome and speaks nationally about behavior analysis and deafblind education.

Jane N. Erin, Ph.D., is Professor Emerita at the University of Arizona at Tucson, where she coordinated the Programs in Visual Impairment since 1994 until her retirement in 2015. She is co-editor of *Foundations of Low Vision: Clinical and Functional Perspectives* (2nd edition); *Diversity and Visual Impairments: The Influence of Race, Gender, Religion, and Ethnicity on the Individual*; co-author of *Visual Impairments and Learning* and *Transition Issues Related to Students with Visual Disabilities*; author of *When You Have a Visually Impaired Student with Multiple Disabilities in Your Classroom: A Guide for Teachers* among her numerous books, chapters, journal articles, and conference presentations. She is a former Editor-in-Chief of the *Journal of Visual Impairment & Blindness* and a former executive editor of *RE:view*. Dr. Erin was a recipient of the Margaret Bluhm and the Mary K. Bauman Awards for contributions to education in visual impairment, both from AER.

Diane Fazzi, Ph.D., a certified orientation and mobility specialist, is Associate Dean, Charter College of Education, and Coordinator of the Orientation and Mobility Specialist Training Program, California State University, Los Angeles. She is co-editor of *Early Focus: Working with Young Children Who Are Blind or Visually Impaired Children and Their Families* (2nd edition) and co-author of *Imagining the Possibilities: Creative Approaches to Orientation and Mobility Instruction for Persons Who Are Visually Impaired*, as well as the author of numerous book chapters, journal articles, and conference presentations on working with young children who are visually impaired.

Elizabeth Hartmann, Ph.D., a certified teacher of students with visual impairments and multiple disabilities, is Assistant Professor in the Department of Education at Lasell College in Newton, Massachusetts. Dr. Hartmann is co-author of *Developmental Guidelines for Infants with Visual Impairments: A Guidebook for Early Intervention*. Her research interests include universal design for learning, teachers' collaborative practice, and the development of symbolic understanding in learners with deafblindness and multiple disabilities.

Robyn Herrera, Ph.D., is an orientation and mobility specialist with the Anaheim Union High School District in Anaheim, California, specializing in providing services to individuals with blindness and visual impairment and additional disabilities, and previously served in that role for the State of California. Dr. Herrera was a fellow of the National Leadership Consortium in Sensory Disabilities and participated in the workgroup that revised the Guidelines for Programs Serving Students with Visual Impairments.

Stacy M. Kelly, Ed.D., is an associate professor in the Visual Disabilities Program at Northern Illinois University in DeKalb. Dr. Kelly is also a certified orientation and mobility specialist, teacher of students with visual impairments, and a certified school administrator, and was previously a disability policy researcher in Washington, DC, for the American Foundation for the Blind. She has published book chapters, position papers, and journal articles on the topic of assistive technology for people with visual impairments and has recently been appointed as a Certified Assistive Technology Instructional Specialist Subject Matter Expert by the Academy for Certification of Vision Rehabilitation and Education Professionals.

Frances Liefert, M.Ed., is an orientation and mobility specialist and teacher of students with visual impairments who taught for over 20 years at the Oakland Unified School District and the California School for the Blind in Fremont, where she also coordinated the Low Vision Program and was a member of the Assessment Program. Ms. Liefert is one of the authors of *Collaborative Assessment: Working with Students Who Are Blind or Visually Impaired, Including Those with Additional Disabilities*.

Angela Martyn, M.A., is a teacher of students with visual impairments and an orientation and mobility specialist and is Principal of Education at the California School for the Blind in Fremont.

Betsy L. McGinnity, M.Ed., is Executive Director, Training and Educational Resources Program at Perkins School for the Blind in Watertown, Massachusetts, where she has provided information and training to teachers, professionals, and families with children who are visually impaired with additional disabilities for more than 30 years. She is a contributing author to *Deafblindness: Educational Service Guidelines* and has published book chapters and position papers on the topic of deafblindness and educational programming for students who are deafblind. Ms. McGinnity is a recipient of the Virginia M. Sowell Award from the AER.

Derrick W. Smith, Ed.D., is Chair, Department of Curriculum and Instruction, and Associate Professor at the University of Alabama in Huntsville. Dr. Smith is a certified orientation and mobility specialist and a certified braille transcriber. He is co-author of the *MathBuilders* set of curricula from the American Printing House for the Blind and has presented and published book chapters and journal articles on the topics of assistive technology, teaching mathematics to students with visual impairments, dual certification, and Nemeth code. Dr. Smith is a past president of the Division on Visual Impairments and Deafblindness of the Council for Exceptional Children.

Therese Rafalowski Welch, Ph.D., is Associate Professor of Pediatrics in the Division of Neurodevelopmental and Behavioral Pediatrics at the University of Rochester Medical Center (URMC) in New York and the Education Coordinator for URMC's Leadership Education in Neurodevelopmental and Related Disabilities Program. She previously served as coordinator of the national consortium for the AFB Deaf-Blind Project and co-editor of its publication, *Hand in Hand: Essentials of Communication and Orientation and Mobility for Your Students Who Are Deafblind.* Dr. Welch has been a teacher, state administrator, consultant, and trainer focusing on autism, educational program development for children and young adults with multiple disabilities, including sensory and developmental disabilities, and teaching individuals with deafblindness and multiple disabilities non-symbolic and early symbolic communication.

Other Contributors

Megan Mogan, M.S., is a speech-language pathologist at the Arizona State Schools for the Deaf and Blind in Tucson and a trainer with the Arizona Deafblind Project's Intervener TEAM Training Program. She specializes in working with students who are early communicators, including deafblind learners and visually impaired students with multiple disabilities. Ms. Mogan is an instructor and presenter for Perkins eLearning and a regular contributor to the Paths to Literacy website.

Carolyn Monaco is a professor in the Intervenor for Deafblind Persons Program at George Brown College in Toronto, Ontario, Canada. She is also the President of the Canadian Deafblind Association and a management committee member of Deafblind International. Ms. Monaco has published book chapters on working with students and individuals who are deafblind.

Maureen P. Reardon, J.D., is an attorney in Redwood City, California, and former Director of Student Information Services at the California School for the Blind in Fremont.

Introduction

* *

Keys to Educational Success: Teaching Students with Visual Impairments and Multiple Disabilities was undertaken to address a widespread concern among professionals who work with children who are blind or visually impaired. Teachers of students with visual impairments and orientation and mobility (O&M) specialists are challenged by the diversity of their caseloads and the student population they serve. Many of the students they work with have complex challenges, which may include intellectual, neurological, physical, or behavioral disabilities that influence the amount and intensity of services they receive. Teachers of students with visual impairments and O&M specialists are called on to provide direct services within a variety of school settings, and they may act as consultants to special education teachers, general education teachers, or related service personnel.

Despite the need for support in working with this diverse and complex population, the availability of literature and curricular materials related to students with visual impairments and multiple disabilities is limited. In addition, teachers of students with visual impairments and O&M specialists often receive only one course in their teacher preparation programs that focuses on the needs of these students. *Keys to Educational Success* was designed to help fill this gap and to provide in one text valuable and practical information to assist professionals in their practice. At the same time, this book will be useful to special education teachers, other members of the educational team, and administrators, many of whom may not be familiar with the unique needs of children with visual impairments or how visual impairments interact with other disabilities. Family members and caregivers, too, will find practical information on how they can support their children, and all will be guided on the collaboration that is necessary to provide the best possible education for students with visual impairments and multiple disabilities.

When we undertook this joint project between Perkins School for the Blind and AFB Press, we wanted readers to have information and resources that could be implemented directly with students. While we recognize that theoretical constructs and research provide a foundational understanding that supports practice, this book focuses on the practical aspects of teaching students with visual impairments and multiple disabilities. The contents of this publication include specialized strategies, assessment techniques and tools, curricular resources, strategies for collaboration among professionals, and an array of resources to support students with visual impairments and multiple disabilities in a variety of school settings. The chapters contain practical tips and suggestions, checklists, and lesson-planning ideas that can be implemented by professionals.

The textbook is divided into five distinct sections. Part 1, "Students with Visual Impairments Who Have Multiple Disabilities: Who They Are and How They Are Served," gives the reader an overview of this unique student group, including historical aspects of serving these students, information about causes of visual impairments and other disabilities, and the impact of visual and multiple disabilities on learning. In addition, roles and responsibilities of teachers of students with visual impairments and O&M specialists within a variety of service delivery models are described, and an overview of team models as well as strategies for effective collaboration are presented.

Part 2, "Assessment," describes how formal and informal assessments can be used for initial placement and ongoing instructional planning for students with visual impairments and multiple disabilities. A variety of assessments and their functions are described to assist the reader in effectively using the assessment process to drive instruction.

Part 3, "Instructional Planning and Design," provides an overview of the Individualized Education Program (IEP) process, with information regarding eligibility for special education services, placement, and program planning as it relates to students with visual impairments and multiple disabilities. A variety of curricular strategies and instructional modes are provided in this section, including information about the expanded core curriculum and its critical importance for students with visual impairments, including those with multiple disabilities. Also included in this section is information about both individualized and universal instructional strategies that must be considered when planning a program for a child who is visually impaired and has multiple disabilities.

The next section of this text, "Essential Areas of Instruction," provides specific content related to teaching students with visual impairments and multiple disabilities. These areas include communication skills, functional literacy, orientation and mobility, social competence, independent living skills, assistive technology, and positive strategies for behavioral intervention. Each chapter in Part 4 provides assessment and instructional strategies that can be applied in home, school, and community settings.

The final section of *Keys to Educational Success*, Part 5, "Preparing for Life Before and After School," describes the unique educational needs, service delivery models, and instructional practices for two groups of children who have visual impairments and multiple disabilities: infants, toddlers, and young children, and transition-aged students.

To make this book as useful as possible, an array of pertinent resources is included in each chapter, and general resources are provided at the end of the book.

It is our sincere hope that *Keys to Educational Success: Teaching Students with Visual Impairments and Multiple Disabilities* will provide readers with the information and resources they need to offer the best educational services possible for students with visual impairments and multiple disabilities.

Part 1

. . . .

Students with Visual Impairments Who Have Multiple Disabilities: Who They Are and How They Are Served

Chapter 1

Educating Students with Visual Impairments Who Have Multiple Disabilities: An Overview

Sharon Z. Sacks

Key Points

- 🔑 Characteristics of students with visual impairments who have multiple disabilities
- 🔑 Historical perspectives that have shaped educational programs and instruction for students with visual impairments and multiple disabilities
- 🔑 Common eye etiologies and syndromes among students who have visual impairments and multiple disabilities
- 🔑 Ways other disabilities affect learning for students with visual impairments and multiple disabilities
- 🔑 How various learning styles among students with visual impairments and multiple disabilities affect instruction
- 🔑 Influence of collaborative efforts among professionals and families on the learning and independence of students with visual impairments and multiple disabilities

---

Eight-year-old Samantha was born prematurely. She weighed 1 pound, 8 ounces at birth. As a result, Samantha developed mild cerebral palsy and retinopathy of prematurity. In addition, it is believed that Samantha has cerebral visual impairment. While Samantha is considered legally blind, she has good useful vision for academic tasks in school and for functional activities in the community.

While Samantha's parents want her to attend her neighborhood school, they recognize the importance of her receiving specialized support from her teacher of students with visual impairments, orientation and mobility (O&M) specialist, occupational therapist, and physical therapist. Samantha receives support in a special day class for students with learning disabilities, and she is included in a general education classroom for social

This chapter was based in part on Sacks, S. Z. (1998). Educating students who have visual impairments with other disabilities: An overview. In S. Z. Sacks & R. K. Silberman (Eds.), *Educating students who have visual impairments with other disabilities* (pp. 3–38). Baltimore: Paul H. Brookes Publishing Co. Adapted by permission.

studies and hands-on science activities. Samantha receives daily support from a teacher of students with visual impairments to work on maximizing her visual functioning, social interactions with peers, study and organizational skills, use of assistive technology, use of adaptive devices and materials, and activities of daily living. Samantha also receives weekly instruction from an O&M specialist, and consultation from an occupational therapist and a physical therapist to work on adaptations for eating and personal care skills.

One of Samantha's greatest challenges is problem solving and making decisions. Her educational team is also concerned about Samantha's ability to generalize information learned in class to other environments. The team, along with Samantha's family, meets regularly to discuss strategies that will support Samantha in school, at home, and in the community.

When teachers of students with visual impairments describe their caseloads, more often than not, the majority of students they serve have a range of disabilities. These may include visual impairment, hearing impairment, physical disabilities, and cognitive challenges. Many students exhibit learning disabilities and behavioral challenges. It is not uncommon to have students who may have autism spectrum disorders. Some students may have acquired a visual impairment as a result of a traumatic brain injury subsequent to an accident or medical intervention. It is important to note that not all students with visual impairments and multiple disabilities have cognitive challenges. However, much of the information included in this book will address the unique educational needs of students with visual impairments who also exhibit some level of cognitive disability (mild to severe).

It is estimated that, of students whose primary disability is visual impairment or blindness, 40–70 percent have multiple disabilities (Silberman, Bruce, & Nelson, 2004). Miller, Menacker, and Batshaw (2002) found that one-half to two-thirds of students with developmental disabilities have a visual impairment. Given the heterogeneity of this population, teachers of students with visual impairments, O&M specialists, related service personnel, special education teachers from other disciplines, and families may not have the skills or resources to serve this group in a comprehensive manner. Typically, teachers of students with visual impairments and O&M specialists receive minimal training to work with students who have multiple disabilities. Professionals from other disciplines may not have the knowledge to understand how vision loss affects learning, or the skills needed to adapt the environment or modify instruction to support students with visual impairments and multiple disabilities in the classroom or in the community. As a result, these students may not be receiving the quality and quantity of services needed to adequately support academic and functional growth.

This chapter begins by providing a historical perspective that establishes a strong rationale for the importance of specialized programs for students with visual impairments and multiple disabilities, as well as an overview of the current legislation that regulates services for these students. The chapter then describes the visual conditions that are most common among students who are visually impaired and have other disabilities as well as other disabilities that often coexist with visual impairments and examines how visual impairments and other disabilities affect learning. Finally, the chapter presents models of service delivery for students with visual impairments and multiple disabilities. This chapter provides a foundation for understanding the information presented throughout the rest of this book.

HISTORICAL PERSPECTIVES

Programs and services for students with visual impairments and multiple disabilities have evolved over time. It was not until the late 1950s and early 1960s that students with visual impairments and multiple disabilities were educated in public school settings. Until the 1960s, even specialized schools for students with visual impairments tended to serve students who only had a visual impairment (Hatlen, 2000). The rubella epidemic of the 1960s forced special educators to create programs to serve students with visual impairments and multiple disabilities in a range of school placements, including schools for the blind and general education programs. In 1967 the Helen Keller National Center for Deaf-Blind Youths and Adults and regional centers for the deafblind were created. These programs provided technical assistance and support for educators and families serving students who were deafblind. As a result,

many schools for students who were blind or visually impaired created programs for deaf-blind students and for students with multiple disabilities.

Landmark legislation in the 1970s established guidelines and regulations for serving all students with disabilities. The Education for All Handicapped Children Act of 1975, renamed the Individuals with Disabilities Education Act (IDEA) in 1990, mandated free appropriate public education (sometimes referred to as FAPE) for students with disabilities. The law also stipulated that students be educated in the "least restrictive environment," which meant that students would be educated in general education classrooms unless their needs indicated otherwise. Advocacy groups and families believed that educating students with disabilities alongside their non-disabled peers provided opportunities for socialization and acquisition of academic skills. (More information about the provisions of IDEA appear later in this chapter.)

A similar shift occurred in early intervention services with the enactment in 1986 of amendments to an earlier law, the Education of the Handicapped Act of 1970. While many excellent early intervention and preschool programs for young children with visual impairments already existed, this law mandated services from birth to 3 years of age, and created programs emphasizing instruction in the child's natural environment, such as the home and integrated classrooms.

As more students with visual impairments and multiple disabilities were included in general education settings, a philosophical debate occurred between special educators, who believed that all students with disabilities should be educated in inclusive environments, and those with expertise in educating students with visual impairments, who believed that a model featuring a continuum of services, including specialized schools for students who were blind or visually impaired, resource programs, and general education classes, allowed students to gain greater independence and acquire academic and disability-specific skills. Proponents of specialized services worked tirelessly in the late 1990s and early in 2000s to create *The National Agenda for the Education of Children and Youths with Visual Impairments, Including Those with Multiple Disabilities* (Huebner, Merk-Adam, Stryker, & Wolffe, 2004). This document established 10 national goals for achieving program excellence for students with visual impairments, as listed in Sidebar 1.1.

Hatlen (1996, 2003) established a framework for providing instruction in disability-specific skills—those that students need to learn specifically because of their visual impairment—via the nine areas of the expanded core curriculum (ECC). These nine areas, which need to be taught in addition to the academic core curriculum that all students are taught, are the following:

1. compensatory access, including communication modes, instruction in braille, use of abacus and other mathematical devices, organization and study skills, and listening skills
2. sensory efficiency
3. assistive technology
4. orientation and mobility
5. independent living skills
6. social interaction
7. recreation and leisure
8. career education
9. self-determination

(See Chapter 5 for a more in-depth discussion of the ECC.) As a result of implementation of the ECC, specialized schools for students who are blind or visually impaired, in particular, changed their focus from strictly providing an academic curriculum to integrating many areas of the ECC. Many began to implement short-term programs, and enhance outreach services to local school districts.

The Elementary and Secondary Education Act (ESEA) of 2001, also known as No Child Left Behind, held all students, including those with visual impairments and other disabilities to a higher educational standard. Not only were these students expected to acquire ECC skills, they were required to achieve academic competence close to or at their grade level in school. For teachers of students with visual impairments, O&M specialists, and classroom teachers, trying to balance both outcomes-based programs and a functional curriculum has posed a real challenge. Educators and families have to prioritize what skills are essential for success in school and into adulthood. Educators grapple with ensuring that goals for students with visual impairments and multiple disabilities formulated under IDEA mandates (see the next section) are measurable and based on performance outcomes derived from state content standards. Just like No Child Left Behind, the new Every Student Succeeds Act of 2015, the latest version of the ESEA, continues to emphasize the importance of academic achievement through evidenced-based and measurable

Goals of the National Agenda

The National Agenda for the Education of Children and Youths with Visual Impairments, Including those with Multiple Disabilities sets forth in clear and concise terms a vision and plan of action for the future of the education of children who are blind or visually impaired, as well as those who are visually impaired and have other disabilities. The agenda consists of 10 goals.

1. Students and their families will be referred to an appropriate education program within 30 days of identification of a suspected visual impairment. Teachers of student with visual impairments and orientation and mobility (O&M) instructors will provide appropriate quality services.

2. Policies and procedures will be implemented to ensure the right of all parents to full participation and equal partnership in the education process.

3. Universities with a minimum of one full-time faculty member in the area of visual impairments will prepare a sufficient number of teachers and O&M specialists for students with visual impairments to meet personnel needs throughout the country.

4. Caseloads will be determined based on the assessed needs of students.

5. Local education programs will ensure that all students have access to a full array of service delivery options.

6. All assessments and evaluations of students will be conducted by or in partnership with personnel having expertise in the education of students with visual impairments and their parents.

7. Access to development and educational services will include an assurance that instructional materials are available to students in the appropriate media and at the same time as their sighted peers.

8. All educational goals and instruction will address the academic and expanded core curricula based on the assessed needs of each student with visual impairments.

9. Transition services will address developmental and educational needs (birth through high school) to assist students and their families in setting goals and implementing strategies through the life continuum commensurate with the student's aptitudes, interests, and abilities.

10. To improve student learning, service providers will engage in ongoing local, state, and national professional development.

Source: Huebner, K. M., Merk-Adam, B., Stryker, D., & Wolffe, K. (2004). *The national agenda for the education of children and youths with visual impairments, including those with multiple disabilities* (Rev. ed.). New York: AFB Press.

outcomes. However, the Every Student Succeeds Act allows for more flexibility in how state standards are achieved and places greater emphasis on providing instruction based on each student's individual learning needs.

Although great strides have been made in providing educational programs for students who have visual impairments and multiple disabilities, it is incumbent on professionals to understand the unique learning needs of such a diverse and complex population. By doing so, programs and services can be expanded and enhanced to ensure excellence and quality.

IDEA BASICS

Over the course of time there have been many challenges to the legislation described in the previous section, as different interest groups sought clarification of the protections afforded them. As a result, the current legislation (which was renamed the Individuals with Disabilities Education Improvement Act of 2004) reflects some specific protections for students who are blind or visually impaired.

Defining Disabilities

To be eligible for special education services, a child must be evaluated and found to have one of the 14 disabilities identified by IDEA as a qualifying condition for special education (see Sidebar 1.2). In particular, the definitions in the legislation that pertain specifically to students with visual impairments, deafblindness, and multiple disabilities are essential for guiding states as they seek to identify the needs of these students. For more information about definitions and categories of disability under IDEA, see the Resources section at the end of this chapter.

The Education Team and the IEP

IDEA mandates that that public school districts must develop an Individualized Education Program (IEP) for each student who is eligible for special education services. An IEP is a written plan defining the education program that is designed to meet the unique needs of the student. An IEP is written by a team of professionals and is based on assessments (see Chapter 3) that each professional on the student's education team is responsible for completing on a yearly basis. The IEP contains goals developed for the student based on his or her needs and abilities. (See Chapter 4 for more information about the education team and the IEP and a detailed consideration of some of the provisions of IDEA.)

For very young children up to 3 years of age, the team works directly with the family as well as the child, and develops an Individual Family Service Plan to detail the services that are needed to meet the needs of both the child and the family as a whole. Once the child turns 3 years old, special education services will be offered in a preschool setting, which means a change in the membership of the educational team. At that point the team will focus on the student's individual educational needs and will write an IEP that outlines the educational goals and the services needed to meet them.

Disabilities as Defined by IDEA

IDEA identifies the following 14 disability terms as meeting the criteria of a "child with a disability":

1. **Autism:** a developmental disability significantly affecting verbal and nonverbal communication and social interaction, generally evident before age three, that adversely affects a child's educational performance.
2. **Deafblindness:** concomitant hearing and visual impairments, the combination of which causes such severe communication and other developmental and educational needs that they cannot be accommodated in special education programs solely for children with deafness or children with blindness.
3. **Deafness:** a hearing impairment so severe that a child is impaired in processing linguistic information through hearing, with or without amplification, that adversely affects a child's educational performance.
4. **Developmental Delay:** for children from birth to age three (under IDEA Part C) and children from ages three through nine (under IDEA Part B), the term developmental delay, as defined by each State, means a delay in one or more of the following areas: physical development; cognitive development; communication; social or emotional development; or adaptive [behavioral] development.
5. **Emotional Disturbance:** a condition exhibiting one or more of the following characteristics over a long period of time and to a marked degree that adversely affects a child's educational performance:
    a. an inability to learn that cannot be explained by intellectual, sensory, or health factors
    b. an inability to build or maintain satisfactory interpersonal relationships with peers and teachers
    c. inappropriate types of behavior or feelings under normal circumstances
    d. a general pervasive mood of unhappiness or depression
    e. a tendency to develop physical symptoms or fears associated with personal or school problems
6. **Hearing Impairment:** an impairment in hearing, whether permanent or fluctuating, that adversely affects a child's educational performance but is not included under the definition of "deafness."
7. **Intellectual Disability:** significantly subaverage general intellectual functioning, existing concurrently with deficits in adaptive behavior and manifested during the developmental period that adversely affects a child's educational performance.
8. **Multiple Disabilities:** concomitant impairments, the combination of which

(continued)

(Sidebar 1.2 continued)

causes such severe educational needs that they cannot be accommodated in special education programs for one of the impairments. This term does not include deafblindness.

9. **Orthopedic Impairment:** a severe orthopedic impairment that adversely affects a child's educational performance.

10. **Other Health Impairment:** having limited strength, vitality, or alertness, including a heightened alertness to environmental stimuli, that results in limited alertness with respect to the education environment.

11. **Specific Learning Disability:** a disorder in one or more of the basic psychological processes involved in understanding or in using language, spoken or written, that may manifest itself in the imperfect ability to listen, think,

speak, read, write, spell, or to do mathematical calculations.

12. **Speech or Language Impairment:** a communication disorder such as stuttering, impaired articulation, a language impairment or a voice impairment that adversely affects a child's educational performance.

13. **Traumatic Brain Injury:** an acquired injury to the brain caused by an external physical force, resulting in total or partial functional disability or psychosocial impairment that adversely affects the child's educational performance.

14. **Visual Impairment, Including Blindness:** an impairment in vision that, even with correction, adversely affects a child's educational performance. The term includes both partial sight and blindness.

Source: Individuals with Disabilities Education Improvement Act of 2004 (34 C.F.R. § 300.8[c]).

As students with visual impairments move into adolescence, greater emphasis is placed on providing educational activities in natural environments and community-based settings. For example, IDEA mandates transition planning for students at age 16. The transition plan portion of the IEP (sometimes referred to as an individual transition plan) becomes the student's roadmap for determining the focus of his or her educational program throughout high school and post-secondary programs. Based on assessment, the team, including the student, determine academic, career, independent living, and community goals. Coordination with state agencies such as the department of rehabilitation and developmental disability services provides opportunities for supported work and living options for students with multiple disabilities who may not be able to live independently. (See Chapter 15 for an in-depth discussion of transition services.)

VISUAL IMPAIRMENTS AND MULTIPLE DISABILITIES

Visual Impairments

As described earlier in the chapter, students with visual impairments and multiple disabilities exhibit a range of visual functioning. Some students with good visual acuity may have difficulty with some visual tasks, while others may be legally blind (defined as possessing visual acuity of 20/200 or less with best correction, or having a visual field that is no greater than 20 degrees), but have the ability to read printed material, move safely through the physical environment, and recognize people and identify objects. Other students may have no vision at all, or vision that is limited to the perception of lights and objects.

For students with multiple disabilities whose learning needs require adaptations that use auditory and tactile modes of instruction, visual impairment will be considered their primary disability. For other students, disabilities other than visual impairment may have a more significant impact on the ways they learn or function. However, a visual impairment that is considered a secondary disability may still play a significant role in how a student accesses information (Silberman et al., 2004). It can be difficult to determine if a visual impairment is the primary disability in a student with multiple disabilities. Professionals and families need to understand the common causes of visual impairments among students who have multiple disabilities in order to understand how best to construct appropriate educational programs. (Causes of visual impairments are also discussed in Chapter 10 from the point of view of very early childhood.)

The three leading causes of visual impairment among students with visual impairments and multiple disabilities, in order of prevalence, are cortical visual impairment, retinopathy of prematurity, and optic nerve hypoplasia (Hatton, 2001; Hatton, Ivy, & Boyer, 2013; Silberman et al., 2004):

- *Cortical visual impairment* (CVI), which is also sometimes referred to as *cerebral visual impairment,* is the result of damage to the visual cortex or posterior visual pathways in the brain. It has a number of causes, including anoxia (lack of oxygen) at birth, infection of the central nervous system, traumatic head injury, stroke, tumor, optic atrophy, optic nerve hypoplasia, and abnormalities of the retina. CVI is common in neurological disorders such as cerebral palsy, epilepsy, hydrocephalus, and learning disabilities. CVI usually does not affect color vision. A student's vision may improve over time after the initial onset or injury (Roman-Lantzy, 2007). Students who have CVI may experience fluctuations in visual functioning, and may exhibit spatial confusion (especially when there is visual clutter or crowding) and inattention to visual stimuli (Lueck & Dutton, 2015), preferring to explore objects by touch. Students with CVI may bring objects close to their eyes in order to block out extraneous visual information and may exhibit light gazing. High-contrast materials in simplified formats are recommended for students with CVI.
- *Retinopathy of prematurity* (ROP) is caused by abnormal blood vessel growth

in premature infants that can eventually lead to retinal detachment. The condition can result in minimal to complete visual impairment; students with ROP may have reduced visual acuity, severe myopia, strabismus (eye muscle imbalance), peripheral vision loss, nystagmus, and an increased susceptibility to retinal detachment, cataracts, and glaucoma. Some students with ROP may also have periventricular lukomalasia (a type of brain injury) or CVI. A combination of auditory, tactile, and visual modes of instruction is recommended for students with ROP.

- *Optic nerve hypoplasia* (ONH) is a nonprogressive congenital disease that results in the underdevelopment or absence of the optic nerve. Neurological and endocrine problems are common among students with ONH. ONH can result in mild to severe visual impairment, with an increased incidence of nystagmus and a range of visual field deficits. Some students may demonstrate behavioral and intellectual challenges, requiring a structured learning environment where students can anticipate changes in routine in a consistent manner. Also, students who have ONH may exhibit difficulty with regulating their body temperature and may require growth hormones.

Additional information about these conditions in relationship to development in very early childhood is found in Chapter 14.

Aside from these most common causes of visual impairments in students with multiple disabilities, a range of other eye diseases may result in visual impairment, including simple refractive etiologies that can be corrected with eyeglasses—like myopia (nearsightedness), hyperopia (farsightedness), and astigmatism (uneven curvature of the cornea)—as well as other eye diseases that may be inherited or caused by chromosomal abnormalities. A description of common eye diseases found in students with visual impairments and multiple disabilities is provided in Appendix 1A.

Students with multiple disabilities may also experience visual impairment as a result of an inherited or acquired syndrome. These students may or may not exhibit a visual impairment when first diagnosed. Appendix 1B provides descriptions of syndromes commonly found among students who have visual impairments and multiple disabilities.

Other Disabilities That Affect Learning

Along with visual impairments, other disabilities affect learning and development. An understanding of other disabilities is required to make sound decisions regarding assessment, school placement, and instruction. Because it can be challenging to determine how to comprehensively serve a student with visual impairment and multiple disabilities, a clear understanding of other disabilities is critical for the design of meaningful instruction that maximizes student performance. (For additional discussion of these disabilities, see Silberman et al., 2004.)

Hearing Impairment

Like visual impairment, hearing impairment can be congenital or acquired, and can range from mild to profound. Hearing loss can be caused by genetic anomalies, infection (encephalitis), premature birth, or trauma. There are four general types of hearing loss: conductive disorders; sensorineural disorders; mixed losses (a combination of conductive and sensorineural disorders); and central auditory disorders. *Conductive hearing loss* refers to any condition that impedes sound waves from being conducted from the outer ear through the middle ear, to the inner ear. A *sensorineural hearing loss* occurs when there is damage to the inner ear. Hearing loss is typically classified by the frequency of the loss (measured in hertz), or the pitch of the sounds the individual has difficulty hearing, and by the intensity (loudness or softness) of the sound the person is able to hear (measured in decibels). (See Chapter 14 for a discussion of hearing screening and evaluation.)

Students with hearing impairments require a range of adaptations and instructional strategies to optimize learning (Sacks, 1998; Silberman et al., 2004). Students with mild hearing losses may require classroom adaptations like amplification, front row seating, and auditory training. Students with moderate hearing impairments may be assisted by hearing aids, amplification systems, and (particularly in cases of sensorineural loss) cochlear implants, and often require support from a teacher of students with hearing impairments, a speech-language pathologist, and an audiologist. Students who have severe to profound hearing losses (usually sensorineural) require specialized instruction by a teacher of students with hearing impairments, and are often served in specialized schools for the deaf where they receive intense instruction in sign language, lip reading, and other communication modes. Students who have mixed hearing loss (conductive and sensorineural) may require a range of services and equipment including speech therapy, sign language instruction, support from an audiologist to provide instruction in the use of hearing aids and assistive listening devices, and support from a teacher of students who are deaf and hard of hearing to provide modifications in the classroom setting.

Students with *central auditory disorders*, sometimes referred to as *auditory processing disorders*, have difficulty processing auditory information. Such students may not necessarily have a hearing loss, yet may be unable to interpret or understand the information they hear. Some students with multiple disabilities that include a central auditory disorder become overly stimulated when a certain level or intensity of sound is present in the environment. Such a student may, for example, become overwhelmed or confused when more than one person is talking or when extraneous noise is present. Behavioral manifestations of confusion or feeling overwhelmed include inattention, physical aggression, or attempts to block out the sound source (by covering the ears and similar efforts).

Deafblindness

Students who are deafblind have both hearing and vision losses. It is relatively uncommon for a student to exhibit total deafness and total blindness. Deafblindness can result from a number of causes. Students who have Usher syndrome, for example, experience a loss of hearing during childhood, and develop retinitis pigmentosa in adolescence or early adulthood. Students who acquire the rubella virus or encephalitis usually experience a range of disabilities including vision and hearing losses and severe cognitive challenges. Students with CHARGE syndrome experience a variety of additional anomalies including gastrointestinal disorders, behavioral challenges, cognitive delays, and other medical conditions (see Appendix 1B for more detailed information about CHARGE syndrome). It is important to note that not all students who are deafblind have cognitive disabilities.

Physical Disabilities and Other Health Impairments

The wide range of possible physical disabilities makes them difficult to categorize. Generally speaking, physical disabilities are structural or neural in nature, or are the result of traumatic brain injury.

Many students with physical disabilities and visual impairments have cerebral palsy, which affects muscle coordination, motor function of the limbs, and neurological functioning of the brain and central nervous system. It can be caused by anoxia (lack of oxygen to the brain), birth trauma, environmental teratogens, or abnormal development of the brain or neural tube.

Other physical disabilities that students with visual impairments may have include muscular dystrophy, spina bifida, and physical disabilities resulting from stroke. These students require services from a teacher of students with visual impairments as well as support from physical and occupational therapists, speech-language pathologists, and special education teachers from other disciplines.

Professionals who work with students who have visual impairments and physical disabilities will want to be aware of the use of adaptive devices to assist with independent movement (walking, sitting, and standing) and devices for eating. Also, professionals need to be trained on how to best position and handle students with physical disabilities. (See Chapter 9 for more information on motor development, positioning and handling, and adaptive devices for students with physical disabilities and visual impairments.)

Many students with visual impairments and multiple disabilities may also experience seizures. Seizures are sudden changes in behavior, motor function, or sensation caused by electrochemical changes in the brain (Freeman, Vining, & Pillas, 2003). Seizure disorders can be caused by inadequate oxygen, low levels of blood glucose, toxic substances, very high fevers, tumors, and traumatic incidents causing brain bleeds. Epilepsy is a condition in which seizures usually occur repeatedly and spontaneously over time. Seizures are not caused by another medical condition. Students with seizure disorders often exhibit cognitive disabilities; students who exhibit more severe multiple disabilities tend to have seizure disorders (Freeman et al., 2003). Table 1.1 provides the reader with descriptions of the types of seizure disorders, along with first aid guidance handling students during and after a seizure (Thuppal & Sobsey, 2004). Educators should be aware of medical procedures for seizures outlined in the health care plan of any student with a seizure disorder.

Table 1.1
Classification of Seizures and First Aid Procedures

Type of Seizure	First-Aid			
Partial-Onset Seizures	*Do (During)*	*Do (After)*	*Do Not (During)*	*Do Not (After)*
Simple Partial Seizure				
Individual remains conscious. Individual may engage in repeated or stereotyped behavior. Typically lasts a few seconds to a few minutes. May include blinking.				
Complex Partial Seizure (Previously called temporal lobe epilepsy)				
Consciousness is impaired. Aura or prodrome is common. Often includes staring, automatisms (such as chewing, lip smacking, mumbling, or fumbling with hands), and posturing (turning to one side or unusual position of one arm). Typically lasts about 60–90 seconds and is followed by a brief period of confusion.	Remove hazards from area or pathway. Supervise until fully conscious.		Restrain movements. Approach, if agitated, unless necessary.	Give foods or fluids until fully conscious.
Secondary Generalized Seizure				
Begins as simple partial or complex partial seizure. May sometimes generalize to tonic-clonic or other type of generalized seizure.				
Generalized Onset Seizures	*Do (During)*	*Do (After)*	*Do Not (During)*	*Do Not (After)*
Absence Seizures (Previously called petit mal seizure)				
Impairment of consciousness. Typically lasts 2–20 seconds.	Protect from environmental hazards.			Give foods or liquids until fully conscious.
Tonic Seizure				
Sudden onset. Impairment of consciousness. Rigid extension or flexion of the head, trunk, and/or extremities. Typically lasts several seconds, occasionally longer.				

Source: Adapted with permission from Thuppal, M., & Sobsey, D. (2004). Children with special health care needs. In F. P. Orelove, D. Sabsey, & R. K. Silberman (Eds.), *Educating children with multiple disabilities: A collaborative approach* (4th ed., pp. 324, 335). Baltimore: Paul H. Brookes Publishing.

(continued)

(Table 1.1 continued)

Type of Seizure	First-Aid			
Generalized Onset Seizures	*Do (During)*	*Do (After)*	*Do Not (During)*	*Do Not (After)*
Clonic Seizure				
Impairment of consciousness. Rhythmic, motor, jerking movements of arms, legs and body. Typically lasts more than a few seconds.				
Myclonic Seizure				
Impairment of consciousness may be hard to identify due to brevity. Jerking, motor movements that last less than a second.				
Primary Generalized Tonic-Clonic Seizure (Previously called grand mal seizure)				
Impairment of consciousness. Generalized tonic extension of the extremities lasting a few seconds. Clonic, rhythmic movements may last from 10 seconds to several minutes.	Ease to floor. Remove hazards. Cushion vulnerable body parts.	Position for clear airway, if required. Check for injuries. Allow to rest.	Put anything in the person's mouth. Move the person, unless absolutely necessary. Restrain the person's movements.	Give food or fluids until fully conscious.
Atonic Seizure				
Impairment of consciousness. Brief loss of postural tone, often results in falls and sometimes in injuries.				
Unclassified Seizures				
Do not fall into the existing categories.				

Traumatic Brain Injury

It is not unusual for teachers of students with visual impairments and O&M specialists to work with students who have experienced traumatic brain injuries (sometimes abbreviated TBI). Traumatic brain injuries are the result of any insult to the brain as a result of events such as severe blows to the head, gunshot wounds, brain tumors, brain hemorrhages, and strokes. Students who have experienced traumatic brain injuries can have blurred or double vision, visual field deficits, and lack of binocular vision. When a traumatic brain injury is experienced shortly after birth, blurred and double vision usually resolve; if the injury occurs later in childhood these deficits may persist. Students with traumatic brain injury can experience a variety of visual perceptual difficulties (Mira, Tucker, & Tyler, 1992). Depending on the nature of the injury, some students may exhibit hearing loss or an auditory processing problem. Some students may become easily frustrated if too much information is presented in a visual or auditory manner. The following characteristics are common among students with traumatic brain injury (Padula, Shapiro, & Jansin, 1988, cited in Smith & Levack, 1999, p. 225):

- difficulty with binocular function (strabismus, oculomotor dysfunction, convergence, and accommodative abnormalities)
- difficulties with accommodation
- low blink rate
- inability to perceive spatial relationships between and among objects (spatial disorganization)
- poor fixation and pursuits

- abnormal posture (often to accommodate a visual impairment)
- double vision
- clumsiness
- stationary objects appear to move
- poor concentration and attention
- poor visual memory
- inability to perceive an entire picture or to integrate its parts (simultanagnosia)
- inability to read despite the ability to write (elexia without agraphia)
- failure to attend to objects in the affected hemisphere (visual neglect)
- inability to recognize objects presented visually (visual agnosia)
- inability to distinguish colors (achromatopsia)
- inability to visually guide limbs (optic ataxia)

Sidebar 1.3 provides strategies to assist students who have traumatic brain injury and visual impairments in the classroom and in the community.

Cognitive Challenges

Students who have intellectual disabilities or who exhibit varying degrees of developmental delay in the areas of cognitive, social, communication, and motor skills may learn at a slower rate compared to peers who do not have these types of disabilities. Students with intellectual disabilities and developmental delays may demonstrate difficulty with generalizing and transferring skills from one environment to the next. Often students with visual impairments who have severe developmental delays also have additional disabilities.

Suggestions and Interventions for Students Who Have Visual Impairments and Traumatic Brain Injury

The following suggestions include ways to address the needs of students with traumatic brain injury in the classroom:

Spatial Organization

- Reduce clutter.
- Increase spacing.
- Add environmental cues (such as outlines to indicate placement of objects, color contrast and light enhancement to draw attention to certain places).
- Use a paperclip or eraser to mark a place on the page.
- Establish a routine for tasks and ensure that it is set up the same way everyday.
- Place a ruler under the line of text a student is reading.
- Cut a window in a piece of paper that can be moved from word to word, from line to line, or picture to picture.

Communication

- Keep instructions short and concrete.
- Ask students to repeat instructions to assess comprehension.
- Teach students to request repetition if instructions are not clear.
- Minimize the use of idioms or figurative speech in communication.
- Teach specific idioms or figurative speech that students are likely to encounter.

New Information

- Relate new information to previously learned concepts.
- Stress the relevance of new information to specific interests or events.
- Encourage students to overlearn new information.
- Allow opportunities for students to practice application of new information through explaining to another student.
- Carefully structure new learning so that students do not have the opportunity to learn incorrectly (variation of precision teaching).
- Correct errors early and thoroughly as new learning occurs.

Spatial Orientation

- Design specific areas for accomplishment of activities.
- Use external cues and materials to mark designated areas.
- Structure these cues and materials so that students can self-evaluate their accuracy.

Attention and Concentration

- Minimize environmental distraction through careful classroom placement.
- Eliminate unnecessary auditory distractions, such as excessive talk.
- Build scheduled breaks into your class period.
- Allow opportunities for physical movement on a scheduled basis.

- Focus on the positive attending behavior rather than punishment for distractibility.
- Break tasks into small sequences that a student can complete in shorter time segments.

Task Completion

- Develop systems, such as notebooks and calendar systems, that allow students to self-monitor their work.
- Develop a nonverbal cue that is mutually agreed upon to signal that students are off task and to redirect them to the present task.
- Provide a consistent way for students to indicate that your help is needed.
- Close each lesson with discussions about accomplishments of the day.
- Assist students in carrying over incomplete activities or tasks to their calendar or notebooks that they can independently initiate the next day.
- Provide external cues that students may use to mark task completion, such as a box in which they put finished work as they complete each segment of a task (a calendar box).

Impulse Control

- Provide a reasonable amount of structure within the classroom and be certain that physical reminders of these rules are apparent.

- Ask students to provide suggestions as to how you should give feedback when you see that it is becoming difficult to control impulses.
- Minimize any tendency to see impulse control as simply a behavioral problem.
- Focus on teaching students to recognize when incidents are likely to occur. Help students develop more adaptive coping strategies.

Dealing with Anger

- Be sensitive to signs that a student is experiencing frustration that is likely to lead to outbursts.
- If possible, redirect the student from the frustrating task to a less difficult one.
- If the student becomes increasingly frustrated, attempt to diffuse the anger by engaging the student in some type of physical activity (such as a trip to the gym, taking a walk, shredding paper).
- Avoid discussing the reasons for the anger or alternative behaviors while the student is still upset and immediately thereafter.
- Don't ridicule the student for reacting with anger to a relatively trivial incident. Frustration and fatigue are often the key factors for the response, rather than the significance of the incident.

Source: Reprinted with permission from Loftin, M. (1999). Suggestions for classroom techniques. In M. Smith & N. Levack (Eds.), *Teaching students with visual and multiple disabilities: A resource guide* (pp. 230–232). Austin: Texas School for the Blind and Visually Impaired.

Cognitive challenges can be caused by a variety of circumstances, including genetic anomalies, premature and postmature births, the presence of teratogens, poor maternal health, viruses acquired through the birth process, and traumatic injuries during or after birth. Students who have visual impairments and who exhibit developmental delays often require an educational program that focuses on respect for individual potential, rather than on achieving developmental milestones. Educational programs for these students are best when they maximize meaningful hands-on learning experiences in natural contexts and promote functional learning experiences. Educators who provide services to students with cognitive challenges and visual impairment will want to give consideration to how they present instruction to these students. Using auditory and tactile cues to teach a concept may be more effective than pictures or gestures. Also, recognizing each student's biobehavioral state (see "Behavior Disorders and Emotional Disturbance" later in this chapter) is essential for understanding his or her readiness for instruction.

Learning Disabilities

Students with visual impairments and multiple disabilities may exhibit a range of learning challenges. These may include difficulty with visual, tactile, and auditory perception and problems with visual memory, visual motor skills, and spatial orientation. Students may reverse letters and words in braille and in print, may lack phonemic awareness, and may have difficulty understanding abstract concepts integral for acquiring proficiency in

mathematics. Determination of a specific learning disability requires collaborative assessment from a school psychologist, general education teacher, special education teachers certified to teach students with learning disabilities, and the teacher of students with visual impairments. It is important for teachers of students with visual impairments to conduct a learning media assessment and, when appropriate, a functional vision assessment in order to inform the team about a student's preferred reading medium and functional vision (see Chapter 3 for more information about these assessments).

Many students with visual impairments, particularly students who were premature at birth, may appear academically and socially competent, but require support and intervention in the area of *executive function*, the ability to organize and problem solve. Executive function has three elements (Katz, 2014, pp. 1–5):

1. *Working memory* is the ability to keep information in mind long enough to complete and initiate tasks. Working memory helps with the planning and organization required to follow rules or directions, keeping track of materials and assignments, and solving problems with multiple steps.

2. *Inhibitory control* refers to the ability to control one's behavior in a variety of settings or situations. It is often referred to as *impulse control* and is essential for regulating emotions.

3. *Cognitive* or *mental flexibility* refers to the capacity to shift gears, to determine options when responding to a given

situation, to adjust to change, and to revise plans with flexibility and ease.

Behavior Disorders and Emotional Disturbance

When students with visual impairments and multiple disabilities are unable to communicate their needs or establish control over their environment, or encounter changes in their routine that are unexpected or unwanted, they may be susceptible to a range of behavioral challenges, including verbal outbursts, temper tantrums, impulsive behavior, autistic-like behavior, aggressive or assaultive behavior, or extreme withdrawal. Some students with visual impairments may feel threatened by unfamiliar people or activities that are not explained or announced in advance. Students with visual impairments and multiple disabilities also may exhibit self-stimulatory behaviors such as rocking, twirling, hand or finger flicking, or light gazing as a way to regulate their emotions or feelings or to establish neurological or vestibular balance. Depending on the severity or complexity of a student's concomitant disabilities, the ability of the student to regulate his or her behavior may be affected by his or her neurological status. Some students may have a chemical imbalance that requires medication in order to regulate or control certain behaviors or emotions (Smith & Levack, 1999). For example, students with depression may have inadequate serotonin levels in the brain, and students who exhibit assaultive or self-injurious behaviors may have elevated levels of dopamine (Smith & Levack, 1999). Regardless of cause, it is important for educators and family members to collaborate and conduct a functional behavior assessment to determine how best to work with a student who exhibits a behavior disorder or emotional disturbance. By implementing a functional behavior assessment, all members of the team can initiate a consistent approach by developing and following a behavior support plan. (See Chapter 13 for more information about challenging behaviors.)

Behavior disorders and emotional disturbance are often measured by the frequency and intensity of unwanted behavior or behaviors. Students with visual impairments who have multiple disabilities may exhibit aggressive and injurious behavior on themselves (such as head banging or eye poking) or on others (such as hitting, pinching, biting, or kicking). Understanding a student's biobehavioral state may assist professionals with working more effectively with the student. A student's *biobehavioral state* is the level of his or her arousal that can be influenced by biological circumstances including hunger, tiredness, comfort, and health. Emotions, motivation, and environmental events can also influence a student's level of cooperation and participation in activities. According to Smith and Levack (1999), understanding, assessing, and manipulating biobehavioral states is essential in determining how best to serve students with visual impairments who have severe multiple disabilities. Smith and Shafer (1996) provide an excellent biobehavioral status assessment that allows the educator to evaluate food and liquid intake, medication information, seizure information, and the student's state during each interval of observation (including time, position, specific external stimulus available, ambient conditions, social conditions, and level of alertness).

Although, as stated previously, students with visual impairments may exhibit autistic-like behaviors (atypical eye gaze, limited eye contact, visual avoidance, use of lateral gaze to view objects, and inefficient pursuit of moving objects [Gense & Gense, 2002]), they may not be on the autism spectrum. Conversely, students with visual impairments who may be diagnosed with autism spectrum disorder will demonstrate atypical characteristics in communication, social interaction, and responses to sensory information. Diagnosis of autism spectrum disorder is usually made by a developmental pediatrician or psychologist who has extensive training in working with children and adults with autism.

Recent research has shown a strong connection between autism spectrum disorder and the causes of some visual impairments, including optic nerve hypoplasia, microphthalmia, anophthalmia, and periventricular lukomalasia (Fink & Borchert, 2011; Miller et al., 2004). While some students with visual impairments and multiple disabilities may be diagnosed with autism, there is a range of abilities and skills for performing functional tasks or academic activities. Again, it is essential for a collaborative assessment to take place to determine a definitive diagnosis of autism spectrum disorder. Table 1.2 compares development of a range of behaviors in students who are sighted and typically developing, blind or visually impaired, and visually impaired with autism. Understanding the differences in behavior among these groups may assist professionals in designing appropriate educational programs.

LEARNING PREFERENCES, NEEDS, AND ABILITIES

To provide effective instruction to students with visual impairments and multiple disabilities, educators will want to consider the role that vision plays in learning. For students with vision, a great deal of learning takes place incidentally—by watching someone else perform a task or use an object. Students with sight can learn about the world through observation and imitation, and they are stimulated, via visual cues, to explore their environments independently and learn about the objects and people they see.

Students with visual impairments, including students with visual impairments and multiple disabilities, do not have the same access to incidental learning and visual information that sighted students do. Students with visual impairments must rely on caring adults and peers to actively bring the world to them, as well as to interpret experiences through auditory, tactile, and visual cues. A student's particular set of disabilities will influence his or her learning preference—auditory, tactile, visual, or a combination—along with his or her access to the core and expanded core curricula.

The elements that follow, among others (such as biobehavioral state, mentioned earlier in this chapter), may influence the instruction of students with visual impairments and multiple disabilities (Sacks, 1998).

Generalization of Skills

Students with visual impairments and multiple disabilities may have difficulty generalizing skills from one environment to the next.

Table 1.2

Comparison of Development among Children Who Are Sighted and Typically Developing, Blind or Visually Impaired, and Blind or Visually Impaired with an Autism Spectrum Disorder

Typical Development	Blind or Visually Impaired	ASDVI
Communication Behaviors		
Makes cooing and gurgling sounds (3–6 months). Copies speech sounds (6–12 months).	The process of acquiring speech and language appears to be the same for visually impaired children as it is for typical children, but slower physical development, a more restricted range of experiences, and the lack of visual stimulation may cause a child's language development to be slower.	Language develops slowly or not at all. Development is frequently "splintered"; language development may or may not be consistent with typical developmental norms or sequences. May show no interest in communicating.
Uses much jargon (unintelligible speech) with emotional content. Is able to follow simple commands (18 months). Has a vocabulary of 150–300 words (24 months).	Speech is echolalic but for a short duration. Language may be delayed if experiences are limited, but is not distorted. Responds appropriately to language requests; enjoys communication "give and take."	Exhibits concrete understanding and use of language; has difficulty with generalizations. Echolalic; often has difficulty breaking this pattern. The echolalia often leads to patterns of verbal perseveration with idiosyncratic meanings. Has difficulty initiating and engaging in meaningful conversations. The range of "topics of interest" is narrow. Has difficulty maintaining a topic chosen by others; exhibits limited or no conversational reciprocity.
Understands most simple questions dealing with his or her own environment and activities (36 months). Relates experiences so that they can be followed with reason. May briefly exhibit pronoun reversals. Takes part in simple conversations (2–3 years).	Vocabulary is built through concrete experiences. Can experience difficulty with abstract language because of limited concrete experiences. May reverse pronouns, but such reversals are brief in duration. Difficulties with concepts are common because of the lack of a visual model; once understood, concepts can be generalized. Language development usually follows developmental norms.	Uses words without attaching the usual meanings to them. Uses nonconventional or non-traditional behaviors (such as gestures, pulling) as a form of communication. Has long-term difficulty using pronouns appropriately.

Source: Reprinted from Gense, M. H., & Gense, D. J. (2005). *Autism spectrum disorders and visual impairment: Meeting student's learning needs* (pp. 32–37). New York: AFB Press. Adapted with permission from Taylor & Francis from Gense, M. H., & Gense D. J. (1994, Summer). Identifying autism in children with blindness and visual impairments. *RE:view, 26*(2), 55–62.

(continued)

(Table 1.2 continued)

Typical Development	Blind or Visually Impaired	ASDVI
Communication Behaviors		
Follows a logical pattern of concept development from the concrete to the abstract.	Language development is based on concrete "hands-on" experiences.	Has apparent lack of common sense; may be overly active or passive. Has difficulty with abstract concepts and often focuses on "irrelevant" information; has a literal translation of language; a literal or concrete understanding of concepts makes generalizations difficult.
Develops language from experience and interaction with the environment; can adjust the topic of interest from an early age.	Learns language from an early age; adjusts the topic of conversation. Had difficulty with abstract concepts for which there is limited "hands-on" experience. Develops a broader understanding based on experiences; is able to generalize information with instruction.	If verbal, may converse but focus on a topic of perseverative interest. Has difficulty generalizing information, even with instruction.
Social Interactions		
Responds to his or her name (6–9 months).	Responds to his or name; responses are more defined when paired with tactile contact. Needs to learn that a world exists beyond reach; may exhibit social interest through changing or shifting posture (leaning or turning).	Appears not to hear; does not orient toward sound.
Takes turns while playing with an adult (for example, using actions, sounds, or facial expressions) (6–12 months).	Engages in social give-and-take; seeks to share information or experiences with others.	Has limited, if any, social interests. Has a limited understanding of social give-and-take.
Makes simple choices among toys. Mimics another child's play (18–24 months).	Play is sometimes observed to be less "imaginative" and more concrete because of the lack of a visual model. Redirection of an activity is possible.	Plays repetitively; often does not use toys for their intended purpose.
Often indulges in make-believe (48 months).	Because of limited visual references, may have difficulty in observing, organizing, and synthesizing the environment; imitative and make-believe play may be delayed, but can be specifically "taught." Requires a variety of opportunities to learn and to generalize; needs feedback to understand and comprehend some social situations.	Does not engage in spontaneous or imaginative play or initiate pretend play. Perseverative behavior is a problem, and a redirection of activities may be difficult.

Typical Development	Blind or Visually Impaired	ASDVI
Social Interactions		
Enjoys playing with other children (3–4 years).	Enjoys playing with other children. Shows social curiosity; is curious about the environment (for example, may ask who may be in the room or where a peer may be).	Prefers to spend time alone, rather than with others; peer relationships are often distorted. Exhibits little social curiosity; may find interactions with others to be unpleasant.
Is able occasionally to use feelings to explain reasons (48 months).	Demonstrates empathy; is able to comprehend another's feelings.	May treat other people as objects; has a limited ability to understand another's feelings.
Enjoys playing organized games with other children (5–6 years).	Enjoys playing organized games with other children. Has difficulty observing, organizing, and synthesizing the environment; requires a variety of opportunities.	Is often anxious and uncomfortable in social situations; prefers to follow routines and rituals. Has difficulty adapting to change.
Demonstrates empathy toward others.	Will acknowledge emotions of self and others. Seeks out others if hurt, sick, sad, or angry.	Appears to ignore when someone is hurt. Shows little bonding with family members.
Restricted, Repetitive, and Stereotyped Patterns of Behavior		
Reaches for a toy (3–6 months). Puts in and dumps objects from containers (12–18 months). Looks at storybook pictures with an adult (18–24 months).	Stereotypic behaviors (rocking, eye-poke) may occur in novel and unfamiliar situations; management of these behaviors can be accomplished with redirection into meaningful activities that provide sensory feedback; the child learns to control these behaviors when older. Interests may be limited because of limited exposure; demonstrates an interest in a variety of toys or objects once they are experienced. Historically, stereotypic behaviors have been attributed to the lack of stimulation of the vestibular system. These behaviors occur more in young children and lessen as the children learn to interact with the environment.	Plays repetitively; toys are not used as intended. May perseverate on a specific feature of a toy (such as spinning the wheel of a car) or may engage in a repetitive action with a toy or objects. The interruption of a favorite activity or of a stimulatory motor behavior (such as hand flapping or rocking from one foot to another) is often met with extreme resistance.
Helps with simple tasks (2–3 years). Follows two-step directions. Uses materials and toys to make things (3–4 years).	Interest may be limited to toys, tasks, or objects that were previously experienced; is able to engage in a variety of activities with adults and peers. Redirection of an activity is possible; response to changes are easier with greater experiences.	Has highly restricted interests; has difficulty being redirected from high-interest toys or objects. Exhibits an extreme interest in one part of an object or one type of object.

(continued)

(Table 1.2 continued)

Typical Development	Blind or Visually Impaired	ASDVI
Restricted, Repetitive, and Stereotyped Patterns of Behavior		
Shifts attention from one person, item, or activity to another.	Exhibits typical flexibility in managing changes in routine.	Challenging behaviors escalate when changes in routine or structure are experienced; demonstrates inflexibility when transitioning between activities. Stereotypic behaviors occur throughout life and are difficult to break. Behaviors increase with anxiety and with stressful situations and can be difficult to redirect. May perseverate on a single item, idea, or person; may rigidly perform a seemingly nonfunctional routine. May engage in aggressive or violent behavior or injure himself or herself; may throw frequent tantrums for no apparent reason.
Responses to Sensory Information		
Turns head toward sounds (3–6 months). Feeds self with spoon; drinks from a cup (12–18 months). Moves body in time to music (18–24 months). Puts on clothing with a little help (4–5 years). Jumps, runs, throws, and climbs using good balance (3–4 years). Tolerates a normal range of touch, movement, sounds, and smells. Attends to relevant stimuli.	Often has poor posture because of the lack of a visual model; learns to orient to sounds with instruction. Interests may be restricted because of the lack of vision; interests expand with experiences. Exhibits little delay in motor development until the onset of locomotion. Can be easily engaged. Because of the lack of visual stimulation, often creates his or her own stimulation; can usually "redirect" the stimulatory behavior. Uses residual senses to gain information. Attends to relevant stimuli.	Has unusual reactions to physical sensations, such as being overly sensitive to touch or underresponsive to pain; sight, hearing, touch, pain, smell, and taste may be affected to a lesser or greater degree. Unusual postures and hand movements are common and can be difficult to redirect. Commonly perseverates various sensory stimuli. Tactile defensiveness is common and is usually not overcome with time. Often appears not to hear or focus.

Students are better able to learn and maintain new skills if they are taught in real and natural environments, For example, teaching a student how to undress and dress himself before and after a swimming activity will give more meaning to the lesson than teaching these skills without such context. In addition, if the student enjoys swimming, using this context will provide motivation for maintaining and improving these skills.

Structure and Routines

Students with visual impairments and multiple disabilities benefit from consistency in their daily lives. Providing structure and organization in the classroom and in work environments helps students anticipate changes in activities and provide opportunities for students to complete tasks with greater independence. Students with visual impairments will not have as much access to anticipatory visual cues as sighted students, and may have difficulty transitioning from one activity to the next. Providing consistent verbal or tactile cues to students so they will know when one activity will end and when another will begin helps students with visual impairments anticipate and adapt to the transition. Students who are given time to process changes in their routines are more likely to engage in activities with greater focus and attention.

Concrete versus Abstract Learning

Students with visual impairments often learn best when activities are experiential in nature. Sighted children can acquire concepts through incidental learning, by observing the activities and objects around them. Students with visual impairments who don't have the benefit of incidental learning may require a different approach. For example, a sighted student may understand that there are different colors of apples because she sees them when she goes to the grocery store with her father. A student who is visually impaired, on the other hand, may have little or no knowledge about different varieties of apples unless he or she is given the opportunity to explore and taste the difference between red, green, or yellow apples. Also, a student with a visual impairment may not realize that apples can be cooked and made into applesauce, or that oranges can be squeezed into juice, unless she is given the opportunity to engage with and participate in hands-on activities that demonstrate these processes.

When students with visual impairments have learning challenges, grasping abstract mathematical or scientific concepts can be difficult. Often, these concepts have little relevance to real life activities. These students may be able to memorize math facts, for example, but when given an equation to solve, or when asked to manipulate geometric formulas, the task requires a deeper understanding than memorization affords. Students may be able to follow a step-by-step process, but not fully understand the concepts behind the steps. For example, some students may not have the math skills to make change or to give the appropriate coins or bills when making a purchase. These students may be taught to use the next highest dollar strategy, in which, when making a purchase for an uneven dollar amount, they learn to give the cashier the next highest even number of dollars, instead of trying to provide the exact amount of dollars and cents; for example, if a purchase is $5.40, the student would give the cashier $6.

In a similar manner, complex problem-solving activities or higher-order thinking skills like planning a travel route in the community may pose a challenge to students who have visual impairments and multiple disabilities as they may not understand the nuances of complex language or idioms without an explanation from a teacher or family member. For example, terms like "parallel," "perpendicular," "traveling on the diagonal," or "traffic surge" may require hands-on experiential instruction in order for students to understand and acquire these skills.

Attention Span and Distractibility

It is important to know how long a student with visual impairments and multiple disabilities can attend to an instructional activity without supervision. Many students with multiple disabilities require a variety of prompts (verbal, physical, tactile, or a combination) to attend to a given task. Some students may only be able to attend for a few minutes at a time, while others can maintain their attention for long periods. When designing instruction it is important for teachers of students with visual impairments and O&M specialists to frame lessons so that the student can achieve success by limiting the time in which a given student is engaged in a lesson, and building in natural reinforcements (verbal and physical praise such as a "high five," a pat on the back, or a hug) to extend instructional time.

Often, students with visual impairments and multiple disabilities are highly distract-ible. Loud noises, the hum from fluorescent lights, overly active classrooms (verbal commotion by others), or too much visual stimuli in the classroom can cause students to lose interest, become overly stimulated, or exhibit disruptive behavior. Students with visual impairments and multiple disabilities do best in an environment that is structured, organized, and predictable. As discussed earlier in this chapter, auditory, tactile, and visual cues help these students anticipate transitions from one activity to the next, but an overload of visual, tactile, or auditory cues can cause students to withdraw or become non-compliant.

Learning Preferences: Auditory, Tactile, or Visual

Some students with visual impairments and multiple disabilities may use a combination of visual, tactile, and auditory skills to access their environment. Some students may be able to depend on their hearing to acquire academic and functional skills, but for others, perceiving information through auditory modes may be difficult. Such students may have normal hearing but be unable to effectively process auditory information. The type and amount of auditory or verbal information offered to these students may require consideration. Some students, for example, need a quiet place to work while completing classroom activities, while others may need verbal and auditory information presented at a slower pace or in smaller chunks.

For tactile learners, how information is presented can affect learning outcomes. Some students may require simple, straightforward, uncluttered presentations of information in two- and three-dimensional formats. Other students may be able to tolerate a greater variety of textures, forms, and shapes. Teachers of students with visual impairments will want to work closely with their students' occupational therapists to determine the most effective way to introduce tactile information. Also, assessment of tactile skills by the educational team is important when considering the introduction of braille. (See Chapter 3 for further information regarding tactile assessment.)

Students who have some functional vision may use visual cues (pictures, familiar landmarks, or survival words such as "Exit", "Open," "Closed," and "Men/Women") to access information and to learn new skills. Students who have experienced a decline in visual functioning can use visual memory to make sense of the world around them. More often than not, however, students with some functional vision use a combination of auditory and visual skills to access learning opportunities in the classroom and in the community.

Tactile Defensiveness versus Tactile Exploration

Many students with visual impairments and multiple disabilities, particularly those students who have severe cognitive and physical challenges, or those who were born prematurely, may demonstrate *tactile defensiveness,* or an aversion to touching certain types of objects or textures, or to eating certain foods. These students may also be resistant to being touched or held, particularly when the touch is gentle or light.

Many of these students have immature vestibular systems, and have experienced trau-

matic medical interventions and numerous hospitalizations. Often these students respond well to a consistent routine, so they can anticipate daily activities. Trusted professionals and family members can help these students gain the motivation to explore and experience the world around them. *Coactive movement,* where the student touches objects and moves together with a trusted adult or adults, can encourage the student to engage with objects, toys, and unfamiliar tasks without feeling threatened. This can lead to the student feeling more motivated to participate in activities.

The hand-under-hand technique, in which the student's hand rests on top of the adult's hand rather than being manipulated by the adult, is a good way to introduce unfamiliar tactile stimuli (objects, toys, food, academic materials). Whenever an adult wants to take a student's hand to demonstrate a task or explore an object, it is important to request permission before doing so. In cases where the student is not able to respond to this type of request, an auditory or tactile anticipatory cue should be provided before taking the student's hand. Also, when students understand the purpose and function of an activity, and the learning environment is structured so that the student can enjoy exploration through touch, the result is more likely to be positive. Seeking support from an occupational therapist to provide strategies to reduce aversion to being touched can help some students. Activities may include vestibular stimulation and a "sensory diet" of brushing the arms.

Motivation

Like other students, students with visual impairments and multiple disabilities exhibit a range of personality types. Some students are more passive and shy, while others are more outgoing and willing to take risks. When family members and professionals have low expectations for students to learn or to master a variety of skills, students can develop a sense of dependency on others. For example, instead of attempting an activity independently, the student may wait for a teacher to do the activity. This level of dependency is referred to as *learned helplessness* (Seligman, 2007) and occurs when individuals are not provided with opportunities to gain control or experience a range of activities independently. Stimulating motivation in students with visual impairments and multiple disabilities requires that professionals encourage students to make choices and solve problems within multiple settings throughout the school day.

To motivate students, professionals and family members alike must have high, yet realistic, expectations for their academic and social performance. Students with visual impairments who also have severe cognitive or physical challenges may be seen as needing assistance with all tasks or as being unable to learn, when this isn't necessarily the case. It is essential for professionals to determine the preferences, learning styles, and activities that reinforce each student's desire to acquire and maintain new skills.

Achieving independence may be difficult for some students with visual impairments and multiple disabilities. It may be more realistic to expect some students to achieve *interdependence*—the ability to perform tasks with the support of caring adults or peers.

Using Prompts

Stepping back and allowing students to accomplish academic and functional tasks on their own or with limited support can be difficult for both family members and professionals. It's important to determine how much time to give a student before providing a prompt (known as *wait time)*, and to identify the minimum level of prompt necessary for the student to perform an activity with relative independence.

Using a *prompt hierarchy* can help professionals and family members determine the minimum level of prompt necessary for a student to proceed with a task independently. The prompt hierarchy starts with the least intrusive prompt accessible to a student and increases the level of prompting, as necessary.

- gestures = G (pointing, nodding)
- indirect verbal = IV (What do you need to do?)
- direct verbal = DV (Drink your juice.)
- partial physical = PP (touching a student's elbow to prompt the student to turn the page of a book)
- full physical = FP (grasping the students wrist to turn the page of a book)

To maximize student motivation and minimize learned helplessness, professionals and family members will want to determine a number of student characteristics, including the following:

- The student's preferences (likes and dislikes): observe the student in a variety of environments and conduct interviews with caregivers to see what the student responds positively and negatively to.

- Wait time: how much time is needed after making a request or giving a prompt before a response can be expected or, if a response is not forthcoming, before intervening with the student.
- Processing time: how long it takes for the student to process information.
- Level of prompt: using the prompt hierarchy, identify the lowest level of prompt necessary for the student to attempt an activity.

Once these elements have been determined, teachers and family members will want to keep the following in mind when instructing the student:

- Ensure that the information given to the student is clear, concise, and consistent.
- Slow the pacing of information so that the student can process and understand the directions or information.
- Allow an appropriate amount of time for the student to process information and before intervening or prompting.
- Always use the lowest level of prompting required, as identified by the prompt hierarchy.
- Be consistent across environments (home, school, community) regarding the prompts that are given to the student.

These strategies are used during the assessment process to determine the level of prompting needed for instruction, as well as during instruction, as an efficient way to determine the level of progress made over time.

Chapter 3 provides more detailed information regarding assessment techniques for students with visual impairments and multiple disabilities and provides an example of a data sheet using the prompt hierarchy.

COLLABORATION AND TEAMS

Students with visual impairments and multiple disabilities need clear and consistent information in order to grow, access the world around them, and acquire academic and functional skills. In order to provide this level of consistency, it is essential that families and professionals communicate and collaborate well. Though it may not be easy to do so at all times, the educational team, including the family, needs to share information and make educational decisions based on consensus and honesty. All members of a student's educational team must be willing to leave their personal biases and feelings about the student at the door. The best decisions will be based on sound assessment practices rather than subjective views. The following suggestions can assist professionals and families toward achieving positive collaboration and communication (Chapter 2 provides a more detailed discussion about collaboration, communication, and team functioning):

- Provide a realistic view of the student's strengths and limitations.
- Respect the family's view of the student, yet provide honest feedback about observations and assessment information.

- Respect each family's values and beliefs regarding their student's disabilities and prognosis for future achievement.
- Educate families about their student's accomplishments through regular communication that is informative and instructional.
- Provide information in the family's native language and at the family's educational level.
- Develop a proactive attitude about the student's level of performance and potential for accomplishing tasks.
- Maintain realistic, high expectations for student performance.
- Consider each student as an individual who acquires skills in his or her own way; avoid generalizations about disabilities and academic performance.
- Create opportunities to share information and student work samples (video clips can be an effective way to show families how students perform activities and skills).

SUMMARY

The population of students with visual impairments and multiple disabilities is quite diverse. Supporting these students requires knowledge beyond understanding how blindness or low vision affects a student's learning and development.

Teachers of students with visual impairments and O&M specialists are, more often than not, placed in a leadership role in helping the educational team understand how blindness and visual impairments impact a student's ability to acquire academic and functional skills. These professionals must be knowledgeable about the accommodations and modifications that can be made for students with visual impairments, and they must be able to demonstrate and share strategies that maximize a student's participation in school and community settings.

The information provided in this chapter lays the groundwork for understanding the unique educational needs of students with visual impairments and multiple disabilities. With an enhanced knowledge base, professionals can apply the more detailed information found in subsequent chapters in their work with students. Sharing curriculum models and innovative strategies, assessment tools, and techniques with professionals and families who may not have expertise in providing services to students with visual impairments and multiple disabilities will help promote positive educational outcomes for this unique population.

REFERENCES

Education for All Handicapped Children Act, Pub. L. No. 94-142 (1975).

Education of the Handicapped Act Amendments, Pub. L. No. 99-457, Part H (1986).

Elementary and Secondary Education Act (No Child Left Behind), Pub. L. No. 107-110 (2001).

Every Student Succeeds Act, Pub. L. No. 114-95 (2015).

Fink, C., & Borchert, M. (2011). Optic nerve hypoplasia and autism: Common features of spectrum diseases. *Journal of Visual Impairment & Blindness, 105*(6), 334–338.

Freeman, J. M., Vining, E. P. G., & Pillas, D. J. (2003). *Seizures and epilepsy in children: A* guide (3rd ed.). Baltimore: Johns Hopkins University Press.

Gense, M. H., & Gense D. J. (1994, Summer). Identifying autism in children with blindness and visual impairments. *RE:view, 26*(2), 55–62.

Gense, M. H., & Gense, D. J. (2002). *Autism spectrum disorders in learners with blindness/vision impairments: Comparison of characteristics.* Washington, DC: Heldref Publications.

Gense, M. H., & Gense, D. J. (2005). *Autism spectrum disorders and visual impairment: Meeting student's learning needs.* New York: AFB Press.

Hatlen, P. (1996). The core curriculum for blind and visually impaired students, including those with additional disabilities. *RE:view, 28*(1), 25–32.

Hatlen, P. (2000). Historical perspectives. In M. C. Holbrook & A. J. Koenig (Eds.), *Foundations of education: Volume I. History and theory of teaching children and youths with visual impairments* (2nd ed., pp. 1–54). New York: AFB Press.

Hatlen, P. (2003, December). *Impact of literacy on the expanded core curriculum.* Paper presented at the Getting in Touch with Literacy Conference, Vancouver, British Columbia, Canada.

Hatton, D. D. (2001). Model registry of early childhood visual impairment: First-year results. *Journal of Visual Impairment & Blindness, 95*(7), 418–433.

Hatton, D. D., Ivy, S. E., & Boyer, C. (2013). Severe visual impairments in infants and toddlers in the United States. *Journal of Visual Impairment & Blindness, 107*(5), 325–337.

Huebner, K. M., Merk-Adam, B., Stryker, D., & Wolffe, K. (2004). *The national agenda for the education of children and youths with visual impairments, including those with multiple disabilities* (Rev. ed.). New York: AFB Press.

Individuals with Disabilities Education Act (IDEA), Pub. L. No. 101-467 (1990).

Individuals with Disabilities Education Improvement Act (IDEA), 20 U.S.C. § 1400 (2004).

Katz, M. (2014, Summer). Executive function: What does it mean? Why is it important? How can we help? *The Special EDge, 27*(3), 8–10.

Levack, N., Stone, G., & Bishop, V. (1994). *Low vision: A resource guide with adaptations for students with visual impairments* (2nd ed.). Austin: Texas School for the Blind and Visually Impaired.

Loftin, M. (1999). Suggestions for classroom techniques. In M. Smith & N. Levack (Eds.), *Teaching students with visual and multiple disabilities: A resource guide* (pp. 230–232). Austin: Texas School for the Blind and Visually Impaired.

Lueck, A. H., & Dutton, G. N. (Eds.). (2015). *Vision and the brain: Understanding cerebral visual impairment in children.* New York: AFB Press.

Miller, M. M., Menacker, S. J., & Batshaw, M. L. (2002). Vision: Our window to the world. In M. L. Batshaw (Ed.), *Children with disabilities* (5th ed., pp. 165–192). Baltimore: Paul H. Brookes Publishing Co.

Miller, M. T., Stromland, K., Ventura, L., Johansson, M., Bandim, J. M., & Gillberg, C. (2004). Autism with ophthalmological malformations: The plot thickens. *Transactions of the American Ophthalmological Society, 102,* 107–122.

Mira, M. P., Tucker, B. F., & Tyler, J. S. (1992). *Traumatic brain injury in children and adolescents: A sourcebook for teachers and other school personnel.* Austin: ProEd.

Padula, W. V., Shapiro, J. B., & Jansin, P. (1988). Head injury causing post traumatic vision syndrome. *New England Journal of Optometry, 41*(2), 16–20.

Roman-Lantzy, C. (2007). *Cortical visual impairment: An approach to assessment and intervention.* New York: AFB Press.

Sacks, S. Z. (1998). Educating students who have visual impairments with other disabilities: An overview. In S. Z. Sacks & R. K. Silberman (Eds.), *Educating students who have visual impairments with other disabilities* (pp. 3–38). Baltimore: Paul H. Brookes Publishing Co.

Seligman, M. E. P. (2007). *The optimistic child: A proven program to safeguard children against depression and build lifelong resilience.* New York: Houghton Mifflin.

Silberman, R. K., Bruce, S. M., & Nelson, C. (2004). Children with sensory impairments. In F. P. Orelove, D. Sobsey, & R. K. Silberman (Eds.), *Educating children with multiple disabilities: A collaborative approach* (4th ed., pp. 425–528). Baltimore: Paul H. Brookes Publishing Co.

Smith, M., & Levack, N. (1999). *Teaching students with visual and multiple impairments: A resource guide* (2nd ed.). Austin: Texas School for the Blind and Visually Impaired.

Smith, M., & Shafer, S. (1996). Assessment of biobehavioral states and analysis of related influences. In M. Smith & N. Levack, *Teaching students with visual and multiple impairments: A resource guide* (pp. 239–254). Austin: Texas School for the Blind and Visually Impaired.

Texas School for the Blind and Visually Impaired, Curriculum Department. (2015). Unpublished document.

Thuppal, M., & Sobsey, D. (2004). Children with special health care needs. In F. P. Orelove, D. Sobsey, & R. K. Silberman (Eds.), *Educating children with multiple disabilities: A collaborative approach* (4th ed., pp. 311–378). Baltimore: Paul H. Brookes Publishing Co.

RESOURCES

For additional resources, see the General Resources section at the back of this book.

Organization

Center for Parent Information and Resources
c/o Statewide Parent Advocacy Network
35 Halsey St., Fourth Floor
Newark, NJ 07102
www.parentcenterhub.org

Serves as a central resource of information and products to a network of parent training and resource centers that focus on serving families of children with disabilities. Provides a listing of categories of disability under IDEA.

Specific Eye Conditions, Their Effects on Vision, and Related Educational Considerations

Eye Condition	Effects on Vision	Educational Considerations
Achromatopsia (color deficiency, colorblindness, achromacy, or rod achromacy) Cone malformation, macular deficiency, and partial or total absence of cones.	• Limited or no color vision • Colors may be seen as shades of gray • Loss of detail • Decreased acuity • Central field scotomas • Normal peripheral fields • Associated with nystagmus and photophobia	• Adapted color-dependent activities • Alternate methods for matching clothing • Support of eccentric viewing • High-contrast materials • May need to use sunglasses, visors, or hats outdoors and indoors as well • Reduced or diffused lighting • Supplement vision with auditory and tactile information
Albinism Total or partial absence of pigment, causing abnormal optic nerve development Lenses and tinted lenses may be prescribed.	• Decreased acuity • Photophobia • Increased sensitivity to glare • High refractive error • Astigmatism • Central scotomas • Nystagmus • Muscle imbalance • Eye fatigue with close or detailed work • Reduced depth perception	• Magnification (e.g., handheld magnifier, electronic magnifier, screen enlargement software, telescope, etc.) • Close viewing • High-contrast materials • May need to use sunglasses, visors, or hats outdoors and indoors as well • Lighting from behind • Reduced glare • Line markers and templates; placeholders • Frequent breaks
Amblyopia (was anopsia, called "lazy eye") *See also Strabismus* Reduced visual functioning in one eye, which causes the person to use one eye instead of both.	• Monocular vision • Reduced visual field • Reduced depth perception • May develop blindness in one eye	• Frequent breaks • Seating should favor functional eye • Familiarization with new environments • Time to adjust in new situations

Source: Reprinted with permission from Texas School for the Blind and Visually Impaired, Curriculum Department. (2015). Unpublished document.

Note: See Appendix 1B for more information about syndromes.

(continued)

Eye Condition	Effects on Vision	Educational Considerations
With young children, eye exercises, occlusion, or patching of one eye or surgery may help.	• Reduced visual-motor abilities • Eye fatigue with close or detailed work	• May need adaptations for activities requiring visual-motor coordination
Aniridia A rare genetic disorder that causes absence of all or part of the iris, usually affecting both eyes It also causes the cornea to lose clarity over time by inhibiting the stem cells that "refresh" it with new, clear epithelial cells. Aniridia is often associated with amblyopia, cataracts, the development of closed angle glaucoma, and sometimes, displaced lens, under-developed retina, and nystagmus. Contact lenses with an artificial iris, tinted spectacles, or bioptic glasses may be prescribed. Iris and stem cell implant surgeries are now possible. Hereditary aniridia is associated with Gillespie syndrome. Sporatic aniridia may cause nephroblastoma (Wilms' tumor), and it is associated with WAGR syndrome.	• Decreased acuity • Photophobia • Large pupil that may be misshapen • Generally, respond very well to use of low vision devices • Corneal involvement: scattered light, increased glare, blurred vision, and further reduction of acuity • If cataracts develop: further reduction of visual acuity, blurred vision, and decreased color vision • Fovial involvement: loss of detailed (fine) vision • If glaucoma develops: fluctuating visual functioning, field loss, poor night vision, and decreased sensitivity to contrast	• Vision stimulation for infants to maximally develop the visual cortex • May need to use sunglasses, visors, or hats outdoors and indoors as well • Allow time for adjustment to lighting changes • Provide seating in the front of the classroom with back to windows • Reduced glare • Provide lighting from behind • Reduced or diffused lighting • Lamps with rheostats and adjustable arms • Magnification (e.g., handheld magnifier, electronic magnifier, screen enlargement software, telescope, etc.) • Use of a black chalkboard and bold chalk • If white board is used, bold black markers are recommended over other colors • Felt-tipped pens and tinted paper with bold lines • Place paper/worksheets on a dark/black background (e.g., blotter, construction or butcher paper, posterboard, etc.) • Provide copies of materials presented on the board. • Use black backgrounds and white sans-serif fonts in slide presentations

Anophthalmia
Absence of one or both eyeballs
 	
Causes can be heredity, injury, or secondary to disease. Prosthetic eyes are prescribed to preserve the health of the eyelids and surrounding tissues.
	• Monocular vision:
	  ◦ Reduced fields
	  ◦ Reduced depth perception
	• Blindness
		• May need visual efficiency training to develop scanning skills
		• Seating and presentation of materials should favor functional eye
		• May need tactile and auditory learning media

Eye Condition	Effects on Vision	Educational Considerations
Aphakia Absence of the lens Although it can be caused by injury, aphakia is usually a result of cataract surgery. Treatments include lens implants, contact lenses, and/or glasses.	• Inability to accommodate to varying focal distance • Inability to accommodate to lighting changes • Reduced depth perception • May have peripheral field distortions	• Support wearing of any prescribed lenses • High-contrast materials • Magnification (e.g., handheld magnifier, electronic magnifier, screen enlargement software, telescope, etc.) • Enlarged printed materials • Close viewing • Adequate lighting (e.g., lamps with rheostats and adjustable arms) • May need to use sunglasses, visors, or hats outdoors and indoors as well • Allow time for adjustment to lighting changes
Astigmatism Irregularity in the curvature of the cornea and/or lens, which prevents light rays from being properly focused on a single point on the retina Astigmatism commonly occurs with myopia and hyperopia. It also can be associated with albinism and keratoconus. Corrective lenses may be prescribed.	• Blurred vision at any distance (uncorrected) • Distorted vision • Tendency to squint to create a pinhole effect • Visual fatigue associated with close work	• High-contrast materials • Adequate lighting (e.g., lamps with rheostats and adjustable arms) • Frequent breaks from close/detailed work
Buphthalmos (infantile glaucoma) Enlarged eyeballs Caused by congenital glaucoma; hereditary; onset from birth to three years; can cause enlargement and increased depth of the anterior chamber, damage to the optic disc, and/or increased diameter and thinning of the cornea; requires surgery, and blindness occurs if left untreated.	• Photophobia • Reduced central acuity • Corneal opacity • Excessive tearing • Refractive error • Eye pain	• May need to use sunglasses, visors, or hats outdoors and indoors as well • Reduced or diffused lighting from behind • Sunglasses, visors, or hats may be worn indoors • Allow time for adjustment to lighting changes • High-contrast materials • Magnification (e.g., handheld magnifier, electronic magnifier, screen enlargement software, telescope, etc.) • Enlarged printed materials • Close viewing

(continued)

37

Eye Condition	Effects on Vision	Educational Considerations
Cataracts Opacity or cloudiness of the lens, which restricts passage of light to the retina; usually bilateral Opacity increases over time until "mature" cataracts can obscure the fundus and the pupil may appear white. Mature cataracts are usually removed surgically, requiring lens implants or contact lenses.	• Reduced visual acuity • Blurred vision • Reduced color discrimination • Photophobia • Associated with nystagmus • Visual ability fluctuates according to light • If cataracts are centrally located, near vision will be reduced • Increased sensitivity to glare	• Support of the wearing of any prescribed lenses • Magnification (e.g., handheld magnifier, electronic magnifier, screen enlargement software, telescope, etc.) • Enlarged printed materials • Close viewing • Support of eccentric viewing • May need to use sunglasses, visors, or hats outdoors and indoors as well • May need reduced or diffused lighting • Lighting from behind • May need lamps with rheostats and adjustable arms • Reduced glare
Chorioretinitis Posterior uveitis, or an inflammation of the choroid that spreads to the retina This can be caused by tuberculosis, histoplasmosis, or toxoplasmosis.	• Blurred vision • Photophobia • Distorted images • Central scotomas	• Support of eccentric viewing • Magnification (e.g., handheld magnifier, electronic magnifier, screen enlargement software, telescope, etc.) • Enlarged printed materials • Close viewing • Diffused, less intense light to enlarge the pupil • Telescope • May need to use tinted lenses, sunglasses, visors, or hats outdoors and indoors as well • High-contrast line markers or templates for reading, finding math problems, or locating other information
Coats' Disease (exudative retinitis or retinitis telangiectasia)	• Decreased central acuity • Loss of detail	• Avoid contact sports and other high risk activities to prevent retinal detachment

Eye Condition	Effects on Vision	Educational Considerations
A congenital, nonhereditary, and progressive disorder that is characterized by abnormal development of the blood vessels behind the retina Coats' occurs mostly in males. Symptoms typically appear in children around six to eight years old but they can appear in infancy. Coats' usually affects only one eye. Severity depends on the size and number of affected blood vessels. Leakage of blood and fluids cause retinal swelling and detachment. Cryotherapy and laser photocoagulation sometimes are used to stop the progression of blood vessel growth and leakage.	• Progressive central field loss • Reduced night vision • Loss of color vision • May develop strabismus • May have iritis • May have glaucoma • May develop cataracts • May be blind in one eye • Peripheral fields can be affected	• Seating and presentation of work should favor more functional eye • Visual efficiency training to develop scanning skills
Coloboma Hereditary birth defect that causes a notch or cleft in the pupil, iris, ciliary body, lens, retina, choroid, or optic nerve A "keyhole" pupil often occurs. It can be associated with refractive error, cataracts, nystagmus, strabismus, and glaucoma (later in life).	• Decreased acuity • Photophobia • Muscle imbalance • Restricted fields (if retina is affected) • Reduced depth perception	• High-contrast materials • Magnification (e.g., handheld magnifier, electronic magnifier, screen enlargement software, telescope, etc.) • Average to bright light • Reduced glare • May need to use sunglasses, visors, or hats outdoors and indoors as well (if iris is affected) • High-contrast line markers and templates may be helpful for reading, finding math problems, or locating other information
Color Deficiency (colorblindness) *See Achromatopsia*		
Cone Monochromacy *See Achromatopsia*		
Corneal Ulcer, Corneal Opacities, Corneal Scarring, Keratitis,	• Photophobia • Fracturing of light (like looking through broken glass)	• May need to use sunglasses, visors, or hats outdoors and indoors as well

(continued)

Eye Condition	Effects on Vision	Educational Considerations
Interstitial Keratitis An open sore or scarring on any part of the cornea It can be caused by bacteria, viruses (herpes), fungi, vitamin deficiency, injury, a hypersensitive reaction, diabetes, or severe dry eye. Superficial ulcers (called abrasions) usually heal quickly and completely, but deep ulcers cause growth of scar tissue or new blood vessels that impair vision. Corneal ulcers are usually quite painful, and other symptoms may include vision loss, squinting, and tearing (watering). Early diagnosis and treatment are crucial. With extensive scarring, a corneal transplant may be necessary. There are promising results with use of artificial corneas, which seem to be less likely to be rejected.	• Increased glare • Blurred vision • Reduced acuity • Blindness	• Reduced or diffused lighting • Sunglasses, visors, or hats may be worn indoors • Seating in front of room with back toward windows • Reduced glare • High-contrast materials • Diffused lighting from behind • Lights with rheostats and adjustable arms are helpful for close work • Magnification (e.g., handheld magnifier, electronic magnifier, screen enlargement software, telescope, etc.) • Enlarged printed materials • Frequent breaks from visual tasks • Support of eccentric viewing • May need auditory materials for longer reading assignments
Cortical Visual Impairment (CVI) A neurological visual disorder resulting from damage to the optic nerve and/or parts of the brain that process and interpret visual information (i.e., visual cortex)	• Fluctuation in visual functioning • Reduced visual fields • Photophobia • Fatigue has a negative impact on visual performance CVI is characterized by: • Specific color preference, especially for red and/or yellow • Attraction to movement • Visual field preference, especially for peripheral fields • Visual latency: delayed visual processing—in directing gaze, identification, recognition, and/or discrimination • Difficulties with discrimination and interpretation of complex visual information	• Use of movement to increase visual attention • Use of preferred color to increase visual attention • Present visual information in preferred visual field • Present visual information on a solid background (e.g., black or white cloth) • Use of bright, high-contrast materials • Increase line spacing and white space on a page of text and/or images to reduce visual clutter and complexity • Use high-contrast templates to reduce the amount of information seen at one time • Close viewing • Vision efficiency training • Frequent breaks from visual tasks

Eye Condition	Effects on Vision	Educational Considerations
	• Poor visual attention • Atypical visual responses (e.g., looking at something while appearing not to look) • May not look at an object and reach for it simultaneously (look first, then look away while reaching) • Better visual performance with familiar objects/settings • Unique visual features (i.e., light gazing and non-purposeful gaze)	• High illumination from behind • Sunglasses, visors, or hats may be worn indoors • Support use of one sense at a time • Reduce visual, auditory, and tactile distractions • Extra time to respond • Extra time to adjust to new environments • Use of consistent language • Use of color coding as visual cues for recognition • Use of consistent visual cues across settings
Diabetic Retinopathy Changes in the blood vessels of the retina, causing hemorrhaging in the retina and vitreous It is caused by juvenile or type 2 diabetes. It may lead to retinal detachment and blindness.	• Increased sensitivity to glare • Lack of accommodation • Floating obstructions in the vitreous • Fluctuating acuity • Diminished color vision • Reduced visual fields • Double vision • Blindness	• Adequate high quality lighting (e.g., lamps with rheostats and adjustable arms) • High-contrast materials • Magnification (e.g., handheld magnifier, electronic magnifier, screen enlargement software, telescope, etc.) • Large button/key technology may be helpful • Training in use of auditory materials may be needed due to loss of vision and tactile sensitivity • Training in use of speech recognition input software may be helpful • Precautions related to decreased sensitivity in hands and feet (e.g., burns, cuts, falls)
Diplopia Muscular defect that restricts the ability of the eyes to work together It causes double vision, as the image from one eye is imposed on the image from the other eye. Left untreated, this condition can develop into amblyopia. Corrective lenses may be prescribed.	• Visual confusion • Double vision • Dizziness • Suppression of the image from one eye, causing monocular vision • Eye fatigue • Blurring of print	• High-contrast materials • Reduced glare • Extended time to adjust to new situations • Frequent breaks from visual tasks

(continued)

Eye Condition	Effects on Vision	Educational Considerations
	• Headache • Loss of place in visual tasks	• High-contrast line markers or templates for reading, finding math problems, or locating other information • Familiarization with new environments
Dislocated Lens The lens is not in its natural position It is sometimes associated with coloboma, Marfan syndrome, or Weill-Marchesani syndrome. Also, it may be associated with diplopia or cataracts.	• Blurred vision • Double vision • Visual fatigue during close or detailed visual tasks	• Frequent breaks from visual tasks • High-contrast materials • Adequate lighting (e.g., lamps with rheostats and adjustable arms) • Reduced or diffused lighting • High-contrast line markers or templates for reading, finding math problems, or locating other information
Enucleation The anterior chamber or the entire eyeball is surgically removed from the orbit (eye socket) Prosthetic eyes or scleral shells are usually recommended.	• If one eye is removed, there is no depth perception • Monocular vision • Reduced visual field • Effects of any eye condition(s) of the remaining eye • Blindness • Affects visual-motor skills, especially reach and negotiation of steps and drop-offs	• Training in care of prostheses • Vision efficiency training (i.e., scanning) • Considerations related to the visual impairment of the remaining eye • Considerations related to possible changes in learning media
Esophoria, Esotropia, Exophoria, Exotropia *See Strabismus*		
Glaucoma An eye disease which causes increased pressure in the eye because of blockage in the normal flow of the fluid in the aqueous humor Causes include changes in the lens or uveal tract, trauma, reaction to a medication, surgical procedures, and heredity. Eye pain and headaches are associated with glaucoma.	• Fluctuating visual functioning • Field loss • Poor night vision • Photophobia • Difficulty reading • Difficulty seeing large objects presented at close range • Decreased sensitivity to contrast • Eye redness	• Support use of sunglasses, visors, or hats in bright sunlight and bright lighting indoors • Allow time for adjustment to lighting changes • Reduced glare • Adequate lighting (e.g., lamps with rheostats and adjustable arms) • High-contrast materials

Eye Condition	Effects on Vision	Educational Considerations
Prescription eye drops to reduce pressure must be used regularly, and surgery may be necessary. Untreated, glaucoma can lead to degeneration of the optic disk and blindness.	• Hazy cornea • Wide open pupil • Stress and fatigue have a negative effect on visual performance	• May benefit from magnification (e.g., handheld magnifier, electronic magnifier, screen enlargement software, telescope, etc.) • May need visual efficiency training to develop scanning skills • Frequent breaks from visual tasks • May need instruction in tactile learning and braille • Teachers must be alert to signs of pain and increased ocular pressure
Hemianopia (hemianopsia) Blindness or impaired vision in one half of the visual field in one or both eyes If both eyes are affected, vision loss may occur on the same side in both nasal fields, or in both temporal fields. Visual acuity in the unaffected field(s) remains unchanged. Hemianopia can be caused by stroke, other brain trauma, tumors, infection, or surgery.	• Field loss • May be unaware of missing visual information	• Visual efficiency training to develop scanning skills • Use markers at the beginning and/or ending of each line of text to facilitate reading the entire line
Histoplasmosis (presumed histoplasmosis syndrome [POHS]) This is a syndrome affecting the choroid and retina, which is characterized by peripheral atrophic chorioretinal scars, maculopathy, and atrophy or scarring adjacent to the optic disc. Vision loss is secondary to macular and choroidal neovascularization (CNV). POHS is most likely caused by a fungal infection acquired through exposure to spores in bird droppings and bat guano. Treatments include steroids to treat the initial infection, laser, anti-vascular endothelial growth factors, and photodynamic therapy. Prism lenses may be prescribed.	• Distorted vision • Blind spots • Macular damage or central scotomas cause "patchy" fields, central vision loss, and reduced color vision • Peripheral damage causes loss of night vision	• Lamps with rheostats and adjustable arms • High-contrast line markers or templates for reading, finding math problems, or locating other information *Central damage:* • Eccentric viewing • Magnification to enlarge an image beyond the scotoma • Enlarged printed materials • Close viewing • Adapted color-dependent activities • Alternate methods for matching clothing

(continued)

Eye Condition	Effects on Vision	Educational Considerations
		• Diffused, less intense light to enlarge the pupil so that more area can be viewed
		• Closed-circuit television (CCTV) with reversible foreground and background (white on black)
		Peripheral damage:
		• High illumination
		• NOIR lenses or overlay filters may be helpful
		• CCTV for maximum contrast
		• Night vision devices (e.g., Streamlight flashlights, Third Generation Night Vision Devices, etc.)
		• Visual efficiency training in organized search (grid) patterns
		• May need to be seated farther away from the front to see more of the viewing area (e.g., board, screen, chart, etc.)
Hyperopia (farsightedness) A refractive error in which the focal point for light rays is behind the retina It is caused by the eyeball being too short from front to back. Corrective lenses are usually prescribed.	• Distance acuity is better than near acuity • Uncorrected, close visual tasks may cause headache, nausea, dizziness, and eye rubbing	• Support use of prescription lenses for close visual tasks • Magnification for near tasks (e.g., handheld magnifier, electronic magnifier, screen enlargement software) • Frequent breaks from close visual tasks • Alternate near and distance visual tasks
Hyperphoria, Hypertropia, Hypophoria, Hypotropia *See Strabismus*		
Hypoplasia *See Optic Atrophy*		
Keratitis *See Corneal Ulcer*		
Keratoconus (KC) Degenerative disorder in which the cornea thins and takes on a conical shape	• Slightly blurred vision in early stages, increasing as KC progresses	• Avoid activities that could cause corneal damage, such as contact sports and swimming in heavily chlorinated water

Eye Condition	Effects on Vision	Educational Considerations
Keratoconus is often bilateral but not symmetrical, so vision may be significantly better in one eye than the other. Vision deteriorates at varying rates (sometimes quite rapidly), and plateaus of stable vision can occur. Although it seems to be hereditary, keratoconus is typically diagnosed in adolescence. It is sometimes associated with retinitis pigmentosa, Down syndrome, Marfan syndrome, and aniridia. Treatments include prescription lenses and various surgeries: intrastromal corneal ring segments, cross-linking, mini asymmetrical radial keratotomy, and corneal transplants. There are promising results in transplants with use of artificial corneas, which seem to be less likely to be rejected.	• Distortion of entire visual field, which worsens in low light • Decreased visual acuity, especially distance vision • Irregular astigmatism (parts of the field are in focus, and parts are out of focus) • Increased sensitivity to glare • Decreased night vision • Multiple images • Flaring of images • Streaking • Stationary objects/lights may appear to move • May develop photophobia • Cornea can rupture • Can lead to blindness	• Reduced glare • Diffused lighting • Lamps with rheostats and adjustable arms • High-contrast materials • High-contrast line markers or templates for reading, finding math problems, or locating other information • Magnification (e.g., handheld magnifier, electronic magnifier, screen enlargement software, telescope, etc.)
Leber's Congenital Amaurosis (LCA) A rare hereditary disorder that leads to degeneration of the macula LCA becomes evident within the first few months of life. Progressive central field loss can occur, although vision is generally stable. LCA is a subset of retinitis pigmentosa with at least 13 described types that are distinguished by genetic cause, patterns of vision loss, and associated eye conditions. Nystagmus, keratoconus, photophobia, extreme hyperopia, and sluggish (or absent) pupillary response to light are often present with LCA. Excessive rubbing of eyes (also poking or pressing) is a characteristic behavior.	• Decreased acuity • Reduced night vision • Progressive central field loss • Loss of color vision • Loss of detail • Peripheral fields can be affected	• May need visual efficiency training to develop scanning skills • Support of eccentric viewing • Magnification (e.g., handheld magnifier, electronic magnifier, screen enlargement software, telescope, etc.) • High-contrast materials • High-contrast line markers or templates for reading, finding math problems, or locating other information • Enlarged printed materials • Close viewing • Adapted color-dependent activities • Alternate methods for matching clothing • Lamps with rheostats and adjustable arms • Support use of sunglasses, visors, or hats in bright sunlight

(continued)

Eye Condition	Effects on Vision	Educational Considerations
		• Seat in the front of the room with windows behind back • May need frequent breaks from visual tasks • May need instruction in use of auditory materials • May need instruction in tactile learning and braille

Leber's Hereditary Optic Neuropathy (LHON) (Leber's Optic Atrophy)
 	
It is a rare hereditary disease caused by a mitochondrial mutation and passed on by the mother. It is characterized by rapidly progressive and severe optic nerve degeneration (atrophy).
 	
It occurs in young men and, rarely, young women. Onset is usually in young adulthood. Most often, there is acute vision loss in one eye and then, a few weeks or months later, in the other eye, but vision loss sometimes occurs in both eyes simultaneously. It can include other types of central nervous system involvement.
	• Reduced central acuity
	• Vision may be blurred
	• Fluctuating visual performance
	• Color vision may be impaired
	• Visual perception may be impaired
		• High illumination
		• High contrast materials
		• Enlarged printed materials
		• Magnification (e.g., handheld magnifier, electronic magnifier, screen enlargement software, telescope, etc.)
		• Avoid visual clutter:
		  ◦ Present visual information in isolation
		  ◦ Avoid busy backgrounds
		• Avoid wearing patterned clothing when presenting visual information

Macular Degeneration (macular disease, congenital macular disease, and age-related macular degeneration) Progressive (degenerating) damage to the central part of the retinal cones The dry form involves yellow deposits (cellular debris) on the macula and eventually, thinning of cells in the macula, which leads to tissue death. In the wet form, there is abnormal growth of blood vessels in the choroid underneath the macula. These blood vessels leak blood and fluid into the retina, causing distortion, blind spots, loss	• Reduced central acuity • Peripheral vision is not affected • Central scotomas • Distorted vision • Blurred vision • Decreased color vision • Slow recovery from changes in light • Loss of contrast sensitivity • Visual fatigue	• Support of eccentric viewing • Support use of sunglasses, hats, or visors in bright sunlight • Allow time for adjustment to lighting changes • Adequate lighting (e.g., lamps with rheostats and adjustable arms) • Diffused lighting may allow the pupil to enlarge so that more area can be viewed • Close viewing • Magnification (e.g., handheld magnifier, electronic magnifier with light text on dark background, screen enlargement software, telescope for distance viewing, etc.)

Eye Condition	Effects on Vision	Educational Considerations
of central vision, retinal scarring, and risk of retinal detachment. Macular degeneration is the leading cause of blindness in people over 60, but it also can occur in children below age 7. Factors contributing to the development of the disease include heredity, diabetes, head injury, nutritional deficits, high cholesterol, smoking, and exposure to sunlight without eye protection. There is no cure, but treatment can slow progress of the disease. Treatments include nutritional supplements, laser therapy, and medication.		• Reduced glare • High-contrast materials • High-contrast line markers or templates for reading, finding math problems, or locating other information • Seating in front with back to window • Adapted color-dependent activities • Alternate methods for matching clothing • Frequent breaks from visual tasks • Avoid standing in front of a light source when speaking to the student
Microphthalmia (microphthalmos, nanophthalmia, nanophthalmos) A hereditary, developmental disorder that causes one or both eyes to be abnormally small It may occur with other congenital abnormalities such as club foot, additional fingers or toes, webbed digits, polycystic kidneys, and cystic liver. This disorder can be associated with Patau syndrome, triploid syndrome, or Wolf-Hirschhorn syndrome. It may result in cataracts, glaucoma, aniridia, and coloboma.	• Decreased visual acuity • Photophobia • May have fluctuating visual abilities	• High contrast • Reduced glare • Average to bright light • May need magnification (e.g., handheld magnifier, electronic magnifier, screen enlargement software, telescope, etc.) • Expectations may need to be adjusted due to the frustration related to fluctuating visual abilities • Frequent breaks from visual tasks • Instruction in strategies for stress reduction and dealing with frustration related to fluctuating visual abilities
Muscle Imbalance *See Strabismus and Amblyopia*		
Myopia (simple and degenerative myopia, nearsightedness) A refractive error in which the image of a distant object is formed in front of the retina and cannot be seen distinctly; eyeball is elongated from front to back	• Reduced distance acuity • Near vision is better than distance vision • May squint and frown when trying to see at a distance	• High illumination • Reduced glare • May need to be seated closer to the front in order to see written information, videos, and demonstrations

(continued)

47

Eye Condition	Effects on Vision	Educational Considerations
Degenerative myopia is progressive, causing increasingly severe nearsightedness, so that visual acuity often cannot be corrected to normal with lenses. It can lead to retinal detachment, choroidal hemorrhages, reduced central vision, opacities in the vitreous, macular swelling, and cataracts. Treatments include corrective lenses and LASIK surgery.		• If myopia is progressive, take precautions to protect the retina
Nystagmus Involuntary eye movements, which can be horizontal, vertical, circular, or mixed Causes can be heredity, neurological disorders, toxicity, pharmaceutical drugs, alcohol, inner ear disturbance, or unknown. Nystagmus can be increased by stress, spinning, and rhythmic movements.	• Inability to maintain steady fixation • Reduced visual acuity • Visual fatigue • Vertigo (rare) • Stripes and other patterns may increase the rate of the nystagmus	• Shifting gaze or tilting the head may help to find the null point at which the nystagmus slows • Frequent breaks from close visual tasks • Vary visual tasks • Adequate lighting • Good contrast • Line markers, rulers, typoscopes, and other templates may be helpful for keeping the place on a page • Instruction in stress reduction strategies
Optic Atrophy (optic nerve atrophy) Hereditary or acquired damage to the optic nerve that limits or stops transmission of visual information from the eye to the brain It is evidenced by a pale optic disc and reduced pupillary response. Acquired optic atrophy can be caused by disease, pressure on the optic nerve, trauma, glaucoma, or toxicity. Type 1 optic atrophy is progressive.	• Fluctuating visual performance • Color vision may be reduced • Night vision may be reduced • Visual perception may be impaired • May have photophobia	• Visual stimulation in infancy and early childhood • Low vision training in early childhood to help the child interpret visual information • Supplement visual information with tactile and auditory information • High illumination *If photophobia is present:* • May need to use sunglasses, visors, or hats outdoors and indoors as well • Provide adequate lighting through use of lamps with rheostats and adjustable arms • High contrast • Enlarged print • May need magnification (e.g., handheld magnifier, electronic magnifier, screen enlargement software, telescope, etc.)

Eye Condition	Effects on Vision	Educational Considerations
		• Avoid visual clutter:
		○ Present visual information in isolation
		○ Avoid busy backgrounds
		○ Avoid wearing patterned clothing when presenting visual information
		• May need adapted color-dependent activities
		• May need alternate methods for matching clothing
		• May need instruction in tactile learning and braille

Optic Nerve Hypoplasia (ONH)
 	
ONH and septo-optic dysplasia (SOD) are related disorders of early brain development. ONH is a congenital, nonprogressive condition in which the optic nerve is under-developed and small.
 	
It may affect one or both eyes, and when both are affected, side-to-side nystagmus is frequently present. During the first few years of life, vision may improve as the brain continues to develop. The incidence of strabismus is increased with ONH. It is one of the three defining characteristics of septo-optic dysplasia, which is also called de Morsier syndrome. Learning disability, autism, cerebral palsy, and intellectual developmental delays can occur with ONH and SOD. Possible causes include young maternal age, genetic mutation, fetal alcohol syndrome, trauma, and viral infection.
	• May have decreased visual acuity
	• May have better acuity in one eye than in the other
	• May have nystagmus
	• May have strabismus
	• May have variable field restrictions
	• Visual perception may be impaired
		• High illumination
		• High contrast materials
		• Enlarged printed materials
		• May need magnification (e.g., handheld magnifier, electronic magnifier, screen enlargement software, telescope, etc.)
		• Avoid visual clutter:
		   ○ Present visual information in isolation
		   ○ Avoid busy backgrounds
		   ○ Avoid wearing patterned clothing when presenting visual information
		• Provide opportunities to confirm or clarify visual information through tactile exploration
		• May benefit from verbal descriptions to help make sense of visual information
		• May need adapted color-dependent activities
		• May need alternate methods for matching clothing
		• May need instruction in tactile learning and braille

(continued)

Eye Condition	Effects on Vision	Educational Considerations
Peters Anomaly A congenital, genetic disorder that involves clouding (opacity) and thinning of the cornea It is caused by abnormal development of the front third of the eye (anterior segment), and central opacities are most common. The iris may or may not be attached to the cornea (type 1), and cataracts and other lens abnormalities may be present (type 2). It is very common for amblyopia and glaucoma to develop. This condition can be associated with Peters plus syndrome.	• Blurred vision • Decreased central acuity • May have scotomas in peripheral fields • Photophobia • Increased sensitivity to glare • Reduced color discrimination • Visual ability fluctuates according to lighting • May have reduced near vision	• Support of eccentric viewing • May need visual efficiency training to develop scanning skills • May need to use sunglasses, visors, or hats outdoors and indoors as well • Adequate lighting from behind using lamps with rheostats and adjustable arms • Reduced glare • Seat with back to windows • Magnification (e.g., handheld magnifier, electronic magnifier, screen enlargement software, telescope, etc.) • Enlarged printed materials • High-contrast materials • High-contrast line markers or templates for reading, finding math problems, or locating other information • Close viewing • May need adapted color-dependent activities • May need alternate methods for matching clothing • Frequent breaks from visual tasks
Photophobia Abnormal sensitivity to light (any type) It is usually associated with an eye disease or disorder (e.g., iritis, ocular albinism, aphakia, aniridia, dislocated lens, cataracts, glaucoma, etc.). However, many people experience mild photophobia that is unrelated to another eye condition. Other causes include corneal inflammation, some medications, and eye injuries. Severe photophobia can be quite painful, even in relatively dim light.	• Squinting • Closing the eyes • Eye pain • Headaches • Eye fatigue	• May need to use sunglasses, visors, or hats outdoors and indoors as well • Reduced or diffused lighting • Provide lighting from behind • Use of shielded lamps with rheostats and adjustable arms • Reduced glare • May benefit from use of NOIR sunglasses and/or filters (colored overlays) when reading • May need breaks from visual tasks or rest periods in a darkened area

Eye Condition	Effects on Vision	Educational Considerations
Phthisis Bulbi Abnormally low intraocular pressure, which can cause shrinkage of the eye It may occur as a complication of eye surgery, or it can be caused by eye diseases, serious and long-term inflammation, or injury. Low pressure damages the macula. The tissues inside the eye deteriorate, become disorganized, and scar tissue is formed. In some cases, the eye can become completely nonfunctional. Sometimes a scleral shell prosthesis is prescribed for proper lid function, eyelash direction, healthy tearing, protection of the cornea, and aesthetics.	• Reduced central acuity • Reduced color vision • Blindness	• Average or bright light • Reduced glare • May need high contrast materials • May need magnification (e.g., handheld magnifier, electronic magnifier, screen enlargement software, telescope, etc.) • May benefit from use of high-contrast line markers or templates for reading, finding math problems, or locating other information • May need some materials presented via auditory modes • May need instruction in tactile learning and braille
Presbyopia The gradual loss of flexibility of the lens that occurs with age It results in inability of the eye to focus at near distance. Presbyopia generally begins to noticeably affect visual functioning around age 40, and people often need prescription lenses by age 45. Options for prescription lenses include glasses for near-distance tasks, bifocals, transition lenses, and monovision contact lenses. Vision also can be corrected by reshaping the cornea using lasers (LASIK), radio waves (conductive keratoplasty [CK]), or gas bubbles (IntraCor). Other surgical treatments include artificial lens implants, corneal inlays, and corneal overlays.	• Blurred vision at normal reading distance • Headaches from doing close visual tasks • Further compromises the vision of aging adults who have existing visual impairments	• Adequate lighting • High contrast materials • Frequent breaks from near-distance visual tasks
Ptosis Drooping (sagging) of the eyelid It may affect upper and/or lower lids and one or both eyes. Ptosis is usually due to weakness of the	• Severe ptosis obscures the upper visual field • Long-term reduction of visual field can cause amblyopia	• May need visual efficiency training to develop scanning skills • Ensure access to information that is elevated (bulletin boards, black/white boards, video screens, etc.)

(continued)

Eye Condition	Effects on Vision	Educational Considerations
muscles that control the eyelids, damage to the nerves that control these muscles, or very loose skin of the upper eyelids. Commonly associated with the aging process, ptosis also can be congenital and hereditary, or caused by injury or disease. A ptosis crutch may be prescribed to elevate the eyelid. Medications may be prescribed for those who have myasthenia gravis. Children with severe ptosis need eyelid lift surgery early in life to ensure normal visual development and to prevent amblyopia.		
Retinal Detachment An emergency situation in which parts of the retina pull away from the underlying tissue that nourishes it and from the supporting structure of the eye Detachments can be repaired if treated within 24–72 hours, but detached parts deteriorate rapidly. Any detachment endangers the entire retina. Detachments are caused by retinal tears, fluid under the retina, or shrinkage of the vitreous. These conditions may be due to injury, inflammatory eye disorders, advanced diabetes, degenerative myopia, and other retinal disorders.	• Field loss • Blind spots (scotomas) • Blurred vision • Possible loss of central vision • May develop myopia and/or strabismus	• Avoid contact sports and other high risk physical activity to prevent retinal detachment • Magnification (e.g., handheld magnifier, electronic magnifier, screen enlargement software, telescope, etc.) • May need visual efficiency training to develop scanning skills • Support of eccentric viewing • High illumination • Reduced glare • High-contrast line markers or templates for reading, finding math problems, or locating other information • Seating in front with back to window • Adapted color-dependent activities • Alternate methods for matching clothing • Frequent breaks from visual tasks
Retinal Dysplasia A rare, hereditary disorder resulting in abnormal development or growth of the retina and characterized by retinal folds, overgrowth of cells, and rosettes of retinal tissue	• Field loss • Blind spots (scotomas) • Blurred vision	• Nighttime orientation and mobility evaluation • Magnification (e.g., handheld magnifier, electronic magnifier, screen enlargement software, telescope, etc.)

Eye Condition	Effects on Vision	Educational Considerations
It can be associated with Meckel syndrome.	• Possible loss of central vision • Reduced visual functioning at night or in dimly lit places	• Visual efficiency training to develop scanning skills • Support of eccentric viewing • Lamps with rheostats and adjustable arms • Reduced glare • High-contrast line markers or templates for reading, finding math problems, or locating other information • Adapted color-dependent activities • Alternate methods for matching clothing • Frequent breaks from visual tasks
Retinitis Pigmentosa (RP) A group of hereditary disorders causing degeneration of the retina It is characterized by progressive loss of vision and reduction of visual fields, usually from the periphery inward. However, in some cases, central vision is affected first. RP may be associated with Usher syndrome, Leber's congenital amaurosis, and Laurence-Moon-Bardet-Biedl and Bassen-Kornzweig syndromes.	• Loss of peripheral vision • Night blindness • Tunnel vision • Decreased acuity • Decreased depth perception • Blind spots (scotomas due to retinal scarring • Photophobia • May develop cataracts • May become totally blind • May be associated with myopia, vitreous opacities, cataracts, and keratoconus	• Avoid contact sports and other high risk physical activity to prevent retinal detachment • High illumination • Reduced glare • NOIR lenses or overlay filters may be helpful • Video magnifier for maximum contrast • Night vision devices (e.g., Streamlight flashlights, Third Generation Night Vision Devices, etc.) • Visual efficiency training in organized search (grid) patterns • Orientation and mobility evaluation at night and in dimly lit places • For central vision loss: magnification (e.g., handheld magnifier, electronic magnifier, screen enlargement software, telescope, etc.) • For peripheral field loss: increase viewing distance to see more area

(continued)

Eye Condition	Effects on Vision	Educational Considerations
Retinoblastoma A rare type of cancer in which malignant cells grow in the retina It usually develops in early childhood. The majority of children who develop this cancer have mutations only in eye cells (non-germinal). They will not pass on the mutation, and usually, retinoblastoma develops only in one eye. When the mutation occurs in all body cells (germinal retinoblastoma), the disease is hereditary. These children are more likely to develop retinoblastoma in both eyes, pineal brain tumors (trilateral retinoblastoma), and other forms of cancer anywhere in the body. Current treatments include surgery, radiation, and chemotherapy. Retinoblastoma can become life threatening if the tumor extends beyond the eye, so enucleation is frequently necessary.	• Strabismus is one of the first signs of retinoblastoma • Restricted fields due to removal of tumors • Blind spots (scotomas) due to removal of small tumors • With monocular vision, there is no depth perception and visual field is restricted • Blindness • Medications can negatively affect residual vision	• Avoid contact sports and other high risk physical activity to prevent retinal detachment • Orientation and mobility evaluation at night and in dimly lit places recommended • May need visual efficiency training to develop scanning skills • Support of eccentric viewing • May need magnification (e.g., handheld magnifier, electronic magnifier, screen enlargement software, telescope, etc.) • May benefit from access to auditory materials • May require instruction in tactile learning and braille
Retinopathy of Prematurity (ROP) (retrolental fibroplasia) Incomplete development of the blood vessels of the retina It occurs in premature infants. The vessels also may grow abnormally from the retina into the back of the eye. They may bleed into the eye, scar tissue may develop, and retinal detachment may occur. The major risk factors are degree of prematurity and low birth weight. There are five stages of ROP, ranging from mildly abnormal blood vessel growth in stage one to retinal detachment in stage five. ROP may be associated with other issues caused by incomplete development. Lasers or freezing (photocoagulation and cryotherapy) may be used to stop the abnormal blood vessels from continuing to grow. Also, surgery may be done to re-attach the retina.	• Retinal scarring • Decreased visual acuity • Severe myopia • Field loss • Partial or complete retinal detachment • Blind spots (scotomas) • Strabismus • Total blindness • May develop glaucoma	• Early intervention and sensory stimulation • Avoid contact sports and other high risk physical activity to prevent retinal detachment • Nighttime orientation and mobility evaluation • May need visual efficiency training to develop scanning skills • Visual efficiency training in organized search (grid) patterns • Adequate to high illumination (e.g., lamps with rheostats and adjustable arms) • Reduced glare • High-contrast line markers or templates for reading, finding math problems, or locating other information

Eye Condition	Effects on Vision	Educational Considerations
		• Frequent breaks from visual tasks
		• May benefit from access to auditory materials
		• May need instruction in tactile learning and braille
		• May benefit from magnification (e.g., handheld magnifier, electronic magnifier, screen enlargement software, telescope, etc.)
		• Reduced glare
		• Night vision devices (e.g., Streamlight flashlights, Third Generation Night Vision Devices, etc.)
		• Balance need for a larger viewing area with the need for magnification
		• Balance need for close viewing against the need for increased distance and a larger portion of the text/pictures
		• Adapted color-dependent activities
		• Alternate methods for matching clothing
		• Support of eccentric viewing
Retinoschisis A degenerative disorder in which the retina splits into two separate layers, resulting in progressive loss of vision, beginning in the fields that correspond to the areas where the retina splits The hereditary form (juvenile X-linked retinoschisis) affects mostly boys and young men. The more common form can affect both men and women, and it usually is acquired in middle age or older (senile retinoschisis). Both forms may be associated with cysts (sack-like blisters) that form a spoke-like pattern in the retina. Retinal detachments can occur, and if	• Strabismus • Nystagmus • Peripheral field loss • Reduced visual acuity • Reduced color discrimination • Blind spots (scotomas) • Blindness	• Avoid contact sports and other high risk physical activity to prevent retinal detachment • May need visual efficiency training to develop scanning skills • Central field loss • Adequate lighting (e.g., lamps with rheostats and adjustable arms) • Reduced glare • High-contrast line markers or templates for reading, finding math problems, or locating other information • Frequent breaks from visual tasks • May benefit from access to auditory materials

(continued)

Eye Condition	Effects on Vision	Educational Considerations
detected early, they sometimes can be repaired with surgery. Prismatic glasses may be prescribed to increase field of vision.		• May need instruction in tactile learning and braille *For central vision loss:* • Nighttime orientation and mobility evaluation • Magnification (e.g., handheld lighted magnifier, electronic magnifier, screen enlargement software, telescope, etc.) • High illumination • Night vision devices (e.g., Streamlight flashlights, Third Generation Night Vision Devices, etc.) • Adapted color-dependent activities • Alternate methods for matching clothing *For peripheral field loss:* • Increase viewing distance to see more area • Support of eccentric viewing • Balance need for a larger viewing area with the need for magnification
Rod Achromacy *See Achromatopsia*		
Scotoma A portion of the visual field that is blind or partially blind and surrounded by relatively normal vision, depending on the presence of other eye conditions Scotomas can occur in any part of the visual field. They can be caused by retinal disorders, tumors, stroke, or traumatic brain injury.	• May affect central or peripheral fields • Reduced acuity • May cause loss of detail • May cause photophobia • May cause reduced color vision	• Visual efficiency training to develop scanning skills • Support of eccentric viewing • Seating and presentation of work should favor more functional eye • May need to use sunglasses, visors, or hats outdoors and indoors as well • Reduced glare • May need lighting from behind using adjustable lamps with rheostats and adjustable arms

Eye Condition	Effects on Vision	Educational Considerations
		• Magnification (e.g., handheld magnifier, electronic magnifier, screen enlargement software, telescope, etc.) • May benefit from enlarged printed materials • May benefit from close viewing • High-contrast materials • High-contrast line markers or templates for reading, finding math problems, or locating other information • May need adapted color-dependent activities • May need alternate methods for matching clothing
Septo-Optic Dysplasia *See Optic Nerve Hypoplasia*		
Strabismus (muscle imbalance) Abnormal alignment of the eyes; an inability to look at the same point in space with both eyes at the same time It can be caused by a defect in the extra-ocular muscles or in the part of the brain that controls eye movement. It can be hereditary, and it may be associated with brain tumors, cerebral palsy, Down syndrome, extreme farsightedness, cataracts, or having much better vision in one eye than in the other. Strabismus includes: • phorias: muscle imbalances that are controlled by the brain's efforts toward binocular vision. Not always present, they tend to manifest when the person is tired. • tropias: observable deviations that the brain cannot resolve. They are always present.	• Impaired ability to achieve binocular vision • Decreased depth perception • Affects eye-hand coordination • Difficulty fixating • May have difficulty scanning, tracking, and tracing • Difficulty following fast-moving objects • Difficulty making eye contact	• Orientation and mobility evaluation recommended, specifically for negotiation of drop-offs and stairs in unfamiliar places • Vision efficiency training in scanning, tracking, and tracing

(continued)

Eye Condition	Effects on Vision	Educational Considerations
• eso: turned inward/nasal (esophoria and esotropia) • exo: turned outward/temporal (exophoria and exotropia) • hyper: turned upward (hyperphoria and hypertropia) • hypo: turned downward (hypophoria and hypotropia) Treatments can be effective for young children: eye exercises, occlusion of the better eye, medications, and surgery. Prismatic glasses may be prescribed to increase field of vision.		

Toxoplasmosis
 	
Congenital or acquired inflammation of the retina and choroid (retinochoroiditis), which can cause retinal scarring
 	
Toxoplasmosis is caused by infection with the toxoplasma parasite found in animal feces and unpasteurized milk. Unborn babies are most vulnerable to the infection, and it can cause damage to the brain, eyes, or other organs. Treatments include anti-inflammatory medications, photocoagulation (laser) therapy, and cryotherapy (freezing).
	• Scotomas
	• Peripheral field loss
	• Central field loss
	  ○ Loss of visual acuity
	  ○ Decreased color vision
	  ○ Photophobia
	• Increased sensitivity to glare
		• Visual efficiency training to develop scanning and eccentric viewing skills
		• Reduced glare
		• May need lighting from behind using adjustable lamps with rheostats and adjustable arms
		• Magnification (e.g., microscopic lenses, electronic magnifier, screen enlargement software, telescope, etc.)
		• May benefit from enlarged printed materials
		• May benefit from close viewing
		• High-contrast materials
		• High-contrast line markers or templates for reading, finding math problems, or locating other information
		• May need adapted color-dependent activities
		• May need alternate methods for matching clothing

Trachoma A contagious bacterial infection of the eyes and eyelids, causing scarring and buckling of the eyelids	• Photophobia • Fracturing or scattering of light (as in looking through a broken windshield)	• Sunglasses, visors, or hats outdoors, and indoors as well • Reduced or diffused lighting from behind (e.g., lamps with rheostats and adjustable arms)

Eye Condition	Effects on Vision	Educational Considerations
This causes the eyelashes to turn under, which leads to corneal scarring. Repeated and prolonged infection causes permanent visual impairment and blindness. Trachoma is spread through direct contact with secretions from the eyes, eyelids, or nose of an infected person. It is the leading cause of preventable blindness worldwide.	• Increased glare • Blurred vision • Reduced acuity	• Front row seating with back toward windows • Reduced glare • High-contrast materials • Magnification (e.g., handheld magnifier, electronic magnifier, screen enlargement software, telescope, etc.) • Enlarged printed materials • Frequent breaks from visual tasks • Support of eccentric viewing • Auditory materials for long reading assignments • May need instruction in tactile learning and braille
Uveitis Inflammation of the uveal tract (middle layer of the eye), which consists of the iris, choroid, and ciliary body The most common form affects the iris, and it may be called anterior uveitis or iritis. The cause may be unknown. Known causes include autoimmune disorders, infection, toxoplasmosis, tuberculosis, and histoplasmosis. Complications can cause glaucoma and damage to the retina or cornea, leading to permanent vision loss.	• Photophobia • Blurred vision • Floaters • Decreased acuity • Glaucoma • Retinal scarring • Corneal damage	• High-contrast materials • Reduced glare • Allow additional time for adjustment to new visual conditions • Use of lamps with rheostats and adjustable arms • May need visual efficiency training to develop scanning and eccentric viewing skills
Wilms' Tumor (nephroblastoma) Rare abnormalities of the eye, especially aniridia, related to a malignancy of the kidneys Although the cause is sometimes unknown, this form of cancer can be caused by genetic changes, which also can be hereditary. Pinhole contact lenses and sunglasses may be prescribed.	• Decreased acuity, further reduced by other conditions • Photophobia • Large pupil (misshapen) • With corneal involvement: fractured light, increased glare, blurred vision • With cataracts: blurred vision, decreased color vision	• Vision stimulation for infants to develop the visual cortex • Sunglasses, tinted contact lenses, visors, or hats in bright light outdoors and indoors • Allow time for adjustment to lighting changes • Front row seating with back to windows

(continued)

(Appendix 1A continued)

Eye Condition	Effects on Vision	Educational Considerations
	• Fovial involvement: loss of detail vision • With glaucoma: fluctuating visual functioning, field loss, poor night vision, decreased sensitivity to contrast • May have nystagmus • May have ptosis	• Reduced glare • Provide reduced or diffused lighting from behind • Lamps with rheostats and adjustable arms • Magnification (e.g., handheld magnifier, electronic magnifier, screen enlargement software, telescope, etc.) • Use a blackboard and bold chalk • Use of bold, black markers on a white board • Felt-tipped pens and tinted paper with bold lines • Use of dark/black background • Provide copies of materials presented on the board

Ocular Syndromes

Name	Main Characteristics
Bassen-Kornzweig syndrome	An inherited disorder in which fat is not properly used, causing degeneration of the light sensitive cells in the periphery of the retina, night blindness, tunnel vision, decreased acuity, and photophobia. It may lead to total blindness and damage to the central nervous system. It is a rare form of retinitis pigmentosa. Can be reversed in the early stages with large doses of vitamin A.
Batten disease (or Batten-Mayou or Spielmeyer-Vogt-Sjogren-Batten disease)	Pigmentary retinopathy, involving the macula most severely, causes loss of central vision, optic atrophy, and seizures. Occurs between ages 5 and 10.
CHARGE syndrome	Colobomas ranging from an isolated iris coloboma with no related visual impairment to clinical anophthalmos. Retinal coloboma is most common. It may also include heart disease, absence of the opening between the nasal cavity and the back of the throat, retarded growth and development, and central nervous system abnormalities.
Coats' disease	A malformation of the retinal blood vessels, causing dilations and leakage in the peripheral retina leading to retinal detachment. It usually occurs in male children and young adults.
Cri-du-chat syndrome	A chromosomal defect that can cause intellectual disability, microcephaly, hypotonia, strabismus, myopia, glaucoma, microphthalmos, coloboma, optic atrophy, and corneal opacity.
Crouzon syndrome	A rare hereditary deformity (autosomal dominant) causing exophthalmos, enlargement of the nasal bones, abnormal increase in space between the eyes, optic atrophy, strabismus, and nystagmus.
De Grouchy syndrome	A chromosomal defect that causes ptosis, strabismus, myopia, glaucoma, microphthalmos, coloboma, optic atrophy, and corneal opacity as well as intellectual disability, microcephaly, and midface hypoplasia.
de Morsier syndrome	A congenital brain malformation (absence of the septum pellucidum) characterized by shortness of stature, nystagmus, and optic nerve hypoplasia.
Down syndrome	A chromosomal abnormality causing high refractive errors, strabismus, nystagmus, esotropia, cataracts, keratoconus, moderate to severe developmental delays, possible cardiac abnormalities, and distinct physical characteristics.

Source: Adapted with permission from Levack, N., Stone, G., & Bishop, V. (1994). *Low vision: A resource guide with adaptations for students with visual impairments* (2nd ed.). Austin: Texas School for the Blind and Visually Impaired.

(continued)

Name	Main Characteristics
Duane syndrome	A genetic (usually autosomal recessive) unilateral or bilateral eye muscle problem in the ability to move the eye(s) horizontally. The visual impairment is seldom severe.
Edwards syndrome	A chromosomal abnormality (autosomal dominant) causing ptosis, corneal opacities, microphthalmos, glaucoma, uveal colobomas, hypopigmentation of the skin and hair, decreased growth, intellectual disability, congenital heart disease, and cleft lip and palate. Most children die within the first year.
Galactosemia	An autosomal recessive deficiency of the enzyme that processes galactose, causing sugar cataracts, liver and spleen enlargement, and developmental delays. Can be reversed if treated with a galactose-free diet.
Goldmann-Favre syndrome	A rare disorder causing peripheral retinoschisis.
Hallermann-Streiff syndrome	A congenital condition that causes mandibular-hypoplasia, feeding problems, and cataracts that mature rapidly in infancy.
Hermansky-Pudlak syndrome	An autosomal recessive form of albinism.
Hurler's syndrome	An inherited disorder (autosomal recessive) in which carbohydrates are not digested properly. Causes skeletal deformities, especially in the face, dwarfism, enlarged spleen and liver, and progressive physical and mental deterioration. The corneas show a diffuse haziness that progress to a white opacity. Other signs include slight ptosis, larger thickened eyelids, strabismus (esotropia), and glaucoma. Death usually occurs before 10 years of age.
Laurence-Moon-Bardet-Biedl syndrome	An autosomal recessive disorder characterized by degeneration of the light sensitive cells in the periphery of the retina causing night blindness, tunnel vision, decreased acuity, and photophobia. Other conditions include obesity, hypogonadism, developmental delays, spastic paraplegia, and renal disorders.
Lowe syndrome	An X-linked recessive disorder causing severe eye involvement including cataracts, microphakia, and congenital glaucoma, as well as intellectual and physical disability with hypotonia and usually early death.
Marfan syndrome	An autosomal dominant connective tissue disease that causes dislocated lens, strabismus, severe refractive errors, cataracts, secondary glaucoma, uveal colobomas, retinal detachments, and multiple pupils. It is characterized by increased length in the long bones of the arms, legs, fingers, and toes; scanty subcutaneous fat; cardiovascular problems; and muscular underdevelopment.
Moebius syndrome	A disorder that causes paralysis on both sides of the face, causing lack of horizontal eye movements, other nervous system disorders, speech problems, and other defects of arms and legs.

Name	Main Characteristics
Norrie disease	An X-linked recessive disorder consisting of bilateral blindness from retinal detachment. Intellectual disability and deafness can possibly develop later.
Patau syndrome	A congenital condition causing microphthalmos, colobomas, cataracts, retinal dysplasia, corneal opacities, optic nerve hypoplasia, as well as congenital heart disease, hernias, intellectual disability, seizures, deafness, and microcephaly. Life expectancy is usually only a few months.
Peters anomaly	Central corneal opacity and adhesions on the iris and cornea that usually result in glaucoma.
Refsum disease	An inborn error of metabolism causing retinal pigment epithelium degenerations, nystagmus, ptosis, small pupils, and possibly nerve deafness; a form of retinitis pigmentosa.
Reiter's syndrome	A triad of symptoms of unknown etiology comprising urethritis (an infection of the urethra often causing bladder and kidney infections), conjunctivitis, and arthritis (the dominant feature). It is usually found in men and there is no satisfactory treatment.
Rubella syndrome	When the German measles virus is transmitted to the fetus by the mother during pregnancy. It can cause damage to the eyes, ears, heart, and brain. Eye damage can include congenital glaucoma, congenital cataracts, microphthalmos, decreased visual acuity, colobomas, nystagmus, strabismus, and constricted visual fields.
Scheie syndrome	An autosomal recessive disorder that causes corneal clouding, and sometimes retinal pigment degeneration and optic atrophy.
Spielmeyer-Vogt-Sjogren-Batten disease	An autosomal recessive determined enzyme deficiency that results in pooling fats in the brain (lipid storage disease). Severe mental and physical deterioration occurs, causing death within a few years. Optic atrophy and retinal pigment changes also occur.
Stargardt disease	An autosomal recessive disease causing pigment change in the macula resulting in a large scotoma in the central field of vision and nystagmus which occurs between the ages of 6 and 20.
Stevens-Johnson syndrome	A disease of the mucous membranes and the skin causing bilateral conjunctivitis, ocular lesions, iritis, uveitis, corneal ulcers, and photophobia. It may lead to corneal scarring and blindness. Pulmonary, renal, intestinal, and cardiac involvement may occur and may lead to death in severe forms.
Still's disease	A form of rheumatoid arthritis that usually affects the larger joints of children under the age of 16 and is more commonly found in girls. Accompanying eye complications include uveitis (iridiocyclitis), strabismus, cataracts, secondary glaucoma, and macular edema

(continued)

Name	Main Characteristics
Sturge-Weber syndrome	A congenital disease of the nerves of the skin characterized by port-wine noncancerous tumors on the face and eyes. It can cause infantile glaucoma, multicolored irises, seizures, contra-lateral hemiplegia, and intracranial calcification.
Tay-Sachs disease	A genetically determined (autosomal recessive) enzyme deficiency that results in pooling fats in the brain, causing severe mental and physical deteriorations. Vision begins deteriorating around 6 or 7 months of age, and blindness usually occurs by 18 months. Most children die between 2 and 4 years of age.
Turner syndrome	A chromosomal abnormality marked by the absence of one X-chromosome which is found in females. It can cause dwarfism, ptosis, strabismus, blue sclera, eccentric pupils, cataracts, color deficiency, coloboma, as well as abnormal development of reproductive organs, spatial confusions, and learning disorders.
Usher Syndrome	An autosomal recessive condition that causes hearing loss and degeneration of peripheral vision.
Weill-Marchesani syndrome	A rare hereditary disorder characterized by multiple skeletal and eye abnormalities including dislocated lens, myopia, glaucoma (which resists treatment), and poor prognosis for vision.
Zellweger syndrome	An autosomal recessive condition that causes "Leopard spot" peripheral retinal pigmentation, cataracts, congenital glaucoma, an optic nerve hypoplasia, as well as severe intellectual disability. Life expectancy is usually less than a year.

Chapter 2

The Role of the Teacher of Students with Visual Impairments with Students Who Have Multiple Disabilities

Jane N. Erin

Key Points

🗝 Roles that teachers of students with visual impairments take when serving students with multiple disabilities

🗝 Ways in which educational teams vary in structure, including features of multidisciplinary, interdisciplinary, and transdisciplinary teams

🗝 Factors to be considered when making service decisions, including experience level of the team and the characteristics, age, and preferred communication modes of the student

🗝 Advantages and disadvantages of indirect, flexible, and direct services and the learning needs that would be met most effectively by each model

🗝 Effective collaboration with other team members

Anita was looking forward to her first job as an itinerant teacher of students with visual impairments. She was pleased to find that she would be working with students who had multiple disabilities. The previous year she had been a student teacher at the state school for students with visual impairments, and she had particularly enjoyed working with students with multiple disabilities. Discovering how to communicate with each child was a challenge she enjoyed; figuring out what motivated each student was like solving a puzzle.

Now that she was an itinerant teacher, however, she felt that she had little control over each student's daily routine. She saw most of her students for only two or three short sessions each week, and she knew that was not enough to teach a new skill to students who learned slowly and needed consistency. As the weeks went on, she began to feel that she could be more effective if she included other adults and students in activities. She often invited paraeducators to join her student sessions, and occasionally she took photos to leave with the classroom teachers so they could see how to position the students to best use vision during a task or how to arrange a visual environment in order to provide good contrast. Anita realized that her students would only learn if all members of their teams were working toward the same goals.

Although the services provided by teachers of students with visual impairments are individualized for every student, there may be some differences in the services needed by students with multiple disabilities as compared with the child who only has a visual impairment. Often, students with multiple disabilities communicate in a variety of ways that include picture or tactile symbols, and they may not be able to learn to read or to learn advanced language and speech. They may have physical or cognitive limitations that affect their learning abilities, and activities carried out with the student need to be tailored to their level of learning. This usually means that learning goals for students with multiple disabilities will be more functional (have a clear application), more concrete (use familiar and tangible materials and actions), and more focused on outcomes that the child can anticipate. Learning often takes place through consistent and frequent routines, which are sequences of activity that allow the student to anticipate familiar elements and produce consistent responses. Teachers of students with visual impairments who work with students who have multiple disabilities become skilled in establishing appropriate

expectations based on a student's current ability and his or her past evidence of progress.

As an advocate for quality services, the teacher of students with visual impairments may need to spend more time in identifying the student's needs that result from visual impairment. Since most children with multiple disabilities also have intellectual disabilities, formal assessments are often not possible. The teacher of students with visual impairments should conduct extended observations of the student's use of vision, touch, and hearing during a variety of activities; interview parents and caregivers who know the student well; and review medical records, which will often include conflicting information about the extent and type of vision the student has. If these sources suggest that visual impairment limits the student's access to learning beyond what would be possible given his or her other disabilities, then it is the obligation of the teacher of students with visual impairments to explain to the family and team members what services and adaptations are needed related to visual impairment. Many people assume that one-to-one instruction provides better learning outcomes, even though there is little research support for this belief. Therefore, when consultation or group instruction appears to be a more appropriate service approach, the teacher of students with visual impairments will need to make this recommendation to the team by showing how consultation may ensure greater consistency and generalization in learning. The ability of the teacher of students with visual impairments to communicate and interpret behaviors related to visual impairment will be a key element in identifying each student's instructional needs.

ROLES OF THE TEACHER OF STUDENTS WITH VISUAL IMPAIRMENTS

Teachers of students with visual impairments have varying roles with students with multiple disabilities, even though their common purpose is to facilitate students' learning. Sidebar 2.1 outlines the role and function of the teacher of students with visual impairments within a variety of educational settings and models of instruction. (See also "Types of Instructional Service" later in this chapter for more details on the role of the teacher of students with visual impairments in different situations.)

Itinerant Teachers

The majority of teachers of students with visual impairments are itinerant teachers (teachers who travel to students' school sites to provide service), and in that role they are supporting professionals, not the main teacher for any student they serve. They may work with the student's educational team or the student several times a week or only occasionally, and they often facilitate learning by adapting the learning environment and working with team members who do not have extensive background in visual impairment. Frequent, collaborative contact with the general education teacher and paraeducators is essential so the teacher of students with visual impairments can be responsive to the general education teacher's goals and routine in the classroom and understand the general education curriculum so that the student's access to the curriculum can be ensured. The teacher of students with visual impairments plays an essential role in providing information about the following areas to the general education teacher, the paraeducator, and other professionals who work with the student:

- the student's visual impairment
- how the student uses adaptive devices like low vision aids or assistive technology
- ways to position and seat the student to maximize the use of his or her vision
- the presentation of tactile materials, including the use of textures
- the basic braille code (uncontracted braille)
- the use of real objects versus representations to present concepts
- maintenance of consistent classroom organization that is free of both visual and auditory clutter
- basic orientation and mobility (O&M) skills, including human guide and protective techniques (see Chapter 9)
- methods for approaching students with visual impairments when engaging with them (such as identifying yourself, asking the student for permission to take his or her hand before doing so to demonstrate something)

In addition, the itinerant teacher may encourage classmates to interact with students with visual impairments, modeling such interactions, and may share some instructional

The Role of the Teacher of Students with Visual Impairments in Various Settings

Teachers of students with visual impairments function in several different settings and may take on different roles and responsibilities in each.

Public School Itinerant Teachers

- support instruction of the general education curriculum by teaching skills that provide access to the general curriculum, including braille and use of low vision devices
- make regular contact with general education teachers and paraeducators to ensure that materials and learning activities included in the general curriculum are accessible
- guide general education teachers and paraeducators in appropriate learning strategies for visually impaired students, and provide useful instructional resources
- consult with teachers and paraeducators in specialized subjects such as physical education and science to adapt activities and curriculum
- assess skills and provide direct instruction to students in areas of identified need related to visual impairment, including the expanded core curriculum
- obtain materials necessary for student access to educational program
- participate as a team member with families and educators to make decisions regarding student educational needs

- complete annual APH registry information and state reporting forms to provide information on student qualifications for services related to visual impairment

Public School Resource Teachers

- support instruction of the general education curriculum by teaching skills related to access, including reading and writing braille and the use of low vision devices
- make regular contact with general education teachers and paraeducators to ensure that materials and learning activities included in the general curriculum are accessible
- guide general education teachers and paraeducators in appropriate learning strategies for visually impaired students, and provide useful instructional resources
- provide intensive assessment and direct instruction in core academic areas such as reading and mathematics
- provide assessment and direct instruction in areas of identified need related to visual impairment, including the expanded core curriculum
- obtain materials necessary for access to educational program
- participate as a team member with families and educators to make decisions regarding students' educational needs, particularly with regard to sub-

ject areas that require direct instruction in the resource room

- encourage learning among groups of students who have visual impairments, and support modeling and group instruction of skills related to visual impairment
- complete annual APH registry information and state reporting forms to provide information on student qualifications for services related to visual impairment

General Education Teachers in Specialized School

- assess students and provide direct instruction in all major subject areas (usually elementary) or in a subject area of focus such as social studies or mathematics (usually secondary)

- integrate instruction in appropriate reading media and technology into subject area instruction
- obtain appropriate materials related to subject expertise
- develop skills related to subject expertise, and provide information and guidance to other professionals as appropriate in the school and visual impairment professional community
- participate with family members, other educators, and residential staff as a member of the educational team in making educational decisions, including the need for a continued specialized placement
- provide annual APH registry information and other reporting information to school representatives

responsibilities with the general education teacher. The teacher of students with visual impairments who works in the role of a supporting professional in the classroom with children with multiple disabilities needs to be efficient in his or her communication with others, since learning skills related to visual impairment depends on cooperation by all team members. It's not realistic to expect improvement in these skills if prompting and practice is restricted to the two or three sessions a week that the student spends with the teacher of students with visual impairments. Learning goals related to a student's visual impairment need to be closely linked to the student's practical daily needs and activities.

For example, a student who is learning to shift his gaze from near to distant objects will be more successful if he is prompted to use the skill during morning circle, at lunchtime, on the playground, and when preparing to go home than if he simply practices shifting gaze with two objects in a classroom. A student working on improving tactile discrimination skills can do so while selecting silverware at lunch, sorting coins during a math lesson, and separating different sized blocks at playtime. Effective communication is required so all members of a student's team take appropriate advantage of these learning opportunities throughout the student's day.

Resource Room Teachers

In some school districts students with visual impairments and multiple disabilities may be served in a special class—often referred to as a resource room or special day class—for students who have visual impairments. Students in these classes may spend all or part of a school day with a teacher of students with visual impairments to meet their disability-specific needs.

Teachers of students with visual impairments who work at specialized schools or in self-contained classrooms in one location may serve as classroom teachers who have the same students for the majority of the school day, especially at the elementary level. In such cases they are the professionals who organize the students' educational day, and they often supervise one or more paraeducational staff members who also work directly with students. The classroom team (teacher of students with visual impairments and paraeducational staff) will carry out the main activities related to the student's Individualized Education Program (IEP) goals (discussed in Chapter 4), and ensure consistency in their approaches to the same goal. Like itinerant teachers, teachers of students with visual impairments who work at specialized schools or in single locations will want to make sure that skills are practiced frequently and applied across contexts, but because these teachers spend more time with their students they are better able to directly observe examples of skill learning at various times of day.

Teachers of students with visual impairments typically serve as the case managers on the educational team for students with visual impairments. In that role, they gather information from specialists who provide related services, including O&M specialists, occupational therapists, physical therapists, speech-language pathologists, adaptive physical educators, audiologists, assistive technology personnel, and others who provide services that allow a student to benefit from education. General education teachers are responsible for conveying information about related service recommendations to others on the team as needed.

Teachers in Specialized Schools

When teachers of students with visual impairments work as general education teachers in specialized schools for students with visual impairments, they enjoy a breadth of expertise from other professionals with experience in visual impairment. In spite of this shared expertise, however, the general education teachers may need to guide the team to set priorities when team members have different ideas about how to implement a goal. Assessments of children who have severe and multiple disabilities (see Chapter 3) often depend on subtle and infrequent behaviors, and it can be more difficult for team members to agree on the significance of these behaviors if there is not a clear framework for data gathering and decision making.

Sometimes teachers of students with visual impairments work as general education or supporting teachers in a specialized school for children with various disabilities. In that capacity, they may be either the primary educator on the team or, if they move among several classrooms, they may function as a supporting professional, as they would as an itinerant teacher. Regardless of whether they serve as general education teachers in a class where all students have a visual impairment or they support the classroom teacher, their professional community is in a separate educational setting for students with other disabling conditions.

Teachers in Mixed Roles

Teachers of students with visual impairments may also teach in self-contained classrooms in public or private schools that include students who are not disabled as well as those with other disabilities. In these settings, the teacher of students with visual impairments will have a broader role in including students with visual impairments in the greater school community. This may involve inviting other students to participate in classroom activities and teaching nondisabled students appropriate interactions with their peers who have disabilities. In a few cases, teachers of students with visual impairments serve in roles that combine features of supporting and general education teachers: part of their time is spent in an itinerant role, and the remaining time they work intensively in one or two classrooms.

Teachers and Paraeducators

Most classrooms that include students with visual impairments who have multiple disabilities are supported by one or more paraeducators who support students' learning and assist them with daily routines. The teacher of students with visual impairments in a general education role may directly su-

pervise paraeducational personnel or may organize the daily classroom responsibilities of the paraeducator even though he or she does not serve as that person's direct supervisor. If the teacher of students with visual impairments is itinerant, it is important to talk with the general education teacher about which paraeducators have responsibilities with the student who has a visual impairment and how the teacher of students with visual impairments can arrange to spend time with these individuals to talk about how to integrate learning into daily routines.

Similarly, when working collaboratively with related service professionals, the teacher of students with visual impairments plays an integral role in providing support and information to these individuals, and may participate alongside them during assessments and instruction. Sidebar 2.2 describes the role and function of related service professionals who support students with visual impairments and multiple disabilities.

TEAM MODELS

Professional literature often defines classroom teams as either *multidisciplinary* (individual specialists working directly with the student at specific times), *interdisciplinary* (specialists working with the student and collaborating with each other), or *transdisciplinary* (specialists working through a main teacher, who implements the recommendations through integrated routines in functional settings) (Cloninger, 2004). Teams in specialized schools are more likely to function like interdisciplinary teams because they

Roles and Responsibilities of Professionals Serving Students with Visual Impairments Who Have Multiple Disabilities

Robyn Herrera

Each member of the educational team plays a significant role in educating students with visual impairments and multiple disabilities. Each provides expertise that can be shared with other professionals. The following are some of the professionals with whom teachers of students with visual impairments may collaborate and an overview of their roles and responsibilities:

General Education Teacher

- demonstrates knowledge of general education curricula
- has skills in teaching reading, mathematics, science, and social sciences
- understands typical child development and can apply this information to specific age groups and ability levels of students
- organizes and initiates classroom activities and daily routines for students
- supervises paraeducators across the school day when students with visual impairments and multiple disabilities are included in the general education classroom

Special Education Classroom Teacher

- demonstrates knowledge and skills in teaching students with intellectual challenges
- demonstrates knowledge and skills in teaching students who have learning challenges such as reading disabilities, auditory processing disorders, or behavioral challenges
- provides direct instruction in the general education curriculum
- coordinates and facilitates consultation and instruction from a range of related services professionals

School Administrator

- sets the tone for providing a positive school environment for students with visual impairments and multiple disabilities
- facilitates collaborative efforts among the teacher of students with visual impairments and other professionals
- provides space for the teacher of students with visual impairments to work with his or her students
- facilitates opportunities for the O&M specialist to work with students on campus and in the community
- assists in ensuring that program goals are undertaken by all staff involved with the student, when the teacher of students with visual impairments and the O&M specialist provide specialized instructional information related to the student's visual impairment
- supports students with visual impairments and multiple disabilities by encouraging independence and

applauding students when they use their devices like a long cane or monocular to travel around the school campus
- plays an active role as an IEP team member in making decisions about program modifications or educational placement

Physical Therapist
- provides information and training to the educational team including the teacher of students with visual impairments and the O&M specialist on posture, balance, purposeful movement, and gait
- supports the classroom teacher and paraprofessional by teaching positioning and handling techniques so that students who exhibit physical disabilities can be transferred in a safe and supportive manner
- trains staff in proper lifting techniques to prevent musculoskeletal injuries, such as strained back muscles
- provides ambulation training to attain or maintain functional walking within the educational environment
- enhances mobility development by teaching the use of a variety of powered or wheeled devices like wheelchairs or walkers within the educational and community environment
- facilitates the development of transfer skills so that students can manage physical change inherent in moving from one supporting surface (such as a wheelchair) to another surface

(such as a classroom desk, chair, or toilet)
- facilitates appropriate positioning of the student so that the student is situated in such a way that he or she is stable and posture is aligned for functional use of the extremities and maximal use of vision, allowing student attention to be focused on educational and functional tasks
- provides information and training on attention to joint mobility and muscle flexibility to prevent deformities that might interfere with the functional use of the extremities required for educational tasks
- provides training and support to students in strengthening the muscular and respiratory systems, allowing them to gradually increase physical endurance and tolerance to facilitate a longer and more productive school day
- provides recommendations for selection, adaptations, and training in the use of equipment, materials, and seating to allow the student greater independence within the educational setting

Occupational Therapist
- assesses student's classroom accessibility, play, sensorimotor integration, fine motor skills, and daily living skills such as eating and dressing skills
- teaches students daily living skills to promote greater independence with personal care skills such as eating, dressing, and toileting

(continued)

- provides instruction to enhance sensorimotor and perceptual skills which are prerequisites for coordinated gross motor and fine motor skills such as using a pencil for writing or scooping food when eating
- supports students by teaching them organization and planning of motor skills in the educational environment, such as cutting with scissors, keyboarding, and manipulation of art and school supplies within a designated work space
- provides adaptations within the classroom to facilitate student attention and success, such as using a specially adapted chair or therapy ball for seating instead of a standard chair, or using an adapted spoon or plate to promote greater independence
- provides information to the educational team about prevention and long-term effects of a disability on a student's future performance related to energy conservation, joint protection, positioning, and ergonomics

- provides information and training to improve oral motor skills like chewing food and drinking from a straw
- provides assessment and training in the use of augmentative and alternative communication (AAC) devices
- supports the classroom teacher and other team members in teaching social pragmatics and social skills to enhance communication with peers and adults
- introduces students with visual impairments and multiple disabilities who are English language learners to real-life language experiences in collaboration with other professionals on the educational team (for example, on an outing to a grocery store, the speech-language pathologist and the teacher of students with visual impairments may introduce the student to a variety of fruits and vegetables and the O&M specialist may help the student use language to support the use of customer service)

Speech-Language Pathologist

- assesses language and speech acquisition, and provides information to the educational team regarding the student's use of receptive and expressive language, production of speech, and any abnormalities (such as hearing loss, neurological disorders, or maxial-facial disorders like cleft palate) that affect the production of speech

Audiologist

- screens and assesses student's hearing
- provides information to the education team about the student's type and severity of hearing loss
- supports students in the fitting and use of hearing aids and assistive hearing devices
- provides information and support with cochlear implants

Source: Information about occupational and physical therapists is adapted from Neal, J., Bigby, L., & Nicholson, R. (2004). Occupational therapy, physical therapy, and orientation and mobility services in public schools. *Intervention in School and Clinic, 39*(4), 218–222.

can more easily hold direct meetings among staff as well as provide students with regular sessions of direct service. Public school settings that include students with multiple disabilities usually follow a transdisciplinary model, in which the general education teacher and staff implement classroom routines such as hanging up coats and morning greetings, with support as needed from specialists such as the teacher of students with visual impairments. This is usually the preferred model because children with significant cognitive and memory difficulties do not easily generalize skills learned in one context to other settings and people (Smith, 2007; Turnbull, Turnbull, & Wehmeyer, 2007).

In reality, most teams have features of more than one model at different times. Applying a specific model is not as important as having an understanding with team members, including the family, about how goals will be implemented and who will be responsible for documenting and supporting each goal. Specialized schools for students with visual impairments often have established routines for team meetings and service delivery. However, the majority of students with visual impairments are served in public schools, where support services related to their visual impairment are addressed by itinerant teachers of students with visual impairments who are not available throughout the school day. The educational team, including the family, will decide the extent and type of services that best meet the student's complex educational needs. Although the decision should address the needs of the individual student, it can be complicated by practical factors such as the itinerant teacher's caseload and travel time.

SERVICE DELIVERY DECISIONS

Decisions about how to provide effective services to a student with visual impairment and multiple disabilities are complex. Each student's individual needs and goals should be considered, but teams should also have a plan for consistent service delivery to students of similar ages with similar needs. A variety of individual factors will inform the team's decision about the amount of specialized services needed and the setting in which they will be provided. Teams will need to decide on how the teacher of students with visual impairments can most effectively meet the student's needs, including instructional service type (whether the service will be direct instruction or indirect) and service time needed from the teacher of students with visual impairments. (See Chapter 4 for additional discussion of service delivery and placement recommendations in the IEP.)

Setting

After the student's educational goals are established, an important initial decision will be the setting in which education services will be delivered. Consideration should begin with the least restrictive environment (see Chapter 1) in the child's neighborhood school. Even children with the most severe disabilities can benefit from educational experiences with peers who are not disabled. If a more restrictive setting is selected, the team should also consider ways in which contact with peers who are not disabled will be arranged as part of the student's experiences.

Sometimes a student with a visual impairment can receive the most effective education in a setting where he or she spends all or most of the day with other students who have visual impairments and where all of the staff members have training in working with children who have visual impairments. This setting may be a resource room or self-contained classroom for students with visual impairments in a public school, or in a classroom in a specialized school for children who are visually impaired. This setting allows for regular practice of new skills, and, when the setting is a residential school, includes an emphasis on daily living skills.

Types of Instructional Service

Not only does the educational team make decisions about how much service the teacher of students with visual impairments will provide, but it also determines whether the teacher of students with visual impairments will serve as a supporting teacher to general education classroom staff or will provide direct instruction to the student on a regularly scheduled basis. Some teachers of students with visual impairments will provide direct instruction as classroom teachers in special schools for children with visual impairments.

Indirect Instruction

Indirect instruction, in which the teacher of students with visual impairments does not directly instruct the student but instead sup-

ports other personnel and family members in providing instruction, is often the most effective way to provide services since general education classroom personnel have more regular contact with students and are more familiar with the student's learning and communication styles. The teacher of students with visual impairments who provides indirect service is often called a *consultant*. As a provider of indirect instruction, a consulting teacher of students with visual impairments may monitor a student's program, observing the student and making occasional contact with the family and classroom teacher to determine that the classroom-based program continues to meet the student's needs related to visual impairment. If new materials or procedures are needed, the teacher of students with visual impairments works with classroom staff to provide those. For example, the teacher of students with visual impairments may ensure that appropriate tangible or visual objects are available for learning activities, that learning materials have appropriate contrast for viewing, and that the child's positioning allows for the most effective use of vision. Does the general education teacher describe visual information to the learner who is blind, and is the paraeducator aware of when something needs to be presented for exploration to a student with visual impairments? When a student's program is monitored by a teacher of students with visual impairments, general education teachers should be able to ask questions or request a classroom visit via telephone and e-mail. Many teachers of students with visual impairments provide a one-page introductory letter that includes a description of their role and may sometimes include a list of key adaptations that are needed by the student in the classroom to provide a convenient reminder of educational adaptations. Sidebar 2.3 is an example of such a letter.

A consulting teacher of students with visual impairments may make regular visits to assess the child, observe classroom routines such as group lessons and lunch, talk with classroom staff about adaptations and progress monitoring, and demonstrate instructional procedures or use of materials. Often, the teacher of students with visual impairments will transfer a skill to another professional through *role release*, a term that describes the process of implementing instruction with a student, demonstrating it to another teacher or paraeducator, and then releasing some responsibility to the other professional by providing feedback to that individual as he or she takes responsibility for instruction (Sacks, 1998).

Indirect services are often appropriate for students who have the most severe multiple disabilities due to variations in physical state, alertness, and communication responsiveness that make it more likely that familiar staff working on a flexible time schedule can implement consistent practice on skills. Also, indirect services are often appropriate for older students with severe multiple disabilities who have received more intensive services from a teacher of students with visual impairments during the preschool and elementary years and are now moving toward more integrated classroom goals. The consultant may sometimes schedule short-term direct instructional sessions with a student for assessment, introduction of a new skill, or demonstration of an instructional strategy.

If the student's classroom teacher and team members have not had previous experience with students who have visual impairments, more intensive initial service by a teacher of students with visual impairments may be appropriate at the beginning of the school year. The teacher of students with visual impairments may provide feedback on classroom arrangements and visual characteristics, appropriate methods of prompting and communication, and the extent to which the child can use vision in regular activities. Members of the team, including the family, should be aware if the team is planning to recommend reductions in the intensity of service provided by the teacher of students with visual impairments after the general education staff gains an understanding of how to adapt classroom activities.

The consulting teacher of students with visual impairments works mainly to support the classroom staff in carrying out educational goals, providing feedback, and making suggestions that can be implemented by those who see the student every day. Since the term *consultation* is interpreted variably by different school districts and educational agencies, it is important that all members of the team, especially family members, understand the nature and frequency of consultative services, and that they realize how services will be provided.

Direct Instruction in a General Education Setting

Direct instruction by a teacher of students with visual impairments in a general education setting may be either flexible or scheduled, depending on the student's needs. The

Sample Letter from a Teacher of Students with Visual Impairments to a General Education Teacher

Dear Mr./Ms. _____,

My name is Sarah Ramirez and I am contacting you because your class includes a student who has a visual impairment. As a teacher of students with visual impairments, I will be available to assist in providing adaptations and specialized instruction for your student, _____ [student's name], and I will help make sure he/she learns along with his/her classmates.

My job is to support your student's learning in the following ways.

- Find ways to create the best learning environment for your student, including positioning, lighting, contrast in visual materials, and auditory background.
- Assess your student in specific skills related to visual impairment (how he/she uses vision in daily activities, what reading medium he/she will use if reading is a goal, and the like).
- Instruct your student at regularly scheduled times if he/she needs to learn special skills related to visual impairment (reading and writing braille, using tactile objects that represent ideas, performing daily living routines, using appropriate social skills, using learning technologies, and the like).
- Identify and obtain any special materials that your student needs because of his/her visual impairment.
- Make regular contact with you to see if there are concerns or questions you have about how to teach this student.

I look forward to working with you to make this a productive year for _____ and to support your skills as a teacher. I appreciate that your school day is very busy, but I would like to arrange a brief meeting in the next week or two. I'd like to discuss the most convenient ways for us to communicate, and also would like to provide you with some specific information about _____'s needs related to visual impairment. **Attached you will find a listing of classroom adaptations that are required under his/her IEP; we can review these further when we meet.**

Although this may be the first child with a visual impairment you have taught, I think you will find that teaching him/her does not require many changes from the way you teach your other students. I look forward to working with you during the coming school year.

Sincerely,

Sarah Ramirez, Teacher of Students with Visual Impairments
Desert Hills Schools District
sramirez@sampleemail.edu, cell phone: 999-123-4567

amount and schedule of service is designated on the student's IEP to ensure a common understanding of the role of the teacher of students with visual impairments. A flexible schedule—12 hours monthly, as arranged with the general education teacher, for example—allows for direct instruction by the teacher of students with visual impairments, with an emphasis on the integration of skills into classroom routines. In other cases, a fixed schedule—for instance, 2 hours weekly, Monday and Thursday 9:00–10:00 a.m.—may best ensure regular instruction of a skill specific to visual impairment. Skills specific to visual impairment might include use of low vision devices, braille, tangible symbols, technology that is needed because of the visual impairment, active use of vision in accomplishing a task (such as searching or scanning), orientation in the classroom and school, or activities of daily living. Students with significant cognitive disabilities will not learn a new skill if they only practice it two or three times a week, so when the teacher of students with visual impairments provides flexible services, a skill can be practiced at first during scheduled sessions with the teacher of students with visual impairments and then during classroom activities, which the teacher of students with visual impairments can support and monitor.

Sometimes a classroom includes more than one child with multiple and visual impairments, and the supporting teacher of students with visual impairments will directly instruct several children in small groups. Professionals and family members sometimes believe that one-to-one instruction results in the most effective learning outcomes, but research offers little to support this belief; interaction with other students offers opportunities for modeling as well as additional motivation (Correa-Torres, 2008; Tomasik, 2007). Grouping students also allows the teacher of students with visual impairments flexibility in using service time: if one child is absent, sleepy, or unresponsive on a given day, that time can be devoted to a classmate who is physically available for learning.

A supporting teacher of students with visual impairments may also work with a larger classroom group that includes a student who has a visual impairment during regularly scheduled classroom activities. If the student can tolerate some distraction, it is preferable to provide services in the classroom, ideally in small groups with one or two other children. Not only does this provide an opportunity for other students to learn new skills and interact with their classmates, but it also increases the likelihood of generalizing the skill to other activities (Downing, 1996). The student who learns to scan for the picture of a classmate when the teacher holds it up during morning group may associate it with that classmate, who is sitting nearby. Recognizing the picture and associating it with a classmate will make the student more motivated to practice scanning when using an array of pictures to find classmates than when using pictures that are presented in isolation and are unrelated to daily experiences.

Direct instruction by a supporting teacher of students with visual impairments is appropriate when students have short or long term educational needs that can only be met by a teacher with intensive preparation in visual impairment. Direct instruction should be especially considered when the child has recently acquired a severe visual impairment or when the child needs a skill such as braille or use of tactile symbols that require daily, frequent practice during the early learning stages. Specialized skills taught in separately scheduled time periods must also be reinforced and practiced during classroom routines outside of scheduled sessions with the teacher of students with visual impairments. For example, if the teacher of students with visual impairments is teaching a student to use vision to recognize photographs of familiar people and preferred play items, then the same photos should be used in the classroom and at home to offer choices and reinforce communication.

Direct Instruction in Special Settings

In special settings such as a resource room or self-contained classroom in a public school or a specialized school for children who are visually impaired, general education teachers are usually required to be certified as teachers of students with visual impairments, and they often have other teaching certifications in an academic subject area, in elementary education, or in another area of special education. Their work as teachers of students with visual impairments is supported by services that are delivered by professionals who are also familiar with the needs of students with visual impairments.

These support services (referred to in the Individuals with Disabilities Education Improvement Act, or IDEA, as "related services") may include audiology, counseling, occupational therapy, O&M, physical therapy, psy-chological services, rehabilitation counseling, school health services, speech-language pathology, therapeutic recreation, and transportation (IDEA, 2004, 34 C.F.R. § 300.34). In a special school where the teacher of students with visual impairments is a general education teacher, he or she will serve as the central educator who coordinates the recommendations of support service personnel and ensures that they are integrated into classroom routines.

Instructional Time

In addition to the service type, the amount of time needed to accomplish the goals for the student will need to be determined by the team and the teacher of students with visual impairments. This decision should be made after the student's goals are established; the best educational setting for the student is determined, and the appropriate type of service delivery (direct or indirect) is identified. When the teacher of students with visual impairments is not the primary classroom teacher, the number and type of service hours are included on the student's IEP, and the teacher of students with visual impairments will need to keep a regular record of time spent serving the student as well as any deviations from the scheduled time due to absences or other schedule changes.

There is no substantive research about how the amount of time and type of service provided to a student with a visual impairment who has multiple disabilities is related to that student's educational outcomes. The team will need to consider the individual student's needs and learning preferences when making this decision and the teacher of students with visual impairments should maintain regular records of skill progress to determine whether their services are resulting in improved functioning. The caseload of the teacher of students with visual impairments should not determine service time for individual students; if time constraints prevent a student from receiving sufficient service, the teacher of students with visual impairments should notify his or her supervisor. The formal guidelines and scales provided in the next section may help teams decide on the appropriate amount of time for students with visual impairments and multiple disabilities who require support from a teacher of students with visual impairments.

Guidelines and Ratings Scales

Some teams use rating scales or formal processes to help them decide what type and amount of service each student requires. A planned process for making service decisions will help to ensure consistency for students who have similar needs. Several such processes are described in the Caseload Analysis Guidelines chapter of the online Administrator's Toolbox from the Texas School for the Blind and Visually Impaired (n.d.). The educational team is responsible for monitoring the progress of their students over time to ensure that students are receiving appropriate services according to their assessed need.

Using a rating scale or template such as the Michigan Vision Services Severity Rating Scale for Students with Additional Needs (Michigan Department of Education, 2013) will ensure that each student receives services based on objective criteria that are understood by the team. This scale provides a template for evaluating the needs of students with multiple disabilities according to a variety of characteristics, including communication and developmental delays, sensory use, daily living skills, and preparation of materials.

Another tool, *VISSIT: Visual Impairment Scale of Service Intensity of Texas* (Texas School for the Blind and Visually Impaired, 2015) provides a multidimensional tool for determining service delivery, uniquely including family support as a component of service delivery. More information on the Michigan and Texas rating systems can be found on the website of Texas School for the Blind and Visually Impaired (see the Resources section at the end of this chapter for more information). The state of Colorado also provides guidelines to assist teachers of students with visual impairments in determining service time for students with visual impairments based on a range of factors, including the student's need for adaptation and the student's preferred literacy media (Colorado Department of Education, 2003).

Educational teams that are trying to achieve consistency in decision making might review existing caseload documents before establishing a service delivery process for students with visual impairments who have multiple disabilities. When a student has multiple disabilities, professionals may unconsciously react emotionally; they may be unaware that their recommendations are shaped by such factors as a student's difficult behaviors, parental concerns, their own discomfort in teaching children with severe disabilities, or a preference for students who progress more rapidly. Establishing district or agency guidelines for delivery of services that are needed because a student has a visual impairment will make it more likely that each student will receive the support that is appropriate to his or her needs as a learner with visual impairment.

Characteristics of the Student

Students' individual characteristics are important to consider when making decisions about service delivery. Some students will respond consistently to a structured activity conducted by the teacher of students with visual impairments. Others will be more likely to respond to familiar people such as the classroom paraeducator, and they may learn better if the teacher of visual impairments provides suggestions to the paraeducator about ways to prompt the use of vision. The following characteristics should be given particular consideration when deciding about the most appropriate service for a student.

Ability to Generalize

Students who are not able generalize a skill learned with one person in one place to another situation with a different person in a different place may be better served by a teacher of students of visual impairments in a consulting role.

Alertness and Behavioral Patterns

Some students are also dominated by unpredictable physical patterns, including seizure activity and periods of sleeping or unresponsive behavior. If no pattern of alertness can be identified, indirect services may be more appropriate so that a familiar staff member can integrate skills related to visual impairment into activities when the child is responsive. In addition, students with behavioral inconsistencies that can limit attention and responsiveness may be better served through a consultant model.

Skills and Experience of Classroom Team

Some classrooms for students with visual impairments and multiple disabilities may have staff who have experience teaching students with visual impairments and multiple disabilities. Such staff members may require only limited training and direct instruction from a teacher of students with visual impairments on how to teach a student with visual impairments effectively.

Age of the Student

In many settings, more intensive service is provided by a teacher of students with visual impairments during a student's preschool and early elementary years. Less direct service may be needed as a student grows older and his or her educational program emphasizes functional activities, and goals and adaptations related to visual impairment become integrated into the student's classroom routines. Intensive activities related to vision usage may be more appropriate during the preschool years, when a child's visual and neurological systems are still developing. Reduced service may be appropriate for some students as they grow older, but others may need intensive services for short periods to achieve specific goals or to facilitate transitions. Service needs related to new age-appropriate goals should be reconsidered each year during the student's IEP conference. For example, if a teenager's goals include observing working adults in different jobs, more time from a teacher of students with visual impairments may be required to accompany the student on observations and to facilitate a student's understanding of the job role.

Previous Services

The frequency, length, and type of service delivery appropriate for an individual student needs to be determined by the educational team. When a student moves from one program to another, families and professionals often assume that the intensity of services appropriate for that student should be based on previous placement decisions. However, determination of services should be based on the student's assessed needs, not prior assessments or philosophical or personal perspectives.

Communication Modes

Students who use a communication system other than spoken language may learn more effectively when a classroom team member is involved in the implementation of goals related to visual impairment. The teacher of students with visual impairments and a classroom staff member such as a general education teacher or paraeducator who is familiar with the student work together until the communication system is understood by the teacher of students with visual impairments. Alternatively, the teacher of students with visual impairments may provide feedback to a classroom team member who is carrying out the activity. Occasionally it is effective for the teacher of students with visual impairments and the speech-language pathologist to conduct collaborative sessions or to observe one another at work. When the student has low vision and is using visual materials to aid in communication, the teacher of students with visual impairments can provide information on appropriate visual symbols as well as lighting, color, or contrast (Downing, 2005). When the student uses a communication system such as tactile symbols or assistive technology, the teacher of students with visual impairments can provide input related to use of touch or hearing in the communication process. Chapter 8 provides more information on communication options.

Individual versus Group Instruction

Some students with severe visual impairments and multiple disabilities may function best with individual instruction. Students who are easily distracted, require consistent communication support from an intervener (a person who works directly with deafblind students to enhance and interpret communication, discussed later in this chapter), or exhibit frequent and intense behavioral outbursts may not be able to tolerate a group setting for instruction.

Vision Characteristics

The extent and use of vision in students with multiple disabilities should be considered in service decisions, just as it is for students with visual impairments who do not have other disabilities. In most cases, students with more severe vision loss will be considered for more intensive service, as indicated in the rating forms described earlier in this section. Students with a progressive vision loss or those who have recently lost vision are usually also considered for more intensive service.

Need for Specialized Skills

A student who needs direct instruction in specific skills related to visual impairment must receive services from a teacher of students with visual impairments. This professional is the only qualified instructor for reading and writing braille, using assistive technology, and using vision efficiently in a school setting. The teacher of students with visual impairments can also instruct the student in basic orientation and mobility techniques such as human guide and classroom orientation. However, the services of an orientation and mobility instructor are needed for advanced instruction in orientation and mobility, including cane travel and community-based instruction. Although general skills such as daily living activities and socialization may be taught by other special educators, a teacher of students with visual impairments is often the appropriate instructor if skill needs are mainly related to visual impairment.

Transition to a New Setting

Often students with visual impairments and multiple disabilities require more intense support and services when moving to a new school environment. Teaching staff and other support personnel may need the specialized skills of a teacher of students with visual impairments to support a student's preferred learning modes.

ASSESSMENT AND INSTRUCTION

New teachers of students with visual impairments are often concerned about what services they can provide to students who have visual impairments and multiple disabilities, especially since the skills a student needs often relate to his or her cognitive and physical differences as well as his or her visual impairment. Initial assessment can help determine the student's needs related to visual impairment and provide the basis for setting goals, which in turn provide the foundation for instruction.

Assessment

Assessments that are routinely conducted by the teacher of students with visual impairments include environmental assessment, functional vision assessment, developmental assessment, and establishing the student's present levels of functioning. (See Chapter 3 for an in-depth discussion of assessment.)

Environmental Assessment

One of the most practical roles that the supporting teacher of students with visual impairments plays in a classroom is to assess the educational setting with regard to the student's visual, tactile, and auditory abilities. General education teachers may organize the classroom environment to be colorful, appealing, and lively, especially for elementary-level classes. General education teachers may not realize that walls and shelves are visually cluttered, or that busy backgrounds make identifying an object or picture held up by an adult more difficult for a student with a visual impairment. Erin and Topor (2010) provide a format for environmental analysis of classroom settings. Sidebar 2.4 provides a listing of environmental features that might be considered when creating an optimal learning environment for a student with visual impairment. The teacher of students with visual impairments can also consider and describe to the general education teacher how the background appears from the student's point of view, especially if the child is lying down for any part of the classroom day.

Tact and understanding are required when communicating with the general education teacher about adjustments to displays and arrangements in his or her classroom. Movable partitions or fabric curtains are easy ways of masking crowded backgrounds for students with low vision. Feedback about the tactile and auditory features of the classroom, including suggestions about controlling sounds and establishing tactile floor and wall surfaces that will provide orientation cues, will be helpful for students who are blind. Assessment of the classroom environment can result in a few minor changes that can affect students' ability to learn.

Functional Vision Assessment

The teacher of students with visual impairments conducts regular vision assessments with students who have multiple disabilities, although the nature and frequency may vary. The functional vision assessment (FVA; see Chapter 3 for a discussion of this assessment) is often conducted by itinerant teachers of students with visual impairments in public schools because they are the only team member with the expertise to do so, whereas in specialized schools a low vision specialist may be responsible for performing the FVA in partnership with the general education teacher and other team members.

When assessing the vision of students with multiple disabilities, it is useful to conduct frequent, short observations at different times of day. Levels of attention vary, and the teacher of students with visual impairments needs to depend on observed behaviors since students may not have the ability to convey their experiences verbally. Formal assessment of visual acuity may not be possible in cases where a student is unable to speak, point, or match, so many conclusions from the FVA are based on repeated observations. Involvement of a student's classroom team, including interviewing teachers and paraeducators, will be important in deciding what behaviors are related to a student's visual experiences. Videotaping, with appropriate permissions from parents and schools, will provide the opportunity to re-examine fleeting visual responses and to review observations; videos will also provide a basis for comparison as skills are taught.

Developmental Assessment

General education teachers of young students with multiple disabilities often rely on developmental assessments to identify goals and measure progress. The teacher of students with visual impairments can be a participant in completing these assessments, and may offer to review developmental competencies in sensory use and motor development. It may be helpful for the teacher of students with visual impairments to talk with general education teachers about the possibility of delays in

Environmental Features to Assess to Improve Access for Students with Multiple Disabilities

In conducting an assessment of the classroom environment for a student with multiple disabilities, identify the locations and positions in which the student spends time for different purposes, and consider the characteristics of each location. The teacher of students with visual impairments will want to request a copy of the daily schedule from the general education teacher and, if possible, spend time in the classroom at different points throughout the day. The following considerations might be helpful in identifying features of the classroom that may help or hinder learning.

Visual Considerations

- What are the general qualities of lighting, color, and contrast, and do these features change over the day (such as shifts in light and shadow)?
- In places where the child views objects or materials, is there a background surface that is neutral and solid (not patterned)? Do classroom staff members hold materials in front of a contrasting background (including their own clothing)?
- Are there options for increasing or decreasing lighting in some areas of the classroom, as needed?
- Are window shades or blinds adequate for light control when needed?
- Are there visually distinct spaces for placing and storing toys and the student's personal items?

- Do main classroom areas have distinct visual characteristics so that a student with low vision can recognize, for example, the blue carpet in the music corner, as compared to the red tablecloth on the snack table?

Auditory Considerations

- Is there continuous background noise during activities? (Consider both indoor and outdoor noises.)
- Are there areas in which echoes or muffled sounds are notable?
- Is there a stationary source of sound that the child might use for orientation (such as a ticking clock or an air conditioner vent?)
- Is the classroom free of annoying or distracting sounds such as clicking fluorescent lights?
- Are there times of day when startling sounds, such as bells or announcements on loudspeakers, occur? If they are bothersome to the student, is there a way to prepare him or her for the sounds?

Tactile Considerations

- Is the temperature in the classroom constant, or are there warmer and colder areas? Does the temperature change at different times of day?
- If the student is ambulatory, do the floor textures vary (such as carpet in one area and tile in another?) Can

these provide a useful cue for identifying different areas of the classroom? Is the surface stable enough to allow the student to maintain balance when walking?

- Do changes in wall and counter surfaces provide clues about the student's location in the classroom?
- Are there sharp corners or tactilely unpleasant surfaces that the student should be aware of or that should be altered to protect the student?
- Are there surfaces and materials in the room—such as carpeting, curtains, and textured walls—that might be pleasant or unpleasant to the touch?

- Is air flow evident in certain areas of the room (such as vents and open windows)?
- Do play materials include items with a variety of tactile qualities that may appeal to students with a range of tactile preferences (such as solid, smooth, textured, furry)?

Olfactory Considerations

- Are there areas of the classroom that have a distinctive smell, such as a snack area or a newly painted wall?
- Are there times of the day during which odors provide useful information about events that are occurring?

---

motor development with students who have visual impairments, and general education teachers may also welcome suggestions from the teacher of students with visual impairments about how to adapt assessment tasks, such as substituting real objects for pictures or presenting small test items in a container or tray. (See Chapter 14 for more information about early development and assessment of young children with visual and multiple disabilities.)

Present Level of Functioning

The itinerant teacher of students with visual impairments will have a different role than general education teachers in establishing the student's present *level of function* (skill and ability level for acquisition of academic and functional tasks) as a foundation for the student's IEP goals. It is important for the

general education teacher to have this information so that appropriate goals and instructional planning can take place for each student. Sometimes activities that occur during assessment can form the basis for later instruction. Having the student perform a task during assessment can help the teacher of students with visual impairments determine where instruction should begin. For example, the teacher of students with visual impairments may compare a child's ability to perform a task with and without an adaptive strategy such as visual placement of materials. The teacher of students with visual impairments may also work on a skill related to visual impairment that requires intense instruction but is not a regular part of a classroom routine (for example, scanning for food items or locating pictures on a schedule board). Because these skills are not routine, they would not have been observed by the classroom teacher. As the team leader, the general education teacher will work to integrate both content skills and sensory adaptations throughout the classroom day, encouraging consistency by all personnel.

Identification of IEP Goals

While some schools are now using prepared listings or banks of goals for students with visual impairments, these should be closely associated with the student's identified level of function and the goals identified for the general education program as well as the child's individual learning needs. Creating isolated goals related to visual skills makes it unlikely that the goals will be integrated into classroom routines when the teacher of students with visual impairments is not present. Ideally, he or she should collaborate with the general education teacher and related service providers to write the full IEP, and should know what goals are being recommended by the other team members before identifying skills related to visual impairment. Skills taught by the teacher of students with visual impairments should be based on general education classroom goals. For example, if the student is learning to eat with a spoon, a logical skill for the teacher of students with visual impairments to teach is to visually search for and locate the spoon. If the child is learning to dress him- or herself, the teacher of students with visual impairments can work with the child on visually identifying garments or on recognizing tactile identifiers on clothing.

Schools vary in their expectations of how goals should be established for students with visual impairments. Some schools expect teachers of students with visual impairments to come to the IEP conference with separate goal statements, while others prefer that the goals related to visual impairment be included on the listing of goals on the classroom IEP. Regardless of how the paperwork is prepared, it is important that all team members have an understanding of how the goals recommended by the teacher of students with visual impairments will fit into the student's home and classroom routines. For example, if the teacher of students with visual impairments is working with a student to turn his or her head slightly to the right when scanning, the parents can encourage the student to do this when looking at picture books at home and the general education teacher can place snack items slightly to the right of center to encourage the student to do a complete search. Skills that are well integrated with home and classroom activities are more likely to be learned and retained.

Areas of Instruction

Instructional activities addressed by the teacher of students with visual impairments may vary by setting as well as by individual needs. In a specialized school, teachers of students with visual impairments who serve as general education teachers may regularly address many areas of the expanded core curriculum (ECC), nine skill areas in which students with visual impairments may need specialized instruction (see Chapters 1 and 5 for more on the ECC). In a specialized setting, an elementary teacher may be responsible for reading instruction, including the standards established by the state for all students, as well as the adaptations that are needed for a visually impaired student to read in print or braille.

Itinerant teachers of students with visual impairments usually have more specific goals for each student than teachers in specialized settings, who are responsible for the entire curriculum; itinerant teachers focus mainly on skills related to the ECC, with an emphasis on linking those with classroom goals. Although they may address general education standards, itinerant teachers of students with visual impairments are primarily concerned with skills that are needed because a student has a visual impairment. For example, an itinerant teacher of students with visual impairments may assist the classroom teacher in developing a calendar system related to the daily classroom routine so that a student with a visual impairment can anticipate activities to come by identifying iconic tactile symbols, or he or she may work with a student who is blind to recognize play options during recess so the student can choose an activity. In either setting, the goals include both adaptations and instruction, but the itinerant teacher in a public school will work closely with the general education team to build the expanded core skills into an established general curriculum while the teacher at a specialized school works within a curriculum that is adapted for students with visual impairments.

SPECIAL POPULATIONS
Students with Cortical or Cerebral Visual Impairment

In both public schools and specialized settings, teachers of students with visual impairments often work with students whose visual impairments are caused by *cortical* or *cerebral visual impairment (CVI)*, in which the basis for the visual impairment is dysfunction in the structures of the brain rather than the eye (see Chapter 1). This has now become the most common cause of visual impairment among students in the United States (Roman-Lantzy, 2007). Assessment of visual impairment in a student with CVI can be complex. Traditional measurement of acuity may not be possible due to the student's physical and communication characteristics, and, because the ocular system is not atypical, eye specialists may not diagnose a visual impairment. Roman-Lantzy (2007) and Lueck and Dutton (2015) provide information about assessments for students with CVI.

A student's eligibility for vision-related educational services should be based on functional evidence of that student's visual impairment. The student's educational team should have clear guidelines based on state standards for determining educational need due to visual impairment in a student with minimal responsive behaviors due to cognitive or physical differences. While some states require that students have an acuity that falls below a particular level (20/70, for instance) to be eligible for educational services, many also allow eligibility for students whose prognosis for stable vision is poor or who demonstrate functional difficulties in using vision, even though their acuities may be difficult to measure. Most states also require an ophthalmological or optometric report. For students with multiple disabilities, the FVA must contain clear evidence that the visual impairment affects educational function for the child to be deemed eligible for services. Teachers of students with visual impairments need to include specific information about skills such as fixating, scanning, tracking, shifting gaze, and responding to objects to support conclusions about eligibility for services.

Roman-Lantzy (2007) and Lueck and Dutton (2015) have developed detailed procedures for facilitating the use of vision in students with CVI through structured assessment and measurement, emphasizing the importance of early intervention with students who have this diagnosis, given the likelihood of visual improvement during the preschool years. Although students with this diagnosis have some distinctive visual characteristics and responses, the question of how the teacher of students with visual impairments should be involved in the student's education still depends on the goals that are identified after assessment. Many students with CVI receive flexible direct services from a teacher of students with visual impairments during the first year after the visual impairment is identified; this allows for assessment and intensive intervention. However, over time, the teacher of students with visual impairments can usually release his or her instructional role to the general education team as the instructional program is established. Under these circumstances, the teacher of students with visual

impairments will need to continue with regular assessment and program monitoring, especially during the early elementary years. Like all students who have visual impairments and multiple disabilities, it is important for students with CVI to learn the use of vision in routine activities throughout the school day, rather than in isolation, in order to facilitate the student's skill retention and generalization. All professionals who work with a student who has CVI should be using the same strategies for teaching skills across school environments; participation of the educational team is vital as the student advances in school.

Students Who Are Deafblind

Students with deafblindness are usually supported by an educational team that includes a teacher of students with visual impairments. Due to the complexity of their sensory disabilities, these students may need specialized professionals and paraprofessionals on their educational team. A student's team may include *interveners*, paraprofessionals who support deafblind students in educational settings. Interveners are trained to interpret the environment to allow maximum participation by the student. Their work may include communicating with students about what is taking place around them, guiding students to explore and understand materials, interpreting social interactions, presenting learning materials, or modifying lessons. (See the Resources section at the end of this chapter for more information about interveners.)

Interveners are not teachers, and the educational team for a student who is deafblind should also include a teacher of students with visual impairments and, ideally, a certified teacher who has specialized background to serve students with deafblindness. At this time, only Utah and Illinois have specific certification or endorsement for teachers of deafblind students (C. Robinson, personal communication, September 12, 2012), although some universities offer specialized courses and programs to help teachers develop expertise in this field. Many states also participate in federally funded deafblind projects (see the Resources section at the end of this chapter), and the teacher of students with visual impairments should become familiar with any such services in his or her state so that appropriate support can be provided to learners who are deafblind.

WORKING EFFECTIVELY WITH THE EDUCATIONAL TEAM

New teachers of students with visual impairments are often surprised at how much time they spend communicating with other professionals. Initially this may be disappointing since most teachers select their profession because they enjoy working directly with students. Over time, however, many teachers of students with visual impairments find increased satisfaction in the gains students make as a result of their team working together to support their educational goals. For most new teachers, learning to be effective as a consulting teacher and a team member requires learning how to communicate with other professionals. Itinerant teachers of students with visual impairments report that effective communication skills are essential in their job role, with emphasis on listening and conveying technical ideas clearly (Correa-Torres & Howell, 2004). Efficient communication is especially important when the teacher of students with visual impairments is an itinerant and does not have daily contact with the classroom team. Sidebar 2.5 provides some suggestions for fostering effective communication with other members of the team.

Consistent communication with the classroom team is a vital skill in conveying information about how a student's learning relates to visual impairment. Ideally, this should begin with a meeting with the general education teacher, during which the teacher of students with visual impairments can find out about preferred ways of communicating (e-mailing, telephoning during specific times of day, leaving notes after sessions with the student). A letter like the one shown in Sidebar 2.3 can be especially helpful when the student has multiple disabilities because the responsibilities of the teacher of students with visual impairments may not be clearly understood by the classroom teacher.

Teachers of students with visual impairments should consider the greater classroom environment when making decisions about when to communicate; conversing with other adults in the classroom while the general education teacher is conducting a lesson demonstrates indifference to the learning needs of other children and to the efforts of the classroom teacher. A teacher of students with visual impairments who interrupts a lesson or disrupts an activity may not be welcomed by the general education teacher (Downing, 1996).

Suggestions and Strategies for Facilitating Collaboration among Educational Team Members

Recognize and solicit the expertise of other team members, especially paraeducators who may know the student's day-to-day patterns of behaviors. Although teachers of students with visual impairments may have an understanding of the effects of visual impairment, students are influenced by many factors and their learning styles vary widely. Making time to recognize the accomplishments of other team members and the challenges of their roles will support development of a unified team.

Verify the preferred time and place for communication with others, especially the general education teacher, who has responsibility for a large number of students. Face-to-face meetings may not always be an option, and e-mail, notes, texts, or scheduled phone calls may be preferred by different team members.

When opinions vary, listen fully to others' perspectives. If a team member seems upset, ask questions to clarify that person's position before moving forward with a decision. Use clarifying statements to acknowledge their viewpoints: "It sounds like you think that Maria needs more opportunities to learn with her peers instead of being separated so much."

Consider using videotapes or photographs of a student performing an activity to provide consistency among team members. If the teacher of students with visual impairments implements an instructional strategy that needs to be generalized to the home or to other parts of the school day, showing the student performing the activity to the other team members will increase the possibility that it will be implemented similarly by all members of the team. Videos can be useful in demonstrating an instructional strategy, demonstrating the proper positioning of a child during an activity, or for collecting data on a specific behavior.

If agreement cannot be reached on a specific issue, set a short-term goal and measure progress. "Let's agree to ignore her outbursts for about three weeks, and Mary will collect data on how often the outbursts happen each day. Then we can get together and see if there has been any change in the frequency with which they occur. This will help us decide if we are paying too much attention to them."

Be willing to "lend a hand" in the classroom when necessary. The busy general education teacher will appreciate the teacher of students with visual impairments who can help out during a bathroom emergency, comfort an upset classmate, wipe up a spill, or take over the class for a moment while the teacher gathers materials for an activity.

When appropriate, include other students in activities or lessons with the child with a visual impairment. Not only does involving classmates promote social skills and reduce the isolation of the student with a visual impairment, but it also disrupts the perception that the teacher of students with visual impairments only works with individual children. The teacher of students with visual impairments who brings materials to be shared with the class as a whole is reflecting the belief that the student with a visual impairment is a member of the class.

Provide reading materials and resources for team members that help them understand why specific strategies are appropriate. If the information is complex and requires considerable time to read and understand, the teacher of students with visual impairments can include a short summary of the key issues and why this information is useful for the team.

The general education teacher needs to understand that the role of the teacher of students with visual impairments is to address skills that are needed because of the student's visual impairment, even though these skills may be integrated into activities and routines of the regular classroom. Recently, many teachers of students with visual impairments have effectively used photographs and videos as tools for communicating with general education teachers and paraeducators. For example, providing the teacher with a photo of a student's best position for scanning materials or a video that shows the child selecting a tactile object from an array can provide information that staff members can review together when time permits. Observing someone else working with the student allows the educational staff to create opportunities for additional practice since they can repeat the activity they have observed being carried out by the teacher of students with visual impairments; this opportunity may also prompt them to ask questions or share perspectives about a student's progress.

Time for direct communication may be necessary when role release is taking place,

as responsibilities for teaching or supporting a skill are transferred to a different team member. For example, when a teacher of students with visual impairments and a speech-language pathologist at a residential school have worked with a student on selecting photographs on a communication board (a flat surface that contains pictures, icons, or words the student can select to convey ideas), they will then show the residential staff how to present and position the board so that the student can use it to communicate outside the school day. The teacher of students with visual impairments and the speech-language pathologist may also arrange to visit and observe at a later date to make sure that the board is being used consistently to allow the child to make requests or respond to questions.

Once an instructional program has been implemented, it is important that the team communicate regularly about the outcome of the instruction. Often team members spend more time in initial assessment and program planning than they do in assessing progress and evaluating program changes. For example, a student who is learning to scan and reach for an object may consistently scan and reach for a spoon at mealtime, but is inconsistent in reaching for his or her toothbrush and ignores a ball that is rolled toward him or her at playtime. By making time to compare data on different activities, the team can identify inconsistencies and consider what can be done to increase appropriate use of the skill. Most itinerant teachers of students with visual impairments do not have frequent opportunities for face-to-face meetings with other team members, but e-mail, document sharing, and video meetings offer alternatives for communication about observations and data related to a student's progress.

The teacher of students with visual impairments who can work in a supportive role within classroom routines and shows an understanding of the skill that it takes to choreograph a school day will be more successful in communicating with general education staff about the needs of the student with a visual impairment. Most general education teachers will welcome an offer from an itinerant teacher to include one or two classmates in activities that are planned for the student who is visually impaired, and working with others on a learning activity can provide an extra incentive for students with and without disabilities to participate. Some itinerant teachers may conduct an occasional demonstration lesson with a small group. Not only does this allow the general education teacher a rare opportunity to observe his or her own students, it also allows the teacher of students with visual impairments to demonstrate how to adapt the activity for the child with a visual impairment. For example, the general education teacher may notice that, during the lesson, the teacher of

students with visual impairments always places the learning materials for the student with a visual impairment on a high-contrast background and seats the student in the middle of the student group while doing a cooking project so that the student will have maximum contact with materials and procedures. Not only can these adaptations result in learning opportunities for the general education teacher, but the teacher of students with visual impairments who leads the lesson will have greater appreciation for the challenges of managing groups of children.

The involvement of paraeducators in the process of instruction and assessment is especially important when students have multiple disabilities. Many learning activities are not complex, but they require an evenly paced, enthusiastic presentation that will capture a student's attention. Consistent prompts and cues included in learning routines will allow a student with a visual impairment to anticipate and respond to the sequence of events. Skilled paraeducators who are with a student for many hours a day can incorporate these teaching strategies if they understand the student's learning goals and the instructional plan. Although paraeducators are not responsible for the development of new goals or the documentation of long-term progress, their effectiveness in implementing routines makes a difference in whether or not students are able to achieve their goals.

The teacher of students with visual impairments can also help paraeducators to understand that the constant presence and guidance of an adult can discourage a student from learning and dampen his or her motivation. Skilled paraeducators know when to move away from the student and how to encourage independent interaction with other students. Research has demonstrated that one-to-one assignment of paraeducators to students with multiple disabilities can decrease students' initiative and inhibit social interactions (Giangreco, Edelman, Broer, & Doyle, 2001; Giangreco, Edelman, Luiselli, & MacFarland, 1997). Paraeducators often guide or direct students because they want to be useful, and the teacher of students with visual impairments can recommend other activities—such as the preparation of materials or the recording of student behaviors—that can contribute to a student's program but do not require interaction when the student does not need assistance. While in exceptional circumstances a staff member may be assigned one-to-one with a student who has specialized medical or behavioral needs, in most cases the constant presence of one adult does not enhance learning. The teacher of students with visual impairments who makes time to reinforce the capabilities of a classroom paraeducator may not only improve the success of the students they share but also influence the success of future students who are served by that paraeducator.

SUMMARY

Many more children with severe and multiple disabilities are included among the population of visually impaired students than was the case 50 years ago, but some teachers of students with visual impairments enter their profession lacking confidence in their ability to teach students with multiple disabilities. Although the role of the teacher of students with visual impairments varies widely across educational settings, both classroom teachers and itinerants who serve in a supporting role can provide essential opportunities for learning for children who have visual impairments. Balanced and clear communication with an educational team, consistent and frequent skill practice, and regular progress monitoring will result in successful learning for most students with visual impairments and multiple disabilities.

REFERENCES

Cloninger, C. J. (2004). Designing collaborative educational services. In F. P. Orelove, D. Sobsey, & R. K. Silberman (Eds.), *Educating children with multiple disabilities: A collaborative approach* (4th ed., pp. 1–29). Baltimore: Paul H. Brookes Publishing Co.

Colorado Department of Education, Resource Allocations Committee. (2003). *Guidelines for a caseload formula for teachers certified in the area of visual impairment.* Denver, CO: Author. Retrieved from http://www.cde.state.co.us/sites/default/files/documents/cdesped/download/pdf/guidelines_for_caseload_formula.pdf

Correa-Torres, S. M. (2008). The nature of the social experiences of students with deaf-blindness who are educated in inclusive settings. *Journal of Visual Impairment & Blindness, 102*(5), 272–283.

Correa-Torres, S. M., & Howell, J. J. (2004). Facing the challenges of itinerant teaching: Perspectives and suggestions from the field. *Journal of Visual Impairment & Blindness, 98*(7), 420–433.

Downing, J. E. (1996). Working cooperatively: The roles of adults. In J. E. Downing (Ed.), *Including students with severe and multiple disabilities in typical classrooms: Practical strategies for teachers* (pp. 147–162). Baltimore: Paul H. Brookes Publishing Co.

Downing, J. E. (2005). *Teaching communication skills to students with severe disabilities* (2nd ed.). Baltimore: Paul H. Brookes Publishing Co.

Erin, J. N., & Topor, I. (2010). Functional vision assessment of children with low vision, including those with multiple disabilities. In A. L. Corn & J. N. Erin (Eds.), *Foundations of low vision: Clinical and functional perspectives* (2nd ed., pp. 339–397). New York: AFB Press.

Giangreco, M. F., Edelman, S. W., Broer, S. M., & Doyle, M. B. (2001). Paraprofessional support of students with disabilities: Literature from the past decade. *Exceptional Children, 68*(1), 45–63.

Giangreco, M. F., Edelman, S. W., Luiselli, T. E., & MacFarland, S. Z. C. (1997). Helping or hovering? Effects of instructional assistant proximity on students with disabilities. *Exceptional Children, 64*(1), 7–18.

Individuals with Disabilities Education Improvement Act (IDEA), 20 U.S.C. § 1400 (2004).

Lueck, A. H., & Dutton, G. N. (Eds.). (2015). *Vision and the brain: Understanding cerebral visual impairment in children.* New York: AFB Press.

Michigan Department of Education, Low Incidence Outreach. (2013, January). *The Michigan vision services severity rating scale for students with additional needs.* Lansing, MI: Author. Retrieved from https://mdelio.org/sites/default/files/documents/BVI/SRS/VSSRS+.pdf

Neal, J., Bigby, L., & Nicholson, R. (2004). Occupational therapy, physical therapy, and orientation and mobility services in public schools.

Intervention in School and Clinic, 39(4), 218–222.

Roman-Lantzy, C. (2007). *Cortical visual impairment: An approach to assessment and intervention.* New York: AFB Press.

Sacks, S. Z. (1998). Educating students who have visual impairments with other disabilities: An overview. In S. Z. Sacks & R. K. Silberman (Eds.), *Educating students who have visual impairments with other disabilities* (pp. 3–38). Baltimore: Paul H. Brookes Publishing Co.

Smith, S. (2007). Cognitive and developmental disabilities. In E. L. Meyen & Y. N. Bui (Eds.), *Exceptional children in today's schools: What teachers need to know* (4th ed., pp. 223–244). Denver: Love Publishing Company.

Texas School for the Blind and Visually Impaired. (n.d.). Workload analysis: Caseload analysis guidelines. In *Administrator's toolbox.* Austin, TX: Author. Retrieved from http://www.tsbvi.edu/tb-workload

Texas School for the Blind and Visually Impaired. (2015). *Guidelines and standards for educating students with visual impairments in Texas.* Austin, TX: Author. Retrieved from http://www.tsbvi.edu/attachments/EducatingStudentswithVIGuidelinesStandards.pdf

Texas School for the Blind and Visually Impaired. (2015). *VISSIT: Visual impairment scale of service intensity of Texas.* Austin, TX: Author. Retrieved from http://www.tsbvi.edu/vissit

Tomasik, M. (2007). Effective inclusion activities for high school students with multiple disabilities [Practice Report]. *Journal of Visual Impairments & Blindness, 101*(10), 657–659.

Turnbull, A., Turnbull, R., & Wehmeyer, M. L. (2007). *Exceptional lives: Special education in today's schools* (5th ed.). Upper Saddle River, NJ: Prentice Hall.

RESOURCES

For additional resources, see the General Resources section at the back of this book.

Rating Scales

Michigan Vision Services Severity Rating Scale for Students with Additional Needs (VSSRS+)
Michigan Department of Education, Low Incidence Outreach
https://mdelio.org/sites/default/files/documents/BVI/SRS/VSSRS+.pdf

Developed to assist the teacher consultant or teacher of students with visual impairments in making recommendations and determining delivery times for services to students who are blind or visually impaired in the state of Michigan. Each of the seven categories listed on the VSSRS+ Severity of Need Profile is structured in terms of the impact on vision functioning as it relates to the student's educational program.

Visual Impairment Scale of Service Intensity of Texas (VISSIT)
Texas School for the Blind and Visually Impaired, Outreach Programs
http://www.tsbvi.edu/vissit

Designed to guide teachers of students with visual impairments in determining the type and amount of itinerant services to recommend for students on their caseloads. Provides a multidimensional tool for determining service delivery, uniquely including family support as a component of service delivery.

VISSIT—How-to Webinar
Texas School for the Blind and Visually Impaired, Outreach Programs
http://library.tsbvi.edu/Play/8630

Provides a brief overview and demonstration of the Visual Impairment Scale of Service Intensity of Texas (VISSIT) that demonstrates how to complete the document, using data from a real-world student scenario.

Website

Intervener.org
http://intervener.org/

Provides information about the role of the intervener with students who are deafblind.

Organizations

National Center on Deaf-Blindness (NCDB)
345 N. Monmouth Avenue
Monmouth, OR 97361
(503) 838-8754
Fax: (503) 838-8150
info@nationaldb.org
https://nationaldb.org/

A national technical assistance center funded by the federal Department of Education that works to improve the quality of life for children who are deafblind and their families. Runs the Deaf-Blind Project, a federally funded program that provides free technical assistance services to children who are deafblind, their families, and service providers in their state.

National Intervener Association (NIA)
SKI-HI Institute
Utah State University
6500 Old Main Hill
Logan, UT 84322-6500
http://intervener.org/nia-national-intervener-association

Aims to promote quality intervention services for individuals with deafblindness; recognition of interveners at local, state, and national levels and acceptance of the term "intervener" as a unique occupation requiring specialized training in deafblindness; awareness of the impact an intervener can have on a child's learning, communication, and overall development; and support for interveners.

Additional Reading

Texas School for the Blind and Visually Impaired. (2015). *Guidelines and standards for educating students with visual impairments in Texas.* Austin, TX: Author. Retrieved from http://www.tsbvi.edu/attachments/Educating StudentswithVIGuidelinesStandards.pdf

Provides decision makers, including school administrators, educational staff, and family members, with a set of guidelines and standards by which they can determine the quality of their programs serving students with visual impairments.

Part **2**

Assessment

Chapter 3

Assessment of Students Who Have Visual Impairments and Multiple Disabilities

Susan Bruce, Sharon Z. Sacks, and Chris Brum

Key Points

- ✔ The specialized assessment process used for students with visual impairments and multiple disabilities
- ✔ Strategies for effective assessment procedures for students with visual impairments and multiple disabilities
- ✔ Formal and informal assessments used to evaluate students who have visual impairments and multiple disabilities
- ✔ Techniques for conducting functional vision assessments and learning media assessments for students with visual impairments and multiple disabilities
- ✔ Assessments and curricula that emphasize the expanded core curriculum
- ✔ Strategies for interpreting assessment results
- ✔ Strategies and techniques for writing comprehensive assessment reports

---

Jeremy is an 8-year-old student who has optic nerve hypoplasia (ONH). In addition to being functionally blind, Jeremy has difficulty regulating his body temperature, has endocrine anomalies, exhibits perseverative behavior, and when frustrated exhibits behavioral outbursts. While Jeremy is in the third grade, he spends part of his school day in a special education class for students with moderate to severe disabilities, and is included in a general education class for music, library, and hands-on science.

Jeremy receives services from a teacher of students with visual impairments three times per week. He is learning braille and assistive technology, but his progress is very slow. Once per week he receives orientation and mobility (O&M) instruction where he works on campus routes and a neighborhood route from school to his home. When Jeremy travels he is easily distracted and often forgets landmarks or auditory cues to help him remember school routes.

During recess and lunch Jeremy does not engage with his peers. He is easily agitated by loud noises or unpredictable situations. Also, Jeremy is a slow and picky eater. He has an aversion to many textures, especially textures found in food. As a result, Jeremy has to be prompted by adults to chew and swallow his food. When in class or in a social situation, Jeremy will not initiate interactions or tasks unless an adult prompts him to do so. When Jeremy is engaged in a stressful activity or an activity he does not like, his language become echolalic.

Jeremy's family is concerned about his progress in school and at home. They want to know why Jeremy is struggling with learning to read braille and with comprehending information that is provided to him. They also want some strategies for helping Jeremy become more independent in dressing, eating, and self-care skills. During Jeremy's last IEP meeting it was decided that a comprehensive educational assessment conducted by a team of professionals, including professionals who have expertise in blindness and visual impairments, might provide some insight and strategies to assist in modifying Jeremy's educational program.

Assessment plays a critical role in determining eligibility for services, placement, and educational planning for students with visual impairments who have multiple disabilities. Assessment is the foundation upon which teachers determine what should be taught, what methods to use for teaching specific skills and academic content, and which curricula to use to initiate instruction. Teachers of students with visual impairments need to have knowledge about formal and informal assessments so they can provide valuable information about their students' visual impairments and effective strategies for adapting and modifying specific assessment tools. While teachers of students with visual impairments may not administer assessment instruments that are unrelated to their areas of expertise, they do need to be able to communicate to school psychologists, speech-language pathologists, occupational and physical therapists, and classroom teachers how best to maximize a student's potential for successful assessment. Not only do teachers of students with visual impairments need to be familiar with their students' individual learning styles and abilities, they need to be able to share environmental modifications to ensure successful assessment of each student. For example, the teacher of students with visual impairments might recommend that tactile materials be placed in a specific position due to characteristics of a student's visual field. Likewise, he or she might suggest optimal spacing of photographs to reduce visual clutter.

Teachers of students with visual impairments who provide educational services to students with visual impairments who have multiple disabilities need to be able to administer functional vision assessments (FVAs), learning media assessments (LMAs), assessments related to each area of the expanded core curriculum (ECC), as well as assessments pertaining to the common core curriculum, especially in the areas of reading and mathematics. Without this essential knowledge, a solid plan for providing effective instruction cannot be developed for a student with visual impairment and multiple disabilities. The teacher of students with visual impairments plays a critical role in the development of the Individualized Education Program (IEP), ensuring that a student's assessed educational needs are considered with respect to his or her visual impairment.

The purpose of this chapter is to provide the reader with pertinent information and resources to assist in the assessment process. It is assumed that readers of this chapter have basic knowledge and understanding of educational assessment. (Readers seeking general information about assessment can refer to Overton [2016], Pierangelo and Giuliani [2012], and Venn [2014]). Therefore, the focus of this chapter will be on effective techniques and strategies for assessing students with visual impairments who have multiple disabilities. (For information about assessment of very young children, see Chapter 14.) While information regarding strategies for formal assessment is important, greater emphasis will be placed on informal assessment.

THE ASSESSMENT PROCESS

The primary purposes of special education assessment are screening, determination of eligibility, instructional planning and placement, progress evaluation, and program evaluation (Brown, Snell, & Lehr, 2006; Venn, 2014). Assessment is a process involving information gathering and analysis. It provides the educational team with a logical way to make decisions about eligibility, the services that the student requires, where and how frequently services will be provided, and the most effective instructional strategies to employ to maximize a student's educational potential. The Individuals with Disabilities Education Improvement Act (IDEA; 2004) contains provisions about assessment, including nondiscriminatory evaluation, parental consent for assessment, and timelines that must be followed by the educational team (Overton, 2016). The teacher of students with visual impairments plays an important role in all aspects of the assessment process.

Screening

Screenings are short, abbreviated evaluations conducted to identify a potential health issue or to identify a possible disability. The screening process determines if further or more in-depth assessment is needed to determine eligibility for special education services. In the school setting, the teacher of students with visual impairments may support the school nurse in providing vision screenings to students in general education classes. Students with visual impairments who have a suspected hearing loss may be screened by an audiologist to determine the nature and extent of the hearing impairment. A school psychologist may recommend screening a student with a visual impairment for additional disabilities, such as an intellectual disability. These examples of typical school screenings may lead to referral for an initial evaluation to determine eligibility for special education services. Screenings may also lead to referrals about additional suspected disabilities in children who are already receiving special education services.

Determination of Eligibility

To be eligible for special education services, a student must have an identified disability (see Chapter 1). This will be established as part of the initial evaluation. Provisions of IDEA (2004) include that the initial evaluation must be comprehensive and completed within 60 days from the date of parent consent (Overton, 2016). Comprehensive evaluation indicates that the educational team will assess the student in every area that relates to the suspected disability. This means that the team must consider the impact of the suspected disability on the following areas of development and performance (Pierangelo & Giuliani, 2012):

- health
- vision
- hearing
- social and emotional status
- general intelligence
- academic performance
- communicative performance
- motor abilities

When engaging in a comprehensive evaluation, consideration must be given to students' strengths, needs, learning styles, and preferences. It is critical to determine an appropriate method of assessment, and appropriate assessment instruments for each student. This is especially true for students who have visual impairments and multiple disabilities. The educational team must take into account how a student's visual impairment may affect the assessment process. Factors such as attention span, level of fatigue, presentation of tactile or visual materials, positioning of the student, and the student's familiarity with the assessor may influence the outcome of the assessment. The teacher of students with visual impairments can play an integral role in helping to determine the accommodations and modifications needed to conduct a successful assessment for students with visual impairments and multiple disabilities.

Eligibility for students with visual impairments is usually determined by an ophthalmological examination. Diagnoses for additional disabilities may be determined by a neurologist or neuropsychologist, or after a comprehensive audiology exam. Eligibility for students who have cortical (also known as cerebral) visual impairment (CVI) is more difficult to determine. Students with CVI may not have a diagnosed visual impairment, but may experience difficulty interpreting visual information to an extent that affects their ability to perform successfully in an educational setting. For example, they may have good visual acuity, but function like a student who is blind. When determining eligibility for these students, it is important to consider the following questions:

- Does the student's visual functioning impact his or her ability to learn?
- Is the impact on functional vision severe enough to require specialized services from a teacher of students with visual impairments or an O&M specialist?
- Does the student function like a student who is blind or visually impaired?

Instructional Planning and Placement

By using the information gleaned from a comprehensive evaluation, program planning for placement and instruction can occur through the IEP process, as described in Chapter 4. The educational team needs to determine the best fit between a student's characteristics (strengths, needs, and learning approaches) and instructional characteristics (environment, content, challenges, and teaching strategies) (Lewis & Russo, 1998).

The performance of students in the following areas need to be considered when developing the IEP and instructional program for students with visual impairments and multiple disabilities (Hatlen, 1996; Heinze, 2000; Lewis & Allman, 2000):

- cognitive development
- achievement of early milestones and academics, depending on the age of the student
- communication and language abilities
- listening skills
- object handling and play skills
- tactile skills development
- gross and fine motor development
- orientation and mobility skills
- socialization
- independent living skills
- adaptive behavior skills
- leisure and recreation participation
- pre-vocational and vocational skills
- functional vision
- appropriate learning media
- medical/health status
- attention states
- preference assessment
- assistive technology use

While each of the areas is important to consider in program planning for children with visual impairments and multiple disabilities, it is especially beneficial to focus on the interactive relationship between communication and behavior (Bruce, 2011).

Student Progress Evaluation

An IEP that is based on a comprehensive evaluation provides the basis for ongoing evaluation. It is important to monitor and evaluate the student's progress toward the goals and objectives established in his or her IEP (see Chapter 4) to determine if the student's program requires modification or updating (Pavri, 2012). Often, teachers and specialists will use curriculum-based assessments to measure a student's progress in learning academic content like reading or mathematics. Also, checklists or task analyses of specific skills can be effective progress-monitoring documents to determine if an intervention or instructional strategy has changed a student's behavior or skill acquisition.

Program Evaluation

The purpose of program evaluation is to examine how closely the current school program meets the needs of enrolled students. Program evaluations are conducted by the educational team and may include the support of an outside consultant to address the following:

- physical characteristics of the environment in which instruction occurs

- equipment (adaptive equipment and assistive technology)
- individualized curriculum
- student's engagement in the general education curriculum
- knowledge and skills of the educational team
- effectiveness of current instructional methodologies

Program evaluation is an especially important component in assessment for students with visual impairments who have multiple disabilities because these students do not acquire skills incidentally. They are particularly reliant on instructors who can provide effective, direct instruction in the context of carefully engineered learning environments. Such learning environments emphasize experiential learning, acquisition of skills through daily routines, access to a variety of communication systems (including alternative communication modes such as tactile symbols or enlarged line drawings), and instructional strategies that are systematic and organized.

EFFECTIVE ASSESSMENT PROCEDURES

Effective assessment is grounded in consideration of the characteristics of the student, the assessor (including his or her ability to apply professional knowledge), the assessment instruments, along with collaboration with other professionals and the family (Kleinert & Kearns, 2004; Pavri, 2012). In addition, consideration needs to be given to the testing environment, the level of rapport the assessor has with the student, and the availability of accessible testing materials.

Consideration of the Student's Characteristics

The student's suspected or identified disabilities determine what areas of development to assess and help to determine what assessment instruments or approaches need to be considered. In some cases specific questions from the family or the educational team determine the focus of the assessment. When planning an assessment, the team needs to consider the following characteristics of the student (Barclay, 2003):

- medical history and current health status
- age of onset of disabilities (including visual impairment)
- effects of disabilities (and etiology) on the assessment process
- sensory characteristics (vision, hearing, sensitivities to sensory input such as loud noises or too much visual stimuli, aversion to touch, and the like)
- communication needs
- cultural and linguistic background (of the student and the family)
- behaviors (including self-stimulatory and self-injurious)
- experiential history
- educational history
- interaction with others (including peers, family, teachers, and assessors)
- learning style (including pace of learning)
- performance consistency (across time, activities, and environments)
- attention and alertness

- adaptive equipment and assistive technology needs

Loftin (2006) speaks to the need for evaluators to thoroughly understand the student's visual impairment (such as acuity, central or peripheral field loss, and the like) so that appropriate accommodations can be planned. Loftin (2006) and Lewis and Russo (1998) suggest several important considerations to ensure that students with visual impairments are provided with appropriate accommodations for assessments, including:

- lighting
- noise levels
- environment free of visual or auditory distractions
- positioning
- level of fatigue
- presentation of materials (real objects versus pictures, high-contrast materials, and the like)
- use of assistive technology (ensuring that the student has familiarity and knowledge)

Before assessing a student with a visual impairment and multiple disabilities it is important for those who know the student best (such as a teacher, paraeducator, and family members) to provide valuable information about the student's learning styles, learning preferences, behavioral or emotional characteristics, processing time required to respond to questions or activities, and strategies to facilitate optimal assessment. Also, it is important for the assessor to know if the student is shy, anxious, or agitated about the assessment itself. When preparing for a comprehensive assessment, it is essential for members on the educational team to provide collaborative input and to generate specific questions to guide the assessment process.

Consideration of the Assessor's Characteristics

It is critical that those who assess students with visual impairments and multiple disabilities have extensive knowledge and skills in their professional disciplines. These individuals also need to have knowledge about how visual impairments affect the assessment process. For example, school psychologists who use formal instruments to test intelligence or adaptive behaviors need to recognize that the norms established for sighted students may not apply to students with visual impairments. Effective assessment of a student can only occur if the individuals conducting the assessments demonstrate appropriate knowledge and skills including the following:

- general knowledge of assessment instrument characteristics such as reliability, validity, and norming groups
- ability to select or develop appropriate assessment instruments for a specific purpose
- knowledge of the selected assessment instruments and procedures
- knowledge of, and comfort with, interacting with the student
- ability to recognize the impact of the student's visual impairment (such as eccentric viewing)
- ability to communicate with the student in his or her communication forms

- willingness to disclose all test adaptations and their possible effect on test validity
- ability to collaborate with the family and other professionals to ensure accurate assessment results
- ability to effectively communicate assessment results in an understandable manner in a written report or through verbal communication

Assessment Environment and Conditions

Assessment of students with visual impairment and multiple disabilities will need to occur across multiple observation sessions and in multiple natural environments (those environments and locations in which the student typically participates in the activities being observed). It is important to note that when students with visual impairments and multiple disabilities are unfamiliar with the assessor (a school psychologist, teacher, or specialist) or the testing environment, they are less likely to perform to their maximum potential. Providing opportunities for the student to visit the assessor's office or classroom and to develop a rapport with the assessor will help to alleviate any fears and establish expectations.

It is not uncommon for assessors to conduct a portion of their assessment in the home environment to obtain a more complete picture of the student's performance. This is particularly true when assessing young children with visual impairments and multiple disabilities. Students often perform differently in their homes than at school. They may be more relaxed and demonstrate tasks not observed in the school setting. Conversely, students may not be willing to perform skills acquired in school or in the community at home, because of distractions from family members, lack of generalization of skills from one environment to the next, or a lack of encouragement to perform activities in the home. When observations are conducted in the home, it is important for the assessor or teacher to adhere to the following guidelines (Kritikos, LeDosquet, & Melton, 2012):

- Develop a rapport with the family prior to the home observation, explaining the purpose of the observation and seeking prior input from family members about the student's skills and activities in the home.
- Consider the impact of the family's first language on the assessment process and their child's performance.
- Respect the family's culture, values, and physical environment. Try not to make judgments about a family's level of support or expertise by the way they engage with their child or by their surroundings.
- Engage in friendly conversation prior to a more formal interview or observation.
- Determine the decision maker(s) or leaders of the family unit. Learn who makes the decisions about the child and his or her education.
- Understand the family's views about disability and the expectations they have for their child.
- Understand the family's daily routine and their child's involvement in daily chores or activities in the home.
- Understand the family's expectations related to their child's behavior and discipline.

- Learn how the family views their child's future and level of support.
- Encourage the family to ask questions and to share the strategies they use to teach their child certain skills or tasks.
- Develop a sense of trust with the family by including them in the assessment process and sharing information gained during the observation.

Whether directly testing the student or recording observations in the context of typical lessons, it is important to offer optimal conditions when performing an assessment, including the following (Chen, Calvello, & Friedman, 2015; Loftin, 2006):

- All materials are readily available and in the format that is most appropriate for the student being assessed (including considerations such as appropriate enlargement and positioning of materials).
- The student's schedule is taken into account. Assess the student at the time of day when he or she performs best. Some students require a series of shorter testing sessions to increase on-task behavior.
- The student is given time to explore the environment and become comfortable with the surroundings if the assessment is occurring in an unfamiliar environment.
- The testing environment is free of auditory and visual distractions, including the type of clothing worn by the assessor or teacher (for example, a solid-colored shirt may be less distracting than a shirt with a pattern).
- The student's response time is taken into account. Many students with visual impairments and multiple disabilities are slow to respond. They may process information (including visual information) slowly and may not produce information at the rate one might expect.
- The student is allowed breaks within the test session. Offer the opportunity to move or stretch, access an outdoor environment, or engage in a play activity for a brief period.

In addition to these conditions, it is important that the assessor understand that students with visual impairments and multiple disabilities may not provide typical responses to questions or tasks on normed instruments. Responses may not exactly match specified items; in some cases the items may not be relevant to the student because of the visual impairment or intellectual challenges.

FORMAL ASSESSMENT

Formal assessment instruments include explicit instructions that outline who the test was designed to be used with, how the test should be administered, qualifications for those administering the instrument, procedures for scoring individual items, time limitations, and procedures for evaluating a student's performance. Formal assessment instruments may or may not include norming data (which may compare the performance of groups with specific characteristics to the performance of individuals without disabilities). While teachers administer formal assessments, more often school psychologists take a leading role in administering these tests, or may collaborate with the educational team to assist in administration.

Many formal assessments are standardized on large numbers of sighted students, so that a consistent level of performance is determined across settings and students. While standardized tests can be used to provide a baseline of performance for students with visual impairments and multiple disabilities, results of these types of tests should be evaluated carefully, taking into account the impact of the student's visual impairment and other disabilities.

Students with visual impairments and multiple disabilities may be given a variety of formal assessments including intelligence tests, development scales, adaptive behavior scales, social and emotional evaluations, and academic achievement tests. While many of these assessments are typically conducted by a school psychologist, other tests can be administered by members of the educational team. The Resources section at the end of this chapter provides information about formal assessments that may be appropriate for students with visual impairments and multiple disabilities and provides a description of each instrument, its purpose, and who may administer it.

Venn (2014) suggests that the most effective assessment instruments for students with multiple disabilities have the following characteristics:

- adaptable response modes (students can express knowledge in more than one way)
- flexible administration procedures (team members can collect data in a variety of ways, such as via the teacher's day-to-day knowledge of the student's performance, observation, testing, and interviewing others who are in contact with the student)
- provision for partial credit for partial performance or emerging skills (includ-

ing measurement of prompting levels required)
- provision of many items (to capture small increments of development that may guide instructional decisions about what to teach)
- procedures to develop lessons to ensure linkages from the assessment process to instruction

When assessing students with visual impairments and multiple disabilities it is important to keep in mind that the assessment process is highly individualized for each student being assessed. The selection of appropriate assessment instruments must be individualized to the needs of each student. Also, when administering formal assessments, good evaluators observe the student carefully, noting the student's level of motivation, behavior, interests, and attitudes. This information can be used to assist the evaluator in interpreting the meaningfulness of the test results derived from the test session.

INFORMAL AND ALTERNATIVE ASSESSMENTS

The majority of assessments that teachers of students with visual impairments and other members of the educational team will undertake with students who exhibit visual impairments and multiple disabilities are more informal in nature. Informal assessments are connected to what a student is actually learning. Informal assessments tend to be more responsive to individual contexts and learners and may include checklists, child-guided assessments, curriculum-based assessments (such as ecological inventory and task analysis), questionnaires, interviews, rating scales, and portfolios (including those used for alternative assessment). These assessments allow teachers to focus on the individual learning needs of the student while determining specific strategies for intervention. The Resources section at the end of this chapter lists a few selected informal assessments and materials that may be helpful to planning the instructional program.

Checklists

Many informal assessments are presented in a checklist format. Such checklists can provide the evaluator with useful information about a student's levels of skill acquisition. For example, *PAIVI: Parents and Their Infants with Visual Impairments* (Chen et al., 2015), includes a checklist intended for use with young children in the home setting. Along with evaluating family needs, the instrument evaluates young children's skill acquisition in typical home activities. Another tool commonly used to evaluate students with visual impairments who have multiple disabilities including deafblindness is the *INSITE Developmental Checklist* (Morgan & Watkins, 1989). It assesses cognition, social-emotional, communication, fine motor, gross motor, self-help, and tactile skills. Other checklists used to assess basic self-help skills, recreation and leisure skills, and vocational skills can be found in *Basic Skills for Community Living* (Levack, Hauser, Newton, & Stephenson, 1997). This comprehensive guide provides the teacher with a way to measure students' progress over time, and offers curricular activities and strategies to teach a variety of essential skills.

Child-Guided Assessment

Child-guided assessment is a form of dynamic assessment meaning that what is assessed and how it is assessed emerges in direct interaction with the student. Child-guided assessment respects the student's interests, preferences, and level of alertness (behavioral state) (Kritikos et al., 2012). It is based on Vygotsky's (1978) principles of the *zone of proximal development* (the difference between what a learner can accomplish with assistance and what the learner can do on his or her own) and *scaffolding* (an instructional strategy that assists students in learning a skill by providing the correct type and amount of support).

In child-guided assessment, the teacher or evaluator creates a learning environment and then follows the student's lead, observing what interests the child. The evaluator may interact *coactively* (moving with or guiding) the student when engaging in learning tasks. For example, the teacher might introduce a new musical toy to a student and observe as the student taps it and turns it over, but does not turn it on. The teacher may then model how to turn on the musical toy. If modeling is not sufficient, the teacher may offer the student his or her hand so that the two of them may coactively turn the toy on. After a few repetitions of this coactive behavior, the student is able to operate the toy independently. Thus, in this child-guided assessment, the evaluator is assessing the kinds of adult supports that elicit desired behaviors. Child-guided assessment is especially suitable for students with the most severe disabilities.

One of the most well-known proponents of child-guided assessment is van Dijk. His assessment procedures provide structure for evaluating the following components (Nelson, van Dijk, Oster, & McDonnell, 2009):

- behavioral states (level of alertness)
- orienting responses
- learning channels
- approach-withdrawal
- memory
- social interactions
- communication
- problem solving

Van Dijk's approach is offered in an assessment kit by the American Printing House for the Blind (APH) (Nelson et al., 2009; see the Resources section at the end of this chapter). This child-guided assessment process includes observation of the specified component areas to note a student's strengths, determination of what the student is ready to learn in each area to guide the development of instruction, and suggestions and recommendations to guide the development of specific instructional strategies. A parent interview is also part of the process.

Ecological Inventory

Ecological inventories assist educational teams in the identification of functional skills to be taught in authentic environments. For example, a teacher may want to evaluate a student's ability to dress him- or herself. An appropriate place to assess these skills might be during gym class or a swimming activity.

The following steps are involved in an ecological inventory (Silberman & Brown, 1998):

- identify curricular domains (such as home, school, or community)
- identify relevant current and future environments within each domain (such as the grocery store for the community)
- identify sub-environments (such as the bathroom or kitchen in the home or the produce section or check-out counter at the grocery store)
- determine appropriate activities for each sub-environment (such as tooth brushing or face washing in the bathroom, selecting fruit from a shopping list, or making a purchase at the check-out line)
- identify the skills that are necessary to perform a specific activity

Activity Analysis

An *activity analysis* measures a student's performance on a set of skills identified in the ecological inventory against those of students without disabilities. The comparison between students with and without disabilities is known as a *discrepancy analysis;* this term is also sometimes used to refer to the entire activity analysis, and the analysis is sometimes also known as a *student repertoire inventory* (SRI). The following steps may be included in an activity analysis (see Figure 3.1 for an example of an activity analysis):

- List the skills performed by students without disabilities to accomplish a specific activity.

Figure 3.1
Sample Activity Analysis

ACTIVITY ANALYSIS

Student: _Brian_   Teacher: _Mrs. B._   Grade: _K_   Date: _1/4/16_

Activity: _Independent writing in journal_   Subject: _Literacy_

Directions:

Sequence steps in the activity analysis to depict the way in which a child or youth of the same age as the targeted student who is not disabled typically performs the activity. In the Student Performance column, mark "+" if the student performed the step independently and a "−" if the student did not perform the step independently (the Discrepancy Analysis and Recommended Adaptations columns depict supports needed for the student to perform steps marked with a "−").

Activity Analysis Steps	Student Performance	Discrepancy Analysis	Recommended Adaptations
Listen to directions	+	None	Ask him to repeat directions to check for understanding.
Go to seat	−	Dependent on paraeducator to prompt to go to seat	Teach to go to own seat by recognizing his name.
Sit in seat	+	None	None
Open journal to right page	−	Dependent on paraeducator, opened to wrong page	Teach to open to next blank page with visual steps.
Create tactile drawing or paste pictures	−	Does not know what to do; relied on paraeducator repetition of instructions	Teach to ask peer what he is supposed to do. Teach to ask for clarification prior to sitting at table. Provide visual of steps for writing.
Write word or words	−	Dependent on paraeducator to tell him what to write	Teach him to dictate words to paraeducator and copy words in braille or print into journal. End goal is to have him write words on his own.
Close journal	−	Dependent on paraeducator for repetition of directions	Teach to close journal when finished writing by referring to visual or steps for writing.

- Observe and record the level of performance of the student with a visual impairment and multiple disabilities in the skills needed to accomplish the activity.
- Perform a discrepancy analysis to determine which steps in the activity the student can accomplish independently and which steps require additional support. When performing a discrepancy analysis, the teacher of students with visual impairments or other specialists may want to consider the following questions:
  - Can the student perform the activity independently?
  - What steps in the activity can the student perform without support?
  - What level of prompting (such as physical prompt, direct verbal prompt, indirect verbal prompt, or gestural prompt) does the student require to perform the activity?
- Determine what adaptations or interventions need to occur in order for the student to fully participate in the activity.

Routine Task Analysis

Once target activities are selected, professionals can develop a task analysis for instruction. A *routine task analysis* breaks down the skills required within a selected routine or activity for more targeted instruction. The teacher of students with visual impairments and other professionals determine the steps involved in performing the activity, measure a student's individual performance on each part of the routine, determine the natural cues that allow the student to engage in the activity, and evaluate the effect or outcome of the cues on the student's performance for each step of the routine (Silberman & Brown,

1998). For example, a natural cue for starting the school day routine might be the bell ringing. The critical effect or outcome might be the student entering the classroom and saying, "Good morning" to his or her favorite classmate. Figure 3.2 provides an example of a routine task analysis.

When performing a routine task analysis it is important for the evaluator to observe and determine how long it takes for a student to perform each step of the task analysis, what level of prompting is needed before a student will perform each step of the task, and the amount of time that elapses between the delivery of a prompt and the student's response.

Preference Assessments

Preference assessment is a unique area of assessment that is especially useful for students with more severe disabilities (Bruce, 2011). This is because many students with severe disabilities and visual impairments are prelinguistic (have not acquired language), so it is more difficult to determine what they prefer. Having preferences and expressing preferences are components of self-determination (Lohrmann-O'Rourke & Gomez, 2001). By performing preference assessments, professionals are better able to determine which activities and experiences students will readily participate in. Preference assessment is part of person-centered planning, a collaborative approach to planning for a student's future that involves the student as well as his or her family and other individuals in the school and community. For secondary students as part of transition planning, person-centered planning addresses preferences for living and working conditions (see Chapter 15).

Figure 3.2

Sample Routine Task Analysis and Prompt Hierarchy Data Collection Sheet

TASK ANALYSIS AND PROMPT HIERARCHY DATA COLLECTION SHEET

Student:	*Colin*	**KEY**
Teacher:	*Ms. Shelia Hagerty*	5 – Independent
Objective:	*When provided with and oriented to the required ingredients and utensils, Colin will prepare his own toast independently (no prompts) on 80% of opportunities over a 2-month period. (Note: This would be a score of 40/40 on 80% of opportunities on this task analysis.)*	4 – Verbal Prompt 3 – Gesture/Model 2 – Physical Prompt 1 – Refusal
Task:	*Making toast with jam. (Colin's favorite. He does not like butter.)*	

Directions: Enter the date of the task analysis and the evaluator's initials in the top row. Below that, enter the student's score or rating for each step in the task, based on the key provided for the prompt hierarchy.

	Score/Rating								
Steps	*6/15/15* *SH*								
Untwist the bread bag	2								
Remove one slice of bread	5								
Place bread slice in toaster	5								
Push toaster button "on"	4								
After toaster pops up, remove slice of toast	4								
Place toast on plate	5								
Scoop up jam with knife	2								
Spread jam on toast	2								
TOTALS	29								

Professionals and families may want to believe that they know a student's preferences by observing and interacting with him or her. However, research clearly documents discrepancies between parents' and teachers' reports of preferences and results of direct preference assessments (Logan & Gast, 2001). Students with severe disabilities change their preferences more often than their nondisabled peers (Lohrmann-O'Rourke & Gomez, 2001), and their preferences are more context specific, meaning that something might be preferred in one context (within a specific activity or with a certain person) and not preferred in another.

Systematic preference assessment involves observing students' behavioral and physical reactions (such as approach, withdrawal, or engagement time) when presented with a sampling of objects, experiences, and activities.

The stimuli may be offered one at a time, in pairs, or in larger arrays, depending on what is most appropriate for each student. Systematic preference assessment is the grounding for authentic choice-making opportunities. Allowing students to make choices for specific toys, games, or activities in a variety of contexts provides students with a sense of control over their lives and their environments.

When performing preference assessments, the following strategies need to be considered:

- Present objects, experiences, and activities in multiple contexts.
- Repeat the presentation of the same stimuli over a period of days to see if the student's response changes.
- Provide stimuli in multiple forms (such as auditory, tactile, olfactory, kinesthetic).
- Present the object, activity, or experience over time (such as in weekly or monthly intervals) to determine if the student continues to demonstrate a consistent response or choice to the stimuli presented.
- Observe how the student determines a preference (such as touching an object, gesturing or pointing to an activity card, making a verbal response, or making a noise indicating a positive or negative response).

An off-shoot of preference assessment is *learning styles assessment* (Silberman & Brown, 1998). This informal evaluation allows the teacher of students with visual impairments and other professionals to determine which learning modes (such as visual, audi-tory, or tactile channels) best suit each individual student. Through observation and interviews with students, their teachers, and family members, the assessor can determine how best to deliver instruction. For example, many students with visual impairments and multiple disabilities require an anticipatory verbal or physical cue before tactile information is introduced. Students with low vision and other disabilities may prefer instruction delivered using a combination of visual (real photographs) and auditory cues paired together.

Portfolio Assessment, Student Profiles, and Video Résumés

Portfolio assessment is one of the most effective forms of assessment for students with visual impairments and multiple disabilities. In a portfolio assessment, the teacher collects a sampling of student work over time as evidence of the student's level of performance in one or more areas of the curriculum (Overton, 2016). Portfolios can be a collection of student work and photographs or videos of the student involved in a variety of learning situations. They may feature the student's best work, or more typical work. Students are generally involved in the selection of portfolio items. Portfolios are commonly submitted as a form of alternate assessment to a state's traditional high-stakes testing requirement (Kritikos et al., 2012). Usually there are stringent requirements for submission of portfolios in lieu of formal testing.

Like portfolios, *student profiles* communicate what a student can do. Profiles do not include work samples, but they can include valuable information about the student's abilities or the student's visual impairment and other disabilities, or his or her level of performance in a specific learning area like literacy or daily living skills. Student profiles can be formatted as a narrative report, a narrated video, or a digital slide presentation. Sometimes student profiles can be generated from formal assessments like the Vineland Adaptive Behavior Scales (Sparrow, Cicchetti, & Saulnier, 2016). Student profiles help new team members, job coaches, and community liaisons gain familiarity with the student's present levels of performance, behavioral needs, and effective strategies for instruction.

Another form of assessment used with adolescents and young adults with visual impairments and multiple disabilities is video résumés. A video résumé allows a potential employer to observe a student performing in a variety of work settings, engaged in a variety of work tasks. It can offer insight into how best to set up the work environment, determine what adaptations are needed for the student to perform the job tasks successfully, and understand how to effectively communicate and interact with the student.

Communication Assessment

Some students with visual impairments and multiple disabilities are pre-linguistic communicators. When assessing these students' communication needs, it is critical to observe them in the context of regularly scheduled activities and with their typical communication partners (Downing, 2005). While many formal and informal communication assessments provide valuable information about a student's language and communication needs, few focus on pre-linguistic development.

The *Communication Matrix* (Rowland, 2004, 2011) assesses seven levels of communication (from pre-intentional communication to early language) across four functions of communication: refuse, obtain, social interactions, and providing and seeking information. See Chapter 14 for additional discussion and resource information about the *Communication Matrix*.

The four aspects of communication (form, function, content, and context) (Bruce, 2002) can be used to organize structured informal assessment by developing questions that relate to each communication aspect. For example, the educational team might design questions related to what functions of communication (such as requests or comments) the student currently uses (Bruce, 2010). The assessment findings may then be expressed in a communication profile using the aspects of communication as headings.

Crook, Miles, and Riggio (1999, p. 100–101) provide a comprehensive list of visual questions to consider when assessing students' communication needs:

- At what distance can the student receive information clearly?
- Where is the student's most functional field of vision?
- How does lighting affect the student's vision?
- How much detail can the student see?
- At what pace can the student follow movement?
- Does the student have any problem focusing? If the student has glasses, does he or she wear and use them consistently?

- Does the student look at people and their faces?
- Does the student visually track people as they move around?
- Does the student give any indication of recognizing people?
- Does the student's use of vision support or interfere with his or her learning?
- Is it easy or hard to attract the student's visual attention?
- Can the student maintain good visual attention to an activity or does he or she constantly shift what he or she is looking at?

For more detailed information about enhancing communication skills for students with visual impairments and multiple disabilities, please see Chapter 7.

Tactile Skills Assessment

Many students with visual impairments and multiple disabilities are resistant to touch or have difficulty discriminating information through touch. Touch perception, or *haptic perception,* provides students with information about objects in their environment (such as hardness, softness, texture, temperature).

McLinden (2004) asserts that assessment of tactile skills can provide information about a student's independent hand use for exploring objects, the student's use of both hands together to gather information about objects and toys, and the student's ability to discriminate two-dimensional objects like raised-line drawings or symbols on a page. Tactile skills assessment provides valuable information about how a student engages with the environment, and helps to determine the

likelihood of a student using braille as a learning medium. The sensorimotor section of the *Reynell-Zinkin Scales: Developmental Scales for Young Visually Handicapped Children* (Reynell & Zinkin, 1979) is particularly useful for assessing hand function. Examples of tactile assessment items included in the Reynell-Zinkin Scales are "hand-mouth exploration of objects" and "getting small object out of a simple round box with lid."

An extension of tactile skills assessment is object handling and play assessment. While Chapter 10 explores several forms of assessment for play and socialization, object handling is an important pre-play skill. Assessing Interactions with Objects is an important component of the *PAIVI: Parents and Their Infants with Visual Impairments* assessment (Chen et al., 2015), which includes items like "hitting objects" or "attempts to tear paper." Other assessments examine object handling as a function of play and tactile awareness. These include the *Oregon Project for Preschool Children Who Are Blind and Visually Impaired* (Anderson, Boigon, Davis, & deWaard, 2007) and *Independent Living: A Curriculum with Adaptations for Children with Visual Impairments* (Loumiet & Levack, 1993). Assessment items for the Oregon Project include "plays with own feet and hands" (p. 1) and "actively explores objects" (p. 25). Items from the Independent Living curriculum focus more on assessing play or leisure activities. Sample items include "play with several hand-held toys" and "engage in a variety of solitary leisure activities for one hour or longer" (p. 135).

When assessing students' ability to use their hands for exploring the environment or for play, Crook et al. (1999) suggest using the following questions when assessing students' hand use:

- How well does the student use his or her hands?
- Is the student alert to vibration and touch?
- Does the student reach out to find the source of a tactile stimulus?
- Does the student handle objects with some caution?
- Is the student interested in differences in texture and detail?
- Does the student explore with curiosity?
- Does the student recognize objects through touch?
- Does the student have some tactile means of identifying people?
- Does the student interact with you physically?
- Does the student allow you to manipulate his or her body in order to show him or her things?

FUNCTIONAL VISION ASSESSMENT AND LEARNING MEDIA ASSESSMENT

Once students with visual impairments and multiple disabilities are eligible for services from a teacher of students with visual impairments or an O&M specialist, it is important for these professionals to conduct a functional vision assessment (FVA) and a learning media assessment (LMA). These assessments provide the basis for determining how to best provide services to these students.

Functional Vision Assessment

The FVA provides valuable information about how a student sees and uses his or her vision in a variety of educational and community settings. The teacher of students with visual impairments usually begins this assessment by obtaining an eye report from an eye care specialist (optometrist or ophthalmologist). The eye report should provide information about a student's visual diagnosis and basic information about the student's visual acuity, visual fields, eye motility, and any medical condition that has an impact on a student's visual function (such as cataracts or glaucoma). Because many students with visual impairments and multiple disabilities are unable to communicate verbally or cannot provide accurate information during an eye examination, many eye care specialists find it difficult to provide useful information about the visual abilities of students in this population. Unless the student is examined by an eye care specialist who has experience working with students with multiple disabilities, the information provided in an eye report may be limited.

Teachers of students with visual impairments and O&M specialists have specialized training to conduct FVAs and to provide valuable information to the educational team and family members about a student's visual function. While school nurses may conduct general vision screenings, teachers of students with visual impairments and O&M specialists need to work collaboratively with medical professionals in sharing vital information about how to maximize a student's visual abilities in school, at home, and in the community.

An FVA includes the following elements:

- measurement of visual acuity for near and distance vision
- a general measurement of visual field
- information about color vision
- information about contrast sensitivity
- information about eye motility and use of eyes together or separately
- information about ocular motor behavior (locating objects, fixation, tracking)
- information about visual motor behavior (reaching for objects in the visual field)
- depth perception
- information about visual perception (visual discrimination, visual memory, figure-ground perception, form constancy)

For students with visual impairments and multiple disabilities much of the information in an FVA will be obtained by observing the student in a variety of environments, over an extended period of time. During an observation, the teacher of students with visual impairments or O&M specialist will want to pay attention to the following questions:

- Does the student turn his or her head when looking at people, objects, or printed materials?
- Does the student prefer working in bright or dim light?
- How long can the student engage in a visual task? What is the student's level of fatigue?
- What level of contrast does the student require for looking at pictures or printed materials?

- What impact does crowding of objects, pictures, or words have on the student's ability to see comfortably?
- How close does the student get to view objects, pictures, or printed materials?
- How does the student maneuver when walking in outdoor environments? How does bright or dim lighting affect his or her mobility?

After a thorough assessment is completed, a report with recommendations is generated to assist the team in providing high-quality services to the student. An FVA should be conducted every three years, especially for students with visual impairments and multiple disabilities.

An example of an FVA form is provided in Figure 3.3. Many states and individuals have created similar assessment forms. For example, see *ISAVE: Individualized Systematic Assessment of Visual Efficiency* (Langley, 1998), the *FVLMA: Functional Vision and Learning Media Assessment for Students Who Are Pre-Academic or Academic and Visually Impaired in Grades K-12* (Sanford & Burnett, 2008), *ToAD: Tools for Assessment and Development of Visual Skills* (Kitchel, 2008), and CVI Range and CVI Resolution Chart (Roman-Lantzy, 2007).

Learning Media Assessment

After an FVA is completed, a learning media assessment is conducted to determine what mode of learning (tactile, visual, auditory, olfactory, or kinesthetic) is best suited for a student with visual impairments and multiple disabilities. A comprehensive LMA as outlined by Koenig and Holbrook (1995) includes information about a student's visual

Figure 3.3
Sample Functional Vision Assessment Form

FUNCTIONAL VISION ASSESSMENT
YOUNG CHILDREN AND STUDENTS WITH ADDITIONAL DISABILITIES

Assessor: _____ Assessment Date(s): _____

Student's Name: _____ Birth Date: _____

School: _____ Program: _____ Grade: _____

REVIEW OF RECORDS

Visual Diagnosis: _____

Visual Prognosis: ☐ stable ☐ deteriorating ☐ capable of improvement ☐ unknown

Eye Doctor: Name: _____ Phone: _____

    Address: _____

    Date of most recent assessment: _____

Visual Acuity without correction from doctor's report:
    OD (right): _____ OS (left): _____ OU (both): _____

Visual Acuity with correction from doctor's report:
    OD (right): _____ OS (left): _____ OU (both): _____

Eyeglasses Prescribed: ____ Near ___ Distance

Contacts: _____ yes _____ no

Sunglasses: _____ yes ___ no

Visual Field from doctor's report: _____

Surgeries: _____

Doctor's recommended activity limitations: _____

OTHER RELEVANT HEALTH/MEDICAL/EDUCATIONAL INFORMATION:

1. INTERVIEW (Parent and/or Educator)

Does the student communicate about what he or she sees? Provide examples or behaviors.

_____

_____

Source: Reprinted with permission from Sacks, S. Z., & Wittenstein, S. E. (2014). Guidelines for programs serving students with visual impairments (Rev. ed., pp. 179–187). Sacramento: California Department of Education. Retrieved from http://www.csb-cde.ca.gov/Documents/VI%20Guidelines/VI_Guidelines_110314.pdf

(continued)

(Figure 3.3 continued)

Does the student take medication regularly? Do you notice if he or she is visually affected by the medication?

What materials does the student prefer for leisure activities? Provide examples or behaviors.

When is the student most alert?

What is the student's preferred position?

Does the student demonstrate unusual sensory response, such as a startle, tactile defensiveness, or visual attraction?

---

2. OBSERVATION

2A. UNUSUAL VISUAL BEHAVIORS

☐ Presses eyes   ☐ Head tilt when viewing   ☐ Light flicks
☐ Pokes eyes   ☐ Twirls or spins objects   ☐ Shakes head side to side
☐ Other

Comments: _____

_____

_____

2B. SOCIAL BEHAVIORS DEPENDENT UPON VISION CUES

☐ Identifies people from distance (specify distance):

_____

☐ Identifies facial expressions (specify distance):

_____

☐ Maintains appropriate social distance when talking (specify distance):

_____

☐ Uses appropriate gestures (*for school-age students*):

_____

☐ Recognizes gestures of others:

_____

☐ Uses eye contact:

_____

Comments: _____

_____

_____

2C. BEHAVIORAL IMPRESSIONS

☐ Responds to simple verbal requests
☐ Communicates verbally   ☐ communicates non-verbally only
☐ Responds more readily to familiar people
☐ Responds more readily in familiar places
☐ Has limited hand use (specify) _____
☐ Has limited mobility (specify) _____
☐ Requires minimal environmental distractions to stay on task

Comments: _____

_____

2D. PREFERRED AREA OF VIEWING

Observe the student's visual behaviors during usual activities for preferred areas of viewing. Pay attention to direction and distance. For students with physical impairments, it is important to determine if responses are due to physical or visual limitation or both.

(continued)

(Figure 3.3 continued)

Responds and/or reaches for objects or people based on vision alone:

☐ To the right ☐ to the left ☐ above ☐ below ☐ directly in front

2E. PREFERRED DISTANCE OF VIEWING

Natural viewing distance for viewing up close: _____

Natural viewing distance for viewing far away: _____

Describe head tilts when viewing *(These postures may be adopted to achieve the null point for nystagmus, to compensate for a peripheral field loss, or to view eccentrically if there is a central scotoma):*

_____

☐ Must first touch or hear object before vision is used to investigate it.

Comments: _____

_____

_____

2F. BRIGHTNESS SENSITIVITY

Be sure to observe lighting needs of students who must lay on their backs in the classroom; in some cases, overhead lights may be uncomfortable for them.

Outdoors, student prefers to use: ☐ baseball cap ☐ visor ☐ sunglasses
☐ Student requires tinted lenses indoors
☐ Student squints in bright light ☐ student avoids looking toward bright light
☐ Student visually disoriented for _____ minutes when going from indoors to outdoors
☐ Student performs near tasks more accurately or easily with directional light on tasks
  (based on information from observation and/or tests of visual acuity)

Comments: _____

_____

_____

_____

3. DIRECT ASSESSMENT

3A. APPEARANCE OF EYES

List any unusual appearance of the eyes that should be evaluated by an eye doctor.

_____

_____

3B. SHIFT OF GAZE

Present two lights or two objects to the student in the positions indicated below. Shine, blink, or shake one object, then pause and do the same with the second object. Additional response time may be needed for students who have motor coordination or motor planning difficulties.

Shifts gaze from one light source to another: _____

Shifts gaze from one object to another: _____

Comments: _____

_____

3C. FOLLOWING (TRACKING)

Use a small object or light source that holds the student's attention. Move object or light slowly—while it is within the student's range of vision. Try objects first, use a light if not successful with an object.

Object/Light used: _____

Follows object or light source: □ left □ right □ up □ down Distance: _____
Follows a person's movement: □ within 3 ft. □ within 10 ft. □ within 25 ft.
Following is: □ smooth □ jerky
Follows across midline: □ Yes □ No
Follows with: □ head □ head and eyes □ both eyes □ RE only □ LE only

Comments: _____

_____

3D. PERIPHERAL VISUAL FIELDS

(Note: Color in area where targets are **not** seen)

When moving, often bumps into objects: □ to the left □ to the right □ above □ below

(continued)

(Figure 3.3 continued)

Comments: _____

_____

_____

3E. DISTANCE VISUAL ACUITY

Only test if appropriate to student's cognitive level and ability.

Test Administered: _____

Distance Presented: _____ Symbol Size Read: _____

Visual Acuity (Test Distance/Symbol Size): _____

Converted to Equivalent Snellen Acuity: _____

Comments: _____

3F. NEAR VISUAL ACUITY USING SYMBOLS (OPTOYPES)

Only test if appropriate to student's cognitive level and ability.

Test Administered: _____

Distance Presented: _____ Symbol Size Read: _____

Recognizes Pictures *(if appropriate)*

☐ Recognizes simple pictures: smallest size _____
☐ Recognizes complex pictures: smallest size _____

Comments: _____

_____

3G. CONTRAST SENSITIVITY

Test Administered: _____

Describe Lighting: _____

Comments: _____

3H. STEREOPSIS

This pertains to fine nearpoint tasks such as threading needles, pouring liquids, and reaching for objects within arm's reach. For activities such as walking, climbing stairs, and stepping down from curbs, the major cause of reported difficulties is poor contrast sensitivity rather than poor stereopsis.

Activity Observed: _____

Comments: _____

_____

_____

31. COLOR

☐ Selects or points to named primary colors:

_____

☐ Matches primary colors:

_____

☐ Demonstrates color preferences (specify colors):

_____

Test Administered: _____

Comments: _____

_____

_____

functioning, sensory learning channels, indicators for reading readiness, reading preferences, and tests of reading skills (such as phonological abilities, fluency, comprehension, and listening skills).

The first step of an LMA is to gather information about the student's visual functioning. It is important to observe the student performing academic and functional activities in the home, school, and community. By doing so, the teacher of students with visual impairments can determine what mode of learning the student uses to perform a variety of tasks throughout the day. Teachers of students with visual impairments, O&M specialists, and families can complete a sensory learning channels inventory, as part of the LMA developed by Koenig and Holbrook (1995).

The sensory learning channels assessment allows the evaluator to determine a student's primary and secondary mode for learning across activities. Figure 3.4 provides an example of a sensory learning channels form adapted from Koenig and Holbrook (1995), and developed at the California School for the Blind (Manning, Waugh, Barclay, & Sacks, 2006).

Once a student's preferred learning medium is determined, the teacher of students with visual impairments needs to determine his or her potential for accessing literacy activities. Figure 3.5 provides an example of a checklist that can be used to evaluate a student's potential for learning to read and write.

In some cases the educational team may determine that a pre-braille or early braille skills assessment should be conducted. The *Assessment of Braille Literacy Skills (ABLS)* (Koenig & Farrenkopf, 1995) measures emergent literacy, academic literacy, and functional literacy. The emergent literacy section includes items such as "sorts by objects" (p. 13) and "uses objects/materials or braille to convey

Figure 3.4
Sample Sensory Channels Form

USE OF SENSORY CHANNELS

This assessment is designed to examine the student's most efficient way of taking in information.

Instructions:

Arrange for three observations of 15 to 20 minutes. Observations should be conducted: 1) in the classroom, 2) during an outdoor activity, and 3) in a familiar location. Observations should also be conducted at various times of the day (i.e., morning, afternoon).

Document observable behaviors. Place a CIRCLE around the <u>primary sensory channel</u> and, if appropriate, a BOX around the <u>secondary sensory channel</u>.

Key: V=Visual, T=Tactual, A=Auditory, O/G=Olfactory/Gustatory (smell/taste), K=Kinesthetic (movement)

Mark "P" if the observed behavior occurred due to *prompting* or mark "S" if it occurred *spontaneously*.

Teacher: _____   Student: _____

Observation # _____   Date: _____   Time: _____   Setting/Activity: _____

Observed Behaviors	Sensory Channel		P-S
	Learning	Additional	
	V T A	O/G K	
	V T A	O/G K	
	V T A	O/G K	
	V T A	O/G K	
	V T A	O/G K	
	V T A	O/G K	
	V T A	O/G K	
	V T A	O/G K	
	V T A	O/G K	
	V T A	O/G K	

Probable Primary Channel: _____ Probable Secondary Channel(s): _____
Additional Sensory Channel (O/G or K) if appropriate: _____

Source: Reprinted with permission from Manning, J. Z., Waugh, J., Barclay, L., & Sacks, S. Z. (2006). Form B-2. In *Assessment of learning media* (2nd ed.). Fremont: California School for the Blind. Retrieved from http://www.csb-cde.ca .gov/csb_assessmentlearmningmedia.html

Permission granted from Texas School for the Blind and Visually Impaired to incorporate the concept of the form "Use of Sensory Channels" from Koenig, A. J., & Holbrook, M. C. (1995). *Learning media assessment.* Austin: Texas School for the Blind and Visually Impaired.

Figure 3.5

Sample Checklist for Evaluating a Student's Potential for Learning to Read and Write

---

INDICATORS OF READING READINESS

This form is designed to generate discussion about the student's ability to display prerequisite skills deemed necessary for reading.

Instructions:

Read each statement in the following sections and mark "Yes" if the student regularly and independently demonstrates the skill in the statement. Mark "No" if the student does not regularly demonstrate the skill or if the student requires assistance to complete the skill. Mark "No Op" if the student has not had an opportunity to demonstrate this skill. If the skill appears to be EMERGING, place an "E" in the "No" column.

_____ Check if the following applies: This form does not have to be completed if, for two consecutive years, the student has earned scores on the English Language Arts section of the state mandated test within or above the basic range.

Teacher: _____   Student: _____

Prerequisites for Reading

Cognitive/Language Development

Yes   No   No Op.

___   ___   ___   Cognitive ability is determined to be at 5 years of age or above, as determined by a cognitive assessment.

___   ___   ___   Touches top, bottom, front, back, and sides of an object on request.

___   ___   ___   Knowledge of left and right on his or her own body and on a page.

___   ___   ___   Understanding of "same" and "different" in a variety of contexts.

___   ___   ___   Ability to follow one-step directions, independently.

___   ___   ___   Curiosity about books (print or braille) is evident. (Pretends to read, touch braille, spontaneously looks at pictures, turns page.)

Advanced Cognitive/Language Development

Yes   No   No Op.

____   ____   ____   Uses expressive vocabulary of several hundred words (may be oral, signed, or with use of an augmentative communication device).

Source: Adapted with permission from Manning, J. Z., Waugh, J., Barclay, L., & Sacks, S. Z. (2006). Form C. In *Assessment of learning media* (2nd ed.). Fremont: California School for the Blind. Retrieved from http://www.csb-cde.ca.gov/csb_assessmentlearmningmedia.html

(continued)

(Figure 3.5 continued)

____ ____ ____ Understands that abstract symbols (may be tactile) or pictures represent words and experiences. Meaning has to be attached to experiences.

____ ____ ____ Ability to follow two-step directions that are sequential but not necessarily related. (i.e., "Pick up the ball and get your coat.")

____ ____ ____ Awareness of the phonological properties of speech, such as rhyming and syllabification (ability to form or divide a word by syllables).

Development of Focused Attention

Yes   No   No Op.

____ ____ ____ Attention span is at least 10 minutes when engaged in an activity of interest.

____ ____ ____ Shows interest in, and attentiveness to, stories told or read aloud and to songs sung.

____ ____ ____ Ability to remain engaged in a task for 10 minutes while seated at a table.

Tactile Skill Development

Yes   No   No Op.

____ ____ ____ Willingness to touch a variety of materials, including a line of braille on a page.

____ ____ ____ Sufficient finger strength and dexterity to form braille characters, using a Perkins Braillewriter, notetaker, or slate and stylus.

____ ____ ____ Shows skill dexterity in making a majority of the various hand movements.

Please circle: pushing, pulling, twisting, poking, tracing squeezing, separating, joining, picking up, putting down, holding, cutting, and pasting

____ ____ ____ Ability to use each hand independently in a coordinated manner to complete a task.

Please check if student will only be using one hand to read braille
____ Right Hand   ____ Left Hand

Summary Page for Indicators of Reading Readiness
Results from previous pages should be tallied and numbers filled in below. Using this information, complete the Summary Analysis.

Cognitive/Language Development
Student demonstrates ____ out of ____ of these skills.

Advanced Cognitive/Language Development
Student demonstrates ____ out of ____ of these skills.

Development of Focused Attention
Student demonstrates ____ out of ____ of these skills.

Tactile Skill Development
Student demonstrates ____ out of ____ of these skills.

Summary Analysis
Based on the above analysis the student . . .

    a) is ready to begin/continue a reading program

OR

    b) should continue to work on pre-reading skills

        1. This assessment should be completed again in _____.

        Focus on pre-reading to include:

        _____

        _____

OR

        2. Functional literacy forms will be used to examine skills and progress

---

meaning" (p. 15), making this highly appropriate for students with visual impairments who exhibit severe cognitive challenges. The academic literacy section includes book orientation and placement, hand movement, tracking, understanding descriptions of pictures, as well as items related to the braille code (such as identification of braille letters, contractions, and punctuation). The functional literacy section examines the functional use of braille for a variety of tasks in the home, school, and community settings. Examples include using a calendar, sending greeting cards, and signing documents. In addition to braille, this tool considers the use of recordings as a literacy medium.

Determining a student's reading preferences and reading level is the final step in the

LMA. It is important for the teacher of students with visual impairments and the general education teacher to know at what level the student is reading, the level of reading fluency, the student's comprehension level, and the student's listening abilities. The *Basic Reading Inventory* (Johns, 2010) is widely used to measure these skills for students with visual impairments and multiple disabilities, many of whom may exhibit significant reading disabilities. They may have auditory processing difficulties that prevent them from interpreting and understanding what is being read. In addition, students who exhibit neurological visual impairments may have difficulty with crowding, letter reversals, or visually identifying letters either in print or braille. When conducting an LMA, it is important to evaluate a student's ability to comprehend what is being read, and to evaluate his or her level of listening comprehension. Many students with visual impairments and multiple disabilities are able to read and decode braille, but their ability to understand what they have read may be limited. While some students may not be able to read efficiently, either in braille or in print, their ability to listen and obtain information via the auditory channel may be a strength.

ASSESSMENT OF EXPANDED CORE CURRICULUM SKILLS

In addition to the framework for assessment already provided in this chapter, it is important to note that it is the role of the teacher of students with visual impairments and the O&M specialist to assess each area of the expanded core curriculum (ECC). As explained in Chapter 1, the ECC plays an essential role in educating students with visual impairments and multiple disabilities and provides a solid foundation for preparation for adult life. Many of the chapters in this book provide specific information for conducting assessments in ECC content areas such as compensatory skills (functional literacy), O&M, daily living skills, social skills, self-determination, career development, and assistive technology.

When assessing students with visual impairments and multiple disabilities in each area of the ECC, using observation and checklists provide teachers of students with visual impairments and O&M specialists with valuable insights into how students perform a variety of functional tasks. This information can be shared and analyzed by the educational team to determine what areas of the ECC need to be prioritized for instruction. *ECC Essentials: Teaching the Expanded Core Curriculum to Students with Visual Impairments* (Allman & Lewis, 2014) provides a variety of assessment tools and curricular suggestions for teaching the ECC to students with visual impairments and multiple disabilities. In addition, a number of excellent resources for supporting instructional planning are available to assist professionals and families (see the Resources section at the end of this chapter).

INTERPRETING AND APPLYING ASSESSMENT RESULTS

The analysis and interpretation of student assessment findings is critical to effective instructional planning. Initially, it is important for team members to discuss their findings and to determine if there are specific areas of concern that need to be addressed in a student's educational assessment report. When analyzing the assessment data, educational teams may find it useful to create an analysis document that organizes a student's skills and abilities by domains, such as literacy or math skills or daily living or social skills. By using this format, teams can identify consistent patterns for student performance that otherwise might be missed. The data in the analysis document can be categorized with "achieved" and "needs to learn" headings. The items can be taken directly from the assessment instruments used by the team or from observations and interviews. When listing items in either category it is not necessary to provide an exhaustive list, rather list the higher-order achieved skills, and prioritize those skills that require immediate instruction. The example in Figure 3.6 demonstrates how such an analysis could be organized.

The achieved items in the analysis document can be used to frame the evaluation summary or the present levels of performance section in the student's IEP. Whenever possible, it is important to include the family in determining what skills or activities in the "needs to learn" category need to be included in the student's IEP. Sometimes students may have partially achieved independence on a skill or activity requiring further instruction. The analysis document and collaborative discussion among team members can help to support the writing of the assessment report, development of individualized curriculum, and selection of IEP goals and objectives.

When assessment data are being analyzed, it is important to take into account why particular skills were not mastered. A student may not have had the opportunity or experience to attain a set of skills because the classroom placement or skill set of the teacher may not match his or her educational needs. Also, many students with significant neurological and physical challenges who have visual impairments may have significant medical issues that prevent them from consistently attending school. In similar cases, students who exhibit severe behavioral challenges may require structured behavioral interventions in order for instruction to occur in a

Figure 3.6
Sample Analysis of Student Assessment

DOMAIN OF LEARNING: TACTILE DEVELOPMENT	
Student: *Sara*	
Achieved	**Needs to Learn**
Discriminates rough and soft textures	*Does not yet sort textures*
Expresses pleasure when touching soft textures (independent)	*Does not yet name textures*

meaningful way. Closely analyzing assessment data allows the educational team to prioritize and determine how best to ensure that students are learning and progressing despite individual challenges.

REPORTING ASSESSMENT RESULTS

The reporting of assessment results is accomplished through written and oral reports shared with colleagues and the family. Pierangelo and Giuliani (2012) suggest the following sections for written reports:

- identifying information about the student (such as name, address, date of birth, school district, teacher, testing dates)
- reason for referral or assessment
- background history (description of family, developmental history, academic history, social history, hobbies, interests, preferences, social life, parent's concerns)
- observation of student's behavior
- description of tests and procedures
- results and findings
- conclusion or summary of assessment
- recommendations to school, teacher, and family

Even though formal assessment instruments may provide normative data and yield comparative scores relevant to the student's performance, it is important to recognize that these assessments should be used as a baseline to measure individual student progress over time. Reporting of this information should be done cautiously, emphasizing how the results impact a student's academic and social performance. According to Bradley-Johnson and Morgan (2008), information regarding formal test results is best reported in percentiles and standard scores rather than gender and age equivalents. Psychologists and other professionals who analyze this information will want to explain how the student's visual impairment and other disabilities influence the assessment outcomes in a way that is useful and meaningful to the family and the educational team. Rather than emphasizing scores or grade equivalents, the assessment report needs to focus on what the student can do, is not yet doing, and what would be most valuable to teach.

The level of collaboration in writing an assessment report will vary depending on several variables including time constraints, access to team members, and a willingness among team members to share information. At a minimum, team members will want to review each other's reports and collaboratively discuss inconsistencies in findings. Some professionals will be required by their school districts to submit individual reports, while others are required to submit a blended report that reflects the findings of the team as a whole. In either case the team needs to share the report with family members prior to the student's assessment meeting, IEP meeting, or triennial evaluation. Sharing the report prior to formal meetings is especially important in the case of initial identification or when the family is to be presented with sensitive information. If a family disagrees with the assessment findings, they may choose to write a dissenting report or seek outside consultation.

SUMMARY

Comprehensive educational assessment for students with visual impairments and multiple disabilities is the basis for determining eligibility, placement, and educational planning for effective instruction. This chapter provided suggestions and strategies for conducting effective assessments to assist with individualized program development and evaluation for student progress. Both formal and informal assessment approaches assist teachers of students with visual impairments, O&M specialists, families, and related service personnel in determining how to prioritize skills and activities for instruction. A variety of commercially produced assessment instruments is available. These instruments provide insight into students' development and potential for living and working independently. Assessment procedures such as ecological inventories, routine task analysis, preference assessments, portfolio assessments, and child-guided assessments help determine what skills need to be taught to a student and allow monitoring of the student's progress over time. For students with visual impairments and multiple disabilities, assessments to determine use of functional vision and learning media provide a basic foundation for determining strategies to enhance literacy instruction.

Collaboration with professionals and families is a key element of effective assessment for students with visual impairments and multiple disabilities. Summarizing data from assessments provides an effective way to interpret and understand assessment results. Educational teams need to work together to ensure that families are included in the assessment team and that findings and recommendations are shared across disciplines.

REFERENCES

Allman, C. B., & Lewis, S. (Eds.). (2014). *ECC essentials: Teaching the expanded core curriculum to students with visual impairments.* New York: AFB Press.

Anderson, S., Boigon, S., Davis, K., & deWaard, C. (2007). *Oregon project for preschool children who are blind or visually impaired* (6th ed.). Medford: Southern Oregon Education Service District.

Barclay, L. A. (2003). Preparation for assessment. In S. A. Goodman & S. H. Wittenstein (Eds.), *Collaborative assessment: Working with students who are blind or visually impaired, including those with additional disabilities* (pp. 37–70). New York: AFB Press.

Beck, J. S., Beck, A. T., & Jolly, J. B., & Steer, R. A. (2005). *Beck youth inventories (BYI-II)* (2nd ed.). San Antonio, TX: Harcourt Assessment.

Blaha, R. (2001). *Calendars for students with multiple impairments including deafblindness.* Austin: Texas School for the Blind and Visually Impaired.

Bradley-Johnson, S., & Morgan, S. M. (2008). *Psychoeducational assessment of students who are visually impaired or blind: Infancy through high school* (3rd ed.). Houston, TX: Region IV Special Services.

Bridgeo, W., Caruso, B., D'Andrea, L., Fitzgerald, D., Fox, S., Gicklhorn, C., . . . Zatta, M. (2014). *Total life learning: Preparing for transition. A curriculum for all students with sensory impairments.* Watertown, MA: Perkins School for the Blind.

Bridgeo, W., Gicklhorn, C., & Zatta, M. (2007). *School-to-work: Developing transition portfolios for students with significant disabilities.* Watertown, MA: Perkins School for the Blind.

Brown, F., Snell, M. E., & Lehr, D. (2006). Meaningful assessment. In M. E. Snell & F. Brown (Eds.), *Instruction for students with severe disabilities* (6th ed., pp. 67–110). Upper Saddle River, NJ: Pearson.

Bruce, S. M. (2002). Impact of a communication intervention model on teachers' practice with children who are congenitally deaf-blind. *Journal of Visual Impairment & Blindness, 96*(3), 609–622.

Bruce, S. M. (2010). Holistic communication profiles for children who are deafblind. *AER Journal: Research & Practice in Visual Impairment & Blindness, 3*(3), 106–114.

Bruce, S. M. (2011). Severe and multiple disabilities. In J. M. Kauffman & D. P. Hallahan (Eds.), *Handbook of special education* (pp. 291–303). New York: Routledge.

Bruininks, R. H., Woodcock, R. W., Weatherman, R. F., & Hill, B. K. (1996). Short form for the visually impaired. In *Scales of independent behavior—revised (SIB-R).* Boston: Houghton Mifflin Harcourt.

Bull, K., Lind-Sinanian, S., & Martin, E. (2008). *Clean to the touch: Housekeeping for young people with visual impairments.* Watertown, MA: Perkins School for the Blind.

Chen, D., Calvello, G., & Friedman, C. T. (2015). *PAIVI: Parents and their infants with visual impairments* (2nd ed.). Louisville, KY: American Printing House for the Blind.

Cohen, M. (1997). *Children's memory scale (CMS).* San Antonio, TX: Pearson.

Conners, C. K. (2008). *Conners 3* (3rd ed.). North Tonawanda, NY: Multi-Health Systems.

Connolly, A. J. (2007). *Keymath-3 diagnostic assessment.* San Antonio, TX: Pearson.

Crook, C., Miles, B., & Riggio, M. (1999). Assessment of communication. In B. Miles & M. Riggio (Eds.), *Remarkable conversations: A guide to developing meaningful communication with children and young adults who are deafblind* (pp. 93–123). Watertown, MA: Perkins School for the Blind.

Delis, D. C., Kramer, J. H., Kaplan, E., & Ober, B. A. (2000). *California verbal learning test (CVLT-II)* (2nd ed.). San Antonio, TX: Pearson.

Downing, J. E. (2005). *Teaching communication skills to students with severe disabilities* (2nd ed.). Baltimore: Paul H. Brookes Publishing Co.

Dykes, M. K., & Mruzek, D. W. (2012). *Developmental assessment for individuals with severe disabilities (DASH-3)* (3rd ed.). Austin, TX: Pro-Ed.

Elliott, C. D. (2007). *Differential ability scales (DAS-II)* (2nd ed.). San Antonio, TX: Pearson.

Gioia, G. A., Isquith, P. K., Guy, S. C., & Kenworthy, L. (2000). *Behavior rating inventory of executive function (BRIEF).* Lutz, FL: PAR Inc.

Hagood, L. (1997). *Communication: A guide for teaching students with visual and multiple impairments.* Austin: Texas School for the Blind and Visually Impaired.

Harrison, P., & Oakland, T. (2003). *Adaptive behavior assessment system (ABAS-II)* (2nd ed.). San Antonio, TX: Pearson.

Hatlen, P. (1996). The core curriculum for blind and visually impaired students, including those with additional disabilities. *RE:view, 28*(1), 25–32.

Heinze, T. (2000). Comprehensive assessment. In A. J. Koenig & M. C. Holbrook (Eds.), *Foundations of education: Volume II. Instructional strategies for teaching children and youths with visual impairments* (2nd ed., pp. 27–60). New York: AFB Press.

Individuals with Disabilities Education Improvement Act of 2004 (IDEA), 20 U.S.C. § 1400.

Jaffe, L. (2009). *Woodcock-Johnson III tests of achievement—braille adaptation.* Louisville, KY: American Printing House for the Blind.

Johns, J. L. (2010). *Basic reading inventory: Pre-primer through grade twelve and early literacy assessments* (10th ed.). Dubuque, IA: Kendall Hunt Publishing.

Kitchel, E. (2008). *ToAD: Tools for assessment and development of visual skills.* Louisville, KY: American Printing House for the Blind.

Kleinert, H. L., & Kearns, J. F. (2004). Alternate assessments. In F. P. Orelove, D. Sobsey, & R. K. Silberman (Eds.), *Educating children with multiple disabilities: A collaborative approach* (4th ed., pp. 115–150). Baltimore: Paul H. Brookes Publishing Co.

Koenig, A. J., & Farrenkopf, C. (1995). *Assessment of braille literacy skills (ABLS).* Houston, TX: Region IV Education Service Center.

Koenig, A. J., & Holbrook, M. C. (1995). *Learning media assessment of students with visual impairments: A resource guide for teachers* (2nd ed.). Austin: Texas School for the Blind and Visually Impaired.

Kovacs, M. (2010). *Children's depression inventory (CDI 2)* (2nd ed.). North Tonawanda, NY: Multi-Health Systems.

Kritikos, E. P., LeDosquet, P. L., & Melton, M. E. (2012). *Foundations of assessment in early childhood special education.* Upper Saddle River, NJ: Pearson Education.

Langley, M. B. (1998). *ISAVE: Individualized systematic assessment of visual efficiency.* Louisville, KY: American Printing House for the Blind.

Levack, N., Hauser, S., Newton, L., & Stephenson, P. (1997*). Basic skills for community living: A curriculum for students with visual impairments and multiple disabilities.* Austin: Texas School for the Blind and Visually Impaired.

Lewis, S., & Allman, C. B. (2000). Educational programming. In M. C. Holbrook & A. J. Koenig (Eds.), *Foundations of education: Volume I. History and theory of teaching children and youths with visual impairments* (2nd ed., pp. 218–259). New York: AFB Press.

Lewis, S., & Russo, R. (1998). Educational assessment for students who have visual impairments and other disabilities. In S. Z. Sacks & R. K. Silberman (Eds.), *Educating students who have visual impairments with other disabilities* (pp. 39–72). Baltimore: Paul H. Brookes Publishing Co.

Loftin, M. (2006). *Making evaluation meaningful: Determining additional eligibilities and appropriate instructional strategies for blind and visually impaired students.* Austin: Texas School for the Blind and Visually Impaired.

Logan, K. R., & Gast, D. L. (2001). Conducting preference assessments and reinforce testing for individuals with profound multiple disabilities: Issues and procedures. *Exceptionality, 9*(3), 123–134.

Lohrmann-O'Rourke, S., & Gomez, O. (2001). Integrating preference assessment within the transition process to create meaningful school-to-life outcomes. *Exceptionality, 9*(3), 157–174.

Loumiet, R., & Levack, N. (1993). *Independent living: A curriculum with adaptations for students with visual impairments* (2nd ed.). Austin: Texas School for the Blind and Visually Impaired.

Manning, J. Z., Waugh, J., Barclay, L., & Sacks, S. Z. (2006). *Assessment of learning media* (2nd ed.). Fremont: California School for the Blind. Retrieved from http://www.csb-cde.ca.gov/csb _assessmentlearmningmedia.html

Martin, N. A., & Brownell, R. (2005). *Test of auditory processing skills (TAPS-3).* (3rd ed.). Novato, CA: Academic Therapy Publications.

McLinden, M. (2004). Haptic exploratory strategies and children who are blind and have additional disabilities. *Journal of Visual Impairment & Blindness, 98*(2), 99–115.

Morgan, E., & Watkins, S. (1989). *INSITE developmental checklist: Assessment of developmental skills for young multidisabled sensory impaired children.* North Logan, UT: Hope Publishing.

Nelson, C., van Dijk, J., Oster, T., & McDonnell, A. (2009). *Child-guided strategies: The van Dijk approach to assessment for understanding children and youth with sensory impairments and multiple disabilities.* Louisville, KY: American Printing House for the Blind.

Newland, T. E. (1969). *The blind learning aptitude test.* Washington, DC: U.S. Department of Health, Education, and Welfare.

O'Connell, C. (2007). *Beyond pegboards: A guide for teaching adolescent students with multiple disabilities.* Watertown, MA: Perkins School for the Blind.

Overton, T. (2016). *Assessing learners with special needs: An applied approach* (8th ed.). Upper Saddle River, NJ: Pearson Education.

Parks, S. (2006). *Hawaii early learning profile (HELP).* Menlo Park, CA: Vort Corporation.

Pavri, S. (2012). *Effective assessment of students: Determining responsiveness to instruction.* Upper Saddle River, NJ: Pearson Education.

Pierangelo, R., & Giuliani, G. A. (2012). *Assessment in special education: A practical approach* (4th ed.). Upper Saddle River, NJ: Pearson Education.

Piers, E. V., Harris, D. B., & Herzberg, D. S. (2002). *Piers-Harris children's self-concept scale (Piers-Harris-2)* (2nd ed.). Torrance, CA: WPS Publishing.

Reynell, J., & Zinkin, P. (1979). *Reynell-Zinkin scales: Developmental scales for young visually handicapped children.* Slough, UK: NFER-Nelson Publishing.

Reynolds, C. R., & Kamphaus, R. W. (2004). *Behavior assessment system for children (BASC-2)* (2nd ed.). San Antonio, TX: Pearson.

Reynolds, C. R., & MacNeill Horton, A. (2006). *Test of verbal conceptualization and fluency (TVCF).* Austin, TX: Pro-Ed.

Reynolds, C. R., & Richmond, B. O. (2008). *Revised children's manifest anxiety scale (RCMAS-2)* (2nd ed.). Torrance, CA: WPS Publishing.

Reynolds, C. R., & Voress, J. K. (2007). *TOMAL-2: Test of memory and learning* (2nd ed.). Austin, TX: Pro-Ed.

Reynolds, C. R., Voress, J. K., & Pearson, N. A. (2008). *DTAP: Developmental test of auditory perception.* Austin, TX: Pro-Ed.

Reynolds, W. M. (1987). *Reynolds adolescent depression scale (RADS-2)* (2nd ed.). Lutz, FL: PAR Inc.

Roman-Lantzy, C. (2007). *Cortical visual impairment: An approach to assessment and intervention.* New York: AFB Press.

Rowland, C. (2004). *Communication matrix.* Portland: Oregon Health and Science University.

Rowland, C. (2011). Using the communication matrix to assess expressive skills in early communicators. *Communication Disorders Quarterly, 32*, 190–201.

Sacks, S. Z., & Wittenstein, S. E. (2014). *Guidelines for programs serving students with visual impairments* (Rev. ed.). Sacramento: California Department of Education. Retrieved from http://www.csb-cde.ca.gov/Documents/VI%20 Guidelines/VI_Guidelines_110314.pdf

Sanford, L., & Burnett, R. (2008). *FVLMA: Functional vision and learning media assessment for students who are pre-academic or academic and visually impaired in grades K-12: Practitioner's guidebook.* Louisville, KY: American Printing House for the Blind.

Schrank, F. A., McGrew, K. S., & Mather, N. (2014). *Woodcock-Johnson IV tests of cognitive abilities.* Boston: Houghton Mifflin Harcourt.

Shannon, S. (2008). *Help yourself: Mealtime skills for students who are blind or visually impaired.* Watertown, MA: Perkins School for the Blind.

Sheslow, D., & Adams, W. (2003). *Wide range assessment of memory and learning (WRAML2)* (2nd ed.). Torrance, CA: WPS Publishing.

Silberman, R. K., & Brown, F. (1998). Alternative approaches to assessing students who have visual impairments with other disabilities in classroom and community environments. In S. Z. Sacks & R. K. Silberman (Eds.), *Educating students who have visual impairments with other disabilities* (pp. 73–98). Baltimore: Paul H. Brookes Publishing Co.

Sparrow, S. S., Cicchetti, D. V., & Saulnier, C. A. (2016). *Vineland adaptive behavior scales (Vineland-3)* (3rd ed.). San Antonio, TX: Pearson.

Stephenson, P. (2008). *Basic skills for community living: Activity routines.* Austin: Texas School for the Blind and Visually Impaired.

Stillman, R. D., & Battle, C. (1985). *Callier-Azusa scales (Editions G & H).* Dallas: The University of Texas at Dallas, Callier Center for Communication Disorders.

Venn, J. J. (2014). *Assessing students with special needs* (5th ed.). Upper Saddle River, NJ: Pearson Education.

Vygotsky, L. S. (1978). *Mind in society: The development of higher psychological processes* (M. Cole, V. John-Steiner, S. Scribner, & E. Souberman, Eds.). Cambridge, MA: Harvard University Press.

Wagner, R. K., Torgesen, J. K., Rashotte, C. A., & Pearson, N. A. (2013). *CTOPP-2: Comprehensive test of phonological processing* (2nd ed.). Austin, TX: Pro-Ed.

Wechsler, D. (2008). *Wechsler adult intelligence scale (WAIS-IV)* (4th ed.). San Antonio, TX: Pearson.

Wechsler, D. (2009). *Wechsler individual achievement test (WIAT-III)* (3rd ed.). San Antonio, TX: Pearson.

Wechsler, D. (2014). *Wechsler intelligence scale for children (WISC-V)* (5th ed.). San Antonio, TX: Pearson.

Zatta, M. C. (2014). *Alternate routines: Adapting orientation and mobility techniques.* Watertown, MA: Perkins School for the Blind.

RESOURCES

For additional resources, see the General Resources section at the back of this book.

Formal Assessments

Developmental Assessments

These assessments are based on the sequence of development for children without disabilities. Usually, developmental scales have many items and capture small increments of development. It is important to recognize that the developmental sequence of acquiring a range of skills for students with visual impairments and multiple disabilities may be different from their sighted peers. They aim to provide a baseline of skills, strengths, and limitations and information about the student's developmental levels in cognitive, linguistic, motor, and social development. Can be administered by school psychologists, teachers of students with visual impairments, or family members.

Callier-Azusa Scales, Editions G & H
Ages: 0–10 years
Source: Stillman, R. D., & Battle, C. (1985). *Callier-Azusa scales (Editions G & H).* Dallas: The University of Texas at Dallas, Callier Center for Communication Disorders.

Developmental Assessment for Individuals with Severe Disabilities, 3rd Edition (DASH-3)
Ages: 6 months to adulthood
Source: Dykes, M. K., & Mruzek, D. W. (2012). *Developmental assessment for individuals with severe disabilities (DASH-3)* (3rd ed.). Austin, TX: Pro-Ed.

Hawaii Early Learning Profile (HELP)
Ages: 0–6 years
Source: Parks, S. (2006). *Hawaii early learning profile (HELP).* Menlo Park, CA: Vort Corporation.

Oregon Project for Preschool Children Who Are Blind or Visually Impaired
Ages: 0–6 years
Source: Anderson, S., Boigon, S., Davis, K., & deWaard, C. (2007). *Oregon project for preschool children who are blind or visually impaired* (6th ed.). Medford: Southern Oregon Education Service District.

Reynell-Zinkin Developmental Scales
Ages: 0–6 years
Source: Reynell, J., & Zinkin, P. (1979). *Reynell-Zinkin scales: Developmental scales for young visually handicapped children.* Slough, UK: NFER-Nelson Publishing.

Intelligence Tests

These norm-referenced assessments are based on acquisition of cognitive skills by students who are sighted and measure a student's level of cognition, including activities of thinking, understanding, learning, and remembering. May include information about a student's problem-solving, abstract reasoning, social judgment, long-term memory, and verbal comprehension and expression skills. Caution must be given when administering these tests as they may reflect cultural bias. They aim to acquire a baseline of cognitive abilities based on age-equivalents; provide information about the student's general cognitive abilities, including abstract reasoning skills, long- and short-term memory skills, visual processing skills, and auditory processing skills; and provide information related to multiple aspects of a student's learning potential. Usually administered by school psychologists.

Blind Learning Aptitude Test
Ages: 6–16
Source: Newland, T. E. (1969). *The blind learning aptitude test.* Washington, DC: U.S. Department of Health, Education, and Welfare.

Differential Ability Scales, 2nd Edition (DAS-II)
Ages: 2–17
Source: Elliott, C. D. (2007). *Differential ability scales (DAS-II)* (2nd ed.). San Antonio, TX: Pearson.

Wechsler Adult Intelligence Scale, 4th Edition (WAIS-IV)
Ages: 16–90
Source: Wechsler, D. (2008). *Wechsler adult intelligence scale (WAIS-IV)* (4th ed.). San Antonio, TX: Pearson.

Wechsler Intelligence Scale for Children, 5th Edition (WISC-V)
Ages: 6–16

Source: Wechsler, D. (2014). *Wechsler intelligence scale for children (WISC-V)* (5th ed.). San Antonio, TX: Pearson.

Woodcock-Johnson IV Tests of Cognitive Abilities (WJ-IV Cog)

Ages: 2–90+

Source: Schrank, F. A., McGrew, K. S., & Mather, N. (2014). *Woodcock-Johnson IV tests of cognitive abilities.* Boston: Houghton Mifflin Harcourt.

Auditory Processing

These assessments measure a student's ability to process and understand auditory information, including auditory comprehension, auditory reasoning, phonological processing, and memory for auditory information. They aim to provide information regarding a student's ability to understand and utilize auditory information as well as possible phonological- or language-based learning disabilities, such as dyslexia. Can be administered by school psychologists or speech-language pathologists.

Comprehensive Test of Phonological Processing, 2nd Edition (CTOPP-2)

Ages: 4–24

Source: Wagner, R. K., Torgesen, J. K., Rashotte, C. A., & Pearson, N. A. (2013). *CTOPP-2: Comprehensive test of phonological processing* (2nd ed.). Austin, TX: Pro-Ed.

Developmental Test of Auditory Perception (DTAP)

Ages: 6–18

Source: Reynolds, C. R., Voress, J. K., & Pearson, N. A. (2008). *DTAP: Developmental test of auditory perception.* Austin, TX: Pro-Ed.

Test of Auditory Processing Skills, 3rd Edition (TAPS-3)

Ages: 4–18

Source: Martin, N. A., & Brownell, R. (2005). *Test of auditory processing skills (TAPS-3).* (3rd ed.). Novato, CA: Academic Therapy Publications.

Memory

These assessments measure a student's ability to encode, store, and retrieve new information. Usually include measures of both long- and short-term memory skills as well as active-working memory skills. Many tools also include measures of the ability to store small versus large amounts of information. They aim to provide information regarding a student's ability to learn and recall new information. Usually administered by school psychologists.

California Verbal Learning Test, 2nd Edition (CVLT-II)

Ages: 16–89

Source: Delis, D. C., Kramer, J. H., Kaplan, E., & Ober, B. A. (2000). *California verbal learning test (CVLT-II)* (2nd ed.). San Antonio, TX: Pearson.

Children's Memory Scale (CMS)

Ages: 5–16

Source: Cohen, M. (1997). *Children's memory scale (CMS).* San Antonio, TX: Pearson.

Test of Memory and Learning, 2nd Edition (TOMAL-2)

Ages: 5–59

Source: Reynolds, C. R., & Voress, J. K. (2007). *TOMAL-2: Test of memory and learning* (2nd ed.). Austin, TX: Pro-Ed.

Wide Range Assessment of Memory and Learning, 2nd Edition (WRAML2)

Ages: 5–90

Source: Sheslow, D., & Adams, W. (2003). *Wide range assessment of memory and learning (WRAML2)* (2nd ed.). Torrance, CA: WPS Publishing.

Assessments of Executive Functioning

These assessments measure a student's executive functioning skills, including processes such as planning, problem solving, initiating, judgment, decision making, flexibility of thought, and self-monitoring. They aim to provide information regarding a student's ability to guide, direct, and manage his or her own behavior in order to accomplish a goal. Usually administered by school psychologists.

Behavior Rating Inventory of Executive Function (BRIEF)
Ages: 5–90
Source: Gioia, G. A., Isquith, P. K., Guy, S. C., & Kenworthy, L. (2000). *Behavior rating inventory of executive function (BRIEF)*. Lutz, FL: PAR Inc.

Test of Verbal Conceptualization and Fluency (TVCF)
Ages: 8–89
Source: Reynolds, C. R., & MacNeill Horton, A. (2006). *Test of verbal conceptualization and fluency (TVCF)*. Austin, TX: Pro-Ed.

Achievement and Academic Assessments

These assessments measure a student's academic performance in the areas of reading, writing, and mathematics. They aim to provide a baseline of academic skills, including areas of strength and areas of weakness; areas in need of remediation; and information for writing appropriate academic goals and objectives. Can be administered by school psychologists, teachers of students with visual impairments, resource specialists, or reading or learning specialists.

Basic Reading Inventory (BRI)
Source: Johns, J. L. (2010). *Basic reading inventory: Pre-primer through grade twelve and early literacy assessments* (10th ed.). Dubuque, IA: Kendall Hunt Publishing.

Keymath-3 Diagnostic Assessment (Keymath-3 DA)
Ages: 4–21
Source: Connolly, A. J. (2007). *Keymath-3 diagnostic assessment*. San Antonio, TX: Pearson.

Wechsler Individual Achievement Test, 3rd Edition (WIAT-III)
Ages: 4–19
Source: Wechsler, D. (2009). *Wechsler individual achievement test (WIAT-III)* (3rd ed.). San Antonio, TX: Pearson.

Woodcock-Johnson III Tests of Achievement (Braille Adaptation)
Ages: 2–90+
Source: Jaffe, L. (2009). *Woodcock-Johnson III tests of achievement—Braille adaptation*. Louisville, KY: American Printing House for the Blind.

Adaptive Behavior

These assessments measure a student's personal and social proficiency, including the performance of daily activities necessary to take care of him- or herself, communication skills, and social skills. It is important to recognize that students with visual impairments and multiple disabilities may develop these skills at a different rate than their sighted age-mates. Most adaptive behavior assessments involve gathering data from individuals in the student's life, including teachers and parents. They aim to provide a baseline of daily living skills, including areas of strength and areas of weakness; areas in need of remediation; and information for writing appropriate adaptive behavior goals and objectives. Usually administered by school psychologists.

Adaptive Behavior Assessment System, 2nd Edition (ABAS-II)
Ages: 0–89
Source: Harrison, P., & Oakland, T. (2003). *Adaptive behavior assessment system (ABAS-II)* (2nd ed.). San Antonio, TX: Pearson.

Scales of Independent Behavior—Revised (SIB-R) (Short Form for the Visually Impaired)
Ages: 0–80+
Source: Bruininks, R. H., Woodcock, R. W., Weatherman, R. F., & Hill, B. K. (1996). Short form for the visually impaired. In *Scales of independent behavior—revised (SIB-R)*. Boston: Houghton Mifflin Harcourt.

Vineland Adaptive Behavior Scales, 3rd Edition (Vineland-3)
Ages: 0–90
Source: Sparrow, S. S., Cicchetti, D. V., & Saulnier, C. A. (2016). *Vineland adaptive behavior scales (Vineland-3)* (3rd ed.). San Antonio, TX: Pearson.

Social, Emotional, and Behavioral

These assessments measure a student's social skills, emotional state, and behavioral functioning. Although some social, emotional, and behavioral assessment tools involve direct assessment of the student, many involve gathering data from individuals in the student's life, including teachers and parents. They aim to provide information regarding possible behavioral or mental health difficulties; assess the need for social, emotional, or behavioral interventions; and provide information for writing appropriate social, emotional, and/or behavioral goals and objectives. Usually administered by school psychologists.

Beck Youth Inventories, 2nd Edition (BYI-II)
Ages: 7–18
Source: Beck, J. S., Beck, A. T., & Jolly, J. B., & Steer, R. A. (2005). *Beck youth inventories (BYI-II)* (2nd ed.). San Antonio, TX: Harcourt Assessment.

Behavior Assessment System for Children, 2nd Edition (BASC-2)
Ages: 2–25
Source: Reynolds, C. R., & Kamphaus, R. W. (2004). *Behavior assessment system for children (BASC-2)* (2nd ed.). San Antonio, TX: Pearson.

Children's Depression Inventory, 2nd Edition (CDI 2)
Ages: 7–17
Source: Kovacs, M. (2010). *Children's depression inventory (CDI 2)* (2nd ed.). North Tonawanda, NY: Multi-Health Systems.

Conners 3, 3rd Edition
Ages: 6–18
Source: Conners, C. K. (2008). *Conners 3* (3rd ed.). North Tonawanda, NY: Multi-Health Systems.

Piers-Harris Children's Self-Concept Scale, 2nd Edition (Piers-Harris-2)
Ages: 7–18
Source: Piers, E. V., Harris, D. B., & Herzberg, D. S. (2002). *Piers-Harris children's self-concept scale (Piers-Harris-2)* (2nd ed.). Torrance, CA: WPS Publishing.

Revised Children's Manifest Anxiety Scale, 2nd Edition (RCMAS-2)
Ages: 6–19
Source: Reynolds, C. R., & Richmond, B. O. (2008). *Revised children's manifest anxiety scale (RCMAS-2)* (2nd ed.). Torrance, CA: WPS Publishing.

Reynolds Adolescent Depression Scale, 2nd Edition (RADS-2)
Ages: 11–20
Source: Reynolds, W. M. (1987). *Reynolds adolescent depression scale (RADS-2)* (2nd ed.). Lutz, FL: PAR Inc.

Informal Assessments

Assessment of Braille Literacy Skills (ABLS)
Source: Koenig, A. J., & Farrenkopf, C. (1995). *Assessment of braille literacy skills (ABLS)*. Houston, TX: Region IV Education Service Center.

This assessment provides teachers with a tool for meaningful assessment of braille literacy skills and measures emergent literacy, academic literacy, and functional literacy.

Child-Guided Strategies: The van Dijk Approach to Assessment for Understanding Children and Youth with Sensory Impairments and Multiple Disabilities
Source: Nelson, C., van Dijk, J., Oster, T., & McDonnell, A. (2009). *Child-guided strategies: The van Dijk approach to assessment for understanding children and youth with sensory impairments and multiple disabilities.* Louisville, KY: American Printing House for the Blind.

This assessment kit includes a manual that provides guidance about what to record when assessing the student (component areas to observe, strengths demonstrated by the student in each observed area, determination of what the student is ready to learn in each observed area, and suggestions and recommendations to guide the development of specific strategies used for instruction). Also includes a parent interview structure and observation worksheets. Two DVDs with assessment examples are provided to assist in understanding the assessment process.

Communication Matrix
Source: Rowland, C. (2004). *Communication matrix.* Portland: Oregon Health and Science University.
www.communicationmatrix.org

This assessment instrument is appropriate for use with students whose communication levels range from pre-intentional communication to emerging linguistic. It measures communication performance across four functions of communication: refuse, obtain, social interactions, and seeking information.

CVI Range and CVI Resolution Chart
Source: Roman-Lantzy, C. (2007). *Cortical visual impairment: An approach to assessment and intervention.* New York: AFB Press.

An assessment instrument designed specifically for children with cortical visual impairment to determine a child's level of visual functioning and the effect of the various characteristics of CVI. Can be used by a teacher of students with visual impairments to determine whether a child requires educational vision intervention in living and learning settings.

FVLMA: Functional Vision and Learning Media Assessment for Students Who Are Pre-Academic or Academic and Visually Impaired in Grades K-12
Source: Sanford, L., & Burnett, R. (2008). *FVLMA: Functional vision and learning media assessment for students who are pre-academic or academic and visually impaired in grades K-12: Practitioner's guidebook.* Louisville, KY: American Printing House for the Blind.

This assessment tool for practitioners is used to gather, store, track, and analyze information regarding students' functional vision and appropriate learning media. This instrument provides a framework for systematic and thorough assessment of a student's visual functioning and the student's needs for adapted educational media.

Independent Living: A Curriculum with Adaptations for Students with Visual Impairments
Source: Loumiet, R., & Levack, N. (1993). *Independent living: A curriculum with adaptations for students with visual impairments* (2nd ed.). Austin: Texas School for the Blind and Visually Impaired.

This curriculum that can be used as an assessment will help in assessing, teaching, and evaluating students from school age to adulthood who will live independently or with minimal assistance in social, self-care, and leisure skills.

INSITE Developmental Checklist: Assessment of Developmental Skills for Young Multidisabled Sensory Impaired Children

Source: Morgan, E., & Watkins, S. (1989). *INSITE developmental checklist: Assessment of developmental skills for young multidisabled sensory impaired children.* North Logan, UT: Hope Publishing.

This detailed checklist was especially designed for children with visual impairments or deaf-blindness who have multiple disabilities. It measures skills that typically develop between 0 and 6 years of age.

ISAVE: Individualized Systematic Assessment of Visual Efficiency

Source: Langley, M. B. (1998). *ISAVE: Individualized systematic assessment of visual efficiency.* Louisville, KY: American Printing House for the Blind.

A comprehensive functional vision assessment for children ages 0 to 5 who are cortically impaired, have diagnosed low vision or blindness, or who are at risk of low vision or blindness. Primary purpose is to determine instructional entry level and programming strategies for facilitating functional application of existing degree of visual functioning.

Parents and Their Infants with Visual Impairments (PAIVI)

Source: Chen, D., Calvello, G., & Friedman, C. T. (2015). *PAIVI: Parents and their infants with visual impairments* (2nd ed.). Louisville, KY: American Printing House for the Blind.

This kit includes materials for practitioners and parents. The practitioner's manual includes an ecological inventory, parent observation protocol, assessment guides, information on braille, and how to conduct home visits. The parent booklet includes information on home routines, preparation for preschool, and braille.

ToAD: Tools for Assessment and Development of Visual Skills

Source: Kitchel, E. (2008). *ToAD: Tools for assessment and development of visual skills.* Louisville, KY: American Printing House for the Blind.

This set of standardized tools, toys, and puzzles aids the educator in performing functional vision evaluations and visual skills development activities.

Resources to Support Instructional Planning

Alternate Routines: Adapting Orientation & Mobility Techniques

Source: Zatta, M. C. (2014). *Alternate routines: Adapting orientation and mobility techniques.* Watertown, MA: Perkins School for the Blind.

A self-paced training manual for O&M instructors, parents, and teachers of students with visual impairments consisting of six modules with video segments, readings, and assigned activities to demonstrate theories and best practices for adapting O&M techniques for students with additional disabilities that may affect their ability to master traditional techniques.

Basic Skills for Community Living

Source: Levack, N., Hauser, S., Newton, L., & Stephenson, P. (1997*). Basic skills for community living: A curriculum for students with visual impairments and multiple disabilities.* Austin: Texas School for the Blind and Visually Impaired.

A guide designed for students between the ages of 6 and 22 who have visual impairments combined with other disabilities, such as hearing impairments or dual sensory impairments and/or severe developmental delays, and particularly students who learn best within highly structured routines and who have great difficulty generalizing what they learn to new situations.

Basic Skills for Community Living: Activity Routines

Source: Stephenson, P. (2008). *Basic skills for community living: Activity routines.* Austin: Texas School for the Blind and Visually Impaired.

A companion book to *Basic Skills for Community Living* for the domestic, recreation/leisure, and vocational domains, it includes activity routine discrepancy analysis forms preprinted with routine steps with permission to copy.

Beyond Pegboards: A Guide for Teaching Adolescent Students with Multiple Disabilities

Source: O'Connell, C. (2007). *Beyond pegboards: A guide for teaching adolescent students with multiple disabilities.* Watertown, MA: Perkins School for the Blind.

A practical guidebook that a uses a theme-based approach to create meaningful learning opportunities for students with multiple disabilities, it provides activities that are easy to replicate and can become a springboard for more activities and ideas.

Calendars for Students with Multiple Impairments Including Deafblindness

Source: Blaha, R. (2001). *Calendars for students with multiple impairments including deafblindness.* Austin: Texas School for the Blind and Visually Impaired.

A guide written for students who need help structuring and organizing their time and activities, it includes information about the benefits of calendar systems; calendar programming based on individual students' needs and skills; the continuum of calendars available for expanding students' skills; communication and time; the benefits of anticipation calendars, daily calendars, and expanded calendars; and assessing and evaluating with a calendar.

Clean to the Touch: Housekeeping for Young People with Visual Impairments

Source: Bull, K., Lind-Sinanian, S., & Martin, E. (2008). *Clean to the touch: Housekeeping for young people with visual impairments.* Watertown, MA: Perkins School for the Blind.

A teaching manual containing systematic, easy-to-use, step-by-step techniques that can enable people with visual impairments to accomplish a wide range of housecleaning and housekeeping tasks easily, safely, and effectively.

Communication: A Guide for Teaching Students with Visual and Multiple Impairments

Source: Hagood, L. (1997). *Communication: A guide for teaching students with visual and multiple impairments.* Austin: Texas School for the Blind and Visually Impaired.

A resource guide discussing how deafblindness and visual impairment in children with severe disabilities can affect their communication. Provides approaches for assessing and teaching communication skills, describes a standard tactile symbol system, and offers reproducible forms.

Help Yourself: Mealtime Skills for Students Who Are Blind or Visually Impaired

Source: Shannon, S. (2008). *Help yourself: Mealtime skills for students who are blind or visually impaired.* Watertown, MA: Perkins School for the Blind.

A manual with step-by-step instructions, accompanied by dozens of photos, on how to teach children who are blind or visually impaired to safely and confidently pour liquids, cut and serve food, use utensils and condiments, and more.

School-to-Work: Developing Transition Portfolios for Students with Significant Disabilities

Source: Bridgeo, W., Gicklhorn, C., & Zatta, M. (2007). *School-to-work: Developing transition portfolios for students with significant disabilities.* Watertown, MA: Perkins School for the Blind.

A guide for developing meaningful vocational activities as well as a template for creating transition portfolios for adolescent-age students with significant disabilities.

Total Life Learning: Preparing for Transition: A Curriculum for ALL Students with Sensory Impairments

Source: Bridgeo, W., Caruso, B., D'Andrea, L., Fitzgerald, D., Fox, S., Gicklhorn, C., . . . Zatta, M. (2014). *Total life learning: Preparing for transition. A curriculum for all students with sensory impairments.* Watertown, MA: Perkins School for the Blind.

A curriculum that provides teachers with goals, objectives, and activities in the following content areas: work skills, organizational skills, self-advocacy skills, personal care/daily living skills, employment, and secondary education.

Part 3

Instructional Planning and Design

Chapter 4

Eligibility and IEP Development

Mary C. Zatta

Key Points

- 🔑 Critical importance of an appropriate Individualized Education Program (IEP) for students who have visual impairments and multiple disabilities
- 🔑 Role of the professional in ensuring that the IEP is appropriate
- 🔑 Information and data the professional needs to know to develop an appropriate IEP
- 🔑 Essential information to include in the IEP

Ian is a 4-year-old boy with a cortical visual impairment and cerebral palsy. He is non-ambulatory, uses a wheelchair, and is nonverbal. Ian understands spoken communication and communicates with body language, gestures, facial expressions, and vocalizations. In addition, he uses 15–20 objects—symbolizing people, activities, things, and feelings—to communicate. Ian enjoys participating in a preschool program that focuses on communication, daily living skills, and social skills. Ian enjoys swimming, eating, parties, and helping out at home.

Karen is 10-year-old girl who is totally deafblind (no vision and no hearing). Karen uses tactile sign language, tactile symbols, and uncontracted braille to communicate expressively and receptively. Karen has recently transitioned from a theme-based curriculum to an early academic curriculum with a focus on academic content. Karen enjoys being active, cooking, and playing with her brother and sister.

Eric is an 18-year-old young man with a visual impairment, a hearing impairment, and cerebral palsy. As a result of his cerebral palsy, Eric uses a wheelchair. He is nonverbal and uses sign language and a dedicated augmentative communication device to communicate expressively. Receptively, Eric understands sign language, pictures, and written communication. Eric has basic math and reading skills (first grade level) and participates in a functional curriculum that includes communication, functional academics, career

education, independent living skills, and social skills instruction. Eric enjoys video games, going into the community, and swimming.

It is critical for parents and professionals alike to be informed about eligibility for special education services to ensure that a student with a visual impairment and multiple disabilities receives the appropriate educational services. The Individualized Education Program (IEP; see Chapter 1) is a powerful tool that, when used effectively, can make a significant difference for the student.

This chapter will review the process for establishing eligibility for special education services and how the IEP can ensure that a student's specific disability areas are addressed. Also included are descriptions of each of the components of the IEP, along with suggestions on how to incorporate the requirements needed to meet a student's specific visual and other disability needs.

DETERMINATION OF ELIGIBILITY FOR SPECIAL EDUCATION

The Initial Evaluation

The Individuals with Disabilities Education Improvement Act of 2004 (IDEA) requires that a student receive an initial evaluation before any special education and related services can be provided to him or her (34 C.F.R. § 300.301). Prior to receiving services, the student's eligibility must first be determined by ascertaining that the student has a dis-

ability as defined by IDEA, as described in Chapter 3. (See Chapter 1, Sidebar 1.2 for definitions of the 14 qualifying disabilities.) An evaluation for special education services can be requested by the parents or the school system and must be "sufficiently comprehensive to identify all of the child's special education and related service needs" (IDEA, 2004, 34 C.F.R. § 300.304 [c][6]). (Note that in the legislation, the term "evaluation" is used as the name for the overall process of determining students' eligibility for services as well as their abilities and educational needs, while "assessment" is used for specific tests or methods used in the evaluation.)

For a student with a visual impairment, the evaluation for eligibility must be determined through assessments conducted by professionals with expertise in assessment and program development for individuals with visual impairments, most typically teachers of students with visual impairments. It is important that professionals with the appropriate expertise participate in the evaluation process in order to ensure that the evaluation results are an adequate reflection of a student's abilities and needs. For a student with a visual impairment and multiple disabilities, other related service professionals will need to be involved in the determination of eligibility. For example, if a student has an intellectual impairment, a psychologist will be involved in the assessment; if a student has a physical disability, a physical or occupational therapist, or both, will be involved.

Determination of Eligibility

Once a student's evaluation is complete, the educational team reviews the results and determines whether or not the child is eligible for special education services.

The determination of eligibility is based on two things:

1. The determination that there is a disability.
2. The impact the disability has on the child's educational progress.

A student with a visual impairment is deemed eligible for special education services if it is determined that he or she has a disability *and* is not able to make effective progress in school without special education.

If a student is eligible for special education services, the next step for the educational team is to identify what services are needed and what placement can appropriately provide those services. All of this information, as well as specific goals and objectives, must be included in the student's IEP, which is to be developed by the educational team. Specific information about members of the educational team is discussed later in this chapter.

INCORPORATING EVALUATION RESULTS INTO THE IEP

Evaluation is time-consuming; it is critical that the evaluation process be relevant, worthwhile, and as useful as possible. When done properly, the evaluation process facilitates meaningful IEP development, with a focus on goals and objectives that enhance learning and promote progress for the student.

The results of the evaluation process must be the basis for the IEP, and the evalua-tion results, including the student's strengths, must be written into the IEP document at the outset. It is critical to address the student's specific vision-related and other disability needs in the IEP. The IEP should aim to remediate and compensate for areas that are challenging for the student while ensuring that the student's strengths are considered in the planning process to promote success.

THE EDUCATIONAL TEAM

Without a doubt, writing—and implementing—an effective IEP requires teamwork. Under IDEA, the educational team has a central role in developing and implementing the IEP for the student with an identified disability. The team consists of the parents of the student and the professionals who work with the student and plan his or her education program. The involvement of the parents in the educational team is very important. Their input is critical to the process, and they should be encouraged to contribute based on their knowledge of their child, rather than to defer to the professionals.

Every student's team may be different, depending on the particular needs of that student and the family. The IEP must also specify the types of professionals who should be involved in providing the educational services, as well as the types of specialized knowledge and expertise those professionals should have to address those needs.

IDEA (34 C.F.R. § 300.344) mandates that school districts ensure that the IEP team for a student with a disability includes the following members:

- the parents of the student
- not less than one general education teacher of the student (if the student is, or may be, participating in the general education environment)
- not less than one special education teacher of the student, or where appropriate, not less than one special education provider for the student
- a representative of the school district (who has certain specific knowledge and qualifications)
- an individual who can interpret the instructional implications of evaluation results (may be one of the other listed members)
- at the discretion of the parent or the school district, other individuals who have knowledge or special expertise regarding the student, including related services personnel as appropriate
- whenever appropriate, the student

For students with visual impairments and multiple disabilities including deafblindness, consideration should be given to additional personnel as described in the following sections.

Teachers of Students with Visual Impairments

Teachers of students with visual impairments have specific training to work with students with visual impairments and are certified or licensed as such. They can provide direct services or consultation services (see Chapter 2). Teachers of students with visual impairments can help a student use optical (low vision) and nonoptical devices (such as reading stands);

identify or modify visual materials (for example, providing large print); and acquire educational materials available with federal funds from the American Printing House for the Blind (see Sidebar 4.1).

Teachers of students with visual impairments are specialized teachers with unique competencies to meet the diverse needs of the visually impaired. They work within the special education system but address the unique needs of students with visual impairments. In addition to working with the students (usually in a one-to-one relationship), teachers of students with visual impairments work closely with other teachers, parents, and people and organizations in the community.

Deafblind Specialist

A deafblind specialist is a teacher with specific training and experience with students who are deafblind. A deafblind specialist can provide direct services or consultation services. The deafblind specialist understands the unique effects of combined vision and hearing loss in communication, learning, orientation and mobility, social skills, and the like.

Orientation and Mobility Specialist

Orientation and mobility (O&M) specialists provide students with the skills to understand and navigate their environment, including developing independent travel skills.

Intervener

An intervener is a one-to-one service provider with training and specialized skills in deafblindness. An intervener facilitates access to

---

✏ Sidebar 4.1

The Federal Quota Program

Students are able to obtain books and other educational materials produced by the American Printing House for the Blind (APH) through a federal program, known as the Federal Quota Program, first enacted in 1879. The program is administered by APH through designated agencies in each state, including the state department of education, the state instructional resource center, residential schools, and other agencies serving people with visual impairments. Congress appropriates an annual amount, allocated on a per capita basis, depending on an annual census of eligible students. Individuals of any age are eligible to obtain materials through the program if they fit the definition of legal blindness and are students working below the college level.

Materials available from APH include textbooks in braille, large type, electronic media, and recorded form; assessment materials; braille teaching programs; talking computer software; low vision simulation programs; infant intervention materials; and commercially unavailable educational aids, tools, and supplies, such as adapted audio recording equipment, devices for writing braille, talking computer hardware, and consumable materials like braille paper, bold-line paper, and special binders and notebooks.

Source: Adapted from Holbrook, M. C., & Koenig, A. J. (2000). Basic techniques for modifying instruction. In A. J. Koenig & M. C. Holbrook (Eds.), *Foundations of education: Volume II. Instructional strategies for teaching children and youths with visual impairments* (2nd ed., p. 189). New York: AFB Press.

---

environmental information usually obtained through vision and hearing as well as the development and use of receptive and expressive communication skills and positive relationships to promote social-emotional well-being.

Paraprofessionals

Transcribers, readers, and aides who facilitate the education of students who are visually impaired within the general education classroom are part of the paraprofessional staff. Paraprofessionals may also be involved in addressing student health or behavioral concerns. They will need training from the professionals on the educational team to assist the student to develop skills for independence rather than dependence. A student's IEP should specify whether he or she requires one or more paraprofessionals throughout the entire day or for particular classes or transitions, as well as any training the paraprofessionals need. The IEP should provide a clear description of paraprofessionals' responsibilities and specify the educator who will supervise them.

Administrators

Administrators are responsible for providing appropriate facilities, technical assistance, and educational service delivery to students with visual impairments. Administrators may need training related to the specific needs and essential interventions associated with a student's visual impairment. They may also need assistance in locating the resources needed to implement high-quality programs.

Additional Professionals

The education team might also include one or more additional professionals:

- psychologist
- special education teacher
- social worker
- pediatrician or other medical personnel
- low vision specialist
- audiologist
- assistive technology specialist
- speech-language pathologist
- physical therapist
- occupational therapist

For example, a student with a visual impairment and a physical disability may have a physical therapist on his team, but because the student does not have a hearing impairment, an audiologist will not be part of the team. At the same time, a speech-language pathologist may play a significant role on the team of a student who is nonverbal. (See Sidebar 2.2 in Chapter 2 for more information about the roles and responsibilities of these professionals.)

To write an effective IEP for a student with a visual impairment, the student's education team must come together at a meeting and review the child's unique needs. The individuals on the team combine their knowledge, experi-ence, and commitment to design an educational program to help the child be involved in, and progress in, the general education curriculum—that is, the same curriculum followed by students without disabilities—with appropriate accommodations and modifications. The IEP must include the information that will guide the delivery of special education, related services, and supplementary aids and supports for the student.

PROCEDURAL SAFEGUARDS AND PARENT'S RIGHTS

As part of the responsibilities required by IDEA (2004), every state must issue rules or regulations that provide guidance on the implementation of IDEA within the state (34 C.F.R. § 300.503). At a minimum, state regulations must provide all of the protections contained in IDEA. These regulations are typically referred to as *procedural safeguards*. The procedural safeguards articulate the protections afforded to parents and the student with a disability. Schools are required to provide parents with a full explanation of the procedural safeguards available to them. The procedural safeguards are often distributed at IEP meetings or prior to an evaluation. Sidebar 4.2 lists the components that are generally included in the procedural safeguards.

Parents' participation in the special education decision-making process is vitally important. The most important way parents can ensure that their child's rights are protected is by being involved with their child's educational team. The team is charged with making educational decisions for the student, including decisions such as eligibility, evalua-

---

✎ Sidebar 4.2
IDEA Procedural Safeguards

The Procedural Safeguards Notice that must be provided to parents detailing their rights must include information about the following guarantees in IDEA (Part E, 34 C.F.R.§ 300.504[c]):

- Parents' rights to obtain independent educational evaluations.
- Parents' rights to receive prior written notice any time the school district plans to evaluate the student, schedules a meeting where decisions will be made about the student's eligibility or educational placement, or refuses to evaluate or change the student's plan or placement.
- Parents' rights to consent to evaluations and to the school providing special education services.
- Parents' rights to have access to their child's educational records.

- Parents' rights to present and resolve a complaint through the due process complaint and state complaint processes.
- Students' rights regarding the process to determine if they can be placed in an interim alternative educational setting.
- Parents' rights regarding unilateral placement in private schools at public expense.
- Parents' rights in due process hearings.
- Parents' rights to state-level appeals of decisions made in due process hearings.
- Parents' rights to bring civil actions against the school district or state.
- Parents' rights to reimbursement of attorneys' fees under specific circumstances.

---

tion, and program content, and parents are a critical part of this team. Teachers play an important role in engaging parental participation. By supporting the parents and providing them with the information they need to be good advocates, teachers can help to ensure that the student receives the appropriate instruction and services.

SECTION 504 PROTECTIONS

If a child has a disability but does not require modifications to the educational con-

tent, he or she may not qualify for special education and related services under IDEA, but may qualify for protections under different legislation, commonly known as Section 504. Section 504 of the Rehabilitation Act of 1973 protects individuals with disabilities from discrimination for reasons related to their disabilities. Section 504 is a federal civil rights law, under which a child with a disability may receive accommodations that are not available to children who are not disabled.

Accommodations are changes made by classroom teachers and other school staff to allow for the student's disability and enable the student to benefit from his or her educational program. Examples of such accommodations include:

- an extra set of textbooks for home use
- adjusting the student's seating
- study guides and organizing tools
- a peer tutor or helper
- recorded books
- school counseling
- untimed tests or oral tests
- use of an organizer
- training for the student in organizational skills
- spellchecker
- calculator
- transportation

For example, a student who needs accommodations in order to make progress in school but does not need specially designed instruction (such as braille instruction, O&M instruction, and the like) will not qualify for services under IDEA but will receive protections under Section 504 of the Rehabilitation Act. Those protections may include accommodations for statewide testing or curricular accommodations, but will not include any modifications to educational content. If a student qualifies for protections under Section 504 but not under IDEA, a 504 plan would need to be developed to articulate the specific accommodations needed by the student as well as what instructional personnel will be responsible for providing the accommodations. However, Section 504 does *not* include the procedural protections that are available under IDEA.

In most cases, it is likely that students with visual impairments who have multiple disabilities will in fact require specially designed instruction, and therefore, a 504 plan would not apply. However, it is important for educators to understand the difference so that they make the appropriate recommendations. (More information related to specially designed instruction is described later in this chapter.)

COMPONENTS OF THE IEP

To ensure that the student's vision-related and other disability needs are addressed in the IEP, it is important to make sure that all components of the IEP are addressed:

- the present level of educational performance of the student
- measurable annual goals, objectives, and benchmarks that will be used to track the student's progress
- service delivery the student will receive
- related services to be provided to the student
- types of accommodations, specially designed instruction, and supplementary aids and services required by the student
- the student's participation in statewide assessment
- extended school year services to be provided to the student
- transition needs of the student
- age of majority rights that will transfer to student, if appropriate (see the section on age of majority later in this chapter)
- progress evaluations and reports for the student

- results from the student's reevaluations
- the student's placement

Figure 4.1 provides a checklist to assist the teacher of students with visual impairments in ensuring that all of the components of the IEP are completed.

Present Level of Educational Performance

The *present level of educational performance,* sometimes referred to as present level of performance (and sometimes abbreviated as PLEP or PLOP), is a section of the IEP that describes the student's current achievement in the areas of need as determined by an evaluation. Along with current achievement, the present level of educational performance summary includes information for the student on the following items:

- learning style
- adaptive behavior
- rate of progress in acquiring new skills
- knowledge in development in subject and skill areas including activities of daily living
- academic strengths
- preferences
- interests
- academic and functional needs including consideration of parental concerns
- social and physical development
- social and physical needs
- disability and its impact on educational progress (see following section)

For students with visual impairments and multiple disabilities, it is important to include a description of how a student's disabilities affect his or her participation or progress in the general curriculum. This might include:

- ways the student's vision loss and other disabilities impact his or her learning
- specific, measurable, and objective information for each area of need affected by the disability (as determined in the evaluation process)
- links between (1) the evaluation results, (2) the expectations of the general curriculum and the expanded core curriculum, and (3) the goals for the student
- transition needs (for older students) in the areas of instruction, employment, post-school adult living, community services, and related services

Measurable Annual Goals, Objectives, and Benchmarks

There is a direct relationship between goals and the areas of need identified in the present level of educational performance summary. *Annual goals* are descriptions of what a student can reasonably be expected to accomplish within a 12-month period with the provision of special education services. There must be at least one need area identified for each goal. In other words, if a student's need areas are English language arts, math, social skills, O&M, physical education, and independent living skills, each goal listed on the IEP must identify at least one of these areas.

The educational team will want to consider the following questions when writing goals for the IEP:

Figure 4.1
IEP Checklist

INDIVIDUALIZED EDUCATION PROGRAM CHECKLIST

☐ Student's eligibility has been determined (initial evaluation for special education)

☐ IEP meeting includes the appropriate personnel and parents

☐ Parents have been informed of the procedural safeguards (provided by the school district)

☐ Most recent evaluation results are incorporated into the IEP and include the student's strengths and specific vision-related and other disability needs

☐ IEP identifies the appropriate personnel

☐ IEP is aligned with the common core and the expanded core curricula

☐ Present level of educational performance summary contains the appropriate information

☐ Annual goals are measurable and appropriate

☐ An annual goal is stated for each identified need area

☐ Objectives or benchmarks include the appropriate information

☐ Objectives or benchmarks pass the "dead man's test"

☐ Service delivery section includes all the appropriate information

☐ Related services section includes all the appropriate information

The IEP includes appropriate information for the following areas pertaining to the student:

☐ Accommodations

☐ Specially designed instruction

☐ Supplementary aids and services

☐ Assistive technology needs

☐ Participation in the statewide assessment system (including accommodations needed to effectively participate in the statewide assessment system)

☐ Extended school year needs

☐ Transition needs (if over 16 or, in some states, 14)

☐ Age of majority rights transfer (if appropriate)

☐ Progress reports

☐ Reevaluation results

☐ Placement determination

1. Is the goal clear and understandable?
2. Is the goal positively stated?
3. Is there at least one need area for each goal?
4. Can the goal be justified on the basis of the information in the student's present level of educational performance summary?
5. Is the goal practical and relevant to the student's academic, social, and vocational needs?
6. Is the goal practical and relevant when the student's age and remaining years in school are considered?
7. Does the goal reflect appropriate growth within the instructional area?

8. Can the goal be accomplished within one year?

Objectives or *benchmarks* serve as a means of measuring the student's progress and determine if the student is making sufficient progress toward attaining an annual goal. *Short-term objectives* are the intermediate steps required to achieve a goal and benchmarks are the major milestones a student must attain to achieve the goal. Either is acceptable in an IEP. When writing objectives or benchmarks it is important to ensure that the following information is included:

- performance of a specific behavior
- conditions or circumstances under which the behavior is performed
- criteria for attainment or level of performance
- evaluation procedures

As an example:

> Eric will independently make a purchase in the community using his communication system 75 percent of the time.

Using the criteria outlined in the steps above, we can break this objective down to ensure that it is written appropriately:

- behavior: make a purchase in the community
- conditions: using his communication system
- criteria: independently
- evaluation: 75 percent of the time

Another standard that is often used to ensure that goals and objectives are written appropriately is to make sure they are S.M.A.R.T.:

Specific
Measurable
Attainable
Realistic
Timely

The S.M.A.R.T standard makes sure that goals and objectives specify what the student is expected to achieve, what criteria will be used to measure achievement, and how progress will be measured.

Goals, objectives, and benchmarks must be measurable so that it is possible to evaluate students' progress. Goals must be student-based and specify the skills that the student will develop.

Here is an example of an inappropriate objective:

> Student will be presented with three choices.

This is actually an objective for the staff because the action required (presenting three choices) is an action for the staff.

Here is an example of how this objective can be written appropriately:

> Given a choice of three activities, the student will indicate her preference by pointing toward the activity she wants.

This is an appropriate objective because it shows an action on the student's part.

When writing objectives and benchmarks it is often helpful to apply the "dead man's test": if a dead man can do it, there is no action required of the student and it is not a student-based objective or benchmark. Applying this test to the previous example, producing "a dead man will be presented with three choices," demonstrates the point.

In the past, benchmarks or short-term objectives were required elements in every student's IEP. As of IDEA 2004 (34 C.F.R. 300.347[s][2]), this is no longer true. Now, benchmarks or short-term objectives are required *only* for children with disabilities who take alternate statewide assessments. Students who are unable to take the standard statewide assessments even with accommodations will take their state's alternate assessment. Since many students who are visually impaired with multiple disabilities participate in the alternate assessment system, their IEPs must include benchmarks or short-term objectives.

Service Delivery

Determination of appropriate service delivery for students with visual impairments is discussed in Chapter 2. The service delivery section of the IEP includes the following information:

- *what* services the student will receive
- *how often* the student will receive the service(s) (number of times per day or week)
- *how long* each "session" will last (number of minutes)
- *where* services will be provided (in the general education classroom or another setting such as a special education resource room)
- *when* services will begin and end (starting and ending dates)
- *who* will provide the service (what personnel)

In addition, the service delivery section articulates the following:

- whether the service method will be *direct* or *indirect/consulting* (see Chapter 2)
- if the service will be provided in the *regular education classroom* or *outside the regular education classroom*
- if the service will be provided in *English* or *another language*
- how large a *group size* the service will be provided to
- the *IEP goal(s)* the service corresponds to (a minimum of one goal is required for each service)

Figure 4.2 provides an example of one possible configuration of services for a student with a visual impairment. In this example, the service delivery grid delineates that the student's need areas are English language arts, functional academics, O&M, physical therapy, and social skills. The grid shows the frequency and duration of the instruction in each area as well as whether the service is a direct or consulting service. The student will receive both direct and consulting services (to the special education teacher and the parents) in several need areas: O&M, physical therapy, social skills. Also note that the personnel column does not name specific professionals but instead names the professional title.

Related Services

IDEA (2004) defines the term *related services* as "transportation and such developmental, corrective and other supportive services as are required to assist a child with a disability to benefit from special education. . . ." (34 C.F.R. § 300.34[a]). Related services can include, but are not limited to, any of the following:

Figure 4.2

Example of a Service Delivery Grid

	SERVICE DELIVERY GRID					
Goal	Service	Frequency	Duration (per session)	Location	Start/End Date	Personnel
Direct Services						
1	English language arts (including braille and communication)	5x/week	30 minutes	Special education classroom	9/6/16– 6/22/17	Teacher of students with visual impairments
2	Functional academics	3x/week	1 hour	Special education classroom	9/12/16– 6/17/17	Special education teacher
3	Orientation and mobility	3x/week	30 minutes	Springfield Elementary campus	9/12/16– 6/17/17	O&M specialist
4	Physical therapy	2x/week	30 minutes	Therapy room	9/20/16– 6/15/17	Physical therapist
5	Social skills	3x/week	30 minutes	Special education classroom	9/19/16– 6/17/17	Teacher of students with visual impairments
Consultation Services						
1	Orientation and mobility	1x/month	30 minutes	Springfield Elementary campus	9/16– 6/17	O&M specialist
2	Physical therapy	1x/month	30 minutes	Special education classroom	9/16– 6/17	Physical therapist
3	Social skills	1x/month	30 minutes	Special education classroom	9/16– 6/17	Teacher of students with visual impairments

- speech-language pathology
- audiology services
- interpreting services
- psychological services
- physical therapy
- occupational therapy
- recreation, including therapeutic recreation
- assistive technology services
- counseling services, including rehabilitation counseling
- O&M services
- medical services for diagnostic or evaluation purposes
- school health services and school nurse services
- social work services in schools
- parent counseling and training

The evaluation process is intended to provide the team with the information needed to identify the related services a student will need. In addition to identifying the related services areas, the service delivery section of the IEP must also specify the following for each recommended service:

- start date
- anticipated frequency (how often)
- anticipated location (where)
- anticipated duration (how long)

Accommodations, Specially Designed Instruction, and Supplementary Aids and Services

Students with visual impairments frequently require supplementary aids and services, ac-

commodations, and specially designed instruction in order to access the educational environment.

Accommodations

Accommodations are practices and procedures intended to reduce or even eliminate the effects of a student's disability. Accommodations do not reduce learning expectations. Accommodations change *how* the student will be taught or expected to learn, but not *what* he or she needs to learn. Accommodations are commonly categorized in three ways: presentation, response, and setting/timing/scheduling.

Presentation Accommodations. *Presentation accommodations* allow students who are blind or visually impaired to access information in ways that do not require them to visually read standard print. These alternate modes of access are auditory, multisensory, tactile, and visual. For the student with a visual impairment and multiple disabilities, presentation accommodations are critical to educational success. Examples of presentation accommodations include the following:

- total communication (multiple forms of communication including pictures, objects, sign language, etc.)
- enlargement devices (electronic video magnifiers, handheld magnifiers)
- braille
- large print
- voice output devices
- picture symbols, picture sequences
- object symbols
- amplification, hearing aids, FM systems

- sign language
- written material presented orally or via audio recording
- directions presented to meet student need
- behavior support plan
- adapted environment to meet student's visual needs
- adapted environment to meet student's auditory needs
- predictable environments

Response Accommodations. *Response accommodations* allow students to complete activities, assignments, and assessments in different ways. Examples of response accommodations include the following:

- use of a scribe
- use of a template
- use of assistive technology
- increased response time
- use of a switch
- signing, pointing, use of a communication board
- use of cues
- individualized response format (yes/no, multiple choice)
- use of behavior support plan (motivation)

Setting/Timing/Scheduling Accommodations. *Setting/timing/scheduling accommodations* change the location or the conditions of the instructional setting. The allowable length of time to complete an assignment may be increased or the way the time is organized may be changed. The following are some examples:

- extended time
- material presented in short blocks of time
- time of day taken into account
- flexible schedule
- time added to master material
- shortened day or lengthened day
- individual schedule
- small group
- distraction-free environment
- preferential seating

Effective decision making about the provision of appropriate accommodations begins with making good instructional decisions. When making decisions about accommodations, the IEP team attempts to level the playing field so that students with disabilities can participate in the general education curriculum on the same level as their peers without disabilities. Accommodations are not meant to give an unfair advantage to a student with disabilities.

Good decision making is facilitated by gathering and reviewing valid data and information regarding the student's disability, present level of academic achievement, and functional performance in relation to district content standards. The IEP team must record each appropriate accommodation in the student's IEP. Students must be provided the selected accommodations during instructional situations that necessitate the use of those accommodations. Teachers and staff of students with visual impairments and multiple disabilities must be familiar with the appropriate accommodation strategies required for each individual student in order to ensure that the students have equal opportunities to achieve academically.

Specially Designed Instruction

Specially designed instruction in its simplest form is "what the teacher does" to instruct, assess, and re-teach the student. Specially designed instruction affects the instructional content, method of instructional delivery, and the performance methods and criteria. Specially designed instruction defines the specific *modifications to instruction* (alterations to educational content) that are necessary to assist the student in making meaningful educational progress. This instruction is designed by or with an appropriately credentialed teacher of students with visual impairments, special education teacher, or related service provider. Unlike accommodations, a modification changes *what* a student is taught or expected to learn.

The IEP team should determine whether modifications to instruction should be included in a student's IEP. Generally, if a methodology is an essential part of what is required to meet the individualized needs of the student, the methodology should be included in the IEP.

Modifications are divided into three categories: modification of content, modification of delivery, and modification of methodology. The following are examples of each category:

Modification of Content
- key concepts/essence
- alternate content
- functional skills
- access skills
- content at [a designated] grade level
- reduced assignments

Modification of Delivery
- integrated team approach
- natural environments
- natural routines
- structured routines
- consistent routines

Modification of Methodology
- objects and manipulatives
- experience-based learning
- hand-under-hand and hand-over-hand techniques
- demonstration
- social reinforcement
- tangible reinforcement
- imitation
- modeling
- inquiry-based communication
- consistency across settings
- clear beginning, middle, and end
- partial participation
- cues, prompts, and physical assistance
- frequent comprehension checks

Considering the case studies presented at the beginning of this chapter and using the list of modifications just presented, the recommendations that may be made for specially designed instruction for each student include the following:

Ian
- teach key concepts
- provide alternate content
- incorporate instruction in functional skills
- teach access skills
- use a team approach

- teach in natural environments and within natural routines
- provide structured routines
- use objects and manipulatives
- provide experience-based learning
- use demonstration and modeling
- provide social reinforcement
- provide opportunities for partial participation
- include frequent comprehension checks

Karen

- provide modified content to the 1st/2nd grade level
- teach key concepts
- use a team approach
- use manipulatives
- use demonstration and modeling
- ensure consistency across settings
- provide frequent comprehension checks

Eric

- teach key concepts
- incorporate instruction in functional skills
- provide alternate content
- use a team approach
- teach in natural environments and within natural routines
- use objects and manipulatives
- provide experience-based learning
- use demonstration and modeling
- provide social reinforcement
- provide opportunities for partial participation
- provide cues, prompts, and physical assistance

Supplementary Aids and Services

Supplementary aids and services are often critical elements in supporting the education of children with disabilities in regular classes and their participation in a range of other school activities. *Supplementary aids and services* as defined by IDEA (2004) reads:

> Supplementary aids and services means aids, services, and other supports that are provided in regular education classes, other education-related settings, and in extracurricular and nonacademic settings, to enable children with disabilities to be educated with nondisabled children to the maximum extent appropriate. . . . (34 C.F.R. § 300.42)

Supplementary aids and services can include direct services and supports to the child, as well as support and training for staff members who work with that child. Therefore, determining what supplementary aids and services are appropriate for a particular child must be done on an individual basis. Supplementary services should be considered in the following areas (Center for Parent Information and Resources, 2013):

- levels of staff support needed (such as consultation, stop-in support, classroom companion, one-on-one assistance; and type of personnel support: behavior specialist, health care assistant, instructional support assistant)
- planning time for collaboration needed by staff
- child's specialized equipment needs (such as wheelchair, computer, software,

voice synthesizer, augmentative communication device, utensils/cups/plates, restroom equipment)
- training needed for personnel
- supports to address environmental needs (such as preferential seating; planned seating on the bus, in the classroom, at lunch, in the auditorium, and in other locations; or altered physical room arrangement)

Considering the case studies presented at the beginning of the chapter, the following recommendations may be made for supplementary aids and services in each student's IEP:

Ian
- communication systems
- switch-activated devices
- communication boards, books, or cards
- picture-based communication
- relaxation strategies
- gestures and visual cues
- sensory issues addressed
- recorded books with appropriate pacing
- environmental modifications
- study carrel
- one-to-one and small group instruction

Karen
- sign language
- augmentative communication devices
- educational interpreter
- graphic organizers
- braille
- manipulatives
- access to technology
- tactile graphics
- braille watch

Eric
- sign language
- high technology communication device
- educational interpreter
- large print
- visual prompts
- cue cards
- self-monitoring checklists
- simple directions
- highlighted material
- access to technology
- schedule
- positive feedback and praise

Assistive Technology

Assistive technology enables children or youth with disabilities to participate more fully in all aspects of life (home, school, community) and helps them access their right to free appropriate public education in the least restrictive environment. The IEP team must determine whether an individual student needs an assistive technology device or service, and if so, what technology is needed. It is important that an assistive technology evaluation be conducted to determine the student's needs. The need for assistive technology must be determined on a case-by-case basis as part of related services or supplementary aids and services, and any needs identified must be reflected in the student's IEP.

In conducting an assistive technology assessment, the team will want to carefully consider the following:

- the environments the student accesses
- the tasks the student is asked to accomplish
- the challenges the student has in accomplishing the tasks

The answers to these questions will determine the current educational needs of the student. Then, the question must be asked, "Would assistive technology enable the student to meet the goals outlined in the IEP?"

It is important to remember that consideration of assistive technology and its role in the education program of a student is an ongoing process. As the student's environment, tasks, and abilities change, it is likely that the student's needs will change as well. The consideration of assistive technology needs is required to be a part of every annual IEP (IDEA, 34 C.F.R. § 300.346[a][2][v]). (See Chapter 12 for more information regarding assistive technology for students with visual impairments and multiple disabilities.)

Student Participation in Statewide Assessment

Federal laws, including IDEA (34 C.F.R. § 300.160[a]) and the Every Student Succeeds Act (2015), mandate that students with disabilities participate in the general education curriculum and in testing programs to the maximum extent possible for each student. Because of these laws, schools have become accountable in new and significant ways for the education of all students with disabilities.

Students may participate in statewide assessments in one of three ways:

1. Participate in the statewide assessment without accommodations.
2. Participate in the statewide assessment with accommodations.
3. Participate in an alternate statewide assessment with or without accommodations.

It is the responsibility of the IEP team to determine how a student will participate in the statewide assessment process. Within the IEP meeting, the team will discuss the strengths and abilities of the individual student and what, if any, accommodations are needed for participation in the statewide assessment or in an alternate statewide assessment. This information should be recorded in the IEP.

Federal law requires the use of accommodations for students with disabilities when necessary. The challenge for educators and families is to decide which accommodations will help students demonstrate what they've learned. The IEP team is responsible for determining *if* a student requires accommodations as well as *what* accommodations need to be provided to the student in statewide testing. It is critical for students with visual impairments to be appropriately assessed, which means ensuring that they receive the appropriate accommodations and/or modifications as specified in the IEP. Table 4.1 provides a checklist of the most frequently allowed accommodations that students with visual impairments might request on a statewide assessment; the specific accommodations vary from state to state.

Students who are unable to participate in the regular statewide assessment system will participate in an alternate assessment. *Alternate assessments* provide an assessment mechanism for students with the most significant cognitive disabilities and for other students with disabilities who may need alternate ways to access assessments in order to be included in the educational accountability system.

The primary purpose of alternate assessments in state assessment systems is to ensure that *all* students are included in the statewide

Table 4.1

Checklist of Accommodations for Statewide Assessment Systems

Type of Accommodation	Accommodation Needed	Accommodation Not Needed	Comments
Presentation Accommodations			
Test in uncontracted braille, by special request			
Test in contracted braille			
Test in regular print with magnification device			
Oral reading of test directions or other allowable portions of the test			
Test in audio format with braille or large print text and graphics (to be used with or without magnification devices)			
Test in audio format with regular print text and graphics (to be used with or without magnification devices)			
Test on computer with refreshable braille display			
Test on computer with screen enlargement software			
Test on computer with large monitor			
Test on computer with screen magnifier in front of regular monitor			
Test on computer with speech output			
Test on computer with complete copy of braille/tactile graphics test			
Test on computer with complete copy of large-print test			
Test on computer with complete copy of regular print test, as allowed by the state			
Subtests given in different order if necessary			
Signing of appropriate parts of the test for deafblind students			
Administration in native language			
Response Accommodations			
Present answers orally to a test proctor			
Tape record answers			
Write answers in test booklet			
Write answers on separate paper			
Use word processors, braillewriters, or notetakers to write responses			

Type of Accommodation	Accommodation Needed	Accommodation Not Needed	Comments
Setting Accommodations			
Individual administration			
Small group administration room			
Ample table space for testing materials and writing tools			
Special lighting			
Adaptive or special furniture			
Distraction-free space in a separate room			
Scheduling Accommodations			
Extended time for test completion			
Several brief testing sessions			
Testing at a different time of the day			
Additional break options			
Testing over a longer period of time (within the testing window)			
Special Tools Accommodations			
3-D objects, as allowed			
Abacus			
Talking calculator			
Large-print calculator			
Braille ruler or protractor			
Large-print ruler or protractor			
Graphing tools and paper			
Bold-lined paper			
Line markers and place holding templates			
Magnification devices			
Tape recorder for audiotaped version of test, including headphones			
Computer with speech output and/or refreshable braille display, braillewriter and paper, or notetaker for recording responses			

accountability system, which increases the ability of large-scale accountability systems to create information about how a school, district, or state is doing in terms of overall student performance.

Extended School Year Services

The IDEA regulations define *extended school year services* as special education and related services that are provided to a student as follows:

- beyond the normal school year of the school district or public agency
- in accordance with a student's IEP
- at no cost to the parents of the student
- in such a way as to meet the requirements of the State Educational Agency (34 C.F.R. § 300.106)

Eligibility for extended school year services is determined by the IEP team annually at the student's IEP meeting; with the decision based on the needs of the student. The most widely used criteria for determining the need for extended school year services are regression and recoupment. *Regression* determines if a student is likely to lose critical skills during the time when services are not delivered. If the likelihood of regression is established, then the IEP team must determine whether the time the student will require to re-learn the skills lost (*recoupment*) will be excessive.

Extended school year services are not necessarily a continuation of the same instructional program and related services the student receives during the normal school year. Some students may need only certain instruction or related services (such as reading instruction or speech-language therapy) outside the normal school year. Once the IEP team agrees that a student is eligible for extended school year services, a description of those services should be included in the student's IEP.

Transition

IDEA mandates schools use the IEP as the vehicle for planning for anticipated individual student needs beyond the completion of secondary education. Beginning at age 16—or younger if deemed appropriate by the IEP team, state regulation, or both—the IEP must contain the following:

- appropriate measurable postsecondary goals based upon age-appropriate transition assessments related to training, education, employment, and independent living skills
- transition services (including course of study) needed to assist the student in reaching the stated postsecondary goals

The IEP team must determine, to the extent appropriate, if any other public agency must be invited to the IEP meeting because they are likely to be responsible for providing or paying for transition services for the student (34 C.F.R. § 300.321[b][3]). If a transition service provider fails to provide the transition service it has agreed to provide, the school must reconvene the IEP team to identify alternative strategies to meet the transition objectives. (See Chapter 15 for more information about planning an effective transition.)

Age of Majority

Age of majority is the legal age established under state law at which an individual is no longer a minor and, as a young adult, has the right and responsibility to make certain legal choices that adults make. When people use the term "age of majority," they are generally referring to the age at which a young person is considered to be an adult. Depending on the state in which the student lives, the age of majority is usually between 18 and 21. Once a student has reached the age of majority, the state may transfer educational rights from the parents to the student. This means that the student becomes his or her own guardian. Not all states transfer rights at the age of majority. However, in many states, the rights and responsibilities that parents have had under IDEA will transfer to the student at that time. This can be a tricky concept for parents who may not understand that their rights as guardians are terminated when their child reaches the age of majority.

Beginning at least one year before the student reaches the age of majority, this topic must be discussed and the IEP must include a statement that the student has received notice and been told about the rights (if any) that will transfer to him or her.

Progress Reports

Another component of the IEP that IDEA requires is the specification of how the student's progress toward meeting the annual goals will be measured. This statement should include the following information:

- how the student's progress will be measured

- when the student's progress will be measured (reporting period)
- the evaluation criteria (how well a student must perform)

The information on how well a child must perform and how his or her progress will be measured is often called *evaluation criteria.* Well-written evaluation criteria are stated in objective, measurable terms. For example:

> Jessica traveled the prescribed route from the classroom to the bathroom using her cane without assistance 25 percent of the time as documented by teacher observation.

Reevaluation

After the initial evaluation, the student must have a reevaluation every three years (or more often if needed) in order to determine the following:

- if the student continues to have a disability that requires special education and related services
- what the student's educational needs are
- if any changes need to be made to the student's program to help him or her
  - meet annual goals and objectives
  - participate, as appropriate, in the general curriculum

When it is time for reevaluation, the team must review the information and any test results that have been gathered on the student (observations, classroom-based assessments, and the like) and determine the following:

- if there is a need for additional information to determine whether the student continues to be a child with a disability in need of special education and related services

- the student's present level of educational performance
- the student's educational needs

It may be determined that no additional information is necessary for the team to make their decision. Conversely, it may be determined that more information is needed, in which case the parents will be asked to give permission for testing. If the team determines that the student no longer needs special education services, the parent has the right to request that an evaluation be conducted. If the team finds that the student continues to have a disability that requires special education and related services, they can proceed with developing a new IEP for the upcoming year.

Placement

Many teams make the mistake of discussing placement before developing the IEP. Decisions about placement are best made after the student's IEP is developed. Once the IEP has articulated the student's abilities and needs, the team can then determine what setting (placement) is the most appropriate (the least restrictive environment that can meet the student's educational needs). Placement decisions for all students with disabilities must be determined annually by the IEP team based on the student's IEP (34 C.F.R. § 300.116[b][c][d][e]).

If the regular education classroom cannot appropriately meet the requirements of the IEP, other options must be considered.

School districts are to make available a range of placement options, known as a *continuum of alternative placements*, to meet the unique educational needs of children with disabilities (34 C.F.R. § 300.115[a]). The continuum of options should include:

- instruction in general education classes
- special classes
- special schools (day and residential)
- home instruction
- instruction in hospitals

This requirement for a continuum of options reinforces the importance of an individualized approach, not a "one size fits all" approach, in determining which placement is the least restrictive environment for each student with a disability.

Courts have held that schools may not predetermine placement. The placement decision must be made by the IEP team. It is critical to follow the process as intended, as failure to do so may result in litigation.

SUMMARY

This chapter has taken an in-depth look at the IEP—how it came to be and how the IEP can address the needs of students with visual impairments and multiple disabilities. This information is a critical resource for parents and professionals involved in the process of developing and implementing educational programs for students with visual impairments and multiple disabilities and is meant to serve as a reference tool in this regard. The IEP is a powerful tool that can ensure that students with visual impairments and multiple disabilities receive appropriate educational services.

REFERENCES

Center for Parent Information and Resources. (2013). Supplementary aids and services. Newark, NJ: Author. Retrieved from http://www.parentcenterhub.org/repository/iep-supplementary/

Every Student Succeeds Act, Pub. L. No. 114-95 (2015).

Holbrook, M. C., & Koenig, A. J. (2000). Basic techniques for modifying instruction. In A. J. Koenig & M. C. Holbrook (Eds.), *Foundations of education: Volume II. Instructional strategies for teaching children and youths with visual impairments* (2nd ed., pp. 173–195). New York: AFB Press.

Individuals with Disabilities Education Improvement Act (IDEA), 20 U.S.C. § 1400 (2004).

Rehabilitation Act of 1973, 29 U.S.C. § 701 (1973).

Chapter 5

Curriculum for Students with Visual Impairments Who Have Multiple Disabilities

Mary C. Zatta

Key Points

- Why curriculum is important
- How to align curriculum with the Common Core State Standards
- The importance of the expanded core curriculum for students with visual impairments and multiple disabilities
- The importance of a functional curriculum
- The importance of a theme-based curriculum
- Appropriate curricula combinations given the age and abilities of the student

---

The word "curriculum" evokes many different meanings and is often a source of confusion and misunderstanding. The goals of this chapter are not only to clarify what curriculum is, but also, more important, to show how a defined curriculum is critical to the provision of an effective educational program for students who have visual impairments and multiple disabilities as well as how teachers can use curriculum to provide that effective program.

The word "curriculum" is defined in many ways, including the following:

- "[T]he means and materials with which students will interact for the purpose of achieving identified educational outcomes." (education.com, n.d.)

- (a) "The aggregate of courses of study given in a school, college, university, etc." (b) "The regular or a particular course of study in a school, college, etc." (Dictionary.com, n.d.)

- "The courses that are taught by a school, college, etc." (Merriam-Webster Online Dictionary, n.d.)

Thus, the word "curriculum" can be described on one level as the lesson plans and materials a teacher uses and on another level as the overall school plan for instruction. In this chapter we will look at curriculum first at the school level as we examine the Common Core State Standards, expanded core curriculum, functional curriculum, and theme-based curriculum; and then at the classroom level as we explore instructional strategies.

"The educational goal for every student is to become an active participant and contributing member of society" (Ford et al., 1989, p. ix). This is the goal that all educators seek for their students, and they are challenged to determine how best to achieve this goal for students with visual impairments and multiple disabilities. Providing students with visual impairments and multiple disabilities with the appropriate curriculum is an essential part of meeting this challenge.

Critical to achieving the goal of becoming contributing members of society is how to achieve the quality of life to which we all aspire as we become adults, including where we live, whom we live with, and the nature of our living environment. *Quality of life* includes the components of living, loving, working, and playing. It is the teacher's job to ensure that students develop the skills necessary to develop the ability to live in a manner of their choosing. Curriculum can assist teachers in incorporating these important skills into their daily instructional planning.

Most students with visual impairments and multiple disabilities are unable to progress through the typical academic curriculum at the same pace and in the same manner as their peers. Typically, these students require a "personalized" (Browder, 2001, p. 3) curriculum that meets each student's individual needs.

Teachers often lack an articulated curriculum—one that incorporates a logical, sequential progression of learning objectives—for students with visual impairments and multiple disabilities, particularly those students with more complex disabilities. However, a specific instructional plan (curriculum) is necessary in order to ensure that each student with a visual impairment and multiple disabilities maximizes his or her potential.

This chapter will explore curriculum at the school level, focusing on the Common Core State Standards (CCSS), expanded core curriculum (ECC), functional curriculum, and theme-based curriculum. This discussion will include the focus of each curriculum and how each can complement the others to meet the educational needs of students with visual impairments and multiple disabilities.

The chapter will also look at curriculum at the classroom level via instructional strategies, including specific ideas and resources for curriculum implementation. This chapter will explore ways to ensure that each student with a visual impairment and multiple disabilities can be provided with a "personalized" or "individualized" curriculum despite the fact that the range of abilities among this population is so varied. In particular, this chapter will assist teachers in considering such factors as the student's age and ability to determine the appropriate curriculum for their students. These tools and resources will assist teachers in helping each of their students reach his or her full potential.

THE IMPORTANCE OF CURRICULUM

When people take a road trip, they generally have some idea of how to get to the destination, using a reference tool that have the necessary information—a map, a GPS, written directions, or the like. Similarly when teachers think about what they want to teach their students they need to have a plan—a course of action. Curriculum is that plan of action.

Curriculum can be thought of as a map or blueprint for a designated course of study that spans the ages of the students in the school. Not only does curriculum provide an outline of this course of study, it also provides direction regarding the route that students must travel so that they learn the same skills along the way. Without a school curriculum, each teacher would be left to his or her own devices to determine what to teach, when to teach it, and how to teach it. Under those circumstances, students would end up in different places and have taken very different routes to get there; that is, they would finish school with varying sets of knowledge and having learned different skills than their schoolmates. Curriculum is necessary to ensure a continuity of educational service for all students, including those with visual impairments and multiple disabilities.

For students with visual impairments and multiple disabilities it is even more critical that the curriculum be appropriate and clear. These students have more content to learn than their sighted peers (such as braille, orientation and mobility, assistive technology, and other skills). In addition, this group of students may take longer to learn than their sighted peers.

INCLUSION IN THE GENERAL EDUCATION CURRICULUM

In today's educational climate there is a tremendous emphasis on including students with disabilities in the general curriculum. The *general curriculum*, also known as the *general education curriculum* or the *core curriculum*, contains those subject areas that are considered to be the general academic content areas: math, science, English language arts, social studies, fine arts, physical education, health, economics, and the like.

The Every Student Succeeds Act (ESSA; 2015), like its predecessor, the Elementary and Secondary Education Act of 2001 (commonly known as No Child Left Behind [NCLB]), requires that *all* children receive a high-quality education and demonstrate proficiency on state achievement standards and assessments. In addition, the Individuals with Disabilities Education Improvement Act of 2004 (IDEA) indicates that Individualized Education Program (IEP) goals should enable students to make progress in the general curriculum and meet educational needs. However, these mandates have resulted in states developing differing standards and assessments for their students. This lack of uniformity led to the Common Core State Standards (CCSS) initiative (n.d.).

The Common Core State Standards

The CCSS initiative is a state-led effort that established a single set of educational standards for kindergarten through 12th grade in English language arts and mathematics in order to adequately prepare students to graduate from college and pursue careers. The "common core," as these standards have come to be known, has been adopted by more than 40 states. These states also collaborated to develop common assessments aligned to the standards, which replaced the individual state assessment systems. The CCSS resulted in a movement toward a nationally unified educational system—a significant shift from how states had previously thought about curriculum.

Alignment with the Core Curriculum

School districts were mandated by NCLB and ESSA to align their curriculum with state standards, and the states that have adopted the common core have mandated that districts align their curriculum with the CCSS. Alignment "refers to the extent of content match" (Browder & Spooner, 2006, p. 2). Alignment does not mean that all of a student's educational goals must link to academic content standards, but that there be sufficient alignment to prepare students for participation in statewide assessment systems. Rather, it "is the process of matching two educational components, which then strengthens the purpose and goals of both" (Courtade & Browder, 2011, p. 12). This chapter is concerned with alignment of the school curriculum and the CCSS for students with a visual impairment and multiple disabilities.

The undertaking teachers face when including students with visual impairments and multiple disabilities in the core curriculum is how to provide them with a challenging yet meaningful education. Teachers struggle to balance instruction in academic areas along with instruction in other content areas needed to prepare the student for life after school. While seeking alignment with the core curriculum, it is important for teachers to make curriculum decisions on an individual basis, in response to each student's needs. Dymond, Renzaglia, Gilson, and Slagor (2007) recommend the following:

- Make connections between the general curriculum and transition goals.
- Make decisions about curriculum access on an individual basis.
- Ensure that access to the general curriculum does not preclude access to other types of curriculum.
- Embed access to the general curriculum across settings.

In addition, teachers need to continuously look for ways to embed the core curriculum within the student's daily routines and environments. It is important to remember that accessing the core curriculum does not mean that other curriculum areas should be ignored. For students with visual impairments and functional disabilities, the ECC and a functional curriculum (both covered later in this chapter) are also necessary components of their educational program.

Accessing the Core Curriculum

Students with visual impairments and multiple disabilities can access the core curriculum in a variety of ways, including access at grade level with accommodations only; access at entry points; and development of access skills.

Access at Grade Level with Accommodations Only

Some students access the general curriculum at grade level with accommodations only. In this case, the student is typically included in a general education classroom setting and receives support from the general education teacher and a teacher of students with visual impairments to ensure that he or she has the accommodations necessary to access content. Accommodations are practices and procedures that are intended to reduce or even eliminate the effects of a student's disability (see Chapter 4 for a detailed discussion of accommodations and a list of accommodations that may be appropriate for a student with a visual impairment and multiple disabilities).

For example, a third-grade student who is blind with learning disabilities may require the following accommodations in order to access the curriculum:

- braille or written material presented orally or on recording
- use of a scribe
- increased response time
- individualized response format
- extended time to allow the student to master the material
- materials presented in short blocks of time
- distraction-free environment

Access at Entry Points

Some students access the general curriculum at an entry point below grade level. *Entry points* are suggested points of access for students that are aligned with learning standards for a student in that grade. They are modifications of the standard and are below grade-level expectations. Also known as the "essence" of the standard, entry points are:

- aligned with the grade-level standard(s) on which they are based
- modified below grade-level expectations
- listed on a continuum approaching grade-level complexity (i.e., from less to more complex)
- used to identify measurable outcomes for a student

Figure 5.1 from the Massachusetts Department of Elementary and Secondary Education (2015) 6th grade level provides an example of a continuum of entry points aligned to one of the standards in the state curriculum in the area of English language arts.

Developing Access Skills

Some students are learning the prerequisite skills needed to access the curriculum. Most students with significant disabilities will be able to access the curriculum through an entry point, or "essence" of the standard. However, a small number of students with the most complex and significant disabilities may not yet be ready to address academic content directly, even at the lowest levels of complexity. In such cases, students may instead need to address *access skills*, which target social, communication, and/or motor skills that will eventually allow them to explore instruction tools and materials and academic content. These nonacademic skills can be addressed as part of in-

Figure 5.1

Example of Entry Points Aligned with State Learning Standards

Standard

The standard in the Massachusetts state curriculum, as written for Reading and Literature 8.4 (Grade 8), is as follows:

> Determine the meaning of words and phrases as they are used in a text, including figurative and connotative meanings; analyze the impact of specific word choices on meaning and tone, including analogies or allusions to other texts.

Entry Points

The entry points to this reading standard for literature in grades 6–8 are as follows:

Less Complex  More Complex

1. Word Meaning:	1. Word Meaning:	1. Word Meaning:
The student will:	The student will:	The student will:
• Cite examples of imagery in a literary text (story, poem, or drama) • Cite examples of figurative language in a literary text (story, poem, or drama)	• Determine the meaning of imagery in a literary text (story, poem, or drama) • Determine the meaning of figurative language in a literary text (story, poem, or drama)	• Describe how imagery and figurative language are used to set the tone of a literary text or drama (e.g., sad, mysterious, playful)

Source: Massachusetts Department of Elementary and Secondary Education. (2015, Fall). *Resource guide to the 2011 Massachusetts curriculum frameworks for students with disabilities. English language arts and literacy, pre-kindergarten–grade 12.* Malden, MA: Author. Retrieved from http://www.doe.mass.edu/mcas/alt/rg/ELA.pdf

structional activities based on the learning standards. For example, a student may participate in a science activity by addressing the access skill of grasping and releasing the objects or materials in the lesson (motor skills), or by hitting a switch that activates an electronic communication device when it is his or her turn to participate (communication skill).

Practicing access skills in the context of academic instruction benefits students in the following ways (Massachusetts Department of Elementary and Secondary Education, 2015):

- It provides exposure to the general education curriculum for students with the most significant disabilities.
- It prepares many of these students to address academic skills and content in the future.

- It exposes these students to challenging new ideas, content, skills, and materials. It provides additional opportunities for students to practice targeted skills in a variety of settings and using a range of instructional approaches.

EXPANDED CORE CURRICULUM

As stated earlier in this chapter, instruction in the general or core curriculum alone is not sufficient for students with visual impairments and multiple disabilities. It is necessary that these students receive instruction in all the traditional areas of academics as well as instruction in areas that are directly affected by the student's visual impairment. "Without these critically important skills, students who are visually impaired cannot access the standard core curriculum or engage in many of the activities that are basic to their own well-being" (American Foundation for the Blind, n.d.b).

As noted in Chapter 1, the expanded core curriculum comprises skills in the following nine content areas:

1. compensatory access and functional academic (including communication modes)
2. orientation and mobility (O&M)
3. social interaction
4. independent living
5. recreation and leisure
6. career education
7. assistive technology
8. sensory efficiency
9. self-determination

See Parts 4 and 5 of this book for in-depth discussion of teaching skills in many of these areas with students who are visually impaired with multiple disabilities.

Compensatory Access

Compensatory access skills include those necessary for accessing all areas of the existing core curriculum. This ECC area includes concept development, spatial understanding, organizational skills, study skills, and communication modes. A wide variety of learning experiences and adaptations are necessary to teach these skills.

Concept Development

Sighted children often learn in "whole-to-part" fashion, meaning that they gain an understanding of the big picture before they begin to attend to the details. Because of their lack of vision, students with visual impairments tend to learn in a "part-to-whole" manner; they experience individual parts of the world and then need to learn how to put the parts together in a meaningful way.

Spatial Understanding

This area refers to basic concepts such as *in, out, on, behind,* and *underneath.* Spatial understanding is a critical skill for all areas of the common core curriculum. Reading left to right, understanding math and science tables and graphs, and being able to use a map in geography or understand a timeline in history are all examples of spatial understanding applied to common core areas. In addition, students need spatial understanding for O&M and proprioception. "Students who have a solid understanding of spatial concepts and how objects in the environment are related to their own bodies will be able to follow directions and travel independently in home, school and playground environments" (Expanded Core Curriculum Advocacy, n.d.).

Organizational Skills

Sighted students learn many organizational skills incidentally via observation of others or through casual conversations. In school, students become interested in how classmates organize their school supplies—what type of notebooks they use, how they keep track of their assignments, and the like. Students with visual impairments must be provided with direct instruction in organizational skills. Organizational skills are even more critical for students with visual impairments, who often cannot look around to easily find the things they require.

Study Skills

Students with visual impairments must also learn strategies for taking notes using their own learning media as well as the way textbooks are organized (titles, chapter and section headings, and so on) so that they can locate information quickly.

Communication Modes

Students' communication needs vary "depending on the degree of functional vision, effects of additional disabilities, and the individual task" (Gannon, 2007). Communication modes may include:

- braille
- large print
- speech
- print with use of optical devices
- regular print
- tactile symbols
- real objects
- sign language
- recorded materials
- picture symbols
- writing

Many students may use a combination of the modes listed above, known as a *total communication approach.*

Orientation and Mobility

Students with visual impairments need to develop the O&M skills to negotiate the various environments they experience and to travel as safely and independently as possible. Teachers who have been specifically prepared to teach O&M to students with visual impairments are necessary in the delivery of this curriculum. Early O&M instruction generally develops concepts of body image and space, then includes the child's immediate environments and expands outward. As students get older, O&M lessons begin to focus on travel in school, home, and the community, including travel in residential, city, and rural areas. The development of motor skills, physical coordination, and stamina as well as the use of appropriate mobility tools (such as a long white cane) are also included in O&M.

Social Interaction Skills

Since nearly all social skills are learned by observation of the environment and people, this is an area where students with visual impairments and multiple disabilities need careful, conscious, and explicit instruction. Without the opportunity to learn appropriate social interaction skills, students with visual impairments are at high risk for social isolation at school and beyond. Social interaction skills include the following skill sets:

- *self-awareness:* recognizes self, identifies likes and strengths, identifies personal information and possessions, is aware of abilities and needs, identifies emotions
- *self-management:* accepts assistance, follows rules and routines, manages transitions and change, seeks assistance and support appropriately, uses organizational skills, completes assigned chores and jobs, follows through on schedule and commitments
- *social awareness:* is aware of others, understands appropriate touch and distance, identifies familiar and unfamiliar people, participates in activities with others, uses active listening, understands public versus private behaviors, recognizes the needs of others
- *relationship skills:* acknowledges the presence of others, shares items or activities with others, maintains meaningful relationships, uses humor and responds to it appropriately, initiates, develops, and concludes conversations, practices conflict management, expresses affection appropriately, names family members
- *responsible decision-making skills:* makes choices, identifies problems, identifies solutions, initiates problem-solving

Independent Living Skills

This area includes the tasks and functions students perform in daily life to optimize their independence, such as personal hygiene, food preparation, money management, and household chores. Many independent living skills are learned incidentally by students with sight. Independent living skills include being able to take care of oneself and one's environment. When a student can take care of his or her personal needs, it lessens the need for support from others and provides the student with greater freedom and more choices. Independence in this area also has an impact on the student's social status and acceptance. The major areas included in independent living skills are as follows (Allman & Lewis, 2014):

- organization
- personal hygiene and grooming
- dressing
- clothing care
- time management
- eating
- cooking
- cleaning and general household tasks
- telephone use
- money management

Recreation and Leisure Skills

Recreation and leisure includes skills that support students developing interests and preferences for how they spend their free time. Having time to play and have fun is a part of having a good quality of life. Students with visual impairments and multiple disabilities need to be exposed to and taught a range of recreational and leisure activities so that ultimately they can develop preferences and interests for how they want to spend their free time. When thinking about leisure and recreation skills for students with visual impairments and multiple disabilities teachers will want to consider four different scenarios:

1. indoor individual leisure and recreation activities such as hobbies, craft projects, reading, computer games, and exercise
2. indoor group leisure and recreation activities, such as card games, craft projects, parties, restaurants, coffee shops, and exercise at a gym
3. outdoor individual leisure and recreation activities such as swimming, walking, and bike riding
4. outdoor group leisure and recreation activities such as sports and walking clubs

Career Education

Career education is important for students with visual impairments and multiple disabilities of all ages. This content area provides students with the opportunity to learn about community services and the work that people do in various jobs in the community. Through this exposure, students will learn the concepts and specific skills that are needed to be successful in those jobs. Once again, these are things that most sighted students learn through observation. This curriculum content provides the student with opportunities to explore their strengths and interests in a systematic, well-planned manner.

"Because unemployment and underemployment have been the leading problem facing adult visually impaired persons in the United States, this portion of the expanded core curriculum is vital to students, and should be part of the expanded curriculum for even the youngest of these individuals" (American Foundation for the Blind, n.d.a). It is important to include career education skills in instruction for young students with visual impairments because these skills have their roots in skills learned before adolescence, including helping out and doing chores, communicating with others, understanding appropriate behavior, understanding physical abilities, and practicing organization, mobility, and self-advocacy.

When considering the implementation of a career education curriculum for students with visual impairments and multiple disabilities, teachers will want to include the following content areas (note that the sections marked with asterisks are applicable to students of all ages from pre-K through 12th grade):

- work skills*: work habits, communication, work behaviors, physical capacities, mobility and transportation
- organizational skills*
- self-advocacy skills*: interests, abilities and preferences, legal issues, age of majority, knowledge of and access to community resources, self-preservation and safety in the community
- employment: career exploration and decision making, job searching, job retention
- post-secondary education

Assistive Technology

"Technology occupies a special place in the education of blind and visually impaired students" (Iowa Department of Education, 2007, p. 11). The legal definition of an assistive technology device is "any item, piece of equipment, or product system, whether acquired commercially off the shelf, modified, or customized, that is used to increase, maintain, or improve functional capabilities of individuals with disabilities" (IDEA, 2004, 34 C.F.R. § 300.5). Assistive technology (AT) includes both low- and high-tech solutions that increase independence and efficiency. In addition, IDEA (2004) mandates that the IEP team consider whether a student requires assistive technology and services and document those needs in the IEP.

Sensory Efficiency Skills

This content area focuses on developing the skills students need to make use of all their senses—functional vision, hearing, touch, smell, and taste—to access the world around them. This area also encompasses learning how to use assistive devices such as optical devices, hearing aids, and augmentative communication devices.

Examples of sensory efficiency skills that a student may learn include the following:

- use of optical devices to enhance remaining vision
- use of augmentative and alternative communication (AAC) devices
- use of touch and functional vision to identify personal items
- use of tactile, gustatory, and olfactory input to identify food
- use of hearing to identify familiar people

Development of sensory efficiency skills is best practiced through meaningful activities, such as these:

- A student practices using an optical device at the grocery store when trying to locate a particular item.
- A student practices using an AAC device to make a request at mealtimes.
- A student practices using his or her hearing upon entering the classroom to identify the teacher's voice.

Self-Determination

It is important for students with visual impairments and multiple disabilities to learn self-determination strategies and for teachers to help these students develop a concept of their abilities, strengths, interests, needs, and goals, along with how to advocate for their needs effectively. Self-determination involves many skills including the following:

- choice making
- exploration of possibilities and options
- self-advocacy
- development of self-esteem
- goal setting and planning

Self-determination skills are most effectively taught within real-world experiences. When offering these real-world experiences teachers must also be prepared to allow the student to experience failures as they occur. The experience of failure helps the student understand the consequences of their actions and decision making. It also assists them in developing an understanding of the control they can have over their lives. Although it may be difficult for teachers to allow a student to experience failure, it is an important component in developing self-determination skills. (See Chapter 10 for more information about self-determination.)

Incorporating the ECC Into a Student's Instructional Program

In addition to assessing students and being prepared to provide instruction in each area of the ECC, teachers of students with visual impairments must be able to incorporate the ECC into students' IEPs and to integrate the ECC into their other instruction. As discussed in Chapter 2, the role of the teacher of students with visual impairments in instruction can vary from direct instruction to consultation, yet it remains the responsibility of the teacher of students with visual impairments to ensure that ECC instruction is included in the student's program. Regardless of who is doing the instruction, it can be a struggle to find enough time to provide instruction in this area. It is important to explore alternative methods of providing instruction in ECC such as summer programs, after-school programs, and short-term placements. It is critical for students to have ECC instruction incorporated into their IEP as well as their daily schedules in order for them to successfully participate in the world around them.

Understanding how the ECC curriculum can be included in the core curriculum and vice versa can be helpful. Many areas taught under the core curriculum include skills that overlap with the ECC, such as working in groups (social skills), learning about different jobs (career education), and managing money (independent living skills).

In addition, many ECC skills can be practiced naturally throughout the day. It is important to take an ecological approach to looking at the school day. When using an ecological approach, teachers perform a careful assessment of the school day and all the environments that the student accesses during the day, including transition periods, lunch, and recess, to identify the areas where a student performs well and the areas that are challenging for the student. By taking this approach, many opportunities for instruction can be identified and incorporated into the student's current schedule. For example, during the transitions between classes, the student can practice the following skills:

- *O&M:* spatial understanding and travel skills
- *social:* seeking assistance and appropriately interacting with peers, recognizing own abilities and needs, managing transitions and change, demonstrating awareness of others, practicing appropriate touch and distances, developing problem-solving skills
- *communication:* seeking assistance, asking questions, interacting with peers
- *self-advocacy:* making needs and preferences known to others
- *assistive technology:* communicating with others and negotiating the environment
- *sensory efficiency:* negotiating the environment
- *self-determination:* demonstrating self awareness, practicing problem solving and self-advocacy, participating in goal setting and planning

During lunchtime the student can practice the following skills:

- *O&M:* spatial understanding and travel skills
- *social:* seeking assistance and support appropriately, interacting with peers, recognizing abilities and needs, demonstrating awareness of others, demonstrating appropriate touch and distance, practicing problem solving, identifying likes and strengths, participating in an activity with others, practicing active listening, developing relationship skills
- *communication:* requesting assistance, asking questions, interacting with peers
- *career education:* demonstrating self-advocacy skills, developing work behaviors (taking a break appropriately)
- *assistive technology:* communicating with others and negotiating the environment
- *sensory efficiency:* negotiating the environment
- *self-determination:* self-awareness, problem-solving and self-advocacy, choice-making
- *independent living:* eating

It is also necessary for teachers to explain the importance of the skills and concepts of the ECC to administrators, parents, and other educators who may not understand the need for spending time and resources on teaching the ECC. For ECC instruction to be effective, the entire educational team needs to support the instruction so that the team can work together in a cohesive manner and ensure that there is adequate instruction and practice. IEP teams must ensure that students with visual impairments and multiple disabilities access the core curriculum as well as address the unique needs relating to the student's blindness or visual impairment as defined by the ECC.

FUNCTIONAL CURRICULUM

If, as stated earlier, "the educational goal for every student is to become an active participant and contributing member of society" (Ford et al., 1989, p. ix), then students must learn the skills required to participate in the world around them. In other words, the functional outcome of education is the ability to live and work as part of the community in a satisfactory manner. Thus, a curriculum must be functional.

It is important for students with visual impairments and multiple disabilities to benefit from a functional curriculum that focuses on the student and the skills he or she needs to learn to be an active, engaged member of the school, home, and community. A functional curriculum prepares students for participation in an integrated community life and provides instruction in critical skills that are central to the success of the student now and in their adult life. To determine if a skill is critical, teachers can ask, "If the student doesn't learn this, will someone else have to do it for him or her?"

A functional approach to curriculum planning must "begin with the end in mind" (Covey, 2004), meaning the teacher must take a longitudinal approach to curriculum planning. The teacher must look beyond the current school year or the current placement and consider the student's current and future quality of life. When a student is 5 years old, it may be difficult to imagine what he or she will be doing as an adult, but it *is* possible to imagine where that student will be in five years. Doing so forces the teacher to continuously look forward to think about whether what he or she is teaching today will (or will not) provide the student with the skills needed to reach that level of ability. Considering the student's future compels the teacher to determine the instructional priorities for the present, ensuring that today's instruction will assist the student achieve his or her desired life outcomes. Functional curriculum isn't taught *instead* of the general curriculum or the expanded core. Using a functional approach to curriculum planning means ensuring that teaching strategies and instructional practices provide the student with functional skills that will help him or her interact successfully with the world.

Given this description, it is clear that many skills that are taught within the core curriculum and ECC can be classified as "functional." There is clearly overlap among the curricula. However, in a functional curriculum there is much more emphasis on *how* and *where* the instruction happens than there is in either the ECC or the core curriculum. Because learning happens more quickly when it can be applied in real life, a functional curriculum emphasizes instruction in natural settings, within environments and activities that are meaningful. For the student with visual impairments and multiple disabilities whose life experiences are already limited by the sensory impairment, learning in a meaningful environment within a meaningful activity means that he or she will be more likely to develop concepts and

skills faster *and* be able to generalize those concepts and skills more easily to other environments and activities. For example, the meaning of money is much clearer when a student is able to go to a store and spend money purchasing what he or she wants. At first, this activity teaches a student that money (coins or bills) is needed to trade in order to get something he or she wants. Over time, the hope would be that the student will learn about the value of money; however, the first step is to make money meaningful to a student. Counting coins or bills in a classroom provides no connection to the actual meaning of money; therefore learning will be much more difficult.

A functional curriculum meets the following guidelines:

- is structured around activities
- is focused on meaningful activities
- takes place in natural environments
- includes natural routines (with instruction embedded within routines)
- is age appropriate
- contains a clear beginning, middle, and end
- takes place in a communication-rich environment
- is ecologically oriented
- incorporates students' interests and strengths
- emphasizes both independence and interdependence
- supports partial participation

Activity-Based Instruction

It is important for students with visual impairments and multiple disabilities to be actively engaged in all learning activities. As has been stated earlier in this book, these students do not have as much opportunity to learn incidentally through observation, as sighted students do, because of their reduced functional vision and multiple disabilities (sensory, intellectual, physical, and the like). These disabilities can interfere with students' comprehension of or experience with the world around them. The lack of incidental learning is even more significant for students whose multiple disabilities include a hearing impairment.

Lack of incidental learning impacts a student's concept development—the ideas he or she has about things, people, and places in the world. Students with visual impairments and multiple disabilities often do not have the same concepts as their sighted peers and often have difficulty developing concepts because they do not have the same experience of the world.

In order for these students to learn about the concepts that are the building blocks for understanding the world around them, they need to be specifically taught the skills that sighted children learn just by looking around them. The best way to teach these skills is by having the student actively involved in the instruction. An *activity-based approach* to teaching maximizes learning by providing opportunities for students to practice skills throughout the day over multiple activities. This approach promotes the generalization of skills and provides students with an opportunity to see the application or meaning of the learning activity.

For example, suppose a student is going to have a smoothie for snack. This activity could consist of the student sitting at the snack table and the teacher bringing the smoothie to the student. However, there are a number of ways that this activity can be expanded to increase the active involvement of the student. Using the students described in the case studies in Chapter 4, here are examples of how activity-based instruction could be incorporated into their daily routines and activities.

> *Ian*, a preschooler, can help to gather the items needed for the smoothie (the fruit and yogurt from the refrigerator, a cup and a napkin from the cabinet), set the table, and participate in clean up.
>
> *Karen*, an elementary school student, can make the smoothie during a cooking activity and share it with her friends at snack time.
>
> *Eric*, a secondary school student, can go to the store to purchase the ingredients needed to make the smoothie, make the smoothie during a cooking activity, and then serve the smoothie at lunch or during a break at school or work.

Meaningful Activities

To have the biggest impact, learning activities must be meaningful to the student. A *meaningful activity* is one in which the student understands the purpose of the activity and how it "fits" into the world. Using the example of the smoothie activity, the activity becomes much more meaningful when the student learns about where the smoothie is stored (the refrigerator), how smoothies are made (cooking activity) and where the ingredients come from (the store). Each iteration of the activity provides another level of concept development, expands the student's understanding of the world around them, and increases the meaning of the activity.

Natural Environments

Another important consideration for teachers is the importance of teaching in natural environments or settings. These are places in which the student is familiar, feels at ease, and can more easily anticipate activities. This anticipation is critical to learning as it demonstrates the development of memory. In addition, it is important to teach skills to students with visual impairments and multiple disabilities within the environments where the skills will be used because these students often have difficulty generalizing from one environment to another. Practicing the skill in the setting where it is normally applied helps students retain the skill and enhances the meaning of the activity.

Sighted children often learn and practice skills via pretend play, prompted by the concepts they have developed by observation. For example, a sighted child might pretend to make a purchase at a store, thereby practicing money skills, because of the concepts she has developed by observing her parents making purchases. However, students with visual impairments and multiple disabilities often do not have the ability to engage in this type of play because they have not developed these concepts through observation. A student with a visual impairment and multiple disabilities will most effectively learn money skills by actually going to a store to make a purchase and going through the routine of taking money out of a wallet, handing the money to the cashier, receiving change, and leaving with her purchase. Repeating this activity in a variety of stores will develop the concept that money can be used in many different ways to make many different types of purchases. Often this is referred to as *community-based instruction*—using the real, natural environment in the community to teach the skill. Similarly, teaching how to set a table at snack time in the place where snack time happens, as in the smoothie example, as well as cooking in a kitchen environment and shopping in a grocery store are further examples of teaching in natural environments.

Embedding Instruction in Natural Routines

Embedded instruction is an approach used to promote student engagement, learning, and independence in everyday activities, routines, and transitions. *Embedded instruction* is accomplished by identifying times and activities when skill instruction can be implemented in the context of ongoing, naturally occurring activities. Embedded instruction maximizes a student's motivation by following his or her interests, and promotes generalization and maintenance of skills by providing instruction in a variety of settings. When a teacher selects a regularly occurring routine in which to embed instruction the student is able to learn the skill more readily because it is placed within a context that is familiar to him or her.

As a result, the student is more likely to remember the skill and will have a greater understanding of the function of the skill.

Using the student's daily schedule, the teacher can easily find numerous routines in which to embed instruction. For example, snack time is not just about eating skills (independent living), but can also include a focus on social skills and communication skills.

Age-Appropriate Instruction

Just as the teacher seeks to embed instruction into natural routines, he or she must also ensure that activities are chronologically age appropriate. This can become challenging when working with an older student whose skills development is at a very young level. *Chronologically age-appropriate activities and instruction* directs the instruction and materials at the student's actual chronological age rather than to a student's developmental age.

Age-appropriate activities are those activities normally found in a student's culture and geographic location that are typical of the student's chronological age. It is important for the teacher to observe other students of the same chronological age to determine what activities are appropriate.

The smoothie activity can be used as an example of how an activity can be constructed to be age appropriate. For preschoolers, the activity is centered around setting the table for a snack. For elementary age students the activity is expanded to the cooking activity of making the smoothie. Finally, for secondary students the activity is expanded further by going to the grocery store, buying the items needed to make the smoothie, and consuming the smoothie as part of a break within a work routine or other activity.

It is also important to consider other aspects of the students' lives, such as how they dress, how their bedroom is decorated, and the like. Particularly when working with students with visual impairments whose multiple disabilities include a cognitive disability, there may be a tendency to have expectations for the student that are more appropriate for a student of a much younger age. In these situations, it is not unusual to find students dressed like a younger child, with the toys of a younger child, and participating in the learning activities of a younger child. The expectations for these students must match the expectations of nondisabled students of the same age to the greatest extent possible.

Clear Beginning, Middle, and End

It is essential that routines have clear beginnings, middles, and ends. Students with visual impairments and multiple disabilities need to experience activities from start to finish so that they are able to understand the larger context of the activity. For example, if a student is preparing a sandwich it is important that he or she obtain all the ingredients from the place where they are stored (the refrigerator, the cabinet)—the beginning of the activity. Likewise, when the student is finished preparing the sandwich, he or she should participate in cleaning up and putting away the food items—the end of the activity. If the student does not experience the gathering of ingredients and the clean up, the student's concept of where the sandwich comes from may be that it just "appears" or "drops out of the sky."

As the student progresses, the definition of beginning, middle, and end can become broader and broader to allow the student to further develop their concepts. Using this same example, the student can go to the store to shop for the food items and to learn where the food comes from. To take it a step further, the student can go to a farm to learn about how animals are raised.

The smoothie activity provides an additional example of how the definition of beginning, middle, and end can be broadened as the student's concept development increases. Ian learns that smoothies come from the refrigerator and how to set a table for snack time. Karen learns what ingredients are needed to make a smoothie and how to make one. Eric learns what ingredients must be purchased to make a smoothie and how to find the ingredients in a grocery store. Each of these examples further expands the students' concepts related to food, thereby making their world bigger and bigger.

Communication-Rich Environment

It is also important to ensure that the learning environment for students with visual impairments and multiple disabilities is rich in communication. Hartmann (2000) describes how space, time, and people "give environments structure and make them more conducive to meaningful communication" (p. 3). Making the learning space accessible means ensuring that the student is able to connect to the people, things, and events that motivate the student to communicate. This can be accomplished by structuring the environment and then "adapting the structure in small but creative ways" (Hartmann, 2000, p. 7). Some examples of how to create a communication-rich environment include the following:

- Make a communication system available; teach the student how to access the communication system.
- Label the students' shelves, cabinets, and personal spaces so that they know where their things are and how to get them.
- Place preferred items in places where students need to request assistance to obtain them, encouraging students to communicate.
- Find ways to increase the number and variety of communication partners within the classroom and school environment; create reasons for students to need to communicate with each other (passing items to each other, taking turns with an activity, and the like).
- Ensure that professionals and peers know the students' communication systems and how to use them effectively.
- Allow time to interact with students in non-structured and playful ways. Show interest in the students' topics of interest and encourage students to talk more about their interests.
- Create reasons for students to communicate; give students the opportunity to ask for what they want.

See Chapter 7 for more information on communication.

Environmentally Oriented Instruction

Assessing a student's school and community environments helps teachers identify the skills, activities, and environments in which the student participates and the activities that are interesting and motivating to the student. This information helps the teacher determine what skills the student needs to develop to have greater success in these activities.

Using the smoothie activity as an example, there are three environments to assess: the snack area, the kitchen, and the grocery store. To assess these environments, the teacher asks the following questions:

- What skills are needed for the student to be successful in this environment and activity?
- Which of these skills does the student have?
- Which of these skills does the student need to learn?

In addition, the teacher needs to make the following observations:

- What is in the environment?
- Where are things located in the environment?
- How does the student communicate in the environment?
- How does the student understand the environment?
- How does the student interact in the environment?

Developing an understanding of a student's abilities within a specific environment offers insight into his or her learning needs and communication abilities. Looking at the case study examples again, such observations can identify skills the teacher may want to focus on developing:

Ian at snack time: Ian enjoys eating but needs to develop his communication and social skills. His teacher can incorporate specific components to this activity that will help him develop his skills. He can set the table with a peer so that he has to interact with someone else. He can serve the smoothie. He can practice asking for more, asking for help, and the like.

Karen in cooking class making a smoothie: Karen needs to learn where things are located in the kitchen, how to ask for help when needed, and how to communicate with her peers when cooking as a group.

Eric at the grocery store: Eric needs to learn how to communicate with people who work in the grocery store so that he can get the assistance he needs.

Student Interests and Strengths

Curriculum and instructional decisions must be made individually for each student based on the identified needs, strengths, and abilities of the student. It is important for teachers to identify each student's interests and strengths and make a concerted effort to develop instructional activities that incorporate these student characteristics. A student's motivation is likely to be higher when learning experiences and activities are related to things he or she is interested in, and that motivation can result in increased learning. This is true for students at a very young age who have just begun school and need to learn that school is a positive place, as well as for older students who are nearing graduation.

Independence and Interdependence

Teachers of students with visual impairments and multiple disabilities generally are skilled in developing students' independence and typically have a strong understanding of the benefits of doing so. This type of instruction is generally quite concrete (getting dressed, preparing a meal, making a purchase at a store) and lots of ideas are available for how to teach many of these skills. However, the idea of independence often implies that a student can either do something or cannot, that the student is either independent or dependent. The truth, though, is that everyone needs support at certain points in their lives, and while there is a sense of pride in being independent, most people are really quite *inter*dependent. Having the skills to access assistance in an appropriate and effective manner is critical for all students.

The smoothie activity demonstrates how independence and interdependence are part of everyday activities. Ian learns how to be independent in locating the smoothie in the refrigerator, but is interdependent in setting the table when he needs assistance counting out the right number of place settings for snack time. Karen is independent in cutting up the bananas and strawberries but needs assistance in measuring the milk. Eric requires assistance traveling to the grocery store as well as in finding the strawberries and bananas, but he knows what he needs to purchase and can make the transaction with the cashier independently.

Partial Participation

The principle of *partial participation* is based on the idea that all students can acquire skills that enable them to participate at least to some extent in many environments and activities. Students with visual impairments and multiple disabilities may have difficulty learning certain skills, but rather than denying them access to activities, environments, or instruction for that reason, the principle of partial participation is based on the premise that with adaptations they may be able to participate in most, or even all, activities at least partially.

There are various ways that partial participation can occur, including adapting the task or activity, providing personal assistance, changing or adapting the rules of an activity, or adapting the physical environment, as shown in the following examples:.

- **Adapt the task or activity** by using alternative materials and devices.
  - The student can use a switch to operate an appliance or device.
  - The student can use picture, tactile, print, or braille communication cards when making a purchase at the store.
  - The student can use a debit card instead of cash when making a purchase, or use a bus pass instead of coins to pay a fare.
  - The student can use a tactile or picture recipe.

- **Provide personal assistance** for part or all of a task or activity.
  - Peers can push a student's wheelchair to help deliver the attendance records.
  - The teacher can take bread out of the bag and place it in the toaster prior to

having the student press the lever on the toaster.

○ The teacher can place the item to be cut into the adapted scissors while the student uses her arm to press the adapted lever for the scissors.

○ The student can put on his coat but ask for assistance with the zipper.

• **Change or adapt rules** to meet the needs of individual students.

○ Allow the student to eat lunch in two lunch periods if he or she is a slow eater due to physical disabilities.

○ Allow the student to be first in line (if waiting is difficult) or to leave ahead of the class (if she needs extra time).

○ Allow the student to take frequent breaks (if sitting for long periods is difficult).

• **Adapt the physical environment.**

○ Wheelchair ramps can be incorporated into the environment.

○ The teacher can reduce clutter and distractions in an environment.

○ The teacher can add extra lighting.

○ The teacher can provide special "jigs" to help students complete tasks (such as for counting).

THEME-BASED CURRICULA

To address the curricular needs of young students with visual impairments and multiple disabilities, the core curriculum, the expanded core curriculum, and a functional curriculum approach are all appropriate, as long as the content presented is appropriate for their age and ability.

A thematic approach to curriculum planning means that each skill area of the curriculum is connected to a particular topic, or theme. Thus, a student's learning and development in the content areas of language and literacy, math, science, and social studies as well as the developmental areas of independent living and fine and gross motor skills are all integrated by being taught through activities related to the theme. Focusing on themes enables teachers to meaningfully link different disciplines so that students will learn to develop big ideas or concepts. This integrated approach promotes wider coverage of the curriculum since it encourages teachers to create learning activities that fulfill numerous purposes.

In a theme-based approach, students typically engage in hands-on experiences using materials that are age-appropriate and address a range of learning styles and abilities. Themes can vary in nature and scope, though they should be motivating to students and relevant to their lives. A student's skills and knowledge are best developed when she participates in meaningful activities related to her interests and life experiences.

The theme may be chosen by the teacher or in collaboration with the students. Themes may also be based on seasonal activities, holidays, or a wide range of topics. Many teachers have their favorite themes that they like to use in their classrooms; other teachers may wish to develop themes that spontaneously emerge from a student's play or special interests. Figures 5.2 and 5.3 show theme-based plans for two units (collections of lessons).

Figure 5.2
Sample Thematic Unit Plan: Thanksgiving

Science

- Mix as recipes require
- Talk about changes that occur when something is cooked
- Discuss the meaning of Harvest: What foods for the meal were harvested? How are those items harvested today?

Independent Living Skills

- Find items on grocery list in the store
- Find items in kitchen to make a specified dish (given a recipe)
- Follow a recipe
- Set the table for the Thanksgiving dinner

Orientation and Mobility

- Travel to food pantry safely
- Travel within the grocery store safely
- Follow the rules for travel

Math

- Measure ingredients as needed for cooking
- Pay for items at the grocery store
- Determine how many people will be eating Thanksgiving dinner

Thanksgiving

K–2

Social Skills

- Display appropriate behavior in the grocery store
- Ask for help as needed in an appropriate manner

English Language Arts

- Read a shopping list
- Read a recipe
- Read stories about Thanksgiving
- Make place cards for the Thanksgiving dinner table

Social Studies

- Collect food items for a food pantry
- Bring food donations to a food pantry
- Discuss what it means to be a "Native" American and what that means in the world today

Dramatic Play/Arts

- Make pilgrim hats, Indian headdresses and turkey decorations, as appropriate
- Dress up in Native American or early settler costumes
- Create a play about Thanksgiving

197

Figure 5.3
Sample Thematic Unit Plan: Community Helpers

Science

- Find out why some community helpers wear protective clothing: What protective clothing do they wear and what is the function of that clothing?

Math

- Find out the number of policemen on the police force; do the same for other community helpers
- Create a bar graph showing how many policemen are at the police station, how many firemen, and so on
- Compare the numbers of community helpers at each location

Independent Living Skills

- Make cookies for community helpers
- Identify where restrooms are located in public places and how to distinguish the men's room from women's room
- Carry a library card in a secure place
- Make a purchase at the post office (buy a stamp for a thank you letter [see "Social Skills"])

English Language Arts

- Read stories about community helpers
- Write experience stories about visiting the fire station, police station, post office, library, and other locations
- Write a poem about a community helper

Community Helpers
K-2

Orientation and Mobility

- Travel safely to community locations
- Travel safely within community buildings
- Follow travel rules
- Discuss emergency procedures and what they are for

Social Skills

- Greet community helpers
- Engage with community helpers (pre-determined questions)
- Demonstrate appropriate behavior in the community
- Write a thank you note to community helpers

Social Studies/Career Exploration

- Visit a fire station, police station, post office, library, and other locations
- Have a class discussion about community helpers and how they help
- Describe the job of a policeman, fireman, postal worker, librarian, and other community helpers

Dramatic Play / Arts

- Make a collage of community helpers
- Try on different uniforms of community helpers
- Create a play about community helpers

One is based on the theme of "Thanksgiving" and the other is based on the theme of "Community Helpers." These examples demonstrate how general education curricular areas can be incorporated into the activities. Assistive technology and sensory efficiency skills should be embedded throughout all activities.

Planning a Thematic Unit

Following are the steps involved in developing a thematic unit:

1. Choose a theme
2. Plan ahead
   a. Set objectives
      i. General or core curriculum
      ii. Expanded core curriculum
      iii. Functional curriculum
   b. Determine evaluation strategies
   c. Divide planning responsibilities
   d. Set deadlines for completion of planning
   e. Gather and locate resources
   f. Plan activities
      i. Introductory activity to kick off the unit
      ii. Class activities
      iii. Small group activities
      iv. Individual projects or assignments
      v. Culminating activity to mark the end of the unit
      vi. Reach out to the community for assistance
   g. Map out the entire unit using weekly planning templates
   h. Put the plan into action
   i. Evaluate and celebrate

Connecting a Theme-Based Curriculum with a Functional Curriculum

The unit plans for the Thanksgiving and Community Helpers units (Figures 5.2 and 5.3) demonstrate how a theme-based curriculum can align with the ECC and the core curriculum. The ideas of a functional curriculum can also be incorporated into these themes. Consider the following activities in the Thanksgiving unit:

Students shop for and prepare a Thanksgiving dinner. This activity spans English language arts, math, science, independent living, and fine and gross motor skills areas. Functional approaches that can be implemented in this activity include the following:

- activity-based instruction
- meaningful activities
- natural environments
- chronologically age-appropriate activities
- clear beginning, middle, and end
- communication-rich environment
- ecologically oriented instruction
- incorporation of students' interests and strengths
- inclusion of independence and interdependence
- support for partial participation

Students collect food to be distributed to needy people in the community. This activity spans social studies, fine and gross motor skills, and independent living areas. Functional approaches that can be implemented in this activity include the following:

- activity-based instruction
- meaningful activities
- natural environments
- chronologically age-appropriate activities
- clear beginning, middle, and end
- communication-rich environment
- ecologically oriented instruction
- incorporation of students' interests and strengths
- inclusion of independence and inter-dependence
- support for partial participation

Students do art projects to make pilgrim hats or turkeys. This activity spans art and fine and gross motor skills areas. Functional approaches that can be implemented in this activity include the following:

- activity-based instruction
- meaningful activities
- natural environments
- chronologically age-appropriate activities
- clear beginning, middle, and end
- communication-rich environment
- ecologically oriented instruction
- incorporation of students' interests and strengths
- inclusion of independence and interde-pendence
- support for partial participation

Students read stories about Thanksgiving. This activity includes the English language arts area. Functional approaches that can be implemented in this activity include the following:

- activity-based instruction
- chronologically age-appropriate activities
- clear beginning, middle, and end
- communication-rich environment
- ecologically oriented instruction
- incorporation of students' interests and strengths
- inclusion of independence and interde-pendence
- support for partial participation

Students dress up in costumes of Native Americans or early settlers. Functional approaches that can be implemented in this activity include the following:

- activity-based instruction
- natural environments
- chronologically age-appropriate activities
- clear beginning, middle, and end
- communication-rich environment
- ecologically oriented instruction
- incorporation of students' interests and strengths
- inclusion of independence and interde-pendence
- support for partial participation

Students "write" and stage their own Thanksgiving play. This activity includes the English language arts area. Functional approaches that can be implemented in this activity include the following:

- activity-based instruction
- natural environments
- chronologically age-appropriate activities
- clear beginning, middle, and end

- communication-rich environment
- ecologically oriented instruction
- incorporation of students' interests and strengths
- inclusion of independence and interdependence
- support for partial participation

Using a theme-based curriculum approach is a holistic way to plan education for young students with visual impairments and multiple disabilities. This type of approach also demonstrates how other curricular areas can be embedded into the activities. There is no need to delineate a time for English, a time for science, a time for social skills, and so on. Instead, the teacher looks at the activities that are planned for that unit and determines how each activity can take a functional approach to address multiple areas of content spanning the common core and the expanded core.

SUMMARY

Providing a student with a quality of life that includes helping him or her be "an active participant and contributing member of society" (Ford et al., 1989) is a tremendous task, though it is no larger than the excitement a teacher feels when witnessing a student's achievements.

Teachers will only reap these rewards with appropriate and thoughtful instructional planning. Academic skills alone do not make a student successful, nor does the ECC on its own. The combination of the two, along with a functional approach to instructional design gives students a robust program of learning. A theme-based curriculum added to this combination provides a fun, interesting, and developmentally appropriate approach for young students.

REFERENCES

Allman, C. B., & Lewis, S. (Eds.). (2014). *ECC essentials: Teaching the expanded core curriculum to students with visual impairments.* New York: AFB Press.

American Foundation for the Blind. (n.d.a). The expanded core curriculum for blind and visually impaired children and youths. New York: Author. Retrieved from http://www.afb.org/info/programs-and-services/professional-development/teachers/expanded-core-curriculum/the-expanded-core-curriculum/12345

American Foundation for the Blind. (n.d.b). Expanded core curriculum: Resources for you from AFB Press. New York: Author. Retrieved from http://www.afb.org/info/expanded-core-curriculum/ecc-resources/45

Browder, D. M. (2001). *Curriculum and assessment for students with moderate and severe disabilities.* New York: The Guildford Press.

Browder, D. M., & Spooner, F. (Eds.). (2006). *Teaching language arts, math, and science to students with significant cognitive disabilities.* Baltimore: Paul H. Brookes Publishing Co.

Common Core State Standards Initiative. (n.d.). English language arts and mathematics standards. Retrieved from http://www.corestandards.org/

Courtade, G., & Browder, D. M. (2011). *Aligning IEPs to the common core state standards for students with moderate and severe disabilities.* Verona, WI: Attainment Company.

Covey, S. R. (2004). *The 7 habits of highly effective people: Powerful lessons in personal change.* New York: Free Press.

Dictionary.com. (n.d.). Definition of "curriculum." Retrieved from http://dictionary.reference.com/browse/curriculum

Dymond, S. K., Renzaglia, A., Gilson, C. L., & Slagor, M. T. (2007). Defining access to the general curriculum for high school students with significant cognitive disabilities. *Research and Practice for Persons with Severe Disabilities, 32*(1), 1–15.

Education.com. (n.d.). Curriculum definition. Retrieved from http://www.education.com/reference/article/curriculum-definition

Elementary and Secondary Education Act (No Child Left Behind), Pub. L. No. 107-110 (2001).

Every Student Succeeds Act, Pub. L. No. 114-95 (2015).

Expanded Core Curriculum Advocacy. (n.d.). Compensatory skills and the expanded core curriculum. New York: American Foundation for the Blind and Perkins School for the Blind. Retrieved from http://www.eccadvocacy.org/section.aspx?FolderID=13&SectionID=143&DocumentID=6101

Ford, A., Schnorr, R., Meyer, L., Davern, L., Black, J., & Dempsey, P. (1989). *The Syracuse community-referenced curriculum guide for students with moderate and severe disabilities.* Baltimore: Paul H. Brookes Publishing Co.

Gannon, C. (2007). *Tip sheet #2: The expanded core curriculum.* Concord: New Hampshire Development Center for Vision Education.

Hartmann, E. (2000). Creating communication rich environments. *reSources, 10*(8).

Individuals with Disabilities Education Improvement Act (IDEA), 20 U.S.C. § 1400 (2004).

Iowa Department of Education. (2007, May). *Iowa expanded core curriculum (ECC) resource guide.* Des Moines, IA: Author.

Massachusetts Department of Elementary and Secondary Education. (2015, Fall). *Resource guide to the 2011 Massachusetts curriculum frameworks for students with disabilities. English language arts and literacy, pre-kindergarten–grade 12.* Malden, MA: Author. Retrieved from http://www.doe.mass.edu/mcas/alt/rg/ELA.pdf

Merriam-Webster Online Dictionary. (n.d.). Definition of "curriculum." Retrieved from http://www.merriam-webster.com/dictionary/curriculum

RESOURCES

For additional resources, see the General Resources section at the back of this book.

Additional Readings

Allman, C. B., & Lewis, S. (Eds.). (2014). *ECC essentials: Teaching the expanded core curriculum to students with visual impairments.* New York: AFB Press.

A comprehensive book for teachers working to meet the unique learning needs of their students with visual impairments. Provides the rationale, suggestions, and strategies necessary to implement instruction in each area of the ECC. *ECC Essentials* gives teachers a road map for helping their students achieve success in school and life. Model learning activities show how to integrate a variety of ECC areas into one activity for different ages and ability levels.

Bridgeo, W., Caruso, B., D'Andrea, L., Fitzgerald, D., Fox, S., Gicklhorn, C., . . . Zatta, M. (2014). *Total life learning: Preparing for transi-*

tion. A curriculum for all students with sensory impairments. Watertown, MA: Perkins School for the Blind.

A curriculum for students ages 3–22 who are blind, visually impaired (including those with additional disabilities), or deafblind for the development of life and career goals that maximize independence, self-determination, employ-ability, and participation in the community. Provides teachers with goals, objectives, and activities in work skills, organizational skills, self-advocacy skills, personal care/daily living skills, employment, and secondary education. Emphasizes the importance of beginning instruction on foundation skills in these areas at a young age.

Chapter **6**

Instructional Strategies: A Universal Design for Learning Approach
. . . .

Elizabeth Hartmann

Key Points

- ✏ The importance of instructional strategies in teaching
- ✏ Balancing individualized and universal instructional strategies
- ✏ Incorporating universal design for learning in instructional strategies
- ✏ How to engage and motivate students
- ✏ Supporting students' perception and comprehension
- ✏ Encouraging students to show what they know

As discussed in Chapter 5, curriculum functions as a plan of action because it maps out the ways for students to meet their goals. In this chapter, the focus shifts to one of the most important parts of curriculum, instructional strategies. *Instructional strategies* are the methods teachers use to teach, or *how* they provide students with meaningful opportunities to learn. Using the analogy of a road trip, if curriculum is a road map, instructional strategies are the different ways a traveler has to get to a destination. When planning a road trip, part of the fun of is exploring options to find those that best fit the traveler's needs on the journey. Back roads, highways, frequent stops, and the fastest route are all options for structuring a trip. Instructional strategies are similar in that they give

teachers options for how to implement curriculum for students with visual impairments who have multiple disabilities.

The art of teaching is figuring out how to implement curriculum, or, in other words, finding the most appropriate instructional practices that support students with visual impairments and multiple disabilities to achieve their fullest potential (Bransford, Brown, & Cocking, 2000). A teacher can teach literature using objects or large print or both. Students can work together or individually during math. Community-based instruction can be incorporated into the social studies unit. There are many ways to plan instruction to minimize the barriers to learning that students may face. This chapter will provide guidance on navigating these many options.

BALANCING INDIVIDUALIZED AND UNIVERSAL INSTRUCTIONAL STRATEGIES

There is no easy answer to the question of what instructional strategies are best for students with visual impairments and multiple disabilities because instruction is intimately connected to other important factors, such as school and classroom materials, curriculum goals, and students' individual support needs. How teachers instruct students with visual impairments and multiple disabilities can only be understood by knowing who these students are, how they are assessed, what they need to learn, and where they learn.

The diversity of this student population adds to the complexity of the discussion of how to best teach students with visual impairments and multiple disabilities. When considering the array of learning needs of students with visual impairments and multiple disabilities, it may be helpful to think about instruction as being both individualized and universal. Instructional strategies can be individualized, that is, based on the specific needs of the child. Instruction can help students to meet individualized learning goals in their Individualized Education Programs (IEPs) and be tailored to their specific strengths and needs. Likewise, instruction can be universal, or based on what we know works well in teaching all students. The balance between instructional strategies that are individual and universal is important, especially as students with visual impairments and multiple disabilities are increasingly given access to general education curriculum in inclusive settings.

It is not uncommon for teachers who do not have a background in visual impairments and multiple disabilities to realize that the instructional strategies thought to be individualized for or specific to students with visual impairments can be used to teach all children. For example, providing students with nonvisual cues, such as real-life objects and tactile representations of mathematical concepts, is an instructional strategy that may be necessary for students who are blind or visually impaired, but it also improves outcomes for other students. Therefore, instructional strategies for students with visual impairments and multiple disabilities can be seen as practices that are both individualized or unique, in that they can unlock the potential of these students, but also universal in that they are an important part of teaching all children well, regardless of their support needs.

A UNIVERSAL DESIGN FOR LEARNING APPROACH TO INSTRUCTION

In this chapter, the wide range of instructional strategies that teachers can use to support students with visual impairments and multiple disabilities are organized using the framework of Universal Design for Learning, or UDL, as developed by CAST (2011). The UDL framework is an important tool in understanding instruction for all students, which most certainly includes those with visual impairments and multiple disabilities. In the UDL framework, teachers must consider three important principles to ensure that students are expert learners, or in other

Table 6.1

Expert Learners and Universal Design for Learning

Characteristics of Expert Learners	What Instruction Needs to Provide Students with for Them to Become Expert Learners	Examples of Instructional Strategies
Motivated and purposeful: they want to learn	Multiple means of engagement	Minimize threats in the learning environment using routines when teaching lessons and throughout the school day
Resourceful and knowledgeable: they know a lot and can generalize what they know	Multiple means of representation	Activate students' background knowledge using accessible media
Strategic and goal-directed: they know how to learn and can use what they learn	Multiple means of action and expression	Infuse instruction with assistive technology and allow students to show what they know using augmentative and alternative communication systems and multiple media tools

Source: Adapted from CAST. (2011). *Universal design for learning guidelines, version 2.0.* Wakefield, MA: National Center on Universal Design for Learning. Retrieved from http://www.udlcenter.org/aboutudl/udlguidelines

words, to ensure that students are achieving their full potential and learning what is needed to lead a fulfilling life. It is important to note that all students can be expert learners, even those with the most complex support needs. These three UDL principles help to guide curriculum design and development and, more important, support instruction that is effective and inclusive for all students (CAST, 2011). The three UDL principles are (CAST, 2011):

1. provide multiple means of engagement
2. provide multiple means of representation
3. provide multiple means of action and expression

(See the Resources section at the end of this chapter for sources of information about UDL.) Table 6.1 shows how these principles can lead to instructional strategies.

In the rest of this chapter, these three principles are used to organize best practices in the instruction of students with visual impairments and multiple disabilities. Although not exhaustive, these instructional practices are important for teachers to consider and will show how to teach students with visual impairments and multiple disabilities.

ENGAGING AND MOTIVATING STUDENTS

No matter how important or well-developed a lesson or curriculum is, students need to be engaged to learn. If students are engaged, they will be motivated to learn and enjoy school. Likewise, if they are not engaged, they may become indifferent to learning. This is why student engagement and motivation is a good place to start when thinking about instructional strategies. Students with visual impairments and multiple disabilities are engaged when teachers leverage or make the most of what gets their attention and keeps it, even when the students are bored and frustrated. What might motivate one learner is often drastically different than what motivates another. Therefore, it is important for teachers to design and implement instruction that taps into each student's interest, sustaining his or her effort and supporting the ability to make choices for him- or herself (Hall, Meyer, & Rose, 2012). There are three elements to consider when planning for motivation and engagement: encouraging students' interest, sustaining students' effort and persistence, and providing opportunities for students to direct and regulate their own learning.

Encouraging Interest in Learning

Students with visual impairments and multiple disabilities, like all children, have unique needs, preferences, and enthusiasms that become rich material for crafting instruction (Brown, 2009a). A first step for teachers who want to use students' motivators to recruit interest is to understand their students' interests and strong personal preferences (Blaha, 1996; Rowland & Schweigert, 2000). Teachers can "follow the child" to understand their motivators (Nelson & van Dijk, 2001) and use these motivators to inform instruction. Following the child involves careful observation of what interests or drives him or her. Students' interests or motivators

are specific and only understood after close observation and collaboration with others who know them well. Although these interests may be unconventional (such as light gazing or hand flapping), teachers can use them to build a positive relationship with students that will lead to more conventional interactions and instruction (MacFarland, 1995; Nelson & van Dijk, 2001).

Teachers who incorporate students' interests into instruction communicate to their students that their preferences are valued. In addition, teachers' use of these interests may provide students with a sense of ownership in their classroom (Hall et al., 2012). Students' interests or motivators, if not too distracting, can be strategically used in instruction as content for lessons and learning activities (Brown, 2009a). For example, consider a student who is fascinated with bracelets. This student's love of bracelets can be used to learn a variety of concepts, skills, and knowledge by integrating this topic into the student's work. Bracelets can be counted, purchased, and made into a variety of shapes in the context of math instruction, they can be designed and represented in the context of art instruction, and styles of bracelets during specific periods of time can be researched and written about during instruction in humanities.

It is equally important for teachers to acknowledge not only what motivates their students but also when instruction is not possible because students feel threatened or are distracted (Blaha, 1996). Teachers can consider what causes students to disengage or avoid instruction, as this information is just as important as figuring out what motivates them to persist. Students with visual impairments and

Table 6.2

Examples of Instruction that Engages Students

Student[a]	Threatening Instruction	Engaging Instruction
Ian is a 4-year-old boy with a cortical visual impairment and cerebral palsy. Receptively, Ian understands spoken communication and expressively he communicates with body language, gestures, facial expressions, and vocalizations.	Ian often becomes overwhelmed in his integrated preschool classroom, especially during unstructured playtime, causing him to vocalize loudly. His stress is more pronounced on Mondays and he will not settle into the classroom activities.	Ian's teachers develop a small communication board that gives him three play centers to choose from during unstructured playtime. He is able to use the board to make a choice and his anxiety is reduced. Other students in the class see Ian using his communication board and use it with him. Ian's teachers have used instruction strategies to *sustain his effort and persistence*.
Karen is a 10-year-old girl who is totally deafblind—no vision and no hearing. Karen uses tactile sign language, tactile symbols, and uncontracted braille to communicate expressively and receptively.	Karen becomes increasingly frustrated when learning science content. Although the teachers have developed a theme-based unit around her interest in cooking, she is often frustrated when her teacher uses new signs that represent concepts she doesn't know. She has started to bite her hand during instruction in frustration.	Karen discusses her frustration with her teacher and together they realize that she learns new concepts best after hands-on application, not during. Together they ask her science teacher to change instruction to suit Karen's needs. Together, Karen and her teacher have helped her to *self-regulate her learning*.
Eric is an 18-year-old young man with a visual impairment, a hearing impairment, and cerebral palsy (CP). As a result of his CP, Eric uses a wheelchair. He uses sign language and a dedicated communication device to communicate expressively. Receptively, Eric understands sign language, pictures, and written communication.	Eric struggles during his instruction in the community. At the start of the school year, he enjoyed learning career skills at a local pizza restaurant, but in recent weeks he has become detached and bored on the job. Nothing seems to motivate him to work and he has started to ask to stay home from school on the days when he knows he will be in the community.	After consulting with Eric and his parents, his teachers decide to change the setting of instruction to a local community center that has arcade-style video games. They also incorporate more opportunities for Eric to socialize during instruction. Eric can develop and learn the same career skills in this new environment and he can play video games with peers after his work is done. Eric's teachers have *recruited his interest* by building instruction off of his interests.

[a] See Chapter 4 for complete student descriptions.

multiple disabilities, like all students, need to feel safe in their environment and valued before they can be expected to learn. Teachers cannot expect students to be engaged with their instruction until basic personal needs such as physical needs (positioning), nutrition, comfort, and students' anticipation of these needs being met are appropriately planned for and provided (Brown, 2009b). Nor can students be expected to work at the threshold of their sensory functioning. In other words, they can't learn when their environment is overwhelming or causes them anxiety (Brown, 2011). Students can only be expected to engage with instruction if they feel like they can truly trust and relate to their teacher (Miles & McLetchie, 2008). Table 6.2 offers some examples of how instruction that is threatening to a student can become instruction that engages the student, using the examples of the students Ian, Karen, and Eric, introduced in Chapters 4 and 5.

Another way that teachers can use students' interests in instruction is by embedding learning opportunities into students' everyday experiences, a teaching strategy referred to as embedded instruction (see Chapter 5). Teachers can embed instruction by using real objects, routines, and events to explain concepts, rather than referring to them in the abstract (Miles & McLetchie, 2008). For example, if teachers wanted to embed instruction of money identification they would have students use money at stores in their community to purchase items they need. When students are involved in authentic tasks that occur in their typical or expected everyday experiences, the natural environment helps them to understand what they are learning and the purpose of learning. Some additional suggestions for engaging students' interest appear in Sidebar 6.1.

Sustaining Effort and Persistence in Learning

When students with visual impairments and multiple disabilities are interested in learning, a next step in designing instruction is to consider how to sustain this effort and encourage persistence in learning. The most important strategy that teachers can implement to support students' effort and persistence isn't even an instructional support, but rather a belief or mindset. It is crucial that teachers believe that students with visual impairments and multiple disabilities can be purposeful and motivated when given access to instruction that supports their learning (Janssen, Riksen-Walraven, & van Dijk, 2003). When teachers believe that students can learn, they often do. Put another way, students with visual impairments and multiple disabilities need teachers to embrace what is called the "least dangerous assumption" (Jorgensen, 2005, p. 5). This is the assumption that students' failure to learn is related to inadequate instruction rather than any deficits the students are perceived to have. Exposing students to meaningful instruction is almost never harmful, but keeping them from it almost always is (Jorgensen, 2005).

Another key instructional strategy to support effort and persistence is the use of flexible instructional supports within embedded instruction and routines. Varying the instructional supports used, varying who provides them, and giving students options to choose their supports can be excellent ways to sustain effort and persistence in learning. Flexible and natural instructional supports help us to provide students with meaningful instruction that is not too hard or easy. Students with visual impairments and multiple disabilities are often educated in learning environments where there are a wide range of academic, social, and communication abilities. The challenge for teachers in these classrooms is to find what Ayers (1989, as cited in Brown, 2008, p. 24) referred to as "the just

---

🔑 Sidebar 6.1

Instructional Strategies for Engaging Students' Interest

Following are some suggestions for engaging students' interest:

- Be a skilled, caring, and responsive conversation partner.
- Use language to talk about a concept the moment you think the learner has that concept on his or her mind.

- Become curious about the student's stories and his or her understanding of the world.
- Provide motivating and interesting materials that encourage exploration.
- Use the students' own interests as a basis for concept development; build instruction on the students' ideas about the world and how things work.

Source: Adapted from Miles, B., & McLetchie, B. (2008, February). *Developing concepts with children who are deaf-blind.* Monmouth, OR: National Center on Deaf-Blindness. Retrieved from https://nationaldb.org/library/page/1939

---

right challenge" or what Vygotsky would refer to as the zone of proximal development (Flavell, Miller, & Miller, 2002; see also Chapter 3). In other words, instruction needs to be appropriately balanced, both challenging and offering support, to ensure learning (Hall et al., 2012). When planning their instruction, teachers can optimize effort and persistence by asking themselves the following questions (Miles & McLetchie, 2008):

- How do I find balance for my students with visual impairments and multiple disabilities? Is my instruction making this lesson too easy or boring? Is my instruction making this lesson too difficult or frustrating?
- How can I maximize my students' efforts to learn and reward their persistence?
- How can I use routines and structure throughout the school day and within

lessons to clarify expectations and encourage participation?
- How do I ensure there is adequate time to communicate with students and enjoy conversations that support learning?
- How do I incorporate opportunities to communicate what *will* happen before instruction, what *is* happening during instruction, and what *has* happened after instruction?

Another instructional strategy for teachers to consider is utilizing a variety of supports available naturally in the classroom (Hartmann, 2006; Jorgensen & Lambert, 2012). Although it is important to provide students with visual impairments and multiple disabilities with instruction that is both routine and consistent, teachers also need to ask the following questions:

- When do the routines and structure provided to students with visual impairments and multiple disabilities hinder more than help?
- Does instruction rely on a one-to-one aide or paraeducator when small group work with peers that is facilitated by an aide would provide greater opportunities for authentic and engaged learning?

The use of natural supports that leverage the resources of the learning environment, in particular the use of student collaboration and community can help both students and paraeducators (Giangreco, Edelman, Luiselli & MacFarland, 1997; Peterson & Hittie, 2010). It is not common for both teachers and paraeducators to find that they are caught in tired routines of overreliance that hinder their students' engagement (Hartmann, 2006). When this occurs, it is often helpful for the teacher to stop and consider if he or she is choosing to teach in this way because it's always been done it this way, or if the teacher is choosing to teach in this way because it helps students learn.

There may be instances when instruction should focus more on supporting peers and other community members to interact with students with visual impairments and multiple disabilities and less on direct instruction by an instructional assistant or teacher. Research has found that the improper use of one-to-one instruction can inadvertently hinder students' independence, thwart social opportunities, and cause instructional assistants to become overprotective and take on too much of the students' responsibility for academics (French & Chopra, 1999; Hart-

mann, 2016). Teachers can avoid the overuse of one-to-one support by carefully thinking about what the student can do without a paraeducator, what the student can do with peer or natural supports, and what the student can do with the teacher or with instructional supports. When teachers and paraeducators are aware and actively mindful of the kinds of supports they provide, instructional decisions that reward effort and persistence can become more coordinated.

Encouraging Self-Direction and Self-Regulation in Learning

Students with visual impairments and multiple disabilities also need opportunities to learn about their strengths, needs, and how they learn best. Like all people, students with visual impairments and multiple disabilities who live high-quality lives are interdependent—they are neither overly dependent nor overly independent (Belote, 2011; Rodriguez-Gil, 2011). To achieve this interdependence, they need access to instruction that helps them to understand how they can succeed, how they can cope, and how they can advocate for themselves as learners.

Instructional strategies that teach children to be interdependent and cope are important for all students but especially those with disabilities, as the research has found that learners with special needs have fewer opportunities to make choices and express their personal autonomy (Chambers et al., 2007). All students, whether they have special needs or not, use a continuum of supports throughout their lives and these supports are as unique as their motivators and interests. It is important to note that students who self-regulate their learning are not in complete control of their lives, because no one is in complete control of his or her life. Rather, students who are able to self-regulate know when and how to ask for assistance.

To maximize a learner's interdependence, teachers can ask themselves the following questions:

- How can I instruct my students so that they develop self-knowledge, self-confidence, and self-determination?
- How does my instruction respect who the students are and what they can do?
- How do I encourage students to learn about themselves and take risks?
- How can I introduce the concept of self-determination to students, their families, and other educators and ensure that all are aware of the importance of instruction that considers how and when the student will take the lead in their learning (Morgan, Bixler, & McNamara, 2002)?
- How can I teach interdependence in social situations, such as leisure and recreational activities?

For example, imagine a very social student with visual impairments and multiple disabilities who is learning how to communicate in her local community setting. Her teacher is embedding her communication instruction into her preferred everyday experiences, and using the natural environment to encourage her to express herself. Instruction that encourages the student to be more independent or self-directed in her learning might involve supporting the student to identify key people in the community that she could approach if she needs assistance, such as a cashier or the owner of the local café. The teacher might think about how to fade her support and use their instructional time in a way that will help the student to cope and be successful in the community. If the student is involved in choosing the people in her community who she can ask for assistance, she will be better prepared and empowered to make these kinds of decisions later in life.

SUPPORTING STUDENTS' PERCEPTION AND COMPREHENSION

Although it may seem obvious, when students can access the concepts that are being taught, learning will take place. Likewise, if instruction is focused on traditional representations or ways of delivering content (such as through text and speech), students with visual impairments and multiple disabilities may not learn. This is why consideration of representations—or the media, symbols, and concepts we use to teach—are so important. Consistent and meaningful access to representations is an obvious barrier faced by students with visual impairments and multiple disabilities. Teachers need to represent information in a way that not only provides access to content and but also supports student comprehension of the content. Teachers achieve this by providing students with instruction that has multiple means of representation. How students perceive and comprehend these different representations is largely dependent on their characteristics (such as the extent of their visual impairment, and also their personal experiences and background knowledge) (Hall et al., 2012). For example, some students may need visual representations that are customized, some may need auditory representations, others may need to touch to understand concepts, and some students may need a combination of all three representations. (See Chapter 7 for additional discussion of representations.)

When thinking about access to and perception of instructional content, teachers may want to consider the following questions:

- How can I ensure that students perceive what is taught through multiple means of representation?
- How can I improve students' symbolic understanding?
- How can I encourage students to apply and generalize what they are learning?

Ensuring Perception of Teaching

Students with visual impairments and multiple disabilities, like all children, need to have access to information before they can be required to fully understand it and act on it. For example, without access to calendars and language or symbols that represent the days of the week, it is not realistic to expect a student to understand what "Monday" is. Visual impairment and blindness can greatly reduce a student's access to the primary forms of media used in classrooms today: text and pictures. Teachers of students with visual impairment and multiple disabilities need to think about two key questions when designing their instruction to provide options for perception:

- How do I optimize my instruction so that students can, if possible, use their functional vision to access representations?
- How do I optimize my instruction to use senses other than vision to help students access information?

Using Visual Representations

A first step for teachers is to consider how they can maximize visual media and representations used in class so that students with visual impairments can use their functional vision, if it is possible and meaningful for them to do so. Teachers who understand their students' visual impairments and the functional implications of their visual impairments can use this information to ensure their instruction supports authentic and efficient access to visual representations (Lueck, Chen, Kekelis, & Hartmann, 2008). For example, teachers can provide additional time for their students to explore visual representations presented in the classroom. Providing students with visual impairments and multiple disabilities with representations used in class (for instance, the materials used in a science experiment or the photos to be shown in a presentation) before the lesson helps them to access and make sense of them on their own terms. Providing students with preferred seating or assistive technology (such as low vision devices or a video magnifier) will also increase their access to visual information in class.

Using Auditory Representations

The use of auditory representations may be a good alternative to vision in that it allows students to access information at a distance. However, auditory representation is qualitatively different from visual representation in that it is not as easily accessed and is processed in a different way. For example, consider a teacher who is showing a picture of a turtle to her class. The visual representation has permanence and can be accessed throughout the lesson by students who can perceive it. In addition, a quick glance at the picture gives students a holistic view of the turtle and his features. In contrast, if the teacher verbally describes the turtle to a child who is visually impaired, this explanation is impermanent—the teacher's verbal description occurs once in time and cannot be easily accessed again without asking someone to repeat the information. In addition, the teacher's verbal description of the turtle would be a list or serial presentation of the features of the turtle, in contrast to the holistic information provided by looking at the picture of the turtle (Lueck et al., 2008; Warren, 1994). Thus, though the use of auditory and visual representations can each be effective, teachers need to consider the strengths and weaknesses of each representation when planning instruction.

Using Tactile Representation

There is a bias toward providing information using auditory and visual representations in classrooms because these two sensory channels, although different, are easiest to use when teaching students. Visual and auditory representations work well in environments where information is continuously presented and exchanged. Another option is the tactile representation of information. Tactile representations are not accessible from a distance like visual and auditory representations are, but they do provide information in a way that is concrete and accessible for repeated exploration (Lueck et al., 2008; Warren, 1994). For example, take the same example of a teacher presenting the concept of a turtle. If the teacher has an actual turtle shell, students can touch it to understand what a turtle is. In almost every situation, the use of a real object or representation, even if it only partially represents the concepts (as the turtle shell does in this example) is preferable to using a plastic representation or miniature object. Plastic representations (such as plastic food or tools) typically can only be understood if students have the vision to notice the visual similarities between the real object and the plastic object. The same is true of miniature objects, like a toy boat or train. Touching these abstract representations of real objects is a qualitatively different experience than seeing them.

When thinking of how to represent instruction, teachers will want to consider the following information:

- Touch provides rich information not usually obtained in other ways and when touch is used in conversations (such as a reassuring pat on the back or the use of tactile sign language) it can be a highly personal and social representation (Nicholas, 2010).
- Movement, or the vestibular sense, is an important component to touch. The use of movement is often overlooked, but can be excellent at supporting learning (Brown, 2006).
- Coactive movement strategies (such as movements that occur jointly or reciprocally between teacher and student) that use movement, gesture, vibration, and tactile exploration of tangible materials

can provide students with visual impairments and multiple disabilities access to people and important information (Bruce, 2005; van Dijk,1967).

- When using tactile modes of instruction, view students' hands with respect and ensure that information is presented in a non-controlling way that does not obstruct the students' experiences (Hartmann, 2011; Miles 2003).

In all, these three different options for perception—visual, auditory, and tactile representations—have different strengths and weaknesses and it is these affordances and hindrances that teachers must carefully consider when they plan instruction for students with visual impairments and multiple disabilities. At the same time, teachers must consider how their students perceive and comprehend information given their individual strengths and needs. Teachers' instructional decisions about what combinations of representations should be used can be instrumental in deciding whether students gain the knowledge and skills they need. Table 6.3 offers examples of instructional strategies that support perception and comprehension.

Improving Symbolic Understanding

Providing basic sensory access to information is never enough. For students to begin to deepen their understanding of the world, they need instruction that supports their understanding of symbols. Similar to the bias given to visual representation as a primary means for instruction, it is equally important for teachers to consider symbol systems used in classrooms and whether their students have the access they need to comprehend these systems. For example, the use of English is often a barrier for non-English language students or students with hearing impairments. The use of mathematical or scientific notations can be equally challenging for students with difficulties decoding or students with dyslexia and dyscalculia (Hall et al., 2012). It is not enough for instruction to provide access to standard symbolic systems and notations and assume that students will make sense of these. Teachers of students with visual impairments and multiple disabilities need to invest high-quality instruction time into teaching nonconventional symbol systems and use instruction as a context to expand on their students' use of symbolic understanding.

Students with visual impairments and multiple disabilities who do not yet have access to or comprehension of conventional symbol systems, like print or braille, may benefit from access to alternative symbol systems. For example, many students with visual impairments and multiple disabilities benefit from instruction that uses tactile representations, like objects of reference or line drawings and pictures (Bruce, 2005; Hartmann, 2011; Miles & McLetchie, 2008). The use of these systems is only effective when teachers embed them into the natural and cultural context for learning (see Hartmann, 2011). Teachers can further empower their students by modeling the use of these systems to all the students in the class, making these objects important for all the students to explore and share with the student with a visual impairment and multiple disabilities. For example, if a teacher uses a series of objects to represent the components

Table 6.3

Examples of Instruction that Supports Perception and Comprehension

Student[a]	Traditional Instruction	Accessible Instruction
Ian	Ian does not sit still during calendar time at his preschool. As the teachers go through the days of the week and weather, he fidgets, touches other students, and gets up to touch the calendar, which is not allowed. When a teacher of students with visual impairments watches Ian, it is clear to her that he cannot see the calendar.	Ian's teachers decide to give him preferred seating near the right side of the calendar. They also decide to give him his own small calendar that he can hold. He is able to see his personal calendar and the classroom calendar better and begins to enjoy morning circle. Other students in the class see Ian using his calendar and use it with him. Ian's teachers have *ensured he is able to perceive information* by tailoring instruction to the efficient use of his residual senses.
Karen	Karen is in a class that uses the common core curriculum to guide instruction. The literacy instruction in her class will focus on the common core English language arts standard, "Determine the main idea of a text and explain how it is supported by key details; summarize the text" (Common Core State Standards Initiative, n.d.). The teachers have decided to introduce a new informational text to teach this standard. Karen struggles to understand the informational text used, even though she can read it using uncontracted braille.	Karen's teachers realize that the informational text is too abstract for her and although she can understand the words, she cannot comprehend the concepts in the text, making it impossible for her to identify the main ideas. Her teachers decide that instead of using a new text, Karen should show her competency in this standard using a familiar informational text on a preferred subject. Together, Karen and her teacher have helped her to *better comprehend and apply* what she is learning.
Eric	Eric has a difficult time differentiating the names of the three women who assist him in the community at his vocation placement in the community center. His teacher reviews their names (Megan, Melissa, and Jessica) by speaking them and encourages him to practice their name signs on the bus ride to the center, but Eric doesn't seem to remember their names when he greets them minutes later.	In collaboration with Eric, his teachers create a small picture album of all the people he commonly meets in the community. Each page has the person's picture, high-contrast print of his/her name, and a brief description of the person's name sign. Eric enjoys looking at this book during his free time, and over time it supports his understanding of Megan, Melissa, and Jessica's names. Eric's teachers have used instructional strategies to *enhance his symbolic understanding.*

[a] See Chapter 4 for complete student descriptions.

of a classroom activity, such as a shared story-book reading, it is important for the teacher's instruction to make explicit connections between these objects and the more abstract symbolic representations (in this example, print, pictures, and speech) for all students in the class. Journals, poetry, and experience books can all be used as meaningful contexts for learning symbol systems (Miles, 2003; see Chapter 7 for more on the use of symbols).

Another important part of instruction is to highlight the important features, ideas, and relationships (Hall et al., 2012) for their students. Students need opportunities to actively engage in learning and efficiently use or apply new information in context. For example, teachers need to explicitly teach new vocabulary from a shared storybook and also provide instruction that supports students' use of the vocabulary. A tactile representation, a drawing, an object, will only be used by a student if he or she can do so in a meaningful way. Often the best way for teachers to use instruction to support the use of symbolic systems is to follow these guidelines:

- Ensure the student has multiple opportunities to use symbol systems in the context of natural conversations.
- Ensure the student has access to teachers and children who can model and share their experiences with these representations.
- Ensure the student has the opportunity to use symbols that represent their interests and memories (Miles & McLetchie, 2008).
- Ensure that the student is involved in deciding what symbols will be used or added to his or her communication or calendar system.
- Ensure that the learning environment is conducive to symbol use. Remove clutter and distractions and make symbols accessible and available.

Application and Generalization

Accessing information and learning about symbols is only useful if students can apply what they are learning in meaningful ways. To apply information or knowledge, students need to generalize or be able to understand what is being taught in a way that they can retain and use the information in the future. Teachers need to provide students with vi-

sual impairments and multiple disabilities with ways to process information and to support deep understanding of that information. To do so, teachers can design instruction that focuses on supporting ways for their students to process information. This may require that they give their students extra time and highlight key features of the curriculum. Students who access the general curriculum need teachers to make strategic decisions and plan instruction so that the most important and relevant information of the instructional content is presented (Browder & Spooner, 2011). The focus of instruction must always be on concepts and representations that students can use and understand (Hall et al., 2012).

Teachers can also support comprehension through activating their students' background knowledge before instruction begins. New concepts should always be related to or built on students' previous experiences (Miles & McLetchie, 2008). Students with visual impairments and multiple disabilities may not have the typical or conventional experiences that other school-aged children have; they may experience the world in unique ways. For example, a student with a visual impairment might experience and think of rain as a smell or feeling in the air, instead of the experience of seeing raindrops hit the windows. Instruction that builds on students' background experiences and knowledge naturally supports their generalization of learning.

Another important way for teachers to focus instruction on comprehension is to use preferred and natural environments. *Preferred, natural environments* are the places with which the student is familiar, and in which he or she feels at ease and can more easily anticipate the activities that are going to occur. Preferred, natural environments allow students to comprehend information in context. Instruction in natural environments that allows students to anticipate and apply what they are learning is critical. Students who are able to develop and apply their knowledge within natural environments are better able to generalize what they are learning from one environment to another. As previously mentioned, students with visual impairments and multiple disabilities can learn money skills by actually going to a store to make a purchase and going through the entire routine of paying. Repeating this activity in a variety of stores develops the concept that money can be used in many different ways to make many different types of purchases. This type of embedded is also called community-based instruction—using the real, natural environment to teach the skill and strengthen students' comprehension.

Teachers can consider how their instruction builds on understanding that leads to lifelong learning by using the following strategies (Miles & McLetchie, 2008):

- Model how the world works (social routines, cause and effect).
- Show the student where things come from, how they are used, arranged, and sequenced.
- Include the student in the whole process of an activity.
- Use the student's experiences as the foundation for understanding.
- Use routines and natural social situations as a context for learning.

ALLOWING STUDENTS TO SHOW WHAT THEY KNOW

For students with visual impairments and multiple disabilities to comprehend what they've learned, they must be given the opportunity to act on and express what they know. Teachers can encourage their students to be active and strategic by using instruction that gives students different options or avenues for demonstrating what they know (Hall et al., 2012). In other words, teachers will want to use instruction that provides students with multiple means of action and expression. As with each of the other UDL principles, how students act on what they know is largely dependent on their individual characteristics, their strengths, and their areas of need. When given instruction that supports the expression of what they know, students can become more independent and organized in their learning. The following questions can help teachers to ensure their students are strategic and goal-directed in school.

- How can I encourage students to be active and move?
- How can I infuse student expression and communication into instruction?
- How can I implement instruction so that students take more responsibility for their learning?

Being Active and Moving

Students with visual impairments and multiple disabilities face many physical barriers in their classrooms. As previously mentioned, visual impairments can limit students' access to information from a distance, often requiring them to find ways to move closer to visual information to access what other students can easily glance at. This kind of movement around the classroom may not be encouraged or seen as appropriate, especially in traditional educational settings that value student compliance over student expression.

Now consider the challenges of students with visual impairments and multiple disabilities that include physical impairments. These students may not be able to compensate by moving in the way their peers with only visual impairments can, further complicating how these students access information (Lueck et al., 2008). Instruction must allow students to act on what they are learning. Movement is a key component for comprehension, and when students who have visual impairments and multiple disabilities are given opportunities to actively engage, move, and show what they know, they learn.

Physical Environment

When planning and implementing instruction, teachers need to ensure that their students can actively express what they know and that their students are not limited by the physical environment of the classroom. A variety of school professionals are critical in helping teachers consider the physical barriers in their classrooms or in their instruction. Orientation and mobility (O&M) specialists provide expertise on how students with visual impairments and multiple disabilities move within the classroom, and have an understanding of how important it is for students to be both oriented in their environment and able to easily navigate in the classroom. Occupational therapists and phys-

ical therapists provide specific expertise on fine and gross motor abilities respectively, and can suggest ways in which natural skill development and learning supports can be incorporated into instruction. They also can address important issues related to seating and movement. Assistive technology specialists and augmentative and alternative communication specialists can provide specific expertise on how physical barriers can be lessened in the classroom through the use of technology. Each of these professionals can provide important information on how to maximize students' physical efforts to ensure more authentic and active learning within the classroom. Careful consideration of the physical environment and how to optimize the physical abilities of students through instruction will ensure that students can have multiple opportunities to act on what they know. The following are ways to improve the physical environment for students with visual impairments and multiple disabilities:

- Reduce clutter and distractions in the learning environment.
- Add extra or specific task lighting if needed.
- Ensure students have space to navigate around their learning environment.
- Provide students with options for seating that support learning in a variety of locations in the environment.

Minimizing Physical Demands

Teachers can also minimize the physical demands placed on students, so that their energy can be spent on learning, not coping. Adaptations that will improve physical action in the classroom include the following:

- Allow students to complete physically complex lessons over longer periods of time.
- Allow students to be first in line (if waiting is difficult) or to leave ahead of the class (if extra time is needed).
- Allow students to take frequent breaks (if sitting for long periods is difficult).

When appropriate and possible, teachers can focus instruction on physical action that leads to comprehension and learning, and away from physically taxing tasks that do not lead to learning by providing personal assistance for part or all of some tasks in school. Examples of this type of adaptation include the following:

- When watering plants as a classroom job, a small pitcher can be used instead of a larger watering can.
- A big button switch can be connected to a blender to make it easier to turn on.
- Students can put on their shoes but ask for assistance with tying the laces.

Partial Participation

Finally, as mentioned in Chapter 5, the use of partial physical participation may be appropriate when students are learning new skills in new environments. Focusing on one or a few key ways for the student to act or participate partially in many environments and activities, and supporting the other skills with teacher or peer assistance that is slowly faded may be appropriate. Using instruction that allows for partial participation is especially important when teaching students with visual impairments and multiple disabilities who may have difficulty learning certain skills or concepts. Rather than denying access to activities, environments, or instruction, partial participation allows for a few, key adaptations or supports to be implemented that will allow students to participate at least partially. There are various ways that partial participation can occur during instruction, including the following:

- When making a smoothie, the student can tell the teacher which item goes into the blender next, and the teacher will put the item into the pitcher.
- When setting the table, the student can put the plates and cups on the table while a peer puts out the silverware.
- In a game of Simon Says when the teacher says, "Touch your toes," the student can move his hands in the direction of his feet.

Table 6.4 provides some examples of how to provide instruction that encourages students' action and expression rather than instruction that limits action.

Infusing Expression and Communication into Instruction

Traditional instruction is often delivered in a way that encourages the passive learning of content and privileges certain forms of expression, such as worksheets, tests, and term papers. In contrast, contemporary instruction values providing options for students to actively approach learning tasks and providing multiple and customized options for how students can express themselves. This is especially true when instruction considers how

Table 6.4

Examples of Instruction that Encourages Students' Action and Expression

Student[a]	Instruction that Limits Action	Instruction that Encourages Action
Ian	Although Ian is usually a very active child, he is very passive during shared storybook readings. Whereas other students contribute to the teacher's questions and repeat rhyming words, Ian is left to vocalize. During a reading of *Circus Ship* by Chris Van Dusen, Ian rocks and hand flaps.	Ian's teachers decide to give him preferred seating near the right side of the teacher. They also decide to give him a box of stuffed animals that relate to each of the zoo animals in *Circus Ship*. After five readings of the book, Ian proudly holds up each stuffed animal when the teacher reads about them in *Circus Ship*. Ian's teachers have infused *expression and communication into his instruction.*
Karen	Karen, like all the students in her class, is assigned to complete a science fair project that will be showcased in the school's science fair. Karen is adamant that she wants to ask everyone in her town what they like better, cats or dogs, but she only has four weeks to complete the project.	Karen's teacher's first impulse is to tell her that her idea for a project is not possible. Instead, she and Karen determine that the population of the town is 32,000 people. They then try to fit scheduling for 32,000 interviews into Karen's calendar. Karen is still adamant and continues on with her plan, but after a day of interviewing people in the community, she realizes her project is unrealistic. Upset, Karen goes home to come up with a new project. The next day, Karen decides to survey the 50 students in her grade. Karen's teacher has helped her to *take more responsibility for her learning.* She let Karen plan, fail, learn, and then adjust, which helped Karen be more strategic.
Eric	Eric is exhausted by his vocational training in the community, so much so that he often will fall asleep on the bus ride home. His educational team worries that they are pushing him too hard, despite the fact that his trips to the community center are becoming the highlight of his school week.	In collaboration with Eric's O&M specialist and physical therapist, his educational team has decided that his motorized wheelchair will help him to better navigate his environment, encourage independence, and allow him to use more of his energy to communicate and complete his vocational training. Eric's teachers have *considered his physical needs in their instruction.* A month after his new motorized chair is used during his vocational training, community members remark that Eric is more communicative and engaged at the center.

[a] See Chapter 4 for complete student descriptions.

students communicate what they know and how instruction that supports communication can be gradually faded to encourage students to be active and independent in the classroom (Hall et al., 2012).

The population of students with visual impairments and multiple disabilities is extremely diverse, and so are the options that they use to act on what they know and to express or communicate this knowledge in the classroom. Some of these students develop verbal or language skills (such as the use of sign language and tactile sign language) to communicate what they know. Some may develop written skills using print, assistive technology, or tactile media, such as braille, or tangible objects. When planning instruction, teachers can optimize their students' expression and communication by asking themselves the following questions:

- How will I provide my students with multiple options to help them develop expressive communication skills that they can use both now and later in life?
- For these students, and especially those who are emerging symbol users, how does every learning activity naturally encourage active participation and expressive communication?
- How can instruction build on how these students are already expressing what they know (Janssen et al., 2003), even if that communication is unconventional?
- How can I use instruction to model various communication forms, representations, and symbolic systems in the classroom?
- How can I embed instruction in everyday routines to maximize the students' understanding and independence?

(See Chapter 7 for more information on communication.)

Encouraging Responsibility for Learning

For students with visual impairments and multiple disabilities who are actively communicating and expressing themselves during instruction and who are ready to be more independent, teachers can think about supporting executive functioning as a next step. *Executive functioning* is the skill set that involves setting goals, making plans, strategizing, organizing, and evaluating (Hall et al.,

2012). Teachers who want to support executive functioning through their instruction need to provide ways for their students to actively plan and organize their learning in the classroom.

Many students, regardless of their impairments and disabilities, need support and explicit instruction to develop knowledge and skills for strategic thinking. For certain populations, such as students with CHARGE syndrome (see Appendix 1B) or adolescents with visual impairments and multiple disabilities, instruction that provides options and supports for executive functioning is almost always a cornerstone of their individualized educational needs. This does not imply that progress for these students in this area is not possible, but rather that teachers need to carefully consider instruction that explicitly builds skills and knowledge that encourages these students to become strategic and goal directed.

Instruction that supports executive functioning is only possible when students feel confident and competent in their learning environment. Therefore, a first step in teaching executive functioning is ensuring that students with visual impairments and multiple disabilities can actively participate and anticipate what will happen in school and the community. As previously mentioned in this chapter, the use of calendars, object schedules, and routines naturally support anticipation so that students' participation is possible. A critical and perhaps overlooked next step in the use of these calendar supports is to use them as a way for students to express and plan what they want to do and accomplish. Students with visual impairments and multiple disabilities need to be actively involved in the maintenance and creation of these calendar systems with the goal of instruction being that the students will use these supports in meaningful ways throughout their life (Hartmann, 2011; Rowland & Schweigert, 2000). For example, a student with visual impairments and multiple disabilities can be given the opportunity to make choices about how she will organize her time and plan her actions both in and outside of school. She can be supported in making active choices about the order in which she will complete a multistep assignment. Instead of being told what she needs to accomplish each day, she can be supported to set her own learning goals and track her own progress. In the community, she can be given support to strategize about in which order she should buy her groceries and supplies. In all, these types of teaching strategies help students to take charge of their learning in meaningful ways.

SUMMARY

This chapter has provided an overview of instructional strategies for students with visual impairments and multiple disabilities using the UDL framework. The use of UDL to organize what works for students with visual impairments and multiple disabilities helps teachers to maximize learning and minimize barriers that are inherent in curriculum that is often designed for students who are not visually impaired. In addition, the UDL framework helps teachers to shift their instruction away from providing students with visual impairments and multiple disabilities access to a standardized curriculum that doesn't help them to achieve their fullest potential.

Instead, it helps teachers to focus instruction on what will lead to deep and sustained learning. UDL helps teachers to focus on the kind of instruction that supports all students, including students with visual impairments and multiple disabilities, to be expert learners who are motivated, purposeful, resourceful, knowledgeable, strategic, and goal-directed (CAST, 2011). Finally, it provides a common language for all teachers (including general educators, special educators, teachers of the students with visual impairments and students who are deafblind, and therapists) on how to best plan and implement instruction.

REFERENCES

Belote, M. (2011). Part 2: Developing and maintaining community connections and friendships. *reSources, 16*(3).

Blaha, R. (1996). Thoughts on the assessment of the student with the most profound disabilities. *SEE/HEAR, 1*(4), 13–21. Retrieved from https://www.tsbvi.edu/seehear/archive/thoughts.htm

Bransford, J. D., Brown, A. L., & Cocking, R. R. (Eds.). (2000). *How people learn: Brain, mind, experience, and school.* Washington, DC: National Academy Press.

Browder, D. M., & Spooner, F. (2011). *Teaching students with moderate and severe disabilities.* New York: The Guilford Press.

Brown, D. (2006). The forgotten sense—proprioception. *DbI Review, July–December 2006*, 20–24.

Brown, D. (2008). The sensory integration perspective and what it offers us in the field of deafblindness (Part 1). *DbI Review, July–December 2008*, 22–26.

Brown, D. (2009a). Helping children want to do things: Identifying and using motivators. *reSources, 14*(2), 1–6.

Brown, D. (2009b). The sensory integration perspective and what it offers us in the field of deafblindness (Part 2). *DbI Review, January–June 2009,* 4–9

Brown, D. (2011). Self-determination is for babies, too! *reSources, 16*(2).

Bruce, S. M. (2005). The impact of congenital deafblindness on the struggle to symbolism. *International Journal of Disability, Development and Education, 52*(3), 233–251.

CAST. (2011). *Universal design for learning guidelines, version 2.0.* Wakefield, MA: National Center on Universal Design for Learning. Retrieved from http://www.udlcenter.org/aboutudl/udlguidelines

Chambers, C. R., Wehmeyer, M. L., Saito, Y., Lida, K. M., Lee, Y., & Singh, V. (2007). Self-determination: What do we know? Where do we go? *Exceptionality, 15*(1), 3–15.

Common Core State Standards Initiative (n.d.). English language arts standards. Reading: informational text, grade 4.2. Retrieved from http://www.corestandards.org/ELA-Literacy/RI/4/2/

Flavell, J. H., Miller, P. H., & Miller, S. A. (2002). *Cognitive development* (4th ed.). Upper Saddle River, NJ: Pearson Education.

French, N. K., & Chopra, R. V. (1999). Parent perspectives on the roles of paraprofessionals. *Research and Practice for Persons with Severe Disabilities, 24*(4), 259–272.

Giangreco, M. F., Edelman, S. W., Luiselli, T. E., & MacFarland, S. Z. C. (1997). Helping or hovering? Effects of instructional assistant proximity on students with disabilities. *Exceptional Children, 64*(1), 7–18.

Hall, T. E., Meyer, A., & Rose, D. H. (Eds.). (2012). *Universal design for learning in the classroom: Practical applications.* New York: The Guilford Press.

Hartmann, E. (2006). It's only natural: Interveners and natural supports for learner with deafblindness. *reSources, 12*(2), 5–7.

Hartmann, E. (2011, September). Universal design for learning [Practice Perspectives]. *National Consortium on Deaf-Blindness, 8.*

Hartmann, E. (2016). Understanding the everyday practice of individualized education program team members. *Journal of Educational and Psychological Consultation, 26*(1), 1–24.

Janssen, M. J., Riksen-Walraven, J. M., & van Dijk, J. P. M. (2003). Contact: Effects of an intervention program to foster harmonious interactions between deaf-blind children and their educators. *Journal of Visual Impairment & Blindness, 97*(4), 215–229.

Jorgensen, C. (2005). The least dangerous assumption: A challenge to create a new paradigm. *Disability Solutions, 6*(3), 1, 5–11.

Jorgensen C., & Lambert, L. (2012). Inclusion means more than just being "in:" Planning full participation of students with intellectual and other developmental disabilities in the general education classroom. *International Journal of Whole Schooling, 8*(2), 21–35.

Lueck, A. H., Chen, D., Kekelis, L., & Hartmann, E. (2008). *Developmental guidelines for infants with visual impairments: A guidebook for early intervention* (2nd ed.). Louisville, KY: American Printing House for the Blind.

MacFarland, S. Z. C. (1995). Teaching strategies of the van Dijk curricular approach. *Journal of Visual Impairment & Blindness, 89*(3), 222–228.

Miles, B. (2003, October). *Talking the language of the hands to the hands.* Monmouth, OR: National Consortium on Deaf-Blindness. Retrieved from https://nationaldb.org/library/page/1930

Miles, B., & McLetchie, B. (2008, February). *Developing concepts with children who are deaf-blind.* Monmouth, OR: National Center on Deaf-Blindness. Retrieved from https://nationaldb.org/library/page/1939

Morgan, S., Bixler, E., & McNamara, J. (2002, July). *Self-determination for children and young adults who are deaf-blind* [Briefing Paper]. Monmouth: OR. National Technical Assistance Consortium for Children and Young Adults Who Are Deaf-Blind.

Nelson, C., & van Dijk, J. (2001). *Child-guided strategies for assessing children who are deafblind or have multiple disabilities* [CD-ROM]. St. Michielsgestel, Netherlands: Instituut voor Doven and AapNootMuis Productions.

Nicholas, J. (2010). *From active touch to tactile communication: What's tactile cognition got to do with it?* Aalborg: Danish Resource Centre on Congenital Deafblindness.

Peterson, J. M., & Hittie, M. M. (2010). *Inclusive teaching: The journey towards effective schools for all learners* (2nd ed.). Upper Saddle River, NJ: Pearson Education.

Rodriguez-Gil, G. (2011). The intervener's motto: Do with, not for [Fact Sheet]. *California Deaf-Blind Services Newsletter, 42,* 1–3.

Rowland, C., & Schweigert, P. (2000). Tangible symbols, tangible outcomes. *Augmentative and Alternative Communication, 16*(2), 61–78.

van Dijk, J. (1967). *The non-verbal deaf-blind child and his world: His outgrowth toward the world of symbols.* St. Michielsgestel, Netherlands: Instituut voor Doven.

Warren, D. H. (1994). *Blindness and children: An individual differences approach.* New York: Cambridge University Press.

RESOURCES

For additional resources, see the General Resources section at the back of this book.

Website

Paths to Literacy
Perkins School for the Blind and Texas School for the Blind and Visually Impaired
www.pathstoliteracy.org

An online hub that provides information related to literacy for students who are blind or visually impaired, including those with additional disabilities or deafblindness. The Strategies section focuses on instructional strategies in a variety of content areas.

Organizations

CAST
40 Foundry Street
Wakefield, MA 01880
(781) 245-2212
cast@cast.org
www.cast.org

A nonprofit education research and development organization that works to expand learning opportunities for all individuals through Universal Design for Learning by providing professional education, publications, and technical assistance on the development and distribution of inclusive, effective learning materials.

National Center on Universal Design for Learning
40 Harvard Mills Square, Suite 3
Wakefield, MA 01880-3233

(781) 245-2212
udlcenter@udlcenter.org
www.udlcenter.org

A program of CAST that supports the effective implementation of UDL by connecting educators and providing resources and information about UDL basics, advocacy, implementation, and research.

Additional Reading and Viewing

Hartmann, E. (2015). Universal design for learning (UDL) and learners with severe support needs. *International Journal of Whole Schooling, 11*(1), 54–67. Retrieved from http://www.wholeschooling.net/Journal_of_Whole_Schooling/articles/11-1%20Hartmann.pdf

Presents the UDL framework as one way to understand how to support learners with severe disabilities, how to support their access to authentic and appropriate curricula that improves their quality of life, and how UDL can be used to support reform for this population and how this will improve education for all learners.

Hartmann, E. (n.d.). Universal design for learning [Webcast]. Watertown, MA: Perkins School for the Blind e-Learning. Retrieved from http://www.perkinselearning.org/videos/webcast/universal-design-learning

Presents the three principles of Universal Design for Learning.

Part 4

. . . .

Essential Areas of Instruction

Chapter 7

Communication Skills

Therese Rafalowski Welch

Key Points

🔑 The impact of visual impairments and multiple disabilities on communication

🔑 The stages of communication development

🔑 Forms of communication

🔑 Other key components of communication

🔑 Ways to support communication development

🔑 Establishing communication goals

🔑 The communicative value of challenging behaviors

Alex is 6 years old and attends his neighborhood school. He is a quiet young boy who prefers to be by himself. Even with corrective lenses, Alex is very nearsighted. He also was recently diagnosed with autism spectrum disorder. The speech-language pathologist on his educational team has recommended that his teachers initiate a picture-based communication system with Alex to supplement the few words he uses. The speech-language pathologist also wants to consider acquiring a voice output device for Alex. His general education teacher is concerned that the pictures in her available collection are likely too small to be used effectively for this new communication system and will be difficult for Alex to see. The teacher recognizes that some adaptations need to be made so that the system can truly be accessible.

Shauntika is an engaging 12-year-old girl who is deafblind. Medical reports indicate that she has light perception only. She wears hearing aids for a moderate hearing loss in her left ear and a profound loss in her right ear. Shauntika has always been highly communicative. From the start, she let her caregivers know what she liked and did not like. Once oriented to her environment, she would take familiar adults by the hand to whatever

---

The author thanks Carolyn Monaco for her advice and consultation in the preparation of this chapter.

object she wanted or activity she wanted to do. In school, her educational team developed a system of object symbols, which they also shared with her family. In addition, Shauntika's teachers use tactile sign language with her, and she is beginning to use more signs herself.

Antonio is a 16-year-old boy who is often out of school for extended periods of time due to frequent respiratory infections. He has significant motor impairment and requires full assistance for all his needs. Antonio was diagnosed with severe developmental delay as a very young child. Later it was discovered that he had cortical visual impairment (see Appendix 1A). Antonio's family members and school personnel talk to him all the time, but are not sure whether he understands what is being said. They use tactile and sensory cues to let him know what is going on and what they may be doing with him. His parents say that since they started using the cues, Antonio seems calmer and is rarely agitated.

Communication is the very essence of personal relationships, social interactions, access to information, and learning. It is also key to assuming and maintaining control over various aspects of a person's life—from the simplest or most mundane (such as what to eat) to the most critical (such as how to live one's life). In addition, communication is a major outlet for relieving emotional tension (Downing, 2005). In light of these factors, the development or enhancement of communication skills is perhaps the most important goal in the instruction of students with visual impairments and multiple disabilities.

Although Alex, Shauntika, and Antonio have very different profiles, they share several features in common: some type of visual impairment or blindness, multiple disabilities, and the need for specialized means of communication. However, just as no single instructional approach is appropriate for every student's specific educational needs, no single means of communication is appropriate for each of these students' specific communication needs.

IMPACT OF VISUAL IMPAIRMENT AND MULTIPLE DISABILITIES ON COMMUNICATION

The impact of multiple disabilities on communication can seem daunting to teachers. A visual impairment alone can present challenges to successful communication. Often, nonverbal forms of communication—facial expressions, body positions, and gestures—are critical components of both sending and receiving messages, and may even be at odds with the words spoken (for example, rolling one's eyes while saying, "Yes, I'll do that."). If such nonverbal elements are missed, the interpretation of a verbal statement may, in fact, be inaccurate. Not having access to nonverbal cues, such as a head nod to signal that it's time for a student to take his or her turn, or a turn away from a student to signal the end of a conversation, can also impede simple social interactions. In addition, visual impairments can present challenges to the acquisition and development of concepts, which ultimately can affect a common understanding of vocabulary.

When one or more additional disabilities combine with visual impairment, the challenges are compounded: the addition of a hearing loss may prevent a student from following a conversation, receiving a spoken message, or recognizing a speaker's tone of voice. A physical disability can further limit the means a student may use to express him- or herself, such as gesturing, signing, or accessing augmentative and alternative communication devices. An intellectual disability may affect overall comprehension, as well as the rate of communication processing and production. A neurodevelopmental disorder, such as autism, may result in an apparent disinterest in interaction in general.

These communication challenges are significant for both the student and his or her educational team, but they can be overcome. It takes a strong commitment from teachers to persevere and to be consistent in their approach to supporting the student's communication. Most important, teachers need to view students with even the most severe disabilities as communicators, and to act on that belief.

DEVELOPMENT OF COMMUNICATION

A common misperception equates communication with language. Obviously, language is the primary means that most people use to communicate; however, it is certainly not the sole means. Individuals communicate in a broad variety of ways, from simple behavior to complex language. The stages through which communication develops are known as preintentional communication, intentional communication, and symbolic communication. (For more information about communication with very young children, see Chapter 14.)

Preintentional Behaviors

At the earliest stages of development, a young child communicates through vocalizations, body movements, and facial expressions. These various behaviors are primarily indications of the child's current state (comfortable, hungry, happy, and the like). At this stage, the child's communication is considered to be *preintentional* (Rowland, 2004; Rowland & Stremel-Campbell, 1987). That is, the behaviors are not purposely directed at another person with the intention of affecting the behavior of that person. For example, a baby may fuss and cry out, but initially she does not realize that it will cause her caregiver to come over to her. Essentially, she may be fussing because she is uncomfortable or bored, not purposely doing so to get the attention of her caregiver. In such cases, it is the child's caregiver who assigns meaning or intention to specific behaviors. "Oh, Maria is fussing, she must want something. I'll go and see."

When a student has a visual impairment and multiple disabilities, he or she may remain at this stage for a longer period of time than is considered typical. The combination of disabilities can impede the student's awareness that his or her behavior affects what others do. The work of the student's teachers is to capitalize on the behaviors and support the student's progression to intentional communication.

Intentional Communication: A Major Milestone

By consistently interpreting and responding to specific behaviors, caregivers help the child learn that what she does can cause others to do something in return. When the child makes that connection, she is at the stage of *intentional communication* (Bates, Camaioni, & Volterra, 1975). The child carries out the behaviors with the intent of communicating something to someone else. A simple way to determine if a student's behavior is at the intentional or preintentional stage of communication is for the teacher to ask, "Would she be doing this even if I were not involved with her here?" If the answer is "No," it is most likely that the behavior is intentional. Intentionality is a critical turning point in the development of communication, "a huge leap" (Rowland & Schweigert, 2004). At this stage, the child is connecting with another individual in a very significant way, and the response from the individual provides motivation to continue to interact, to communicate. As a result, the child's role in the relationship makes a major shift, from a passive role to a much more active one.

Because a child's intentional communicative behaviors can be very idiosyncratic or child-specific, their meanings may only be understood by caregivers or others who have frequent contact with the child. For example, to let family members know she wants an activity to stop, the child arches her back; when she wants more to eat, she moves her hands quickly back and forth on the tabletop. Over time these idiosyncratic behaviors, referred to as *nonconventional behaviors*, can be shaped or may simply evolve into more generally understood, *conventional, behaviors* (such as pointing to, touching, or looking toward something; nodding or shaking one's head; or performing greeting gestures). The very use of conventional behaviors helps expand the number of people with whom the child can communicate.

The following are some suggestions for supporting the progression from preintentional to intentional communication:

- Observe the student carefully and frequently. Some behaviors may be quick or very subtle, and thus may be easy to miss. This can result in the teacher missing opportunities to support the student's communication development.

- Document the interpretation of the student's current behavior by developing a chart that lists each behavior and its meaning (for instance, arching head back = "I don't want that"). Educational team members need to work collaboratively with the student's family and caregivers to accurately identify the interpretation of behaviors. Documentation can better ensure that the professionals who work with the child will respond consistently (see Figure 7.2 later in the chapter for a sample documentation chart).

- Imitate the student's vocalizations and movements to foster turn-taking. Likewise, pay careful attention to the student's hands, as what she is touching may be the source of interest to her at the time. Sharing that interest tactilely with the student, by following her lead, provides an opportunity for joint attention, or, more specifically, mutual tactile attention (Chen & Downing, 2006; Miles, 2003). Such interactions are conversations, at a most basic level.

- Provide the student immediate feedback to indicate that her behavior is the cause of your response. For example, if the student's educational team assumes that the student wants more juice when she bangs the palms of her hands on the table, teachers can help the student make the connection between that behavior and getting more juice. One way to provide this feedback is for the teacher to slip her hands under the student's, bang her palms on the table, then—through visual or tactile means—immediately show the student that more juice is being poured into her cup. (At a later point in time, a more conventional way of requesting juice can be taught.)

- Use *behavior chain interruption*, also known as *interrupted routines* (Carter & Grunsell, 2001; Siegel-Causey & Downing, 1987), to encourage behaviors from the student that indicate she wants an activity to continue (sometimes referred to as *signaling behaviors)*. Here, the teacher engages the student in a favored activity, then unexpectedly stops the activity and waits to see if the student gives any indication that she wants the activity to continue. The response from the student may be any type of body movement or vocalization. The teacher interprets the behavior as a signal to continue, acknowledges the student's signal (saying, gesturing, signing, or otherwise responding "Yes"), and restarts the activity. Some students may

require prompting and direct instruction to produce a consistent, observable response (Chen, 2014).

- Use a somewhat similar approach to encourage the student to indicate that she wants more of an item, or wants help to do or get something. Create a need for the student to communicate her desire. For example, at meals or snack times provide small portions of food items, or when working or playing with preferred materials, provide only a few at a time (Hancock & Kaiser, 2006). When using this technique with a student with a visual impairment, it is particularly important that she is made aware that more of what she wants is available but not attainable without assistance (Rowland & Schweigert, 2004). By responding to a student's anticipated need before the student has had a chance to communicate that need, a teacher can inadvertently squelch the student's motivation to communicate.

- Provide opportunities for the student to make choices. Begin by presenting to the student a highly desirable item along with a less desirable or neutral one. (Remember that a student who has a visual impairment may need tactile contact with these items in order to choose.) The student may indicate her choice by various behaviors, such as touching, gazing at, or reaching toward an item. Although it may be known that the student prefers one of the items, her initial response to both items may simply be random. If the student selects the less-favored or neutral item, allow her to have it for a brief period of time, then present the choices again. (See

Chapter 12 for more information on choice making.)

Symbolic Communication: Another Major Milestone

Another major leap in communication takes place when a child begins to use symbolic communication in addition to intentional, nonsymbolic communication such as behaviors, vocalizations, body movements, and facial expressions. *Symbolic communication* may include spoken and signed words, object and picture representations, and written and brailled words. The use of symbols can be limitless, progressing from simple, single-symbol usage to complex language structures. Likewise, the content of communicated messages can broaden from concrete, "here and now" topics to abstract concepts and information about past and possible future experiences.

Forms of Communication

Communication involves two fundamental processes: taking in information (*receptive communication*) and conveying information (*expressive communication*). In a communicative exchange or conversation, each individual engages in both processes, alternating roles as the sender and receiver of information. In supporting a student's development of communication, teachers need to address both receptive and expressive processes.

Typically, people use a variety of communication forms receptively and expressively in their daily interactions. Several factors simultaneously influence the types of forms an individual may use:

- the individual's abilities, skills, and preferences, including physical and cognitive abilities and communication skills
- the communication partner's abilities and skills
- the demands and supports present in the physical environment, such as lighting, acoustics, and access to aids and devices
- the demands and supports of the social environment, such as the cultural appropriateness of the communication form chosen, and the appropriateness of the form for the particular activity

Many—but not all—students who have visual impairments and multiple disabilities can and do use speech as their primary form for both receptive and expressive communication. To effectively instruct a student who has a visual impairment and multiple disabilities, teachers need to be familiar with a broad array of communication forms. Additional key forms of communication are discussed in the following sections.

Tactile and Other Sensory Cues

A *cue,* defined in the broadest terms, is anything that serves as a signal for a student to do something or that something relevant to the student is about to be done. Tactile and other sensory cues are most often used with students who are at the early levels of receptive communication skills. These cues are a form of receptive communication for the student, and negate the statement too often used in reference to students with multiple disabilities: "There is no way to communicate with him." Tactile and other sensory cues can provide:

- information (for example, who is with the student, which activity is about to begin, that a position change is about to happen)
- directives about what the student is expected to do (for example, "Open your mouth.")
- feedback regarding what the student is doing (for example, "Good work.")

Tactile cues include both touch cues and object cues. Such cues can be combined with speech to reinforce the spoken message. Rowland, Schweigert, and Prickett (1995) note the essential features of these cues and describe how and why they are made:

- directly onto an individual's body
- specifically for an individual's receptive communication needs
- the same way each time by every person who uses them with that individual
- immediately preceding an action or activity
- to alert the individual that something will follow the cue
- to focus the individual's attention on the interaction or event that follows
- to help the individual begin to anticipate what will follow and begin to make associations of meaning between the cue and the event or action
- with the expectation of a response from the individual, perhaps not initially, but after repeated cuing over time

Touch Cues. *Touch cues* are made on the student's body by the teacher to indicate a specific message. These cues are individualized for each student; there is no universal list or dictionary of cues. In selecting touch cues for a particular student, teachers must take into consideration several factors: where on the body the student has sensation, whether touching a particular area may trigger a reflex that would interfere with an activity or routine, whether touching a particular area is associated with a negative or distressing experience for the student, and the social and cultural appropriateness of touching a particular area on the student's body.

Object Cues. Objects or parts of objects from a student's daily activities can serve as *object cues* to inform the student about what will be taking place. When using object cues, generally an object that is part of a particular activity is brought under the student's hand for her to touch, or the teacher guides the student's hand to touch the object, immediately before a related action is to take place. For example, while in the locker room preparing to play in the gym, a teacher may bring one of the student's sneakers under his or her hand or guide the student's hand to touch his or her sneakers as the cue to change shoes before going into the gym. In the gym, the teacher may lead the student to the climbing ropes, then bring one of the ropes under the student's hand to indicate that climbing is the first activity. In some cases, an arbitrary cue is needed, such as a piece of textured fabric to indicate the student's desk, locker, or closet hook. As with touch cues, object cues are individualized for each specific student.

Other Sensory Cues. For a student with a considerable amount of usable vision, object cues can be presented visually. At times, olfactory (scents) or auditory information may provide more prominent cues than tactile cues: the scent of popcorn may alert the student that it is time for a break, or the sound of a bell may signal the end of the school day. Teachers need to make their students aware of these general environmental cues and teach their specific meanings, based on each student's sensory capacities. As with tactile cues, consistent use is key. Figure 7.1 offers a sample chart for documenting the tactile and sensory cues used with an individual student, including the purpose and meaning of the cues.

The following are some suggestions and reminders about using tactile and other sensory cues for communication:

- Tactile and other sensory cues support the mindset that teachers and caregivers need to communicate with students, not just meet their physical needs. For example, it is not acceptable to move, feed, dress, or otherwise handle a student without first letting him or her know what will be happening. A simple cue in an accessible and understandable format can provide that information.

Figure 7.1

Sample Chart for Documenting Touch Cues, Object Cues, and Sensory Cues

COMMUNICATION DOCUMENTATION: TOUCH CUES, OBJECT CUES, AND SENSORY CUES					
For: _____					
	Date Initiated	Message to be Conveyed	Informative or Directive	Touch/Object/ Sensory Cue	Instructional Description
1.	3/14/14	I'm going to put your hearing aid in your right ear	Informative	Touch Cue	Tap right ear (where hearing aid mold would be) twice with index finger
2.	3/14/14	Please open your mouth	Directive	Touch Cue	Touch student's bottom lip with object to be placed in mouth (spoon, straw, toothbrush)
3.	3/14/14	I'm going to put your shoe on	Informative	Object Cue	Encourage student to manipulate entire shoe with both hands
4.					
5.					
6.					
7.					
. . .					

Source: Developed by Carolyn Monaco.

- Tactile cues, in particular, are an effective means of identifying yourself to a student. When greeting a student, the teacher can guide the student's hand to touch a distinctive ring, bracelet, or watch that is consistently worn, to help confirm the teacher's identity. Likewise, some teachers may use a distinctive touch cue, such as a double squeeze of the student's shoulder or a quick rub of the upper arm, to identify themselves.

- Generally, teachers simultaneously speak and present tactile or sensory cues, especially for students with hearing abilities. It is important to keep in mind that some students, such as those with cortical visual impairment (CVI), may not be able to make use of more than one sensory mode at a time. In such cases, it is better to present the cues without speaking, or to sequentially offer speech and then a cue, allowing for processing time in between.

- A major goal in using tactile and sensory cues is for students to make the connection between the presentation of the cue and what is to happen next. After consistent use of tactile and sensory cues, teachers will detect connections being made as they observe the student perform behaviors that indicate that she is anticipating what will follow the cue. For example, if given a cue to stand up, the student may start to ready herself by changing her posture and may require less assistance. If a student's gym bag is the tactile cue for going to the pool—and swimming is a favored activity for the student—when presented with the bag, the student's behavior or facial expression would likely indicate that he or she is happy.

Body Movements, Vocalizations, and Facial Expressions

The previous section explained how body movements, vocalizations, and facial expressions are a child's first means of expressive communication. It also described their possible progression from preintentional communication to intentional communication.

For some students, these earliest forms of expression are their sole means of expressive communication. Teachers must be careful to recognize the importance of this basic form of communication and to work closely with family members and other caregivers to ensure that everyone is accurately and consistently interpreting and responding to the student. It is essential for teachers to also recognize that body movements, vocalizations, and facial expressions are not only expressive forms of communication for students but also means for receptive communication. That is, students who have visual and multiple disabilities also "read" the body movements, vocalizations, and facial expressions of their caregivers and teachers. The way a teacher touches or moves the student, the teacher's tone of voice, and, for those students with sufficient vision, the teacher's facial expression, all provide information—positive, negative, or neutral—as to how the teacher regards the student. Such seemingly simple aspects of interaction provide the foundation for the relationship between the teacher and the student.

Figure 7.2 offers a sample chart for documenting the body movements, vocalizations, and facial expressions of an individual student, along with the assumed meanings of these communications.

Gestures

As a student's intentional expressive communication progresses, she may use a variety of gestures. If the student wants to engage in a particular activity, she may let others know by mimicking or pantomiming motor movements associated with that activity. For example, she might indicate that she wants to use the stationary exercise bike by imitating the back and forth pumping movement of its handles. A student communicating at this level may use the same gestures to relay the experience to others, telling them what she did or remembering a shared activity. Gestures derived from the movements a student experienced in an activity provide an excellent basis for shaping those gestures into more formal signs in the future.

Another type of gesture involves moving the teacher's hand or leading the teacher to obtain a desired object, to get the teacher's help (such as with opening a container), or to initiate an activity together. Learners who have sufficient usable vision may engage in more typical or conventional gestures like pointing or waving hello and goodbye. Figure 7.3 offers a sample chart documenting the expressive gestures of a particular student and their meanings.

Figure 7.2

Sample Chart for Documenting Body Movements, Vocalizations, and Facial Expressions

		COMMUNICATION DOCUMENTATION: BODY MOVEMENTS, VOCALIZATIONS, AND FACIAL EXPRESSIONS		
For: _____				
	Date	Description	Type	Interpretation of Message
1.	3/19/14	Top lip is quivering	Facial expression	Move me
2.	4/24/14	Head is tilted upwards	Body movement	I'm trying to look at something directly in front of me
3.	5/5/14	Rocking movement back and forth (front to back) from one foot to the other	Body movement	I am feeling nervous or anxious
4.				
5.				
6.				
7.				
...				

Source: Developed by Carolyn Monaco.

The following are some suggestions and reminders about using gestures for communication:

- When a student uses a gesture to communicate a request, acknowledge the gesture by imitating it and modeling a more conventional way of expressing the message. For example, a student may indicate that she wants to play with a ball by making the motions of bouncing a ball and then nudging the teacher. The teacher can imitate

the student's gesture and say or sign, "Yes, you want to play ball," or simply, "Play ball."

- Keep in mind that gestures may be a way that the student is "thinking out loud" and remembering an experience. Teachers need to maintain the mindset that students' gestures are meaningful—and are not always requests. Again, the teacher will want to use the same practice of imitating and modeling, as well as helping the student to recount the experience. For example, a student may be remembering

Figure 7.3
Sample Chart for Documenting Gestures

COMMUNICATION DOCUMENTATION: GESTURES					
For: _____					
	Date Initiated	Description	Interpretation of Message	Receptive Gesture Acquired	Expressive Gesture Acquired
1.	4/8/14	Both arms extended directly in front and bounced up and down	Receptive: it is time to bounce the large therapy ball Expressive: student wants to bounce the large therapy ball	5/15/14	4/8/14
2.	4/24/14	Rocking movement of upper body forward and backward	Receptive: Expressive: student wants rocking horse to move back and forth		4/24/14
3.	5/27/14	Palm of right hand moves in a circular motion over left wrist and top of hand area	Receptive: it is time to put hand lotion on Expressive:	10/12/14	
4.					
5.					
6.					
7.					
...					

Source: Developed by Carolyn Monaco.

the experience of making a cake with her teacher by moving her hand in a circular motion just above the tabletop. Ideally, the teacher also remembers the experience and then goes through a sequence of gestures (visual or tactile), such as, "Yes, mixing the cake was fun. We poured it in the pan and put it in the oven. We waited and then ate the cake."

Tangible Symbols

The term "tangible symbols" may be unfamiliar to many teachers, but, in fact, most teachers have likely used various types of tangible symbols, especially pictures, as a communication option or support for their students. *Tangible symbols* include three-dimensional symbols such as objects or parts of objects, and two-dimensional symbols such as pictures, photographs, or line drawings. Tangible symbols are considered *concrete* symbols because they have a direct and obvious physical relationship with what they represent (Rowland & Schweigert, 2000). Some students who are not able to use abstract symbols (such as speech, sign language, written words, or braille) can make use of concrete tangible symbols. Some students may use tangible symbols as a primary means of expressive communication; for others, tangible symbols may serve as a means of support for bridging the transition to more abstract symbols.

Figure 7.4 offers a chart documenting the tangible symbols used with an individual student.

The following are some suggestions and reminders about using tangible symbols for communication:

- Before developing a tangible symbols communication system, consider the student's experiences, cognitive skills, and level of vision before deciding whether to begin with three- or two-dimensional symbols and which types of symbols to include in the system. Consider a general progression from most concrete to most abstract, such as: 1) the whole object, 2) a piece of the object, 3) a picture or drawing of the object.

- Individualize three-dimensional tangible symbols based on the particular student's experience. For example, a piece of chain may be used to represent a swing for a student in one program, while a piece of rope may be used for a student in a different program, depending on the type of swing at each student's school.

- Use miniatures (such as toy buses, toy chairs, and the like) only with students who can understand what they represent. In most cases, it is not advisable to use miniatures as symbols. However, some students who comprehend more abstract information may be able to make use of miniatures, after direct instruction pairing the miniatures to the object they are to represent (their *referents*). It is important that the student shows evidence of understanding the concept of size—a concept critical to the generalization of using miniatures to represent other referents—before using miniatures in his or her tangible symbol system.

- Mounting objects on a backing of cardboard or other sturdy surface helps establish the representational function of the object. Figure 7.5 provides a clear example; the mounted toothbrush serves as the *symbol* for brushing teeth, while another toothbrush is used in the actual routine of brushing teeth.

Figure 7.4

Sample Chart for Documenting Tangible Symbols

COMMUNICATION DOCUMENTATION: TANGIBLE SYMBOLS							
For: _____							
	Date Initiated	3D	2D	Description	Represents	Receptive Symbols Acquired	Expressive Symbols Acquired
1.	4/8/14	X		Toothbrush mounted on black cardboard	Brushing teeth	5/16/14	
2.	4/12/14		X	Picture of a group of five different colored markers	Coloring with markers	6/10/14	
3.	5/2/14	X		Plastic lid from a container mounted on black cardboard	Recess snack	5/26/14	6/24/14
4.							
5.							
6.							
7.							
…							

Source: Developed by Carolyn Monaco.

Figure 7.5

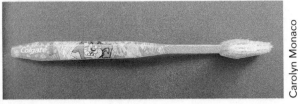

Carolyn Monaco

The toothbrush is mounted on heavy cardboard to emphasize its function as a representation for the activity. The learner will use a different, personal toothbrush for brushing her teeth.

- Students who initially use three-dimensional tangible symbols may come to use to two-dimensional symbols. Teachers can implement a variety of methods to systematically make the transition, such a tracing the object symbol, coloring the outline, and using that line drawing as the new symbol. They can also pair the object with a photograph, line drawing, or commercial picture while gradually decreasing use of the object.

- Students may use a mix of three- and two-dimensional symbols. Students who have transitioned to pictures for familiar, frequently occurring activities may use objects as symbols for new activities.

- As appropriate for the student, label tangible symbols with print or braille plus print. Labeling can serve as a means of exposure to a more abstract form of representation for the student, as well as confirmation of the meaning of the symbol for the teacher or other professional.

- When using two-dimensional symbols, consider the optimal visual features for each individual student, including size, contrast, color, and detail.

Manual Communication Systems

Manual communication forms used by students with visual impairments and multiple disabilities include visual signing and tactile signing. Both can be used receptively and expressively.

Visual Signing

Sign language is primarily a visual form of communication that uses shapes, positions, and movements of the hands; body movements; and facial expressions to convey messages. Learners with sufficient vision may be able to access visual sign language. Often these individuals may still require some adaptations based on their specific abilities. A student with low vision may need his or her communication partner to reduce the size of the hand and arm movements, change position, or adjust the distance from the student to accommodate the student's visual field. Likewise, a student with low vision and physical disability may need to alter the formation of signs because of movement limitations.

Tactile Signing

Students who are deafblind (those with significant hearing loss and whose level of vision precludes the receptive use of visual signing) may use tactile signing as a primary receptive communication option. To receive sign language tactilely, the student places one or both hands on the hands of the person who is signing to her. When the student is signing expressively, she will generally sign visually, without the tactile component, unless the individual she is communicating with is also deafblind.

Figure 7.6 shows communication between a student who uses tactile sign language and a sighted teacher. (The student's right hand is on top of the teacher's hands. The student also is responding to the teacher by using visual signing.)

The following are some suggestions and reminders about using manual communication systems:

- Sign language has some distinct advantages over spoken language: the hand positions for many signs (for instance, "mother") can be paused and yet remain intact, allowing a student additional processing time, as well as a stable model for imitation. In contrast, spoken words quickly "disappear," and extending the time for uttering a word distorts it ("mooothherr"). It is also easier to help a student form a sign by manipulating the student's hands than it is to help a student form a spoken word.

- As a student is learning to use sign language expressively, teachers may guide the student's hands in forming signs, particularly when the student is blind or has very low vision. This is known as *coactive signing*. Teachers will want to taper off such assistance as quickly as possible.

- Students with processing disabilities may need to have the pace of signing slowed to allow for more time to interpret a message, as well as to plan and carry out their response.

- According to Chen (2014), four criteria determine the signs students are likely to produce initially. The more criteria the signs meet, the more likely the student will be to produce them.

Figure 7.6

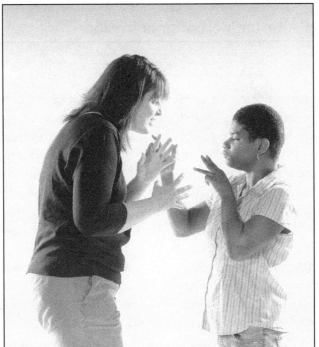

Mary C. Zatta

Example of communication between a student who uses tactile sign language and a sighted instructor. The student's right hand is on top of the instructor's left hand. The student is also responding to the instructor using visual signing with her left hand.

- Signs that represent preferred objects, favorite activities, and familiar people.
- Signs that are used for daily routines.
- Signs that are easily produced, touch the body, and/or have symmetrical movements (such as "home," "eat," "more").
- Signs that look or feel like what they represent (such as "eat," "wash," "sleep").

Augmentative and Alternative Communication Devices

Learners with visual impairments and multiple disabilities may use augmentative and alternative communication (AAC) devices. Most common are voice output communication aids (VOCAs) for expressive communication. These can range from simple single message devices to complex tablet- or computer-based systems. Devices can be adapted in a variety of ways, such as attaching three-dimensional tangible symbols to the message buttons of simpler devices or adjusting the size and contrast levels of picture icons and letters or words on complex devices. Sidebar 7.1 provides more details about AAC systems.

It is essential that students with visual impairments and multiple disabilities undergo

🖋 Sidebar 7.1
Augmentative and Alternative Communication

Megan Mogan

The term *augmentative and alternative communication (AAC)* is sometimes only associated with complex, high-tech AAC devices. In fact, many students with visual impairment and additional disabilities already utilize alternative and augmentative communication forms such as objects, picture symbols, drawings, photographs, and tactile symbols. "AAC includes all forms of communication (other than oral speech), that are used to express thoughts, needs, wants, and ideas" (American Speech-Language-Hearing Association, n.d.a). AAC systems are tools for *any* learner whose speech is not effectively meeting his or her communication needs (Burkhart, 2008).

Types of AAC Systems

AAC can be divided into two types of systems (American Speech-Language-Hearing Association, n.d.a):

1. **Unaided communication systems** rely on the user's body to convey messages. Examples include gestures, body language, and/or sign language.
2. **Aided communication systems** require the use of tools or equipment in addition to the user's body. Aided communication methods can range from paper and pencil to communication books or boards to devices that produce voice output (speech-generating devices or SGDs) and written output. Electronic communication aids allow the user to use picture symbols, letters, and words and phrases to create messages. Aided AAC systems can be classified into three general categories:

    a. **no-tech: does not require a power source**
    b. **low-tech or light-tech: has a power source**
    c. **high-tech: computer-based**

Common Reservations about AAC Systems

Some providers or family members may be concerned that a potential AAC candidate does not have an already established set of communication skills. When it comes to AAC however, there are no prerequisite skills required. In fact, some learners with severe sensory and motor needs must first have access to an alternative form of communication to demonstrate their cognitive skills.

Family members or educational team members may be concerned that learning how to use an AAC system will eclipse a student's learning to talk. This concern can lead to an AAC device being one of the last options for a student with a visual impairment, after every other therapy has been attempted and significant delays in expressive communication continue to exist (Romski & Sevcik, 2005), sometimes in the form of negative behaviors. One of the greatest, but often-overlooked features of AAC is that it is not meant to replace speech. AAC is truly multimodal, permitting a child to use every mode possible to communicate messages and ideas (Romski & Sevcik, 2005).

The Role of the Teacher of Students with Visual Impairments in Communication Assessment

Students who have visual impairments and multiple disabilities may have educational teams that include a classroom teacher, a physical therapist, an occupational therapist, a speech-language pathologist, an orientation and mobility specialist, and a teacher of students with visual impairments. When a student with visual impairment is a candidate for using an AAC device, it is essential to seek every team member's input and expertise in each of these domains in order to carry out effective assessment.

The teacher of students with visual impairments has much to offer the educational team with regard to the impact of a visual impairment on the development of communication and language, and thus AAC intervention. He or she can provide information critical to a comprehensive communication assessment, including the following:

- functional vision assessments (visual acuity and field; oculomotor function; light sensitivity; color perception; icon/print size and contrast)
- learning media assessments
- interpretation of vision reports and medical history
- observations and reports related to the student's abilities, to help guide decisions regarding input and output options

- information regarding orientation and placement of AAC materials and devices

Options and Terminology Related to AAC Systems and Devices

The following information offers an overview of some of the most common options provided in AAC systems and devices and the terms used to describe them, but it is not exhaustive. (For a more comprehensive list of AAC terminology, see American Speech-Language-Hearing Association, n.d.b.)

The messages within aided AAC systems can be displayed in two different ways:

1. static display: messages are in a tangible format and are "fixed"
2. dynamic display: options or vocabulary change when a device is activated in a certain location

Aided AAC systems may require differing methods of access:

- Direct selection: requires physical contact with the message location to activate.
- Scanning: a form of indirect selection for users who cannot use motor skills to access devices directly; requires the user to utilize an alternate source (such as a switch). The device lights up or gives auditory cues to messages in sequential order. The user activates the switch when he or she sees or hears the desired message.

Aided AAC devices have different types of output:

(continued)

(Sidebar 7.1 continued)

- digitized speech: more natural sounding because it is a recorded voice
- synthesized speech: computer-generated speech
- visual output: pictures or print

Message storage on an AAC device varies:

- single button/single message: one message is recorded onto the device
- single button/multiple messages:
  - sequenced: a single-button device in which the output expresses multiple single messages in a specific order when activated
  - randomized: a single button device in which the output expresses multiple single messages in a random order when activated
  - multiple cells: a single display offers the user access to different messages of varying cells or units
  - single level: each cell or button represents a single message
  - multiple levels: the cells or buttons on the device can represent more

than one message (depending on the level setting)

Conclusion

There are several key points to remember when considering an AAC device for a student with visual impairment and multiple disabilities. AAC includes many modes of communication. AAC can be considered in the framework of an overall "communication system," rather than a single device or mode.

Students learn AAC systems in the same way they learn verbal skills: through modeling and scaffolding in natural contexts. Just as in any other intervention for a student with a visual impairment, motivation is a key factor.

While the multitude of options and features of AAC technology can seem overwhelming at times, educational teams can consider ways in which access to augmentative and alternative forms of communication provides students the potential for meaningful interactions with others. This is, after all, the overall goal for any communication intervention.

---

a thorough AAC assessment to determine which device or devices would be most appropriate. When a student has multiple disabilities, the assessment process necessitates a team approach, as discussed in Chapters 3 and 4. The composition of the team will be based on the individual student's specific needs. In addition to an assistive technology specialist, the team may include a speech-language pathologist to assist with the se-

lection and organization of messages, an occupational therapist or physical therapist whose charge is to determine the best way for the student to access the device, and the student's teachers to help identify the student's relevant messages. When a visual impairment is present, a teacher of students with visual impairments can advise the team regarding the visual, tactile, and aural abilities and needs of the student (see Sidebar 7.1).

Written Language and Braille

Some students with visual impairments and multiple disabilities can use written forms of language or braille. In recent years, special education programs have promoted the development of literacy skills for all students, including those with multiple disabilities. The efforts are often met with very positive results. (Literacy is discussed in depth in Chapter 8.)

Selecting the Appropriate Forms of Communication

As mentioned previously, the form or forms of communication a student will use will depend on her attributes and needs, those of her communication partners, and environmental factors. Educational team members will want to carefully consider these three essential criteria when selecting communication forms for each individual student.

The following are some suggestions and reminders about selecting the appropriate form or forms of communication for a student with a visual impairment and multiple disabilities.

- Typically, individuals use several communication forms within a conversation or communicative exchange. For example, a person might combine speech, body language, various gestures, touch, and even objects such as photographs or items. Instructors of students with visual impairments and multiple disabilities need to teach all relevant communication forms to their students. Different circumstances and different stages of cognitive development call for different forms of communication.

- Combining forms of communication can be used to assist a student in learning a new communication form. This essentially serves as a form of *scaffolding* (teaching at a level that is clearly understood by the student, then building on that understanding). For example, to teach sign language to a student who is deafblind and who already uses tangible symbols for communication, a teacher can pair the appropriate sign with the tangible symbol. In this way, the teacher is presenting information at a level that the student comprehends (the tangible symbol) while exposing the student to the new form (the sign). If the teacher were to begin using the sign without first establishing its association with the known object, the student would likely become frustrated. Over time, with sufficient exposure and modeling, the sign may be presented without the tangible symbol.

- When a student has a visual impairment and multiple disabilities, the form or forms she uses for receptive communication (taking in information) may be different from the form or forms she uses for expressive communication (conveying information). For example, if the student's multiple disabilities include severe motor impairment or severe autism, she may take in information primarily through speech, but be unable to produce speech. Instead, she may use simple gestures, an electronic voice output device, tangible symbols, or all three. Teachers must be careful to model all of the receptive and expressive communication forms a student will use. Students cannot be expected to expressively use a form that is not frequently modeled or to which they do not have frequent exposure. In addition, teachers should not eliminate a particular communication form because it cannot be used both receptively and expressively by a student.

SUPPORTING COMMUNICATION

Functions and Content

The forms of communication are *how,* or the various ways, a student communicates. Equally important, and perhaps even more important, are *why* and *what* the student communicates.

Functions of Communication

Why is the purpose or function for communicating. Some of the earliest communicative functions include protesting or refusing, seeking attention or interaction, requesting continuation, and indicating a preference—all of which can be expressed without the use of symbols. Functions such as greeting, commenting, and asking questions develop later. Many of these functions also can be expressed without symbols, via gestures, directed gaze, body positions, facial expressions, and the like. In most cases, however, detailed expressions of these later functions use symbols.

Content

What is the content of a message, the vocabulary and phrases used. Content can be expressed through a variety of forms. In order for students to express themselves using symbols—speech, pictures, objects, sign language, and similar modes—they must first have exposure to the words or messages, and, most often, learn them receptively. When building a student's vocabulary, priority should be given to symbols representing the student's preferred activities, objects, and people; frequently occurring activities (such as eating, going home, and dressing); and family preferences. Jungle animals, often taught to young children, should be much, much farther down the list!

Experiences

The *why* and *what* of communication are directly related to a student's experiences. It is through the student's specific experiences with others and the environment that she is motivated to communicate—to protest, to request that an activity or interaction continue, and so on. Likewise, the labels, general vocabulary, and phrases the student learns are based on her experiences. Overall, the student's "bank," or collection of experiences, provides the frame of reference for making sense of what others express to her, and also forms a basis for the student's expressive communication.

Use of Routines

Routines have been used with students with visual impairments and multiple disabilities as a means to encourage communication. Certainly, routines that a student finds enjoyable will be the most motivating. Routines include simple greeting rituals or more complex daily activities, such as making a snack. Because routines have clear beginnings, set sequences of steps, and clear endings, they provide good contexts for modeling, teaching, and reinforcing communication, especially more formal or symbolic communication. The predictability of the steps involved in a given routine also allows the student to focus more attention on communication. It can be helpful for teachers to write a *task analysis* (the sequence of steps) for a routine and to identify related receptive and expressive communication targets, including the appropriate vocabulary and the various forms used to represent the specific labels, actions, and concepts involved in the task.

Instructors, however, need to be cautious and ensure that a student does not get "stuck" in a particular routine. Once the student learns a routine, she needs to be taught to generalize what she has learned to other situations that include similar actions and materials. For example, a snack routine of making microwave popcorn might be changed to include air-popped popcorn, so a different device and a different form of packaging would be used. The popcorn might also be made in a different kitchen, or used to make popcorn balls instead of being buttered and placed in a bowl. From the perspective of communication, the activity and meaning of "making popcorn" has expanded, and the meanings of familiar vocabulary and labels have broadened.

Use of Calendar Systems

Calendar systems are composed of a series of symbols arranged in sequential order representing the activities of an individual's day. Calendar systems are a means for orienting students to their day's activities and serve as a kind of agenda for the day. Items representing the activities may be three-dimensional objects and symbols (including whole or partial objects) or two-dimensional symbols (including photos, pictures, and line drawings), according to the student's most appropriate communication form or forms. In some cases, a calendar may contain a mix of three- and two-dimensional objects. For example, a student who comprehends two-dimensional representations may initially require a more concrete form to represent new activities until those become familiar.

A routine can be built around the use of the calendar. Sidebar 7.2 outlines a typical calendar system routine. (See Chapter 8 for some examples of calendar systems. For detailed information about calendar systems and video examples of their use see Blaha, 2001 and the website of the National Center on Deaf-Blindness, n.d.)

Use of Experience Books

Experience books are tactile books whose contents are directly related to a student's specific experiences (Lewis & Tolla, 2003). The format of the contents is based on the level of representation that the student most easily comprehends: three-dimensional objects and symbols or two-dimensional symbols. Sidebar 7.3 outlines the characteristics and purposes of experience books, and Figure 7.7 shows an example. The pages of experience books can be captioned in print, braille, or both for the student, as well as for accurate interpretation by the teacher or other literate communication partners.

Experience books address several early literacy objectives for students with visual impairments and other disabilities. The books also provide a source for conversation and practicing vocabulary. (See chapter 8 for further information on experience books.)

✎ Sidebar 7.2

A Typical Calendar System Routine

Carolyn Monaco

The following is a typical routine for using a calendar system with a student who has a visual impairment and multiple disabilities.

1. Together, the student and the teacher arrange the items for the calendar in the sequence of the day's activities.
2. The teacher encourages the student to touch, handle, and/or look at each item. The teacher and the student have a conversation about the activities, which may consist of simply naming the activities or may involve a discussion about them, such as what the student will be doing during each activity, the participants involved in each activity, the locations involved, which activities are preferred by the student, and the like.
3. In sequence the student takes the associated item to the specific activity it represents, confirming what she will be doing. The simple act of carrying the item can also serve as a reminder for the student of where she is going. (The area or room where the activity takes place can be labeled with an identical item. The student can then confirm that she is at the correct location by matching the item she is carrying to the identical one in the room or area.)
4. When each activity is completed, the student returns with the item to the calendar and places the item in a designated "finished" container near the calendar. The teacher and the student may talk about which activities are done (touching or looking at the empty spaces) and what is yet to come (touching or looking at the remaining items).
5. The student selects the next item in the calendar and begins the routine again at step 3.

COMMUNICATION PARTNERS

Teachers

In addition to a student's family members, a student's teachers will be among the most important, and often among the most frequent communication partners. There is much that teachers can do to ensure that their communication with students who have visual impairments and multiple disabilities is successful and enjoyable:

- **Be attentive and present.** A student deserves the full attention of her teacher when the two are interacting. A responsive communication partner is likely to elicit more communication from the student. If not focused on the student during an activity, a teacher runs the risk of missing subtle behaviors that could

Experience Books

Key Characteristics
- handmade rather than commercially produced
- based on the specific experiences of a particular student (for instance, going to a store in the neighborhood, visiting family members, making a pizza, and so on)
- designed to be easily understood by the student (the level of representation of the content is appropriate for the student who will use the book)

Contents
Experience books can include any of the following:

- objects (whole or partial) used by or experienced by the student within a specific activity
- pictorial representations, such as photos, drawings, and pictures from magazines, brochures, or packaging
- textured materials
- printed text
- braille

How Students Use Experience Books
- for comfort (such as recalling a familiar experience)
- for information
- for directions (step-by-step instruction)
- to repeat and practice communication skills
- as an independent recreational activity

- as a means to anticipate an upcoming activity or event
- as a tool for interaction and socialization with others
- as a means for other individuals to gain insight into the student's personality
- as a three-dimensional option to store memories, especially for students who cannot access photos or videos

What Experience Books Can Teach
- receptive and expressive communication
- the concept of representation
- the sequence of steps in an activity
- time concepts: past, present, and future
- fine motor skills
- early literacy skills
- social skills
- independence

Suggestions for Using Experience Books
- Start with books about pleasurable experiences.
- Include the student in as many aspects of making the books as possible.
- Make the books interactive (for example, include things that can be manipulated, opened, removed, and counted).
- Keep in mind that the concepts represented in the books will become better understood as the student has more opportunities for repetition of the experiences.

Figure 7.7
Example of an Experience Book

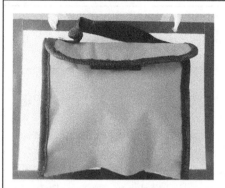

Front Cover: A replica of the student's snack bag, representing the beginning of snack time.

Page 1: A washcloth that represents washing hands prior to having a snack. The cloth is attached to the backing with Velcro and can be removed to model the skill, practice the skill, or talk about the activity.

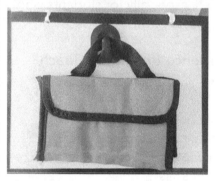

Page 2: A replica of the student's snack bag on a hook that represents removing the bag from the hook where it is kept. The bag can be removed from the hook to model the skill, practice the skill, or talk about the activity.

Page 3: A replica of the student's snack bag that represents opening and closing the bag. The top of the bag can be opened and closed to model the skill, practice the skill, or talk about the activity.

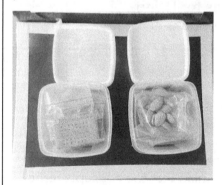

Page 4: Two containers identical to the ones used in the student's snack bag, each with a different snack inside, that represent selecting a snack. The containers are attached to the backing board with Velcro. Once the lids are removed, the two snacks can be viewed or felt, the options discussed, and a choice made.

Photos by Carolyn Monaco

Page 5: A garbage bag with the empty snack bag inside that represents the snack bag being thrown away. This is the final step in the process.

begin to be shaped into intentional communication, or the student's attempt to get attention. Not only are these lost opportunities for advancing communication skills, but, according to basic behavioral principles, such behaviors can be extinguished simply by being ignored.

- **Allow for processing time and response time.** Multiple disabilities present challenges for students in first accessing information, taking in the information, accurately interpreting the information, devising a motor plan for responding, and then carrying out the plan as a response. Consider the impact on this process of visual impairments, in combination with other possible sensory impairments, physical impairments, intellectual disabilities, or neurological disabilities. A skilled and responsive communication partner is patient and resists the urge to intervene too soon.

- **Attend to positioning.** How the student is positioned, how the teacher is positioned, and how the materials or devices the student needs for communication are positioned, will either foster or hinder communication. Teachers must ensure that students are comfortably and stably positioned, and have easy sensory and physical access to communication partners and materials or devices. If a student is not properly positioned, her efforts to stabilize herself and gain access to partners, information, and materials may supersede her efforts to communicate. Functional sensory assessments (see Chapter 3) and input from members of the educational team can provide valuable information for optimum positioning.

- **Be mindful of students' energy levels.** When a student has multiple disabilities, a great deal of effort goes into interactions, such as trying to focus attention, holding the best positions for information access, carrying out the motor aspects of communication, and the like. A student's reluctance to communicate or to participate in an activity may be due to fatigue. Teachers can plan the school day to balance high demand, high attention activities with less demanding ones or breaks.

- **Learn new ways to communicate.** Students with visual impairments and multiple disabilities are a heterogeneous group, so different forms of communication will need to be used with individual students who have different profiles. It is likely, then, that teachers who work with these students will need to acquire a variety of communication forms and strategies. The student's needs are the priority, and should be the guiding factor in what communication forms the teacher will need to understand and teach.

- **Teach communication skills in context.** Teaching forms of communication, vocabulary, and phrases within students' "real life" situations and settings can help support students' acquisition and use of these skills. The elements of the actual context can strengthen the association between what students do or what materials are used, and the related receptive and expressive communication means and labels.

Peers and Other Partners

Expanding the number of individuals with whom students with visual impairments and multiple disabilities can communicate should be a major goal in educational programs. To realize such a goal, teachers serve as liaisons between a student, other adults in the school, student peers, and perhaps individuals in the larger community. Generally, teachers will need to teach a student's peers and other adults specific skills for interacting and communicating with the student. In some school programs, teachers conduct mini in-service training sessions for staff and students to teach them the appropriate communication skills. The student herself may be able to participate in the training, adding a personal perspective. It is also possible for the student to make a contribution without being physically present, such as making a video showing how she uses a tangible symbols system. In other programs, small groups of interested students may work directly with teachers and the student to acquire the needed skills, and then in turn teach their friends. Often, student peers become strong advocates for the student, and develop creative approaches for including him in a broad variety of activities.

Some educational programs involve community-based activities with more occasional contact with members of the local community. In most cases, teachers do not have the same opportunities for training community members, so the focus must be on finding strategies that allow the student to communicate in ways that she knows and understands, and that at the same time can be understood by the community member. For example, a student who wants to order a chocolate drink at a fast food restaurant, and who uses either three- or two-dimensional tangible symbols, may hand the symbol to the clerk. On the reverse side of the symbol can be written, "Chocolate drink, please."

ESTABLISHING COMMUNICATION GOALS

This chapter has presented information on forms of communication (*how* a student communicates), communication functions (*why* a student communicates), communication content (*what* a student communicates), experiences to support communication, and communication partners. Communication is a dynamic process with all of these elements interwoven within a single interaction. Meaningful communication goals for a student can address one or more of these elements: receptive and expressive forms, functions, content, experiences, and partners.

Goals for any student generally evolve from the student's needs as based on his or her current skills (otherwise known as "present levels of performance" on the student's Individualized Education Program [IEP], as discussed in Chapter 4). Ideally, decisions are made following a careful examination of information from several sources: data collected from daily programs, teacher observations, family and student input, and assessment results (see Chapter 3). The same is true for students with visual impairments and multiple disabilities. As much as teachers would like to have one formal, comprehensive assessment instrument that addresses all the key communication elements for these students, such an instrument unfortunately does not (yet) exist. Teachers frequently make use of portions of various assessments, but encounter problems with standardization when adaptations are made for different disabilities, age range parameters, and the like. Perhaps even more useful and informative are resources that provide a framework for a relevant assessment process. One such resource is *Assessing Communication and Learning in Young Children Who Are Deafblind or Who Have Multiple Disabilities* (Rowland, 2009). This manual makes use of what the authors label an "authentic" approach to assessment, which essentially involves collecting needed information within a specific student's typical environments and during his or her typical routines.

The following are suggestions and reminders for establishing communication goals for students with visual impairments and multiple disabilities:

- When outlining communication goals for a student, be sure to address the supports he or she needs to successfully meet each specific goal. These may include positioning, materials, environmental conditions, characteristics of communication partners, opportunities for practice, and so on.

- Another means for supporting attainment of a particular goal is to minimize the demands of related communication elements. Sometimes a particular element may be singled out and made a priority of a student's program. In such cases, keeping the other elements unchanged allows the student to focus on the new skill within familiar scenarios. For example, if the goal is to learn sign language, which would be a new communication form for the student, teachers can teach the new form while using already known functions (for example, requesting and commenting), familiar partners (for example, teachers and family members), and familiar activities (for example, meal time and games). The content of messages would also remain unchanged, but they would be expressed in sign language.

- If the use of abstract communication forms is a goal for a student, make sure he or she has a solid foundation in intentional communication, demonstrates a variety of communication functions, and can make sense of more concrete symbols. As one experienced practitioner stated, "It's not a race to get every student to use the most abstract communication forms, whether it's speech, sign language, or some complex level AAC device. It's pointless if students don't actually understand what they're using" (C. Monaco, personal communication, August 11, 2005).

- Progress as related to communication can be a matter of *quality*, not just a matter of adding new skills. Qualitative indicators of progress include (Rowland, 2009):
  - increased consistency of response
  - increased frequency of response
  - increased clarity of response
  - increased independence or decreased need for assistance (cues, for example)
  - more sustained attention
  - faster response time

CHALLENGING BEHAVIORS AND COMMUNICATION

In recent years, the field of special education in particular has sought to better understand and better address students' challenging behaviors. The latest reauthorization of the

Individuals with Disabilities Education Improvement Act in 2004 includes provisions for a functional behavior assessment and resulting behavior intervention plan when a student exhibits behaviors that interfere with his or her learning or the learning of his or her classmates (see Chapter 13). The rationale behind a functional behavior assessment is the recognition that behaviors serve a purpose for the student—to attain something, avoid something, self-regulate, and so on. Essentially, behaviors carry a message and may serve as a means of communication. In fact, various practitioners and researchers emphatically claim that all problem behaviors are communication.

Communication is a powerful means to gain some control over one's environment and influence other people. Often, individuals who have severe disabilities, including students who have visual impairments and multiple disabilities, may have very limited or no formal communication options. As a result, a student's challenging behaviors can influence others to provide the student's desired outcomes, such as attention or a break from work. Even when students do have formal communication skills, they may find that challenging behaviors are the most effective means for getting what they want. In either case, teachers are charged with providing the students more conventional ways of expressing the same messages. Teachers simultaneously must work to reduce and ultimately eliminate the power of the problem behavior for achieving the student's desired outcome (Carr & Durand, 1985). For example, if it is determined that a student throws materials when she is frustrated and needs help with her work, the teacher may set up a single message communication device with the message, "I need help please," and teach the student to use it when she needs assistance. The teacher will go to help the student when he hears the message, and, unless other class members are being disturbed, he will not respond to the student's throwing. In addition, the teacher will likely become more aware of the tasks that the student finds frustrating and the student's body language that signals she is becoming frustrated, allowing the teacher to intervene before the problem behavior is carried out.

It is important to remember that from the perspective of communication, problem behaviors may be preintentional or intentional. As previously discussed, preintentional communication is simply a reaction to the student's current circumstances or an expression of his or her current state. It is not directed toward another person. Intentional communication is deliberately directed at another person in order to affect that person's behavior. Using the example above, the same approach could be used whether or not the student's communication is preintentional or intentional, as the goal is to change the student's behavior.

SUMMARY

The communication needs of students who have visual impairments and multiple disabilities are diverse and often complex. Teachers play a major role in addressing those needs. Most likely, to effectively communicate with their students, as well to teach them, teachers are required to recognize and learn new communication forms and strategies. The Communication Bill of Rights, developed by the National Joint Committee for the Communication Needs of Persons with Severe Disabilities (see Sidebar 7.4), can serve as a standard and reminder for teachers as to their ultimate goals. The importance of supporting the development of communication skills for a student who has a visual impairment and multiple disabilities cannot be overestimated, as communication is inextricably tied to the student's quality of life.

🔑 Sidebar 7.4

Communication Bill of Rights

All people with a disability of any extent or severity have a basic right to affect, through communication, the conditions of their existence. All people have the following specific communication rights in their daily interactions. These rights are summarized from the Communication Bill of Rights put forth in 1992 by the National Joint Committee for the Communication Needs of Persons with Severe Disabilities.

Each person has the right to:

- request desired objects, actions, events, and people
- refuse undesired objects, actions, or events
- express personal preferences and feelings
- be offered choices and alternatives
- reject offered choices
- request and receive another person's attention and interaction
- ask for and receive information about changes in routine and environment
- receive intervention to improve communication skills
- receive a response to any communication, whether or not the responder can fulfill the request
- have access to AAC (augmentative and alternative communication) and other AT (assistive technology) services and devices at all times
- have AAC and other AT devices that function properly at all times
- be in environments that promote one's communication as a full partner with other people, including peers
- be spoken to with respect and courtesy
- be spoken to directly and not be spoken for or talked about in the third person while present
- have clear, meaningful, and culturally and linguistically appropriate communications

---

Source: Reprinted with permission from National Joint Committee for the Communication Needs of Persons with Severe Disabilities. (1992). Guidelines for meeting the communication needs of persons with severe disabilities. *ASHA, 34*(Suppl. 7), 2–3.

REFERENCES

American Speech-Language-Hearing Association. (n.d.a). Augmentative and alternative communication (AAC). Retrieved from http://www.asha.org/public/speech/disorders/AAC/

American Speech-Language-Hearing Association. (n.d.b). Augmentative communication: A glossary. Retrieved from http://www.asha.org/public/speech/disorders/AAC-Glossary/

Bates, E., Camaioni, L., & Volterra, V. (1975). The acquisition of performatives prior to speech. *Merrill-Palmer Quarterly of Behavior and Development, 21*(3), 205–226.

Blaha, R. (2001). *Calendars for students with multiple impairments including deafblindness.* Austin: Texas School for the Blind and Visually Impaired.

Burkhart, L. J. (2008). *Key concepts for using augmentative communication with children who have complex communication needs* [Handout]. Retrieved from http://www.lburkhart.com/hand_AAC_OSU_6_08.pdf

Carr, E. G., & Durand, V. M. (1985). Reducing behavior problems through functional communication training. *Journal of Applied Behavior Analysis, 18*(2), 111–126.

Carter, M., & Grunsell, J. (2001). The behavior chain interruption strategy: A review of research and discussion of future directions. *Research and Practice for Persons with Severe Disabilities, 26*(1), 37–49.

Chen, D. (2014). Promoting early communication and language development. In D. Chen (Ed.), *Essential elements in early intervention: Visual impairment and multiple disabilities* (2nd ed., pp. 395–462). New York: AFB Press.

Chen, D., & Downing, J. E. (2006). *Tactile strategies for children who have visual impairments and multiple disabilities: Promoting communication and learning skills.* New York: AFB Press.

Downing, J. E. (2005). The importance of teaching communication skills. In *Teaching communication skills to students with severe disabilities* (2nd ed., pp. 1–26). Baltimore: Paul H. Brookes Publishing Co.

Hancock, T. B., & Kaiser, A. P. (2006). Enhanced milieu teaching. In R. J. McCauley & M. E. Fey (Eds.), *Treatment of language disorders in children* (pp. 203–236). Baltimore: Paul H. Brookes Publishing Co.

Individuals with Disabilities Education Improvement Act (IDEA), 20 U.S.C. § 1400 (2004).

Lewis, S., & Tolla, J. (2003). Creating and using tactile experience books for young children with visual impairments. *Teaching Exceptional Children, 35*(3), 22–28.

Miles, B. (2003, October). *Talking the language of the hands to the hands.* Monmouth, OR: DB-LINK and The National Information Clearinghouse for Children Who Are Deaf-Blind.

National Center on Deaf-Blindness. (n.d.). Learning and instruction: Calendar systems. Retrieved from https://nationaldb.org/library/list/50

National Joint Committee for the Communication Needs of Persons with Severe Disabilities. (1992). Guidelines for meeting the communication needs of persons with severe disabilities. *ASHA, 34*(Suppl. 7), 1–8.

Romski, M., & Sevcik, R. A. (2005). Augmentative communication and early intervention: Myths and realities. *Infants & Young Children, 18*(3), 174–185. Retrieved from http://depts.washington.edu/isei/iyc/romski_18_3.pdf

Rowland, C. (2004). *Communication matrix.* Portland: Oregon Health and Science University.

Rowland, C. (Ed.). (2009). *Assessing communication and learning in young children who are deafblind or who have multiple disabilities.* Portland: Oregon Health and Science University, Design to Learn. Retrieved from https://

www.designtolearn.com/uploaded/pdf /DeafBlindAssessmentGuide.pdf

Rowland, C., & Schweigert, P. (2000). *Tangible symbol systems: Making the right to communicate a reality for individuals with severe disabilities* (2nd. ed.). Portland: Oregon Health and Science University, Design to Learn.

Rowland, C., & Schweigert, P. (2004). *First things first: Early communication for the pre-symbolic child with severe disabilities.* Portland: Oregon Health and Science University.

Rowland, C., Schweigert, P. D., & Prickett, J. G. (1995). Communication systems, devices, and modes. In K. M. Huebner, J. G. Prickett, T. R. Welch, & E. Joffee (Eds.), *Hand in hand: Essentials of communication and orientation and mobility for your students who are deaf-blind: Volume 1* (pp. 219–260). New York: AFB Press.

Rowland, C., & Stremel-Campbell, K. (1987). Share and share alike: Conventional gestures to emergent language for learners with sensory impairments. In L. Goetz, D. Guess, & K. Stremel-Campbell (Eds.), *Innovative program design for individuals with dual sensory impairments* (pp. 49–75). Baltimore: Paul H. Brookes Publishing Co.

Siegel-Causey, E., & Downing, J. (1987). Nonsymbolic communication development: Theoretical concepts and educational strategies. In L. Goetz, D. Guess, & K. Stremel-Campbell (Eds.), *Innovative program design for individuals with dual sensory impairments* (pp. 15–48). Baltimore: Paul H. Brookes Publishing Co.

RESOURCES

For additional resources, see the General Resources section at the back of this book.

Organizations

National Center on Deaf-Blindness (NCDB)
345 N. Monmouth Avenue
Monmouth, OR 97361
(503) 838-8754
Fax: (503) 838-8150
info@nationaldb.org
https://nationaldb.org/

A national technical assistance center funded by the Department of Education that works to improve the quality of life for children who are deafblind and their families. Runs the Deaf-Blind Project, a federally funded program that provides free technical assistance services to children who are deafblind, their families, and service providers in their state.

National Joint Committee for the Communication Needs of Persons with Severe Disabilities (NJC)
www.asha.org/NJC/

An interdisciplinary committee consisting of members from numerous associations whose purpose is to advocate for individuals with significant communication support needs resulting from intellectual disability that may coexist with autism, sensory, and/or motor limitations.

Chapter 8

Functional Literacy

Charlotte Cushman

Key Points

- 🔑 The definition of literacy
- 🔑 The continuum of literacy experiences, from concrete to abstract
- 🔑 Strategies to encourage the development of literacy skills in children with visual impairments and additional disabilities
- 🔑 Ways in which books and literacy materials can be adapted for learners with visual impairments and additional disabilities
- 🔑 Opportunities to reinforce functional literacy skills in the natural routine

Juanita is a 5-year-old girl who is totally blind and nonverbal. Her teacher has been looking for ways to include her in activities in the classroom with other students in her kindergarten classroom. Juanita uses objects and tactile symbols to communicate and her educational team has been working together to incorporate literacy goals into her daily routine. Her teacher has created a number of story boxes for the books that are being read aloud in class. Juanita is using tactile symbols to write about her daily experiences.

Omar is 10-year-old boy with cortical visual impairment and severe cerebral palsy. He enjoys looking at lights and prefers materials that are red. He has limited use of his hands, but is learning to operate a switch that is mounted on the headrest of his wheelchair. He is able to identify common objects in his daily routine, such as a red cup, a red toothbrush, and a red baseball cap. His teacher has been creating books for him with photographs of these objects on a black background, paired with the real objects. He has made progress in his ability to identify two-dimensional representations of three-dimensional objects.

Brittany is a 15-year-old girl with low vision and a severe hearing loss. She has bilateral hearing aids and corrective lenses, although she does not wear them consistently. She

is able to identify familiar words in 18-point font and is highly motivated to read words that are meaningful to her. She enjoys cooking and has been working on reading and writing shopping lists, identifying ingredients in the store and kitchen, and following a simple recipe in large print. She would like to sell the items she bakes and is hoping to be able to earn money by doing so.

The standard definition of literacy refers to the ability to read and write. In recent years, the definition has expanded to include speaking and listening, which reflects society's growing adoption of technology and alternate forms of media, as well as a more inclusive view of literacy. In addition, tactile symbols, pictures, objects, and other systems are now increasingly recognized as forms of literacy. If we think of *literacy* as the ability to communicate and derive meaning from a set of socially recognized symbols, then listening and speaking, as well as the use of objects, pictures, and other symbols, are part of the array. As such, literacy takes many different forms, including braille, print, pictures, objects, speech, sign language, and other symbol systems.

Juanita, Omar, and Brittany are at different stages in the development of literacy skills. Their ages and interests, in alignment with the general education curriculum, determine the focus of their educational programs. For each of them, a key to their success has been identifying activities that are both meaningful and functional, and working with the entire educational team, including their families, to ensure consistency and repeated practice across all settings.

Functional literacy refers to the ability to use literacy skills and tools in the natural context of daily life. This includes being able to read or understand what is being communicated by items in the environment, such as signs, menus, and product information one encounters in daily life, as well as to create notes to oneself and to others. For people with some amount of vision, this may mean being able to recognize packaging of specific items in a grocery store or identifying emergency signs, such as "Exit." For students who are blind, however, functional literacy is more complicated, as recognizing common "sight" words in context is based on much more than the ability to read text. For example, everyone is familiar with the red octagonal stop sign. Even if no words were written on it, people would still be able to recognize it in the context in which it appears. For individuals without vision, however, this type of functional literacy is developed through other tactile cues or symbols, as well as through repeated exposure to objects and information in the natural environment.

For students with significant multiple disabilities, functional literacy can be defined as the ability to communicate and derive meaning from a set of symbols. Literacy includes the skills of reading, writing, listening, and speaking, as well as the ability to use literacy tools of braille, print, auditory materials, pictures, tactile symbols, and objects in any combination to express thoughts. Students with visual impairments and multiple disabilities should not be limited in achieving their potential as literate beings. Functional literacy for these students can include a wide range of skills and tools. For some, it may mean mastering a communication system, while for others it may mean the ability to create a shopping list using a combination of print, braille, photos, and tactile symbols. Others may be able to enjoy reading books as a leisure activity. Educational teams need to keep an open mind when approaching literacy for students with visual impairments and multiple disabilities and to consider all options for each individual student.

Literacy is much more than learning to read braille or print; literacy begins with an understanding of one's environment, including people, activities, and routines. All students must be exposed to meaningful experiences. Communication about these experiences may be through speech, sign language, objects, or some combination, as well as through written forms. Literacy includes expressing thought in spoken, signed, or written words or symbols, as well as receiving messages in spoken, signed, or written words or symbols. Meaningful experiences help enrich students' vocabularies and their conceptual frameworks for understanding the world. For a student with a visual impairment and multiple disabilities, direct hands-on experience really is the best teacher, and helping the student to interpret activities and discuss them is an essential part of a strong foundation in the development of literacy skills.

In this chapter we include mathematical literacy and the recognition of numerals and their values as part of basic literacy. Understanding that numbers have meaning and using them in a functional context to count and compare is one of the goals of functional literacy.

FUNCTIONS OF LITERACY IN OUR CULTURE

As a culture, we have broadened our use of the term "literacy" to convey competence. We use "computer literacy" to refer to a basic knowledge and skill level with computers—how to turn them on, use the keyboard, create a document, or access the Internet. Computer literacy does not mean that we know how to program a computer or assemble the hardware, but rather that we have a basic familiarity with how to use computers. Thus, literacy in the broadest sense conveys a level of competence in expressing and receiving messages and information in a symbolic form.

All students, regardless of any disabilities they may have, should be exposed to literacy activities and be encouraged to achieve the highest level of literacy possible. It should never be assumed that a student is a "nonreader" or that a student with an intellectual disability should not be exposed to print or braille. Careful assessment and adaptations are essential in making literacy accessible to each individual student. Literacy is not a privilege, but rather it is a right for all!

Literacy Is a Framework for Understanding Experiences

Using a variety of formats, such as speech, objects, pictures, symbols, signs, print, and braille, we can help students to know what will happen next, as well as review an experience after it is finished. Showing a student a pumpkin before the class goes on a field trip to pick pumpkins can make the experience more meaningful. Similarly, creating a tactile experience book (introduced in Chapter 7) using tangible objects or parts of objects to recount something that happened can help to reinforce and enrich an experience.

Literacy Builds Self-Esteem and Promotes Independence

Having a sense of belonging and competence helps people feel better themselves and participating in an activity with others can help students build self-esteem. Reading books together, writing a group story or shopping list, or discussing shared experiences are all ways in which students with visual impairments and multiple disabilities can develop literacy skills. Being able to follow a recipe, write a grocery list, or read messages from friends and family are some of the ways in which literacy can help to promote independence. In addition, recognizing packaging in a store or a tactile sign outside of a public restroom will allow an individual to function more independently in the community.

Literacy Allows Connection

When students are able to discuss events in their lives both before and after they take place, they can make sense of them and share them with others. Literacy also gives students a way to refer to events in the past and future, refer to someone who is not present, and communicate about other concepts.

Literacy Is a Source of Pleasure

Literacy can also be a source of pleasure and a means of lifelong learning that all students can enjoy outside of the school environment throughout the course of their lives.

Barriers to Literacy Instruction

Despite the substantial functions literacy serves in our culture, there are a number of barriers to literacy instruction for students with significant disabilities (Downing, 2005), including:

- negative attitudes toward people with disabilities
- low expectations
- limited opportunities
- limited means of accessing literacy
- limited time
- the age factor (students with significant disabilities typically function at a developmental level below their chronological age and may be viewed as too old to begin literacy instruction in their teen years, or they may not have access to age-appropriate materials that are geared to their reading level)

It is the task of educators and advocates to help expand and elevate the attitudes and expectations of these students held by other teachers and the families, and to provide increased opportunities and access to literacy materials so that all students, regardless of age or ability, will have a chance to develop some level of functional literacy skills.

LITERACY AND COMMUNICATION

Literacy Begins at Birth

There is clearly a great deal of overlap between literacy and communication at the earliest stages of development. For students with visual impairments and multiple disabilities, there is very little distinction between literacy and communication, and, for practical purposes, they are the same thing in the beginning. Literacy starts with developing an understanding of the world (including routine events and experiences), communicating wants and needs, and learning to both interpret and send messages. As a student develops, these concepts and the ability to communicate about them become more abstract and symbolic.

Just as communication moves from simple to complex, so too does literacy. As we have seen, a broad definition of literacy includes speaking and listening, signing, and using picture or object symbols. At the most basic level, speaking, signing, or using a symbol system are ways for a student to express his or her immediate wants and needs. These techniques can be a means for a student to convey a message or tell a story. Receptively, messages or information can be taken in by a student in similar ways, including through listening, interpreting sign language, or by recognizing symbols that are presented. These are all examples of forms of communication that are also early literacy tools or methods.

Literacy builds on concepts that a child begins to develop from the very beginning of life, and stretches far beyond an introduction to the alphabet and letter-sound associations. Engaging children in meaningful hands-on experiences is a crucial step in helping them to begin the journey to literacy. This means that children should participate actively in daily events, with objects and actions clearly labeled verbally, through signing, and by touching objects associated with the activity. For example, when changing a child's diaper, it is important to verbally tell the child what is going to happen ("Time to change your diaper."). It is also important to show him or her a clean diaper and let the child touch it and explore it, perhaps experimenting with the ways that the sticky tabs open and close. Then, during the changing routine, the child can hold a clean diaper while the adult refers back to it, saying, "That's your diaper." In this way the child develops vocabulary, as well as an understanding of the sequence of a routine event. For children who are blind or visually impaired with additional disabilities, this is a crucial step in developing the basic concepts that are the foundation for future learning.

Routines are a way of structuring activities in a clear, predictable manner, so that students can begin to anticipate the sequence of events involved in a given task or activity. Gathering items for a meal, bath, or changing routine can help a child to begin to associate certain objects with events (for example, the towel means bath time, the cup and bowl mean mealtime, and the diaper means changing time). As a child repeats the sequence of steps in a routine, he or she will begin to understand what comes next. For example, saying, "After we get your cup out of the cabinet, we will go to the refrigerator and get some juice" as these actions are performed helps the child learn the sequence and eventually develop a sense of anticipation for what comes next in the routine. Creating routines with very young children can help to foster anticipation as well as sequencing and participating in routines.

While routines may not be connected to literacy in obvious ways, for students who are visually impaired with multiple disabilities, routines are at the heart of developing basic language and concepts, such as object identification and an understanding of the functional use of objects. As a child begins to associate these objects with routines, the objects themselves can begin to signal that an activity is about to take place. From there, a simple object calendar or schedule can be developed and the objects themselves can be used to tell a story.

Object Communication

Object communication occurs when actual objects are used to refer to the activity in which those objects are used. For example, a cup or spoon can be used to refer to mealtime, and when attention is called to a cup or spoon during mealtime, a child will begin to associate the object itself (the cup or spoon) with the event (mealtime). Once these associations are made, the child can then use the objects to indicate a request or the desire for an activity. For example, a student may pick up a cup in the classroom and hand it to the teacher, thereby communicating his or her desire for something to drink. In order for this type of communication to occur, the following conditions must be present:

- The child must touch the objects regularly during an activity. If an adult brings a cup to the lips of a child who is totally blind, for example, and the child never touches the cup while drinking, then the cup will have no meaning for the child.
- The child must have access to the objects outside of the activity. This means that the child needs to know where the objects are stored, and needs to be able to travel independently to them. For children who are blind and who have difficulty with independent mobility, the objects should be stored in a predictable location near where the child sits.
- An adult needs to respond to the child's attempts to communicate. This means that when the child presents the cup, the adult should say something like: "That's the cup. Would you like something to drink?"

Once the child recognizes the objects that are used within daily routines and associates them with the events, these objects can be arranged in sequential order to indicate events that will happen during the day. This arrangement of objects is called an *object calendar* or a *calendar box* (see Figure 8.1). As the student masters an understanding of the objects and the ways in which they can be used to refer to events in the past and in the future, then parts of objects (instead of entire objects) can be used in the calendar system. As discussed in Chapter 7, miniature objects should typically be avoided as symbols, since students with visual impairments and additional disabilities may not be able to understand the relationship between the miniature and its referent. A miniature toy school bus may have no meaning to someone who has never seen a bus, and a better choice may be the full-sized buckle of a seatbelt. Object symbols communicate most clearly when they are selected based on the meaning they have from the student's point of view.

The next step in using objects to develop literacy skills is to gather them into a box or bag to facilitate having conversations about

Figure 8.1

This object calendar pairs a real object with a photo of the object and the printed name of the activity.

events. Objects can also be attached to pieces of heavy cardboard or pegboard to make a book. If children have usable vision, photographs can be paired with the objects, eventually replacing the objects as the child learns to identify them. For students who are blind, partial objects or object symbols can be used.

CREATING A LITERACY-RICH ENVIRONMENT

As noted throughout this book, students with visual impairments lack the same access to incidental learning that their sighted peers have. Students with sight are able to observe objects and events in the course of their daily lives, which helps them to develop concepts and an understanding of the world within a natural context. Students with visual impairments often must be directly taught these same concepts, and adults will need to find ways to make language and experience meaningful. Creating a literacy-rich environment can help to increase a student's access to information within a natural context.

The following are some suggestions for creating a literacy-rich environment for a student at school and at home:

- Describe literacy in the daily routine: explain how print, braille, objects, and photos are used throughout the daily routine.
- Identify literacy opportunities in the environment: discuss where print, braille, objects, and photos are found in the environment.
- Ensure access to literacy: label items in a format that is accessible to the child.

- Make literacy materials available: provide access to books and other literacy materials in appropriate formats.
- Read with the student: set aside time to read with the student each day.

Describe Literacy in the Daily Routine

It is essential for adults to let students know about the ways that print, braille, objects, photos, and symbols are used throughout the day. Sighted students can observe people reading the newspaper, surfing the Internet, exchanging e-mail messages, reading labels on boxes or cans of food, and reading signs in stores and on the street. Students with visual impairments are not able to see models of people using reading and writing within the daily routine and thus may not be aware that the world is full of these symbols. Teachers and other adults in these students' lives must give them access to the wealth of literacy in the environment by describing and explaining how print, braille, photos, and objects are used each day. For example, a father might say, "We just finished all the milk. I'm going to write 'milk' on our shopping list so that we'll remember to buy some more when we go to the store this afternoon." Or a mother might say, "Next week is grandma's birthday. Let's make a card for her to wish her a happy day. That way she'll know that we're thinking of her." Children who are blind or visually impaired must be made aware of some of the ways in which literacy is woven into daily life.

It is possible to create similar types of lists or systems for children with visual impairments and multiple disabilities. For example, a student can make a shopping list by putting labels or pictures (cut from packaging or boxes) on a card. A parent can rinse out the empty milk carton and place it in a bag as part of a three-dimensional shopping list while explaining to the child what is happening: "The milk carton is empty. Let's rinse it out and put it in this bag so that we'll remember to buy more when we go to the store." Then, when it is time to go shopping, the contents of the bag can be examined and reviewed as a reminder of what needs to be purchased.

For children who are able to recognize pictures, an adult can call attention to something by "reading" the image. For example, a teacher might say, "I need to find another box of markers in the cabinet. Here's the box with the picture of the markers on it."

Identify Literacy Opportunities in the Environment

Pointing out meaningful images, symbols, and objects in the classroom, home, or community can help children to recognize the information that is available all around them in the natural environment. Adults should discuss throughout the day examples of where print, braille, photos, objects, and symbols are found in functional ways in the environment. For example, "Look what it says here on the door. It says 'Women' in braille and print. We can go in here because we're both women." Or, "Can you push the button on the elevator? See if you can find the one that says '3' since we're going to the third floor."

Photos or objects can be discussed in a similar way. For example, while looking at a menu in a restaurant an adult might say, "I see a picture of a salad on the menu. I think

I'll order the salad." Or while walking down the hallway with a student, a teacher might say, "Here is the water fountain. Would you like a drink of water?" In this way students can begin to look for clues that provide information about important features in the environment.

Ensure Access to Literacy

Teachers will want to label items in the environment using whatever format the student prefers, including a combination of print, braille, and symbols. For example, a student's desk, cubby, chair, and materials should be labeled with print, braille, and a consistent symbol that is unique to that student that the student can learn to recognize as his or her own. For children with cortical visual impairment (CVI), a shiny red ribbon or reflective material may be an appropriate way to label a cubby or desk if that child responds to shiny material and demonstrates a preference for the color red, as many children with CVI do (see Figure 8.2). The child's name can also be included in large print and braille, with a tactile symbol embedded in the card.

In the classroom, plastic bins and similar organizational systems can be labeled with print, braille, and an object so that students can more easily identify what is inside each bin. Similarly, a tactile symbol can be glued to the outside of a box or container, such as a cracker on the outside of a box of crackers. The symbol can then be read by a student with a visual impairment and multiple disabilities, much as a photo on a box can tell people who are sighted what is inside. Tactile symbols can perform multiple literacy func-

Figure 8.2

A child's cubby is marked with a bright red ribbon, as well as his name in print and braille and his tactile symbol.

tions: they can help the student to locate an item and identify its contents; they can be used by the student when creating or reading a shopping list; and they can be used by the student to make requests.

Accessible literacy materials can be incorporated into a student's routine in the classroom, through activities such as using a calendar system, taking attendance, cooking with recipes, and performing specific jobs.

Make Literacy Materials Available

Books and literacy materials should be available to the student at home and in school in a variety of accessible formats (braille, large print, tactile symbols, and pictures) based on the student's literacy preferences and abilities. Teachers can ensure that literacy materials are available throughout the classroom in a variety of ways, including the following:

- Adapt regular books by adding tactile illustrations, braille, or other modifications.
- Create tactile and object books with the student and encourage the student to look at them, share them with other students, and take them home (see Figure 8.3).
- Make audio recordings of books the child has made and make those recordings, as

well as recordings of commercial audio books, available to the student.

- Store the recordings where the student can find them and explore them during both leisure time and structured class periods.
- Make writing materials, including braillewriters and tactile materials (such as clay, Wikki Stix, fabric, and craft supplies) available for the student to explore and experiment with.

Read with the Student

Teachers will want to involve all students in literacy activities, regardless of whether or not a given student is identified as a "reader." Whenever possible, teachers should make a point of setting aside special time each day to read with a student with visual impairments and multiple disabilities. Books or other reading materials should be at a level that is meaningful to the student and in a format that is accessible to the student.

Figure 8.3

Teresa Paglucia

This book has been adapted for a child with CVI by placing a photo of a red bird on a plain black background and adding some feathers. The three-dimensional red bird toy placed in front of the book facilitates the transition from three dimensions to two dimensions.

PLANNING LITERACY ACTIVITIES

Comprehensive Assessment

As with any instructional program, a student's educational team must begin with comprehensive assessment of the student (see Chapter 3), including a functional vision assessment (FVA), a learning media assessment (LMA), and a full evaluation of speech and language, cognition, motor skills, and literacy skills. As described in Chapter 3, these assessments are best performed by members of the team who are skilled and specifically trained in each area, working together as needed. For example, a speech-language pathologist may be an expert on communication, but may not have had experience working with a student with a visual impairment and multiple disabilities. Teachers of students with visual impairments have special training and experience in recognizing the effects of visual impairment on a student's overall performance, as well as in making specific recommendations for individual students. As such, it is important to involve teachers of students with visual impairments in the assessment process to ensure that assessment tools are accessible to the student and that functional vision and the preferred learning medium are taken into careful consideration when planning a literacy program.

Chapter 3 discusses the FVA and LMA in detail, but it is important to mention them briefly here, as they are an essential consideration in literacy instruction for students with visual impairments and multiple disabilities. The FVA assesses what a student can see and how he or she uses near, intermediate, and distance vision in a variety of settings to perform routine tasks. The FVA measures visual acuity and visual fields using the best correction. Recommendations are also included in the FVA, and these typically include environmental modifications (such as lighting, glare, and positioning), as well as adaptations (such as the use of dark markers, green-lined paper, and the like). Magnification and optical aids are often discussed as well.

The LMA offers a framework for the selection of appropriate literacy media (including braille, print, auditory strategies, objects, and pictures) for students with visual impairments. The LMA also assesses a student's learning style, and his or her preferred means of gathering information—through vision, hearing, touch, and other senses, either singularly or in combination.

Both these assessments involve a team process, with active involvement of the student's family. Since vision may change over time, these assessments may be done periodically, depending on the student's specific type of vision condition. The teachers who are responsible for planning literacy instruction for a student should be sure that the student has had both of these assessments and that all members of the team are familiar with the results and understand the implications for the classroom.

Assessment of Literacy Skills

For students with visual impairments and multiple disabilities, assessment is an ongoing process that teachers need to integrate into the students' daily activities. The ability to use skills in the natural environment and in the context of the daily routine is a critical feature of functional literacy. For example, a student may tell about an experience that happened over the weekend and create a story about it. Another child may draw a picture of what he or she did at recess that morning, or use object symbols to make a choice about foods at snack time. These are all examples of literacy activities that can be evaluated as part of the assessment process.

Literacy encompasses a range of skills, including:

- entry-level skills, such as basic concepts, language, and communication development

- motor skills, including fine motor coordination and tactile exploration
- listening skills, including auditory processing and listening comprehension
- speaking skills, including oral language, vocabulary, and verbal expression
- reading skills, including decoding and reading comprehension
- writing skills, including the expression of ideas, as well as the motor skills of using writing tools, such as a braillewriter, slate and stylus, computer, or pencil

Ideally, the appropriate member or members of a student's educational team assesses each of these areas. For example, a speech-language pathologist would be involved in the assessment of language and communication development, as well as speaking skills. An occupational therapist would be involved in the assessment of fine motor skills and tactile development. Assessment may include informal tools, such as checklists, informal reading inventories, and observation. (For more detailed information on assessment, see Chapter 3.)

Determining Goals and Objectives

Once the assessments have been completed, the team should meet to discuss appropriate goals and objectives for the individual student. Goals and objectives must be aligned with the general education curriculum, and will be determined by the student's age and ability level. Literacy goals can and should be included across the curriculum (see Chapter 5 for additional information on curriculum considerations).

STRATEGIES FOR TEACHING LITERACY SKILLS

As noted earlier in this chapter, literacy encompasses a broad range of skill levels and formats. As in all areas of education for students with visual impairments and multiple disabilities, it is important that literacy instruction be individualized according to each student's needs and interests.

Basic Concepts and the Foundations of Literacy

The development of basic cognitive concepts is essential to the foundation of literacy skills. An understanding of matching, sorting, directionality (left to right, top to bottom), positional concepts, quantities (such as more or less), and comparisons (such as same and different) all help to provide a base for literacy. Being able to recognize if an object, letter, or braille cell is the same as or different from another is necessary for beginning readers. Similarly, being able to identify the left and right sides or top and bottom of a page are critical skills for anyone who is learning to read. In addition to these basic concepts, students also need to understand that words have meaning. The development of communication skills is also crucial to expanding literacy skills.

Continuum of Literacy Experiences

Developing meaningful routines and using objects in the functional context of the natural environment are important steps in helping students with visual impairments and multiple disabilities to move forward on the path to literacy. Literacy skills for students with visual impairments and multiple disabilities progress along a continuum of literacy experiences from concrete to abstract, as follows:

1. routines in the natural environment
2. real objects in a calendar box or choice board
3. object book with whole real objects
4. experience book with whole objects or partial objects
5. tactile book with partial objects, textures, or raised lines
6. books in braille or large print

A student begins with a meaningful experience in the real environment. For example, the student makes a fruit salad by putting on an apron and participating in a cooking activity in which the fruit is peeled, cut, and mixed together. Progressing from this first experience, the teacher can move through the continuum this way: an apron can be placed in the student's calendar box to represent cooking class; an object book about cooking class can be created that has plastic bags with small bits of what was prepared in cooking class, such as a piece of dried apple or cinnamon that was mixed into the fruit salad; an experience book can be made with bits of orange peel glued to a page and a description of the activity ("I made fruit salad in cooking class today. I peeled an orange and put it in the bowl."); a tactile book can be made with the outline of a bowl or piece of fruit; and finally, the book can be created in braille or large print.

Instructional Strategies for Beginning Readers

Numerous literacy tools and books that use objects and tactile symbols can be created for early readers as they progress along the continuum of literary experiences, as just described. These include:

- calendar boxes and schedule systems
- choice boards
- conversation or discussion boxes
- story boxes, story bags, or storyboards
- object books
- language experience stories
- tactile books
- PowerPoint books (can be switch-activated)
- journals (tactile journals, daily journals)

Calendar Boxes and Schedule Systems

As mentioned earlier, students begin their literacy journey by developing an understanding of real objects in the natural environment. Once a student has developed that understanding, a teacher can use real objects as symbols of specific activities, in the form of a calendar box, to let the student know the order of activities in his or her day. To use a calendar box, the teacher selects meaningful, associated objects to represent each activity and arranges the objects in a left-to-right sequence (see Figure 8.4). The student goes to the calendar, takes out the first (leftmost) object, carries it to the associated activity, refers to the object during the activity, then places the object in a special "finished" box after the activity has been completed. As the

Figure 8.4

Adam Pulzetti

A calendar box for a beginning reader. A series of boxes are arranged in a left-to-right sequence with an object in each box representing an activity.

student begins to associate the objects with certain activities, he or she may begin to use these same objects to refer to the activities, either to request them or to discuss them afterwards.

As students become familiar with this basic set up, the teacher may begin to use slightly more abstract systems—in which partial objects or tactile symbols replace the full objects—still arranged from left to right. This is helpful to build literacy skills, as it teaches left to right and is a step toward abstract representation. Objects can also be arranged on a board or tray as a transition from separate boxes to a more abstract arrangement (see Figure 8.5).

Students with low vision may begin to use picture symbols once they have a basic grasp of the activities and understand the meaning of the symbols. It is essential to evaluate a student's ability to interpret the images in picture symbols, as well as his or her ability to see them. Many students with CVI, for example, have difficulty with visual complexity, and many picture symbols are very complex. In addition, many picture symbols are very

Figure 8.5

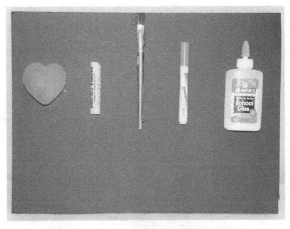

Adam Pulzetti

Objects are arranged on a board to indicate the progression of steps in a crafts activity.

abstract, especially when they depict something other than a noun. Picture symbols for words such as "wait," "want," and "more," may be very challenging for a student with significant visual and cognitive impairments to interpret. It is also important to note that the ability to "see" something that is three-dimensional is not the same as the ability to interpret something that is two-dimensional, even if it is presented at the same distance and is the same size. While picture symbols may be useful for students with some types of multiple disabilities, such as autism spectrum disorder and visual impairment, the educational team should proceed cautiously and determine whether or not potential symbols are accessible and meaningful to the individual student.

Symbols can be arranged in a left-to-right, top-to-bottom sequence, just as print and braille symbols are arranged. With this arrangement, the student begins to read the symbols at the top left, moving across to the right, and then to the next line below. Initially, picture symbols are paired with print. For example, a photo of the cafeteria or a picture symbol of a bowl are accompanied by the word "lunch." After students have developed a clear understanding of the symbols, the print and symbols can be separated and students can begin to match the sight words on their schedules. Students can be given word cards of the items in their daily schedule and asked to match them to the schedule itself, such as "gym," "lunch," and "recess." As students become more proficient, the system can be made more abstract, and it can also be used as a writing activity, in which the students place the words and symbols in the correct sequence (see Figure 8.6).

The schedule can also be used to help teach concepts about time, becoming increasingly complex and abstract as the student demonstrates progress in understanding.

Figure 8.6

A student places word cards with picture symbols on his schedule.

Initially, the time for each activity can be presented to a student as part of his or her schedule, such as: 8:30: Homeroom; 9:15: Cooking; and so on. Later, the student can write in what activity takes place at a particular time (see Figure 8.7). The first option is a reading activity and the second is a writing activity. Both combine an understanding of time concepts, numeracy, and literacy. A similar type of activity can also be done in which the time is written or a clock is shown, and the student can indicate what happens at that time.

Figure 8.7

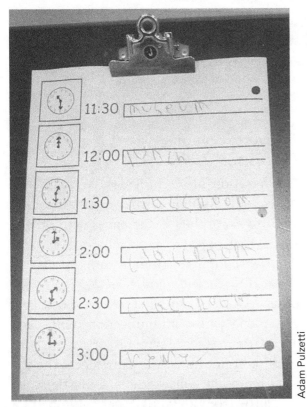

A student with low vision has written each activity of his day next to a picture of a clock showing the time at which it is scheduled to take place.

Choice Boards

A choice board is another early literacy tool that can be used in the classroom. Choice boards use object symbols paired with print and braille to offer a student a selection of items. The boards can be set up to present a student with two or more activities or other items (such as food, musical instruments, or stories, as shown in Figure 8.8). As with the calendar boxes, choice boards begin with real objects and progress through more abstract representations thusly: partial objects to tactile symbols to picture symbols, to just print and braille. Partial objects should also be used in cases where it is not possible to use a whole object. For example, a piece of rope or of chain might be used to represent a swing.

A beginning choice board might include a wrapped granola bar on the left and a bag of crackers on the right. The student can then examine both choices before making a selection. For students without vision, it is important to be sure that they understand what each choice is, as a bag of popcorn can feel a lot like a bag of crackers. A piece of popcorn can be glued to the outside of the bag, so that the student can feel it but still recognize that it is a symbol (and not something to be placed immediately in the mouth).

The teacher will want to make sure that a choice board is placed in a location that is accessible both visually and physically to the student. If a student has limited range of motion or the use of only one hand, then the choice board should be placed where he or she can reach all options the board presents. Similarly, if a student has a limited visual field, it might be preferable to place choices

Adam Pulzetti

Figure 8.8

This choice board can be used during a music activity to choose between listening to a CD or playing a xylophone with a wooden mallet.

above and below each other rather than next to each other.

Choice boards can be made for specific songs or stories, and these boards can be used as part of circle time or another group activity. Separate boards can be made for different circle time songs, using photos, tactile symbols, print, and braille (see Figure 8.9). Objects can also be used to represent a specific story, such as a real or toy turtle being shown to students when reading a story about a turtle. In this case, a child who is not able to read print would be able to select this story by choosing the turtle symbol and giving it to the teacher. Print and braille can be used in addition to the real object to help the student make the step to the next level of literacy.

Conversation or Discussion Boxes

Conversation boxes provide a way for students with limited formal communication skills to share their experiences with others. Using real objects or object symbols, students with limited communication skills can share these objects and refer to them with others. Objects can be stored in a box or a bag, along with communication tools, such as pictures or tactile symbols, or sentences in print or braille about the experiences the objects represent. For example, a plastic straw and a toy from a Happy Meal could be in a box, along with a strip of paper that says, "I went to McDonald's yesterday with my brother. I ate Chicken McNuggets and drank

Figure 8.9

Charlotte Cushman

This choice board uses tactile symbols to present different song options for circle time.

milk with a straw. I got a toy with my meal." The learning objective is to increase communication skills and social interaction, while also building literacy skills. These objects and phrases can later be used in an experience book.

Discussion boxes and theme boxes are similar arrangements, and may be used for a routine activity. For example, a discussion box about bath time may include a towel, shampoo, bath toys, and a bar of soap. These items can be stored in a box or bucket

and reviewed with the child before the activity takes place. This helps prepare the child for the activity, as well as builds vocabulary and develops an understanding of routine events.

Story Boxes, Story Bags, and Storyboards

Story boxes, story bags, and storyboards are wonderful ways to engage students with visual impairments and multiple disabilities in early literacy activities. Each story box or bag contains a collection of real objects that correspond to the items or events in a story. For students who cannot see the illustrations in a story or who may not understand the meaning, story boxes can help them to be active participants in early literacy experiences.

Teachers can begin with very simple stories that describe events from the student's own experience, such as bedtime, bath time, or mealtime. *Little Rabbit's Bedtime* by Alan Baker is a great example of a simple story that can be used for this strategy. Teachers can gather the objects mentioned in the story (a sponge, rubber ducky, fluffy towel, and toothbrush and toothpaste; see Figure 8.10). The objects are then used like illustrations to tell the story and to help a student with a visual impairment and multiple disabilities more fully understand the meaning of the story. Tactile markers (such as a small piece of terry cloth for the towel) can be added to each page of the book, and braille text can also be added, using adhesive pages. Story boxes can be made around a theme, such as Halloween or other holidays, birthdays, gardening, school, and the like. Predictable stories that use fa-

Figure 8.10

Objects from a story box include a sponge, washcloth, and a rubber duck to illustrate a story about bath time.

miliar items often make the best choices for starting out.

At a slightly more abstract level, objects or partial objects can be embedded on cards—with large print and braille words—and placed in the sequence of the story. Similarly, storyboards use objects or picture symbols arranged on cardboard or an easel to supplement the narrative of a story. Students can be asked to arrange the items in sequence or to retell the story using the objects.

Object Books

Object books use real objects collected and arranged in book format, usually about a familiar activity, a routine, sensory experiences, or basic concepts (such as big and little). To make an object book, the teacher and student attach real objects to a piece of heavy cardboard, poster board, or pegboard using hot glue, Velcro, cable ties, or other method, then place the page in a binder. It is best to begin with one object affixed directly to the page, and then slowly add more objects to the page.

Pegboard is sturdy and allows for exploration of the items. Similar groups of objects can be attached to a single page. For example, socks can be attached with cable ties to one page and different types of brushes attached to another page.

Preferred objects or items that are interesting or tactilely distinct often make good beginning books. For example, a small bell can be attached to a foam page and the student can then explore the bell (see Figure 8.11).

Books at this stage should be made with sturdy materials, such as cardboard or notebook binders. As the student becomes famil-

Figure 8.11

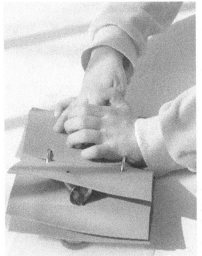

Adam Pulzetti

Real objects can be attached to sturdy pages for the child to explore.

iar with the books, small plastic bags or envelopes containing objects can be attached to the pages. For example, real objects can be collected from bath time, including small bottles of shampoo and bars of soap. The bars of soap can be taken out of the baggie to smell and explore.

A book can be made for lessons in different subjects, such as a science lesson about planting seeds, with a different page for each step of the process. A book about planting might include a plastic bag of soil to be put in a pot, a plastic bag of seeds, a small pot, and a watering can. In this way, an object book can be used to sequence steps in a science lesson.

After the books have been created, they should be made available to the student on a regular basis to share with classmates, read independently, or to take home and share with family and friends.

Experience Stories

Experience stories (sometimes also referred to as experience books) are another way to create meaningful stories with students with visual impairments and multiple disabilities who are beginning to explore books. With experience stories, students discuss events or activities after they have taken place, and their words are used to write a book about their experience, as described in Chapter 7. The experience may be a daily experience, similar to the routines described earlier, or it may be a special event, such as a trip to a restaurant, a birthday party, or a day at the beach.

For example, after a visit to the low vision specialist, an experience story could be created using a small penlight attached with Velcro onto a page, with the text in print and braille saying, "I went to the low vision office" (see Figure 8.12). Having a real object associated with an activity or event attached with Velcro allows the student to take the object off the page, explore it, and then put it back on the page. In this case the student could also turn the light on and off, which would help to make the story relate even more closely to the experience.

The following are some suggestions for creating experience stories:

- When choosing tactile items to attach to a page, be sure to think about each object from the student's perspective. For a student with a visual impairment and other disabilities, it is important to select real items or pieces of items that he or she has touched as part of the experience. In other words, a raised-line drawing to represent a tree is less meaningful than a piece of bark. Cotton balls do not represent clouds to a

Figure 8.12

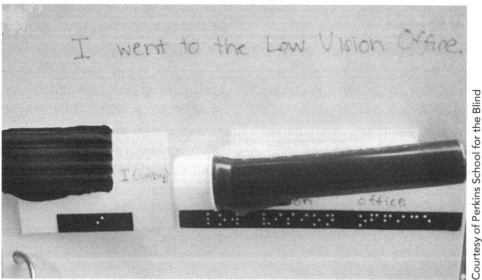

This experience story uses print and braille text, along with a small flashlight that is attached to the page with Velcro, to represent the student's experience.

child who is blind; leaves or a handful of grass may be a better way to represent being outside. Similarly, a matchbox car is visually similar to a real car, but will have little or no meaning to a student with a visual impairment. A better way to represent a car may be the buckle of a seat belt or part of a car seat.

- Include print and braille on every page, even if the child is totally blind. This is important for other people who are reading the book and will help to give the child continued exposure to these symbol systems.

- Have the student participate as much as possible in the creation of the story, including choosing the topic, telling the story, selecting the objects to be included, and attaching the items to the pages.

Tactile Books

Tactile books use textures, partial objects, and raised lines to tell, augment, or illustrate a story. The terms *tactile book* and *object book* are sometimes used interchangeably, but a distinction is being made here to emphasize the difference between books with actual objects, and books that have some textures or raised lines. Tactile books are further along the continuum toward abstract literary experiences than are object books.

Tactile books can be a great way to encourage students with visual impairments and multiple disabilities to explore different textures and to participate more actively in reading activities. While these books can be enjoyable, it is important to keep in mind that for students who have additional disabilities, abstract illustrations in tactile books may not be meaningful.

A student may enjoy feeling different textures, such as sandpaper, satin, and a cotton ball, but interpreting meaning is something else. For example, a piece of orange foam cut in the shape of a Jack-o'-Lantern may look like a pumpkin with a carved face and may have tactile properties that make it interesting to touch, but the orange foam may not signify a Jack-o'-Lantern or have meaning for an inexperienced reader. Therefore, it is crucial to think about a student's understanding of abstract representation and what will be meaningful to him or her.

A child who is able to identify real objects can then move on to partial objects and then to more abstract tactile representations. For example, a student may begin with a real spoon with a distinctive handle, then the spoon may be attached to a page, then just the handle (partial object) is glued or embedded on a page, and finally a raised-line drawing or outline of a spoon may be used in a tactile book. Color and images may also be used if the student has some vision, and print and braille should be added to each page. For a student with CVI, it may be helpful to use his or her preferred color to highlight key features, such as the handle or the outline of the spoon.

Tactile graphics and raised-line drawings are very difficult for beginning readers to interpret, so it is important to provide direct instruction to help the student to understand the intended meaning. Students will benefit from practice matching real objects to tactile representations and from exposure to different textures, noting which are the same.

Accessible PowerPoint Books

Accessible PowerPoint books use technology to make simple stories accessible to all readers. The teacher can upload digital photos and simple text to a PowerPoint presentation, and audio can be added as well. The student can advance pages using a switch. Books may be on any topic, from an "All About Me" book to favorite activities, special events, seasons, animals, or nearly any theme. For example, a PowerPoint book called "Let's Make Macaroni and Cheese" can include the experience of the cooking class and the recipe.

Daily Journals

Daily journals can be done on many different levels, depending on the abilities and interests of the individual student. Some students may be able to write in print or braille, or dictate daily entries. A student may include information such as his or her name, date, what he or she ate for breakfast, what he or she is wearing, his or her schedule for the day, a recounting of something he or she did at home the night before, and what he or she plans to do today. This activity can be as simple or complex as desired and appropriate. A beginning level daily journal could involve the student placing pre-made braille or print labels or tactile symbols in a notebook. For example, if it is known that the student goes bowling every Thursday evening, a picture of people bowling with a large-print label could be selected from an array of pictures to show what he or she did the night before. Other students may be able to write more independently. This is a great time for a student to practice writing his or her name and the date, and to work on vocabulary that occurs regularly.

Tactile journals can be used like experience stories, with students making tactile pictures of something they did that day or the previous day. Again, these can be very simple—for example, gluing some leaves on a piece of paper to signify going for a walk. As the student's abilities increase, the journal entries can become increasingly complex and abstract.

A student can also dictate a journal entry, describing an event aloud, such as getting a haircut or going to restaurant. The teacher, a paraeducator, or a classmate can then write down the text, in both print and braille, and the student can create a tactile illustration using something from the experience, such as a straw similar to one used at the restaurant.

Suggestions for Modifying Existing Books

As has been described, there are many different types of books that can be made for students with visual impairments to encourage active participation in literacy activities. In addition to teacher-made books, there are also ways to adapt existing books, by modifying either the content or the format. Modifying the content involves simplifying the storyline, while modifying the format refers to making the text accessible to a reader with a visual impairment.

Educators working with students with visual impairments and multiple disabilities often adapt materials from the general education curriculum for their students, and efforts should be made to ensure that adapted materials are as age-appropriate as possible.

This means that although a 17-year-old may be reading at a pre-kindergarten level, it would be best to for him or her to read books on topics similar to those being read by other students who are the same age. Thus, instead of reading books about Barney or Big Bird, a book could be made about a popular athlete or pop star, a current movie, or a fashion trend. Typical magazines and books would be above the student's reading level, but pictures could be cut out from a magazine story about the latest hit movie for teens, and the story could be retold with 8 or 10 key ideas written in simple sentences, using pictures or tactile symbols to supplement the text.

Another way to modify content is to change the characters and setting to the student's own experience. The student's name replaces the main character's name, and similar changes can be made for the name of the family members and other characters, the name of the town and school, pets, and so on. Fairy tales and folk tales can be tailored to a student's own background.

The format of a book can also be modified; that is, changes can be made in the book itself to make it accessible to students with visual impairments and those with motor difficulties. Format adaptations include:

- adding textures
- decreasing visual clutter
- increasing font size
- using page fluffers (small pieces of foam or cardboard affixed to the corners of pages that allow students with motor challenges to grasp and turn the pages)

For a student with CVI, for example, a typical picture book that is too visually cluttered for the student to access can be simplified by choosing the key element of the picture and blocking out or deleting the background. For instance, the book *Mouse Mess* by Linnia Riley is popular with many young readers, but is very busy visually. A teacher can reduce the visual clutter by selecting a key part of an illustration (such as Oreo cookies) and then creating a new page with that part of the illustration isolated on a contrasting background. This can be done using a color photocopier, by cutting a page out of the book, or by creating a new photo or image.

Incorporating Literacy Activities into the School Day

Literacy skills can be built into almost any activity throughout the school day. Students who are blind or visually impaired will benefit from repetition and practice across different subject areas and in different learning environments. For example, a student may be learning the word "gym" in braille, print, picture, tactile symbol, sign, or in some combination. The student can practice reading the word in his or her individual calendar or schedule first thing in the morning, then practice reading the word outside of the gymnasium itself, where the door of the area is marked with a print, braille, picture, object, or tactile symbol label. At the end of the day in a home-school notebook, the student can then tell about the day's activities, including the word "gym" in braille, print, or symbols. Reinforcing words and concepts across all subjects and areas will help a student to generalize skills. For example, if a student reads the word "girls" in the classroom and then finds the word "Girls" on the door to the girls' bathroom, the word will have more meaning for the student.

Literacy activities should be as meaningful as possible for all students. In addition to the ideas that were previously mentioned about creating books related to a student's own experience, literacy skills can be built right into activities like cooking, shopping, gardening, making products to sell, and recreational activities. Examples of ways to incorporate literacy into cooking activities include:

- read or write the recipe out (using pictures and tactile symbols, as necessary)
- write a list of ingredients needed to create a shopping list
- read the labels on the cabinets in the kitchen area
- read the label on a box or a can (or match the picture)
- read the ingredients on a label
- write the label for the food after it has been prepared
- write a journal entry about the cooking experience

Youths with visual impairments and multiple disabilities can learn to be more independent as their literacy skills increase, as in the following physical education activity designed for a group of teenagers with deaf-blindness (and residual vision) in the public school system:

The goal of the activity was to encourage the students to be more physically active through basic stretching and simple exercises, while also encouraging them to be as independent as possible. The staff started with a list of exercises for the class to do, but since the students were not able to read the instructions themselves, they were dependent on staff for direction. Staff decided to add line drawings to the list with spaces for the students to make a check mark after they had completed an activity. Each student was able to do the activity at his or her own level. One student practiced keeping track of his own time and later learned to take his heart rate.

Modifications continue to be added according to the needs of each individual student, so that the activity is adapted in an accessible format, including print and image size, while also incorporating reading and other goals.

This is an example of literacy being used across the curriculum in a way that can be adapted and used with students of all ages.

Auditory Strategies

An auditory strategy is any type of listening activity that helps a student to access information. Auditory skills are an important way for students with visual impairments and multiple disabilities to participate in literacy activities, and can be used in combination with print, braille, pictures, or other symbols. Students with visual impairments must be provided with adequate instructional support to interpret and develop literacy skills through auditory materials. It is important to remember that merely providing CDs or reading aloud written text does not ensure a meaningful literacy experience.

Listening skills include:

- listening comprehension (understanding what the student heard)
- sound localization (being able to tell where a sound is coming from)
- auditory discrimination (identifying what a sound is)

(For more information on listening skills, see Barclay, 2012.)

It is extremely important to have each student's hearing tested on a regular basis, as many students with visual impairments are at increased risk for hearing loss.

Strategies to help students develop listening skills include:

- reading aloud
- playing listening games, such as asking the student to point to a particular sound
- playing "I hear with my little ear" to practice identifying particular sounds
- asking students to repeat back what they have heard

Auditory materials are available through a number of sources, including CDs from the library, Bookshare, Learning Ally, and National Library Service for the Blind and Physically Handicapped (NLS). There are numerous sources for free audiobooks online, and sites such as Tar Heel Reader, a collection of free, easy-to-read, and accessible books on a wide range of topics that also allows users to create their own books, and offers a wide range of accessible books for students with special needs. (See the Resources section at the end of this chapter for more information.)

Writing

Writing includes the tools and mechanics of writing, as well as the writing process itself. It is important to teach writing alongside reading right from the very beginning. To establish familiarity and increase engagement, students need to have access to writing tools in appropriate formats from a young age, with braillewriters and tactile materials, along with markers, pencils, and paper all readily available. Commercially available materials are available for emergent writers who are blind, and many students enjoy using Wikki Stix or the Picture Maker: Wheatley Tactile Diagramming Kit from the American Printing House for the Blind (see Resources for more information). Students with visual impairments and multiple disabilities should be encouraged to scribble or use pretend writing at the initial stage, just as their sighted peers are. This means allowing them to play and explore on a braillewriter, just as sighted children scribble with crayons and pencils. In addition, multisensory writing programs, such as Handwriting Without Tears, may be useful for helping students with visual impairments to develop their handwriting skills. (See the Resources section for more information on these products.)

The writing process focuses more on the organization and expression of ideas rather than the mechanics. For students with visual impairments, the first step is to increase their awareness of writing as it occurs around them in the natural environment. It is crucial to let students know when writing is being used, such as when making a shopping list, noting a telephone number, typing an e-mail message, writing a handwritten note, placing an order, or filling out a form.

Many of the strategies discussed earlier in this chapter can be used to develop writing as well as reading skills. Objects and picture symbols can be used to tell stories or discuss events, to make requests, or to review activities. Students can create their own object books or experience stories, and take the lead on deciding about content.

Story boxes or story bags can also be used as beginning writing tools. With this approach, real items are placed in a bag and the student assists the teacher in taking out the objects and arranging them to tell a story. For example, a bag might contain a blanket, a pillow, pajamas, a toothbrush and toothpaste, and a storybook. The student can help the teacher to sequence the objects to tell a story about bedtime. "First we have to put on pajamas, then we brush our teeth, then we get into bed and pull up the blanket and listen to a bedtime story." The student may enjoy pretending to do each step of the sequence.

Students can dictate stories or fill in the blanks in *directed-writing activities*. For example, when writing about a trip to the grocery store, the student can first dictate the story to the teacher or describe the experience with support, as needed. The teacher then writes the story out and gives it back to the student with some blanks, such as "We went to the grocery store and bought some _____." The student then fills in the blanks. Words can be written out in print or braille to be placed in the blanks, or photos or tactile symbols can be used. Students who have difficulty with this activity might be given several choices of objects or pictures, such as a shoe, an apple, and a marker, and then asked to select which one they bought at the grocery store.

A home-school notebook is an excellent way to encourage carryover and to enable students to share their experiences more broadly with people in their lives. Students may use tactile symbols and a recording device to tell what they did during the day in school, and then play the recording back to their families when they get home. For example, a student may carve a pumpkin in school on a day in October. While this event can be written down in a notebook by the teacher and sent directly to the parent, another approach is to have the student be part of this process by creating a page with braille and print sentences saying, "Today I carved a pumpkin in school. I scooped out the seeds and we baked them in the oven. We made a Jack-o'-Lantern for Halloween." The page can be illustrated with some pumpkin seeds glued to the paper. The student can read the page together with his or her family, which allows them to discuss the events of the day, thereby providing greater carryover with communication and literacy experiences in the home and school.

Scaffolded writing is another technique that can be used to provide support to students while they are being challenged to develop a new skill. With this technique, support is provided initially and then withdrawn as learners develop confidence and competence. Scaffolding breaks learning into chunks, and then provides a tool or structure with each chunk. A scaffolded writing project may begin with a student meeting with the teacher to discuss the project and to plan for what will be included and what shape it will take. The teacher may help to make a list of some of the main ideas or support the student in making such a list. The teacher then collaborates with the student during the writing process, providing support and prompts as needed, while also encouraging the student to do as much as possible independently.

The following activities help students to develop writing skills:

- creating object books
- dictating language experience stories
- making entries in daily journals
- contributing content to home-school notebooks
- e-mailing or writing letters to family or friends
- writing recipes
- developing shopping lists

Using Technology to Increase Access to Literacy

There are many types of assistive technology available that increase access to literacy materials for students with visual impairments. Some devices are specifically designed for people with visual impairments, while other devices (such as the iPad) are popular tech-

nological instruments that appeal to a broad audience of diverse users. Students with visual impairments and multiple disabilities can often use assistive technology to increase their access to literacy activities.

The following list highlights a few types of assistive technology that are commonly used to increase access to literacy materials and activities (see Chapter 12 for a detailed discussion of assistive technology):

- Digital talking books: a multimedia presentation of a print publication, rendered in audio with a human voice.
- Screen magnification for computers: software that is loaded onto a computer to magnify the text and graphics displayed on the screen.
- Screen reader: a program that uses text-to-speech software with a speech synthesizer or a braille display to give a computer audio user access to the text on a computer screen.
- Video magnifier: a device that uses a video camera to project a magnified image onto a screen or monitor. Video magnifiers can be used to assist with reading, writing, examining photos, and a wide range of other activities.
- Voice recognition software: a program that translates spoken words to printed text on a computer.
- iPad: a mainstream tablet computer with a built-in screen reader (VoiceOver) and screen magnifier (Zoom). A wide range of applications (apps) are available for students of all ages and ability levels.

LITERACY AND STRUGGLING READERS

Many readers struggle to master literacy skills. A student may be experiencing difficulties for a wide variety of reasons. For students with visual impairments, it is important to look carefully at a variety of factors, including the effects of their visual impairment, a hearing loss, medical issues, motor challenges, a learning disability, or a lack of understanding of English. During the assessment process, educational teams should also look at whether or not there has been a recent change in the student's learning medium (such as from print to braille) and whether or not appropriate modifications have been used. Any of these factors may be considerations in determining what causes the reader to struggle.

Identifying Learning Disabilities in Students with Visual Impairments

For students with visual impairments, a number of indicators may signal a possible learning disability in basic reading, including difficulty recognizing words out of context, confusion of words with similar sounds (such as "pin" and "pen"), and reversals or inversion of letters. In comprehension, potential indicators of learning disabilities include difficulty determining relevant information, challenges with inferential questions, and problems predicting. In writing, difficulty with handwriting and spelling may be indicators, as is written expression far below that of expressive language, both in vocabulary and content (Loftin, 2006; Loftin & Miller, n.d.).

Strategies for Readers with Learning Disabilities

Both fluency and comprehension must be considered during reading instruction. Fluency is the ability to read with speed, accuracy, and proper expression. Strategies for increasing fluency include:

- reading with a partner
- reading while listening to audio
- breaking sentences into smaller chunks
- practicing reading phrases on cards
- repeating readings
- asking student to summarize after reading

Strategies for increasing comprehension include:

- pre-teaching vocabulary and concepts
- asking questions as the student reads
- asking student to re-tell the passage
- asking "wh" questions (who, what, where, when, and why) to review what happened

In addition to the strategies listed above, other methods of working with students who have visual impairments and learning disabilities include the Wilson Reading System (see the Resources section at the end of the chapter) and I-M-ABLE (Individualized Meaning-Centered Approach to Braille Literacy Education; Wormsley, 2016). The Wilson Reading System is a research-based reading and writing program for grades 2 and up (McCarthy, Rowley, & Rines, 2015). It is highly structured, with a systematic and cumulative approach that teaches decoding and encoding using phonemic segments. Specific techniques include controlled vocabulary, sight words, and a multisensory language program with "sound tapping" to segment and blend sounds. The Wilson Reading System approach uses individual letter sounds and blends to build words. The program has been adapted for students with visual impairments and it is now available through the American Printing House for the Blind in large print and braille.

I-M-ABLE (Wormsley, 2016) is an innovative, individualized approach to teaching reading and writing braille that focuses on words that are meaningful to the reader (key vocabulary words). It is not always easy to discover what words are meaningful to students with visual impairments and multiple disabilities, but observation and discussions with members of the child's family will help to identify words that are significant. Key vocabulary words are often not found in most beginning reading programs, but research has shown that students will be motivated to read and write words that are the most meaningful to them. The I-M-ABLE approach introduces whole words that are meaningful to the student and then moves to the individual sounds and letters, going from the whole to the part.

MATHEMATICAL LITERACY

Although this chapter focuses primarily on language-based literacy, such as reading and writing, mathematical literacy is also included here because recognizing numerals and knowing what they mean is part of the array of skills encompassed by functional literacy. *Mathematical literacy* includes numeracy (the ability to recognize numerals), a basic number sense, and a grasp of simple mathematical concepts. Students with visual impairments often do not have the same exposure to numbers or mathematical concepts as their sighted peers and, as a result, they may be behind their age-level peers in understanding these concepts

As they do with other forms of literacy, students with visual impairments need information about how numbers are used in daily life. Because they cannot see price tags, street numbers, telephone numbers, dates—all the ways in which numbers appear all around us—they will need to be told when these occur. Adults will want to tell students when and how they use numbers, for example, with the date: "Yesterday was the 11th, so today is the 12th." Similarly, when walking along, an adult might say, "We're looking for number 239. This building is number 215, so we need to go a little further." Shopping presents many opportunities for using numbers, and introducing students to money and its value is an essential part of mathematical literacy.

Numeracy begins with basic concepts such as more and less, big and little, and other comparative measurements (heavy and light, short and tall). Many students will need repeated practice developing the concept of one-to-one correspondence, in which one number stands for one item. Children learn to count by rote well before they can accurately count the number of items in a given set or create a smaller set of items from a larger array.

It is important to present numbers in accessible formats in the student's preferred learning medium, with labels in print, braille, and tactile symbols. In a typical classroom, for example, the numbers on a calendar can be displayed in print and braille. Many elementary classrooms have number lines, which can also be presented in print and braille. Numbers on classroom doors, clocks, microwaves, and measuring devices can all be labeled in accessible formats.

Strategies for teaching mathematical literacy to students with visual impairments and multiple disabilities include the following:

- Provide frequent opportunities to count everything.
- Offer exposure to numbers in the context of the daily routine.
- Help students to develop an understanding of basic mathematical concepts, such as big and little, and more and less.
- Provide opportunities for students to explore and sort materials to learn about these concepts.
- Create opportunities for children to develop the concept of one-to-one correspondence (the idea that one number stands for one item). For example, one chair for each student, one spoon for each bowl, one sock for each shoe.
- Provide consistent hands-on exposure to concrete items or manipulatives to sort, compare (more and less, bigger and smaller), and count.

In addition to exposure in an accessible environment, students at a beginning level will benefit from repeated practice counting a set of items and matching the print or braille numeral to the set. At a more abstract level, textured items or raised dots can be glued to a card or page and the student can match the print or braille numeral to the corresponding set.

Numeracy can also be incorporated into many functional activities, such as measurement during cooking class, money skills, and time concepts. Educators will want to place emphasis on teaching concepts and skills that will be useful to the student in his or her daily life, with applications in the real world. Rather than just memorizing addition facts or doing worksheets in print or braille, students must practice applying these skills throughout the day. For example, at snack time a student can count how many people are present, and then count out the corresponding number of napkins. The teacher might then say, "There are five children and two adults. How many all together?" This is the type of practice within the routine environment that can help to reinforce skills and make them meaningful.

SUMMARY

This chapter examined a broad definition of literacy, which includes communication, speaking and listening, and expressing and interpreting ideas in a variety of formats—including objects, tactile symbols, and pictures—in addition to the more traditional definition of reading and writing in print or braille. This chapter has discussed the importance of incorporating mathematical literacy into functional activities and routine events. Students who are blind or visually impaired with additional disabilities can and should be active participants in a range of literacy experiences. Functional literacy that draws on students' own experiences and events from their lives can be a meaningful way to expand concepts and skills, and can be used to promote productive and independent lives.

REFERENCES

Barclay, L. A. (Ed.). (2012). *Learning to listen, listening to learn: Teaching listening skills to students with visual impairments.* New York: AFB Press.

Downing, J. E. (2005). *Teaching literacy to students with significant disabilities: Strategies for the K-12 inclusive classroom.* Thousand Oaks, CA: Corwin Press.

Loftin, M. (2006). *Making evaluation meaningful: Determining additional eligibilities and appropriate instructional strategies for blind and visually impaired students.* Austin: Texas School for the Blind and Visually Impaired.

Loftin, M., & Miller, C. (n.d.). Indicators for possible learning disabilities. Retrieved from http://www.pathstoliteracy.org/indicators-possible-learning-disabilities

McCarthy, M., Rowley, R., & Rines, J. (2015). Implementing the Wilson Reading System with braille students. Retrieved from http://www.pathstoliteracy.org/blog/implementing-wilson-reading-system-braille-students

Wormsley, D. P. (2016). *I-M-ABLE: Individualized meaning-centered approach to braille literacy education.* New York: AFB Press.

RESOURCES

For additional resources, see the General Resources section at the back of this book.

Literacy Materials

American Printing House for the Blind (APH)
1839 Frankfort Avenue
P.O. Box 6085
Louisville, KY 40206-0085
(502) 895-2405; (800) 223-1839
Fax: (502) 899-2284
info@aph.org
www.aph.org

Publishes a wide variety of print/braille books with tactile pictures for preschoolers including *On the Way to Literacy* books; the Early Braille Trade Books; and many other braille children's books and early learning materials. Distributes a wide variety of educational products and instructional materials including the Perkins Brailler, slates and styli, and Wikki Stix, as well as a variety of tactile materials such as the Picture Maker: Wheatley Tactile Diagramming Kit. *See also* the organizational listing in the General Resources section at the back of this book.

Bookshare
480 California Avenue, Suite 201
Palo Alto, CA 94306
(650) 644-3400
Fax: (650) 475-1066
info@bookshare.org
www.bookshare.org

Administers the world's largest accessible digital library for persons with print disabilities. Memberships are free for U.S. students with qualifying print disabilities. Members can download books from the website in any of a variety of text or audio formats.

Learning Ally
20 Roszel Road
Princeton, NJ 08540
(800) 221-4792
www.learningally.org

Distributes digitally recorded textbooks and literature titles to empower students with reading-related learning disabilities and visual impairments to reach their full potential.

National Library Service for the Blind and Physically Handicapped (NLS)
Library of Congress
1291 Taylor Street, NW
Washington, DC 20542
(202) 707-5100; (800) 424-8567
Fax: (202) 707-0712
TDD/TTY: (202) 707-0744
nls@loc.gov
www.loc.gov/nls

Administers the Braille and Talking Book Library Service, a free program that loans recorded and braille books and magazines as well as specially designed playback equipment to residents of the United States who are unable to read or use standard print materials. Talking books are delivered to eligible borrowers through local cooperating libraries throughout the United States. It also offers audio, braille, and print/braille books for preschool through grade 8 and periodicals for blind and physically handicapped children.

Seedlings Braille Books for Children
P.O. Box 51924
Livonia, MI 48151-5924
(734) 427-8552; (800) 777-8552
Fax: (734) 427-8552
info@seedlings.org
www.seedlings.org

Publishes and distributes high-quality braille books for children of all ages, including print and braille preschool picture board books and beginning reader print and braille books, including a variety in uncontracted braille.

Tar Heel Reader
http://tarheelreader.org/

Offers a collection of free, easy-to-read, and accessible books on a wide range of topics and allows users to create their own books. It offers a wide range of accessible books for students with special needs. The site can be accessed through a mouse, touch screen, alternative pointing device, AAC device with serial output, alternative keyboard, or switch.

Literacy Curricula

Handwriting Without Tears
806 West Diamond Avenue, Suite 230
Gaithersburg, MD 20878
(301) 263-2700
Fax: (301) 263-2707
info@hwtears.com
www.hwtears.com

A curriculum for teaching handwriting using developmentally appropriate, multisensory tools and strategies, with materials that address all styles of learning.

Wilson Reading System
Wilson Language Training
47 Old Webster Road
Oxford, MA 01540
(508) 368-2399; (800) 899-8454
Fax: (508) 368-2300
www.wilsonlanguage.com

A highly structured, research-based reading and writing program for students with language-based learning disabilities. It has been adapted for students who are blind or visually impaired and is available through the American Printing House for the Blind.

Websites

Literacy for Children with Combined Vision and Hearing Loss
National Center on Deafblindness
http://literacy.nationaldb.org/

A website of NCDB that provides information and resources for teaching and working with children who have complex learning challenges, designed for individual state deafblind projects, teachers, family members, and related services providers interested in beginning or enhancing literacy instruction for children who have combined vision and hearing loss. Content is organized around evidence-based instructional strategies identified as being effective in building emergent literacy skills for children with dual sensory challenges and moving children along a continuum toward independent reading.

Paths to Literacy
Perkins School for the Blind and Texas School for the Blind and Visually Impaired
www.pathstoliteracy.org

An online hub that provides information related to literacy for students who are blind or visually impaired, including those with additional disabilities or deafblindness.

Additional Reading

Wormsley, D. P. (2016). *I-M-ABLE: Individualized meaning-centered approach to braille literacy education.* New York: AFB Press.

Describes an innovative, individualized approach to teaching reading and writing braille, focusing on key vocabulary words that are meaningful to the reader.

Chapter 9

Orientation and Mobility Programs
· ·
Robyn Herrera, Jennifer Cmar, and Diane Fazzi

Key Points

🔑 The impact of visual impairment and multiple disabilities on the development of skills for orientation and mobility

🔑 The roles and responsibilities of orientation and mobility specialists in serving students with visual impairments and multiple disabilities

🔑 The features of orientation and mobility assessment and instruction for students with visual impairments and multiple disabilities

🔑 The role of technology in promoting orientation and mobility skill development for students with visual impairments who have multiple disabilities

---

Angelica is a 4-year-old child who has been blind since birth and also has global developmental delays. She acquired early motor developmental milestones such as sitting and standing about the same time as her older siblings, but struggled more with locomotor movements such as coordinated reaching for objects, crawling in the home, and walking—especially on uneven surfaces. She is now able to walk independently, but needs support transitioning from one floor surface to another and negotiating changes in depth such as ramps, door joints, and stairs and curbs.

Angelica attends an afternoon, half-day class at Evergreen Preschool Monday through Friday. The school is located in a suburban area with regular sidewalks and is in walking distance from her home. Her older sister attends the elementary school across the street and is in the fifth grade.

Tony is in the fourth grade at Rosewood Elementary School. He has low vision (reduced visual acuity in both eyes) and also has intellectual disabilities that impact his daily functioning at home and in school. Tony learns best through repetition and when he is given consistent routines to practice basic O&M skills. Tony is able to communicate his needs to others and complete tasks with multiple steps when given verbal prompts. He is friendly towards his peers, but has a difficult time understanding and following

social cues and often "invades" the physical space of others in his exuberance to join in conversations or learning activities.

Emily is a junior in high school. A summer boating accident the previous year resulted in hemiplegia to the left side and visual impairment. Due to these injuries, she requires a wheelchair for mobility. Her visual field loss makes navigation with her power chair a challenge as she has trouble keeping track of her path of travel, locating drop-offs consistently, and remembering visual landmarks along the way. Emily, her family, and the high school staff are working to adjust to the significant changes that have occurred in her life.

This chapter provides an overview of the impact of visual impairments and multiple disabilities on the development of students' skills for orientation and mobility (O&M). The roles and responsibilities of O&M specialists in serving students with visual impairments who have multiple disabilities, as well as the roles of family members and other professionals, are outlined. Unique features of O&M assessment, instruction, and program evaluation are highlighted, with the importance of team involvement stressed throughout. Finally, the role of technology and O&M devices in promoting O&M skill development is described.

Three vignettes, describing students with multiple disabilities who are of different ages and who are receiving O&M services, are in-

cluded to illustrate the role of the O&M specialist and other team members in promoting independent and semi-independent travel. These vignettes are woven throughout the chapter to provide further concrete examples and to show how various O&M components contribute to a cohesive O&M program for students with visual impairments and multiple disabilities.

ORIENTATION AND MOBILITY

Orientation is the use of an individual's remaining senses to determine their location in an environment, and *mobility* is the facilitation of movement (Jacobson, 2013). The key principles of orientation are (Hill & Ponder, 1976):

- Where am I?
- Where am I going?
- How am I going to get there?

In the Individuals with Disabilities Education Improvement Act of 2004 (IDEA), O&M is identified as a related service for children with disabilities (34 C.F.R. § 300.34[a]). The IDEA Amendments of 1997 define *O&M services* as "services provided to blind or visually impaired children by qualified personnel to enable those students to attain systematic orientation to and safe movement within their environments in school, home, and community" (34 C.F.R § 300.24[b][6]). O&M is further described in IDEA (2004) as the teaching, as appropriate, of the following concepts and skills (34 C.F.R. § 300.34[c][7]):

- spatial and environmental concepts
- use of information received by the senses to establish, maintain, or regain orientation and line of travel
- use of the long cane or a service animal
- use of remaining vision and distance low vision devices
- other concepts, techniques, and tools

O&M instruction is highly individualized, tailored to meet the unique needs of each student. As explained in more detail in Sidebar 9.1, the traditional O&M curriculum encompasses human guide techniques, self-protective techniques, orientation skills, long cane skills, residential area travel, commercial area travel, and other topics not covered in the preceding units. A critical skills model, where O&M skills are taught as needed in natural environments, is an appropriate approach to use with some students who have multiple disabilities (Fazzi & Petersmeyer, 2001).

🔑 Sidebar 9.1

Components of the Traditional O&M Curriculum

- *Human guide techniques:* basic human guide, reversing directions, transferring sides, narrow passageways, accepting and refusing assistance, ascending and descending stairs, doorways, seating
- *Self-protective techniques:* upper hand and forearm, lower hand and forearm, trailing, negotiating open doorways, parallel and perpendicular alignment, search patterns, dropped objects
- *Orientation skills:* landmarks, clues, indoor and outdoor numbering systems, measurement, compass directions, self-familiarization
- *Long cane skills:* diagonal technique, trailing with the cane, ascending and descending stairs, two-point touch technique, contacting and exploring objects, touch and slide technique, touch and drag technique, constant contact technique, three-point touch technique
- *Residential area travel:* car familiarization, refinement of cane skills, straight line of travel, block travel, detecting curbs, shorelining, sidewalk recovery, residential street crossings, street crossing recovery, drop-off lessons
- *Commercial area travel:* Street crossings at traffic lights, pedestrian traffic controls, soliciting aid, bus travel, store travel, escalators, elevators, revolving doors, airports
- *Other topics:* railroad crossings, trains and subways, gas stations

Source: Based on Hill, E., & Ponder, P. (1976). *Orientation and mobility techniques: A guide for the practitioner.* New York: AFB Press.

EFFECTS OF VISUAL IMPAIRMENTS AND MULTIPLE DISABILITIES ON DEVELOPMENT

The presence of visual impairments affects several aspects of typical development. These developmental differences are often compounded for students who have multiple disabilities, having significant implications for early development in general and development of O&M skills specifically.

Vision serves as a motivator for, coordinator of, and refinement tool for the multifaceted components of purposeful movement and independent exploration. Compared to children who are sighted, children with visual impairments may reach motor development milestones in a different pattern or at a later age. Visual impairments may affect early motor development in the following areas (Brambring, 2007; Ihsen, Troester, & Brambring, 2010; Levtzion-Korach, Tennenbaum, Schnitzer, & Ornoy, 2000):

- *Gross motor skills:* rolling, crawling, standing with support, walking with assistance walking independently, walking up stairs, standing on one foot, and jumping on both feet
- *Fine motor skills:* eating, drinking, dressing, simple object manipulations (pushing a toy or pulling up a diaper), and using tools (spoons, cups, drumsticks, and the like)
- *Early reaching:* reaching for silent objects in particular

Children with visual impairments interact with environments using information gathered from hearing, smell, touch, and vision. Children with visual impairments and multiple disabilities may exhibit further differences in motor and sensory development, depending on the extent and complexity of their disabilities. The use of sensory information is a fundamental aspect of O&M instruction for children with visual impairments and multiple disabilities. For example, Tony, the elementary school student in one of the vignettes that opened this chapter, works with his O&M specialist to locate areas at his elementary school. Tony's general education teacher and teacher of students with visual impairments reinforce his use of sensory information by providing verbal prompts during natural routines such as lunchtime. Tony identifies the school cafeteria by hearing the voices and footsteps of other children, smelling pizza, seeing the vending machines near the entrance, and feeling the doorway with his long cane.

The presence of physical, neurological, or other cognitive disabilities in addition to a visual impairment may affect (Rosen, 2010; Rosen & Crawford, 2010; Strickling & Pogrund, 2002):

- early movement and awareness of body position in space
- development of spatial understanding
- tactile sensation
- balance and coordination
- stamina and posture
- gait pattern
- physical activity skills

Children with visual impairments and multiple disabilities may have difficulty with a variety of O&M skills, such as the following (Rosen, 2010; Rosen & Crawford, 2010):

- using proper arm positioning for basic protective techniques
- grasping and moving the long cane
- negotiating stairs and curbs
- walking on uneven surfaces
- maintaining a straight line of travel
- crossing streets

Some of these difficulties are illustrated in the vignette of Angelica by her delays in development of motor skills. Angelica has difficulty transitioning to different surfaces and maintaining her balance on curbs, ramps, and stairs. See Sidebar 9.2 for examples of strategies used to facilitate Angelica's O&M skill development.

The combination of visual impairments and other disabilities affects children's development of skills needed for purposeful movement and exploration. An understanding of the unique implications on each individual child's development will assist teachers of students with visual impairments and other professionals in promoting independent or semi-independent travel to the greatest extent possible.

THE ROLES AND RESPONSIBILITIES OF O&M SPECIALISTS

O&M specialists have diverse roles and responsibilities when serving students with visual impairments and multiple disabilities. O&M specialists are responsible for a com-

> ✒ **Sidebar 9.2**
>
> ## Strategies and Tips for Promoting Early O&M Development
>
> Angelica's team used the following strategies to promote exploration and development of O&M skills:
>
> - encouraging Angelica to use her adaptive mobility device
> - practicing in natural settings, including Angelica's neighborhood, home, and school playground
> - using motivating objects and activities (for example, a preferred toy, a talking pedometer, or games involving music) to encourage movement and exploration
> - reinforcing skills during natural transition times, such as before and after school
> - sharing information about Angelica's progress with all team members through use of an electronic bulletin board

prehensive assessment of students' O&M skills and needs. Assessments typically include interviews with students, families, and key school personnel, evaluation of students' current travel skills, functional vision assessment (FVA), evaluation of travel environments, and determination of goals.

For students with low vision, a functional low vision mobility assessment is an essential component of comprehensive assessment (Geruschat & Smith, 2010). The overall purpose of this assessment is to learn how students use their vision for tasks related to O&M. Components of a functional low vision mobility assessment include (Geruschat & Smith, 2010):

- a review of information from the student's clinical low vision examination
- interviews
- assessment of the student's functional vision
- assessment of the student's mobility in various travel environment
- assessment of the travel environment

Results of the comprehensive assessment will dictate whether O&M services are needed and will guide the extent of services provided. (For additional information about assessment, see Chapter 3.)

O&M specialists are key members of Individualized Education Program (IEP), Individualized Family Service Plan (IFSP), and transition IEP teams. Associated responsibilities include collaborating with teachers of students with visual impairments and other team members to ensure that:

- students' needs are met
- O&M goals and objectives are developed
- individualized instruction tailored to meeting these goals and objectives is provided
- O&M skills are reinforced and
- O&M progress is monitored and communicated with others

O&M specialists are primarily responsible for teaching O&M skills and concepts, but they also provide consultative and support services to other professionals who interact with students. The O&M specialist is a crucial source of information and training for team members, including families (Griffin-Shirley, Kelley, & Lawrence, 2006). The O&M specialist provides support to team members in the form of in-service training sessions on topics such as the use of proper guide techniques, presentations on current orientation devices and mobility tools, and formal and informal collaborative team and student progress meetings.

ROLES AND STRATEGIES FOR PROMOTING O&M FOR STUDENTS WITH VISUAL IMPAIRMENTS AND MULTIPLE DISABILITIES

Students with visual impairments and multiple disabilities often require specialized strategies and modifications to the traditional O&M curriculum. Consideration of the whole child is an essential element of planning and promoting O&M for students with visual impairments and multiple disabilities (Skellenger & Sapp, 2010). Sidebar 9.3 provides a list of strategies for promoting development of O&M skills for students with visual impairments and intellectual disabilities. O&M instruction for these students may require greater repetition, and the students may take longer to attain specific goals than students without multiple disabilities. Overall, O&M instruction facilitates independence to the maximum extent possible in school, home, and community environments for students with

✐ Sidebar 9.3

Strategies and Suggestions for Promoting O&M for Students with Intellectual Disabilities

The following suggestions can help members of the educational team work with the O&M specialist to support students with visual impairments and intellectual disabilities in their O&M instruction:

- **Teamwork:** Collaborate closely with the O&M specialist and other team members, including families, to promote maximum incorporation of O&M skills and techniques into students' lives.
- **Communication:** Consult with the O&M specialist and other team members to learn about students' communication strategies and systems and how to incorporate these strategies and systems into O&M activities.
- **Recordkeeping:** Maintain thorough records of assessment reports, lesson plans, lesson notes, and progress reports, and share relevant progress reports with the O&M specialist.
- **Time considerations:** Share information with the O&M specialist to determine the best time of day for scheduling O&M lessons for each student, considering aspects such as medication, alertness, endurance, and the need for functional lessons.
- **Task analysis:** When reinforcing O&M techniques, use task analysis to divide skills into smaller steps that are more manageable for the student.
- **Sequenced instruction:** Work with the O&M specialist to emphasize functional skills leading up to a manageable goal. Keep in mind that the O&M specialist may not teach all skills from the traditional O&M sequence.
- **Environment:** Be aware of sights, sounds, smells, or activities that interfere with a student's ability to learn, and share that information with the O&M specialist and other members of the team.
- **Motivation:** Work with the O&M specialist to develop a reward system for students who lack interest in practicing O&M skills.
- **Prompting:** Provide appropriate prompting when reinforcing O&M skills and concepts.
- **Choice making:** When reinforcing O&M techniques, allow students to choose activities, routes, and materials as appropriate.

Source: Based on Ambrose-Zaken, G., Calhoon, C. R., & Keim, J. R. (2010). Teaching orientation and mobility to students with cognitive impairments and vision loss. In W. R. Wiener, R. L. Welsh, & B. B. Blasch (Eds.), *Foundations of orientation and mobility: Volume II. Instructional strategies and practical applications* (3rd ed., pp. 624–666). New York: AFB Press.

visual impairments, including those with multiple disabilities.

While the O&M specialist has many important responsibilities to ensure that students with visual impairments and multiple disabilities are learning and using skills for getting around the home, school, and greater community, other professionals also have key roles to play in promoting O&M for these students. Families, teachers, related service professionals, paraeducators, and administrators each contribute to the success of the O&M program. With so many individuals involved in the process of assessment, instruction, reinforcement, practice, and real-life application of skills of O&M, collaboration is key to providing consistency and successful student outcomes.

Collaboration and the Transdisciplinary Approach

Collaboration is a process by which two or more individuals voluntarily come together to achieve shared goals. Collaboration is the cornerstone of a transdisciplinary approach. A *transdisciplinary approach* is a framework used in educational settings that allows for and promotes the active sharing of the knowledge and skills each member of the team possesses in order to collectively determine the services and goals for each student (see Chapter 2 for additional discussion of teamwork). According to Bruder (1994, p. 61):

> The primary purpose of this approach is to pool and integrate the expertise of team members so that more efficient and comprehensive assessment and intervention services may be provided. . . .

Professionals from different disciplines teach, learn, and work together to accomplish a common set of intervention goals for a child and their family.

A transdisciplinary approach is often used when working with individuals with visual impairments and multiple disabilities; therefore, it is important for the teacher of students with visual impairments and O&M specialist to become familiar with the transdisciplinary approach, along with how to promote O&M within this approach. The following sections present strategies and suggestions that can assist educational team members in working with the O&M specialist using a transdisciplinary approach. (See Chapter 2 for a full discussion and additional suggestions for working with teachers, paraeducators, related service professionals, and administrators to ensure that students receive optimal coordinated services.)

Family Members

Angelica receives direct service O&M three times per week at 30 minutes per session. One session is scheduled in the morning before her school day starts, the second session is scheduled during the school day to work on transitions from class to the playground, and the third session is scheduled at the end of the day so that the O&M specialist can work with her and her sister on a semi-assisted routine for walking home one day per week.

On Mondays, Angelica's O&M specialist works with her at home and focuses on activities to improve her balance and confidence in walking on a variety of surfaces such as linoleum in the kitchen, carpet in the living room, grass in the yard, and pavement in the driveway. Angelica's mom participates in these weekly lessons in the home and gives updates on her progress as well as suggestions for how to best adapt the balance activities to keep Angelica's motivation high. Each of these activities is reviewed with the physical therapist to ensure that it is appropriate for Angelica and to make sure that appropriate positioning and handling approaches are always used.

On Wednesdays, when Angelica's lessons are at school, part of the time is spent orienting her to the other play equipment and reinforcing some of her expressive communication goals with other children, as established by the speech-language pathologist. The O&M specialist always checks in at the office to see if anyone has left a message for her and also with the classroom teacher to get a weekly update on Angelica's progress. On Fridays, Angelica and her older sister work with the O&M specialist at the end of the school day to work on walking home together safely in preparation for walking together the following year (one of Angelica's goals).

Angelica works with many specialists during the week, including a teacher of students with visual impairments, physical therapist, and speech-language pathologist. The team has established an electronic bulletin board where they can post weekly updates for team members to review and post questions and answers as needed. Angelica's mother also has access to this website and can participate as she wishes. The team works

together to support successful development in areas important to Angelica's participation in school, readiness for kindergarten, general well-being, and increased levels of independence at home, school, and in the community.

The teacher of students with visual impairments refers Tony to the O&M specialist for assessment. Based on those assessment results, it is determined by the educational team that he will benefit from direct O&M instruction to improve his safe navigation on the school campus, initial travel experiences in the surrounding residential area, spatial and environmental concept development, and increased purposeful use of vision. A major focus of O&M instruction will be incorporating use of vision together with the long cane. A classroom poster is created to remind classmates and teachers of the rules and expectations related to Tony's use of the long cane, including a place for classmates to post pre-written compliments about his weekly progress. A smaller version is duplicated for posting on the refrigerator at Tony's house in order to remind his family of the importance of bringing his cane on community outings.

Families provide a natural support system to children with visual impairments and multiple disabilities. Family members are children's first and primary teachers. Families provide a safe place for children of all ages and abilities to acquire and practice new skills. The teacher of students with visual impairments can promote family involvement in the O&M program by working with the O&M specialist to encourage the family's active involvement in assessments, goal planning, progress evaluations, school meetings, and skill reinforcement and application at home and in the community. See Sidebar 9.4 for guiding questions to promote family involvement in IFSP and IEP meetings.

The teacher of students with visual impairments can accomplish this involvement by building and maintaining a collaborative relationship with families of the children they serve through consistent and planned contact. For example, the teacher of students with visual impairments and O&M specialist in Angelica's vignette provide consistent planned contact with her family through weekly lessons in the home. During these sessions, the teacher, O&M specialist, and Angelica's mom review her progress. During the lesson, her mom provides suggestions on how to keep Angelica's motivation high, and

---

 Sidebar 9.4

Communication Suggestions for Encouraging Family Participation in IFSP and IEP Meetings

Communication is key to success in encouraging family members to participate in educational team meetings. Be prepared to explain the answers to the following questions in plain language *prior* to each meeting:

Assessment

- What is the goal of the assessment?
- Who will conduct the assessment?
- When and where will the assessment be conducted?
- What will the assessment entail (observation, questionnaire, direct assessment, and the like)?
- When will assessment report be available?
- What if there are questions about the report?

Goal Development

- How are goals formulated?
- Who will formulate goals?
- Can the family develop a goal based on their priorities?
- Why is a new goal being developed or an old goal extended or changed?
- Has the child made adequate yearly progress in this area?

Implementation

- Who is responsible for this goal?
- How often will the child be working on this goal?
- Who will be working on this goal with the child?
- Where will the instruction take place?
- How will progress be monitored?
- How often will family members be notified about student progress?
- Is instruction evidenced based?

the teacher and O&M specialist demonstrate how to incorporate activities that are just beyond Angelica's current skill level. In this example, using the transdisciplinary approach, the O&M specialist is also working on balance-related goals from the physical therapist and the teacher of students with visual impairments is working on expressive communication goals from the speech-language pathologist.

Similarly, the teacher of students with visual impairments and O&M specialist in Tony's vignette use consistent planned contact with Tony's family to embed O&M skills throughout his day to promote their acquisition. To encourage Tony to remember to take his long white cane with him whenever he leaves the house, the teacher of students with visual impairments, O&M specialist, and his family have established a consistent storage area near the door for Tony's cane, and the mutual expectation that whenever Tony leaves the house he is to have his long white cane. The teacher monitors and reinforces this expectation during class time. Establishment of routines is particularly important in Tony's case as he learns best through repetition and consistent routines.

The teacher of students with visual impairments and O&M specialist can also encourage families to take an active role in promoting O&M by encouraging families to create opportunities to engage with their child in their local community. These opportunities allow for academic, social, and O&M skill reinforcement, and can be coordinated to align with curricula from other content areas (Barrella et al., 2011). These activities provide opportunities to use a transdisciplinary approach to focus on multiple content areas including the expanded core curriculum (ECC), which families feel is often overlooked (Grimmett, Pogrund, & Griffin-Shirley, 2011).

Through the use of coordinated lessons (see Sidebar 9.5 for an example), the teacher of students with visual impairments can engage in consistent planned contact, work on the ECC, encourage children to be physically active, and help families develop high expectations while easing overprotectiveness (Lieberman & Lepore, 1998; Longmuir, 1998; Nixon, 1988 as cited in Stuart, Lieberman, & Hand, 2006).

Teachers of Students with Visual Impairments

Teachers of students with visual impairments require specialized competencies to address the unique needs of children who have visual impairments and multiple disabilities (Silberman & Sacks, 2007). Depending on the educational setting, roles of the teacher of students with visual impairments can include teacher-consultant, specialized skills instructor, and general education teacher (Spungin & Ferrell, 2007). Regardless of the particular role and setting, the teacher of students with visual impairments can promote O&M throughout the school day.

Teachers of students with visual impairments are responsible for conducting formal assessments, such as functional vision assessments (FVAs), learning media assessments (LMAs), and assistive technology assessments (see Chapter 3 for more on assessments). Whenever possible, teachers of

---

✏ Sidebar 9.5

Coordinated Lesson: Preparing a Favorite Meal

During this activity, the teacher of students with visual impairments is working on multiple content areas and multiple goals. The teacher has coordinated the activity with the O&M specialist and also with the family so that the child prepares the meal after the lesson, making the activity immediately meaningful (see, for example, Sapp, 2011). This activity incorporates many content areas and can be adjusted for many skill levels. The teacher of students with visual impairments, the O&M specialist, and family members each have a role to play as they work with the student in different parts of the activity and in teaching different skills.

Teacher of Students with Visual Impairments

- choose food to prepare (expressive communication, self-determination)
- identify ingredients (soliciting assistance, expressive communication, assistive technology)

- make shopping list (assistive technology, writing, braille, organization)
- cost or budget (math and money management)
- share experience (writing, braille, assistive technology, language arts, self-evaluation, self-determination, public speaking, social skills)

O&M Specialist

- travel to, from, and inside store (O&M, soliciting assistance)
- locate items (visual efficiency, O&M, soliciting assistance)
- purchase items (money management, social skills, math)

Family Members

- prepare meal (math, daily living skills, time management, fine motor skills, expressive and receptive communication, gross motor skills, concept development)
- clean up (daily living skills, fine motor skills, gross motor skills)

---

students with visual impairments and O&M specialists can plan and conduct portions of their respective assessments jointly and should always share results. When working with students with multiple disabilities, teachers of students with visual impairments may use informal assessment techniques (see Chapter 3), such as the following (Silberman & Sacks, 2007):

- ecological inventories
- routine task analyses
- activity analyses
- discrepancy analyses
- functional daily routines (a form of assessment that uses students' everyday activities to gain an understanding of their typical functioning in home and school settings)

- person-centered planning (a collaborative approach that focuses on helping students discover their unique preferences, abilities, and needs; see Chapter 15)
- making action plans (MAPs) (a person-centered approach in which information is gathered about a student's history, dreams, fears, interests, and needs to develop a plan for the future)

Teachers of students with visual impairments also have the responsibility of assisting other professionals, including O&M specialists, in understanding results of these assessments (Spungin & Ferrell, 2007). Because teachers of students with visual impairments and O&M specialists share the responsibility of conducting FVAs for students with low vision, the two professionals may benefit from coordinating their schedules to conduct this assessment together. Co-planning assessments allow greater collaboration and facilitate an exchange of ideas across professions, while taking less time out of students' schedules.

Teachers of students with visual impairments provide reinforcement and encouragement for students to use their O&M skills whenever possible. They also sometimes have specified roles related to teaching O&M basics, as designated by their students' IEPs. There are a variety of ways for teachers to support and reinforce O&M skills and concepts, such as the following (Brauner, 2009; Sapp & Hatlen, 2010; Silberman & Sacks, 2007):

- promoting generalization and maintenance of O&M skills during daily routines

- enhancing visual efficiency
- encouraging independent travel
- using consistent terminology when naming key locations
- collecting data and providing feedback

Sidebar 9.6 offers strategies and suggestions to facilitate collaboration between teachers of students with visual impairments and O&M specialists when serving students with visual impairments and multiple disabilities.

Many professionals in the field of visual impairment and blindness are dual-certified, holding certifications as both teachers of students with visual impairments and O&M specialists. This combination of roles leads to unique benefits, challenges, opportunities, time constraints, and additional responsibilities, such as (Griffin-Shirley, Pogrund, Smith, & Duemer, 2009):

- facilitating IEP meetings
- coordinating assistive technology training
- conducting additional assessments
- participating in additional faculty and parent meetings
- being involved in extracurricular school-sponsored activities

Dual-certified professionals are especially skilled at integrating O&M skills into students' daily routines, such as reviewing O&M techniques with students as they walk to the classroom (Griffin-Shirley et al., 2009). The resulting challenge is making the time to provide the full realm of services needed in both areas in a balanced manner.

✒ Sidebar 9.6

Strategies and Suggestions for Collaboration between Teachers of Students with Visual Impairments and O&M Specialists

- Sit down and talk with the O&M specialist to discuss students' progress, share ideas and resources, and establish mutual expectations for collaboration.
- Observe and participate in students' O&M lessons to learn more about their travel abilities and needs.
- Share information about students' visual impairments and needs with the O&M specialist.
- Co-plan functional vision assessments and community lessons with the O&M specialist.
- Inform the O&M specialist of any changes (in behavior, medication, schedule, mood, alertness, and the like) that may affect students' functioning.
- Communicate with the O&M specialist to ensure that team members use consistent terminology when referring to O&M-related tasks. For example, using phrases such as "trail the wall," "follow the wall," and "shoreline the wall" to refer to the same task may cause unnecessary confusion for students.
- When reinforcing O&M skills, give clear, specific directions to students, consulting with the O&M specialist as needed. For example, say, "the second door on your right" instead of "just a bit further down."
- Confer with the O&M specialist to ensure consistency in travel routes.
- Develop ongoing method of communication with the O&M specialist, such as a physical or electronic bulletin boards, biweekly lunch meetings, e-mails, text messages, weekly conference calls, or a combination.

Paraeducators

Paraeducators are also essential to the transdisciplinary team serving students with visual impairments and multiple disabilities and promoting O&M. For example, after Tony's assessment, the team decides that he will benefit from O&M instruction that is consistent and supported by daily routines. Tony's teacher of students with visual impairments and O&M specialist meet with the paraeducator to provide a copy of Tony's O&M goals and the associated task analysis. The teacher of students with visual impairments and O&M specialist provide any training and support needed so that the paraeducator clearly understands his or her role for encouraging and monitoring Tony's use of O&M skills at school. In some cases, the paraeducator may be included in O&M lessons on a regular basis for support and consistent follow-through.

Related Service Professionals

Similarly, using a transdisciplinary approach, related service professionals such as physical therapists, occupational therapists, and speech-language pathologists can work together to optimize service delivery for students with visual impairments and multiple disabilities. (See Chapter 2 for more in-depth information regarding the roles and responsibilities of related service personnel.)

O&M specialists may consult with physical therapists on positioning and handling approaches to use with students with physical and motor difficulties, such as spasticity or hypotonia. *Positioning* refers to providing support for the student's body and arranging instructional or play materials in special ways. *Handling* refers to how a student is picked up, carried, held, and assisted. Proper handling helps make the student more comfortable and more receptive to instruction. Proper positioning allows the student to perform actions and manipulate materials most efficiently. Teachers of students with visual impairments and paraeducators who work with students with visual impairments and multiple disabilities may also need to be responsible for or assist with positioning and handling students with visual impairments and multiple disabilities. Sidebar 9.7 provides suggestions for professionals on effective positioning and handling techniques. Before any professional engages in positioning and handling of students, he or she should review the district's related policy and receive proper training and information from a physical therapist or nursing staff member.

The physical therapist and O&M specialist can address issues regarding balance and body alignment, which affect a student's ability to attend to sensory information, concentrate on learning experiences, and travel safely and efficiently. The physical therapist and O&M specialist can collaborate to design and choose positioning devices and mobility devices that take comfort, safety, and gait pattern into consideration, and to develop programs and strategies that promote and reinforce attention, concentration, balance, erect posture, stamina, and purposeful movement. For example, when the O&M specialist is assessing what type of mobility device might be prescribed for a student with a visual impairment and an additional motor impairment, it is suggested they contact and collaborate with the physical therapist (Glanzman & Ducret, 2003). The physical therapist and the O&M specialist can schedule a collaborative assessment time so that they can observe the student travel with a variety of mobility devices. During the assessment, the physical therapist can assess the student's stability, posture, and stamina while using each device, while the O&M specialist can assess the student's reaction time and safety. The physical therapist and O&M specialist next compare assessment findings and choose a mobility device that promotes safety and efficiency.

An O&M specialist may collaborate with both a physical therapist and an occupational therapist to determine the best mobility device for a given student. The O&M specialist may determine that a student would benefit from the use of a long white cane to provide advance warning of obstacles and changes in walking surfaces; however, the student's reaction time might be slow, his or her balance fair, and he or she might have difficulty main-

Sidebar 9.7

Positioning and Handling Suggestions for Teachers of Students with Visual Impairments and O&M Specialists

The following are suggestions for positioning and handling students who have visual impairments and physical or motor disabilities:

- Consult with a physical therapist about the student's needs and receive training in how to position and handle the student.
- Consult district lifting policy, for example, about individual weight limits and the use of lifting belts.
- Allow the student to do as much of the movement as possible.
- Pace yourself; go slowly.
- Carry the student (if necessary) to encourage head and trunk control, by using your body to give dynamic support (increasing and decreasing as the student progresses and tolerates).

- Avoid pulling against tightness if a student has spasticity; move slowly and rhythmically.
- Begin movements proximally (trunk-hips-shoulders). In students with low muscle tone this sequence promotes core strength and control, which supports distal use (arms and legs). In students with spasticity, this sequence will indirectly reduce muscle tone distally.
- Remember that students with low muscle tone typically do not like light touch and tire easily.
- Position students with low muscle tone in a semi-reclining position to encourage visual tracking and extension of abdominal muscles.
- Handling should be decreased as the student gains more control.

Source: Adapted from Martin, S., & Kessler, M. (2007). *Neurologic interventions for physical therapy* (2nd ed.). St. Louis, MO: Saunders.

taining his or her grip on the cane. As a result, the O&M specialist can contact a physical therapist and occupational therapist for a collaborative solution. A physical therapist may need to observe the student travel using adaptive mobility devices (AMDs) of varying shapes and then help to determine which device would best encourage the student to walk with an erect posture and support stability and balance when transitioning

from one walking surface to another. An occupational therapist may recommend the best design of the grip on the AMD so that the student can easily hold the device and maintain his or her grasp.

Speech-language pathologists can also work collaboratively with the team and O&M specialists can benefit by becoming familiar with any alternative or augmentative communication (AAC) devices that students may use (see Chapters 7 and 12 for more on AAC devices). Using these devices in the community can be a rich source for promoting communication and encouraging the application of any devices that the student is learning to use.

DEVELOPING THE O&M PROGRAM FOR STUDENTS WITH VISUAL IMPAIRMENTS AND MULTIPLE DISABILITIES

The essential components of successful O&M programs for school-age students with visual impairments are assessment, program planning, implementation, and program evaluation. Discussions of these program components can be found elsewhere in literature (see, for example, Bina, Naimy, Fazzi, & Crouse, 2010). For students with visual impairments who have multiple disabilities, these same components are essential; hence, only aspects of the processes and approaches that might be somewhat different for this population will be addressed here, including assessment, program planning, supporting positive behaviors, opportunities for practice, and ensuring quality services.

O&M Assessment

The school staff is concerned about Emily's use of a power wheelchair on campus and the educational team and family have requested a physical therapist and O&M consult. The physical therapist and O&M specialist coordinated their schedules in order to observe Emily's use of the power chair at school and to talk with Emily, the family, and school staff. Together they determined that Emily was not safe operating the power chair on the school campus. The physical therapist recommended having the speed controls adjusted by the chair manufacturer (eliminating the faster speeds) and the O&M specialist recommended a series of visual training sessions to focus on visual scanning, landmarking, and drop-off detections. The entire team agreed that Emily would be scheduled for O&M lessons to strengthen her use of visual skills.

Depending on the severity and complexity of a student's visual impairment and multiple disabilities and the number of professionals who may be involved, the assessment process can consist of anywhere from a few to many different educational assessments. In many cases, a school psychologist may assist in coordinating these assessments, but with numerous service professionals serving students with multiple disabilities on a consultative or itinerant basis, coordination is a challenge. It is incumbent upon O&M specialists and teachers of students with visual impairments to seek out the information needed for planning before conducting their respective assessments, including developing a schedule of other assessments that will be completed. Whenever possible, it is beneficial to work collaboratively on various aspects of assessments to reduce the time required of students and professionals, as well as to share information and observations. For example, the speech-language pathologist can be invited to conduct a portion of his or her assessment in the community with the O&M specialist. By doing so, the speech-language pathologist can determine how well the student is making use of his or her AAC device in the community, while the O&M specialist observes travel techniques in a local store. At the same time, the O&M specialist can glean additional ideas on how to promote communication in the community to benefit the student's ability to solicit information.

The assessment process can be enhanced through collaboration and communication with family members and other professionals to gain broader perspectives and deeper understanding of the student's abilities and potential for independent and semi-independent travel. In determining the overall effectiveness of the O&M program for a given student, both formative (ongoing) and summative (endpoint) assessments should be considered. The teacher of students with visual impairments can contribute to these ongoing assessments through anecdotal and other observations that are shared with the O&M specialist. The O&M specialist and teacher of students with visual impairments can work collaboratively to establish a tracking system for a given O&M skill to be used on campus. For example, the teacher of students with visual impairments can ensure that a student places a tactile sticker on a daily calendar for each day the student remembers to bring his or her long cane to school. This approach provides a concrete method for establishing an ongoing assessment and can be adapted for a wide variety of skill areas.

Whether in regard to communication strategies, use of hearing aids in noisy environments, physical restrictions, or memory aids needed for remembering routes, gathering input from teachers of students with visual impairments, families, and other involved professionals is an important part of planning for assessment. Naturalistic observations, or unannounced observations of O&M skill usage during typical times of day, are another important tool for gathering assessment information. In Emily's case, the O&M specialist, teacher of students with visual impairments, and physical therapist coordinated their schedules in order to conduct a naturalistic observation of Emily's use of her power wheelchair. By observing her use of the chair during transition from her general education classroom to the cafeteria area, they were able to observe the challenges that she experienced maneuvering the chair during a crowded transition period (both related to her skill level and the behaviors and reactions of her peers) and make an appropriate recommendation.

Similar to all O&M assessments, assessment materials will need to be gathered, assessment areas and routes preplanned, and assessment tools and checklists selected. For students with multiple disabilities, O&M specialists will need to ensure that all devices or auxiliary aids are in good working order (for example, the AAC device is properly charged or the hearing aids are brought to school) prior to starting the assessment. In addition, the general health of the student should be considered and alternative assessment dates and times planned for instances in which a student's health fluctuates frequently. O&M specialists will want to assess students on days that represent their fullest potential and to make any notes about health status, stamina, and well-being on days on which assessments are conducted. For example, when assessing a student who has a visual impairment and a mild hearing loss, it should be noted if the student reports having a head cold, which may negatively impact his or her ability to clearly hear traffic sounds at a given intersection on that particular day. Results should be compared once the student is feeling better to ensure accurate results.

In addition to collaborating with other professionals on planned assessments, there may be instances when a student works with a one-to-one adult assistant and that assistant is present for the assessment either as an observer or participant. A one-to-one adult assistant might be an observer who only provides support as needed, such as performing aspiration (suction) or assisting with handling to transition the student from the vehicle to the wheelchair once the team arrives in the community. As a participant, the one-to-one assistant might facilitate communication using an AAC device or assist in operating a manual wheelchair on campus so that the O&M specialist can assess the student's level of participation in the orientation process as the two move about on the school campus.

While the basic elements of quality O&M assessments remain the same, the role of the teacher of students with visual impairments and involvement of other professionals provide a framework for considering the complex needs for supporting communication, behavior, and the use of other mobility devices when planning and conducting assessments with students with visual impairments and multiple disabilities.

O&M Program Planning

With assessment results in hand, O&M specialists, with input from teachers of students with visual impairments, can create an O&M program that:

- emphasizes skills that will help the child function in a range of environments (such as increasing sound localization skills to help the student locate the drinking fountain)
- enhances the student's levels of independence in getting from one place to another (such as from classroom to bathroom, home to bus stop, or school to after-school community activity)
- increases participation in activities at home, school, and community (such as improving mobility skills on the playground to increase play with others)
- improves overall quality of life (such as encouraging self-determination for transition planning through exposure to a wider range of community activity options)

Not only should the O&M program plan lead to greater levels of independent travel for the student, but it should also support other areas of the ECC such as activities of daily living, communication, use of technology (including GPS), and career readiness. The O&M specialist shares responsibility for these areas of the ECC with the teacher of students with visual impairments, and when O&M goals are discussed and established collaboratively, the opportunity for alignment and reinforcement is enhanced. Creating O&M goals that are easily measured and that have an impact on daily functioning helps the student, teacher of students with visual impairments, family, O&M specialist, and other members of the team readily see the benefits of O&M instruction. In Emily's case, the O&M specialist used a task analysis to determine the skill set that Emily would need to independently operate her power wheelchair. Each success led Emily to the ultimate goal of increased independence in getting around her school campus.

Whether a student's O&M services are provided through direct instruction or consultation, the teacher of students with visual impairments can be assured that the O&M specialist is an essential member of the student's educational team. The frequency (number of lessons or consultative visits per week or month) and duration (number of minutes or hours per lesson or contact) of O&M services are determined based on a student's need and benefit. Services are not determined based on caseload size, availability of the O&M specialist, cost, or convenience. For teachers of students with visual impairments who are dually certified as O&M specialists, the plan for service delivery can be especially challenging due to the presence of students' competing needs. For example, O&M lessons may be planned twice per week, but in the event that the student is having a challenge in an academic class that needs to be addressed, the dual-certified professional may try to juggle the schedule to better meet the student's most immediate needs.

As noted in Chapter 2, the *Visual Impairment Scale of Service Intensity of Texas* (VISSIT; Pogrund, Darst, & Munro, 2015;

Texas School for the Blind and Visually Impaired, 2015) is one tool that teachers of students with visual impairments can use to gauge the service needs of their students. Similarly, the *Orientation and Mobility Severity Rating Scale for Students with Additional Needs* (O&MSRS+; Michigan Department of Education, 2013) can be used to help determine the O&M service needs of students. This scale uses eight categories related to O&M to help determine need and frequency of service, as well as mode of service delivery (direct service versus consultation). These types of validated scales can provide teachers with dual certification with a means for making recommendations for services in both areas for students with visual impairments and multiple disabilities. Such tools provide consistent guidance to IEP teams in making these important educational decisions.

Supporting Positive Behaviors for O&M

In addition to her visual impairment and motor challenges, Angelica is working to increase her receptive and expressive communication skills. She interacts with other children in her class, but frequently engages in aggressive behaviors such as pulling hair and biting others when she doesn't receive attention. She currently needs adult assistance to get to the playground and is focused on solitary time spent on the swing without exploring other play apparatus options.

Students with visual impairments and multiple disabilities may engage in behaviors that have an impact on educational engagement and put the student's or others' health and safety at risk. While challenging, these behaviors are attempts at communication, even when they consist of acts of aggression to the self, others, and property. These behaviors can be of particular concern during O&M lessons as the O&M specialist is often within close proximity to the student; therefore, the O&M specialist can become a target of aggression or be injured indirectly. In addition, O&M instruction is often carried out within the community, which may result in a reduction of additional staff or important environmental supports. Community-based instruction is also subject to a less predictable learning environment, which may, for some students, create additional anxiety and result in increased behavioral expressions.

To support positive behaviors, the school psychologist assesses students with such behavioral difficulties and behavior plans are created often based on the function of the behavior. The psychologist, in collaboration with others, determines *why* the student is engaging in the behavior (for example, is the behavior an attempt to seek attention, escape or avoid an activity, an expression of fear or frustration?). Next, a behavioral intervention plan is created that addresses both the why of the behavior and the behavior itself (see Figure 9.1 for a sample behavioral intervention plan form). Each member of the team, including the teacher of students with visual impairments, is expected to be familiar with the behavioral intervention plan and how, when, and why to implement it. To meet this expectation, teachers of students with visual impairments need to have planned frequent contact with the student's psychologist. Frequent meetings will ensure that the teacher of students with visual impairments is following the student's behavioral intervention plan, and that the student's progress and regression are addressed appropriately and expediently. (Chapter 13 discusses positive strategies for intervention with challenging behaviors in-depth.)

In addition to following the behavioral intervention plan, the teacher of students with visual impairments can use the following practical suggestions and strategies to protect the student and increase personal safety:

- Know the student, including his or her disposition, current level of fatigue, and means for communicating needs.
- Speak with the student and others prior to each lesson to learn how the student's behavior or mood was prior to the lesson.
- Describe the upcoming lesson to the student and gauge his or her response.

When working with a student who displays a particular behavior, it is helpful for the teacher of students with visual impairments to have a few strategies for student protection and self-protection while following through with the lesson (see Sidebar 9.8), as in the following example:

The O&M specialist for 4-year-old Angelica meets with the school psycholo-

Figure 9.1

Sample Positive Behavioral Intervention Plan Form

BEHAVIORAL INTERVENTION PLAN

Student _____ Age _____ Sex _____

Teacher(s) _____ Grade _____

Case Manager _____ Date(s) _____

Reason for intervention plan:

Participants (specify names):

☐ student _____	☐ special education administrator _____
☐ family member _____	☐ general education administrator _____
☐ special educator _____	☐ school psychologist _____
☐ general educator _____	☐ other agency personnel _____
☐ peer(s) _____	_____

☐ other (specify) _____

_____

Fact Finding

1. **General learning environment:** Describe the student's school class schedule, including any special programs or services.

2. **Problem behavior:** Define the problem behavior(s) in observable, measurable, and countable terms (such as topography, event, duration, seriousness, and/or intensity). Include several examples of the behavior.

3. **Setting events:** Describe important things that are happening in the student's life that may be causing the behavior(s) of concern.

4. **Review existing data:** Summarize previously collected information (records review, interviews, observations, and test results) relevant to the behavior(s). Attach additional sheets if necessary.

(continued)

(Figure 9.1 continued)

Possible Explanations

5. Identify likely antecedents (precipitating events) to the behavior(s).

6. Identify likely consequences that may be maintaining the behavior(s).

7. Identify and describe any academic or environmental context(s) in which the problem behavior(s) does <u>not</u> occur.

Validation

8. **Functional assessment:** Do you already have enough information to believe that the possible explanations are sufficient to plan an intervention?

   If yes, skip to Step 9.

   If no, what additional data collection is necessary?
   - ( ) review of IEP goals and objectives
   - ( ) review of medical records
   - ( ) review of previous intervention plans
   - ( ) review of incident reports
   - ( ) ABC (antecedent, behavior, and consequence, across time and situations)
   - ( ) motivational analysis
   - ( ) ecological analysis
   - ( ) curricular analysis
   - ( ) scatter plot
   - ( ) parent questionnaire/interview
   - ( ) student questionnaire/interview
   - ( ) teacher questionnaire/interview (specify who) _____
   - ( ) other (explain) _____

   Summarize data. Attach additional sheets if necessary.

Planning

9. **Formulate hypothesis statement:** Using the table below, determine why the student engages in problem behavior(s), whether the behavior(s) serves single or multiple functions, and what to do about the behavior(s). *Internal* refers to behaviors driven by feelings or emotions. *External* refers to behaviors driven by outside sources.

	Internal	External	Intervention
Obtain something	1. 2.	1.	
Avoid something	1. 2.	1.	

10. **Current level of performance:** Describe problem behavior(s) in such a way that the team will be able to recognize onset and conclusion of behavior.

11. **Replacement behaviors:** Describe replacement behavior(s) that is likely to serve the same function as the behavior(s) identified in Step 9.

12. **Measurement procedures for problem behavior(s) and replacement behavior(s):**
    a. Describe how (such as permanent products, event recording, or scatter plot), when, and where student behavior(s) will be measured.

    b. Summarize data by specifying which problem behavior(s) and replacement behavior(s) will be targets for intervention.

13. **Behavioral intervention plan:**
    a. Specify goals and objectives (conditions, criteria for acceptable performance) for teaching the replacement behavior(s).

    b. Specify instructional strategies that will be used to teach the replacement behavior(s).

    c. Specify strategies that will be used to decrease problem behavior(s) and increase replacement behavior(s).

gist to discuss the results of Angelica's functional behavioral analysis, which was conducted because of her behavior of biting others. It is determined through the functional analysis that Angelica was possibly resorting to biting out of frustration, presumably as a result of difficulties with expressive communication. The speech-language pathologist collaborates with the team to develop a

---

Sidebar 9.8

Strategies and Suggestions for Working with Students Who Have Behavioral Difficulties

Plan for success by knowing:

- your student's moods and behaviors
- the antecedents of the student's behavior, such as increase in vocalizations or agitation
- triggers of the student's behavior, such as noisy environments, hot weather, and thirst
- reinforcers, such as verbal praise, a high five, and stickers
- the student's individual likes and dislikes

To reduce, avoid, or mitigate a student's biting or scratching:

- wear a jacket of sturdy material such as denim or leather for protection (if the student engages in the behavior of biting or scratching him- or herself

during lessons, the student should wear an appropriate lightweight jacket to protect him- or herself)

To reduce, avoid, or mitigate a student's hair pulling:

- wear a baseball cap
- avoid wearing ponytails
- avoid dangling jewelry or name badges

To reduce, avoid, or mitigate a student's aggression or striking out:

- maintain adequate space from the student when agitated
- distract the student
- anticipate the possibility of aggression by knowing student's antecedents and triggers

---

replacement behavior that would increase Angelica's expressive communication competence, thereby decreasing her frustration and eliminating the biting behavior. The teacher of students with visual impairments and the O&M specialist receive training in implementing the behavior plan (what to do when Angelica becomes frustrated or engages in the behavior), embedding the expressive communication goal within instruction, and beginning to wear a lightweight denim jacket for lessons during which Angelica might become frustrated.

Opportunities for Practice and Application of O&M Skills in School, Home, and Community

The importance of practicing and applying O&M skills in daily routines for the maintenance and generalization of skills cannot be overemphasized when working with students who have visual impairments and multiple disabilities. Teachers of students with visual impairments, families, and other professionals can assist in planning for practice and application of essential elements of the O&M program that may not typically happen without a routine or a team plan. For example, Angelica's O&M specialist makes sure to build in practice and application of O&M skills with Angelica by involving family members in O&M lessons that fit within natural routines, such as using her cane to find changes in walking surfaces at the local neighborhood park frequented by her family or pushing the laundry basket from the bathroom to the laundry area while noting the changes in sounds from carpeted areas to linoleum as the basket scrapes along the floor. Checklists and tactile markers can be used to keep track of practice or application routes on a weekly basis.

MOBILITY TOOLS, ORIENTATION DEVICES, AND COMMUNICATION DEVICES

Children with visual impairments and multiple disabilities use a range and combination of mobility tools, orientation devices, and communication devices for independent or semi-independent travel. This section will highlight adaptations, strategies, and instructional considerations that may be used with children who have visual impairments and multiple disabilities. It is not intended to provide a comprehensive description of the available mobility tools, orientation devices, and communication devices. (For more information, see the Resources section at the end of this chapter.)

Mobility Tools

Many students with visual impairments, including those with multiple disabilities, travel using human guide techniques, long canes, dog guides, AMDs, electronic travel aids (ETAs), or ambulatory aids. A student may use one or more of these travel methods, many of which require adaptations to best meet the individual needs of each student. The choice of a travel method depends on numerous factors, such as the age of the student, the nature of the student's disabilities, his or her personal and family preferences, and the student's safety and travel needs. Teachers of students with visual impairments will want to work with O&M specialists to ensure that they are familiar and comfortable with these tools in order to effectively reinforce skill development in the school environment.

Human Guide Techniques

Some children with visual impairments and multiple disabilities require adaptations to standard guide techniques, although a detailed description of guide techniques is beyond the scope of this chapter. See Sidebar 9.9 for a list of commonly used human guide adaptations for children and individuals with multiple disabilities.

Long Canes

Many students with visual impairments use long canes, which facilitate independent travel by providing a preview of objects and surfaces in the travel path (LaGrow, 2010). Some students with multiple disabilities can benefit from adaptations to the long cane and techniques for its use, such as the following:

Adaptations to Human Guide Techniques

The following are some adaptations to human guide techniques that can be used with children in various situations:

- **Preschool-age children:** The child grasps one or two of the guide's fingers.
- **School-age children:** The child holds on to the guide's wrist or arm below the elbow.
- **Children who display aggressive behaviors:** The guide wears gloves or a thick jacket for protection.
- **Children with balance difficulties:**
  - The child links one arm between the guide's arm and body, holding on to the guide's forearm for extra support.
  - The guide makes sure that the child stands on the appropriate side of the guide to facilitate maximum support.
- **Children who use one cane or crutch:** The child uses the traditional human guide grasp by holding on to the guide's arm with the free hand.
- **Children who use two canes or crutches:**
  - The child grasps the guide's arm with one hand while using one cane or crutch with the other hand.
  - The guide carries the extra cane or crutch, or in some cases, the child carries both canes or crutches with the same hand.
- **Children who use wheelchairs:**
  - The guide provides verbal directions while the child propels the wheelchair.
  - The child in the wheelchair either holds on to the guide's elbow or places one hand on top of the guide's forearm, with the guide holding his or her arm parallel to the floor.
  - A child with low vision who can independently detect drop-offs may choose to follow the guide visually.
- **Children who use walkers:**
  - The guide holds on to the child's elbow, applying light pressure to signal whether to turn right, turn left, or stop.
  - The guide places a hand on the child's back, applying light pressure to the shoulder blade to signal turns.
  - The guide places one hand on top of the child's hand, using tactile signals to signify stopping, starting, and turning.
  - The guide provides verbal directions, such as "turn right," "turn left," and "stop."

Source: Based on Rosen, S., & Crawford, J. S. (2010). Teaching orientation and mobility to learners with visual, physical, and health impairments. In W. R. Wiener, R. L. Welsh, & B. B. Blasch (Eds.), *Foundations of orientation and mobility: Volume II. Instructional strategies and practical applications* (3rd ed., pp. 564–623). New York: AFB Press.

- modifying the cane's grip to make it easier to grasp
- modifying the cane's tip to provide additional tactile feedback or making it easier to move from side to side
- prescribing a longer cane to increase the coverage area
- teaching students to use a modified diagonal technique
- exploring use of the long cane in conjunction with an ambulatory aid, such as a wheelchair

As described earlier in the chapter, Tony's O&M instruction involves learning basic cane techniques on his elementary school campus. Tony had difficulty with cane control when using the two-point touch technique, but had greater success learning to use the constant-contact technique. Even with the new technique, Tony's teacher of students with visual impairments and O&M specialist noticed that Tony's arc width was inconsistent, causing him to occasionally bump into objects. Tony works on his cane movement during O&M lessons, and all team members reinforce his skills using consistent verbal prompts.

Dog Guides

Few dog guide schools have programs that serve individuals with visual impairments and multiple disabilities. Information about dog guide schools that serve students with multiple disabilities is included in the Resources section at the end of this chapter. Teachers of students with visual impairments and O&M specialists may share this information and these resources with families of students with visual impairments and multiple disabilities, as appropriate.

Adaptive Mobility Devices

The O&M specialist determines that Angelica will benefit from the use of a long cane to provide advance warning of obstacles and walking surface changes, but her reaction time is slow and she is not able to firmly grasp the cane grip independently. The O&M specialist prescribes an AMD, which provides greater protection from obstacles and is easier for Angelica to grasp. On Wednesdays, O&M lessons are at school and focus on Angelica using her AMD to get from her classroom to the playground during that natural transition time at school.

Since Angelica began using her AMD, her O&M specialist and teacher of students with visual impairments notice a gradual improvement in her balance and posture. On the playground, Angelica spends less time on the swings and uses the AMD to explore new areas as her confidence increases. Once her grip strength, balance, and reaction time improve, Angelica's O&M specialist will begin transitioning her to using a long cane.

AMDs are devices (typically constructed from PVC pipe) that individuals push on the ground in front of them in a similar manner to a walker. Unlike long canes, AMDs provide information about obstacles and surface changes in the area in front of a child's body without the need to move the device from side to side. AMDs are sometimes used in place of long canes for early O&M development to encourage independent movement and exploration. For students with visual impairments and motor impairments, AMDs promote safe travel and optimal gait patterns and posture (Glanzman & Ducret, 2003).

Electronic Travel Aids

A small percentage of students with visual impairments use ETAs. ETAs are electronic devices that provide environmental information through auditory and tactile feedback. ETAs facilitate concept development by providing information about the world that is beyond the reach of traditional mobility devices (Penrod, Smith, Haneline, & Corbett, 2010). Some students with visual impairments and multiple disabilities use ETAs with long canes or ambulatory aids to access information about the environment, such as obstacles, landmarks, and doorways or other open spaces.

Ambulatory Aids

Emily's O&M lessons are scheduled after school on the high school campus so Emily doesn't miss any academic subjects and fall further behind on her studies. The O&M lessons begin with Emily using a manual wheelchair, which the O&M specialist pushes, turns, and stops on Emily's command. Emily's focus is to describe what she sees in front of her and to the sides, predicting turns and stops. Once Emily is able to consistently predict turns and stops along key routes, she and the O&M specialist work with the power chair at its lowest speed until Emily is confident and consistent in its use.

Through practice and repetition, Emily becomes more comfortable maneuvering her motorized wheelchair on her high school campus. Emily's O&M specialist, with guidance from the physical therapist, attaches curb feelers to the front wheels of the wheelchair to help Emily detect objects on the sides. Emily's teacher of students with visual impairments notices that Emily occasionally has difficulty visually judging the depth of drop-offs, especially in situations with poor lighting. The teacher informs the O&M specialist, who wants to introduce a long cane to help Emily in these situations of uncertainty. In prescribing a long cane, Emily's O&M specialist considers the width of the wheelchair and Emily's ability to detect obstacles and react in time to stop at a safe distance. Due to her hemiplegia, Emily is initially unable to control both the long cane and the wheelchair at the same time. With input from Emily, the team—including the teacher of students with visual impairments, O&M specialist, and physical therapist—devise a solution that allows Emily to use the long cane and her wheelchair.

Some students with visual impairments and multiple disabilities use ambulatory aids, such as wheelchairs, scooters, walkers, crutches, and orthopedic canes (Rosen & Crawford, 2010). Canes, crutches, and walkers provide support on one or both sides of a student's body to improve balance, stability, and endurance. Manual and motorized wheelchairs provide full support for some students with physical disabilities, but produce orientation challenges due to a decrease in the student's tactile contact with the environment. See Sidebar 9.10 for orientation strategies for students who use wheelchairs.

Ambulatory aids facilitate independent or semi-independent movement and give students with physical disabilities greater access to the environment. A walker held in front of a student provides some protection from obstacles, but ambulatory aids do not provide adequate protection from obstacles and drop-offs. Ambulatory aids can be used along with a long cane or ETA to provide information about the environment (Rosen & Crawford, 2010). The O&M specialist traditionally prescribes mobility devices, such as the long cane, while ambulatory aids are typically prescribed and fitted by the physical therapist (Glanzman & Ducret, 2003). A team approach is beneficial when a child has needs that overlap the two professions.

Orientation Devices

Four-year-old Angelica uses her Trekker Breeze (a handheld, accessible GPS device) in the car on the way home from school. Angelica has not learned all of the functions of the GPS device, but she enjoys pressing the buttons and listening to the auditory feedback. This type of exploration exposes her to information such as street names and landmarks, the same items that a 4-year-old child without a visual impairment ac-

cesses by looking out of the car window. When Angelica arrives at home with her family, she is excited to create a landmark at the entrance by using the device to record herself saying, "I'm home!"

Before her accident, Emily used an iPad to read school textbooks, browse the Internet, and listen to music. Built-in accessibility features allow Emily to continue using the iPad after the accident. Through lessons with her teacher of students with visual impairments, Emily learns how to adjust the font size, magnification, and contrast on the iPad. The teacher of students with visual impairments also teaches Emily to use the iPad's dictation feature to prepare a grocery list, as she tires easily when typing with one hand. For future lessons, Emily will learn to use her iPad to plan bus routes by using the transit company's website and an electronic maps application to get the information needed to travel to the grocery store.

Numerous orientation devices are available to support the travel needs of students with visual impairments and multiple disabilities. Teachers of students with visual impairments may also incorporate orientation devices and cues within their classrooms. Orientation cues in the classroom might include tactile cues, such as a personalized bell above a storage cubby or a large-print sign to indicate the north wall of the classroom. Orientation devices that support O&M may include:

✏ Sidebar 9.10

Strategies and Suggestions for Promoting O&M for Students Who Use Wheelchairs

Discussions among the teacher of students with visual impairments, O&M specialist, physical therapist, occupational therapist, and other educational team members are essential for fostering uniformity in travel routines, student safety, and consistent expectations for independent or semi-independent travel for students who use wheelchairs. Considerations may include:

- alerting students to orientation information, such as turns and landmarks, to promote active participation and environmental control
- allowing students who are unable to propel a wheelchair independently to exercise control over their environment by providing directions to destinations, for example, "turn left at the water fountain"
- informing the O&M specialist and physical therapist of situations where students have difficulty detecting obstacles or drop-offs during day-to-day travel
- discussing the possibility of having the maximum speed of the motorized wheelchair adjusted by the manufacturer

Teachers of students with visual impairments and other professionals should be aware of the following strategies and adaptations that may be used to promote O&M for children with visual impairments who use wheelchairs:

- use of longer footrests to prevent accidental injury to students' feet
- use of a lap tray as a "bumper" for waist-height obstacle detection
- attachment of curb feelers—flexible wires that stick out to the sides of the chair—to the front wheels to provide warning of objects on the sides
- modification of the hand trailing technique (for example, use of a patting technique in place of sliding the hand) to prevent injury to students who use motorized wheelchairs
- use of a rigid cane with a roller tip, if appropriate, as prescribed by the O&M specialist
- adjustment of cane length to accommodate the width of a wheelchair or the increased speed of a motorized wheelchair, as determined by the O&M specialist

Sources: Based on Bozeman, L., & McCulley, R. M. (2010). Improving orientation for students with vision loss. In W. R. Wiener, R. L. Welsh, & B. B. Blasch (Eds.), *Foundations of orientation and mobility: Volume II. Instructional strategies and practical applications* (3rd ed., pp. 27–53). New York: AFB Press; and Rosen, S., & Crawford, J. S. (2010). Teaching orientation and mobility to learners with visual, physical, and health impairments. In W. R. Wiener, R. L. Welsh, & B. B. Blasch (Eds.), *Foundations of orientation and mobility: Volume II. Instructional strategies and practical applications* (3rd ed., pp. 564–623). New York: AFB Press.

- auditory, tactile, web-based, electronic, and large-print maps
- tactile (or three-dimensional) models
- global positioning systems (GPS)
- optical devices, such as magnifiers, telescopes, and video magnifiers
- large-print, braille, or talking compasses

Functional Considerations

When exploring options for orientation devices, the team should consider how a given device would promote environmental access for the student. Consider the student's cognitive functioning, motor skills, and preferred learning media (visual, tactile, auditory). Teachers of students with visual impairments can consult with O&M specialists to discuss orientation challenges that a student may experience at school, and the two professionals can work together to find an appropriate solution or tool. Independent use of electronic orientation devices (such as GPS or electronic maps) requires problem-solving skills and the ability to seek alternative options if a device gives incorrect directions or does not work properly. These skills should be included in evaluations, taught through explicit instruction, and practiced in authentic travel situations.

Practical Considerations

The team should also consider built-in options and add-ons to devices the student is already comfortable using. For example, touch tablets and accessible personal digital assistants often have built-in GPS capabilities and devices such as mobile phones and touch tablets may have built-in compasses. A software upgrade or application download may provide this added functionality without requiring students to learn and manage a new device. The selection of an orientation device must be based on the student's needs and goals. External factors, such as the availability of a device or the O&M specialist's familiarity with a device, are not considerations in the selection process.

Orientation devices are used in real travel situations and are therefore subjected to adverse weather conditions, drops, spills, and other inevitable accidents. Accordingly, a protective case is an essential consideration for most devices. Furthermore, coordinating numerous O&M devices can easily become an unwieldy juggling act for students. Advanced planning and foresight by the teacher of students with visual impairments, O&M specialist, and other team members can ease this burden. Students need a place to store orientation devices when otherwise occupied with travel tasks. For example, orientation devices may be stored in a hands-free carrying case, a backpack, or on a mount attached to a wheelchair or other ambulatory aid. Any adaptations to ambulatory aids should be made in collaboration with the physical therapist to ensure that the function and safety of the device is not compromised. Students who are cane users will need to develop a strategy for managing the cane while using orientation devices.

Safety and Instructional Considerations

Overreliance on an orientation device can be dangerous. The entire team, including the teacher of students with visual impairments,

O&M specialist, and the student, must share a mutual understanding of the purpose, function, and limitations of the device. In general, an orientation device (Phillips, 2011)

- is not a replacement for mobility tools or foundational O&M skills;
- may be introduced at an early age to allow a child to gain familiarity with a device through exploration and play; and
- can distract a child from sensory information and mask important environmental sounds.

Instructional considerations that may be especially useful for students who have multiple disabilities include the following:

- Instruction on GPS devices and other electronic orientation devices does not have to cover every possible function; even simple functions can provide valuable information to a student (Ponchillia, Rak, Freeland, & LaGrow, 2007).
- Students who have difficulty maintaining focus on the environment while using an orientation device should stop ambulating while interacting with the device.
- Students should not use headphones during outdoor travel (Phillips, 2011).
- Students must be cognizant of appropriate and inappropriate places to stop when using a device.

Promoting the Use of Orientation Devices through Collaboration

Collaboration is essential to encourage functional use of orientation devices in natural settings.

Tony's team uses a collaborative approach to support functional monocular use in multiple environments. Tony's teacher of students with visual impairments introduced him to the monocular, and he uses it in the classroom to view assignments on the blackboard. When Tony goes into the community with his family, they encourage him to bring his monocular. As Tony progresses through his O&M instruction, he will work with his O&M specialist to use the monocular to view menu boards at restaurants. The teacher of students with visual impairments and O&M specialist keep each other updated on Tony's progress in these differing environments.

Teachers of students with visual impairments and other team members need a working knowledge of orientation devices to support student use during functional routines. Training may be provided to the team by the O&M specialist through methods such as informal consultations, presentations, or written materials. A "cheat sheet" of commonly used functions and commands may be shared with all team members who provide support to a student (Phillips, 2011). Teachers of students with visual impairments and O&M specialists can work together to synchronize the incorporation of technology, such as low vision devices, into lessons. Team members should be careful to use consistent terminology when referring to orientation devices to minimize confusion. Sidebar 9.11 provides a list of questions that the team may wish to discuss when a student begins using an orientation device. The questions are by no means exhaustive and are not intended to replace comprehensive assessment by trained professionals.

Family members, teachers of students with visual impairments, and other professionals can support functional use of orientation devices by informing the O&M specialist in advance of field trips, family vacations, and other community outings. The O&M specialist can work with the student ahead of time on skills that may be used during the outing, including preparing a tactile map of the area, teaching the student to generate directions to a new destination, reviewing monocular techniques, or teaching GPS commands for use in a vehicle. Integration of orientation devices into naturalistic settings facilitates learning and increases students' confidence and self-efficacy. For additional information about GPS systems, electronic maps, AMDs, tactile maps, ETAs, and talking pedometers, see the Resources section at the end of this chapter.

Communication Devices

Some students with visual impairments and multiple disabilities use AAC devices to communicate with others. These devices can be helpful in providing increased access in classroom and travel environments. Teachers of students with visual impairments, O&M specialists, and other professionals must be knowledgeable in the operation of students' AAC devices, and may wish to seek training from the speech-language pathologist. The following is an overview of strategies for supporting students who use AAC systems, such as symbols, calendar boxes, communication boards, communication cards, and electronic devices. (See Chapter 7 for a more detailed discussion of communication devices.)

Sidebar 9.11

Considerations for the Selection and Use of Orientation Devices

The following are considerations for the educational team to discuss regarding a student's use of an orientation device:

1. Did the teacher of students with visual impairments, O&M specialist, and other team members consider how the orientation aid will support the student's IEP goals?
2. Were decisions based on the student's needs and not on the availability of devices or the expertise of professionals?
3. What orientation options are available in the devices the student already has?
4. How will the team promote the use of orientation aids during natural routines?
5. Does the student have sufficient O&M skills without reliance on the device?
6. Which safety rules does the team need to enforce?
7. What type of protective covering or case is needed?
8. How will the student carry the device while managing a long cane or ambulatory aid?
9. What type of training is necessary for team members and how will this training be provided?
10. How will team members collaborate to facilitate functional use of the device in appropriate settings?

Students with language impairments may use symbols (or object cues) to communicate with others (Lolli, Sauerburger, & Bourquin, 2010). Symbols, in the form of real objects, photographs, pictures, or abstract signals, help students indicate their desires and anticipate upcoming events (Lolli et al., 2010). For example, a transit pass may be used to indicate an upcoming transition to a bus lesson with the O&M specialist.

Calendar boxes consist of a series of interconnected compartments in which object symbols are placed to represent activities that students engage in throughout the day. Calendar boxes are used with some students with language impairments and those who are deafblind to convey the sequence of daily activities (Lolli et al., 2010). The teacher of students with visual impairments, speech-language pathologist, and O&M specialist can collaborate to integrate O&M-related symbols into students' calendar boxes to help students anticipate O&M lessons and transitions between activities.

Students may also use communication boards in classroom and O&M contexts to express their desires by pointing to representative symbols. Communication boards may be used to:

- facilitate choice making for classroom and O&M activities
- promote student interactions with the teacher of students with visual impairments or O&M specialist during lessons
- present lesson instructions, such as the sequence of a route

- check for student understanding by providing an enhanced means for expressive communication

Consistency in the use of communication boards is important for improving expressive communication, and teachers of students with visual impairments, O&M specialists, families, and other professionals working together with this tool can provide an optimum learning opportunity.

Students who are deafblind may use communication cards and signs to interact with the public during O&M–related tasks. Students can use communication cards to locate businesses, find specific areas or items in stores, order food at restaurants, use public transportation, and cross streets (Bourquin & Sauerburger, 2005). Students with visual impairments and multiple disabilities may also use a vast assortment of electronic devices to facilitate communication. (See Chapter 12 for additional information about electronic devices.) Sidebar 9.12 contains strategies and suggestions for integrating AAC devices into O&M tasks.

The prior section introduced a selection of tools and technologies for promoting mobility, orientation, and communication, with an emphasis on how teachers of students with visual impairments and O&M specialists can work together to consider adaptations, strategies, and instructional plans for students with visual impairments and multiple disabilities. Conferences, workshops, websites, electronic discussion groups, podcasts, and professional journal articles are excellent resources for staying informed of new and emerging technologies.

Sidebar 9.12

Strategies and Suggestions for Promoting O&M for Students Who Use AAC Devices

---

- Meet as a team to discuss each student's communication needs.
- Use symbols and object cues in a clear, consistent manner to avoid confusing the student (Lolli et al., 2010).
- Incorporate an O&M–related object, such as a cane tip, into a student's calendar box to promote anticipation of O&M instruction and facilitate smoother transitions between activities.
- Incorporate TTYs into lessons to allow students who are deafblind to plan public transportation trips or solicit information to prepare for trips into the community (Lolli et al., 2010). A TTY is a device that allows people who have a hearing or speech impairment to use the telephone to communicate, by allowing them to type messages back and forth to another individual instead of speaking and listening. Both parties must have a TTY.
- Make communication cards and signs in bright colors and use large, clear fonts to increase visibility to the public (Bourquin & Sauerburger, 2005).
- Facilitate opportunities for students who are deafblind to practice using communication cards in a variety of contexts, such as asking for directions, locating an item at a store, or purchasing a bus ticket.
- Be aware of backup plans for situations where initial communication strategies do not work as planned (Bourquin & Sauerburger, 2005).
- Consult with the speech-language pathologist to learn proper use of AAC devices used by students.

SUMMARY

While the presence of visual impairments and multiple disabilities has a clear impact on the development of students' abilities to get from one place to another, teachers of students with visual impairments and O&M specialists, working with a team that includes students, family members, and appropriate related professionals, can promote the development of O&M for independent and semi-independent travel. Making full use of mobility tools, orientation devices, and communication devices can support mobility and orientation for students with visual impairments and multiple disabilities in home, school, and community settings.

REFERENCES

Ambrose-Zaken, G., Calhoon, C. R., & Keim, J. R. (2010). Teaching orientation and mobility to students with cognitive impairments and vision loss. In W. R. Wiener, R. L.

Welsh, & B. B. Blasch (Eds.), *Foundations of orientation and mobility: Volume II. Instructional strategies and practical applications* (3rd ed., pp. 624–666). New York: AFB Press.

Barrella, K., Besden, C., Crow, N., Greenberg, M. D., Shrieves, G., Smith, K. A., & Vickroy, M. (2011). Striving to provide innovative orientation and mobility services in times of diminishing resources [Practice Report]. *Journal of Visual Impairment & Blindness, 105*(10), 587–590.

Bina, M. J., Naimy, B. J., Fazzi, D. L., & Crouse, R. J. (2010). Administration, assessment, and program planning for orientation and mobility services. In W. R. Wiener, R. L. Welsh, & B. B. Blasch (Eds.), *Foundations of orientation and mobility: Volume I. History and theory* (3rd ed., pp. 389–433). New York: AFB Press.

Bourquin, E., & Sauerburger, D. (2005). Teaching deaf-blind people to communicate and interact with the public: Critical issues for travelers who are deaf-blind. *RE:view, 37*(3), 109–116.

Bozeman, L., & McCulley, R. M. (2010). Improving orientation for students with vision loss. In W. R. Wiener, R. L. Welsh, & B. B. Blasch (Eds.), *Foundations of orientation and mobility: Volume II. Instructional strategies and practical applications* (3rd ed., pp. 27–53). New York: AFB Press.

Brambring, M. (2007). Divergent development of manual skills in children who are blind or sighted. *Journal of Visual Impairment & Blindness, 101*(4), 212–225.

Brauner, D. (2009). Putting orientation back into O&M: Teaching concepts to young students. *Insight: Research and Practice in Visual Impairment and Blindness, 2*(3), 138–143.

Bruder, M. B. (1994). Working with members of other disciplines: Collaboration for success. In M. Wolery & J. S. Wilbers (Eds.), *Including children with special needs in early childhood programs* (pp. 45–70). Washington, DC: National Association for the Education of Young Children.

Fazzi, D. L., & Petersmeyer, B. A. (2001). *Imagining the possibilities: Creative approaches to orientation and mobility instruction for persons who are visually impaired.* New York: AFB Press.

Geruschat, D. R., & Smith, A. J. (2010). Improving the use of low vision for orientation and mobility. In W. R. Wiener, R. L. Welsh, & B. B. Blasch (Eds.), *Foundations of orientation and mobility: Volume II. Instructional strategies and practical applications* (3rd ed., pp. 54–90). New York: AFB Press.

Glanzman, A., & Ducret, W. (2003). Interdisciplinary collaboration in the choice of an adapted mobility device for a child with cerebral palsy and visual impairment [Research Report]. *Journal of Visual Impairment & Blindness, 97*(1), 38–41.

Griffin-Shirley, N., Kelley, P., & Lawrence, B. (2006). *The role of the orientation and mobility specialist in the public school.* Position paper of the Division on Visual Impairments. Arlington, VA: Council for Exceptional Children.

Griffin-Shirley, N., Pogrund, R. L., Smith, D. W., & Duemer, L. (2009). A three-phase qualitative study of dual-certified vision education professionals in the southwestern United States. *Journal of Visual Impairment & Blindness, 103*(6), 354–366.

Grimmett, E. S., Pogrund, R. L., & Griffin-Shirley, N. (2011). A national study of parents' perspectives on dual-certified vision professionals. *Journal of Visual Impairment & Blindness, 105*(4), 211–221.

Hill, E., & Ponder, P. (1976). *Orientation and mobility techniques: A guide for the practitioner.* New York: American Foundation for the Blind.

Ihsen, E., Troester, H., & Brambring, M. (2010). The role of sound in encouraging infants with congenital blindness to reach for objects. *Journal of Visual Impairment & Blindness, 104*(8), 478–488.

Individuals with Disabilities Education Act Amendments of 1997, Pub. L. No. 105-17 (1997).

Individuals with Disabilities Education Improvement Act (IDEA), 20 U.S.C. § 1400 (2004).

Jacobson, W. H. (2013). *The art and science of teaching orientation and mobility to persons with visual impairments* (2nd ed.). New York: AFB Press.

LaGrow, S. J. (2010). Improving perception for orientation and mobility. In W. R. Wiener, R. L. Welsh, & B. B. Blasch (Eds.), *Foundations of orientation and mobility: Volume II. Instructional strategies and practical applications* (3rd ed., pp. 3–26). New York: AFB Press.

Levtzion-Korach, O., Tennenbaum, A., Schnitzer, R., & Ornoy, A. (2000). Early motor development of blind children. *Journal of Paediatrics and Child Health, 36*(3), 226–229.

Lieberman, L. J., & Lepore, M. (1998). Camp abilities: A developmental sports camp for children who are blind and deaf-blind. *Palaestra, 14*(1), 28–31, 46–48.

Lolli, D., Sauerburger, D., & Bourquin, E. A. (2010). Teaching orientation and mobility to students with vision and hearing loss. In W. R. Wiener, R. L. Welsh, & B. B. Blasch (Eds.), *Foundations of orientation and mobility: Volume II. Instructional strategies and practical applications* (3rd ed., pp. 537–563). New York: AFB Press.

Longmuir, P. (1998). Considerations for fitness appraisal, programming, and counseling of individuals with sensory impairments. *Canadian Journal of Applied Physiology, 23*(2), 166–184.

Martin, S., & Kessler, M. (2007). *Neurologic interventions for physical therapy* (2nd ed.). St. Louis, MO: Saunders.

Michigan Department of Education, Low Incidence Outreach (2013). *The Michigan orientation and mobility severity rating scale for students with additional needs.* Lansing, MI: Author. Retrieved from https://mdelio.org/sites/default/files/documents/BVI/SRS/OMSRS+.pdf

Penrod, W. M., Smith, D. L., Haneline, R., & Corbett, M. P. (2010). Teaching the use of electronic travel aids and electronic orientation aids. In W. R. Wiener, R. L. Welsh, & B. B. Blasch (Eds.), *Foundations of orientation and mobility: Volume II. Instructional strategies and practical applications* (3rd ed., pp. 462–485). New York: AFB Press.

Phillips, C. L. (2011). Getting from here to there and knowing where: Teaching global positioning systems to students with visual impairments. *Journal of Visual Impairment & Blindness, 105*(10), 675–680.

Pogrund, R. L., Darst, S., & Munro, M. P. (2015). Initial validation study for a scale used to determine service intensity for itinerant teachers of students with visual impairments. *Journal of Visual Impairment & Blindness, 109*(6), 433–444.

Ponchillia, P. E., Rak, E. C., Freeland, A. L., & LaGrow, S. J. (2007). Accessible GPS: Reorientation and target location among users with visual impairments. *Journal of Visual Impairment & Blindness, 101*(7), 389–401.

Rosen, S. (2010). Improving sensorimotor functioning for orientation and mobility. In W. R. Wiener, R. L. Welsh, & B. B. Blasch (Eds.), *Foundations of orientation and mobility: Volume II. Instructional strategies and practical applications* (3rd ed., pp. 118–137). New York: AFB Press.

Rosen, S., & Crawford, J. S. (2010). Teaching orientation and mobility to learners with visual, physical, and health impairments. In W. R. Wiener, R. L. Welsh, & B. B. Blasch (Eds.), *Foundations of orientation and mobility: Volume II. Instructional strategies and practical applications* (3rd ed., pp. 564–623). New York: AFB Press.

Sapp, W. (2011). Somebody's jumping on the floor: Incorporating music into orientation and mobility for preschoolers with visual impairments [Practice Report]. *Journal of Visual Impairment & Blindness, 105*(10), 715–719.

Sapp, W., & Hatlen, P. (2010). The expanded core curriculum: Where we have been, where we are going, and how we can get there. *Journal of Visual Impairment & Blindness, 104*(6), 338–348.

Silberman, R. K., & Sacks, S. Z. (2007). *Expansion of the role of the teacher of students with visual impairments: Providing for students who also have severe/multiple disabilities.* Position paper of the Division on Visual Impairments. Arlington, VA: Council for Exceptional Children.

Skellenger, A. C., & Sapp, W. K. (2010). Teaching orientation and mobility for the early childhood years. In W. R. Wiener, R. L. Welsh, & B. B. Blasch (Eds.), *Foundations of orientation and mobility: Volume II. Instructional strategies and practical applications* (3rd ed., pp. 163–207). New York: AFB Press.

Spungin, S. J., & Ferrell, K. A. (2007). *The role and function of the teacher of students with visual impairments.* Position paper of the Division on Visual Impairments. Arlington, VA: Council for Exceptional Children.

Strickling, C. A., & Pogrund, R. L. (2002). Motor focus. In R. L. Pogrund & D. L. Fazzi (Eds.), *Early focus: Working with young children who are blind or visually impaired and their families* (2nd ed., pp. 287–325). New York: AFB Press.

Stuart, M. E., Lieberman, L., & Hand, K. E. (2006). Beliefs about physical activity among children who are visually impaired and their parents. *Journal of Visual Impairment & Blindness, 100*(4), 223–234.

Texas School for the Blind and Visually Impaired. (2015). *VISSIT: Visual impairment scale of service intensity of Texas.* Austin, TX: Author. Retrieved from http://www.tsbvi.edu/vissit

RESOURCES

For additional resources, see the General Resources section at the back of this book.

Rating Scales

Orientation and Mobility Severity Rating Scale for Students with Additional Needs (O&MSRS+)
Michigan Department of Education, Low Incidence Outreach
https://mdelio.org/blind-visually-impaired/severity-rating-scales

Can be used to help determine the O&M service needs of students. Eight categories related to O&M are used to help determine need and frequency of service, as well as mode of service delivery (direct service versus consultation).

Visual Impairment Scale of Service Intensity of Texas (VISSIT)
Texas School for the Blind and Visually Impaired, Outreach Programs
www.tsbvi.edu/vissit

Designed to guide teachers of students with visual impairments in determining the type and amount of itinerant services to recommend for students on their caseloads. It provides a multidimensional tool for determining service delivery, uniquely including family support as a component of service delivery.

Dog Guide Schools

The following dog guide schools have programs specifically for students with multiple disabilities.

Guide Dogs for the Blind
California
350 Los Ranchitos Road
San Rafael, CA 94903
(415) 499-4000; (800) 295-4050
Fax: (415) 499-4035

Oregon
32901 S.E. Kelso Road
Boring, OR 97009
(503) 668-2100
Fax: (503) 668-2141
information@guidedogs.com
www.guidedogs.com

Guide Dogs of the Desert
60735 Dillon Road
Whitewater, CA 90062
(760) 329-6257; (888) 883-0022
www.guidedogsofthedesert.org

Guiding Eyes for the Blind
611 Granite Springs Road
Yorktown Heights, NY 10598
(914) 245-4024; (800) 942-0149
Fax: (914) 245-1609
www.guidingeyes.org

Leader Dogs for the Blind
1039 S. Rochester Road
Rochester Hills, MI 48307-3115
(248) 651-9011; (888) 777-5332
TTY: (248) 651-3713
leaderdog@leaderdog.org
http://leaderdog.org

Southeastern Guide Dogs
4210 77th Street East
Palmetto, FL 34221
(941) 729-5665; (800) 944-3647
www.guidedogs.org

Websites and Articles

Anticipators for Young Children with Visual Impairments: Push Toys, Pre-canes, and Long Canes
http://www.wonderbaby.org/articles/anticipators

Describes the benefits of anticipators, or adaptive mobility devices (AMDs), choosing the right device and the advantages and disadvantages of each, and provides general guidelines in teaching skills with the devices.

Games that Enhance the O&M Experience for Children
Professional Development and Research Institute on Blindness
www.pdrib.com/pages/omgames.php

Provides a list of games and activities to enhance the O&M experience for children.

Mobility Devices for Young Children
www.afb.org/section.aspx?SectionID=40
&TopicID=168&DocumentID=804

Describes the types of canes and mobility devices that children who are blind or severely visually impaired can learn to use, how to decide which devices or canes to use, and where to obtain these products.

Orientation and Mobility for Visually Impaired Persons with Multiple Disabilities Including Deaf-Blindness
www.sauerburger.org/dona/imc.htm

Offers tips and strategies from three experienced orientation and mobility specialists.

Organizations

For professional organizations, see the General Resources section at the back of this book.

Sources of Products

Global Positioning Systems

HumanWare
1 UPS Way
P.O. Box 800
Champlain, NY 12919
(800) 722-3393
Fax: (888) 871-4828
info@humanware.com
www.humanware.com

Manufactures and distributes the Trekker Breeze GPS.

Sendero Group
Davis, CA 95616
(888) 757-6810
Fax: (888) 757-6807
orders@senderogroup.com
www.senderogroup.com

Distributes a number of GPS systems, including BrailleNote, Mobile Geo, and Sense Navigation, as well as Sendero PC Maps software.

Adaptive Mobility Devices, Canes, and Accessories

Ambutech
34 DeBaets Street
Winnipeg, MB R2J 3S9
Canada
(204) 667-6635; (800) 561-3340

Fax: (204) 663-9345; (800) 267-5059
orders@ambutech.com
www.ambutech.com

Offers a wide range of mobility and support canes.

SpecialEd Solutions, Inc.
P.O. Box 6218
San Antonio, TX 78209
(877) 324-2533
Fax: (210) 828-3785
info@SpecialEd.com
www.specialed.com/orientationmobility.html

Provides information about pre-canes and where to purchase them.

Tactile Map Supplies

American Printing House for the Blind (APH)
1839 Frankfort Avenue
P.O. Box 6085
Louisville, KY 40206-0085
(502) 895-2405; (800) 223-1839
Fax: (502) 899-2284
info@aph.org
www.aph.org

Manufactures and distributes a wide assortment of products for creating tactile maps, including the Chang Tactual Diagram Kit, Picture Maker: Wheatley Tactile Diagramming Kit, and Wikki Stix. (See also organization listing in the Resources section at the back of this book.)

Electronic Travel Aids

Bat Advanced Technologies
31/7 Saint Vincent Avenue
Remuera, Auckland 1005
New Zealand
+64 9 522 8872
Fax:+64 9 522 8887
inquiries@batforblind.co.nz
www.ksonar.com

Distributes K-Sonar, which enables blind and visually impaired persons to perceive their environment through ultrasound.

LS&S
145 River Rock Drive
Buffalo, NY 14207
(716) 348-3500; (800) 468-4789
TTY: (866) 317-8533
Fax: (877) 498-1482
LSSInfo@LSSproducts.com
www.lssproducts.com

Distributes the Miniguide Mobility Aid, which uses ultrasonic echolocation to detect objects in its vicinity, vibrating based on the distance to objects.

Sound Foresight Technology Limited
40 Freemans Way
Harrogate HG3 1DH
United Kingdom
+44 (0)1423 359711
www.ultracane.com

Manufactures and distributes the UltraCane, an electronic mobility aid that provides mobility assistance to blind and partially sighted people by emitting ultrasonic waves.

Talking Pedometers

Accusplit
7901 Stoneridge Drive, Suite 350
Pleasanton, CA 94588
(800) 935-1996
www.accusplit.com

Distributes an array of pedometers, including talking pedometers.

Sportline
555 Taxter Road, Suite 210
Elmsford, NY 10523
(914) 964-5200
Fax: (914) 964-1283
www.sportline.com

Manufactures and distributes a talking calorie count pedometer.

Chapter **10**

Promoting Social Competence

. . . .

Sharon Z. Sacks

Key Points

✐ The impact of visual impairments and multiple disabilities on social development

✐ Strategies for assessing social skills and emotional well-being

✐ Instructional strategies for teaching social skills and self-determination

---

Eli is a 12-year-old student who has a severe visual impairment due to optic nerve hypoplasia. His visual acuity is 20/800 in both eyes. In addition to his visual impairment, Eli has additional disabilities that include cognitive challenges, behavioral challenges, difficulty regulating body temperature, and endocrine irregularities. Academically, Eli's literacy skills are at the fourth-grade level, while his math abilities are at the first-grade level. He is in a class for students with mild to moderate learning disabilities and is included in a sixth-grade class for social studies, art, music, and special events. Eli receives services from a teacher of students with visual impairments three times per week for an hour-long session each day, and an orientation and mobility (O&M) specialist one time per week for a 60-minute session.

One of Eli's greatest challenges is engaging with peers and adults in an age-appropriate manner. Eli tends to whine when a task becomes too difficult, and then refuses to engage in the activity. Sometimes Eli's behavior becomes disruptive. He will scream or pinch peers or adults. After completing a social skills assessment and observation of Eli in many different environments, the educational team, including Eli's parents, agreed that teaching Eli to express his emotions and to communicate verbally with others were priorities.

The educational team examined the environments in which Eli was susceptible to disruptive behavior and determined that he becomes disruptive when he does not receive immediate attention from others. Also, the team determined that Eli does not have a high enough level of verbal and cognitive sophistication to express his feelings.

The team works with Eli to develop words and phrases to help him express feelings of frustration, loneliness, and anger. They provide him with emotions cards in braille, and practice using role-play scenarios to assist in self-expression. The team also allows Eli to pick a class buddy to help him check or maintain his behavior.

Teaching social skills to students with visual impairments who have multiple disabilities is especially difficult because of the diversity of the population. The range of skill levels and concomitant disabilities represented in this population make it challenging for professionals to create curricula and activities that suit each student. It is critical that individualized programs be established that allow each student to achieve a level of social competence with peers and adults in a variety of settings including the home, school, and community.

While teachers of students with visual impairments and O&M specialists recognize the importance of teaching social skills, they often report that they do not have the time, resources, or support to teach this critical area of the expanded core curriculum (ECC) (Sacks & Wolffe, 2006b; Wolffe & Kelly, 2011).

Rather than focusing their attention on teaching all areas of the ECC, teachers of students with visual impairments are often directed to work with students on compensatory skills to assist students with the acquisition of academic competencies. Even school programs for students with visual impairments and multiple disabilities tend to emphasize support for academic skills rather than encouraging the acquisition of functional skills (Sacks, Blankenship, Douglass, & Kreuzer, 2014). As a result, students with visual impairments and multiple disabilities may not receive regular instruction in social skills. Special education teachers, teachers of students with visual impairments, O&M specialists, related service personnel, and family

members need to work together to create social skills activities that have meaning and are important to the student. Also, when students learn specific social skills in one environment, it is important that these newly learned skills are transferrable to other settings. In order for students to acquire a repertoire of social skills, they need to be given the opportunity to practice them throughout their day with many different people including teachers, assistants, family members, and peers.

For students with visual impairments and multiple disabilities, developing a set of socially competent behaviors and skills may lead to greater independence and social inclusion with others. While visual impairment alone may create social challenges for students, the presence of additional disabilities adds another component that may influence how others interact with and perceive the abilities of these students. When students exhibit a repertoire of socially engaging behaviors, peers and adults are more likely to engage with and include these students in home, school, or community activities.

The purpose of this chapter is to provide professionals with strategies and activities to support and encourage social inclusion for students with visual impairments and multiple disabilities. While it is important to understand the theoretical basis for teaching social skills and to understand the unique differences in the social development of students with visual impairments and multiple disabilities, the focus of this chapter will be on providing effective methods to enhance the socialization of students with visual impairments and multiple disabilities. Much of what has been written related to the development and instruction of social skills has focused on the needs of students with visual impairments only. Many of the strategies used by teachers of students with visual impairments and O&M specialists to teach social skills are based on the work of Sacks and Wolffe (2006b) and can be adapted for use with students who have visual impairments and multiple disabilities. Expanding on this knowledge base, professionals can add to their toolbox and ensure that their students with visual impairments and multiple disabilities are socially successful and engaged with the world around them.

SOCIAL DEVELOPMENT OF STUDENTS WITH VISUAL IMPAIRMENTS AND MULTIPLE DISABILITIES

Differences in Social Development

Research has clearly documented that there are differences in the way in which children with visual impairments develop socially as compared to their sighted peers. Ferrell (2000), Gold, Shaw, and Wolffe (2010), MacCuspie (1996), Sacks, Wolffe, and Tierney (1998), and Warren (2000) demonstrated that students with visual impairments require support from others to mediate the world around them. Because of their vision loss, students with visual impairments may be reluctant to explore their environment or interact with toys, household objects, or people unless they are familiar with them. As a result, the development of social relationships and the natural process of learning to play and interact with others may be limited. Also, if students are not provided with hands-on experiences and expectations to engage with their world, they may be more likely to be isolated and unwilling to interact socially.

While vision plays a significant role in the social development of students with visual impairments and multiple disabilities, other factors may have an impact on the social development of these students, including the following:

- **Extended hospitalizations:** As a result of medical conditions related to students' visual impairment or other disabilities, many students with visual impairments and multiple disabilities require medical procedures or surgery on an ongoing basis, making it difficult to engage or interact with family and peers.

- **Impact of medication:** Students with visual impairments and multiple disabilities are often prescribed a variety of medications that can influence how they interact with others. Some medications make students lethargic, while others can cause overstimulation and agitation.

- **Neurological stability:** Many students with visual impairments and multiple disabilities are highly sensitive to loud sounds, auditory overload (such as many people talking at the same time), visual clutter, and various textures. Too much or too little auditory, visual, or tactile stimulation can cause students to demonstrate negative or isolative behaviors.

- **Biobehavioral states**: A student's biobehavioral states may affect his or her level of awareness or alertness. Many students with severe multiple disabilities may exhibit periods of fatigue and sleepiness as well as periods of agitation.

In addition, the social development of a student with visual impairment and multiple disabilities is influenced by his or her family's cultural values and the expectations family members have for the student to engage with others in an appropriate manner.

Levels of Social Development

There are three levels of social development, as illustrated in Figure 10.1. The first level requires students to develop an awareness of others and a sense of self-identity. For example, a young child who is deafblind and exhibits cognitive challenges may not respond to family members or siblings in a positive manner unless he is helped to understand the existence of others outside of himself and is provided with a tactile cue, such as a light touch to the arm or shoulder coupled with a

Figure 10.1
Levels of Social Development

> **HIERARCHY OF SOCIAL SKILLS**
>
> **LEVEL I – AWARENESS**
>
> Self-identity + Social awareness
>
> =
>
> Behavioral social skills
>
> **LEVEL II – INTERACTIVE**
>
> Awareness of other people's needs + Strategies for positive interactions
>
> =
>
> Interactive social skills
>
> **LEVEL III – EVALUATIVE**
>
> Interpretation of social situations + Awareness of social needs of others +
> Strategies to enhance social competence
>
> =
>
> Cognitive social understanding

Source: Reprinted from Sacks, S. Z. & Silberman, R. K. (2000). Social skills. In A. J. Koenig & M. C. Holbrook (Eds.), *Foundations of education: Volume II. Instructional strategies for teaching children and youths with visual impairments* (2nd ed., p. 621). New York: AFB Press.

greeting, to alert him to others entering his world.

At the next level, students develop skills and strategies to interact with peers and adults. For example, a student with autism spectrum disorder and a visual impairment may avert his gaze from a conversational partner. This student may need verbal prompts from his teacher and practice starting conversations.

The third level requires a student to be able to interpret social situations, evaluate each social encounter, and use a range of social strategies to engage with others. For example, an adolescent with low vision and a physical disability may not be able to see the facial expressions of his peers. As a result, he may misinterpret nonverbal cues that would help him gain entry into a group. He may need to learn strategies to evaluate a range of facial expressions. It is important to keep in mind that the social development process will vary from student to student. Some students may only achieve an awareness of themselves and those closest to them (family members, teachers, and assistants). Other students may be aware of their social surroundings and initiate social interactions with others. With support and practice, students can develop skills to evaluate social situations and understand the nuances of nonverbal communication. In order for professionals to determine how to teach social skills to students with visual impairments and multiple disabilities, a clear definition of social skills is needed. Also, professionals need to be able to accurately assess students' level of social competence in order to determine how to prioritize activities for instruction.

DEFINITIONS OF SOCIAL SKILLS

Social skills are the behaviors that allow individuals to engage with one another in a variety of situations and environments. These behaviors are based on social norms and cultural values established within communities and families. Many social behaviors are learned incidentally through observation (Sacks, 2006). Other social interaction skills are based on following rules for specific social situations. For example, students in a school environment learn to raise their hands before answering a question rather than spontaneously blurting out a response. During recess, students learn to stand in line and wait their turn before engaging in an activity like playing wall ball or jumping rope. As students mature and gain more social savvy, they learn to evaluate social situations and become aware of how their behavior affects others.

It is important to consider that the effects of a visual impairment and multiple disabilities may influence how a student develops socially competent behavior. The teacher of students with visual impairments also needs to take into account factors such as a student's personality and temperament. For example, if a student seems shy, he or she may not have the desire to interact with peers. Or, if a student's temperament is easygoing and flexible, he or she may be more motivated to play or talk with unfamiliar peers.

The following list of components attempts to define the parameters of social skills and establish a basis for teaching them. Although the list is not exhaustive, it is based on research completed by experts in the field of blindness and visual impairment (Sacks, Kekelis, & Gaylord-Ross, 1992; Sacks & Wolffe, 2006b; Sacks et al., 1998; Wolffe & Sacks, 1997).

- appropriate body language
- communication skills
- cooperative skills and play skills
- social interaction skills
- social etiquette
- development of relationships and friendships
- knowledge of self
- interpretation and monitoring of social behavior

Within each of these components are numerous behaviors and skills to be learned by students with visual impairments and multiple disabilities. For more information on these components and the specific behaviors and skills in each, see Sacks, 2014.

SOCIAL SKILLS ASSESSMENT

Assessment of social skills allows teachers and families the opportunity to determine which skills are most critical for a given student to learn. The assessment process provides a systematic way to evaluate each student's strengths and limitations. When initiating social skills assessment for students with visual impairments and multiple disabilities, the teacher may want to observe sighted students of similar ages to become familiar with typical social behavior, communication styles, language, and activities. While

social skills assessment needs to be based on the individual needs of the student, having baseline information to help establish realistic expectations for student performance is essential. (See Chapter 3 for a general discussion of assessment.)

There are several forms of social skills assessment that provide ongoing information so that student progress can be monitored over time. Assessments include observation, interviews, checklists, and role-play and problem-solving scenarios. Among the behaviors assessed are executive functioning, cognitive behavior, and perspective taking.

Observation

Observation is the primary way in which teachers, families, and other professionals gather information about most students with visual impairments and multiple disabilities. Systematic observation is one of the most powerful tools of assessment available to the educational team (teachers, specialists, and family members) and provides valuable insights into students' social worlds. By observing a student's daily routines, the educational team can begin to objectively interpret behavior in terms of his or her interaction with others (peers and adults) and the influence of the physical and social environment. For example, many students with visual impairments and multiple disabilities may react negatively (by screaming or pinching, for example) if they are in social environments with too much auditory stimulation (such as active classrooms with many people talking).

It is important to observe students with visual impairments and multiple disabilities in a variety of environments including the home, the school, and the community. The keen observer will conduct observations at various times of day, and in multiple environments, including those that are familiar and comfortable for the student and those that are not. Observers can keep anecdotal records of each observation session documenting a student's social growth over time. Often, it is useful for teachers, families, and other professionals to complete individual observations, and then compare their observations with one another to determine how best to teach a specific skill or to determine an effective intervention.

When observing a student with visual impairments and multiple disabilities the following areas may be considered:

- Does the student have awareness of others in the environment?
- Does the student demonstrate interest in others?
- Does the student show an ability to use joint attention?
- How many social contacts are made by the student during the observation?
- What social behavior is effective for the student?
- What social behavior causes obstacles for the student?
- Which environmental factors impede the student's social interaction?
- What is the length of the student's social interactions?
- Does the student demonstrate interest in peers and types of activities that promote engagement?

- Does the student demonstrate an ability to initiate a conversation or greeting (verbal, signed, gestured, or with the use of an augmentative and alternative communication device [AAC])?
- Does the student demonstrate an ability to sustain a conversation (verbal, signed, gestured, or with the use of an AAC) that is age appropriate?
- Does the student express interest in peer culture, such as games, music, dress, social language, and communication?
- Does the student demonstrate an ability to use nonverbal communication, such as gestures or facial expressions?
- Is the student regarded as a peer or as someone to care for by others?

Interviews

Much can be learned by conducting interviews with professionals, peers, and family members who are most familiar with a student's level of social competence. Interviews allow these individuals the opportunity to prioritize which social skills are most critical to teach the student. This is especially true when students are unable to verbalize or communicate their desire to participate with others, engage in games or other social activities, or spontaneously initiate a choice without support from an adult. The following questions provide a framework for interviewing families (Sacks & Barclay, 2006, pp. 289–290):

- How do you view your child's social skills?
- How does your child communicate the activities he or she likes or dislikes?

- How does your child initiate social interactions?
- What are some social behaviors that you think your child might need support to acquire or to improve?
- What does your child like to do for fun or during free time?
- Does your child have friends? What does your child do with his or her friends?
- What would you want to change about your child's social behavior?

The teacher of students with visual impairments, O&M specialist, and teacher of students who are deafblind can promote and facilitate social skills instruction for their students by engaging in a collaborative discussion through guided interview questions. These questions can help the team determine what skills need to be taught. The following interview questions can be used by professionals to assess a student's social competence (Sacks & Barclay, 2006, pp. 291–294):

- How does your student interact with peers? With adults?
- How does your student make choices related to social activities?
- What games or social activities does your student like to participate in when in the classroom, on the playground, and in the community?
- How does your student show frustration or anger?
- How does your student show excitement or pleasure?

- What social skills does your student do well?
- What specific social behaviors does your student need help to learn?

Often, students who exhibit mild to moderate cognitive challenges or learning disabilities and visual impairments but can express themselves verbally or through the use of an AAC may be able to be interviewed to determine their level of social competence. Obtaining a student's perspective allows professionals to gain insight into how the student views his or her own level of social competence. The following questions may be used for student interviews (Sacks & Barclay, 2006, pp. 303–304):

- Do you have friends? What do your friends like about you?
- What do you do with your friends?
- How do you greet a friend? How do you greet an adult?
- How do you let people know you want to play with them or join a group?
- What games or activities do you do with school friends or your brothers or sisters?
- How do you let someone know you are angry or frustrated?
- What do you tell people about your visual impairment and other disabilities?

Social Skills Assessment Checklists

Social skills checklists provide a structured way for professionals and families to observe

Figure 10.2

Social Competence Assessment

INTERACTION WITH FAMILY, PEERS, AND OTHERS				
Age (Years)	Skills	IEP School Year	Competence	Generalized Use
0–1	1. Respond to an adult's attempt to interact.*			
	2. Initiate interactions with an adult.*			
	3. Demonstrate the ability to differentiate between familiar people and strangers.*			
	4. Respond to the presence of a peer.*			
	5. Accept a substitute activity that replaces a socially unacceptable mannerism.			
2–3	6. Demonstrate understanding of approval and disapproval of adults.*			
	7. Address parents or other familiar adults by name.*			
	8. Associate particular adults with routine activities.*			
	9. Engage in same activity as a peer.*			
	10. Comply with simple directions and limits from adults.*			
	11. Interact with peers or siblings.*			
	12. Address siblings by name.*			
4–7	13. Interact with blind, low vision, and sighted peers in common situations.*			
	14. Identify the person in charge in various situations.*			
	15. Identify situations in which an adult should not be obeyed.*			
	16. Initiate interactions with peers.*			
	17. Share toys or other items with a peer.*			
	18. Use a peer as a resource.*			
	19. Indicate preferences in playmates.*			
	20. Discuss the concept of friendship.			
	21. Describe other people.			

*Skills considered essential.

Source: Excerpted with permission from Loumiet, R., & Levack, N. (1993). *Independent living: A curriculum with adaptations for students with visual impairments* (2nd ed.). Austin: Texas School for the Blind and Visually Impaired.

Age (Years)	Skills	IEP School Year	Competence	Generalized Use
4–7	22. Take turns.*			
	23. Determine when it is not appropriate to share something, and communicate it in an assertive manner.*			
	24. Identify the consequences of behaviors in social interactions.*			
	25. Name family members, and discuss the relationship to each of them.			
	26. Maintain contact with parents, guardians, and family members when separated for a long period of time.*			
	27. Respond to humor, and use it in social situations.			
	28. Recognize sarcasm, and respond in an effective manner.			
	29. Interact with blind and low vision adults in a variety of situations.*			
	30. Initiate, continue, develop, and conclude conversations.*			
	31. Discuss the personal likes and dislikes of other people.			
	32. Recognize behaviors that can cause social isolation and demonstrate alternative behaviors that promote social integration.*			
8–11	33. Demonstrate affection in socially acceptable ways, considering the person, place, and situation.			
	34. Demonstrate the ability to resist peer pressure when resistance is necessary or desirable.*			
	35. Demonstrate skills for resolving conflicts with siblings and peers.*			
	36. Deal with personal insults, ostracism, ridicule, or other mistreatment.			
	37. Tolerate some unusual or unexpected behaviors from others.*			
	38. Seek interactions with blind, low vision, and sighted peers and adults in a variety of situations.*			
12–15	39. Interact positively with friends.*			
	40. Discuss some problems that might arise with family members or with friends, and suggest strategies that could be used to resolve them.*			

(continued)

(Figure 10.2 continued)

Age (Years)	Skills	IEP School Year	Competence	Generalized Use
12–15	41. Identify how different friends can meet different needs.			
	42. Demonstrate various aspects of planning and carrying out social activities with friends.*			
	43. Use assertive techniques in appropriate social situations.*			
	44. Discuss the rights and responsibilities of an individual in a relationship.*			
16–21	45. Establish and maintain a variety of friendships.			
	46. Work effectively in various groups that have a defined purpose or structure.			
	47. Discuss the concepts of role model(s) and/or mentor(s) for self.			
	48. Discuss the concept of networking, and demonstrate an understanding of its value.			

SELF-CONCEPT

Age (Years)	Skills	IEP School Year	Competence	Generalized Use
0–1	1. Recognize and respond to name.			
	2. Demonstrate interest in a mirror image.*			
	3. State own first name.*			
	4. Demonstrate a strong desire to perform tasks independently.*			
	5. Demonstrate awareness that his/her behavior has an effect on others.*			
2–3	6. Indicate a preference.*			
	7. Demonstrate recognition of own image in a picture or on a videotape, and/or demonstrate recognition of own voice on an audiotape.*			
	8. Use personal pronouns I, you, and me.*			
	9. Use a variety of methods to get own way.*			

Age (Years)	Skills	IEP School Year	Competence	Generalized Use
2–3	10. Demonstrate an awareness of self as a separate person.			
	11. Show pride in accomplishing tasks.*			
	12. State own first name, last name, and age.*			
4–7	13. Separate own possessions from those of others.*			
	14. Name things that he/she can do now that he/she was unable to do at an earlier age, and name things that he/she will learn to do in the future.*			
	15. State basic information about self.*			
	16. State basic information about family members.*			
	17. Indicate awareness of own visual and other physical abilities, and differences between his/her abilities and those of others.*			
8–11	18. Discuss personal likes and dislikes.*			
	19. Provide basic information as to own ethnic origin, religious preference, and family background.*			
12–15	20. Evaluate own personality traits, and attempt to modify those that are not functional.*			
	21. State own point of view on various specific topics.			
16–21	22. State own social security number.*			
	23. Obtain and use an identification card.*			
	24. Show pride in personal achievements.			
	25. Express realistic views of own capabilities and limitations.*			
	26. Demonstrate confidence in own decisions, values, and beliefs.*			

students' social behavior in many different environments. Checklists allow teachers and families the opportunity to assess students' progress over a period of time. Also, social skills checklists can streamline the observation process by listing behaviors or skills according to a student's chronological age or developmental abilities. The Social Competence Assessment (excerpted in Figure 10.2) from *Independent Living: A Curriculum with Adaptations for Students with Visual Impairments* (Loumiet & Levack,

1993) provides a checklist that includes scales for:

- interaction with family, peers, and others
- self-concept
- recognition and expression of emotions
- nonverbal communication
- values clarification
- personal and social aspects of sexuality
- physical aspects of sexuality
- courteous behavior
- problem solving
- decision making and planning
- scholastic success
- personal and civic responsibility

This checklist allows the evaluator to tie the assessment directly to the student's Individualized Education Program (IEP) or transition plan. It also provides age equivalents to assist teachers and families in determining what skills are appropriate to teach at various age or grade levels.

Another social skills assessment checklist commonly used with students who have visual impairments and multiple disabilities is the *Social Skills Assessment Tool for Children with Visual Impairments: Revised (SSAT-VI:R)* (Sacks & Wolffe, 2006a; see Figure 10.3). This tool allows the evaluator to rate a student's social behavior on a scale from 1 to 6, where 1 is "absent" and 6 is "excellent," in three general areas: basic social behavior, interpersonal relationships, and cognitive social behavior. After the evaluation, the student's educational team can prioritize skills for instruction and determine the most appropriate approach for intervention.

Many students with visual impairments may exhibit autistic-like behaviors (rocking, aversion to touch, and avoidance of eye contact) or have a diagnosis on the autism spectrum. When considering social skills interventions for these students, it is important to consider assessments that examine behavioral characteristics typically exhibited by these students. The Individual Strengths and Skills Inventory (Aspy & Grossman, 2008), shown in Figure 10.4, provides a framework for teachers and families to use when determining social strengths for each student. The evaluator is asked to note specific strengths in each category.

Situational Role-Play and Problem-Solving Scenarios

Role-Play Scenarios

Role-play scenarios allow the evaluator to assess typical social situations encountered by students with visual impairments and multiple disabilities during the school day or in after-school activities at home or in the community. Role-play assessment serves several purposes. It allows the evaluator to target specific social behaviors that are the student's strengths and those that require instruction. In addition, this form of assessment provides the evaluator with a means to determine the effectiveness of instruction over time. It also allows the student with a visual impairment and multiple disabilities to learn from other classmates who may be more socially adept at handling a specific social situation.

Because students with visual impairments and multiple disabilities may have difficulty

Figure 10.3
Social Skills Assessment Tool

SOCIAL SKILLS ASSESSMENT TOOL FOR CHILDREN WITH VISUAL IMPAIRMENTS: REVISED (SSAT–VI:R)

Student: _____ Assessor: _____ Date: _____

Rate each item as: 1 = absent; 2 = poor; 3 = fair; 4 = adequate; 5 = good; 6 = excellent

Basic Social Behaviors

A. Body Language

1. _____ Maintains appropriate eye contact.
2. _____ Demonstrates appropriate body posture.
3. _____ Maintains appropriate personal body space.
4. _____ Uses and responds to gestures and facial expressions.
5. _____ Refrains from engaging in socially unacceptable mannerisms.

B. Communication Skills

1. _____ Positively initiates interactions with others.
2. _____ Exhibits age-appropriate interactions.
3. _____ Maintains age-appropriate conversations.
4. _____ Demonstrates an appreciation of others by giving compliments.
5. _____ Recognizes and responds appropriately to others' feelings.
6. _____ Exhibits the ability to interrupt conversations appropriately.
7. _____ Responds appropriately to positive and negative feedback from peers.
8. _____ Responds appropriately to positive and negative feedback from adults.

C. Cooperative Skills

1. _____ Shows awareness of age-specific activities and interests.
2. _____ Demonstrates ability to play or engage in activity with others.
3. _____ Exhibits turn-taking skills.
4. _____ Demonstrates ability to engage in a variety of play activities.
5. _____ Demonstrates ability to join a group.
6. _____ Demonstrates ability to share in group activity.

Source: Adapted from Sacks, S. Z., & Wolffe, K. E. (2006a). *Social skills assessment tool for children with visual impairments (SSAT-VI)* (Rev. ed.). Fremont: California School for the Blind.

(continued)

(Figure 10.3 continued)

7. _____ Demonstrates ability to sustain group involvement.

8. _____ Demonstrates ability to lead group activity.

Interpersonal Relationships

A. Social Interaction

1. _____ Demonstrates appropriate greetings

2. _____ Maintains interaction with: _____ adult _____ disabled peer
_____ nondisabled peer _____ younger children _____ older children.

3. _____ Demonstrates ability to compromise.

4. _____ Demonstrates appropriate use of social etiquette (manners).

B. Developing Friendships & Relationships

1. _____ Demonstrates an understanding of differences between family, friends, acquaintances, and strangers.

2. _____ Develops friends and is liked by peers.

3. _____ Demonstrates appropriate behaviors for attending social events.

4. _____ Interacts with peers outside of school.

5. _____ Understands the needs of others.

6. _____ Demonstrates an age-appropriate awareness of human sexuality, including concepts of public vs. private, and societal values and attitudes.

7. _____ Demonstrates an age-appropriate awareness of job-related concepts, including assuming responsibility and relating to others in work situations.

Self-Identity & Self-Monitoring

A. Self-Identity

1. _____ Demonstrates understanding of visual impairment.

2. _____ Demonstrates awareness of personal competencies and limitations.

3. _____ Demonstrates awareness of possible adaptations.

4. _____ Advocates for self in school, home, and community environments.

5. _____ Demonstrates assertiveness in appropriate manner.

B. Self-Monitoring

1. _____ Observes and identifies opportunities for social interactions.

2. _____ Interprets social cues and generates strategies for interaction.

3. _____ Anticipates consequences of strategies and selects most desired.

4. _____ Initiates *and* performs appropriate behaviors.

5. _____ Generalizes social skills to a variety of situations.

6. _____ Sustains social competency over time.

7. _____ Demonstrates ability to evaluate and monitor own social performance realistically.

8. _____ Demonstrates ability to adjust own behavior accordingly.

Figure 10.4

Individual Strengths and Skills Inventory

When designing an effective intervention plan, it is important to consider individual strengths. Please describe strengths in the following areas:

Social

- Likes structured interaction with one adult and/or one preferred peer. Is able to remain in a social interaction with one adult for up to five or more turns in an environment with minimal background noise and distractions. In noisy environments, his ability to engage in a social interaction is quite difficult.
- Likes individual attention from adults and his best friend.
- Is aware of others within group learning activities and is beginning basic social interactions with them.
- Loves close personal contact with adults and children he is comfortable with.
- Benefits from adults telling him what they would like him to do versus what he needs to stop doing (negative corrective statements focus on the behavior instead of his underlying characteristics).
- Enjoys community orientation and mobility outings with one-on-one support.
- Loves his mother, father, grandparents, and cousins.

Behavior, Interests, and Activities

- Soothing/rhythmic music, sensory room/activity therapy, physical therapy, speech therapy.

- Likes counting backwards from 100 to 1; he often likes to count backwards during long transitions (i.e., classroom to front of school to catch bus). Counting seems to help him cope with loud noises in hallways.
- Loves earning M&Ms as a reward for attempting new skills; this can be faded to more natural rewards (i.e., verbal praise) on a random/interval basis.
- Likes swimming.
- Responds well to various forms of positive reinforcement.
- Able to transition to new activities better when staff whispers in his right or left ear a reassuring statement such as, "It is going to be okay." This reassurance helps him overcome his fears/anxiety.

Communication

- Able to communicate basic needs and is showing interest in preferred adults and one student in class.
- Likes individual FM system and when adults talk softly into his ear.
- Enjoys using object cues for scheduling and making choices.
- Typically needs approximately 10 to 15 seconds to verbally respond to a question; this wait time is significantly reduced when using an FM system or

Source: Reprinted with permission from Aspy, R., & Grossman, B. G. (2008). *Designing comprehensive interventions for individuals with high-functioning autism and Asperger syndrome: The Ziggurat model* (Textbook ed.). Lenexa, KS: AAPC Publishing.

(continued)

(Figure 10.4 continued)

when his learning environment has minimal background noise and distractions.
- Loves when adults are able to figure out the true intent/message often hidden in his rote communication and guide it in the correct direction (i.e., if Kordell hears a preferred person's voice he may come over and start singing a song to them. The adult then responds to Kordell by saying, "Oh hi Kordell, it is nice to see you also" [recognizing that his singing is actually his greeting]. Kordell often then responds by asking for something he wants.)

Emotional
- Able to regulate self better within highly consistent and predictable routine.
- Able to regulate self better when environment is calm and predictable.

interpreting or understanding a specific social situation, role-play assessment allows the student to take the role of others. It provides students with the opportunity to experiment with how they might react to a given situation. Teachers of students with visual impairments and other members of the educational team can use this information to design instructional strategies that assist students with learning specific social behaviors, like initiating social greetings or using eye contact to gain a person's attention. Examples of role-play scenarios used for assessment with a student may include the following:

- You are in your general education classroom and your teacher is asking students to respond to a question about a story read in class. What do you do to get the attention of the teacher?

- You are waiting for a paratransit pickup. A van stops at the designated pickup spot and the driver gets out, takes your arm, and escorts you to the van. What do you say to the driver?
- You are at the lunch table and need help opening your milk carton. What do you do to get help from a classmate?

Problem-Solving Scenarios

Students must be able to use specific social conventions as well as be able to interpret and understand the consequences of their actions. Problem-solving scenarios assess these higher-order social skills. In order for teachers to use this form of assessment, students need to be able to evaluate a specific social situation, determine what specific social behaviors need to be used, initiate the encounter, and evaluate if the choices made during the social encounter yielded a successful outcome. Problem-solving scenarios allow the evaluator to determine if the student is able to appropriately combine social behaviors for a specific situation.

Problem-solving scenarios provide a natural vehicle for authentic assessment of social skills. Each scenario should reflect situations in which students need to make decisions and choices that are typical in their daily lives. Examples of problem-solving scenarios that can be used with a student include the following:

- You have low vision and do not carry a cane during the day. You are applying for an after-school job and will need to use a magnifier to complete the job tasks. How do you inform your supervisor and coworkers of your specific visual needs?
- On your way to lunch you hear some students talking about you. Their comments are negative. How do you handle this situation?
- On the playground at recess, some kids start calling you names like "blindy" or "stupid." What do you do?

Assessing Executive Functioning

Many students with visual impairments and multiple disabilities find it difficult to figure out social situations. Often these students have challenges interpreting the social nuances of verbal and nonverbal communication. They may misinterpret a person's tone of voice or physical actions. For example, a student may feel that a teacher dislikes him or her because the teacher uses a firm voice. These are issues related to executive functioning, such as problem solving, organization, and self-regulation (see Chapter 1 for additional information). Challenges with executive functioning are particularly apparent when building social relationships, making decisions that involve critical thinking, or developing systems for organizing daily routines that are not consistent. Skills that are required for organization and problem solving require systematic and structured instruction.

The *Behavior Rating Inventory of Executive Function (BRIEF)* (Gioia, Isquith, Guy, & Kenworthy, 2000) examines several aspects of executive functioning and results in a profile of areas where the evaluated student needs additional support. Both teachers and parents complete each form in the assessment. The BRIEF includes two rating scales: behavioral regulation and metacognition. Areas of the behavior regulation scale include the following:

- *Inhibit:* ability to control impulses and to stop engaging in a behavior.
- *Shift:* ability to move freely from one activity or situation to another, tolerate change, and switch or alternate attention.
- *Emotional control:* ability to regulate emotional responses appropriately.

The metacognition scale includes the following categories:

- *Initiate:* ability to begin an activity and to independently generate ideas or problem-solving strategies.
- *Working memory:* ability to hold information when completing a task, when

encoding information, or when generating goals or plans in a sequential manner.

- *Plan/organize:* ability to anticipate future events, set goals, develop steps, grasp main ideas, and organize and understand the main points in written or verbal presentations.
- *Organization of materials:* ability to create order in work, play, and storage spaces (such as desks, lockers, backpacks, and bedrooms).
- *Monitor:* ability to check work and assess one's own performance and to keep track of the effect of one's own behavior on other people.

Cognitive Behavioral Assessment

Cognitive behavioral assessments allow professionals to examine how a student views and interprets his or her social world. For example, is the student able to understand and figure out what is happening in a given social situation and determine the best strategy for engaging in a social exchange? For many students this is a complex process and involves the ability to perceive or take the role of others. For many students with visual impairments and multiple disabilities, abstract concepts or ideas may be difficult to interpret or use in a variety of social situations and they may require the support of professionals and family members.

Winner (2007) presents an "I-LAUGH" model to determine how students use perspective-taking strategies to engage with others. The areas listed are areas in which students need to develop skills and understanding for social interaction:

I = Initiation of language or action

L = Listening with all of your available senses and brain

A = Abstract and inferential language

U = Understanding perspective taking

G = Getting the big picture, gestalt processing

H = Humor and human relatedness

As a result of her initial work, Winner developed a tool to evaluate social skill problems in a wide variety of students with disabilities. The Social Thinking–Social Communication Profile (ST-SCP) provides a systematic way to examine levels of social communication and functioning (Winner, Crooke, & Madrigal, n.d.).

STRATEGIES FOR PROMOTING SOCIAL COMPETENCE AND EMOTIONAL STABILITY

Systematic assessment allows the educational team an opportunity to prioritize those skills that are important for a given student to learn. Often, the component behaviors described earlier in the chapter comprise those activities that allow students to engage with others in a positive manner. Teaching skills that promote social competence, self-determination, and emotional stability is an ongoing process that requires the help and support of caring professionals and family members. As other textbooks have outlined specific methodology for teaching these skills (Crow & Herlich, 2012; Sacks & Wolffe, 2006b), this section will describe strategies that facilitate social competence and emotional well-being for students with visual impairments and multiple disabilities, including:

- developing skills to promote joint attention
- facilitating play through modeling and co-action
- encouraging social initiations through scripts
- identifying and communicating emotions
- teaching the concept of personal space
- teaching personal safety and the concepts of public and private
- developing social etiquette and manners

Developing Skills to Promote Joint Attention

Skills that promote joint attention allow students to become aware of others in their world and facilitate social engagement on a basic level. According to Gense and Gense (2005), joint attention is "the ability to orient and attend to a social partner, shift one's gaze between people and objects, share affect or emotional states with another, follow the gaze and point of another person, and draw another person's attention to objects or events for the purpose of sharing experiences" (p. 96). Successful use of joint attention is highly dependent on the use of vision for imitation and modeling. The creative professional will find alternative ways to develop these skills. Use of verbal cues and physical modeling will assist students in engaging in reciprocal actions to promote social engagement. The following strategies may help to promote joint attention:

- When students elicit verbal utterances, respond with similar verbal utterances. Try to use a variety of intonations that motivate the student to respond.
- Observe a student's facial expressions and eye movements to discern a student's response to a social initiation, and respond back to the student with a physical cue (pat on the shoulder, hand shake, touch cue on the face or arm).
- When in a group (morning circle or meeting), model direction of gaze toward a person or object.
- When partnering with a student, model or co-act his or her movements to help develop a partnering relationship. Games like "London Bridge" for younger students, or dancing with a partner for older students, can elicit joint attention.
- During a snack or meal activity, have students pass food to one another, practicing turning their heads to the person who is speaking and encouraging the use of facial expressions. If a student is unable to pass food independently, assist using the hand-under-hand technique so that the student is completely engaged in the activity. Likewise, if a student cannot provide verbal requests or responses, facilitate or model the language needed.
- Initiate games and activities that promote partnering and promote physical proximity.

Facilitating Play through Modeling and Co-Action

Families and caring professionals are the first teachers to promote and engage students with visual impairments and multiple disabilities in meaningful play. Meaningful play occurs on many different levels depending on the developmental, emotional, and physical abilities of the student. Many students with visual impairments and multiple disabilities prefer engaging in isolative play, while others may enjoy playing alongside others. Engaging a student with a visual impairment and multiple disabilities in play requires the family and educational team to examine several factors, including:

- the student's level of development
- the student's physical ability to engage with toys and people
- the student's desire or motivation to engage with others
- the activities or objects that promote or stimulate play

When determining how best to facilitate play, professionals and family members will want to keep in mind that their concept or expectation of what the student should be doing for play may be very different than what the student actually likes to engage in when play opportunities arise. For example, a 12-year-old student who is blind, exhibits cognitive challenges, and has physical disabilities may enjoy listening to music or experimenting with sounds from a video game in a quiet environment. Another student with similar disabilities may enjoy the excitement of being wheeled in a wheelchair while playing a game of baseball with peers during recess.

While it is important to recognize and be aware of the individual behavioral and physical differences of students with visual impairments and multiple disabilities, it is also important for families and professionals to recognize that for most children, play is highly dependent on the use of vision. Children learn play skills by observing and imitating those closest to them. For students with visual impairments, learning to play requires modeling and facilitation by adults and peers. Providing students with a variety of opportunities to experience the world around them, and encouraging students to explore and become curious about their environment, encourages play and facilitates social interaction with others. Many students with visual impairments and multiple disabilities, particularly students who have severe cognitive challenges or who are deaf-blind, may resist engaging with others or their environment because they are unaware of what to expect from these interactions. These students may be resistant to unfamiliar noises or textures. They may find crowded, cluttered spaces overstimulating. Also, they may be resistant to touching, tasting, or smelling objects or food without anticipatory cues.

The following strategies can help to promote play for students with visual impairments and multiple disabilities:

- Design and facilitate activities that promote reciprocal interactions. Find activities that are enjoyable for students and stimulating for adults or peers.
- Give students the opportunity to take the lead in a play situation. Interpret students' actions by observing facial expressions and behavior. As the play activity continues, provide verbal interpretation of the activity being undertaken. For example, "Oh, you are smiling, you like swinging on the swings."

- Find toys and activities that are motivating for students and will increase the potential for engaged play. Try to find toys and activities that are age-appropriate, yet developmentally desirable for the student. For example, a 16-year-old student may find animal sounds fun. Finding a matching game on the iPad that involves animals may promote interactive play.
- Structure play activities in real environments. Provide students with opportunities to experience authentic events like sports, dances, and field trips even if their participation is facilitated by an adult.
- Give students choices of play activities either with touch cues, tactile symbols, verbal prompts, or photographs of the actual activities.
- Organize environments to promote play and social engagement. For example, create a specific space in the classroom where students can play and relax.
- Model socially appropriate behavior within play activities. Encourage turn taking, sharing, and problem solving. Students may require physical modeling in order to grasp these concepts.
- Develop an understanding of when a play activity begins, ends, and shifts to a new activity. Using anticipatory cues like a timer will help students to know when an activity begins, ends, or changes.
- Through modeling, teach students to engage in pretend play with real objects. For example, if students have cooking utensils, model their use while pretending to cook a meal.
- Teach students to play board games or card games that involve turn taking and building social conversation skills. For example, many older elementary and teenage students love to play Uno.

Encouraging Social Initiations through Scripts

Many students with visual impairments and multiple disabilities have limited communication skills. They may not have the skills to initiate social greetings or the ability to carry on a simple conversation. Scripts, which can be developed by family members or educational team members, give students a structured way to engage with others verbally or through the use of an augmentative communication device. When developing a social script, it is important for the person who is creating the script to be aware of the peer culture, the age of the student, and the environment in which the script will be used. The following strategies can be used when developing and using social scripts with students with visual impairments and multiple disabilities:

- Create scripts that are meaningful and useful for the student, making sure that the language promotes engagement with others.
- Observe students of similar age levels to your student.
- Create a script that is no more than two to three social exchanges. For example, a script could read as follows:

  Student: Hi, Susan.
  Peer: Hi.
  Student: How ya doin' today?
  Peer: I'm good. What did you do last night?

Student: Oh, I watched TV. Want to go play?

Peer: Sure, let's go.

- Provide opportunities for the student to practice the script with a trusted adult or peer. Role-play a variety of social situations where the script could be used. For example, using a social greeting to acknowledge peers could be role-played in a variety of scenarios: walking into the classroom and greeting the classroom teacher, saying hello to a friend on the playground, or greeting friends in the cafeteria at lunch.

- When teaching a student a script, provide opportunities for unexpected responses and offer the student alternate responses. For example, a simple greeting may diverge into a discussion of a favorite TV show or the respondent may not provide any verbal response. In these cases the student needs to practice other ways of engaging the peer.

Identifying and Communicating Emotions

One of the most essential components of teaching social skills is to assist students in identifying and expressing their emotions in a positive and effective manner. In general, children learn to express emotions through observation. They learn about emotional stability by imitating family members and friends. Students with visual impairments, and especially those with multiple disabilities, may not have these experiences. Instead, their frame of reference for learning about emotions may come from listening to others. Students with some usable vision may have challenges identifying body language, facial expressions, or gestures that provide visual cues for understanding a variety of emotions.

When students have a visual impairment and intellectual challenges, their ability to interpret social cues may be skewed. Because many students with visual impairments and multiple disabilities are unable to express themselves verbally, alternative strategies need to be employed, like pairing a tactile symbol with a specific emotion or feeling. Even when students have expressive language, they may have difficulty determining how best to express their emotions. For example, a student may feel frustrated when she is unable to complete a dressing task. Instead of saying, "I'm angry or frustrated," she may choose to cry, scream, or physically throw the piece of clothing.

Teachers of students with visual impairments often find it challenging to interpret the emotions and feelings of students with visual impairments who also exhibit significant intellectual and physical disabilities. These students may lack the motor movements or physical control to express emotions or feelings. Assisting these students in correctly identifying their emotional needs requires that teachers and caregivers understand the students' biobehavioral states (see Chapter 1) and effectively and accurately interpret the meaningful intent of a students' behavior. For example, if a student appears agitated, it may be that the student is tired, hungry, or lacks sleep. However, more in-depth observation by the teacher of students with visual impairments and reporting from the family may show that the student has a long bus ride to school with noisy students.

Identifying the emotion or feeling with the student in a meaningful way and creating a morning routine that allows the student a quiet environment to regulate him- or herself may reduce the student's level of agitation.

When students with visual impairments and multiple disabilities are able to effectively and accurately express their emotions and feelings, they have greater control over their lives and their choices and decisions. In addition, being able to accurately express feelings or emotions allows students to develop skills in self-determination and self-advocacy. The following strategies support students' understanding and use of emotions and feelings in social situations:

- Identify a variety of emotions and feelings (such as happy, sad, angry, and frustrated) and work with students on pairing appropriate facial expressions and physical gestures to the emotions and feelings. This may involve physically modeling the facial expression, physical gesture, or body stance to accurately demonstrate the behavior.
- In a group setting, have students listen to or watch video clips that depict a range of emotions or feelings. Have the students talk about their interpretations of the emotions or feelings depicted in the video clips. Talk about whether these interpretations are correct.
- For students who have difficulty expressing themselves, provide brailled cards or tactile symbols that represent specific emotions or feelings. Teach students to use the cards as a way to communicate feelings.

- Work with the speech-language pathologist to create communication boards or AAC devices that allow students to express their feelings or emotions.
- For students who have low vision, use picture cards that illustrate a variety of emotions. Teachers of students with visual impairments can work with students to help them understand and interpret the emotion being portrayed on the card. Then, students can practice the emotion using the appropriate facial expression or nonverbal cue.

Teaching the Concept of Personal Space

In Western society, there are unwritten social rules regarding personal space. Through observation and imitation, young children learn from their parents that when engaged with another person, it is customary to stand at approximately an arm's length from one another. This allows individuals to establish physical contact by looking at one another when engaged in a social exchange. Students with visual impairments, and especially those with additional disabilities, may not have had the social experiences or family expectations to learn this concept. Many students may come from cultures where close physical proximity is encouraged. Also, for many students with visual impairments and multiple disabilities it is difficult to gain social attention or engagement with another person without physical contact. Despite these obstacles, it is important for students to develop strategies to effectively engage with peers and adults in a socially acceptable manner. The following strategies assist students in understanding personal space when engaging with others:

- Teach students the concept of an imaginary fence at arm's length to help students understand how much space is needed between people when engaging in a social exchange.
- Teach students to ask if they can touch another person or stand or sit in close proximity to another person before engaging in the action.
- Teach students to shake hands with peers and adults. This establishes a natural way to use personal space effectively. It also teaches students the concept of face-to-face contact.
- Model appropriate and inappropriate personal space for students during role-play scenarios. Allow them to determine if the level of personal space in each scenario is acceptable.

Teaching Personal Safety and the Concepts of Public and Private

Many students with visual impairments and multiple disabilities may be at risk for social isolation or may imperil their own personal safety because they do not understand the concepts of public and private. It is critical for students to learn which daily activities can be done in public places and which activities require privacy. Because students with visual impairments and multiple disabilities are unable to visually observe the social behavior of others in a variety of settings, they may miss critical cues that provide valuable information about what is considered public and private. For example, a student with a visual impairment who exhibits intellectual challenges may know that when he uses the bathroom, the door to the bathroom is shut. However, the student may not realize that when he undresses, he needs to close the blinds or curtains in the bedroom.

Likewise, it is important for students with visual impairments to understand that there are considerations to make about the type and amount of information they provide to others. Understanding the difference between a friend, stranger, and acquaintance and knowing how much information it is appropriate and safe to give to other people is critical in social situations. Because students with visual impairments and multiple disabilities want to have friends and be accepted by a peer group, they may place themselves in vulnerable situations by sharing information that is personal. For example, a student may divulge information about him- or herself or family (such as his or her home address or e-mail address) that should only be provided to those peers or adults who are closest to the student. As a result, students with visual impairments and multiple disabilities need to be given opportunities to work with trusted adults who can provide them with accurate information about the individuals with whom they interact. The following strategies can reinforce these concepts:

- Assist students in understanding the concepts of public and private by modeling appropriate social behavior and by giving students scenarios in which they need to determine if a behavior could take place in public or should remain private (for example, undressing, picking one's nose, or hugging another person).

- Assist students in understanding what makes someone a friend, acquaintance, or stranger by providing numerous examples of each type of relationship. For example, would a bus driver in the community who says hello every time the student enters the bus be a friend, acquaintance, or stranger?

- Create a game where students have to categorize people into friend, acquaintance, and stranger categories by listening to scenarios in which a person provides personal information and determining that person's role.

- Have students make a list of the kind of information they might provide to a friend, acquaintance, or stranger.

- Discuss strategies for personal safety in the community, including strategies for keeping track of personal belongings.

- Develop a checklist with students to help them understand what information can be shared when engaging in social media websites.

- Encourage students to participate in a personal safety curriculum that provides units of instruction on personal safety and understanding the concepts of public and private. The *Safe and Sound* curriculum (Besden, Dibble, Dowling, Greenberg, and Tanaka-Libbon, 2007) is an excellent resource for teachers to use with students who have visual impairments and multiple disabilities.

Developing Social Etiquette and Manners

Just like their sighted peers, students with visual impairments and multiple disabilities need to exhibit good manners when interacting with others in the home, at school, and in the community. Without these skills, students may find it difficult to gain entry into groups, be invited to a range of activities like going to restaurants, hanging out at the mall, or being invited to a school dance. It is important for these students to demonstrate a set of skills that will allow them greater access to the environments in which they live.

Demonstrating good manners in a variety of social situations is a skill that all students are expected to acquire. It is important to give feedback and cues to students with visual impairments and multiple disabilities so that they will generalize these behaviors and skills to all aspects of their daily lives. One of the first behaviors sighted children learn is to say "please" and "thank you." Toddlers model this behavior by repeating the cues from their family members in a variety of social situations. Students with visual impairments should be given a variety of opportunities to practice these skills. As with students with unimpaired vision, students with visual impairments and multiple disabilities may require verbal and physical prompts from their teachers or family members to help them know when to use these niceties. For example, a student who is deafblind may need to learn the signs for "please" and "thank you," paired with a tactile cue to reinforce when to sign an appropriate response.

In the same vein, it is important for students with visual impairments to learn and demonstrate appropriate eating skills. Not only do students need to learn techniques for using eating utensils, as discussed in Chapter 11, they need to learn the social rules surrounding eating. Students need to learn which foods are acceptable to eat with their fingers or hands (such as chunks of cheese, crackers, raw vegetables, sandwiches, tacos, and fried chicken), and which foods require utensils. Also, students need to be given experiences to help them learn how to determine how much food should be placed in one's mouth, the importance of closing one's mouth while eating, and appropriate posture when bringing food to one's mouth while seated at a table. Finally, students need to learn the social graces surrounding eating. Because eating can be a social event, students need to learn not to talk with a mouthful of food, to say or sign "excuse me" if one burps or belches, and to use a napkin to wipe food off one's face and hands. It is important to note that for some students with visual impairments and multiple disabilities, especially those with physical disabilities and the most complex cognitive challenges, teachers and family members will need to model these behaviors as well as provide physical and verbal prompts on a consistent basis to assist students in learning these essential skills.

In school, students with visual impairments and multiple disabilities need to learn the social rules of waiting one's turn, raising one's hand to be acknowledged, and sharing toys, games, and materials with classmates. Often students with visual impairments miss nonverbal cues, such as a nod of the head or a wave of the hand, that indicate it is time to answer a question or join a group. Teachers and family members need to assist students by giving them reliable verbal or physical cues to let them know it is okay to answer a question or respond to a request. Also, older students with visual impairments and multi-

ple disabilities need to learn the social rules in work and community settings. For example, students need to learn the culture of the workplace: knowing what is expected during breaks, understanding how to get the attention of others during group meetings, and knowing procedures for meeting with a supervisor.

Reciprocation is a key behavior for students with visual impairments and multiple disabilities to acquire, especially in secondary and postsecondary settings. Students with visual impairments and multiple disabilities need to recognize that they cannot simply assume that they will receive assistance and support from others. Students need to understand that positive social relationships are built on mutual caring and concern. Also, students need to learn the social rules involved in demonstrating genuine appreciation for the assistance and support given by others. If students are perceived by their sighted peers as always needing help and never providing any sort of social reinforcement, it is likely that the student will eventually experience isolation. Providing opportunities for students with visual impairments to learn to reciprocate from an early age is critical. This concept is especially true for students who have visual impairments and multiple disabilities. Often, these students require support for physical movement or positioning, signed interpretation of what the student is communicating, or simplified interpretation of the information the student is providing. Many of these students will need to learn to use an assistant or attendant throughout their lives. While these individuals may be paid employees or family members, students need to recognize that using social amenities and reciprocating is considered a positive and meaningful gesture of appreciation.

The following teaching strategies can assist teachers of students with visual impairments and family members in enhancing social etiquette and manners for students with visual impairments and multiple disabilities:

- Teach students to say or sign, "please," "thank you," and "excuse me" in a variety of social situations with consistent reinforcement. These skills can be taught during mealtime or snack time, when a teacher or family member has assisted the student, or when the student is in the community and is soliciting assistance or bumps into another person accidentally.

- During mealtime or snack time, teach students to use a variety of eating utensils. If needed, introduce students to adapted utensils like a fork with a cutting edge, or a spoon that is weighted. Provide feedback to students and model appropriate posture, mouth closure, and bringing food from the plate to the mouth.

- Provide opportunities for students to eat in a variety of community settings including fast-food restaurants, coffee and tea bars, buffets, and restaurants where food is ordered from a menu.

- In the classroom, on the playground, or during community recreational activities, create opportunities where students have to take turns and wait to experience an activity.

- Encourage students to share toys and personal items like chewing gum, a favorite game, or a treat from home with others.

- Have students write thank you notes, bake a batch of cookies, create a special piece of art, or buy a favorite food item to let helpers know that students recognize and appreciate the help.

- Teach students to reach beyond themselves with a sense of altruism. Developing community service projects, such as sponsoring a canned food drive during the holiday season or collecting food for an animal shelter, teaches students with visual impairments that reciprocation is a two-way street. By giving to others, and by others giving to them, students are using social amenities in a positive manner.

TEACHING SELF-DETERMINATION

The previous sections of this chapter have outlined the skills and strategies necessary for students with visual impairments and multiple disabilities to gain social competence within home, school, and community settings. Many of the skills needed for social and emotional stability are grounded in the tenants of self-determination. Self-determination is a combination of skills, knowledge, and beliefs that allow students to develop skills in knowing one's strengths and limitations, together with a belief in oneself as capable and productive (Wolffe & Rosenblum, 2014).

Self-determination involves a set of skills that prepares students to live and work in their communities (Cleveland et al., 2007). These skills include knowledge of self and others, decision making, problem solving, goal setting, personal advocacy, self-control, and knowledge of how to interact with the environment to achieve desired outcomes. *Empowered: An Activity Based Self-Determination Curriculum for Students with Visual Impairments* (Cleveland et al., 2007) provides 23 units of instruction that focus on each aspect of self-determination.

Having the opportunity to make choices and decisions and having control over one's livelihood are two of the most important aspects of self-determination for students with visual impairments and multiple disabilities. These may be particularly challenging when students have intellectual challenges, physical limitations, or emotional difficulties. It is essential that the educational team incorporate the following into their instruction:

- Respect the student's wishes and desires.
- Recognize and affirm the family's beliefs and expectations about their student.
- Provide opportunities for students to engage in activities that foster self-determination.

The following activities may be considered in teaching self-determination to students with visual impairments and multiple disabilities:

- Create classroom and instructional opportunities where students have to make choices on a daily basis.
- Encourage problem solving by giving students real experiences or activities where they have to make decisions and determine outcomes.
- Encourage students to take responsibility for their belongings, make appoint-

ments, and perform school jobs and chores around the house.
- Provide students with the opportunity to choose peers to perform activities at school (such as assisting the student at lunch or on the playground, or assisting the student with traveling from one class to another).
- Have students create a list of their strengths and their limitations.
- Have students create a list of the activities and tasks they can do well.
- Work with students to establish realistic goals for themselves.
- Help students understand and communicate their visual impairments and other disabilities.

Further discussion of self-determination can be found in Chapter 15.

SUMMARY

The development of social skills and emotional stability for students with visual impairments and multiple disabilities provides a foundation for acquiring skills to foster greater independence within the home, school, and community. Having acceptable social skills helps students build social relationships with peers and gain access to more inclusive school environments, and provides greater opportunities for students to live and work independently.

While acquiring a repertoire of social skills may be challenging for students with visual impairments and multiple disabilities because so much of social behavior is typically learned through visual imitation and modeling, families and educational teams can work collaboratively to provide experiences that teach essential social skills. The assessment procedures provided in this chapter can help prioritize various aspects of social skills instruction, and the chapter also covered a variety of instructional strategies and suggestions to support students in acquiring and maintaining appropriate social behavior.

REFERENCES

Aspy, R., & Grossman, B. G. (2008). *Designing comprehensive interventions for individuals with high-functioning autism and Asperger syndrome: The Ziggurat model* (Textbook ed.). Lenexa, KS: AAPC Publishing.

Besden, C., Dibble, F., Dowling, R., Greenberg, M. D., & Tanaka-Libbon, J. A. (2007). *Safe and sound: A safety awareness curriculum for students who are visually impaired and have multiple disabilities.* Fremont: California School for the Blind.

Cleveland, J., Clinkscales, R. M., Hefner, N., Houghtling, D., Kubacak, C., & Sewell, D. (2007). *Empowered: An activity based self-determination curriculum for students with visual impairments.* Austin: Texas School for the Blind and Visually Impaired.

Crow, N., & Herlich, S. (2012). *Getting to know you: A social skills and ability awareness curriculum.* Louisville, KY: American Printing House for the Blind.

Ferrell, K. A. (2000). Growth and development of young children. In M. C. Holbrook & A. J. Koenig (Eds.), *Foundations of education: Volume 1. History and theory of teaching children and youths with visual impairments* (2nd ed., pp. 111–134). New York: AFB Press.

Gense, M. H., & Gense, D. J. (2005). *Autism spectrum disorders and visual impairment: Meeting students' learning needs.* New York: AFB Press.

Gioia, G. A., Isquith, P. K., Guy, S. C., & Kenworthy, L. (2000). *Behavior rating inventory of executive function (BRIEF).* Lutz, FL: PAR Inc.

Gold, D., Shaw, A., & Wolffe, K. (2010). The social lives of Canadian youths with visual impairments. *Journal of Visual Impairment & Blindness, 104*(7), 431–443.

Loumiet, R., & Levack, N. (1993). *Independent living: A curriculum with adaptations for students with visual impairments* (2nd ed.). Austin: Texas School for the Blind and Visually Impaired.

MacCuspie, P. A. (1996). *Promoting acceptance of children with disabilities: From tolerance to inclusion.* Halifax, Canada: Atlantic Provinces Special Education Authority.

Sacks, S. Z. (2006). Theoretical perspectives on the early years of social development. In S. Z. Sacks & K. E. Wolffe (Eds.), *Teaching social skills to students with visual impairments: From theory to practice* (pp. 51–80). New York: AFB Press.

Sacks, S. Z. (2014). Social interaction. In C. B. Allman & S. Lewis (Eds.), *ECC essentials: Teaching the expanded core curriculum to students with visual impairments* (pp. 324–368). New York: AFB Press.

Sacks, S. Z., & Barclay, L. A. (2006). Social skills assessment. In S. Z. Sacks & K. E. Wolffe (Eds.), *Teaching social skills to students with visual impairments: From theory to practice* (pp. 279–331). New York: AFB Press.

Sacks, S. Z., Blankenship, K. E., Douglass, S., & Kreuzer, D. T. (2014). Aligning the expanded core curriculum with state standards. In C. B. Allman & S. Lewis (Eds.), *ECC essentials:*

Teaching the expanded core curriculum to students with visual impairments (pp. 555–576). New York: AFB Press.

Sacks, S. Z., Kekelis, L. S., & Gaylord-Ross, R. J. (1992). *The development of social skills by blind and visually impaired students: Exploratory studies and strategies.* New York: AFB Press.

Sacks, S. Z., & Silberman, R. K. (2000). Social skills. In A. J. Koenig & M. C. Holbrook (Eds.), *Foundations of education: Volume II. Instructional strategies for teaching children and youths with visual impairments* (2nd ed., pp. 616–652). New York: AFB Press.

Sacks, S. Z., & Wolffe, K. E. (2006a). *Social skills assessment tool for children with visual impairments (SSAT-VI)* (Rev. ed.). Fremont: California School for the Blind.

Sacks, S. Z., & Wolffe, K. E. (Ed.). (2006b). *Teaching social skills to students with visual impairments: From research to practice.* New York: AFB Press.

Sacks, S. Z., Wolffe, K. E., & Tierney, D. (1998). Lifestyles of students with visual impairments: Preliminary studies of social networks. *Exceptional Children, 64*(4), 463–478.

Warren, D. H. (2000). Developmental perspectives—youth. In B. Silverstone, M. A. Lang, B. P. Rosenthal, & E. E. Faye (Eds.), *The Lighthouse handbook on vision impairment and vision rehabilitation: Volume I. Vision Impairment* (pp. 325–337). New York: Oxford University Press.

Winner, M. G. (2007). *Thinking about you, thinking about me: Teaching perspective taking and social thinking to persons with social cognitive learning challenges* (2nd ed.). Santa Clara, CA: Social Thinking.

Winner, M. G., Crooke, P., & Madrigal, S. (n.d.). The social thinking–social communication profile (ST-SCP): Levels of the social mind. Santa Clara, CA: Social Thinking.

Wolffe, K., & Kelly, S. M. (2011). Instruction in areas of the expanded core curriculum linked to transition outcomes for students with visual impairments. *Journal of Visual Impairment & Blindness, 105*(6), 340–349.

Wolffe, K. E., & Rosenblum, L. P. (2014). Self-determination. In C. B. Allman & S. Lewis (Eds.), *ECC essentials: Teaching the expanded core curriculum to students with visual impairments* (pp. 470–509). New York: AFB Press.

Wolffe, K. E., & Sacks, S. Z. (1997). The lifestyles of blind, low vision, and sighted youths: A quantitative comparison. *Journal of Visual Impairment & Blindness, 91*(3), 245–257.

RESOURCES

For additional resources, see the General Resources section at the back of this book.

Assessments

Behavior Rating Inventory of Executive Function (BRIEF)
Source: Gioia, G. A., Isquith, P. K., Guy, S. C., & Kenworthy, L. (2000). *Behavior rating inventory of executive function (BRIEF).* Lutz, FL: PAR Inc.

An 86-item questionnaire for the assessment of executive function behaviors at home and at school for children and adolescents, ages 5–18. Assesses a wide range of difficulties including those related to learning, attention, brain injuries, developmental disorders, and various psychiatric conditions and medical issues. There are separate forms for parents and teachers.

Individual Strengths and Skills Inventory
Source: Aspy, R., & Grossman, B. G. (2008). *Designing comprehensive interventions for*

individuals with high-functioning autism and Asperger syndrome: The Ziggurat model (Textbook ed.). Lenexa, KS: AAPC Publishing.

An inventory that examines behavioral characteristics typically exhibited by students with autistic-like behavior, noting students' strengths in the categories of social interaction; behavior, interests, and activities; communication; and emotional self-regulation.

Social Competence Assessment
Source: Loumiet, R., & Levack, N. (1993). *Independent living: A curriculum with adaptations for students with visual impairments: Volume I. Social competence* (2nd ed.). Austin: Texas School for the Blind and Visually Impaired.

A checklist that allows the evaluator to rate the student on a large range of social competence skills organized into 12 scales. Age equivalents are provided for each skill to assist teachers and families in determining what skills are appropriate to teach at various age or grade levels.

Social Skills Assessment Tool for Children with Visual Impairments (SSAT-VI)
Source: Sacks, S. Z., & Wolffe, K. E. (2006a). *Social skills assessment tool for children with visual impairments (SSAT-VI)* (Rev. ed.). Fremont: California School for the Blind.

A tool that rates a student's social behavior in three general areas: basic social behavior, interpersonal relationships, and cognitive social behavior, using a scale from 1 to 6, where 1 is "absent" and 6 is "excellent."

Social Thinking–Social Communication Profile (ST–SCP)
Source: Winner, M. G., Crooke, P., & Madrigal, S. (n.d.). The social thinking–social communication profile (ST–SCP): Levels of the social mind. Santa Clara, CA: Social Thinking.

https://www.socialthinking.com/Articles?name=Social%20Thinking%20Social%20Communication%20Profile

A profile that provides a systematic way to examine a student's levels of social communication and functioning once he or she has been recognized as having social skills problems.

Curricula

Empowered: An Activity Based Self-Determination Curriculum for Students with Visual Impairments
Source: Cleveland, J., Clinkscales, R. M., Hefner, N., Houghtling, D., Kubacak, C., & Sewell, D. (2007). *Empowered: An activity based self-determination curriculum for students with visual impairments.* Austin: Texas School for the Blind and Visually Impaired.

A curriculum, comprised of 23 units, developed to guide the instruction of self-determination skills, including knowledge of self and others, decision making, problem solving, goal setting, personal advocacy, self-control, and knowledge of how to interact with the environment to achieve desired outcomes. Includes a self-determination evaluation and a materials guide on CD.

Getting to Know You: A Social Skills and Ability Awareness Curriculum
Source: Crow, N., & Herlich, S. (2012). *Getting to know you: A social skills and ability awareness curriculum.* Louisville, KY: American Printing House for the Blind.

A curriculum for grades K-12 in which blind and visually impaired students and sighted students interact and get to know each other. The manual is sold with a kit to implement lessons that engage students who are blind and visually impaired with their sighted age-mates in activities that promote social competence.

Safe and Sound: A Safety Awareness Curriculum for Students Who Are Visually Impaired and Have Multiple Disabilities
Source: Besden, C., Dibble, F., Dowling, R., Greenberg, M. D., & Tanaka-Libbon, J. A. (2007). *Safe and sound: A safety awareness curriculum for students who are visually impaired and have multiple disabilities*. Fremont: California School for the Blind.

This curriculum introduces safety skills and behaviors for a diverse student population, including those who are blind, visually impaired, and deafblind, both with and without multiple disabilities, to practice in the home, school, and community. Includes adaptations for students who are young, have cognitive disabilities, and are English language learners. Provides guidelines to be used by teachers, other staff, and parents and focuses on personal safety.

Chapter 11

Teaching Independent Living Skills

Angela Martyn and Frances Liefert

Key Points

- The importance of teaching independent living skills to students with visual impairments who have multiple disabilities
- The basic categories of independent living skills
- Why maximizing independence in the use of independent living skills is important
- How various skills are taught to a variety of students

Cory is a 9-year-old boy who has been diagnosed with cerebral visual impairment (CVI) in conjunction with cerebral palsy. He uses a wheelchair and has some trouble with hand use and speech. He is accomplished academically. He is easily frustrated when he is asked to do physical tasks like placing assignments in his binder or opening food containers during lunch. Cory is in fourth grade at his local school. He participates in general education classes and is at grade level. Due to his limited hand use and intelligibility issues, he uses an adapted keyboard for writing and communication. Working with a scribe has been tried over the years unsuccessfully due to his speech difficulties. Writing continues to be a laborious, tedious process. Cory has excellent listening comprehension skills and is an attentive student with good retention.

Many aspects of daily living that his peers do quickly and effortlessly are frustrating to him. Navigating his wheelchair in and out of the room requires assistance due to surface elevation changes and the height of the threshold. He cannot gather his own materials, take out his homework folder, or locate materials in his desk without assistance. He requires assistance for transfers and manipulating fasteners on his clothing, so he cannot take trips to the bathroom independently. Cory requires extra time to eat, so that at lunch time, while other students are running on the playground, he is still completing his lunch.

When Cory arrives home after school his mother expects him to remove his jacket and place it on a rack near the door, and remove his shoes and place them on a shelf. He chooses his own slip-on or Velcro shoes. His mom has added a loop to the back necklines of his jackets to make them easy to remove with one hand. Before he leaves the house in the morning he stops at the same location to put on his jacket and shoes. This

369

routine has been in place for many years and is one of the most predictable parts of the day.

Cory's educational team, including his mother, have determined that working with Cory to become more independent with dressing, eating, travel, and organization is essential as he moves into middle school. With the help of his occupational therapist, physical therapist, and mother, Cory's teacher of students with visual impairments and orientation and mobility (O&M) specialist will work with Cory on the following tasks:

- *Developing a route to the bathroom using visual landmarks to help Cory travel independently, and teaching him a technique for hand washing and cleaning his glasses with minimal support.*
- *Using Velcro fasteners to dress and undress with greater independence during toileting and gym class. Cory will also learn to use the support of a personal attendant to assist with personal tasks. The teacher of students with visual impairments will teach Cory effective strategies for asking for assistance in an assertive, proactive manner.*
- *Using an adaptive spoon and fork, along with an eating surface that will prevent his food from moving while he eats. The teacher of students with visual impairments will also monitor the eating environment to ensure that high-contrast materials are presented to Cory at mealtimes.*

Rosa is a 15-year-old girl who is visually impaired as a result of optic nerve hypoplasia. She also has mild autism and diabetes insipidus. She started a new high school this year and participates in a special day class that emphasizes functional skills. Her home is well organized and her mom has encouraged her to participate in household tasks such as laundry and bed making. Although she has asked to help make dinner, her mother is afraid of having her work with the stove and be around knives. When Rosa was younger, her mother had her help in the kitchen and it took so much extra time she decided it was not worth the effort. Now that Rosa is 15 and is learning to use the microwave at school, she is asking more questions about food preparation and wants to learn to cook like her mother.

- *With the support of Rosa's mother, the teacher of students with visual impairments and the O&M specialist want to expand Rosa's experiences with clothing care by having her travel to a local laundromat to do her personal laundry. While there, Rosa will learn to use coin-operated washers and dryers, and will come up with ways to transport her laundry from the laundromat to her home.*
- *Working with her teacher of students with visual impairments, Rosa is learning to use the microwave at school. She wants to help with the cooking at home. She will start by learning the layout of the kitchen, setting the table, and washing dishes. She will also assist her mother with food preparation tasks that involve cleaning fruits and vegeta-*

bles, opening packages, measuring, stirring, and mixing. The teacher of students with visual impairments will create lessons around each one of these independent living tasks during her scheduled time with Rosa.

- *Working together, the teacher of students with visual impairments and O&M specialist will create lessons with Rosa to assist her in understanding and articulating her visual impairment and her other health needs. Rosa will create a resource binder that includes this information, along with the names and addresses of her doctors and dentist, a list of medications and their use, and a list of procedures to be used for medical emergencies.*

THE SIGNIFICANCE OF INDEPENDENT LIVING SKILLS

Independent or daily living skills are essential to independent living. They are an integral part of the expanded core curriculum for all students with visual impairments (see Chapter 1) and may form the backbone of an educational program for a student with a visual impairment and multiple disabilities. Students who are not following an academic curriculum may be more receptive to learning reading, mathematics, and other skills through their practical applications in daily life. For example, learning to follow a recipe may be the best way to present information about fractions to certain students who have cognitive disabilities, and learning to read a shopping list may motivate these students to acquire reading skills.

Living skills include activities that others may take for granted and that students who are sighted often learn through imitation or incidental learning. For example, learning to wash hands, stir honey into a bowl of oatmeal, or find food on a plate with a spoon or fork and bring it to the mouth are all skills which typically developing children observe and then learn through trial and error. Students who are blind or visually impaired do not have the option of seeing these skills performed by others in order to gain knowledge and motivation to try them on their own. Therefore, these skills need to be deliberately and systematically taught. For students with visual impairments and multiple disabilities, these skills may need to be taught with a lot of repetition, in a sequential and systematic manner, and with accommodations and adaptations to ensure successful outcomes. The basic categories of independent living skills include the following:

- personal hygiene
- dressing and clothing care
- housekeeping
- using a personal assistant
- money management
- shopping
- food preparation
- eating skills
- time concepts and management
- learning and using personal information
- communication

Collaboration among teachers of students with visual impairments, families, caregivers, and other educational professionals is imperative in order to build a program that can be reinforced across settings. General education classroom teachers, O&M specialists, occupational therapists, speech-language pathologists, and other specialists will have diverse expertise in a student's acquisition of daily living skills. The role of the teacher of students with visual impairments is to be sure that the visual needs of the student are understood and accommodated appropriately. A functional vision assessment (FVA; see Chapter 3) completed by the teacher of students with visual impairments provides all team members with information regarding how the student uses vision. The teacher of students with visual impairments has knowledge of specialized equipment, tactile labeling systems, systematic teaching techniques, low vision devices, and other specific strategies that contribute to the student's acquisition of independent daily living skills. (Sources of some of the products mentioned in this chapter appear in the Resources section at the end of this book.)

Among the basic instructional strategies the teacher of students with visual impairments can highlight during collaboration with team members are hand-under-hand instruction, how to provide specific verbal directions, and the importance of letting students know before a teacher is going to touch them.

Step-by-step instruction of independent living skills is essential for students with visual impairment and multiple disabilities. Teachers need to emphasize the student's mastery of independent living skills in addition to academic content, and with many students, such daily living skills will be the primary curriculum. When prioritizing goals, educators and caregivers need to think of the impact specific skills will have on the student's quality of life at home and in the future. Given the heterogeneous nature of the population of students with visual impairments and multiple disabilities, it is impossible to address every possible scenario in this chapter. The level of independent daily living skills that a student acquires will depend on his or her cognitive abilities, physical challenges, memory skills, and attention issues, in addition to the nature of his or her visual impairment. For example, students with acquired visual impairment from traumatic brain injury or degenerative disease may have mastered a repertoire of independent living skills, or observed others before their loss of vision, and may retain the basic concepts required for routine tasks of daily living.

Quality of life is enhanced for students with visual impairments and multiple disabilities and their families when the students can take care of their most basic needs unassisted or only partially assisted. For many of these students, mastering daily living skills such as eating and dressing will take years and require deliberate concerted instruction from families and educators in a consistent, systematic manner. Demonstrating and teaching specific skills in a manner that students with visual impairments and multiple disabilities can understand may require adult facilitation, and it may take considerable time for students to attain these skills. Sometimes caregivers or family members are too busy to spend the additional time required for the student to complete a task, or they may feel inadequately trained to teach the skills efficiently and thoroughly. Family members may also be impatient to see the final results and have their child acquire a set of skills, rather than working through the sometimes tedious learning process. Teachers of students with visual impairments play an integral role by providing specialized techniques for teaching independent daily living skills to every member of the educational team, including family members and caregivers.

ESSENTIAL ELEMENTS OF TEACHING INDEPENDENT LIVING SKILLS

Before describing methods for teaching specific independent living skills, it is important to first review components that are common and foundational for all independent daily living skills lessons. These include:

- assessment
- collaboration with occupational therapist
- collaboration with speech-language pathologist
- natural context
- organization
- social appropriateness
- making judgments
- taking responsibility even when independence is not achieved
- establishing priorities
- teaching strategies

Assessment

Before attempting to teach a student new skills it is imperative to perform an assessment of the student's current level of functioning with regard to specific skills. When working on daily living skills, it is important for the team to establish present levels of performance or a performance baseline for each living skills component. This allows educational team members to determine what the student already does with minimal assistance, what is done with some assistance, and what the student does not yet do. Assessment provides guidance for setting priorities for which skills need to be acquired, and for determining which strategies for teaching are most likely to be effective. Assessment results allow all team members, including parents and other caregivers, to pick out which skills will be worked on next by the entire team. Also, finding a way to quantify the beginning skill set and assessing progress at regular intervals will assist the team in determining if the student has learned the skill and has generalized it to a variety of settings.

When determining assessment procedures for daily living skills to be used with students with visual impairments and multiple disabilities, it is important to consider a variety of factors. Sidebar 11.1 provides background information that is important to gather as well as a list of competencies that can be included in such an assessment. (See Chapter 3 for more information about assessment for students who have visual impairments and multiple disabilities.)

A number of living skills assessment checklists are available to assist the educational team in designing effective teaching strategies for teaching daily living skills to students with visual impairments and multiple disabilities. For example, the *Independent Living* curriculum (Loumiet & Levack, 1993)

🔑 Sidebar 11.1

Independent Living Skills Assessment

The following information should be included in an independent living skills assessment for students with visual impairments and multiple disabilities:

Medical, Educational, and Family Background

- vision information from eye care professional
- physical ability to accomplish tasks
- suggested accommodations from observation and physical and occupational therapists' assessments
- cognitive ability from school psychologist's assessment
- communication abilities from speech-language pathologist's assessment

Skills to Assess

- personal hygiene
- dressing and clothing care
- housekeeping
- using a personal assistant
- money management
- shopping
- food preparation
- eating skills
- time concepts and management
- learning and using personal information
- communication

Methods of Assessment

- observation
- interview of caregivers
- interview of student (when possible)
- performance assessment
  Method: Set up a situation in which the student has to demonstrate his or her skills without instruction. Make requests of the student and provide no instruction. For each request, note the student's ability, interventions required, and response times. Examples of requests that can be made as a part of a performance assessment include the following:
  - ○ Request that the student put his or her folder or schoolwork away (to assess level of organization and independence).
  - ○ Request that the student call his or her home.
  - ○ Ask the student to put on clothing, such as a jacket or shoes.
  - ○ Ask the student to clean a counter or sink.

---

includes a comprehensive checklist of skills with suggested age ranges for acquisition. Areas within the self-care evaluation include:

- dressing
- clothing management

- personal hygiene and grooming
- toileting and feminine hygiene
- eating
- food management
- housekeeping
- telephone use

- time concepts
- obtaining and using money
- health and safety
- self-advocacy

Basic Skills for Community Living: A Curriculum for Students with Visual Impairments and Multiple Disabilities (Levack, Hauser, Newton, & Stephenson, 1997) provides a set of basic skills inventories that assist in the task analysis of a range of daily living skills tasks that include personal care and hygiene, eating skills, and dressing skills. The companion guide to that publication—*Basic Skills for Community Living: Activity Routines* (Stephenson, 2008)—provides charts for a variety of daily living tasks. At a more advanced level, *Looking Good: A Curriculum on Physical Appearance and Personal Presentation for Adolescents and Young Adults with Visual Impairments* (Corn, Bina, & Sacks, 2009) includes pre- and post-test assessments.

Collaborating with Occupational Therapists

Students with visual impairments and multiple disabilities often tend to avoid touch and certain textures, dislike particular clothing, and have an aversion to messy materials such as glue, tape or clay. Students may be hypersensitive and resist touching various textures because their tactile sense is overpowering (see Figure 11.1). It may actually hurt to put their hands on certain objects or textures, or to wear certain fabrics. They may also have hypersensitive hearing, taste, and smell. All sensory input may distract theses students from a task set before them by their

Figure 11.1

Frances Liefert

Although this student seems to be using sticky tape without a problem, it can be a challenge for a student who has a high degree of tactile sensitivity.

teacher. Other students may be hyposensitive and have a deficient response to sensory stimulation. These students may appear to be lethargic and unresponsive during instruction. Sidebar 11.2 provides a list of indicators that a student may have sensory integration issues, meaning he or she is either oversensitive or undersensitive to certain stimuli. Students who have these issues may need to be referred to an occupational therapist for assessment.

The teacher of students with visual impairments and occupational therapist collaborate to provide assessment and develop interventions that address the individual student's learning needs. The occupational therapist's

Indications of Sensory Integration Needs

The following findings indicate that a student needs a referral for assessment by an occupational therapist with a specialty in sensory integration therapy.

Overreactions

- Dislikes being touched. Squirms or pulls away when anyone physically attends to him or her.
- Is very picky about clothing and how it feels.
- Dislikes a variety of food textures.
- Hates lotion, glue, or food on his or her skin. Avoids messy tasks.
- Seems afraid to move, has shaky balance.
- Falls out of his or her chair throughout the school day.
- Clings to walls, fences, and railings rather than walking alongside them.
- Has stiff posture.
- Locks his or her joints as he or she moves or tries to stay still.
- If sighted, watches everyone who moves in the room.
- Easily startled by unexpected sounds.
- Distracted by background noises or others' conversations.
- Detects scents sooner and more accurately than most people.
- Intolerant of unpleasant smells.

Underreactions

- Mouths and chews objects frequently.
- Has no reaction or delayed reaction when touched.
- Leaves the clothes he or she is wearing bunched or twisted without trying to pull them straight.
- Leaves food, drool, or mucus on his or her face without attempting to wipe it off.
- Cannot differentiate between textures with his or her fingers.
- Touches items to his or her face when first exploring them.
- Gets too close to others when playing or talking.
- Takes a long time to react to physical contact or to his or her cane contacting an object.
- Is clumsy or lethargic.
- Tires easily, has poor stamina.
- Rocks when sitting or standing.
- Gets turned around easily, even when traveling in familiar places.
- Has a weak grasp.
- Cannot lift heavy objects or maintain his or her arm in raised positions, such as those used for trailing, protective arm techniques, or classic cane techniques.
- Moves body parts in different rhythms; has difficulty moving a cane in time with his or her feet.
- Leans on things when trying to sit or stand still. Hangs on people when being guided.
- Is slow to respond when his or her name is called.
- Seems overwhelmed or oblivious in noisy environments.
- Frequently makes nonsense noises.

Source: Reprinted from Liefert, F. K. (2003). Expanded core curriculum: Orientation and mobility. In S. A. Goodman & S. H. Wittenstein (Eds.), *Collaborative assessment: Working with students who are blind or visually impaired, including those with additional disabilities* (pp. 270–271). New York: AFB Press.

assessment of sensory processing and fine motor skills are essential in determining appropriate programming and accommodations. Sensory issues are best addressed by occupational therapists trained in sensory integration. Teachers of students with visual impairments and O&M specialists may support the occupational therapist's work if they have the opportunity to collaborate. Occupational therapists may have concrete suggestions for the student who resists doing art because he doesn't want to get glue on his hands or for the student who won't put on her swimsuit because the straps are constantly rubbing her shoulders. The occupational therapist may develop customized "sensory diets" for students. This could include brushing and rubbing the students' limbs with firm pressure or allowing breaks for lying on the floor or rolling along a blank wall. It may involve using gross motor equipment such as hammocks or swings. Often, teachers and caregivers can learn a few sensory integration activities that can precede living skills lessons to prepare the student for the activity and make the experience more positive and productive.

Collaborating with Speech-Language Pathologists

Many students who are visually impaired with multiple disabilities have difficulty with communication and eating skills. Speech-language pathologists are specifically trained to address these issues. Working with the student's speech-language pathologist ensures that everyone who works on these areas with the student uses a uniform approach. Speech-language pathologists can be invaluable re-sources when teaching eating skills and when facilitating communication for students. Chapter 7 provides extensive information regarding communication strategies for students with visual impairments and multiple disabilities.

Many students with visual impairments and multiple disabilities have oral-motor difficulties. The speech-language pathologist can design classroom programs to enhance a student's oral-motor skills for speech and eating. Students who experience difficulty with chewing and swallowing and are resistant to foods with certain textures may benefit from oral-motor assessment and training.

Teaching in Natural Contexts

Students with visual impairments and multiple disabilities need to be taught the skills of daily living within appropriate contexts. Learning to wash hands at random times of the day may promote better hygiene and sanitation, but learning to wash hands before eating, after playing outside, before cooking, and after using the toilet puts hand washing into the context of a student's daily routines. Likewise, learning to use a spoon or fork within the context of mealtime, learning to open and apply an adhesive bandage when the student has a cut or scrape, and learning to sweep the floor after an activity that scattered crumbs or scraps provide natural context.

Input from parents and other caregivers about which skills to work on is crucial for having appropriate contexts for practicing the skills. Families who are interested in working with their son or daughter on certain tasks will support them in practicing skills at home. Parents and other caregivers who have been waiting for assistance to teach their son or daughter a specific task will be delighted to reinforce what is being done at school or to have teachers reinforce what they are working on at home. Pleasing families with new skills may actually make the difference between a student being eager to learn or being apathetic about living skills. If it is clear to a student that using independent living skills impresses family members, he or she may be more motivated to work on acquiring the skills.

For effective learning, the student's curriculum should include activities that emphasize the acquisition of a set of independent living skills that are age-appropriate and meaningful for the student and the family. Time for living skills to be taught must be built into lessons of all kinds. For example, a student may take swimming lessons as an adapted physical education activity with an underlying purpose of reinforcing dressing skills, clothing care, and the concept of privacy. Cooking lessons can be expanded to include independent living skills such as shopping, money management, food storage, measuring, eating, and cleaning up, along with literacy skills such as writing a shopping list and reading a recipe.

Routine repetitions of tasks also create effective contexts for learning independent living skills. Many students who are visually impaired and who have cognitive challenges need to have lessons repeated frequently as a part of their daily routine over a period of time. For some students, providing regular routines in which they can practice a specific skill or set of skills on a regular basis promotes generalization. Repetition of routines in appropriate contexts day after day allows the student to master tasks.

Organization

Organization is of paramount importance for individuals who are visually impaired. Students with visual impairments need to rely on being well organized even more than their sighted peers. A student who cannot rely on vision to spot and recognize papers, tools, clothing, and other items must instead have a designated place for each object and remember to return items to their places after each use (see Figure 11.2). Knowing where to find the tools used for each activity is essential for independence. Distinguishing between similar items, as in selecting the proper knife for a cooking project or choosing the right shirt to wear with a pair of pants, is important.

Students who have disabilities in addition to visual impairments may have even more need for learning organizational skills to avoid being dependent on others to find or locate items they need for specific tasks. Students who exhibit cognitive challenges or traumatic brain injuries, for example, may require many repetitions of learning where items are kept because of memory issues. They may need visual or tactile cues, or other organizers to assist them in retrieving items independently. For specific suggestions about organization, see Household Organization on the Vision Aware website (http://www.visionaware.org /info/everyday-living/essential-skills/house hold-organization/125).

Social Appropriateness

Another common factor in many living skills activities is the need for social awareness (as addressed in Chapter 10). Students with visual impairments and multiple disabilities

Figure 11.2

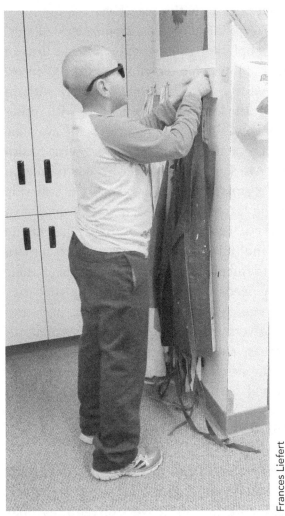

Frances Liefert

Providing predictable and easily accessible storage locations, such as these hooks for painting aprons, facilitates the learning of organizational skills.

may not realize what kind of clothes their peers are wearing and how their peers may react when they wear something very different. They may not be aware that some activities are expected to be performed in private, and may not know how to find private places. They may not distinguish among friends, acquaintances, and strangers or understand who to ask for assistance, who to give personal information to, and when to keep a distance from strangers. Making sound social judgments is important to incorporate into all lessons related to independent living skills.

Making Judgments

Many students with visual impairments and multiple disabilities are rote learners. They acquire a set of skills by practicing routines throughout the day. Often, these students are taught to perform tasks using a step-by-step approach. Because of their cognitive challenges or physical limitations, students may not have the ability or be given the opportunity to make basic choices or decisions. According to Wolffe (1998) and Wolffe and Silberman (2006), students can be categorized into three levels, according to their needs: advocacy level, instructional level, and informational level. Students with visual impairments and multiple disabilities who are at the *advocacy level* require support and possible supervision from teachers, families, or caregivers to make decisions or advocate for them. Despite these limitations, students with visual impairments and multiple disabilities at this level need to be encouraged to make choices or decisions initially in supportive environments, such as the classroom.

Students at the *instructional level* require direct instruction by a teacher or another professional to acquire a skill or a set of skills. These students may need consistent repetition in instruction in order for tasks to be generalized from one environment to the next. Most students, in fact, are at the instructional level.

Some students with visual impairments and multiple disabilities, however, can acquire skills in the same manner as their nondisabled peers and are at an *informational level*, meaning they require very little intervention or support from adults. For some students, however, making sound judgments about important life decisions, such as handling an emergency or making financial decisions, may require adult supervision. Two of the most important skills students can learn are knowing when to ask for assistance and knowing when to refuse assistance that is offered. Students need to be able to evaluate a situation to determine when assistance is needed. For example, if a student cuts him- or herself, the student would need to determine if a bandage is sufficient or whether he or she needs to ask advice about getting stitches at the local hospital or urgent care center.

The educational team needs to take into consideration what level of judgments students are capable of and challenge them to increase that ability while still making sure they take responsibility for getting assistance when it is needed. It is often useful to consult parents and caretakers and school psychologists who are familiar with the students when assessing their capabilities for making sound judgments.

Taking Responsibility

American culture places importance on independence. The ultimate goal for educating students with visual impairments and multiple disabilities is to maximize a student's level of independence whenever possible. The more independent the students are, the more people around them can relax and enjoy their company, allowing more time for playful and productive activities together.

Despite the emphasis on independence, all people are interdependent regardless of their abilities. No one possesses the skills required to live in our modern society without some level of interdependence with other people. We count on groceries being available on the shelves of the local store, visit health care workers as needed, hire mechanics to make sure our cars are working, and ride public transportation staffed by a myriad of workers. Students with visual impairments and multiple disabilities may need even more interdependence with others to meet their daily needs. Rather than insisting that they become totally independent, teachers and caregivers can encourage these students to increase their responsibility for making sure all the needed daily tasks of life are accomplished, with or without assistance.

Establishing Priorities

As discussed in Chapter 3, formal assessments provide information about what skills students do and do not have. Setting priorities for which skills to work on requires input from family members, caregivers, teachers, therapists, and others involved with students. Communication with each other to establish priorities in the area of daily living skills is imperative. Students who are capable of communicating what they want to learn will benefit from being part of the team that decides which skills to prioritize when devising a teaching plan. Family priorities are especially important to consider when students are living with their families. The families' cultural expectations, the importance of a skill in the family system, and the time available at home to address the skill development are all factors to consider. Considering these factors ensures that the student will receive the support at home that is required. For example, if the family will not allow their child near the kitchen stove until they are older, teaching cooking will not be a top priority, and it may be wise to concentrate on fixing a snack or lunch that does not require the stove. For students who are living on their own or in group homes, the culture of the staff caring for them, as well as the time available for teaching, may also need to be considered. If a student is in a group home, for example, and does not have access to his or her own money, it will be important to negotiate with the group home staff before launching into lessons on shopping or managing money.

Teaching Strategies

As discussed in Chapter 6, choosing appropriate strategies to teach specific skills is important for both teacher and student success. Teachers and family members alike need to be consistent in their approach to teaching independent living skills. Determining how to teach a specific living skill is dependent on the individual needs and learning styles of the student. Some students with visual impairments and multiple disabilities learn tasks in a rote manner. Once they learn the skill, attempting to teach an alternate approach may be difficult. From the beginning, it is important for all individuals working with the student to use similar language when teaching a specific lesson. The team needs to consider language that will continue to be appropriate for the student as he or she gets older, making sure there is

carryover to home and community environments. For example, a very young child may ask to go "pee pee," but if that language sticks, it will sound very inappropriate coming from a teenager at a job site. The teacher of students with visual impairments can play an integral role in facilitating a discussion with families about using language with students that will be appropriate for a lifetime.

Teachers and caregivers use varied methods of communicating with each other. Texts, e-mails, phone calls, meetings, and notebooks that go back and forth from school to home can all work to ensure that a student's team is well integrated. Options to videotape daily living activities are readily available. Many students love to see themselves in a video, and if their vision does not allow them to view the screen, they may enjoy the audio. Creating a video of a student participating in an activity can be used as a teaching strategy to motivate and prepare the student to participate in the activity (see Figure 11.3). Digital recordings, both audio and video, can be motivational, used to provide consistency across settings, and be a valuable communication tool for educators and families or caregivers.

When teaching daily living skills to students with visual impairments and multiple disabilities, a variety of teaching strategies can be employed. Depending on the task, teachers may choose to use the following strategies.

- task analysis
- backward chaining
- hand-under-hand
- describe and demonstrate
- modeling (depending on the student's vision and proximity)

Figure 11.3

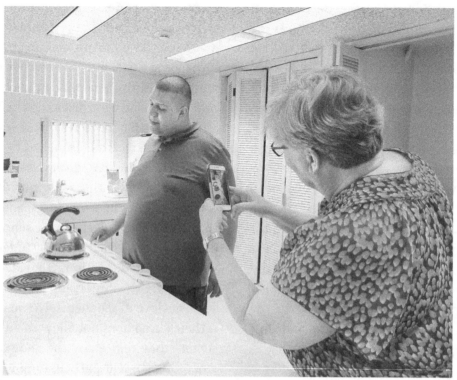

Frances Liefert

Texting or e-mailing short videos of strategies used at school, such as this video of an older student in the kitchen, can help family members follow up at home.

Task analysis, which is the practice of breaking a task into teachable components, is described in detail in Chapter 3 of this book. *Backward chaining* is a teaching technique that begins with the final components of a task. A student gets the reward of completing the task rather than having to learn all the beginning steps before having that satisfaction. (Examples of task analysis and backward chaining are provided in the section on "Washing and Bathing Skills" later in this chapter.) In the *hand-under-hand* teaching method, a teacher or caretaker places his or her hand under the student's hand when demonstrating what is involved in a task. In that way, the student has the security of feeling a familiar hand rather than having his or her hand pulled or pushed toward an unknown object. The student may also easily remove his or her hand if the lesson is overwhelming. Describing and demonstrating tasks is especially important when the visual component of teaching is unavailable. A verbal description and a demonstration, which may be done using hand-under-hand technique, may adequately take the place of visual input for some students. If a student has enough vision, *modeling* an activity, or visually demonstrating it, may also provide valuable instruction on how living skills are performed. When these techniques are employed, the likelihood is greater that students will learn and maintain skills over time.

TEACHING COMPONENTS OF INDEPENDENT LIVING SKILLS

Each of the specific categories of independent living skills listed at the beginning of this chapter encompasses many skills that may need to be adapted for a student who is visually impaired and for his or her additional disabilities. This section gives a basic overview of each area along with specific suggestions and strategies for teaching the skills. (For additional discussion of independent living skills, see Bardin, 2014, and for more information about the products and other resources mentioned in these sections, see the Resources sections at the end of this chapter and the end of this book.)

Personal Hygiene

Privacy

Many students with visual impairments and multiple disabilities have difficulty learning the concept of privacy. They may have relied on assistance with personal hygiene far longer than other people as they grew up, so they are used to people being around as they wash, dress, and use the toilet. Their visual impairment may prevent them from noticing that other people only do certain activities in privacy. They may not realize how to find private spaces or spaces where only select assistants are present. Nevertheless, these students will be expected to abide by the common rules for privacy when they attend school, use a public recreation facility, or go to a restroom in a public place. And for safety they need to be aware of finding privacy in their own homes for certain activities, such as dressing and using the bathroom. Teachers need to be sensitive to a student's need for privacy as the first step in teaching the student to seek out privacy on his or her own.

Students with visual impairments and multiple disabilities need very specific instructions to describe where they may dress and how to close the stall door in a public restroom when using the toilet. Asking before touching a student and describing what the procedure will be before making physical contact is essential when teaching personal hygiene. Teachers may need to discuss with caregivers and others involved with the students how important it is for the students to learn about privacy, especially when they attend school in the general population.

Even when students understand the concept of privacy, they may still need specific examples of what activities are done in complete privacy, what activities may require assistance from a particular person, and what activities are generally accepted in public. For example, a student who is totally blind may not have been aware as a young child that people could see into his bedroom through an uncovered window, and may not even have known where the windows and doors were located in unfamiliar places, such as swimming pool dressing rooms, a new dorm room at school, or at camp. Now that he is a teenager, it is more important that the student understand the concept of privacy not only for personal hygiene activities, but for exploring his budding sexuality as well. If the student grew up in a home where his parents made a point of showing him how to pull the shades before undressing, where to lock the doors of a variety of public restrooms, and what situations, such as a gym locker room or doctor's office, required less stringent privacy to fit cultural expectations, teaching the concept of privacy only builds on those foundations. "Do that in private" means something concrete to such a student, and with this type of guidance, he can avoid embarrassing situations due to misunderstanding which places are appropriate for personal and private activities.

Washing and Bathing Skills

Many children take a casual approach to cleanliness because it can interfere with having a good time or enjoying a delicious meal. As they develop social skills, they realize that they want to be clean and neat in many circumstances to make a better impression on others. They learn rules, such as the importance of washing hands after using the restroom, even though they cannot see the germs they've been exposed to. All personal hygiene is similar to washing off invisible germs for students who are blind or visually impaired. Without seeing their image in the mirror or their peers' faces and hands, these students have to take the word of caregivers and teachers that it makes a difference whether their hair is brushed or their shirt is spotless.

Teaching basic hygiene skills to students with visual impairments and multiple disabilities often entails breaking these skills into small pieces, such as the steps for hand washing as seen in Sidebar 11.3. A similar task analysis can be generated for activities such as hair washing and brushing, bathing, toileting, teeth brushing, and nail care as well. Sidebar 11.4

⚷ Sidebar 11.3

Sample Task Analysis: Hand Washing

The following is a task analysis of the steps required for hand washing:

1. Turn on water faucet.
2. Rinse hands under water.
3. Pick up soap or squirt soap from container.
4. Smooth soap over hands under running water.
5. Rub soapy hand without additional water in the following order:
   - Rub palms together.
   - Rub the back of the hand and wrist on the left hand.
   - Rub the back of the hand and wrist on the right hand.
   - Rub the thumb and each finger on the left hand.
   - Rub the thumb and each finger on the right hand.
6. Rinse front and back of each hand under running water.
7. Turn off water.
8. Find towel and dry hands in this order:
   - Dry back of left hand.
   - Dry front of left hand.
   - Dry back of right hand.
   - Dry front of right hand.
9. Throw away towel if it's paper. Hang up towel if it's cloth.
10. Straighten towel if it's cloth.

Using Backward Chaining to Teach Hand Washing

This example of using backward chaining to teach a daily living skill is based on the steps for hand washing listed in the task analysis in Sidebar 11.3. A disposable towel was utilized in this example. Backward chaining begins by teaching the last step in the routine first, so that the student experiences success each time the routine is performed.

Step 1: After washing and drying the student's hands with verbal and physical assistance, place the towel in the student's right hand and have the student locate the garbage (it should be very close to the sink). Once the student has located the garbage receptacle, have her drop the towel into the container. Say, "Good, you threw away the towel."

Step 2: Once the student has mastered throwing away the towel with verbal assistance only, fade first physical and then verbal prompts for drying her hands. When she dries her hands successfully, say, "Your hands are dry."

Step 3: Once steps 1 and 2 are learned, stand behind the student and, after rinsing her hands with physical and verbal assistance, guide them hand-under-hand to the faucet and demonstrate how to turn the water off. Say, "Water off." Fade physical assistance as the skill is mastered.

Step 4: Once steps 1 through 3 are mastered, it is time to add rinsing the fronts and backs of each hand under running water.

Backward chaining continues until the student completes all the hand-washing steps without physical assistance. It is important to diminish physical prompts during the process of teaching specific skills.

A chart such as the following can be used to monitor the student's progress in learning a daily living skill through backward chaining. In the chart, Step 1 would be the first step the student learns, which is the last step in the task analysis.

BACKWARD CHAINING PROGRESS CHART

Task: _____

Week of: _____	Step Number AM	Level of Assistance* AM	Step Number PM	Level of Assistance* PM
Monday				
Tuesday				

(continued)

(Sidebar 11.4 continued)

Week of: _____	Step Number AM	Level of Assistance* AM	Step Number PM	Level of Assistance* PM
Wednesday				
Thursday				
Friday				
Saturday				
Sunday				

Notes:

_____

_____

_____

*Levels of assistance:

P: Physical and verbal (talking and helping) (both telling the student what to do and doing the step with her)

H: Helping only (doing the step with the student hand-under-hand)

V: Verbal (talking only) (telling the student clearly and simply what to do)

I: Independent (without prompt)

shows how backward chaining can be used to teach a skill, based on the task analysis of hand washing in Sidebar 11.3.

Many basic concepts can be emphasized when teaching students to wash their hands. In addition to cleanliness, emphasis can be placed on positional concepts (in front of you, next to the sink, on the right/left) and other basic concepts (on/off, wet/dry, and in/out). It may take years for some students to become fully independent with hand washing. Some schools have a variety of faucets, and those may all be different from the one used at home. Learning to use one or two faucets at first may help the student adapt to others later on (see Figure 11.4). Likewise, different soap dispensers will give different amounts and textures of soap. The student may benefit from learning how to use just one dispenser at school and just one at home as she starts learning to wash hands independently. In some schools the towel dispensers at different sinks are configured differently. It may be helpful to teach the student to use one set of dispensers at the sink that is used most often, and then to move on to teach the use of other dispensers in other locations routinely visited by the student. Being able to generalize the similarities among the faucets and dispensers and to adapt to the differences is an important life skill. Sidebar 11.5 presents some specific sugges-

Figure 11.4

Once a hand-washing routine is established, the student can be taught to generalize the skills to a variety of situations.

tions and strategies for teaching hand washing, tooth brushing, and toileting.

Teen and Adult Hygiene

As students become teens and young adults it is important to increase the attention to personal hygiene. Young men will require instruction to manage facial hair, whether by shaving or trimming. They may need a list of steps for shaving themselves or they may need to take responsibility for finding someone they can ask to trim or shave their beards regularly. Young women will require direct instruction to recognize their menstrual cycle and to change sanitary pads or tampons. Both

girls and boys may have their nails done in a salon or they may prefer to learn to do their own nails. Both genders are likely to need pointers for attending to cleanliness and the use of deodorant, lotions, and hair products.

The educational team has several roles in this effort. Support for the home caregivers is one important role. Sitting down and generating a list of steps a student needs to learn for good hygiene will seem natural if this same kind of discussion has gone on throughout the student's education. A more direct role in teaching hygiene skills to young adults can be facilitated by arranging situations

Suggestions and Strategies for Teaching Personal Hygiene Skills

The following are some suggestions and strategies for teaching hand washing, tooth brushing, and toileting.

Hand Washing

- Use specific language from the student's perspective. "The sink is in front of you. Reach forward." "The trash can is on your right."
- Offer ample verbal praise throughout the process.
- Prompt the student verbally before physically assisting her. The language used will vary depending on the receptive language skill of the student.
- Describe the actions in simple terms as they are occurring. For example, say, "Hands wet," as the student's hands are placed under the water.
- Most schools have liquid soap; consider using liquid at home to reinforce the action of using the pump properly and obtaining the proper amount of soap.
- Keep the soap and towel in a consistent location so that the student can locate them.
- Recognize that there will be times for the teacher of students with visual impairments to give a hand washing lesson at home, and other times it will need to be done by a caregiver. Consider alternating in the interest of allocating time and energy.

Tooth Brushing

- Establish a routine time or times for brushing teeth such as after a meal or before bed.
- Consider an electric toothbrush that vibrates to provide novelty and assist the process. Be sure that it is the right size for the student's mouth and that she can manage the grip.
- Choose a favorite color for the brush if the student can see color.
- Store the brush in a location that the student can access consistently.
- Find toothpaste that the student likes. There are many flavors available.
- Sometimes getting the right amount of toothpaste is very difficult; try a pump rather than a tube.
- Place one pump of toothpaste on the finger, then put the toothpaste on the toothbrush or directly in the mouth. Or, consider turning the brush sideways so the toothpaste can be placed on the side of the bristles. Alternatively, toothpaste can be put in a wide-mouth jar and the student can dip the brush into it.
- The children's singer Raffi has a fun song called "Brush Your Teeth" that teachers and caregivers can sing while teaching this skill. Or make up a song for the specific student.
- Praise the student—make it fun and offer lots of encouragement!

Toileting

Although toileting is typically taught to students with multiple disabilities during the early years (preschool through elementary school), it is sometimes an important skills for older students to acquire. Basic requirements to determine if a student is ready for toilet training include:

- The student is dry for periods of at least 30 minutes when in diapers.
- The student shows some recognition of wetting and soiling.
- The student displays no fear of being in or around the bathroom, or on the toilet (if fears exist, a desensitization program needs to be done first).
- All medical and physical barriers to toilet training (such as constipation) have been ruled out.

Being able to communicate the need to be taken to the bathroom and the functional ability to independently toilet are *not* required for toilet training. It may be most practical to begin with "habit training," meaning that the child is taken to the toilet on a regular schedule before she begins asking to go as needed.

where using the skills are necessary. Summer school swim lessons or scheduled visits to a local gym to learn lifelong fitness habits offer opportunities built into them for working on hygiene. Classes in family life or sex education may also incorporate instruction on these important skills.

The following are some suggestions and strategies for managing menstruation:

- Collaboration between the school and other caregivers is imperative when instructing a girl to manage menstruation.
- Hand-under-hand guidance may be necessary to teach proper disposal of pads.
- Provide an accessible container in a consistent location for disposal.
- Consult with medical professionals regarding medication to ease discomfort.

- Keep a record or teach the student to keep a record to detect irregularities that may warrant medical attention.

For more suggestions, see Blaha & Moss, 1999.

Care of Eyeglasses and Prostheses

Students with visual impairments and multiple disabilities will have additional personal hygiene tasks to address if they wear eyeglasses or prosthetic eyes. Most teachers are comfortable teaching and reminding students to clean their eyeglasses, and this task can be done routinely at the beginning of the school day, after lunch, and perhaps before going home for the day. Opticians usually advise people to wash eyeglasses in clean water and use a soft lint-free cloth to dry them. Many provide soft cloths specifically made for the purpose. Using soap to clean eyeglasses is not recommended because soap residue may build up around the edges of the lenses. The residue will reduce visual fields, as well as make the glasses look less clean. Students who don't have the motor skills to clean their own glasses can still learn to take responsibility for asking for help to make sure their glasses are clean each day. They may enjoy taking part in the cleaning when there are steps that they can do.

Helping or teaching a student to clean prosthetic eyes makes many members of educational teams uncomfortable. Some feel squeamish about removing an artificial eye. Some may be worried that they will make a mistake or damage the eye. The prostheses are worn in the eye sockets, and infection is not uncommon for students wearing them. Different eye care specialists and ocularists (professionals who create prosthetic eyes) give different instructions for how to clean prosthetic eyes and for how often to clean them. Sometimes family members and caregivers are not aware of how to care for a student's prosthetic eyes. It may be necessary to get parental permission to consult with the prescribing specialist regarding the care of prostheses. Once the ocularist's instructions are obtained, creating a task analysis of the process for teaching the student to care for the eyes can be once again done as a team.

Some students need to clean their prosthetic eyes daily, others every few weeks. Generally, it is recommended that the prosthetic eyes be washed with clean hands in clear water, using very mild soap if needed. Rubbing with a cloth is not a typical practice since the cloth may dull the finish of the eyes and make them look less like real eyes. Taking care to have a soft surface, such as a towel covering the sink, is recommended in case the wet, slippery prosthesis drops into the sink. It is important to rinse off all soap before reinserting the prosthetic eye. Prosthetic eyes need to be replaced approximately every five years (more often when they are for a growing child). Prosthetic eyes are usually polished every six months to a year by an ocularist or optometrist, and older, capable students can learn to take responsibility to make an appointment to take care of that procedure.

Dressing and Clothing Care

Dressing and Undressing

As children grow they generally attain self-help skills such as dressing and undressing primarily unassisted. The age of acquisition of skills is dependent on family customs and parental expectations. Children may begin to take off their clothes before they are 2 years old, yet may not learn to put on all their clothes correctly until they are 5 or 6 years old. Often a typical 6-year-old may put a shirt on backward, or the left sandal on the right foot. Students with visual impairments and multiple disabilities do not develop these skills in the same way as sighted children, who watch the dressing process and gain the knowledge and motivation to dress themselves through visual input. As with other living skills, it is necessary to deliberately teach the steps of dressing and clothing care to students with visual impairments and multiple disabilities. It will generally take longer for these students to acquire these skills than it does for a typically developing child, and assistance may always be required. However, it is important to help these students gain as much independence with these routine activities as possible.

Dressing also offers an opportunity to help the student develop in many areas at once: body awareness, balance, movement, and even language. Generally undressing is an easier skill than dressing, so teach undressing before dressing. Taking socks off is typically easier than putting them on, and removing a jacket is usually accomplished before putting one on.

If a student cannot take his or her clothes off, encourage the student to assist with the process any way he or she can. For example, ask him or her to raise an arm as the shirt sleeve is pulled off. If a student's ability to control movement is limited, he or she can still participate by looking toward or gesturing toward the next item to be removed when asked a question like, "What comes next?" Routine is crucial when learning to dress. Repeating an activity such as undressing or dressing in the same order on a daily basis with the same language will help a student succeed.

Caregiver Positioning. When teaching or helping a student dress or undress, it is important to address the teacher's, parent's, or caregiver's ergonomic concerns. The student should be at a height that will not put strain on the caregiver when assisting with these tasks. The best position for students when being assisted with undressing and dressing is standing. Students should be encouraged to stand holding onto a piece of furniture for support. If they are dressed on the floor, the caregiver should kneel on one or both knees rather than bend over from a standing position. Students with physical limitations, such as cerebral palsy, may be more easily assisted when they are seated on a supportive bench or chair. If the student has poor trunk or head control, he or she may need to be seated in a caregiver's lap.

No matter what position the student is in while dressing, his or her abilities and physical limitations need to be taken into consideration. If a student must be dressed in bed because of a lack of mobility, try to make the bed high enough off the floor so the teacher or caregiver is not straining to reach down while dressing the student. It is necessary to have some kind of side rail or support so that the student will not get hurt by falling out of bed. As students get older, bigger, and heavier, dressing and positioning will pose more obstacles and additional assistance, such as mechanical lifts, may be required.

Concept Building. Dressing presents multiple opportunities to instruct students on many basic concepts. One or two concepts should be emphasized at a time, with new ones added as they are mastered.

Such basic concepts include:

- body parts
- on/off
- up/down
- inside out/right-side out
- left/right

When dressing or undressing students, talking to them and labeling the concept of on/off each time it occurs will help them learn the concept. Clothing, jackets, and shoes will be put on or taken off multiple times over the course of a day; and each time a student takes off a jacket, for example, the teacher or caregiver can say, "Take your jacket off," or "Jacket off." Pairing language with these concepts within natural contexts will help to build the concept of on/off.

Learning the following contributes to a student's awareness of his or her body:

- identification of body parts: naming hands, feet, arms, legs, head, and chest
- spatial awareness and movement of body parts: lift arm up in the air, straighten arm, bend arm at the elbow, lift leg, bend or straighten at knee
- identification of body planes: front of body, back of body, top of head, side of body, and bottom of foot
- demonstration of a functional understanding of the left and right sides of the body

When helping a student dress, talk to him or her about how the parts of the body relate to the clothing: "The hand goes in the sleeve," "The foot goes into the pants," and so on. Once the student can identify body parts, consider adding spatial information and the concepts of left and right: "The left hand goes in the sleeve," "The right foot goes into the pants." Over time, through repetition, students begin to learn language and connect parts of their body to the actions and things around them.

Choosing Clothing. Students can participate in making choices about their clothing from a very early age. They may have favorite colors or textures, or other preferences. Students can be offered a choice between two of the same item of clothing. When offering clothing choices, be sure that both options are acceptable and appropriate for the current weather conditions. Getting dressed also offers an opportunity to expand on weather concepts the student may be learning at school. For instance, if it's snowing out, the teacher can tell the student about the snow and then ask if he or she should put on a pair of shorts or long pants.

If clothing is organized consistently students can learn to choose their own clothing. Put all of the pants in one drawer and all of the tops in another, and encourage the student to choose one of each. Clothing choices can be kept simple by purchasing bottoms in neutral colors—such as pants or shorts (depending on climate) in khaki, denim, black, or blue—that will coordinate with almost any top. Family members can choose clothing that is easy to put on and take off and ensure that any fasteners can be managed by the student. If only one color of sock is purchased, matching will not be an issue. Many children wear white socks (which can be bleached when necessary) with most outfits.

Labeling and Organizing Clothing. Students who would like more information about their clothing can use braille or alternate tactile labels. Braille labels can be used to indicate the color of garments, and there are more elaborate labeling systems in which cards can be brailled to include outfit and accessory options for specific garments.

Labeling clothing is not always necessary. Instead of labeling, the following organizational techniques may be adequate:

- Place matching outfits together on a hanger or shelf; or hanging sweater racks can be used to separate outfits chosen for daily wear.
- Group similar clothing together.
- Establish a place for each item.
- Always keep items in the same place every time.
- Return all items to their designated places when finished using them.
- Use tactile cues, such as texture, cut, style, and button design to identify clothing.

If labeling is still desired, teachers need to be sure to take into account the student's literacy level, memory, and ability to use organizational systems. More practical suggestions for labeling and organization, as well as details regarding braille and tactile labels, can be found at VisionAware (http://www.visionaware.org /info/everyday-living/home-modification -/labeling-and-marking/125).

Laundry: Sorting, Washing, Drying, Matching

Designate a specific place for dirty clothes, such as a basket or hamper. Consider where the student will undress when choosing a location for the hamper. Proximity to the student is important. Teach him or her to drop the clothes in the hamper as he or she takes them off.

Students can participate in the laundry routine from an early age. Concepts of in and out, open and closed, and wet and dry can be reinforced by taking clothes out of the hamper and placing them into the washer, taking clothes out of the washing machine and putting them into the dryer, closing the door on the dryer, opening the door, feeling the clothes when they are wet, and feeling them when they are warm and dry. Even students with limited mobility can enjoy feeling the temperature and tactile differences with the clothes. Many schools have laundry machines available for washing towels and other items utilized in the classroom where these experiences can be provided.

The following are some suggestions and strategies for teaching skills related to doing the laundry and putting clothes away:

- Teach students to put their clothes away. Good organization is essential.
  - Group like items together. For example, have one drawer for socks, another for shirts, another for pants, another for pajamas, and so on.
  - Involve the student in setting up the organization system if appropriate.
- Encourage students to be involved with the laundry process from an early age; they can:
  - open and close the doors,
  - turn on the washer and dryer,
  - listen to the water,
  - learn the concepts of wet and dry, and
  - learn the concepts of in and out (out of the laundry basket, into the washer,

out of the washer into the dryer, and so on).

- Tactile marks such as Hi-Marks or braille labels can be used to mark machine controls; involve the student in the labeling process whenever appropriate.
- Secure matching socks together before placing them in the hamper.
- Place matching socks or outfits in washable clothing bags before laundering (possibly done by the student immediately after undressing).
- Be consistent with the laundry routine and add additional steps as mastery is achieved.

Housekeeping

The overall goal with teaching housekeeping is for students to acquire skills in organizing, cleaning, and maintaining their living space to the extent that they are able. Some of the first tasks that students will learn are to drop trash into a wastebasket; pick up and place toys on a shelf, in a toy box, or in another designated storage space; and hang a towel on a towel rack or hook. The reinforcement of the use of designated locations for toys, dishes, clothing, personal hygiene items, and other daily necessities helps a student to build crucial skills for maintaining his or her living space as he or she grows. Once organizational systems are established, encouraging regular maintenance is imperative to building their use over time.

As with other areas of daily living skills, it is important to start simple and build skills over time. It is never too early to start work-

ing on independent daily living skills. Teachers and family members should take every opportunity to build independent skills within the course of the day. For example, a simple progression of skills needed to clean up after eating may include:

1. Naming the utensils used during a meal.
2. Telling the student where the item is going. "That cup goes in the sink," for example.
3. Requiring the student to put the dirty dishes into a washbasin.
4. Carrying items to the sink or trash.

Later, students can expand on this sequence by learning to wash utensils or load a dishwasher.

Students can learn at a young age to replace an empty toilet paper roll and hang clean towels. Cleaning counters, sinks, and floors should be taught first, and the toilet, shower and tub, and mirrors later added later. A teacher of students with visual impairments can observe routines within the home or school and suggest portions of the skills that can be added to a routine to acquire new skills over time.

In order to efficiently learn to clean a flat surface (such as a floor, countertop, desktop, or table), a systematic approach is optimal to ensure a thorough job. Keep in mind that students who are learning to clean may not do thorough work. They will refine their cleaning skills over time if given detailed, specific feedback and an opportunity to "check their work."

Here are some general principles for teaching cleaning and organization skills:

- Teach systematic patterns by having students clean flat surfaces such as desks or tables in the classroom regularly (see section on "Wiping Surfaces and Dusting").
- Teach students to organize and clean out backpacks, desks, cubbies, or locker areas on a regular basis.
- Provide step-by-step reminders for teaching new skills. Depending on the students' literacy media, these may be brailled, digitally recorded, or pictured.
- Utilize nontoxic, natural cleaners, such as white vinegar for windows or baking soda for cleaning out the refrigerator, whenever possible.
- Provide students with a cleaning schedule so that they learn recommended frequency.

Wiping Surfaces and Dusting

When wiping or dusting a surface, a systematic approach (wiping from left to right, starting at the top edge and working toward the bottom edge) can again be used (see Figure 11.5). A pattern of concentric circles can also be employed, starting with small circles and overlapping as the circles enlarge. Make sure to teach the student to lead with the free hand to ensure that there is nothing in the way. Periodically rinsing a sponge or refolding a cleaning rag ensures a cleaner surface.

Sweeping and Mopping

Start with a small area and familiarize the student with the boundaries of the room. To

Figure 11.5

Frances Liefert

As with most housekeeping skills, establishing a systematic pattern for wiping a flat surface makes cleaning efficient and complete.

begin with, a room with very little furniture (such as the bathroom or kitchen) is preferable to a room full of furniture that requires navigation. Orient the student to the room by exploring the perimeter, and check that there aren't any obstacles or hazards on the floor. Have the student start in a corner opposite a doorway and walk sideways toward the opposite wall while sweeping or mopping. Once the opposite wall has been reached, have the student take a step backward and walk sideways back toward the original side while sweeping or mopping. Have the student step back again and continue side to side and backward until the length of the room has been covered. If mopping, stay off the surface until it is dry. A student can be encouraged to walk barefoot on the floor after sweeping or mopping in order to check the thoroughness of the work.

For some students, it may be preferable to start cleaning a very limited section of a floor on their hands and knees with a cloth, using the same pattern they use when cleaning a flat surface. Once they are familiar with the process of wiping the floor with a rag or cloth, they can be introduced to a cleaning tool such as a mop or broom.

When sweeping, a small handheld broom and dustpan or a portable vacuum can be used to pick up the pile. Electric brooms and disposable products are easier to use than traditional brooms. A variety of products use dry or wet disposable cloths attached to a rectangular pad at the end of a pole. The wet pads are used for mopping and the dry pads are useful for picking up lint. However, these products create more waste then electric brooms.

Cleaning the Bathroom

When approaching an entire room it is a good idea to work from the top down. Start up high with any dusting of light fixtures or cobwebs in the corners. This will require the use of an extension pole and may not be appropriate to teach all students. Most students can learn to clean the counter and toilet before the floor. It is important to in-struct students about the toxicity and purpose of different cleaning products. Natural cleaners, such as white vinegar and baking soda, may be appropriate choices for some. No matter what the personal choice of cleaning products, it is imperative that students learn which ones are used for which purposes. The products should be labeled correctly in a way that the student can access.

Cleaning the Kitchen

Start with one task and add others gradually as skills are mastered. Clearing and wiping tables are generally good places to start. Sinks and floors can be added once the flat surfaces are mastered. Teaching students how to wash dishes and where to store them when they are clean is a large part of cleaning a kitchen. Food storage is also an important skill to learn in order to keep the kitchen clean.

Changing Bedclothes

Use of a comforter rather multiple blankets will simplify the process of making a bed. Instruction can start by encouraging students to strip the bed. The difference between flat and fitted sheets can be shown by teaching students to feel the edges of the sheets to determine which one has the elastic corners. The use of a tactile marker, such as a safety pin, to identify the center of the bottom edge of a flat sheet can be a helpful reference point for centering a sheet on a bed. Changing pillow cases can be practiced over time; students should be encouraged to feel for the seams on the inside of the case to ensure that the case is on right-side out.

Vacuuming

Before using the vacuum cleaner or any other new appliance, encourage the student to examine it thoroughly while it is unplugged. Take it apart and put it back together again. Encourage the student to push it back and forth while it is still unplugged so that he or she can become accustomed to the motions of vacuuming. Utilize procedures similar to those described in the sweeping and mopping section in terms of orientation to the room and application of a systematic approach. Be sure students can demonstrate safety procedures, such as keeping the cord out from under the vacuum, and avoiding tripping on the cord.

Cleaning Windows

As long as students learn the right cleaning products and to utilize a lint-free rag or squeegee to dry the surface, a window can be cleaned by starting at the top corner and working in a systematic manner left to right and down.

Using a Personal Assistant

Some students with visual impairments and multiple disabilities will need assistance throughout their lives for accomplishing personal care tasks, household chores, and work activities. If assessment findings indicate that students will need lifelong assistance, teaching them to use a personal assistant can begin at any age. Students who will be living in group homes or with family members will also benefit from mastering many of the skills involved in hiring a personal assistant.

Strong social skills are required for hiring, directing, and maintaining a good relationship with any employee. Chapters 7 and 10 address the development of good communication skills and essential social behaviors for students who are visually impaired. For students who are likely to need assistance throughout their lives, it is important to stress how to be clear, direct, and polite when working with a personal assistant. It is equally important to learn to express gratitude for the assistance received, a skill which could mean the difference between hiring a new personal assistant each month or maintaining ongoing relationships with a small staff of rotating personal assistants. It is beneficial early on to teach language for refusing assistance and for politely and assertively correcting someone who is not providing the type of assistance that is required.

Giving students the opportunity to take charge of an activity where they must direct a teacher or teaching assistant will allow good practice for the future. Begin with a simple task that students need to do every day, such as arranging tools for a specific task. Teachers can help the students break down the job into select elements. Then they can help students make a list of directions, written or auditory, for another adult to follow. The list may be only a basic template describing the type of assistance that is needed; it can serve as a starting point for students who have never been in the position to direct others before. A lot of play can be involved in these activities, as adults make mistakes, accidentally or on purpose, and students must find tactful ways to correct them.

As students become skilled at directing adults, they can be allowed to have similar activities with older students and then with peers. Activities such as fixing a sandwich for themselves, creating an art project, or recording messages for their families work well in this context. Eventually, it is important for the students to practice giving directions concerning what they want to wear and how they are bathed or assisted in the bathroom. Family members and other caregivers will once again be important teachers of these beginning skills for employing personal assistants.

Personal assistants are not always easy to find. Although people who are eligible for Supplemental Security Income (SSI) from the government may also be eligible for help paying for in-home services, the hourly rate of pay for personal assistants is quite low, and additional money is often needed to pay for their social security and health care. For this reason, family members and family friends are often the most likely to take on the job of personal assistant. Independent living centers, which are located in most cities and some smaller towns, frequently keep resource files of people wanting work as personal assistants for people who are disabled. These centers provide many other resources for people who are disabled, and are a good resource for students who are about to make the transition from school to work or higher education.

Students who will eventually rely on personal assistants will need practice interviewing people for the job. Teachers and caregivers can help the students come up with a list of questions that will determine whether applicants are fit for the job. The questions need to cover the areas of schedule availability and flexibility, physical fitness needed for the job, experience with people who are disabled, whether the rate of pay will be acceptable, and personal preferences students may have for their personal assistants. Having the student role-play the job interview with familiar people is a good first step. Interviewing fellow students for a real assistant job at school, no matter how part-time, will give invaluable experience to students facing the prospect of managing personal assistants in the future.

Money Management

Sorting and Adding Coin Values

From the time students with visual impairments and multiple disabilities enter school until well into adulthood, they spend countless hours working on the skills of sorting coins and adding up their values. For some students this is time well spent. Sorting U.S. coins involves differentiating among the sizes of coins and feeling the edges (the edges of dimes and quarters are rough, while the edges of pennies and nickels are smooth). Additional coins become popular from time to time, and students may benefit from being exposed to them as well so they are not taken by surprise. Using play money is not suitable for teaching students with visual impairments to sort coins because the weight and the edges of play money do not match the salient features of actual coins.

Learning the value of coins is easy for some students with visual impairments and multiple disabilities, and difficult or impossible for others. Having basic arithmetic concepts is required. Fortunately, Thomas Jefferson made sure that our money values are based on the decimal system, making it easier for us to add and subtract coin values once basic concepts are understood. The most efficient way to teach the skill of adding and subtracting values is to have students sort the coins and arrange them from most valuable to least from left to right at their workstation. Containers are helpful to hold the coins. These containers need to be heavy enough not to slide around the work surface when they are touched. Using a nonslip product such as Dycem under the containers is helpful. For students who have significant fine motor issues, consulting with an occupational therapist will be helpful. Once they are sorted, each denomination of coin can be added up before adding the next denomination. It is practical to teach counting by tens and by fives, making adding up the values of dimes and nickels easier, as well as the multiples of 25 to make counting quarters easier.

Plus One Dollar Method

Being able to sort and add up the value of coins is not necessary in order to use money. Students who are unable to sort and add coin values can use another method, called "plus one dollar" or "next highest dollar," for making payments and accepting change. This is actually the method most people use for buying items with cash. The method involves listening for the total amount of a purchase at the check stand, ignoring the number of cents required, and adding one dollar to the dollar amount requested. In other words, if the clerk asks for $3.95, the customer counts out three dollars and then adds one more to cover the

ninety-five cents. One-to-one correspondence is still a required concept in order to use this method successfully and repetition is required for many students to be able to distinguish the dollar amount and ignore the amount of cents. It is important to practice using the variety of language typically used by clerks. Many might say, "Five fifty-two." Others could say, "That'll be ten dollars and fifty-three cents." Still others might say, "A buck fifty." Students preparing to shop independently need exposure to all these different methods of stating prices. They also need to be prepared to ask more than once for the price in order to understand it. The risk of the "plus one dollar" system is that a dishonest clerk might short change the student. However, the student is only risking less than a dollar.

Paper Money

American paper money is not yet accessible to people who are blind, although efforts have been made to increase the accessibility of bills for people who have low vision. Large magenta numbers appear in the corners of some bills to indicate their denominations. For bills that do not have the large numbers and for people who are blind, it is important to develop a system of folding bills or keeping bills separate in order to distinguish among them. Many people use a folding system (see Figure 11.6). Each bill is folded in a manner that is unique to that denomination. Typically ones are kept flat, fives are folded into half their length, tens into half their width, and twenties are folded twice. Larger bills are stored in separate compartments of the wallet to keep them safe and to remind the user of their value. The folding method

Figure 11.6

Frances Liefert

Folding each denomination of bill in a different way is a simple, low-tech way to keep track of amounts of paper money.

requires assistance from a sighted person or an electronic currency reader. Sighted assistance can be solicited from family and friends or from bank tellers and store clerks. Currency readers, which were formerly too expensive for many users, are now appearing as inexpensive applications for smartphones. The iBill Talking Banknote Identifier, EyeNote app, and IDEAL Currency Identifier app are currently available at no cost to eligible Americans through the U.S. Bureau of Engraving and Printing (see the Resources section at the end of this chapter).

Handling Money

Physically handling money can be a challenge for many students with visual impairments and multiple disabilities. It takes good fine motor skills to pick up coins and to fold bills into recognizable shapes. It is also important to have coin purses, wallets, and billfolds that work well for the individual student. Teachers can present a selection of money containers for students to try out. Occupational therapists might also contribute ideas for storing and retrieving money in ways that are acceptable in public for particular students.

Bags that are designed for wheelchair users are available from medical supply businesses. Practice is important for handling money smoothly no matter how the student stores their money. Another skill involved in handling money in public is being discrete. It is essential for students who are visually impaired to understand the temptation presented when money is carried visibly in the hand or is laid on a counter before a clerk is there to collect it. Play acting "thefts" at home or at school can raise students' awareness of how to handle money discretely.

Handling money while in the community is an important skill to teach. Students need to practice inserting and removing money from their preferred money container (wallet, bag) before shopping. As mentioned, locating bills or coins can be quite challenging for some students. A student who struggles with fine motor and communication skills may find it easier to shop using a credit or debit card as he or she gets older. Many grocery stores have gift cards customers can purchase and use for future shopping trips. Using these cards eliminates the need for students to physically handle money.

Role-Playing: Money Management

Students with visual impairments and multiple disabilities have few opportunities to manage money. There are several ways that teachers and caregivers can change this. At school a classroom economy can be created using artificial money, such as copies of real bills with the class's name inserted in place of "United States of America." As mentioned earlier, it is important to use real coins so the students get used to their different textures, sizes, and weights. Students can earn "money" by doing classroom jobs, and can decide how to spend their money with opportunities to purchase healthy snacks, decorative or scented stickers, key chains to attach to their canes or other inexpensive items that appeal to them. Items need to have a variety of prices so that students have to make decisions about saving money for something more expensive or spending it immediately.

Creating Student Businesses

Another way to make money available at school is to hold regular sales for other students and staff members. A weekly bake sale, which involves many skills in addition to handling money, such as shopping, baking, cleaning up, advertising, and talking to customers, will provide some income. Students can then make decisions on how to use the proceeds of the sale each week. Other businesses, such as a flower delivery service or a company selling student-created greeting cards, could also be set up on a weekly basis for students to experience the exchange of money and formal social opportunities, as well as the opportunity to make a little money to manage.

Learning to Estimate Prices

Caregivers and family members have unlimited opportunities to include students in household money management. Students can often participate in shopping trips for clothing, food, hardware supplies, and other family needs. Caregivers can point out the prices of items they frequently buy and give students money to make the purchases. This way the students will learn the relative monetary value assigned to various items they may be interested in buying later in their lives. Playing guessing games with students to estimate the prices of specific items could be an entertaining way of letting them practice their knowledge of prices.

Many O&M specialists provide specific lessons on shopping (discussed later in this chapter), and the ancillary skills required to shop, such as organizing a list, utilizing customer assistance, and handling money.

Managing a Budget

Older and sophisticated students will need to learn more about managing money. Students who are eligible can look into applying for Supplemental Security Income (SSI) (a federal program that pays benefits to adults and children with disabilities who have limited income and resources). Some adults with visual impairments and multiple disabilities are placed under a conservatorship by other family members (discussed in Chapter 15). This is a legal process that declares the adults need various levels of supervision by a specific person or people. If students are not likely to be under a conservatorship as adults and do not expect to have high-income professions, managing their SSI could be a lifelong task.

All students who will be responsible for their own money need to understand the basics of bank services, including what a checking account is and how it differs from a savings account, how to make deposits and withdrawals, how to balance a checking account, and how to use an ATM card. Practicing filling out raised-line or large-print checks or writing checks using computer software will help prepare students for paying bills and making purchases. Students can learn how to pay bills directly from their bank account by setting up a plausible budget and practicing the steps involved in setting up payments electronically. Online banking requires the student to have access to technology with the appropriate software and the skills to operate such a system. Many transactions can also be accomplished over the telephone through the use of automated systems or by speaking directly to a bank's customer service representative.

Introducing young people to credit cards is becoming more and more crucial for responsible money management; some banks now offer student credit cards for just this purpose. Students who have access to money can open a credit account and practice using it with supervision. Students need to understand that they must pay for whatever they charge on a card, and that interest will accrue if the charges are not paid for each month. Having this information before leaving secondary school will provide immeasurable benefits to students who will be responsible for their own finances.

Shopping

Students first learn about shopping by going to the store with their families. As their knowledge of the community develops, they are told the names of the stores they are visiting and what will be purchased there. Over time students develop an awareness of the variety of stores in the community and understand the differences between the grocery store, a gas station, or a clothing store, for example.

When shopping, parents can describe the process in terms that their child can understand, such as: "We are going to get groceries at Safeway, so that we have milk for breakfast," or "We are going to the farmer's market to buy fruit for snacks." Parents are also encouraged to describe the new sounds that students may hear in these environments: the carts, cashiers, electric doors, and voices of other patrons.

Younger students will often ride in a cart during shopping. Parents and other caregivers are encouraged to tell the student that they have a shopping list. If time permits, each item on the list can be identified and handed to the student to explore. As the student grows, prices of each item can be included. A game can be played where the student guesses the approximate cost of various items. If the student is ambulatory, he or she can be taught to hold onto the handle of the cart while a parent or instructor guides the cart from the front or side.

Making a grocery or shopping list can be done using braille, picture cards, or voice recorders. Once students have a list and have gone to the store on multiple occasions, they may be ready to use customer service while shopping. The skills involved in this interaction are often taught by an O&M specialist. To locate customer service in an unfamiliar store, students are taught to locate a cashier and ask for assistance. Students can benefit from frequenting the same store in order to build a rapport with the staff. If scheduling allows, it is best to shop when it is less crowded (the student or teacher may ask when the quiet times of day are at that store). It is easier to maneuver in the aisles with fewer customers in the store, and customer service is often better during quiet times as the employees are less rushed.

Food Preparation

Encourage students to become involved in food preparation from an early age. A very young student can learn to put his or her bowl in the sink and assist with setting a table. In addition to building lifelong habits that will increase independence, many O&M skills and basic spatial concepts can be taught in the kitchen. When taking a bowl to the sink, some of the concepts that can be introduced include:

- Where is the sink? (Above the bottom cabinets, between the counters, under the window, across from the table, and so on.)
- How do you reach the sink? (Someone lifts me up. I stand on the stool, with an adult behind me.)
- Where is the faucet and how is it adjusted?
- Is the sink smooth or rough? Wet or dry?
- Is the water on or off?

Students who use wheelchairs may not have immediate access to the sink because of proximity or physical access to the sink. Before a child takes a dish to the sink he or she may use a simple dish tub placed on the table near his or her seat to clear a dirty dish from the table.

Do not assume that students with visual impairments understand what is going on in the kitchen. For example, a student sitting in the kitchen may hear the water in the sink running, but before he or she is told what the sound is or is brought to the sink to touch the running water, he or she will not understand what the sound signifies. It is important to include students in the kitchen on a regular basis.

Before they learn to prepare a meal, students can be encouraged to obtain their own snacks. Make sure that the snacks are kept in the same location, easily reachable by the students. Designate a shelf in the kitchen or pantry area for kid-friendly snacks such as fruit, granola bars, and crackers. Individually wrapped snacks are opportunities to practice opening packages. Fruits or vegetables can be rinsed and enjoyed as a healthful snack.

Participating with a teacher, class, or parent or other caregiver in food preparation is encouraged. The first food preparation skills students are typically taught include stirring, measuring, pouring, and spreading (see Figure 11.7). As students participate in the cooking process, they learn the names of kitchen tools and appliances and begin to understand their purposes.

As students are learning to pour, it is a good idea to keep their favorite liquids in a small pitcher in a consistent location in the refrigerator. When transitioning from pouring cold liquids to hot, some people prefer to use a liquid-level indicator. These devices hang on the lip of the cup and have sensing prongs that extend into the cup. An audible sound emanates when the liquid in the cup reaches the level of the prongs. Most adults use techniques such as a finger placed inside the lip of the cup, the sound of the liquid in

Figure 11.7

Frances Liefert

Stirring with low vision takes practice.

the cup, and the weight of the cup and liquid to determine fullness when pouring liquids.

It is important to emphasize hygiene when familiarizing a child with the kitchen. Students need to wash their hands before and after eating and before food preparation. It is often difficult for new cooks to refrain from tasting the recipe as they cook. Tasting with a clean spoon and washing hands again if a student licks his or her fingers are important skills to reinforce. Also, dressing for cooking may include a hair band, apron, and the removal of a sweatshirt, jacket, or other garment with loose sleeves to prevent fires, especially if the student is using a gas stove. Students should be familiarized with the stove when it is cold (see Figure 11.8). Tactile indicators on stove knobs can make it easier to find the most frequently used positions. Sidebar 11.6 lists a number of other helpful suggestions for maintaining safety in the kitchen.

Organize the workspace before teaching food preparation. Provide a tray or shallow baking dish on top of a nonskid mat to define the primary workspace and to catch spills. First familiarize the student with the workspace, utensils, ingredients, and recipe before beginning food preparation. Use of a waste bowl or bag allows students to readily dispose of refuse without needing to walk across the room or open cabinets.

Eating Skills

Eating by hand and drinking from a cup are the first eating skills most children master. If a student has low vision, cups or placemats in colors that provide high contrast against the table or plates may be helpful for locating a desired item. Consider unbreakable dishes

Figure 11.8

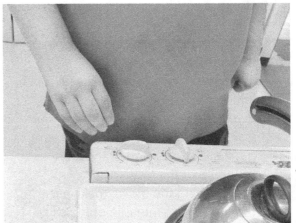

Frances Liefert

Tactile orientation to a cold stovetop is a good first step when learning stovetop cooking skills (top). Marking specific temperatures on the stove with dots of Puffy Paint or other tactile materials may be helpful (bottom).

Basic Safety Tips for Cooks with Visual Impairments

- Close drawers and cabinet doors immediately after use.
- Put away each item after using it.
- Wipe up any spills immediately.
- Work on a tray to help keep track of items and to keep spills under control.
- While cooking, have an open plastic or paper bag near your work area to conveniently collect the garbage.
- Before preparing food to be cooked, gather all the necessary utensils and ingredients and place them on one side of the counter or a tray.
- As you use things, place them on the other side of the counter or tray or in a dishpan to avoid using the same thing twice.
- After using sharp knives, wash and dry them and put them away immediately.
- Do not put knives in the sink or in a dishpan full of water.
- The safest place to store knives is in a knife block.
- If you're keeping your knife on your tray while you're using it, make sure to have the sharp edge of the knife next to the lip of the tray.
- Before using the stove, make sure there are no flammable objects like paper towels, food boxes, or appliance cords on or near the stove.
- Center the pan on the burner, using both hands, before turning on the heat.
- Make sure the pot handle does not stick out into the room or over a counter.
- Use a wooden spoon to locate a pan on the stove, and to locate food in the pan to test for doneness.
- Test the doneness of meat by pushing on it with a utensil to feel how firm it is.
- Lift the far side of the pan lid first to release the steam away from you. This prevents the steam from rising into your face.
- Never leave the stovetop cooking unattended.
- In case of a grease fire, smother the flames with a lid, or use baking soda, and turn the burner off. Never use water to try to put out a grease fire.
- Before putting a pan into a hot oven, place the pan on the counter near the oven and put on two oven mitts. Stand to one side of the oven and open the door. Pull out the top rack partway and place the pan on the rack with both hands. Push the rack in and close the door.
- Use oven mitts only. Don't use pot holders or towels.
- Bend the handle of an aluminum measuring spoon up in the form of a ladle; when measuring, dip the measuring spoon into the ingredient and lift it out.

- Measure over a small bowl to catch spills. Pour spilled ingredients back into the jar by using a funnel.
- If store containers are too small to be useful, transfer the ingredients to clearly marked containers with wide mouth openings.
- Use your sense of smell to tell if something is done.

- Label stove, microwave, and oven dials at common temperatures with tactile substances such as Puffy Paint or Hi-Mark.
- Use a timer; tactile, talking, and large-print styles are available. Timers allow for accurate cooking times and act as reminders to check food or turn off the oven or stove.

when students are first learning to eat independently. To minimize tipping over cups, teach students to place cups to their right and above the plate, and to reach for a cup by sliding their fingers across the table slowly to feel for the base of the cup instead of swatting in the air.

Eating by hand provides opportunities for students to develop tactile discrimination and to become familiar with food textures, temperatures, and tastes. When learning to scoop with a spoon, using a bowl with a suction base to keep it stable can be very helpful. A nonskid placemat may also aid the process, and spoons and forks with bent handles make scooping easier. Hand-under-hand assistance given from behind can be used to help students develop a natural scooping motion. Occupational therapists can provide multiple resources for adaptive utensils and cups, as well as teaching ideas.

When beginning to learn polite eating skills, a student can be encouraged to play with dishes, containers, and utensils in water or sand. Playing with real utensils allows children to explore and experiment with their use at a time when messiness does not matter. Many parents have a low cupboard in their kitchens

designated specifically for items their children can play with. Banging on a pot with a wooden spoon can be great fun and very instructive.

Learning to open packages can be very challenging for students. School lunch offers multiple opportunities to open cartons, take a straw out of its sleeve, and take a wrapper off of a sandwich or other food item. The backward chaining instructional technique (see Sidebar 11.4) can be used to teach students to unwrap packages; the teacher can start the unwrapping and encourage the student to finish. As students are learning to master eating techniques, it is important to supply napkins and teach students where to store them and how to use them. Students may need prompting to wipe their faces periodically throughout a meal.

Family-style dining promotes independence and self-help skills. As students are mastering the skills of pouring and scooping, they are going to spill. It is important for the adults working with them to remain patient and support their efforts. Utensils that are sized appropriately for the student will make the process easier. Smaller pitchers make pouring easier, and utilizing a tray or plate under the glass while the student is pouring will minimize cleanup. Family-style dining can be practiced at home or in a school setting. Suggestions to promote success during mealtime include the following:

- Follow the same routine daily. Make sure the students know what is expected and when.
- Adult explanation and modeling of passing, serving, and proper use of utensils helps children learn what is expected at mealtimes. For a student with a visual impairment, modeling alone is not enough. Specific, detailed explanations, coupled with hand-under-hand assistance, are often required for students to learn socially accepted eating techniques, table manners, and polite table interaction.
- Be prepared for mistakes. Anticipate spills and prepare for how to handle them and remain supportive. Keep paper towels handy, and teach students how to help wipe up the spills that occur.
- Make cleaning up easy by providing a convenient bussing station that includes a tray or sink for plates and utensils and a trash receptacle. Many schools even have compost and recycling bins available.

Managing Time

Managing time is an important aspect of being organized. In order to manage time students must first learn the concepts involved. Creating a schedule that each student can refer to is a first step. Students who read can begin with a schedule that includes morning, lunchtime, and afternoon at school. It is relatively easy to make a written schedule indicating what activities are planned for each portion of the day. At home, caregivers can also write a schedule that allows students to anticipate what their afternoons and weekends will be like.

Develop adapted schedules for students who do not read. The simplest schedule is a basket of objects used in various activities. Students select or are given the object for each activity before the activity begins. This simple action gives them an opportunity to understand that a transition is taking place. Once the activity is finished, the object used is placed in a "finished" box, and the object for the next activity is selected. As students become more sophisticated at recognizing the objects and associating them with activities, the objects can be arranged in a calendar box, a container that lines the objects up from left to right in the order in which they will be used, as discussed in Chapters 7 and 8 (Blaha, 2001; Blaha & Moss, 1997). Eventually, parts of objects or symbols of activities can be substituted for the whole object. The symbols can be attached to a piece of cloth with Velcro so they can be easily removed when the activity begins and returned to a box or envelope when the activity is finished. Students who have enough vision to recognize print symbols can have paper or whiteboard schedules each day and can cross off or erase each activity once it is done.

Using schedules gives students the opportunity to understand the order of their days and to anticipate any change in schedule. This forms the basis for understanding how time passes each day. As students learn their schedules, they can also be introduced to a weekly calendar, a monthly calendar, and the concept of seasons. Marking holidays that are celebrated in public schools, such as Labor Day, Veterans Day, Thanksgiving, Presidents' Day, and Memorial Day, also helps students understand how time passes and seasons change.

The sense of time must also include minutes and hours. Teachers and caregivers can begin work on the concepts of small increments of time by letting students know how much time will be spent on each particular task (discussed in Chapter 8). After the students are familiar with periods of a certain number of seconds, minutes, or hours, they can begin estimating how long certain activities will take. Have the student estimate how long a task will take, set a large-print or audio timer, then see how close the student's estimate was after completing the task is over. The concepts learned this way will benefit students when they need to plan their own schedules, including trips into the community, fixing meals for themselves and others, and being on time to work, medical appointments, and social engagements.

Students who are visually impaired and have other disabilities can learn to tell time in a variety of ways. Talking watches and clocks are readily available from generic electronics shops and stores or catalogues specializing in equipment for people who have visual impairments. Large-print digital watches and clocks are also readily available. Analog watches and clocks can be found in both large print and braille, and may be useful for many students with visual impairments who have the intellectual ability and motor skill to learn to use them. Students who learn how analog clock faces are laid out may use this information for more than just telling time. Traditionally, directions for everything from the location of different food items on a round plate to how to get around a large room or shopping area are given using clock-face orientation.

If students are capable of telling time, the next step will be for them to learn to add and subtract time. This skill is essential for such activities as planning trips via public transportation, knowing when to begin cooking dinner for friends, and scheduling classes in college. Understanding that there are 60 minutes in an hour takes practice since it is very different from the base-ten counting system we use routinely. It is often useful to begin learning to add and subtract time by learning to add and subtract half-hour increments and then 15-minute increments. Learning that these periods of time are referred to as "half hours" and "quarter hours" will benefit students. Students can then use the practice they have in adding and subtracting half hours and quarter hours to learn to add and subtract other quantities of minutes and hours. For example, if a student understands that 15 minutes before ten o'clock is 9:45, it will be easier to understand that 17 minutes before ten o'clock is 9:43. Students who are sophisticated enough in their math skills may enjoy the challenge of planning outings and other events down to the minute once they develop these skills.

Managing Personal Information

It is essential for students who are going to travel in the community to memorize or have access to personal information. In the United States this includes their full names, their birth dates, including the year they were born, their current ages, their addresses, phone numbers, and social security numbers. More sophisticated students may also need to re-member various passwords to open their e-mail accounts, use their ATM cards, and the like. They may also benefit from memoriz-ing the number on their state or school ID card. Students with visual impairments and multiple disabilities may not be able to memo-rize all of their personal information and may need to carry this information in written form instead. It is important for these students to learn to keep the written information with them when traveling in the community in case it is needed. Students need to be able to easily identify cards containing their personal information. A symbol, a certain color, or a clipped corner may be used to remind the stu-dents which card has particular information on it. Using a wallet or a pocket in a backpack or bag to hold a personal information card works well.

Knowing when to share personal infor-mation is the other component that requires work for many students with visual impair-ments and multiple disabilities. Students who have poor judgment may need to learn very specific rules regarding who may have access to their personal information. Categories of people, such as medical workers, police offi-cers, and teachers, can be learned by rote as people students can trust with personal infor-mation. Bus drivers, dial-a-ride drivers, and shopkeepers may need some personal infor-mation from time to time as well. It is impor-tant to stress, however, that these people are acquaintances, not friends or family, and it takes more nuanced judgment calls to decide how much information to give them. Students can prepare for real-life situations by role-playing scenarios in which they are asked for personal information. (See also the discussion of personal safety in Chapter 10.)

Personal Communication

Communication skills are covered exten-sively in Chapter 7. Here we will look at the skills that are needed in routine independent living skills activities by students with visual impairments and multiple disabilities. The earlier discussion about using a personal as-sistant included information about develop-ing interpersonal skills required for hiring and maintaining a good working relationship with an assistant. These interpersonal skills are also important for students who will rely on family or group home caregivers for assis-tance in daily living skills. Students need to learn to request assistance clearly and po-litely, to show appreciation for assistance re-ceived, and to refuse unneeded assistance appropriately.

Students who have the potential to use the telephone for gathering information about community resources, for making social con-tacts with friends and family, or for making medical appointments can begin learning to use the telephone appropriately at a young age. Parents and other caregivers can begin to teach these skills by including students in telephone conversations, and teachers can facilitate calls home or to the school office if arranged prior to the call. Students may struggle to understand that the person on the other end of the telephone is not present in the room and cannot observe everything that people in the room notice. A student can learn to call someone at school and arrange to bring something to them, such as the daily attendance sheet or a note from the teacher. This will increase the student's understanding of the phone call when they walk to the person's office to deliver the message or other item.

Many students who are unable to physically handle the telephone receiver or who cannot hear well enough to use a standard phone can still learn to use the telephone. Government-supported programs are available to make accessible phones available to people who are disabled; dialing 711 puts the caller in touch with a special operator who can help. Accessibility includes telephones with large numbers on the key pads, telephones with amplified sound, telephone devices for the deaf (which can use braille input and braille displays), telephones with custom pictures or symbols on the speed dial numbers, and speaker phones that do not require hand use. Several voice-activated dialing devices are also available. Government programs and nonprofit organizations assist people who are disabled in procuring accessible phones once they are adults. Students who are at least 18 years old can take advantage of these programs in order to obtain a usable telephone while still in school, with the opportunity to learn how to use the phone. Often, programs

that provide accessible phones will provide one to schools that are teaching students to use them.

Cell phones are currently used more than landlines. There are a few cell phones that are made specifically with large-print buttons and displays. Agencies that serve adults who are blind are a good resource for finding current models. Smartphones have auditory features that people who are blind find helpful, and they can be attached to small braille keyboard and display to make them accessible to people who prefer to use braille. The VisionAware website and *AccessWorld* online technology magazine both have many articles about accessible phones and how to use them (see the Resources section at the end of this chapter for more information).

SUMMARY

Students with visual impairments and multiple disabilities need to learn independent living skills whether or not they expect to live on their own in the future. Reaching their maximum level of independence is important for students' self-esteem and for their relationships with others. Teachers, parents, and other caregivers need to spend the time to collaborate on teaching daily living skills at a level at which students are challenged but not frustrated, so that students can meet high, yet reasonable, individual expectations. It is crucial to keep in mind that students need the skills to work with others in achieving personal success. Knowing when to seek assistance and when to refuse assistance are two of the most important skills an independent living skills curriculum will address.

Collaboration among teachers, families, caregivers, and occupational therapists will provide the most efficient and comprehensive living skills education.

REFERENCES

Bardin, J. A. (2014). Independent living. In C. B. Allman & S. Lewis (Eds.), *ECC essentials: Teaching the expanded core curriculum to students with visual impairments* (pp. 283–323). New York: AFB Press.

Blaha, R. (2001). *Calendars for students with multiple impairments including deafblindness.* Austin: Texas School for the Blind and Visually Impaired.

Blaha, R., & Moss, K. (1997, Winter). Let me check my calendar. *See/Hear.* Retrieved from https://www.tsbvi.edu/seehear/archive/Let%20Me%20Check%20My%20Calendar.htm

Blaha, R., & Moss, K. (1999, Summer). Preparing your daughter for her menstrual cycle. *See/Hear.* Retrieved from http://www.tsbvi.edu/seehear/summer99/menstruation.htm

Corn, A. L., Bina, M. J., & Sacks, S. Z. (2009). *Looking good: A curriculum on physical appearance and personal presentation for adolescents and young adults with visual impairments.* Austin, TX: Pro-Ed.

Hauser, S., Levack, N., & Newton, L. (Eds.). (1999). *Functional academics: A curriculum for students with visual impairments.* Austin: Texas School for the Blind and Visually Impaired.

Levack, N., Hauser, S., Newton, L., & Stephenson, P. (Eds.). (1997). *Basic skills for community living: A curriculum for students with visual impairments and multiple disabilities.* Austin: Texas School for the Blind and Visually Impaired.

Liefert, F. K. (2003). Expanded core curriculum: Orientation and mobility. In S. A. Goodman & S. H. Wittenstein (Eds.), *Collaborative assessment: Working with students who are blind or visually impaired, including those with additional disabilities* (pp. 264–297). New York: AFB Press.

Loumiet, R., & Levack, N. (1993). *Independent living: A curriculum with adaptations for students with visual impairments: Volume II. Self-care and maintenance of personal environment.* Austin: Texas School for the Blind and Visually Impaired.

Pogrund, R., Sewell, D., Anderson, H., Calaci, L., Cowart, M. F., Gonzalez, C., Marsh, R. A., & Roberson-Smith, B. (2012). *Teaching age-appropriate purposeful skills (TAPS): An orientation and mobility curriculum for students with visual impairments* (3rd ed.). Austin: Texas School for the Blind and Visually Impaired.

Stephenson, P. (2008). *Basic skills for community living: Activity routines.* Austin: Texas School for the Blind and Visually Impaired.

Wolffe, K. E. (Ed.). (1998). *Skills for success: A career education handbook for children and adolescents with visual impairments.* New York: AFB Press.

Wolffe, K. E., & Silberman, R. K. (2006). Teaching social skills to students with multiple disabilities. In S. Z. Sacks & K. E. Wolffe (Eds.), *Teaching social skills to students with visual impairments: From theory to practice* (pp. 441–474). New York: AFB Press.

RESOURCES

For additional resources, see the General Resources section at the back of this book.

Curricula

Basic Skills for Community Living: A Curriculum for Students with Visual Impairments and Multiple Disabilities

Source: Levack, N., Hauser, S., Newton, L., & Stephenson, P. (Eds.). (1997). *Basic skills for community living: A curriculum for students with visual impairments and multiple disabilities.* Austin: Texas School for the Blind and Visually Impaired.

Designed for students who are between the ages of 6 and 22 who have visual impairments combined with other disabilities, such as hearing impairments, dual sensory impairments, and/or severe developmental delays, and who learn best within highly structured routines and have great difficulty generalizing what they learn to new situations. Includes functional activities and assessment procedures. A companion guide, *Activity Routines,* provides charts created for domestic, recreation/leisure, and vocational domains and includes activity routine discrepancy analysis forms.

Functional Academics: A Curriculum for Students with Visual Impairments

Source: Hauser, S., Levack, N., & Newton, L. (Eds.). (1999). *Functional academics: A curriculum for students with visual impairments.* Austin: Texas School for the Blind and Visually Impaired.

Designed for teachers and instructors who work with adolescents 12 years of age and older for whom the developmental or academic approach is no longer effective, and who have basic academic skills at a kindergarten through second grade level. Describes curriculum content as well as strategies, adaptations, and procedures for planning, teaching, and documenting progress. An activity-based program, it structures students' learning day around daily life activities that are age-appropriate and prepares students for productive adult lives, blending traditional academic work with real-life tasks. Instructors may choose from assessment forms and sample units included.

Independent Living: A Curriculum with Adaptations for Students with Visual Impairments

Source: Loumiet, R., & Levack, N. (1993). *Independent living: A curriculum with adaptations for students with visual impairments* (2nd ed.). Austin: Texas School for the Blind and Visually Impaired.

Helps in assessing, teaching, and evaluating students from school age to adulthood who will live independently or with minimal assistance in social, self-care, and leisure skills. This three-volume curriculum is accompanied by reproducible assessment and ongoing evaluation forms. A booklet of these forms can also be purchased separately. Designed for teaching in public schools, residential schools, and rehabilitation centers.

Looking Good: A Curriculum on Physical Appearance and Personal Presentation for Adolescents and Young Adults with Visual Impairments

Source: Corn, A. L., Bina, M. J., & Sacks, S. Z. (2009). *Looking good: A curriculum on physical appearance and personal presentation for adolescents and young adults with visual impairments.* Austin, TX: Pro-Ed.

Details the potential areas of difficulty that students with visual impairments might experience related to understanding the concepts of physical appearance and personal presentation and offers a curriculum for addressing these challenges. Included are units focused on the importance of physical appearance and presentation; the conventions of nonverbal communication; the significant role of family culture and value on appearance and dress; and the contributions facial appearance, fitness, posture, dress, accessories, and physical movement have to "looking good." Also includes pre- and post-test assessments.

TAPS: An Orientation and Mobility Curriculum for Students with Visual Impairments
Source: Pogrund, R., Sewell, D., Anderson, H., Calaci, L., Cowart, M. F., Gonzalez, C., Marsh, R. A., & Roberson-Smith, B. (2012). *Teaching age-appropriate purposeful skills (TAPS): An orientation and mobility curriculum for students with visual impairments* (3rd ed.). Austin: Texas School for the Blind and Visually Impaired.

Designed for orientation and mobility specialists who serve students ages 3 to 21 who may also have other impairments. This four-part curriculum includes goals, objectives, and teaching strategies as well as functional mobility tasks for the following environments: home/living, campus, residential, commercial and public transportation, as well as an ambulatory devices section.

Currency Identifiers

These devices and applications recognize currency and speak denominations, enabling people who are blind or visually impaired to quickly and easily identify and count bills.

EyeNote (iOS)
Bureau of Engraving and Printing
http://www.eyenote.gov/

iBill Talking Banknote Identifier
Orbit Research
http://www.orbitresearch.com/ibill_details.php

IDEAL Currency Identifier (Android)
IDEAL Group, Inc. Android Development Team
https://play.google.com/store/apps/details?id=org.ideal.currencyid&hl=en

LookTel Money Reader
LookTel
http://www.looktel.com/moneyreader

Note Teller 2
Brytech
http://www.brytech.com/noteteller/

Voice-It-All Money and Color Identifier
Reizen
http://www.reizenusa.com/prodView.asp?status=c&recid=28

Websites

AccessWorld
American Foundation for the Blind
www.afb.org/aw

A free online magazine providing information on assistive technology and reviews of accessible products from the American Foundation for the Blind.

FamilyConnect
American Foundation for the Blind and National Association of Parents of Children with Visual Impairments
www.familyconnect.org

An online, multimedia community for parents of visually impaired children. Provides suggestions about independent living skills for visually impaired children of all ages, including a section specifically for students with multiple disabilities. A searchable database provides link to local resources.

Perkins Scout
Daily Living Skills in Young Children
Perkins School for the Blind
http://www.perkinselearning.org/scout/daily-living-skills-young-children-blind-multiple-disabilities-deafblind#General_Considerations_for_Daily_Living

A searchable database of online resources related to blindness and visual impairment for parents of children who are blind or visually impaired that includes practical suggestions for encouraging greater independence in all areas of daily living such as eating, dressing, bathing, sleeping, and using the toilet.

VisionAware
American Foundation for the Blind
www.visionaware.org

A website directed to adults who are losing their sight to continue to help them live full and independent lives. Provides step-by-step daily living techniques in many areas of use to individuals of all ages with visual impairments.

Sources of Products

For companies that distribute daily living products, see the General Resources section at the back of this book.

Bureau of Engraving and Printing
U.S. Department of the Treasury
14th and C Streets, SW
Washington, DC 20228
(844) 815-9388
meaningful.access@bep.gov
http://www.bep.gov/uscurrencyreaderpgm.html

Launched the U.S. Currency Reader Program, which provides currency readers, free of charge, to eligible blind and visually impaired individuals.

Chapter 12

Assistive Technology

• •

Stacy M. Kelly and Derrick W. Smith

Key Points

�🗝 How assistive technology can be used to increase the academic and functional capabilities of students with visual impairments and multiple disabilities

�🗝 Assistive technology assessment as an ongoing and individualized process that addresses the unique needs of students with visual impairments with multiple disabilities

�🗝 How a wide array of assistive technology devices can be used to teach a variety of fundamental concepts to students with different abilities

�🗝 How technology can be used to facilitate life and pre-academic skills for students with visual impairments and multiple disabilities

---

Jake is a lively, outgoing boy who attends third grade at his local elementary school, where he is performing at the kindergarten grade level. Jake has been receiving special education services since he was three due to having cerebral palsy and visual impairment. He is able to walk short distances, but uses a wheelchair for longer distances or when on uneven ground. Jake's vision fluctuates due to optic nerve atrophy with visual field loss. Although he usually relies on his own speech, he uses synthesized speech produced by a communication device as a backup. He is provided special education and related services from various special education teachers, including a teacher of students with visual impairments and related service providers (occupational therapist, physical therapist, and orientation and mobility specialist).

Jake has difficulties with both his gross and fine motor skills, and his poor hand-eye coordination coupled with his visual impairment make most activities challenging. Jake can push larger buttons and he truly enjoys working with a desktop computer. Jake experiences challenges inputting information into the computer using the standard keyboard. As a result of his visual impairment, it is also difficult for Jake to see information displayed on the computer monitor.

The desktop computer is the extent of technology involved in Jake's school day and it has not yet been adapted to meet his needs. Jake wishes to use many of the same

commonly used devices as his third-grade peers, such as interactive whiteboards and tablet computers, but he does not have the opportunity to do so during the school day. Jake currently does not have an assistive technology plan. It seems that the school district does not have a clear vision of Jake's needs regarding assistive technology.

Jake's use of assistive technology is currently being reviewed by his IEP team, who are considering a range of devices and software to include as an integral part of Jake's daily routines.

Assistive technology is often considered the great equalizer for students with disabilities, especially for students with visual impairments. For students who have visual impairments (and who do not have multiple disabilities), assistive technology offers the tools to overcome the major obstacles they must deal with on a daily basis. For instance, assistive technology provides students with visual impairments access to information, a critical aspect of education, employment, and social interactions. Using screen readers, braille displays, screen magnifiers, electronic braille notetakers, and the classic Perkins Brailler, students have the ability to read and write, gather information, and express themselves. Assistive technology also provides students with the ability to lead independent lives and participate in meaningful experiences. Assistive technology tools, such as audio global positioning systems (GPS), support the ability of students with visual impairments to orient themselves in space and travel independently. Less sophisticated as-

sistive technology tools allow individuals with visual impairments to lead normal lives doing tasks such as cleaning, cooking, watching television, playing games and sports, and the like. Assistive technology is truly the mechanism leading to a normal and successful life for individuals with visual impairments. For students with visual impairments and multiple disabilities, assistive technology is no less important.

As defined in the Individuals with Disabilities Education Improvement Act of 2004 (IDEA; 34 C.F.R. § 300.5):

> Assistive technology device means any item, piece of equipment, or product system, whether acquired commercially off the shelf, modified, or customized, that is used to increase, maintain, or improve the functional capabilities of a child with a disability. The term does not include a medical device that is surgically implanted, or the replacement of such device.

For students with visual impairments and physical disabilities, assistive technology tools such as specialized keyboards for typing, microswitches for controlling devices, speech-recognition software for inputting information on a computer, and custom educational furniture all provide access to education.

Students with visual impairments and cognitive disabilities need opportunities to construct understanding of fundamental concepts in education such as choice making and cause and effect, the connection between an action or behavior and an outcome. At the basic level, a student's understanding that his or her actions lead to some reactions is critical to that student understanding more advanced concepts. A student with a visual impairment and cognitive disability may begin learning the concept of cause and effect by pushing a large button that makes a toy move. Once the student understands this concept, then the idea that pushing a button on a keyboard can "write" a letter on the computer can begin to be developed. Although the activity is modified using the assistive technology, for students who have cognitive disabilities, the experiences are no less important to their learning,

The assistive technology devices and teaching strategies discussed within this chapter are intended to serve as resources for increasing students' functionality, independence, and performance across many life skills. A range of items will be discussed, from simple battery-powered learning tools to high-tech computer software applications, which can all be used to perform simple tasks. *No-technology* or *no-tech* refers to any assistive device that is not electronic and does not have moving parts. No-tech items include the slate and stylus, dark markers, bold-lined paper, and the long cane. *Low-technology* or *low-tech devices* have movable parts which may or may not be electronic, but they do not include highly sophisticated computer components. Examples of low-tech devices include items such as an electronic voice-recording device, a talking calculator, and the manual braille-writer. *High-technology* or *high-tech devices* involve complex, multifunction technology and usually include a computer and associated software (Maushak, Kelley, & Blodgett, 2001). (The Resources section at the end of this chapter provides information about specific products mentioned in this chapter, as well as additional assistive technology resources.)

THE EDUCATIONAL TEAM AND ASSISTIVE TECHNOLOGY

Having the information included in this chapter will assist the educational team in planning for best practices in their delivery of services to their students in the area of assistive technology instruction. The educational team should strive to involve assistive technology tools in learning tasks on a regular basis. Furthermore, assistive technology can only be effective if students with visual impairments and multiple disabilities are provided with devices and services through a coordinated team approach. When all team members are working collaboratively toward common goals, and not in isolation, the delivery of assistive technology–specific services is improved. Although each team member's responsibility for the implementation of assistive technology use may vary, everyone contributes to a coordinated team approach that is designed for each student and his or her family. For example, an audiologist and teacher of students with visual impairments may work together with a classroom teacher to coordinate the most effective use of assistive technology for a student who has a visual impairment and hearing loss.

Individualized Education Program (IEP) team members' corresponding roles with classroom-based assistive technology assessment and assistive technology instruction is unique and important. Particular IEP team members may be more or less involved in the assistive technology assessment and instruction process depending on the individual learning needs of the student with visual impairment and multiple disabilities. An assistive technology specialist is specifically trained to work with assistive technology for individuals with multiple disabilities. Residential schools for students with visual impairments often have assistive technology specialists who have expertise in assessment and instruction in assistive technology for students with visual impairments. Many of these individuals can provide valuable resources, technical support, and assessment services. For all of these reasons, the assistive technology–specific needs of students with visual impairments and multiple disabilities are best served through well-coordinated team approaches.

Teachers of students with visual impairments need to be equipped to work with a large variety of students, including those with multiple disabilities. Each student will require an IEP that may require assistive technology. Therefore, the purpose of this chapter is to provide teachers of students with visual impairments with a basic knowledge of specific content areas in which assistive technology can advance the education of students with visual impairments and multiple disabilities. The chapter will offer an overview of the content and its importance, a listing of tools that address that content, and teaching strategies connected to the use of assistive technology. This information is focused on classroom-based assistive technology used by students with visual impairments and multiple disabilities for learning tasks. (For information about assistive technology for particular modes of communication, such as augmentative and alternative communication [AAC] devices, see Chapter 7; for positioning and O&M, see Chapter 10.) In reading this chapter, it is important to remember that assistive technology is constantly evolving and growing, so the range of tools described here is not exhaustive and is always subject to change. However, the concepts found in this chapter should provide a foundation for teachers of students with visual impairments to use assistive technology with students with visual impairments and multiple disabilities.

There are many challenges in assistive technology instruction and assistive technology use, yet these challenges do not override the advantages. It is important not only to point out several of the most prevalent challenges but also to emphasize that being aware of the challenges helps to overcome them. Prevalent challenges in assistive technology instruction include:

- overload or shortage of necessary information about how to use assistive technology
- shortage of well-trained personnel able to provide effective assistive technology instruction to students with visual impairments and multiple disabilities
- limited compatibility of assistive technology equipment (for example, there is not yet one screen-reading program that works on all available operating systems)
- equipment costs and limited sources of financial assistance
- rapid changes in technology make it difficult to keep knowledge current

As technology quickly evolves, new assistive technology devices will be invented, old assistive technology devices will be reinvented, and a variety of technologies will become obsolete. However, in the end, the best devices will always need to be coupled with a strong team focused on the best interests of the student.

ASSISTIVE TECHNOLOGY ASSESSMENT

As with any aspect of education, assessment is the first step to determine the assistive technology needs of each individual student with a visual impairment and multiple disabilities. When evaluating a student for assistive technology, collaboration with the other professionals who work with the student is vitally important. Teachers of students with visual impairments collaborate with the local education agency (the administrative agency for public schools in the area) and the district educational and assistive technology specialists who oversee the resources and materials that are available to the IEP team. Therefore, a collaborative team approach begins with the assessment and should include the teacher of students with visual impairments, all educators (both general and special), the assistive technology specialist, and other related service providers. (See also Chapter 3 for a general discussion of assessing students with visual and multiple disabilities.)

Collecting Information

Educational team members need to begin the assistive technology evaluation process by collecting and gathering information about the student, his or her educational and functional needs, and the goals established in his or her IEP. This information will identify tasks that should be addressed through the formal assistive technology assessment process. The most widely used framework for gathering information about students' assistive technology needs is the SETT framework. SETT refers to Student, Environment, Tasks, and Tools, the areas that need to be reviewed during the assessment. The SETT planning framework (Zabala, 2005) is a tool that helps teams gather and organize information that can be used to guide collaborative decisions about assistive technology devices and services. Since it focuses on gathering and organizing information, it is referred to as a "planning framework" instead of an assessment tool.

To begin using the SETT framework, the assistive technology assessment team should focus on understanding the student they are serving. Next, the team should consider the student's environment, which plays a significant role in the success of assistive technology for students with visual impairments. This significance multiplies when students have multiple disabilities. The evaluation of tasks focuses on two primary questions: (1) What *specific* tasks occur in the student's natural environments that allow for progress toward mastery of IEP goals and objectives? and (2) What *specific* tasks are required for active involvement in all environments (Zabala, 2005)? Once the assistive technology assessment team has completed an assessment of the student, environment, and tasks, they then can begin to determine what system of tools is needed to support access and increase the achievement of the student, which leads to the need for more robust evaluation measures and instruments. Sidebar 12.1 contains a list of questions that can be used to gather information in each of these areas.

Assistive Technology Assessment Instruments

The SETT framework provides a basic structure that is appropriately applicable to all assistive technology assessments. However, there exist some specific instruments that can be used by an assistive technology assessment team to make specific determinations about a student's assistive technology needs. (See the Resources section at the end of this chapter for more information about these and other technology resources.) For example, the Assessment Package from the Wisconsin Assistive Technology Initiative (WATI) (Reed, 2004) is a process-based, systematic approach to providing a functional assessment of the student's need for assistive technology in his or her natural environment. The WATI is considered *process-based* because it focuses on understanding what is needed to produce specific results, thus addressing the unique needs of the student. The WATI provides a full assessment package that includes referral and question identification guides and additional checklists to determine the assistive technology needs of the student. The robustness of the WATI makes it a valuable assessment tool for students with visual impairments and multiple disabilities. Other valuable instruments include the University of Kentucky Assistive Technology Project's

Assistive Technology Toolkit (2003) and the Dynamic Assistive Technology Evaluation (DATE; Texas Assistive Technology Network, 2009).

Assistive Technology Assessments for Students with Visual Impairments

Presley and D'Andrea (2009) provide a comprehensive guide for assessment of assistive technology needs for students with visual impairments. This text provides a solid framework, numerous checklists, and full explanation of the process of assessment for this population. The assistive technology assessments, combined with the student's functional vision assessment (FVA) and learning media assessment (LMA) (see Chapter 3 for more on these assessments), should provide a comprehensive evaluation of the needs of the student with visual impairments. However, more generic assistive technology assessment tools, like the WATI, could also be used when assessing a student with visual impairments and multiple disabilities, since the broader instruments focus on a larger array of technological needs.

Connecting the Assistive Technology Assessment to the IEP

Since assistive technology must be discussed as part of the IEP development process, the assistive technology assessment must be completed before developing the IEP. The assistive technology assessment should be completed separately from all other assessments and *after* the educational assessments, so that the

Applying the SETT Framework

The following are questions that can be used to gather information using the SETT framework:

The Student

- What is the student's learning medium?
- What abilities does the student possess?
- What impact do the multiple disabilities have in combination with the visual impairment?
- What are the general attitudes of the student toward technology and instruction?

The Environment

- What is the student's current least restrictive environment?
- How is the student able to interact with his or her environment?
- What level of independence does the student have in his or her learning environment?
- What special materials and/or equipment are used for the student to access the core and expanded core curriculum?
- What areas of expertise do the educators and related service providers that work with the student possess?

The Tasks

- What core academic learning activities will the student be engaged in via the curriculum?
- In what expanded core curriculum learning activities will the student be engaged?
- What are the most important aspects of the learning activities where assistive technology may be used?
- What impact will assistive technology have on the student's ability to access the core and expanded core curriculum?
- What goals and benchmarks have been developed for the student by the IEP team?

The Tools

- What type of tools might be used in creating a learning environment to meet the needs of the student?
- What instructional strategies can be used to increase motivation to use appropriate assistive technology for learning?
- How can the use of assistive technology be generalized beyond the classroom?

Source: Adapted from Zabala, J. S. (2005). Using the SETT framework to level the learning field for students with disabilities. Retrieved from http://www.joyzabala.com/uploads/Zabala_SETT_Leveling_the_Learning_Field .pdf

assistive technology evaluator can collaborate with the educational evaluation team to determine what specific areas of need have been identified, such as access to print information, access to the physical environment, or functional independent living skills. The FVA and LMA are both critical pieces in a valid assistive technology evaluation because of the importance of the information they provide regarding the needs of the student. For instance, the FVA may provide information about specific lighting or print color combinations that may influence the use or settings of specific computer software programs (such as inverting the colors on a monitor). The LMA provides invaluable information about which media should be used for learning for a particular student. Knowing whether the student needs braille, large-print, or auditory information will have major implications on many assistive technology decisions.

IEP GOALS FOR ASSISTIVE TECHNOLOGY

Assistive technology services and devices are typically listed within the benchmarks section of the IEP as tools that are used to meet an academic goal. However, for students with visual impairments and multiple disabilities, direct instruction on the use of an assistive technology device may also be an appropriate annual goal. For example, consider Jake, the student in the vignette that introduced this chapter. The evaluation found that Jake has an array of disabilities that have inhibited his use of the computer even though the assistive technology assessment indicates that he has a preference toward using it. Therefore, the IEP team may decide that one of Jake's measurable annual goals may involve learning to use one specific device or even an array of devices to make the computer accessible.

The IEP team will need to determine whether Jake needs a separate annual goal focused solely on the technology or if the goal should be connected directly to academic content. Sidebar 12.2 presents two examples of measurable annual IEP goals and benchmarks for Jake. Annual Goal 1 is focused solely on technology while Annual Goal 2 is focused on academic content. The selection of how much time to spend and how much focus to give the assistive technology device will depend on the student's abilities and the complexity of the tool.

USING ASSISTIVE TECHNOLOGY IN TEACHING

The IEP provides goals for *what* should be taught to the student. However, the assistive technology evaluation provides not only guidance for developing assistive technology goals and benchmarks for the IEP but supports the development of a comprehensive plan for the use and instruction of assistive technology. After the assistive technology evaluation is complete, the teacher of students with visual impairments, along with the local education agency, determines which assistive technology devices need to be acquired to meet the individual needs of the student. In essence, the school provides the student with an assistive technology "toolbox," or a collection

---

✏ Sidebar 12.2

Sample Assistive Technology–Specific Annual Goals and Benchmarks for Jake

---

Measurable Annual Goal 1: Focus on Technology

When provided an IntelliKeys alternative keyboard, Jake will type simple 2–5 word sentences with 80 percent accuracy in 4 out of 5 trials.

- **Benchmark 1:** When provided an IntelliKeys alternative keyboard, Jake will select specific alphabet keys as prompted by the teacher with 80 percent accuracy in 4 out of 5 trials.
- **Benchmark 2:** When provided an IntelliKeys alternative keyboard, Jake will write simple sight words (up to 5 letters) as prompted by the teacher with 80 percent accuracy in 4 out of 5 trials.
- **Benchmark 3:** When provided an IntelliKeys alternative keyboard, Jake will write simple, 2–3 word sentences with 80 percent accuracy in 4 out of 5 trials.
- **Benchmark 4:** When provided an IntelliKeys alternative keyboard, Jake will write simple, 4–5 word sentences with 80 percent accuracy in 4 out of 5 trials.

Measurable Annual Goal 2: Focus on Academic Content

When prompted, Jake will use appropriate assistive technology devices to complete writing assignments with 90 percent accuracy in 4 out of 5 trials.

- **Benchmark 1:** When prompted, Jake will use switches to turn on and off his computer with 90 percent accuracy in 4 out of 5 trials.
- **Benchmark 2:** When prompted, Jake will use his "BIG" mouse to select Dragon NaturallySpeaking with 90 percent accuracy in 4 out of 5 trials.
- **Benchmark 3:** When prompted, Jake will use Dragon NaturallySpeaking to draft a story composed of a minimum of 4 sentences with 90 percent accuracy in 4 out of 5 trials.
- **Benchmark 4:** When prompted, Jake will use his "BIG" mouse to print his assignments with 90 percent accuracy in 4 out of 5 trials.

---

of tools the student can use to access his or her education. Therefore, the remainder of this chapter will focus on tools that might be found in such a toolbox, providing an overview of primary fundamental concepts for students with visual impairments and multiple disabilities, the applicable tools and uses for each concept, and teaching strategies for teachers of students with visual impairments working with these students. The fundamental concepts addressed fall into two domains: assistive technology for fundamental concepts and assistive technology for academic instruction.

ASSISTIVE TECHNOLOGY FOR FUNDAMENTAL CONCEPTS

Students with visual impairments and multiple disabilities need to be exposed to particular fundamental concepts at a young age. The concepts of cause and effect and choice making and skills involving sensory efficiency are among children's earliest learning experiences. A solid understanding of these initial concepts is particularly important to prepare for tasks involving higher-order thinking. Assistive technology devices can provide many meaningful interactions between a student with a visual impairment and multiple disabilities and his or her environment during this stage of development. Switch access to computer activities, toys, and appliances; touchscreen access to computer activities; alternative keyboard access to computer activities; and switch or touch access to communication functions are all examples of assistive technology that can be used to facilitate early concept development and sensory efficiency among students with visual impairments and multiple disabilities.

Assistive Technology for Teaching Cause and Effect

Teaching cause-and-effect relationships in actual situations can be highly beneficial. Cause and effect is the beginning of learning and leads to understanding many other concepts. For example, children must understand the concept of cause and effect before they begin using language skills (Jamieson, 2004). A student can learn cause and effect when he or she engages in an action that causes a consistent response. Concrete experiences with cause and effect are even more important for students with visual impairments and multiple disabilities. Assistive technology can provide many novel opportunities to allow students to establish control, through an understanding of cause and effect, over parts of their everyday activities.

It is important to develop a wide range of tools and devices beyond computer-based options when providing assistive technology instruction. The use of interactive switch-activated toys or appliances is one example of well-established assistive technology that has an important role in concept development for students with visual impairments and multiple disabilities. For some students, battery-operated toys or devices can be an early introduction to cause-and-effect relationships. A switch can be attached to most battery-operated toys or simple appliances.

Tools for Teaching Cause and Effect

Tools for teaching cause and effect include the following:

Switches. Switches are available that can be activated by any body part that can produce consistent and voluntary movement (see Figure 12.1). For example, switches can be activated by pushing, pulling, pressing, blinking, squeezing, puffing, kicking, or touching. Using the type of switch that best meets their individual needs, students with visual impairments

Figure 12.1

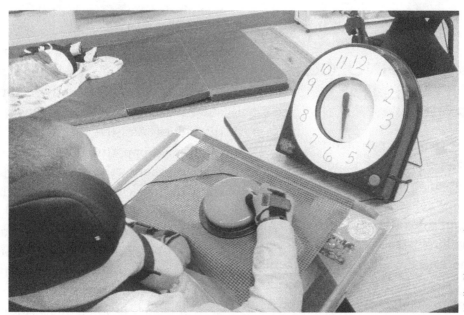

Molly Clesen Pasley

A student using a switch attached to a battery-operated analog clock.

and multiple disabilities can determine when the toy or activity starts and stops or what exactly the toy or activity does when it is turned on.

Software Programs. Software programs or applications that run on standard, adapted laptop or desktop computers may also prove beneficial for cause-and-effect instruction with students with visual impairments and multiple disabilities (see Figure 12.2). Software applications may be of interest to students who are ready to progress beyond the use of basic switch-activated toys or appliances. The accessibility features of Windows and Mac computer operating systems for students with visual impairments and multiple disabilities include:

- alternative keyboards, alternative keyboard layouts, and keyguards (a plate with holes that fits over a keyboard to prevent pressing keys by accident)
- programmable keyboards or onscreen keyboards
- modified mice
- joysticks
- trackballs
- switch access with visual or auditory scanning
- mouth sticks, head pointers, sip-and-puff systems
- voice-recognition capabilities
- speech output
- screen magnification software
- touchscreen access

Figure 12.2

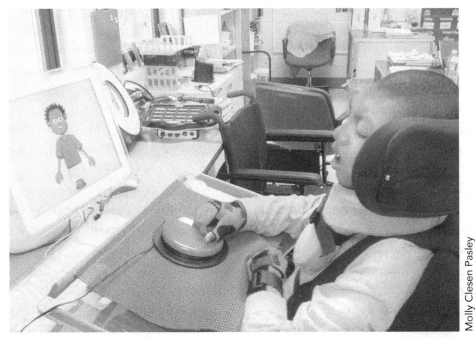

Molly Clesen Pasley

A student using a switch to access a desktop computer software application.

Mobile Devices. Tablet computers, smartphones, and portable media players equipped with wireless Internet connectivity are all examples of mobile devices. Downloads of cause-and-effect software programs to tablets or other mobile devices has become an increasingly popular way to facilitate early learning experiences.

Apps. Apps are programs designed to run on mobile devices. There are thousands of apps on the market that range from free or low cost to $200 or more. Examples of low-cost apps that can be used to teach cause and effect to students with visual impairments and multiple disabilities are presented later in this chapter.

Strategies for Teaching Cause and Effect

Teachers can use switches with a push button to cause a desktop fan to turn on, a kitchen blender to start operating, or a pillow to vibrate. When the student pushes the button, the fan turns on, the blender starts working, or the pillow vibrates. If the student pushes the button again, the switch-activated activity stops. In each of these examples, activating a switch has an impact on the environment, leading to more active participation.

Teaching the use of switches with a push button helps the student learn the concept of cause and effect in a functional way. This is one of the most basic and low-tech methods of providing students with visual impairments and multiple disabilities with the opportunity to practice initiating a cause that results in an effect. The use of simple switches in conjunction with simple battery-powered toys or appliances is the beginning of student empowerment and feelings of autonomy through the fundamental understanding of cause and effect.

Teachers can use many of the widely available software programs to facilitate the early learning of cause and effect through a unique combination of fun and interesting audio and visual output. For preschool students with visual impairments and multiple disabilities, the *Baby Smash* Windows-compatible software download and the *AlphaBaby* Macintosh-compatible software download are examples of many of the available software programs that can be included as a first step in early learning experiences. The user is locked into the *Baby Smash* or *AlphaBaby* software application and out of other computer options or applications. Both programs work in an identical manner, allowing the user to randomly press on any computer key, with the end result being a combination of stimulating colored letters, numbers, or shapes appearing on the screen. The young learner can more safely use the computer to explore cause-and-effect relationships with these free and basic types of early learning software downloads.

For students who may require more age-appropriate teaching strategies for practicing cause-and-effect relationships, a standard or adapted laptop or desktop computer may be considered by the educational team. There are literally thousands of educational software programs to choose from that can be used in combination with many of the computer operating system accessibility features and basic switches presented in this chapter. *101 Animations* is an example of cause-and-effect software and is available for both Windows and Mac operating systems. The software includes animations that can be activated by a switch, space bar, touch screen, or mouse click.

Tablet computers can be equipped with the same switches or buttons as previously discussed with basic toys or simple appliances, although tablet switches are connected by a switch interface rather than plugged directly into the device. The switch interface bridges the connection between the switch and the tablet. A switch can be plugged into the tablet's switch interface to make the switch work with switch-friendly apps. Students with visual impairments and multiple disabilities for whom a traditional control mechanism or required movement may be too difficult can then participate in learning tasks with tablets by using a variety of body movements, or even eye blinks.

For example, *RadSounds* is a cause-and-effect music app designed specifically for students with multiple disabilities. Teachers and students can customize the *RadSounds* playlist by recording or singing new music into an iPad, importing music from the iPad's music library, or using the songs that come with the app. Momentary mode plays music for as long as the user holds his or her finger on the iPad screen. Timed mode plays music for a specified number of seconds upon each activation. In Advanced mode, the user chooses songs by cycling through the playlist.

Tap-n-See Now (formerly known as *Tap-n-See Zoo*) is among the first mobile apps developed specifically for students who have cortical visual impairment (CVI). This simple cause-and-effect app includes basic pictures, colors, and sounds that can all be customized. Teachers can present their students with a red or yellow animal against a black background, for example, and as the student touches or taps the animals (cause), they expand or disappear (effect). Rewarding sounds play to encourage students to interact with this app.

There are many more types of activities that involve the use of apps to facilitate understanding fundamental and more advanced concepts to build on early learning experiences with cause and effect. For example, there are apps that can be used to identify money, light, and color. Surroundings can be explored with GPS applications. Students can routinely check the weather, instant message with friends, or play their favorite games using apps that involve practice with choice making. A listing of additional resources that support practice with life skills through the use of assistive technology is included at the end of the chapter.

It is important to note that the array of available apps changes daily. When providing access to the wide variety of applications that can be used to enhance quality of life for students with visual impairments and multiple disabilities, teachers and other professionals should also be prepared for the regular updates the applications require.

Assistive Technology for Teaching Choice Making

The skill of choice making, which allows students to make decisions for themselves, is a component in building a foundation for self-determination and increasing independence in students with visual impairments and multiple disabilities. Choice making can be taught through regularly encountered daily activities that involve technology. Choice making involves the identification and communication of a preference. Students with visual impairments and multiple disabilities can express their preferences or make requests using assistive technology devices and software.

Tools for Teaching Choice Making

The following are some tools for teaching choice making:

Picture Exchange Communication System (PECS) Symbols. A highly effective method for students with visual impairments and complex communication needs to make requests is to present them with PECS symbols that have been modified to include three-dimensional or tactile features (Murray-Branch, Udavari-Solner, & Bailey, 1991; Rowland & Schweigert, 1989; Turnell & Carter, 1994). PECS was developed nearly 30 years ago for use with students who have autism and related developmental disabilities, but the target audience has since expanded to include many other disabilities that have an impact on functional communication skills. The PECS symbols include both a simple picture symbol and a word below the symbol that captures the intended concept of the symbol. For example, a simple picture symbol of eggs also includes the word "eggs" written in basic typed text directly below the image. The PECS program requires the student to hand the picture of a requested item to his or her communication partner. In exchange for the picture, the student receives the requested activity or item. In this initial phase of the PECS program, the student is using a symbol to express and make his or her desired choice. There are thousands of PECS symbols a teacher can select from when planning a variety of unique choice-making opportunities.

Other Communication Symbols. Boardmaker Picture Communication Symbols (PCS from Mayer-Johnson) and High Contrast Icons (from Enabling Devices) may be used in a similar fashion as the PECS symbols to practice decision making. There is also a PCS collection of high-contrast icons. High-contrast icons are communication symbols specifically designed to be highly visible to support students with visual impairments.

Talking Switches. In addition to the basic switch technology already discussed, talking switches can also be used to evaluate students' preferences and facilitate choice making. Talking switches are switch-activated voice output devices. These devices can be used as a starting place to assist with a means of communication for students who are nonverbal. There are two basic types of talking switches: those that allow the communication of only one thought or message (such as the BIGmack from AbleNet) and those that

allow the communication of a sequence of messages (such as the Step-by-Step Communicator from AbleNet). (Chapter 7 includes additional information on augmentative and alternative communication devices.)

Software Applications. As students advance in concept development, the complexity of the device used to express their choices gradually increases. Technology can assist with this increase in complexity in several ways. PowerPoint, for example, is a software application with considerable potential for use as assistive technology. PowerPoint can support independent practice and provide numerous onscreen choice-making activities, as explained in the next section.

Strategies for Teaching Choice Making

Preference Evaluation. One of the first steps in establishing choice-making opportunities for students with visual impairments and multiple disabilities is for the teacher to implement a preference evaluation. A *preference evaluation* involves the presentation of a variety of objects (such as toys) and recording the student's response to determine a set of the student's preferred and nonpreferred objects. Once the student's preferences are determined, he or she can be presented with a preferred and nonpreferred object using the assistive technology solution most suitable for the individual student. Choosing between objects can develop into choosing between words (such as "yes" or "no") and preferred activities (computer time versus reading a book), the foundation for many educational tasks.

Developing Social Skills. IEP team members can work together to seek social opportunities in which to involve assistive technology in choice-making opportunities. The ability to make simple choices in basic conversations (for instances, whether to work with Mr. Smith or Ms. Kelly) establishes basic social skills.

Adapting Communication Symbols. The communication symbols, such as PECS images, can be modified by educational specialists to include three-dimensional or textured features for students with visual impairments and multiple disabilities. These features are attached directly onto the symbol to provide a meaningful learning experience for students with visual impairments and multiple disabilities. Lund and Troha (2008) explain that three-dimensional objects (either in part or whole) with relationships to the corresponding symbol can work well. Using a part of a chain to represent the concept of "swing" or a whole spoon to represent the concept of "breakfast" are examples of partial and whole objects that have associated or direct relationships with the corresponding symbol. Textured symbols that can be attached directly to the symbols may be related to the concept (such as wax paper to represent the concept of "candy") or more arbitrary in nature (such as a piece of felt to represent the concept of "stop") (Lund & Troha, 2008).

Braille can be put directly on the symbols to provide the same degree of stimulation as the printed word provides sighted students. The text is consistently located in the same location on every symbol, and it would follow that the braille can be consistently located too.

Several of the communication symbols and systems can be used in conjunction with each other. Communication books, communication boards, and communication aprons are examples of ways for students with visual impairments and multiple disabilities to present their communication symbols to their communication partners (peers, family members, teachers, and other educational specialists).

Using Talking Switches. Talking switches can facilitate choice making in a variety of ways. For example, a student with visual impairments and multiple disabilities can be asked a choice-making question by his or her teacher, such as "Would you like to take a break now?" or "Are you ready to go on a walk?" The student is then presented with two talking switches. Each switch is a large button, 5 inches in diameter, to provide the student with a sizable target area. One button has been recorded to speak "yes" when pushed and the other to speak "no" when pushed. The "yes" button is red and has a soft felt circle attached to its surface; the "no" button is yellow with a scratchy sandpaper square attached directly to its surface. After being presented with the question and the two switches, the student then makes a choice by pressing the red talking switch for a "yes" response message or the yellow talking switch for a "no" response message. This choice-making teaching strategy may work as a long-term goal for a particular student. This example also demonstrates how tactile symbols or simple pictures that match the message can be placed directly on a switch for enhanced tactile or visual cueing.

Most talking switches have up to two minutes in available playback time, which allows the teacher the option to facilitate the recording of an entire sentence instead of shorter answers like "yes" and "no." Full sentences allow the student to express a more complete thought about his or her decision. When ordering a meal, for example, the student with visual impairments and multiple disabilities can present his or her order by pressing the talking switch to activate the recorded message on the talking switch: "I'd like eggs, toast, and orange juice, please." This provides practice with many important life skills that involve expressing a personal preference. Students with visual impairments and multiple disabilities who are nonverbal can be assertive with others in this way. Talking switches give these students the opportunity to learn that when they express their choices, they will receive attention or highly preferred things, such as favorite meals, fun opportunities, or a short break from a difficult task. It is important to find and record messages that are motivating to the individual student. A brand new message can be programmed in place of a familiar message when the novelty of a particular message wears off, or a new choice-making task arises.

Using PowerPoint. PowerPoint slideshows are set by default to progress from slide to slide on a mouse click or with a particular keystroke command. To use PowerPoint slides for choice making, rather than using the default slide-to-slide progression, the teacher can set individual slides to progress only when a student selects a certain item (from a choice of two or more) on that particular slide. As the teacher creates the PowerPoint file, the teacher can determine which slide the student will progress to after the choice is made. Sounds can be added to images on PowerPoint slides and made to play as the focus is moved around the screen from one image to another. Students with visual impairments and multiple disabilities can use keystrokes or other adapted methods of computer input—such as a modified mouse, joystick, track ball, or assistive pointer—to make onscreen selections and practice choice making with PowerPoint.

Generalizing across Settings. Each of the choice-making tools and strategies presented here can be generalized by students with visual impairments and multiple disabilities for use in their schools, homes, and communities.

Regardless of the particular teaching strategies used, it is important to use different types of assistive technology to elicit students' choices and responses. Collaboration among members of a student's educational team will help in planning ahead to provide additional opportunities for unique assistive technology–supported choices throughout the student's school day, during the student's community experiences, and at the student's home. In addition, family members of students may have considerable knowledge regarding students' preferences and prior choice-making experiences that may have been facilitated by basic technology tools (including toys) available for the student to use at home. Educational team members can take advantage of this resource by collaborating with families on choice-making tasks and the technology the student uses at home.

Assistive Technology for Teaching Sensory Efficiency Skills

Another component of early development is facilitating the use of sensory efficiency skills, or the use of all the senses to receive information from the environment. Sensory efficiency skills are necessary to comprehend our experiences and surroundings. Most everyday activities involve a combination of input from different senses. Any available sensory information combines together to inform an individual about what is happening in the world around them at any given point in time. For students with visual impairments and multiple disabilities, the development of sensory efficiency skills may need special attention. The tools and activities described next help increase the use of auditory, tactual, and visual skills alone and in combination with each other in order to make sense of the world.

Tools and Strategies for Teaching Sensory Efficiency Skills

The following are some tools that can be used for teaching sensory efficiency skills:

Light Boxes. A light box can be used to assist younger students with visual impairments and multiple disabilities in the use of their residual vision. Materials used with the light box promote basic visual skills, eye-hand coordination, and a number of other developmental milestones related to multisensory input.

Arts and crafts activities are just one example of possible ways to provide instruction using a light box. The use of scented markers on tissue paper, scented Play-Doh for mini sculpture building, and painting with dark colored pudding involve a wide range of sensory tasks. The light box can be covered in clear plastic to protect the light box from substances that might damage it.

Sensory Rooms. Sensory rooms can be used for students with visual impairments and multiple disabilities of all ages and degrees of visual impairment. A sensory room (the room can be a large room or little nook) is a special place that is intended to help students who have difficulty responding appropriately to environmental activity.

Sensory rooms are used to facilitate the exploration and development of senses and sensory skills. They can include features ranging from soft play areas, bean bag chairs, exercise balls, options for listening to music on CD or MP3 players, fragrance sprays, novel visual objects (such as a mirror ball, dazzling lights, lava lamp, or virtual image projected on a padded wall or padded floor), and interactive toys (such as bubble machines or textured gizmos). There are many low cost ways to find products and gather the equipment for learning experiences in a sensory room. Whatever space is selected, the objective in making a sensory room should be to keep it simple to allow students to calm down during their time in the sensory room.

Multisensory Activity Centers. A multisensory learning tool, such as a multisensory activity center, can be used for an entire lesson or included within a sensory room. Each component of an activity center is activated by switches or large buttons. The Visually

Impaired Activity Center from Enabling Devices includes various auditory and tactile experiences, including a radio, a fan, a buzzer, and a vibrating plate. It is designed specifically for students with visual impairments and can be used by a wide range of students, regardless of age or degree of visual impairment.

Other Multisensory Instructional Tools.

Bubble Wrap is a multisensory instructional tool worthy of mention. There are also mobile apps that involve sensory efficiency skills and the concept of Bubble Wrap has been included in this advancement. *BubbleFREE* is a bubble-popping mobile app. The user pops the virtual bubbles that appear on screen and each pop is accompanied by the sound of a Bubble-Wrap bubble popping. Students with multiple disabilities and any degree of visual impairment may find these sorts of apps to be an enjoyable way to practice sensory efficiency skills. Other sensory learning tools may include something as simple as a switch whose surface vibrates when activated.

Sensory Efficiency Considerations for Individual Students

Although students with visual impairments and multiple disabilities may be motivated by the use of assistive technology in combination with sensory efficiency practice, instructional strategies should be sensitive to each student's unique degree of tolerance for stimulation—whether he or she needs extra stimulation to respond or is easily overstimulated. For example, a reflective, shiny Mylar balloon or pom-pom may be useful in motivating a student with CVI to look, but if it

has an added design on it or includes more than two of the student's preferred colors, it may be too complex or stimulating for the student to attend to.

The examples presented here show how the use of assistive technology provides students with access to activities for basic life skills in the areas of cause and effect, choice making, and sensory efficiency. Given the amount of technology that is currently available today, there are many options to provide individualized services in the areas of sensory efficiency and assistive technology. Assistive technology can provide access to meaningful life experiences in different ways.

ASSISTIVE TECHNOLOGY FOR ACADEMIC INSTRUCTION

Once a student with visual impairments and multiple disabilities has developed sensory efficiency skills and an understanding of cause and effect and choice making, he or she possesses the prerequisites to move forward to a robust IEP. Such a program, focused on the unique needs of the student, may include pre-academic, early literacy, and functional skills, as well as standards-based academics. Pre-academic skills include organization and other basic compensatory skills needed to use the technology (for example turning on the software or using a mouse). At this point, the student can also focus on using assistive technology to support instruction in the expanded core curriculum (ECC). It is important for a student with a visual impairment and multiple disabilities to have access to and training with assistive technology that supports their academic skills along with each of the ECC areas (see Chapters 1 and 5).

As the student with visual impairments and multiple disabilities begins to work on academic skills, educational team members should consider the following when selecting assistive technology:

- age of the student
- cognitive ability of the student
- physical ability of the student
- academic standards of the student's school district and state

The educational team must be careful to avoid providing a student with inappropriate technology. For example, for a teenage student with visual impairments and a mild or moderate cognitive disability, it may be inappropriate to always use toys when teaching the student to use a switch. At this age, it would be more appropriate to connect the same switch to a tablet, desktop computer game, or radio.

Assistive Technology for Teaching Organization and Other Pre-Academic Skills

Organization is a key pre-academic skill that affects all aspects of the general education and expanded core curricula. For a student with a visual impairment and multiple disabilities, direct instruction in organization is critical for academic success. Therefore, students need to be provided with the array of tools available to support organization.

Tools for Teaching Organization and Other Pre-Academic Skills

Folders (Color Coded). Students may use no-tech folders with different colors that are able to hold large-print or 11.5 × 11-inch braille folders.

Tactile Stickers and Braille Labels. Tactile stickers or braille labels (homemade or made with a braille label maker) can be used to label everything from folders to books to areas on bookshelves.

Software and Apps. For students with visual impairments and multiple disabilities who are able to utilize a computer or tablet (such as an iPad) for pre-academic tasks and many of the associated daily living skills, there is a large array of software and apps that are available to teach pre-literacy, reading, writing, and numeracy skills. However, each of these programs and applications must be made accessible to the student with the appropriate technology (screen magnifiers, screen readers, switches, specialized keyboards, and the like). Many of these applications, coupled the correct assistive technology, allow students with visual impairments and multiple disabilities to learn distinct academic skills related to their IEP goals and benchmarks.

Strategies for Teaching Organization and Other Pre-Academic Skills

Organization as a skill is fundamental to success in many areas, including employment. Direct instruction can be provided by the teacher of students with visual impairments on how to be organized, especially for students with more severe visual impairments. Therefore, the teacher of students with visual impairments should teach students how to organize their paperwork in folders, how to label folders (using braille labels or tactile stickers), and how to manage delivery of their work from school to home.

Labeling. The skill of labeling is taught in the early grades. However, for students with visual impairments and multiple disabilities, the skill may need to be addressed continually. Students with low vision need to be taught to write large enough so the labeling information is visible at a reasonable distance. Students who have low vision may want to select a specific color to highlight labels for each school subject area. Highlighting the first line of the page near the top of each assignment with the appropriate color may be a simple way for students to keep track of their materials in different content areas. Students who are tactile readers can learn to create their own braille labels using a braillewriter. This includes having the student cut the labels out and paste them on the appropriate folder. Keeping a consistent way of labeling assignments in braille (such as: "first line: name; second line: date; third line: assignment title) is another method of supporting learners in their organization.

Using Software: There are many useful educational software programs that are beneficial for students at all ability levels. In order for students with visual impairments and multiple disabilities to use software, they will need direct instruction on how to turn the computer on, log on to the computer (if applicable), and use the mouse and keyboard. They will also need to know how to insert a software CD into the computer's disk drive or how to select a program from the desktop. Students will need direct instruction on how to use the mouse or keyboard for each program. All of these skills are prerequisite skills for software used to teach pre-academic skills. Many educational games are not accessible with screen-reading software, but many have built-in audio prompts. The accessibility of the program should be evaluated by the teacher of students with visual impairments before providing instruction to the student.

Apps. The use of apps on a tablet computer (such as an iPad) is dependent on the student's ability to use the accessibility features of the tablet and of the app itself. Tablet computers come with many accessibility features built into their operating systems. The iPad comes with built-in accessibility features such as the VoiceOver screen reader and the Zoom screen magnifier that the teacher of students with visual impairments will need to teach students to use effectively. Regardless of a student's degree of visual impairment, tablets are most accessible when paired with a keyboard or braille input-output device. When teaching a student to use a tablet, the teacher of students with visual impairments will need to focus on the most important skills that the student will need to complete specific tasks. For instance, the ability to turn on an iPad, open the word processor app Pages (or any other word processor app), write, save the document, and e-mail the document would be an appropriate skill set for some students. The instruction of these skills is best provided incrementally (as small tasks) with a set procedure that can be followed each time. Again, all of these skills are prerequisite skills required before applications on tablet computers are used to teach pre-academic skills.

Assistive Technology for Teaching Literacy

Literacy is a foundational academic skill for all students, including students with visual impairments and multiple disabilities. (See Chapter 8 for an in-depth discussion of literacy for students with visual impairments and multiple disabilities.) Literacy can be separated into three major skills for these students: reading, writing, and numeracy. Listening skills are fundamental to all three of these major skill areas.

Tools for Teaching Listening and Reading Skills

For students with visual impairments and severe cognitive or physical disabilities, early literacy begins with the development of their listening skills, including their ability to listen and follow instructions and listen to audio materials. The use of switches to turn on and off devices that are used to teach listening skills gives the student some control. Other important pre-literacy skills include recognizing the top and bottom of a page, turning pages, and connecting the text to the illustrations in books. There are many readily available technologies to support the development of listening skills. (For additional information on teaching listening skills to students with multiple disabilities, see Staples, 2012.)

The following are some tools that can be used for teaching listening skills:

- Ordinary CD or MP3 players.
- Apple or Android devices with accompanying apps. Examples of this include the Learning Ally Audio audiobook player app, or Go Read for Android devices.
- DAISY-compliant readers. Examples of this include the Book Wizard Reader from American Printing House for the Blind (APH) and ReadHear from gh, LLC.
- The Book Talker from Enabling Devices turns any book into a switch-adapted audiobook. Between 1 and 16 messages can be pre-recorded. The Bookworm from AbleNet also allows any book to be turned into a switch-adapted audiobook. The Bookworm includes an SD card that is used to store the recorded library of books.
- A scanner, optical character recognition (OCR) software, and speech synthesis program on a computer can be used as an advanced method of converting reading material to audio. OCR systems provide a mechanism for converting print into digital files via a scanner, inputting them into a computer, and using the software to create speech output. There are many OCR systems on the market.
- The Kurzweil 3000 is an excellent example of a comprehensive reading, writing, and learning software system that can provide access to information that is printed, electronic, or on the Internet.

This product, combined with screen magnifiers (such as ZoomText), screen readers (such as JAWS), or both, allow a student with more complex computer access skills to acquire information from a laptop or desktop computer.

While listening may be the primary medium for learning for many students with visual impairments and multiple disabilities, other students will be able to develop the skills to read text. Reading materials will need to be provided in the media appropriate for each student's visual impairment. Conducting a formal learning media assessment (See Chapter 3) is necessary before beginning reading instruction.

The following are some tools that can be used to help students with reading text:

- For students with low vision and multiple disabilities, assistive technology devices to enlarge text include: video magnifiers, handheld or desk magnifiers, and OCR scanning systems combined with screen magnification systems.
- A slant board, desk lamp, or both, may also be needed to help with document positioning and lighting.
- For a student who is blind, reading is a tactile experience. Early reading experiences should begin with storybooks with real objects, different textures, and tactile graphics. Commercial products such as *On the Way to Literacy: Early Experiences for Visually Impaired Children,* a set of read-aloud storybooks containing large-print, braille, and tactile illustrations, from APH are an excellent example of tactile-focused reading materials.

Strategies for Teaching Listening and Reading Skills

Strategies for teaching listening and reading skills include the following:

Listening Basics. Reading instruction begins with developing listening skills. Educators and parents can provide opportunities for students to hear stories being read. This develops vocabulary, makes connections to concepts, teaches the flow of reading, and teaches the importance of books. Students with visual impairments and multiple disabilities need to participate in all reading activities that include listening to someone read. From an assistive technology perspective, there is a large array of ways for students to listen to books using readily available devices that require little or no modification (such as those tools previously listed).

Using Pictures. During early reading, pictures and illustrations play an integral part in the experience. The teacher of students with visual impairments will want to provide descriptions, tactile graphics, or models of the images that are portrayed in the text. This is where items such as the Book Talker or specialized apps that allow the addition of personal audio notes would be appropriately used to support meaningful use of pictures for students who are visually impaired.

Providing Access. The first strategy for teaching actual reading is to ensure that students have access to a large array of reading materials appropriate for their ability levels and accessibility needs. The teacher of students with visual impairments should order accessible books for their students with visual impairments and multiple disabilities, but also be prepared to make books accessible themselves using the aforementioned examples of tools for listening skills alone or in combination with each other.

Supporting Preferences. If the student shows a preference for a particular book, then the teacher of students with visual impairments will want to ensure that the book is available in an appropriate medium, using assistive technology as applicable. For students with cognitive disabilities for whom braille may not be appropriate, objects that go along with the story should be used.

Personalize. In order to teach appropriate social behavior, a *Social Story* (Gray, 2010) can be created using the student as the main character of a text that focuses on social situations. Teachers can create personalized storybooks using apps and websites such as those previously mentioned, based on the age and preferences of the student. Students may enjoy being involved in the authorship of personalized reading material (see Chapter 8). Hagiwara and Myles (1999), for example, found that social stories that involve such assistive technology interventions were highly effective with learners who have autism spectrum disorders and other disabilities.

Tools for Teaching Writing

Writing allows the student to express his or her ideas in a more permanent form. For students with low vision and multiple disabilities, the same tools that are used for reading would typically be used for writing (a video magnifier, for example). However, writing may also involve the use of unique assistive technology tools.

The following are some tools that can be used for teaching writing:

- pens or markers (black or felt-tip)
- paper (tactile or black-lined)
- Perkins Brailler or Perkins SMART Brailler
- Mountbatten brailler
- adapted keyboards
- keyboard overlays
- accessible electronic braille notetakers
- speech-recognition software
- switches
- apps with stylus

Uses of Tools for Teaching Writing

- The student may need to use a black, felt-tip pen (or marker) along with bold-lined paper.
- If the student has problems with fine motor skills, the use of a specialized "pencil grip" may be appropriate.
- Many students with low vision may be able to use the computer to complete writing assignments. Keyboards with larger keys and different color schemes may be appropriate for some students (see Figure 12.3).
- Some students may only need large-print (or braille) sticker overlays to place on a standard keyboard.
- For students who are blind and can use a keyboard, braille stickers or tactile markers can be used to indicate specific keys.

Figure 12.3

Molly Clesen Pasley

A color-coded keyboard with larger keys and large-print letters and numbers can help students with low vision use the computer.

- Another option for such students would be the use of an accessible electronic braille notetaker (such as a BrailleNote or BrailleSense) connected to a computer and an embosser or a printer. However, for many students with severe disabilities, typing while managing the features of an electronic braille notetaker may be quite difficult.
- Speech-recognition software can be used to recognize speech and convert it to print within a computer application (typically a word-processing program). The use of speech-recognition software may be the most applicable to many students with visual impairments and multiple disabilities who are able to speak.
- Another option for access to a computer for writing may be the use of a more sophisticated switch that is color coded or labeled with enlarged images, tactile graphics, or braille.

Strategies for Teaching Writing

The following are some strategies for teaching writing:

For Students with Low Vision and Fine Motor Skill Challenges. Writing may be cumbersome and difficult for students with low vision and multiple disabilities, depending on their unique abilities. Students who have challenges with fine motor skills may need to use a pencil or pen with a larger barrel or use a common pencil grip with a standard pencil or pen. The instruction of writing should follow typical writing strategies including tracing, practice, and correction. However, the materials will need to be made accessible, depending on the student's degree of residual vision; for example, the tracing lines may need to be made larger.

For Students with Low Vision and Cognitive Disabilities. Writing may be a challenging process for students with low vision and cognitive disabilities. It may be appropriate to have the student use magnetic letters or stickers to create words while they learn to write.

For Students Who Use Braille and Have Physical Disabilities. To be able to write in braille, students need to not only have strong fine motor skills but they also need a typical sense of touch. Pre-braille students need exercises to prepare their hands for the demands of pressing the keys on the Perkins Brailler. Other assistive technology devices, such as the Mountbatten brailler, may provide a better alternative if hand strength is an issue. The Mountbatten brailler is basically an electronic brailler that uses the same six-key entry as a Perkins Brailler. The Mountbatten brailler is much easier to type on and has unique features (such as clear audio response and Bluetooth capabilities) that may make it a preferred device.

For Students Who Use Braille and Have Cognitive Disabilities: Braille is very challenging to learn for students with cognitive disabilities. If braille is determined to be a student's appropriate learning medium, ample instruction time must be provided for the student to learn to read the letters. For many students with cognitive disabilities, reading uncontracted braille will be the highest level of braille literacy they will attain. An assistive technology option for teaching braille is to use the Perkins SMART Brailler. This device has a video screen and provides audio feedback to the student as he or she types the braille.

Using Keyboards. If writing using conventional methods is not feasible for a student, a keyboard or adapted keyboard may be the most appropriate tool to use. The use of a modified keyboard that does not have the standard QWERTY keyboard layout may be appropriate for teaching typing. There are many commercially available keyboards that arrange the letter keys alphabetically and offer large-print keys, color-coded vowels, and special keys. IntelliKeys is a programmable alternative keyboard by IntelliTools. They also make a program called Overlay Maker that enables the user to create highly individualized and custom keyboard overlays.

Tools for Teaching Numeracy

Numeracy is the ability to understand and work with numbers (see Chapter 8). Often, numeracy skills are addressed in pre-K through second grade and focus on developing a sense of quantity connected to the abstract concept of a numeral. For students with visual impairments and multiple disabilities, the basic concepts of numeracy need to begin early and use multiple types of assistive technology. Accessible math manipulatives are the most appropriate tools for teaching numeracy. Additional tools for teaching numeracy include:

- counters or manipulatives
- tactilely distinctive counters
- IntelliTools
- apps

Uses of Tools for Teaching Numeracy

- Tools such as counters (bear-shaped counters, tokens, and the like) are universally designed and do not require modification to be used to teach basic counting skills for students with visual impairments and multiple disabilities.

- As students progress from counting to mathematical operations, tactilely distinctive counters (such as Tactile Tokens from APH) can be used. Many of the lessons and manipulatives from the APH MathBuilders kits may be useful to provide access to beginning math concepts.

- IntelliTools products that are highly suitable for the early learning experiences of students with visual impairments and multiple disabilities include the Classroom Suite of software tools (reading, writing, and numeracy skill development programs and activity packages for early students).

Strategies for Teaching Numeracy

Teaching Counting. Teachers should provide students with opportunities to count as frequently as possible. The use of counters is a contrived means of forcing students to count, so this skill should be generalized to other contexts. A variety of apps that focus on teaching students to count may be accessible to most students with visual impairments.

Teaching about Currency. The ability to count money (bills and coins) is an important life skill for all students. Beyond the basic instruction of identifying and counting money, there are various technologies that can identify money for individuals with visual impairments. These include stand-alone devices such as Voice-It-All and Note Teller 2, and apps such as LookTel's Money Reader. (See the Resources section in Chapter 11 for more information on these products.)

Using Calculators. The ability to use a calculator can be a valuable skill. A wide array of talking calculators can be used with instruction in math. Instruction would need to focus on the location of the specific buttons on the calculator (including the unique "repeat" button) and what the operation buttons actually do.

Teaching Measurement. The ability to compute basic measurements will be important for all students, including those with visual impairments and multiple disabilities. Teachers of students with visual impairments will need to teach students to work with accessible rulers for measuring length, audio scales for weight, audio thermometers for temperature, and accessible calendars. However, teaching students to measure ingredients in typical measuring containers is very important. Students need to learn to differentiate among different sized measuring cups whether or not they have accessible labels.

SUMMARY

Assistive technology is often considered a great equalizer for students with any disability, regardless of the degree or type. For students with visual impairments and multiple disabilities, the use of assistive technology is critical for access to education. The educational team must begin with a full and individualized evaluation to determine the educational and functional needs of the student. Based on these needs, the team then determines the type of devices and services that would best meet these needs of the student.

A wide variety of assistive technology devices can be used to meet the diverse needs of students with visual impairments and multiple disabilities. Depending on the student's level of vision and the type and severity of his or her additional disabilities, these devices can provide access to the most basic educational tasks (such as choice making) and the most advanced (such as typing an essay). This chapter provided a sampling of assistive technology devices for students with visual impairments and multiple disabilities.

REFERENCES

Gray, C. (2010). *The new social story book* (Rev. ed.). Arlington, TX: Future Horizons.

Hagiwara, T., & Myles, B. S. (1999). A multimedia social story intervention: Teaching skills to children with autism. *Focus on Autism and Other Developmental Disabilities, 14*(2), 82–95.

Individuals with Disabilities Education Improvement Act (IDEA), 20 U.S.C. § 1400 (2004).

Jamieson, S. (2004). Creating an educational program for young children who are blind and who have autism. *RE:view, 35*(4), 165–177.

Lund, S. K., & Troha, J. M. (2008). Teaching young people who are blind and have autism to make requests using a variation on the picture exchange communication system with tactile symbols: A preliminary investigation. *Journal of Autism and Developmental Disorders, 38*(4), 719–730.

Maushak, N. J., Kelley, P., & Blodgett, T. (2001). Preparing teachers for the inclusive classroom: A preliminary study of attitudes and knowledge of assistive technology. *Journal of Technology and Teacher Education, 9*(3), 419–431.

Murray-Branch, J., Udavari-Solner, A., & Bailey, B. (1991). Textured communication systems for individuals with severe intellectual and dual sensory impairments. *Language, Speech, and Hearing Services in Schools, 22,* 260–268.

Presley, I., & D'Andrea, F. M. (2009). *Assistive technology for students who are blind or visually impaired: A guide to assessment.* New York: AFB Press.

Reed, P. (2004). *The W.A.T.I. assessment package.* Madison: Wisconsin Department of Public Instruction. Retrieved from http://dpi.wi.gov/sites/default/files/imce/sped/pdf/at-wati-assessment.pdf

Rowland, C., & Schweigert, P. (1989). Tangible symbols: Symbolic communication for individuals with multisensory impairments. *Augmentative and Alternative Communication, 5*(4), 226–234.

Staples, S. (2012). Students with additional disabilities: Learning to listen. In L. A. Barclay (Ed.), *Learning to listen/listening to learn: Teaching listening skills to students with visual impairments* (pp. 247–335). New York: AFB Press.

Texas Assistive Technology Network. (2009). The Texas 4-step model: Considering assistive technology in the IEP process. Retrieved from http://www.texasat.net/default.aspx?name=trainmod.consideration

Turnell, R., & Carter, M. (1994). Establishing a repertoire of requesting for a student with severe and multiple disabilities using tangible symbols and naturalistic time delay. *Australia and New Zealand Journal of Developmental Disabilities, 19*(3), 193–207.

University of Kentucky Assistive Technology Project. (2003). UKAT toolkit. Retrieved from http://edsrc.coe.uky.edu/www/ukatii/toolkit/index.html

Zabala, J. S. (2005). Using the SETT framework to level the learning field for students with disabilities. Retrieved from http://www.joyzabala.com/uploads/Zabala_SETT_Leveling_the_Learning_Field.pdf

RESOURCES

For additional resources, see the General Resources section at the back of this book.

Assessments

Dynamic Assistive Technology Evaluation (DATE)
Texas Assistive Technology Network
www.texasat.net/default.aspx?name=trainmod.evaluation

An evaluation loosely based on the SETT framework, it is a brief evaluation checklist that supports the collection and interpretation of assistive technology evaluation data and is intended for personnel and teams who are or will be participating in assistive technology evaluations.

Student, Environments, Tasks, and Tools (SETT) Framework
Joy Smiley Zabata, Ed.D.
www.joyzabala.com

A four-part planning tool intended to promote collaborative decision making in all phases of assistive technology service design and delivery, from consideration through implementation and evaluation of effectiveness.

University of Kentucky Assistive Technology Toolkit
University of Kentucky Assistive Technology Project
http://edsrc.coe.uky.edu/www/ukatii/toolkit/index.html

A toolkit that provides a systematic method of delivering assistive technology services to students in schools by providing guidance to IEP and assistive technology teams in considering the use of assistive technology for a comprehensive evaluation, from referral through implementation.

Wisconsin Assistive Technology Initiative (WATI)
Wisconsin Department of Public Instruction
http://dpi.wi.gov/sites/default/files/imce/sped/pdf/at-wati-assessment.pdf

A process-based systematic assessment approach to providing a functional assessment of students' needs for assistive technology in their customary environment. The full assessment package includes referral and question identification guides and additional checklists to determine a student's assistive technology needs. Can be used for all students, including those with visual impairments and additional disabilities.

Applications and Software Programs

Mobile Applications
Braille Institute of America
www.brailleinstitute.org/digital/mobile-applications.html

A team that researches and develops mobile apps for individuals who are visually impaired and specialists that work with people who are visually impaired. This includes the free ViA app that sorts through hundreds of thousands of apps in the iTunes App Store to locate the most functional apps for people who are visually impaired.

Early Learning

101 Animations (PC and Mac)
RJ Cooper
www.rjcooper.com/101-animations

A cause-and-effect software that includes animations that can be activated by a switch, space bar, touch screen, or mouse click.

AlphaBaby (Mac/iOS)
AlphaBaby
http://alphababy.sourceforge.net/

A software program that provides a safe environment for very young children to play on the computer and helps teach letters. Every time a key is pressed or the mouse is clicked, a letter or shape is drawn, and sounds can be played. An app version is available.

Baby Smash (Windows/PC)
Scott Hanselman
www.hanselman.com/babysmash

A software program that can be included as a first step in early learning experiences. When interacting with the keyboard or mouse, letters, shapes, numbers, or sounds appear on the screen.

RadSounds
RJ Cooper
www.rjcooper.com/radsounds/index.html

A cause-and-effect music program for special needs learners. Users can customize playlists and choose from different modes for playing music. It is switch-friendly for those with physical challenges.

Tap-n-See Now
Little Bear Sees
http://littlebearsees.org/cvi-ipad-app-tap-n-see-zoo/

A cause-and-effect app created specifically for children with cortical visual impairment. Simple, bright animals float on the screen and respond to a tap. All aspects of the app are fully customizable to meet each child's needs, making it possible for the app to adapt to each child's visual and physical abilities.

Reading and Listening Skills

Book Wizard Reader (Windows/PC)
American Printing House for the Blind
http://tech.aph.org/bwr_info.htm

A program to read a wide variety and types of digital talking books. Provides enhanced ability to control and navigate through both structured and unstructured audio files.

Go Read (Android)
Bookshare
www.bookshare.org/cms/help-center/reading-tools/goread

A free, open source e-book reader optimized for visually impaired readers and usable by anyone. The app connects directly to online libraries, such as Bookshare, and allows users to download and listen to e-books.

Kurzweil 3000 (PC and Mac)
Kurzweil Education
www.kurzweiledu.com/products/products.html

An educational software designed to provide literacy support for those who struggle with literacy in the classroom, at home, or in the workplace. Built-in features for reading, writing, and study skills help students become independent learners, active participants within inclusion classrooms or sheltered instruction programs.

Learning Ally Audio (iOS and Android)
Learning Ally
https://itunes.apple.com/us/app/learning-ally-audio/id418888450?mt=8

https://play.google.com/store/apps/details?id=org
.learningally.learningallyaudioandroid&hl=en

An app that allows instant access to Learning
Ally's downloadable DAISY-formatted audiobooks. Learning Ally membership is required
to use this app.

ReadHear (PC and Mac)
gh, LLC
www.gh-accessibility.com/software/readhear-pc
-instant-download
www.gh-accessibility.com/software/readhear
-mac-instant-download

A software reading system designed for reading
NIMAS, DAISY Digital Talking Books, ePub/
HTML, and plain text files while providing multiple sensory output. Provides large-text, recorded
or synthesized speech, and braille output.

Sensory Efficiency Skills

BubbleFREE (Mac/iOS)
Falcon Mobile
https://itunes.apple.com/cv/app/bubblefree
/id284945681?mt=8

A mobile app in which users pop virtual
bubbles, with each pop accompanied by a
sound. Provides an enjoyable way for students
with visual impairments and multiple disabilities to practice sensory efficiency skills.

Communication Systems

High Contrast Icons
Enabling Devices
https://enablingdevices.com/catalog/products
_for_the_visually_impaired/communicators_for
_the_visually_impaired/high-contrast-icons

A set of highly visible communication icons.

Picture Communication Symbols (PCS)
Mayer-Johnson
www.mayer-johnson.com/category/symbols
-and-photos

A set of photos, templates, and layouts to help
create visual materials for the classroom or
home. Designed to fit students' specific learning
and communication needs and to promote
communication, learning, and understanding
through visual representations.

Picture Exchange Communication System (PECS)
Pyramid Educational Consultants
www.pecsusa.com/pecs.php

An augmentative/alternative communication
intervention system originally intended for
individuals with autism spectrum disorder and
related developmental disabilities. Has thousands of picture symbols to choose from.

Technology Resources

Websites

Access World
American Foundation for the Blind
www.afb.org/aw

A free online magazine providing information
on assistive technology and reviews of accessible
products from the American Foundation for the
Blind.

Blind Cool Tech
Blind Cool Tech
www.blindcooltech.com

A podcast that offers interviews, sound-seeing
tours, and discussions on technology.

Center of Excellence in Nonvisual Access to Education, Public Information, and Commerce (CENA)
National Federation of the Blind
https://nfb.org/technology-center

A center that serves to share knowledge regarding web accessibility and access technology in
order to bring about greater accessibility in
government, education, and business and to

promote best practices nationally. Includes a technology resource list, Access Technology blog with tips, and a list of usable consumer electronics.

Equal Access to Software and Information (EASI)

Equal Access to Software and Information (EASI)
http://easi.cc/

A provider that offers online training on accessible information technology for persons with disabilities.

iPad for Children with MIVI

Texas School for the Blind and Visually Impaired Outreach Department
www.tsbvi.edu/tsbvi-blog/ipad-for-children
-with-mivi

A blog that provides a list of iPad apps appropriate for students with visual impairments with multiple disabilities.

Technology and Media Division (TAM)

Council for Exceptional Children (CEC)
www.tamcec.org

A division of CEC that works to promote the availability and effective use of technology and media for individuals with exceptional learning needs. Focuses on improving the results of individuals with disabilities through the selection, acquisition, and use of technology.

Organizations

Assistive Technology Industry Association (ATIA)

330 North Wabash Avenue, Suite 2000
Chicago, IL 60611-4267
(312) 321-5172; (877) 687-2842
Fax: (312) 673-6659
info@ATIA.org
http://atia.org/

Works to ensure the best products and services are delivered to people with disabilities. Provides an annual research journal, online webinars, and an annual conference for professional development. Membership consists of manufacturers, sellers, and providers of technology-based assistive devices and services.

Bookshare

480 California Avenue, Suite 201
Palo Alto, CA 94306
(650) 644-3400
Fax: (650) 475-1066
info@bookshare.org
www.bookshare.org

Administers the world's largest accessible digital library for persons with print disabilities. Memberships are free for U.S. students with qualifying print disabilities. Members can download books from the website in any of a variety of text or audio formats.

Center on Disabilities

California State University Northridge (CSUN)
18111 Nordhoff Street
Northridge, CA 91330
(818) 677-1200
www.csun.edu/cod/index.php

Provides training on assistive technology through its Assistive Technology Applications Certificate Program (ATACP) and its annual International Conference on Assistive Technology and Persons with Disabilities.

Closing the Gap

526 Main Street
P.O. Box 68
Henderson, MN 56044
(507) 248-3294
Fax: (507) 248-3810
www.closingthegap.com

Covers the latest assistive technology news, how-tos and ever-changing technologies and implementation strategies. Provides assistive technology resources and training opportunities through its bimonthly magazine, webinars, and annual international conference.

Learning Ally
20 Roszel Road
Princeton, NJ 08540
(800) 221-4792
www.learningally.org

Distributes digitally recorded textbooks and literature titles to empower students with reading-related learning disabilities and visual impairments reach their full potential.

National Library Service for the Blind and Physically Handicapped (NLS)
Library of Congress
1291 Taylor Street, NW
Washington, DC 20542
(202) 707-5100; (800) 424-8567
Fax: (202) 707-0712
TDD/TTY: (202) 707-0744
nls@loc.gov
www.loc.gov/nls

Administers the Braille and Talking Book Library Service, a free program that loans recorded and braille books and magazines as well as specially designed playback equipment to residents of the United States who are unable to read or use standard print materials. Talking books are delivered to eligible borrowers through local cooperating libraries throughout the United States. It also offers audio, braille, and print/braille books for preschool through grade 8 and periodicals for blind and physically handicapped children.

Sources of Products

AbleNet, Inc.
2625 Patton Road
Roseville, MN 55113-1308
(651) 294-2200; (800) 322-0956
Fax: (651) 294-2259

customerservice@ablenetinc.com
www.ablenetinc.com

Distributes a number of different switches including the BIGmack, a single-message speech generating device, and the Step-by-Step Communicator, a device for recording a series of messages. Also offers the Bookworm, which turns any book into a switch-adapted audiobook. In addition, distributes the Classroom Suite from IntelliTools, a software tool of reading, writing, and numerical skill development programs and activity packages for early learners. Additional tools include IntelliKeys programmable alternative keyboard, Overlay Maker for customizable keyboard overlays, IntelliBraille, and tools that enable teachers to produce their own accessible classroom activities.

Ai Squared
130 Taconic Business Park Road
Manchester Center, VT 05255
(802) 362-3612
Fax: (802) 362-1670
www.aisquared.com

Distributes ZoomText magnification and screen-reading software.

American Printing House for the Blind (APH)
1839 Frankfort Avenue
P.O. Box 6085
Louisville, KY 40206-0085
(502) 895-2405; (800) 223-1839
Fax: (502) 899-2284
info@aph.org
www.aph.org

Manufactures and distributes a wide assortment of educational and daily living products including the Book Wizard Reader; slates and styli; braille paper; *On the Way to Literacy: Early Experiences for Visually Impaired Children,* a set of read-aloud storybooks containing large-print, braille, and tactile illustrations to help young children develop the abilities that form the foundation for literacy; the MathBuilders kit; and Tactile Tokens for learning beginning math concepts. Also distributes the Perkins Brailler and SMART Brailler.

Brytech
1800 Dorset Drive
Ottawa, ON K1H 5T8
Canada
(613) 731-5800
Fax: (613) 731-5812
inquiries@brytech.com
www.brytech.com

Distributes the Note Teller 2, a portable money reader for blind, visually impaired, and deaf-blind individuals.

Enabling Devices
50 Broadway
Hawthorne, NY 10532
(914) 747-3070; (800) 832-8697
Fax: (914) 747-3480
www.enablingdevices.com

Creates innovative communicators, iPad products, adapted toys, multisensory devices, adapted electronics, and capability switches for the physically challenged. Distributes the Book Talker, a 16-position flat switch array that can be placed inside the back of any book to record the story; and the Visually Impaired Activity Center, which activates tactile and auditory features when plates are pressed.

Freedom Scientific
11800 31st Court North
St. Petersburg, FL 33716
(727) 803-8000; (800) 444-4443
Fax: (727) 803-8001
www.freedomscientific.com

Distributes JAWS, a screen reader developed for computer users whose vision loss prevents them from seeing screen content or navigating with a mouse. Provides speech and braille output for the most popular computer applications on the PC.

HIMS Inc.
4616 West Howard Lane, Suite 960
Austin, TX 78728
(888) 520-4467
Fax: (512) 837-2011
sales@hims-inc.com
https://hims-inc.com/

Manufactures and distributes the Braille Sense electronic notetaker.

HumanWare
1 UPS Way
P.O. Box 800
Champlain, NY 12919
(800) 722-3393
Fax: (888) 871-4828
info@humanware.com
www.humanware.com

Distributes a variety of assistive technology products such as the Mountbatten brailler and the BrailleNote electronic notetaker.

Maxi-Aids
42 Executive Boulevard
Farmingdale, NY 11735
(631) 752-0521 (Information); (800) 522-6294 (Orders)
TTY: (631) 752-0738
Fax: (631) 752-0689
Contact form: www.maxiaids.com/store/contactUs.asp
www.maxiaids.com

Distributes the Voice-It-All, a 3-in-1 unit that includes a money identifier, color identifier, and voice recorder. Also sells a variety of talking calculators, keyboard overlays and stickers, and pens and markers, among other independent living products.

Nuance
1 Wayside Road
Burlington, MA 01803
(781) 565-5000
Fax: (781) 565-5001
www.nuance.com/index.htm

Manufactures and distributes the Dragon suite of speech-recognition software.

Perkins School for the Blind
175 North Beacon Street
Watertown, MA 02472
(617) 972-7308; (855) 206-8353
solutions@perkins.org
www.perkinsproducts.org

Manufactures and distributes the Perkins Brailler and the Perkins SMART Brailler, as well as slates and styli. Also distributes a variety of assistive technology, low vision, and daily living products.

TACK-TILES Braille Systems LLC
P.O. Box 475
Plaistow, NH 03865
(603) 382-1904; (800) 822-5845
Fax: (603) 382-1748
www.tack-tiles.com

Manufactures and distributes a line of LEGO-style blocks that provide a path to braille literacy that are available in multiple languages as well as Nemeth code for mathematics, braille code for music notation, and computer braille code. Also provides a computer keypad overlay for IntelliKeys.

Additional Reading

Presley, I., & D'Andrea, F. M. (2009). *Assistive technology for students who are blind or visually impaired: A guide to assessment.* New York: AFB Press.

A foundational text that provides a comprehensive discussion and instruments for assistive technology assessments for students with visual impairments.

Chapter **13**

Positive Strategies for Behavioral Intervention

Laurie Denno

Key Points

- Fundamental aspects of behavioral intervention include positive behavioral interventions and supports (PBIS), functional behavior assessment, and data-based decision making
- The design of individual behavior interventions
- Prevention of challenging behaviors
- The development of a behavior intervention plan (BIP)
- Ensuring the effectiveness of a behavior support team

Morgan, a visually impaired, nonverbal 4-year-old, yells when another child tries to play with her. When this happens, the teacher usually comes over to the children and, after telling Morgan that the other children are allowed to play too and not to yell at them, supervises the children so that they learn to play together. At other times Morgan is removed from the activity and her teacher tries to involve her in another activity.

The teachers are trying to figure out why she engages in this behavior. Some of them think that it is her way of telling the other child to go away, while others think she has a hard time sharing.

Jacoby is 10 years old and has cortical visual impairment. He is also nonverbal. He knows his daily schedule and routines. When a class or activity is cancelled Jacoby often becomes quite upset. When he is upset he will generally bite his hand, stomp his feet, and slap his head.

His teachers are trying to figure out how to help him accept changes in his schedule. They think it is an important life skill for him to be able to tolerate change.

Enrico is 16 years old. He is blind and has a hearing impairment. He understands basic sign language and uses an object calendar. His school program uses a functional

451

curriculum approach and is focused on preparing him for the future. He has a variety of "jobs" that he does at school: delivering mail, collecting recyclables, filling the soda machine, and the like. He is generally accurate in his work but sometimes makes an error that has to be corrected (for instance, putting a soda can in the wrong slot in the soda machine). When Enrico is asked to correct something he often becomes extremely agitated and will strike out at anyone within his reach.

Enrico's teachers are trying to figure out how to tell him that he needs to correct his work without his becoming aggressive.

This chapter provides an overview of current thought on the use of positive behavioral intervention methods for challenging behavior and how they can be applied to students with visual impairments and multiple disabilities. Special education teachers, including teachers of students with visual impairments, often are isolated, physically and educationally, from other educational professionals who, as a result, often do not understand the special challenges involved in teaching students with visual impairments, especially when combined with other disabilities. When students also display challenging behavior in addition to the challenges of the visual impairment and other disabilities, teachers can become overwhelmed. The lack of access to colleagues for collaboration and assistance forces teachers to "go it alone." This chapter seeks to assist teachers to better understand troublesome behavior in their students and to respond to

that behavior with a positive, proactive teaching approach and positive interventions and supports.

HISTORY OF APPLIED BEHAVIOR ANALYSIS

In 1968, the *Journal of Applied Behavior Analysis* was founded, moving the study of how learning takes place into the mainstream. Since that time, thousands of studies have shown that changes in environmental variables change behavior in socially significant ways. In the 1960s and 1970s, the term used most frequently to describe this work was *behavior modification*. Research and application were focused on "modifying" troublesome behavior, usually through consequence interventions, responses that come after the behavior, including reinforcement and punishment. Over time the emphasis shifted somewhat to a more environmentally integrated approach that included both consequence intervention and antecedent intervention—making changes in the environment before the target behavior occurs, thus preventing troublesome behaviors. This allowed for a more proactive and preventative approach to behavior change, often referred to as *behavior management*.

An important breakthrough in the research and application of the behavior management methodology occurred in 1982 with a groundbreaking study on self-injury by Iwata, Dorsey, Slifer, Bauman, and Richman (1982, 1994). This study presented the idea that each individual has a unique learning history and that while troublesome behaviors displayed by different individuals may look the same, they can be caused by different environmental variables. For example, severe self-injurious behavior in one student may function to get attention from the teacher while severe self-injurious behavior in another student may function to avoid less-preferred activities. The researchers posited that in order to design the most effective intervention for an individual student, one must assess the function of each behavior and then design the treatment in response to that function. This fundamental shift away from merely manipulating antecedents and consequences in order to change behavior to evaluating behavior in relation to the total environment is called *applied behavior analysis* (often abbreviated ABA). This is the terminology that will be used throughout this chapter.

CHALLENGING BEHAVIOR IN THE CLASSROOM

Teaching positive, proactive social and academic behavior is a component of all behavioral interventions, and the primary goal of many behavior support programs begins with a request by an educator for assistance in targeting troublesome behaviors that interfere with learning and positive social interactions. Examples of this type of target behavior include:

- being out of one's seat
- talking out of turn
- making rude comments to others
- swearing
- "not listening"

- refusals
- throwing items
- minor and more serious aggression to peers and staff
- self-stimulatory behavior
- self-injurious behavior

These are the behavioral issues that are often observed in children with sensory deficits, who are less able to learn by seeing and hearing what others do and whose access to explicit instruction may be limited by sensory or cognitive delays.

Sometimes teachers attempt to address these difficulties by using a loud reprimand, taking away privileges, and applying other punishment interventions that may temporarily discontinue the behavior. Thus, the teacher is reinforced and uses these techniques again. However, using reprimands and taking away privileges does not teach the student an alternative or replacement behavior. If the disruptive behavior is a means to get attention, the student is likely to re-engage in the behavior, the teacher is likely to re-apply the last successful strategy, and a cycle of challenging behavior and ineffective intervention is built. To interrupt this cycle teachers can use the following strategies:

- Ask more questions about why the student does the behavior.
- Ask what happens before the behavior, what happens after the behavior, and what the student gets or avoids by engaging in the behavior.

The answers to these questions will assist teachers in developing more effective responses to challenging behavior and replacing challenging behavior with more prosocial and acceptable behavior.

COMPONENTS OF BEHAVIORAL INTERVENTIONS

Three key components of behavioral intervention based on the principles of behavioral analysis are positive behavior intervention and support, functional behavior assessment before intervention, and data-based decision making. Each of these is described in the following sections.

Positive Behavior Interventions and Supports

Since the 1990s a vast amount of research has been produced that supports the efficacy of positive behavioral interventions and supports (PBIS) in increasing both academic and prosocial behavior (see, for example, Lewis, Sugai, & Colvin, 1998; McCurdy, Kunsch, & Reibstein, 2007; McCurdy, Mannella, & Eldridge, 2003; Sugai & Horner, 2002; Sugai, Sprague, Horner, & Walker, 2000). The PBIS approach includes four components (Sugai & Horner, 2002):

1. targeting both academic and prosocial behavior for all students
2. using a schoolwide systems approach to increase these behaviors
3. using procedures that are data based and designed to provide specific results
4. using procedures based on well-researched science of behavior

PBIS is specifically cited in the regulations for the Individuals with Disabilities Education Improvement Act (IDEA) of 2004, which state that the IEP team must "In the case of a child whose behavior impedes the child's learning or that of others, consider the use of positive behavioral interventions and supports, and other strategies, to address that behavior" (34 C.F.R § 300.324[a][2][i]). PBIS is a schoolwide system of applying behavioral interventions to increase the academic and prosocial behavior of all students, not just students who display challenging behavior. Usually the program includes a list of three or four prosocial behaviors that are "expectations" across the school population. The expectations are written in positive language such as:

- "Students will be respectful to students and staff at all times."
- "Students will try their best to meet their academic challenges."

Expectations are also defined, such as: "Respectful means that students will use positive language to address others; will not tease, bully, or engage in hurtful comments to others; and will not use vulgar language, swear, or engage in physical confrontations to resolve disputes." All students receive explicit instruction in the behavioral expectations of their school as part of the ongoing curriculum, and receive opportunities to practice through role-play, modeling, and other direct instruction techniques.

In addition, students participate in a schoolwide system of reinforcement for meeting the expectations. Often the reinforcement is in the form of a token or card given to the student when he or she is observed meeting a behavioral expectation that can be exchanged for items or entered in a lottery for prizes such as movie tickets, small electronics, or other items, often donated by the community or parent teacher organization. For groups of students or individual students who continue to display challenging behavior, there is the opportunity to put into place increased behavior supports, including more instruction and practice regarding the behavioral expectations and a higher frequency of prompts, feedback, and reinforcement. Therefore, PBIS is an escalating system designed to address the behavioral needs of *all* students in a school.

Another component of this approach is data-based decision making, discussed in more detail later in this chapter. Schools that use PBIS collect data on some aspect of behavior that indicates to the administration and teachers that the implementation of the schoolwide program is increasing academic and prosocial behavior. Different schools choose to measure different target behaviors. Some schools look for a decrease in detentions and suspensions to indicate success. Other schools measure absenteeism, academic improvement, and the overall number of students who participate in the program. This information allows administration and teachers to make data-based decisions about improvements and changes in the system.

Although the PBIS approach has a number of specifically outlined components, each school or school district that uses this system has wide latitude in designing and implementing the components. Most schools have found it helpful to explicitly teach alternatives to antisocial behavior. Generally there is a separate curriculum designed to teach replacement behaviors to students who continue to display challenging behavior after implementation of the schoolwide program.

The PBIS website (www.pbis.org) has a variety of resources available to individuals and school systems that would like to explore this approach. (See the Resources section at the end of this chapter for more information.) PBIS has been adopted by the State of Virginia, and 18,277 schools in the United States use this system to improve academic and social behavior.

Functional Behavior Assessment

A thorough functional behavior assessment (often abbreviated FBA) of troublesome behavior is the foundation for all behavioral intervention. A functional behavior assessment is conducted to obtain information about the reasons a student engages in troublesome behavior and to form a hypothesis about what variables in the environment make it worthwhile for the student to continue to engage in the behavior. Assessment assists teachers in identifying the environmental variables that may cause and maintain troublesome behavior. An assessment will provide a much more individualized and targeted approach.

IDEA requires school staff to conduct a functional behavior assessment to address challenging behaviors instead of merely applying disciplinary measures such as detention or suspension. Many educational team members have the skills to do an assessment but often a teacher who has a background in using behavioral interventions, a school psychologist, a guidance counselor, or a board-certified behavior analyst (a certification granted by the Behavior Analyst Certification Board) conducts the assessment. Today many schools have a certified behavior analyst on staff, recognizing that this professional designation is a valuable adjunct to the educational team.

Conducting a functional behavior assessment is the foundation of designing effective behavioral interventions to decrease troublesome behavior in students. A functional behavior assessment essentially attempts to discover why a student performs the behavior and what the student receives or avoids after performing the behavior.

Behavior analysts—mental health professionals who apply the principles of behavior analysis in interventions to change behavior—believe that all behavior is lawful and orderly (that is, predictable in its context) and is displayed in relation to other environmental events. In order to do a thorough assessment, one must look at the whole environment, including what happened before the behavior, what happened after the behavior, and what other individuals in the environment may have contributed to the behavior of concern. The old adage "all behavior is communication" is true, because all behavior happens for a reason; and it is the reason for the behavior that a functional assessment seeks to identify.

The reason for the behavior is called its *function*. Behavior analysts believe that all behavior has a function in relation to other variables in the environment. Broadly speaking, most behavior functions to:

- get items or attention (positive reinforcement)
- avoid or escape unpleasant events (negative reinforcement)

More specifically, behavior analysts generally speak about the following four main functions of behavior:

1. To get social attention such as praise, eye contact, nods, reprimands, and high fives.
2. To obtain tangible objects such as toys, games, TV time, and stickers.
3. To get automatic reinforcement. *Automatic reinforcement* is generally sensory feedback that a student gives him- or herself that is self-reinforcing. This can include light gazing, finger flicking, tapping, rocking, and self-injurious behavior. Sometimes these behaviors also are associated with pain or pain attenuation. Especially if these behaviors suddenly appear in the student's repertoire, it is important to follow up the functional behavior assessment with a medical assessment as well. Automatic reinforcement is very common in students with visual impairments.
4. To escape from or avoid events such as a less-preferred lesson or teacher, hard assignments, loud noises, or a bully.

There are two main types of assessments in behavior analysis, a descriptive assessment that includes both direct and indirect assessment, and a functional analysis. A descriptive assessment is most commonly used in education settings. A *descriptive assessment* begins by defining the target behavior of concern in clear and concise terms. The definition must be clear enough so that all people who interact with the student can agree whether or not the behavior has occurred. This requires that the student's educational team agree on the definition. Second, data on the frequency, duration, or intensity of the behavior must be collected.

A *functional analysis* also begins by carefully defining the target behavior of concern. The evaluator then applies different antecedents and consequences to the target behavior in a systematic manner and measures which conditions result in the most and least frequency of the target behavior. This is sometimes called an *experimental* analysis. It is used when the descriptive analysis does not identify the function of the target behavior. It is most often used in a learning clinic setting, but can be used in a school setting if a trained evaluator is available.

Direct Assessment

To conduct a direct assessment, the behavior of concern is defined, and data is collected based on direct observations of the student's behavior. Direct data collection can be done throughout the day or during part of the day. The teacher or another available member of the educational team can perform the data collection. Generally, if the behavior of concern occurs at a low frequency, it can be recorded using a simple count of its frequency. Sometimes, recording the duration of a behavioral difficulty and noting the start time and end time can be instructive.

A recording technique that can be very helpful is that of a scatter plot (Touchette, MacDonald, & Langer, 1985). A scatter plot uses a grid of the student's week by class and/or time. When the behavior of concern occurs, the teacher makes a mark in the appropriate box for that particular class or time. This can be very helpful because it shows patterns of troublesome behavior by day, time, or class with a single glance. A scatter plot is most useful if the behavior of concern is relatively low frequency and has a clear beginning and end.

Teachers and paraeducators often use written notes to document troublesome behavior; they may be asked to write down the flow of events during an episode. However, note taking is not as easy as it sounds and can be cumbersome and time-consuming. Not everyone is an objective observer or careful about recording details. A more complete recording can be made using what is called *ABC recording* (Alberto & Troutman, 2009, pp. 187–189; Cooper, Heron, & Heward, 2007, pp. 53–55). ABC stands for antecedent, behavior, and consequence. Events that happen before the behavior are called *antecedents. Behavior* is the behavior of concern. *Consequences* are events that happen directly after the behavior; they are not punishments. Consequences can include no response by others, looking at the student, talking to the student, moving away from the student, laughing at the student, and a variety of other responses. In this three-section recording system, antecedents are often neglected because staff does not begin to observe the student until the troublesome behavior has started. ABC recording usually requires a dedicated observer or another person besides the teacher to get accurate information.

Indirect Assessment

Indirect methods of data collection also can be helpful. To conduct an indirect assessment, the behaviors of concern are defined and a standardized assessment tool is used to collect information from those with the best knowledge of the student and his or her behavior challenges.

There are many long and short assessment tools that are available commercially or through the behavior analytic literature. These are often paper-and-pencil assessments that can be filled out by anyone who knows a student well. They are helpful for parents as well as a student's educational team. Several commonly used tools are the Functional Analysis Screening Tool (FAST; Iwata & DeLeon, 1996); Functional Assessment Informant Record for Teachers (FAIR-T; Doggett, Mueller, & Moore, 2002); Motivational Analysis Rating Scale (MARS; Wieseler, Hanson, Chamberlain, & Thompson, 1985); Motivational Assessment Scale (MAS; Durand & Crimmins, 1992); and Problem Behavior Questionnaire (PBQ; Lewis, Scott, & Sugai, 1994). (See the Resources section at the end of this chapter for more information.)

After a functional behavior assessment is completed using direct observation and/or one of the indirect assessment tools, the assessor formulates a hypothesis about which function may be maintaining the behavior of concern. This is an educated guess, based on the information collected, about the reason the student engages in the troublesome behavior. Sometimes a behavior has more than one function. This complicates the design of behavioral interventions but it does not preclude effective treatment.

Data-Based Decision Making

In applied behavioral analysis in education, decisions about continuing or changing behavioral interventions are made based on measured data, such as the frequency, intensity, or duration of the target behaviors. When evaluating the effectiveness of an intervention, teachers need to compare data during baseline (before the intervention is put in place) with the same data after the intervention is put in place. Even though the teacher may feel that is clear whether the intervention is either successful or unsuccessful, subjective data are not sufficient to make a real determination of success or failure. The data that are collected tell the real story of success or failure. This data-based approach is complementary to the IEP process, in which measurable educational objectives are tracked over time by the teacher using a variety of data collection approaches including permanent products (completed work samples), percentage of correct answers on tests and papers, frequency of errors, and a variety of other methods (see Chapter 4).

When looking at behavioral interventions, the data tell the teacher whether or not the student's target behaviors are increasing, decreasing, or staying the same. Without concrete data it is impossible to determine if interventions are appropriate for the student and the situation. There are many simple commercial and teacher-made data-collection systems that can be used to assess the success of the intervention. If a student's behavior is not changing, the next step is to reevaluate the intervention and make adjustments.

More and more classroom instructors use video recording, especially for small-group instruction. Video recording allows teachers to go back after a lesson and record data on a student's frequency of interfering behaviors, attention, time on task, rate of response, and percentage of correct responses. Video recording helps teachers look for antecedents to behavior challenges. It also creates a complete record of behavior and academics and allows teachers to observe many behaviors that they may miss when they are actively teaching students. Video recording also is useful when doing a time sample. A time sample divides a longer period of time (for example, 10 minutes) into shorter intervals (such as 30 seconds); an observer records whether or not the target behavior was observed during the shorter intervals, for the whole interval or at the end of the interval. Different intervals are selected depending on the frequency of the target behavior. If video recording is used, the teacher can go back after the time sample has been recorded and score the frequency, duration, and other characteristics of the behavior. This eliminates the need to use another person as a dedicated recorder of the student's behavior.

Behavior analysts prefer direct methods of data collection. Direct methods of data collection provide those conducting a functional behavior assessment with more accurate, objective information that can lead to a better assessment and more effective interventions.

DESIGNING INDIVIDUAL BEHAVIORAL INTERVENTIONS

Once the function of a student's behavior has been determined based on a functional behavior assessment, the teacher can then begin to consider intervention strategies. The following sections consider the functions of challenging behavior and describe potential intervention strategies for each. (See Cooper et al., 2007, pp. 500–523 for more information.)

Behavior Functioning to Get Attention

Obtaining attention is a very common function of challenging behavior. Many students enjoy attention from staff and from peers. In a busy classroom it can be difficult for the adults to spread out their attention in an even manner. Quite often, attention is directed toward the students who engage in troublesome behavior, while students who work quietly at their desks receive minimal attention. This sets up a situation whereby undesirable, inappropriate, and disruptive behavior may occur at a higher rate because it is attended to at a higher rate. Attention can take the form of verbal prompts, verbal reprimands, eye contact, the teacher coming over to the student's desk, or the teacher having a "talk" with the student. Peers may point their fingers, laugh, cry, say they are afraid, or run from the student engaging in the challenging behavior. All of these responses can function as reinforcement for the behavior of concern. There are a few common interventions that can be implemented in this scenario without a lot of difficulty.

Increase Attention for Other Behavior

First, increase overall attention for positive behavior both for the student engaging in the challenging behavior and others. There is some possibility that the challenging behavior will decrease without any other intervention. If attention is truly reinforcing the challenging behavior, receiving attention for other more positive behaviors, especially at a higher rate than the student receives attention for the challenging behavior, may increase the other behaviors and the challenging behavior may fall out of the student's repertoire.

Increase Attention to Other Students Engaged in the Correct Behavior

In addition, offering positive attention to other students for engaging in good student behavior may assist with this change. This is one of the most powerful positive behavior supports and uses only reinforcement.

Use Planned Ignoring

In addition to increasing attention for other more positive behaviors, unless there is a dangerous or extremely disruptive situation, the teacher can add *planned ignoring* for the undesirable behavior. This is the behavioral intervention based on extinction. *Extinction* is when a previously reinforced behavior is no longer reinforced, leading to the frequency of the behavior decreasing over time. Ignoring undesirable behavior is a difficult and unnatural response for many teachers. It takes time and practice to master. Ignoring challenging behavior will not work without a com-

mensurate increase in attention for other behaviors. If attention is truly reinforcing the challenging behavior, when attention is withdrawn, the frequency and duration of the behavior should decrease. Be aware, however, that the behavior may get worse before it gets better. This is a common problem with using extinction. This intervention is a combination of reinforcement and extinction.

Use Time Out

Another strategy that can be implemented when troublesome behavior in the classroom is maintained by attention is to use time out. Time out from reinforcement is a more intrusive intervention but one that can be helpful if a behavior is too disruptive to be ignored. Time out is removing the opportunity for the student to gain access to reinforcement (generally attention) for a designated period of time. Time out for one behavior is always used with reinforcement for another behavior. Reinforcement for acceptable behavior should be frequent. Time out should be brief, 30–60 seconds for young children and 2–5 minutes for other children. Time out is a condition, not a place. Therefore, it can take place while the student is at his or her own desk, in a space away from the group, or in another location out of the classroom. Time out is a restrictive procedure. Restrictive procedures include removal of reinforcement and using fines to decrease target behaviors and are punishment interventions. Time out should not be implemented unless the teacher is thoroughly comfortable and knowledgeable about its use. This intervention is a combination of positive reinforcement and negative punishment. *Negative punishment* occurs when something is withdrawn after a behavior occurs (in this case, attention).

Behavior Functioning to Get Tangible Items

Behavior that functions to get tangible items is also very common, especially in younger children and children with limited communication skills. Students with visual impairments and multiple disabilities may be unaware of the social conventions of sharing and asking because of their sensory deficits. Engaging in troublesome behavior, especially crying and self-injurious behavior, often functions to at least get someone to come to you. Out of desperation, teachers often try to "re-direct" students from these behaviors by offering preferred items, but this sequence actually teaches the students to engage in these behaviors to get the items. For example, a student is crying and the teacher does not know why. The teacher offers the student a vibrating toy. The student stops crying. From a behavioral standpoint, the teacher is reinforced because the student stops crying. The teacher is likely to offer preferred items to stop crying in the future. The student is reinforced for crying by receiving a preferred item. The student is likely to cry in order to get preferred items in the future. There are several ways to address this situation.

Use the Item as Reinforcement

First, use the preferred item as reinforcement for engaging in other behaviors you would like to increase. This will use the motivating value of the item in a positive way. For younger children, offering brief intervals with a pre-ferred item after completing brief intervals of work can build work skills and increase attention. For other students, access to the item can be scheduled after completing a lesson or completing the morning routine. The amount of time that the item is available for reinforcement depends on the student, the setting, and the learning situation. Providing the item as reinforcement for positive behavior alone may decrease the challenging behaviors that the student engages in to receive the item. However, it can be a difficult transition for students and teachers to shift from engaging in challenging behavior to get an item to receiving it as reinforcement. The teacher needs to decide how to respond to the challenging behavior now that the item will not be forthcoming after the challenging behavior occurs. Planned ignoring, described previously, is one of the best strategies to consider. Remember, behavior may get worse before it gets better.

Schedule the Item Independent of Behavior

Another strategy is to offer the item on a regular schedule throughout the day. This will decrease the need for the student to engage in the troublesome behavior, as the item will be delivered *noncontingently*, that is, on a fixed time schedule unattached to the student's behavior. Noncontingent reinforcement is described in more detail later in this chapter under "Changing What Happens before Challenging Behavior Occurs."

Teach the Student to Ask for the Item

Yet another intervention that can be considered when a student engages in challenging behavior to obtain items is to teach the student to ask for the item. If the student could ask for the item, he or she probably would, so it may take some creativity and explicit teaching to help the student learn this skill. This can be a difficult task, especially if the student is nonverbal. The first step is to evaluate the student's communication strengths. How does the student get what he or she wants? What is his or her primary mode of communication? Does the student use words, vocalizations, signs, pointing, gestures, pictures, objects, symbols, or a combination of modes? (See Chapter 7 for more information on communication.) It sometimes can be helpful get an evaluation from a speech-language pathologist.

Once this assessment is complete and the preferred mode of communication has been identified, the teacher and the student can engage in practice sessions where the teacher prompts the student to ask for what he or she wants, the student responds or is prompted to respond, the item is given to the student for a brief interval, and then removed. Another trial is then initiated. Four or five trials once or twice a day may be sufficient to teach the correct communication response in a relatively short time. Along with this procedure, it is recommended that a preference assessment be used to identify items that are highly motivating. While this may seem like a tedious process, once students learn the value of using the communication mode, they are quite likely to use it to get what they want rather than engaging in troublesome behavior. The student expends less effort when he or she uses communication, and the outcome is more certain, therefore teaching communication behaviors is a powerful way to replace challenging behavior.

Use Functional Communication Training

Another similar and well-documented approach is called functional communication training (Durand, 1990). Functional communication training (often abbreviated FCT) establishes communication to compete with the troublesome behaviors by taking over the same function that maintains these behaviors—making the communication and the troublesome behavior *functionally equivalent*. For example, if through a functional behavior assessment it can be determined that a student screams in order to get a snack, the teacher will teach the student to request a snack. When the student begins to scream, the teacher goes over to the student, interrupts the screaming, has the student sign "eat," and immediately gives the student a snack. Given enough opportunities, the student may begin to sign "eat" or an approximation of "eat" before he or she begins to scream. Screaming is replaced by signing. (More information on functional communication training appears later in this chapter in the section "Changing What Happens before Challenging Behavior Occurs.")

Behavior Functioning to Get Sensory Input

Obtaining sensory input is a common function of challenging behavior for students with visual impairments and multiple disabilities. These self-stimulatory or self-injurious behaviors often occur in the absence of social reinforcement, attention, or the presence of others. They can interfere with learning because they are immediately reinforcing and under the control of the student. Students would rather flip their fingers in front of their eyes (immediate reinforcement) than follow the teacher's directions (maybe delayed reinforcement, maybe no reinforcement).

Increase Overall Sensory Input

One approach is to compete with these behaviors by increasing the overall stimulation in the environment. The student should be actively engaged in activities at their educational level throughout the day. For some students, free time is scheduled to engage in self-stimulatory behavior so that it does not interfere with learning.

Use Preferred Sensory Stimulation as Reinforcement

Another approach is for the teacher to give the student sensory input as reinforcement for completing work. Sensory reinforcement can include flashing lights, light that provides warmth, noises, access to a switch that runs a fan that produces a breeze, tickles, high fives, deep pressure, or handshakes. The list is endless. This type of reinforcement is highly individualized but can be very effective. For example, if a student is constantly touching his or her face with taps and rubs to the degree that he or she cannot engage in productive work, the teacher can introduce brief periods of work and follow correct responses (even if they are heavily prompted) with shoulder squeezes (if that is reinforcing to the student) to see if this decreases the amount of face touching and increases

the student's attention. This type of reinforcement also works very well using a discrete trial teaching format—a series of individual teaching attempts—that includes a request for a response, a brief waiting interval, a prompt if no response is made, the response, and then sensory input as reinforcement. (For more information on discrete trial instruction see Ghezzi, 2007; Smith, 2001.)

Shape Disruptive or Stigmatizing Sensory Stimulation into Something More Acceptable

Another tactic to consider if challenging behavior is maintained by sensory input is to shape the challenging behavior into another behavior that is less challenging, less interfering, or less stigmatizing, as in the following example:

> A young man with a visual impairment and autism frequently lifts his arms above his head and waves them wildly around. His hands are not available to engage in academic tasks that he is capable of, and his waving behaviors are stigmatizing in the community. The teacher uses a highly preferred edible reinforcement when the student keeps his waving below his shoulders for 30 seconds. When this change in behavior has been achieved, the student is reinforced when he keeps his waving below his waist for 30 seconds, and then when he keeps his hands at his sides. He still waves his hands around, but the behavior is now less disruptive and more acceptable in the community.

Use Functional Communication Training to Teach the Student to Ask for Sensory Input

Yet another suggestion uses functional communication training. A teacher can interrupt a student engaged in high-frequency self-injurious behavior that is automatically reinforced by teaching him or her to ask for time in the sensory room (see Chapter 12), a specific kind of stimulation, or a box of sensory objects that he or she can manipulate on his or her own. Selecting the exact mode of communication is highly individualized, as previously noted.

Behavior Functioning to Escape or Avoid Something or Someone

Teachers ask students to do a lot of difficult activities during a school day. Although teachers are motivated to follow a curriculum and teach to the students' highest ability, students often do not see the value in the lessons. Lessons may be too long for students' attention levels, jump to material that is too difficult without teaching intermediate steps, or be just plain boring. Some members of the educational team are more positive, more helpful, and more enthusiastic about the material and the students' mastery of it, which makes them more reinforcing than team members who provide mainly negative feedback and corrections, fewer prompts, and less positive feedback. There are many reasons why students may want to escape from or avoid less-preferred team members and less-preferred activities. When challenging behaviors function to escape or avoid in these situations, it is an example of negative reinforcement. Negative reinforcement occurs when an aversive stimulus is present (work or less-preferred team members) and a challenging behavior terminates that stimulus (the work stops or the team member leaves), making the challenging behavior more likely in the future.

This is an area in which evaluation of the antecedent to the behavior is very important. An antecedent is the event that happens directly before a behavior. The answer to the question, "Why does the student want to escape or avoid this situation?" may be the key to identifying the intervention that needs to be implemented. Teachers can ask the following questions to gain further insight:

- What tasks or activities result in the challenging behavior?
- Is the activity too long or too difficult?
- Does the student have all the prerequisite skills for the activity or task?
- Is communication about the task clear?
- Is the student familiar with the format of the task or activity?

Change the Activity Requirement

Answers to the questions just listed may result in the use of shorter tasks, more inviting materials, or reinforcement for completion; teaching at a more basic level; better communication about what needs to be done; or using a different format. The use of very short, easy lessons followed by reinforcement can sometimes overcome challenging behaviors. Once the student is performing the work at this level, requirements can increase gradually. Reinforcement in this situation should be ongoing to prevent reemergence of escape-motivated challenging behaviors.

Offer Choices during Activities

Sometimes escape-motivated troublesome behaviors can be decreased through offering students their choice of activities and materials rather than insisting on the teacher's choice of activities and materials. Sometimes students are more willing to complete a less-preferred activity after they have completed a more-preferred activity, especially if reinforcement is available.

Use Powerful Reinforcement for Activity Completion

Other students are more willing to complete a less-preferred activity if they are reassured that a more-preferred activity will follow. This is called the Premack principle, after the person who did the initial research in this area (Premack, 1959). (Sometimes it is referred to as "Grandma's Law": "First you need to eat your green beans and then you can have dessert.") Essentially all of these suggestions manipulate antecedents or consequences to see what works best for a specific student.

Teach the Student to Ask for a 'Break' or to Be 'Finished'

Another tactic that can be successful in decreasing escape-motivated challenging behavior is to teach a functionally equivalent response that is more appropriate. Teach the student to ask for a "break," ask for "help," or ask to be "finished." One way to do this is to use functional communication training as previously described. When the teacher sees the student fidgeting in his or her seat, looking around the room, talking to another student, or otherwise engaged, the teacher may say to the student, "Do you need a break?" The teacher has the student repeat, "Break please," and models the answer if necessary. Having the student actually make the request and then receive reinforcement in the form of a break is important for increasing that specific behavior in his or her repertoire. Remember, the reinforcer for the student engaging in the challenging behavior is to escape the activity. Asking for a break will serve the same function and thus will also be reinforcing. The teacher allows the student to take a brief break, and then reintroduces the work. Interrupting the challenging behavior and completing the sequence also can decrease challenging behaviors. However, early intervention, before the challenging behavior has occurred, may be more efficient and can prevent escalation to the more disruptive behaviors.

When discussing teaching appropriate escape and avoidance behaviors, teachers often resist this idea. They feel as if students should do the work and if they are allowed to take a break or be finished upon request, they will overuse these requests and avoid all work. Initially this may be the case. But, in fact, if antecedent variables are reviewed carefully and reinforcement for completing work is in place, students usually are able and motivated to complete the work. Allowing students to ask for a break or to be finished may allow for more work to be completed in the course of the day because students are not engaging in disruptive behavior to escape from or avoid the work. This can increase the productivity of the individual student and possibly others in the classroom as well.

Behavior Functioning to Attenuate Pain

As noted earlier, some behaviors that function to obtain sensory feedback can be related to attempts to relieve pain. There is a fair body of research that documents instances when challenging behavior is observed in children in whom an undetected medical condition is present. Often these children cannot communicate effectively about their condition. Behavior analysts conceptualize this troublesome behavior as behavior that "competes" with pain or discomfort and functions as negative automatic reinforcement—behavior that produces escape or avoidance of pain. Correlation has been found between chronic ear infections and self-injurious behavior (O'Reilly, 1997). Other behaviors such as screaming, biting, increased head banging, and hitting others have been linked to urinary tract infections, a broken leg, ear infections, bowel impaction, hernia, undetected tissue damage, and menses (Bosch, Van Dyke, Smith & Poulton, 1997; Gunsett, Mulick, Fernald, & Martin, 1989; Roy & Simon, 1987).

Medical conditions and physical discomfort should be considered, especially if there is a sudden onset of troublesome behavior not seen in the past. While teaching staff is not likely to be in touch with all of the health concerns of students or in contact with their medical providers, being aware of changes in behavior is important. Teachers and other members of the educational team spend many hours each day with students, and any such changes should be reported at once to parents. This reporting should not necessarily refer to the behaviors as troublesome or challenging, but as unusual, out of the ordinary, and just "not right." Enlisting parents to think with you about these issues and to suggest a possible medical component can be helpful. Remember to document behavior changes, including dates and time. This may be useful over the long term. Sometimes it can be helpful to share these notes with the school nurse so the exact information gets into the student's record. While not suggesting that all troublesome behavior is a function of medical conditions, medical conditions can be a component and should be investigated when doing a functional behavior assessment.

Multiple Functions

Many students demonstrate complicated and challenging behavior that is maintained by more than one function. This can be a difficult situation to evaluate for people who are not specifically trained in behavior analysis. If a teacher determines that a behavior functions both to get attention and to escape or avoid work, he or she probably cannot respond to both functions in the same way. The teacher may need to design one intervention for the attention function and another for the escape or avoidance function. A rule of thumb is to select the situation that is most interfering and start there. Sometimes when one situation improves, there is generalization to other situations.

Another intervention is to take a generalized approach to both functions by introducing FCT to get attention and to escape or avoid less preferred activities. For example, when working with a nonverbal student, you can provide a "Talk to me" card and a "Break please" card. Maybe in the short term, the student can be immersed in a functional communication training environment to get all of his or her needs met in this way. In such a classroom environment there can be picture boards placed in strategic locations or iPads available, and everyone, teachers and students alike, can use this communication system.

Although there are strategies a teacher can try when multiple functions of one troublesome behavior are present, it can be very helpful to consult an expert. As noted earlier, many school districts hire board-certified behavior analysts, and a teacher can ask an administrator if there is one available or if one can be hired on a consulting basis. (Listings can be found on the Behavior Analyst Certification Board website, www.bacb.com; see the Resources section at the end of this chapter.) In addition, many school psychology programs are now training their students in functional behavior assessment and behavioral intervention programs, so school psychologists may also provide additional resources.

Changing What Happens before Challenging Behaviors Occur

There are several somewhat generalized interventions, known as antecedent interventions, that can be applied to a variety of challenging behaviors that serve a variety of functions.

Antecedent interventions change behavior not by changing the consequences, as do many of the interventions outlined so far, but by decreasing the effectiveness of the positive or negative reinforcement that maintains challenging behaviors. Their use depends on completing a functional behavior assessment to identify the function that maintains the behaviors. If the function has been identified, two interventions can be considered: *noncontingent reinforcement* (sometimes abbreviated NCR) and *functional communication training*. In this context, they both are somewhat more complicated than the interventions previously outlined, taking more planning, more resources, and more skill to implement. However, they can be highly effective and are wonderful tools for teachers.

Noncontingent Reinforcement

Noncontingent reinforcement identifies the maintaining or reinforcing function of the challenging behavior and makes the reinforcement available noncontingently, which means that the reinforcement is delivered without regard to the behavior of the student. For example, a student talks out of turn, and it has been determined that this behavior is maintained by teacher attention (positive reinforcement) in the form of eye contact, coming over to the student, and reprimands. Therefore, the teacher comes over to and talks to the student once every one or two minutes no matter what behavior the student displays. Another example: It has been determined that a student's self-injurious behavior is maintained by sensory input (automatic reinforcement). Therefore, the teacher gives the student a shoulder squeeze every one or two minutes, no matter what else is going on. A third example: It has been determined that a student's throwing of items is maintained by escape from less-preferred activities (negative reinforcement). The teacher instead gives the student a break after every five minutes of work.

Noncontingent reinforcement is a fixed-time reinforcement schedule. The amount of fixed time depends on the frequency of the troublesome behavior. Usually the noncontingent reinforcement is scheduled in intervals shorter than the average interval at which the troublesome behavior occurs. Most noncontingent reinforcement also uses planned ignoring (discussed earlier in this chapter) as a consequence to the troublesome behavior. This procedure requires ongoing monitoring to ensure that the noncontingent reinforcement is effective in decreasing the troublesome behavior.

Noncontingent reinforcement is easy to use and creates a positive environment filled with reinforcement. It makes the teacher who delivers the noncontingent reinforcement a *conditioned reinforcer*. A conditioned reinforcer is not in and of itself a reinforcer, but, when it is paired with another reinforcing stimulus, takes on the same reinforcing properties. The chance pairing of reinforcement with other positive behaviors may increase these behaviors. There are several disadvantages to noncontingent reinforcement. Free and frequent access to reinforcement may decrease its effectiveness for increasing other behaviors. Also, chance pairing of reinforcement with troublesome behavior may increase the troublesome behavior. This procedure needs to be evaluated carefully during use.

Functional Communication Training

As already described, functional communication training establishes communication behavior to compete with troublesome behavior by taking over the function of the troublesome behavior—it makes both behaviors functionally equivalent. Once the functional behavior assessment has determined the function of the behavior of concern, the next step is to teach the student to ask for what he or she wants or needs in a more acceptable manner. For example, a student talks out of turn and it has been determined that this behavior is maintained by teacher attention (positive reinforcement) in the form of eye contact, coming over to the student, and reprimands. Therefore, the teacher teaches the student to raise his or her hand to get attention that is always reinforced by the teacher coming over and talking to the student. Another example: It has been determined that a student's self-injurious behavior is maintained by sensory input (automatic reinforcement). Therefore, the teacher teaches the student to ask for sensory input by using signs, symbols, or other communication devices, and then delivers these sensory activities whenever the student asks for them. A third example: It has been assessed that a student's throwing of items is maintained by escape or avoidance of less-preferred activities (negative reinforcement). The teacher teaches the student to ask for a break from a less-preferred activity by holding up a "Break" card. The teacher then grants a short break. Functional communication training often uses other procedures such as prompting, planned ignoring, and time out as a consequence to the challenging behavior.

Functional communication training provides a dense schedule of reinforcement and allows for the fading of prompts as skills develop. In addition, teachers can add a "wait time" into this procedure so students can ask for what they want, but learn to wait until after the next activity or class.

Functional communication training fosters good generalization and maintenance of behavior because the student learns to recruit reinforcement. This is an intervention that has high social validity; it is acceptable to teachers and other educational staff. It is relatively easy to implement and can be effective without using other, more restrictive interventions. Functional communication training usually includes planned ignoring, which can be difficult to implement in some settings. In addition, functional communication training can interfere with the learning of others if the requests are frequent and disruptive.

PREVENTING CHALLENGING BEHAVIORS

The strategies described in the previous sections represent ways to intervene with challenging behavior when it occurs in the classroom. The following strategies focus on preventing challenging behavior from arising in the first place.

Positive Behavior Interventions and Supports

As discussed earlier in this chapter, a primary method for preventing challenging behavior is positive behavioral interventions and supports (PBIS). As previously noted, this is a system of rules, reminders, and reinforcements that applies to an entire classroom or an entire school and can be an excellent way to prevent challenging behaviors. Usually three or four rules, stated in positive terms, are the basis of the system. Examples include students will be respectful to classmates and staff; students will work hard at their studies; and students will walk in the hallways and cafeteria. The rules are behavioral expectations. Usually the teacher reviews the rules on a regular basis with the students, along with explicit teaching and examples of what the rules mean. The teacher may give reminders and examples at teachable moments, such as a situation where the rules are in jeopardy. Reminders are prompts about what behavior should be displayed in a specific situation.

Reinforcement is what gives positive behavior supports their power. Along with attention and positive social feedback, a variety of reinforcement systems, as discussed earlier, can be easily implemented in a classroom. Teachers and peer monitors (a position that can be earned as a privilege) can deliver reinforcement. Delivering reinforcement for following the rules is a much more successful and positive approach than delivering reprimands or negative feedback for breaking the rules. It sets a positive tone in the classroom and makes everyone, teachers and students, responsible for encouraging positive social behavior.

Many teachers implement a specific prompt system to encourage prosocial behavior in students. As noted earlier, research indicates that errorless learning can be very effective in teaching new skills (Green, 2001; McCartney & LeBlanc, 1997). This system usually uses a most-to-least prompt system—one that starts with the most intrusive prompt and then fades to less intrusive ones—to teach students the correct response; it is errorless because the student is prompted to provide the correct response before he or she can make a mistake. The teacher begins to teach by stating exactly what the expectation is. Once the student engages in the expectation, the teacher reinforces the student's success. The teacher then adds in a delay before prompting the student. This allows the student an opportunity to respond independently. The prompt hierarchy for teaching social behavior usually consists of the following:

- full verbal prompt (say what you want the student to do)
- partial verbal prompt (say part of what you want the student to do) followed by
- an expectant pause
- a gesture prompt (often initially paired with the verbal prompt)

Sometimes the first prompt is a physical prompt (the teacher helps the student do the behavior). This type of prompt can be used if verbal directions are difficult for the student or the student does not have skills in the area of instruction.

Using Social Feedback as Reinforcement

The role of reinforcement in preventing challenging behavior cannot be overstated. In a busy classroom, it is often easy to overlook the students who are working quietly at their desks in favor of students who are calling out or moving around the classroom when they should be working. It can be very easy to focus attention, and possibly reinforcing attention, on these students. Yet it is difficult to used planned ignoring under these circumstances because the behavior is disruptive in the classroom. One way to get around this dilemma is to specifically reinforce students who are engaged in the correct behavior while other students are engaged in behavior that should be discouraged. For example, if Raul is out of his seat, the teacher can say, "Jane, I like the way you are working in your seat; Serge, I like the way you are working in your seat," while ignoring the student who is out of his seat. This is one way to prompt the student who is out of his seat to do the correct behavior without giving him direct attention for engaging in the incorrect behavior.

Self-Management and Self-Monitoring

Another classroom management strategy that can assist in preventing challenging behaviors is to have students implement self-management interventions. Self-management can be used to monitor following the classroom rules, assist students in meeting personal goals, break up large tasks by setting incremental goals, and change bad habits or interfering behaviors. Students who learn self-management skills can apply them to a variety of behaviors and situations. Self-management skills allow students to work independently and self-direct their own work without relying on the supervision of teachers or others. An example of self-management includes a student giving him- or herself a check on an individual "good behavior" check sheet before lunch and a check before leaving school in the afternoon for being respectful to students, being respectful to teachers, and completing all of his or her assignments. Another example, for a student who is weak in math: The student contracts with her teacher to do 10 math problems correctly every day. The student completes the problems and then checks the problems against a correction sheet from the teacher. Ten correct problems result in 10 extra minutes of recess. In a third example, a student who frequently calls out answers before the teacher calls on him gives himself a star on a chart every time he waits to be called on by the teacher. He takes a full sheet of stars home to share with his parents, who offer positive feedback for his improving school behavior, and maybe take the student to a favorite restaurant.

The last example is one of *self-monitoring,* in which the student (with help from the teacher) identifies a behavior to change and records data on the behavior. Sometimes self-monitoring will change behavior without further reinforcement (the data collection itself changes the behavior, not social feedback or other reinforcers). Another type of self-monitoring intervention may include the student using a checklist of steps to follow in order to produce a desirable behavior, such as the steps in making a new friend. These techniques often require the use of special materials, prompts from the teacher (to start recording and then to become an ac-

curate recorder), a clearly defined target behavior to measure, frequent monitoring or use of short intervals for monitoring, and reinforcement for accuracy.

There are many pre-made materials available for self-management programs. Some of the best can be obtained from KidTools Support Systems (see the Resources section at the end of this chapter for more information), which has a variety of materials for children ages 7 to 14 that address self-management of academic and social behavior, organizational skills, and learning strategies.

Positive behavior supports, frequent and ongoing attention as a reinforcer, indirect prompts to decrease troublesome behavior, peer monitors to deliver reinforcement, and self-management interventions can all assist in preventing challenging behavior and increasing the positive atmosphere in the classroom.

Setting Up a Positive Environment

One of the most important variables in preventing troublesome behavior—and one over which the teacher has considerable control—is the classroom environment. Setting up a positive classroom environment can prevent many behavioral difficulties and avoid the need to use valuable resources to address behavioral difficulties. A few classroom management tools can be very effective:

- Structure the day. Set a schedule and stick to it.
- Make sure there is not too much down time between lessons or activities.

- If there is down time or free time, make sure students have something interesting to do. Provide a variety of free-time activities that will occupy the students.
- Even though the students may have free time, staff should be available to monitor that the rules are being followed and that students are receiving positive feedback for engaging in prosocial behavior.

A routine can be very helpful. It allows students to anticipate the next activity, decreases worry and confusion, and quite often increases compliance with requests. Routines for entering the classroom, leaving the classroom, eating in the lunchroom, and passing in the hallways all can be very helpful. These are times when students are likely to engage in troublesome behavior and identifying the behaviors that students should be doing can decrease problem behaviors. Sometimes the routine can include specific rules and social feedback such as walk on the right in the hallways, keep your hands to yourself, and use an indoor voice. Employing reviews and rehearsals directly before these behaviors are demonstrated and providing positive feedback directly after following the rules can be helpful.

Classroom organization should support structure and routine. Having lessons planned ahead of time, preparing special materials and worksheets in advance, and keeping materials in a designated place can cut down on wasted time and time that students are waiting around while the teacher locates various supplies. Some teachers find learning centers helpful. Learning centers are classroom locations where different activities are conducted. There can be a math center, a reading center, and a social studies center. This allows for efficient placement of materials, books, and worksheets.

If the classroom is using a PBIS system, the rules should be posted in a number of locations, and they should be reviewed and practiced at a specific time every day. The data-collection system should be simple rather than complex. A lottery system of points, checks, stars, or cards is simple and easy to use and does not require a lot of recordkeeping. Some teachers find it helpful to keep a corner or area of the room dedicated to these materials.

Teachers will want to consider using a predesigned curriculum based on direct instruction and active responding whenever possible. There are a number of commercially available direct instruction curricula for math, reading, history, many of the sciences, and social studies (see National Institute for Direct Instruction listing in the Resources section at the end of this chapter for more information). These programs use a *logical instructional design* approach; that is, the programs have been carefully designed to build skills in a stepwise manner, in which progression to new material happens only after the previous material is mastered. This prevents errors, frustration, and the many troublesome behaviors that can occur when students seek to escape or avoid educational material.

Alternating active and passive classroom activities can be helpful for some students. Also, students with sensory deficits may be overstimulated or understimulated in the everyday classroom. Overstimulated students may be inattentive and fidgety. Relaxation exercises or deep breathing can be helpful in restoring their equilibrium. Some teachers have found simple yoga poses helpful for overstimulated students. Understimulated students may be sleepy, tired, and lethargic. Standing up, stretching, moving around, marching in place, giving themselves deep pressure, or dancing a jig may make understimulated students more alert before the next activity.

While this is not an exhaustive list of environmental variables that can assist in preventing behavioral difficulties in the classroom, all of them provide important positive components in a well-ordered and functioning classroom.

DEVELOPMENT OF A BEHAVIORAL INTERVENTION PLAN

Based on the outcome of the functional behavior assessment, schools also are mandated by IDEA to design and implement a behavioral intervention plan (sometimes abbreviated BIP) to teach a student alternatives and replacement behaviors for challenging behaviors demonstrated by the student. The behavioral intervention plan is part of the Individualized Education Program (IEP) and must be approved by the student's parent or caregiver.

Developing a behavioral intervention plan involves the following steps:

1. Define the behavior of concern.
2. Collect direct data or complete an indirect assessment.
3. Make a hypothesis about the function of the behavior.
4. Design an intervention based on the function.
5. Continue data collection.
6. Make adjustments.

The first step in positive behavioral intervention planning is to carefully define the behavior of concern so all people who work with the student can agree on when the behavior occurs. Second, data needs to be collected, either through direct observation or through using an indirect assessment tool. Third, the data is reviewed and a hypothesis formed about the function of the challenging behavior. The hypothesis should be written down in specific terms, for example: "The function of the screaming behavior seems to be to avoid math lessons and occupational therapy."

It is critical that these earlier steps be completed before the fourth step, designing the actual behavioral intervention plan, is undertaken. Performing a thorough assessment will result in a clearer hypothesis about the function of the behavior, lead to fewer errors in treatment design, and result in faster progress and more efficient interventions. Sometimes it is hard to wait to implement behavior interventions. Often teachers are desperate, the classroom is disrupted, and students are not learning as a result. But the groundwork must be done in order to provide the student with a behavioral intervention plan that has the best chance of changing the behavior.

Once the assessment is completed and the appropriate intervention identified, an outline of the intervention should be completed so that all members of the educational team can implement it consistently. The basic outline of a behavioral intervention should answer all of the following questions:

- What is the troublesome behavior in which the student engages? Be specific and define it carefully. This is sometimes called the *behavior to decrease.*
- When, where, and with whom does the behavior occur? Include frequency and duration data if possible. This will be considered baseline—the level of the behavior before intervention.
- What function does the behavior serve? Attention, tangible items, sensory, or escape or avoidance.
- What do you want the student to *do*? This is sometimes called the *behavior to increase.* It is the alternative to, or replacement for, the challenging behavior.
- When, where, and with whom do you want the new behavior to occur? These are program details including reminders, prompts, and directions.
- Why should the student want to do the new behavior? What motivation or reinforcement is in place to encourage the student to learn and do the new behavior?
- What is the direct response to the challenging behavior? This response can include planned ignoring, prompting, response blocking, *response cost* (loss of something previously earned), or a variety of time out procedures.
- What would a crisis consist of, and what should be done about it? This component is optional and only required when students display highly dangerous or disruptive behaviors.

Sidebar 13.1 provides an example of a behavioral intervention plan for a 6-year-old girl with a moderate visual impairment and mild intellectual delay who has begun screaming in her classroom. Chapter 9 (Figure 9.1) also contains a form that can be used to assemble the data and document the behavioral assessment plan.

The following are some suggestions for implementation of a behavioral intervention plan:

- Implement the intervention as written.
- Be alert for trouble spots and procedures that are incomplete or difficult to implement.
- Once the intervention is implemented, adjustments are often required. Do not be afraid to make changes. However, give the intervention some time to work. If you are constantly changing the intervention, the student will not be able to learn the new contingencies.
- Remember, these troublesome behaviors did not appear in one day and it will take more than a day to teach new behavior. For high-frequency behavior, a change may be seen quickly, but for low-frequency behavior, it may take more time.
- Collect some data on the frequency or duration of the troublesome behavior and compare it to the baseline. If there is no change after several weeks, it may be time to reevaluate the intervention, review the assessment, or both.

Sample Behavioral Intervention Plan (BIP) for Susan

Name: _Susan Smith_   **Date of birth:** _8/15/2009_   **Date of evaluation:** _1/16_

Classroom: _Ms. White's special education young elementary classroom (substantially separate)_

Background

Susan Smith is a student with a moderate visual impairment (legally blind in her right eye) and a mild intellectual delay. She lives at home with her parents and is an only child. Although she is 6 years old, she functions as a 4-year-old child. She has delays in academic, communication, and social skills, but is making slow and steady progress. Susan can recite the ABCs, sing familiar songs, listen quietly to stories, take turns and share toys, ask for what she wants, and say "hello" and "goodbye." She is generally pleasant and cooperative.

Last year Susan was in an integrated kindergarten class of 15 students, 1 teacher, and 3 paraeducators and reportedly did very well. Her present class consists of 6 students, a classroom teacher, and 1 paraeducator. Both adults have worked with students who have visual impairments and intellectual disabilities for several years. They have not had much experience working with students who display behavior challenges.

Since September, Susan has displayed an increasing frequency of random screams during classroom activities. Both the teacher and the paraeducator professional have attempted to ask her why she is screaming and what is wrong. She has been unable to say and sometimes she bursts into tears. On oc-

casion they have taken her to the nurse, expecting that she may be ill. Nothing specific has been discovered. Several conversations with her family have resulted in no other clues. She reportedly does not engage in this behavior at home.

Functional Behavior Assessment

Screaming was defined as loud vocalizations that last for one or more consecutive seconds. An example would be loud vocalizations without words. A loud vocalization in response to a friend running a race would not be considered an example of the target behavior.

An assessment was completed using the following tools:

- Functional Analysis Screening Tool (FAST)—This tool includes 16 questions about when the behavior occurs and other information such as frequency, severity, situations where the behavior is observed, and specific times when the behaviors is observed.
- ABC recording—Over the course of one week the teacher and the paraeducator wrote down what happened before the screams and what happened after the screams whenever they could.
- Partial interval time sample—The school guidance counselor came into

(continued)

the classroom for 30 minutes on three separate occasions and recorded the frequency of the screams based on 30-second intervals over the course of observation. One interval was a group activity and the other two intervals included individual seatwork and "play centers."

The results of these assessments indicated the following:

1. The FAST noted the most likely function of the screams was social (attention) reinforcement. The screams were most likely when Susan was not engaged with a staff person, very unlikely when she was engaged in a group or individual activity with a staff person. During individual seatwork, screams often resulted in staff coming over to her to see what was wrong.
2. ABC recording resulted in information similar to the FAST.
3. The partial interval time sample revealed that during the group activity, screams were recorded during only 5 percent of intervals (3 out of 60; 30 minutes). During seatwork, screams were recorded during 25 percent of intervals (10 out of 40; 20 minutes). During "play centers," screams were recorded during 8 percent of intervals (7 out of 80; 40 minutes).

Based on these results, it was hypothesized that the function of the screaming was to get adult attention, especially when an adult was not nearby. This hypothesis was supported by all three assessment tools, but strongly supported by the time sample data. When staff are present, such as during group activities and "play centers" (staff circulated between the three centers), screams were low, only 5–7 percent of 30-second intervals. During independent seatwork, screams occurred during 25 percent of 30-second intervals and often resulted in staff coming over to Susan's seat. The longest amount of consecutive time that Susan went without a scream was 3.5 minutes.

Target Behaviors to Increase

Working/playing quietly—whenever Susan engages in group or individual activities and uses her voice with words and only at a conversational level.

Target Behaviors to Decrease

Screaming—loud vocalizations (without words) that last for 1 or more consecutive seconds.

Behavioral Interventions

- *Noncontingent reinforcement (NCR)*—An intervention whereby reinforcement (attention) is delivered on a fixed time schedule without regard to the occurrence or non-occurrence of the behavior to decrease.
- *Functional communication training (FCT)*—An intervention whereby a student is taught a functionally equivalent behavior (hand raising) to replace the behavior to decrease (screaming).
- *Extinction*—An intervention whereby a previously reinforced behavior

(screaming) is no longer reinforced (by attention).

Reinforcement Procedures

1. Based on the collected baseline data during the functional assessment, it was determined that Susan was most likely to scream during individual seatwork. Therefore, staff will implement a NCR procedure during individual seatwork times. Every three minutes a staff will go up to her desk and give her some form of attention, commenting on her work, offering positive feedback for working hard, or some other attention (pat on the back, thumbs up, etc.).
2. One staff member will be assigned to provide the attention during each individual seatwork activity. The staff member will be able to keep track of the time using a vibrating timer that can be clipped to the waistband or put in a pocket.
3. If, at the exact time the timer goes off, Susan is screaming, the staff member will wait for 30 quiet seconds and then offer attention.

Functional Communication Training

1. Teaching staff will give two lessons per day with all of the students in the class. They will review "How to get attention the right way." This will include modeling (staff doing) and role-playing (students doing). All students will receive at least two to three turns per lesson. Students will be asked, "What can you do to get attention? Show me." A raised hand is the correct response.
2. When students call out during group activities or lunch, staff will say, "How do you get attention the right way?"
3. All students will be reminded before individual seatwork, "How do you get attention the right way?"
4. In addition, there will be a visual aid, a picture of a student with raised hand, posted on the front board and on Susan's desk.
5. Descriptive praise will be given, "Nice job, raising your hand to get attention," whenever any students engage in this behavior, whether prompted or not.

Interventions for Behaviors to Decrease

1. If Susan screams, staff will withhold comments, eye contact, and all attention. Other students should be assisted in doing the same by prompting them to pay attention to their own work and saying, "Do not worry about Susan. She will be okay."
2. It is important to note that when first beginning to extinguish the screaming behavior, there may be a temporary increase in screaming. It may be difficult to ignore the behavior, but it should decrease relatively quickly.

Data Collection and Program Review

1. The baseline was 10 screams in 20 minutes or 0.5 per minute. Staff members will record the frequency of screams during individual seatwork only and divide that number by the

(continued)

(*Sidebar 13.1 continued*)

length of the seatwork interval for a "rate of screams per minute."

2. Data will be reviewed weekly to assess progress.
3. If progress is not made after two weeks, program procedures will be adjusted.
4. It is expected the frequency of screams will decrease during other activities as a result of the functional communication training. Staff should be aware of this and look for a decrease. If it appears that a decrease during other activities is not forthcoming, further data collection (a probe) may be necessary. However, if the behavior does decrease, no further intervention or data collection will be required.

Laurie S. Denno, Ph.D., BCBA-D
Behavior Analyst

BEHAVIOR SUPPORT TEAMS

Many schools or school districts develop behavior support teams. Behavior support teams are designed to assist teachers with identifying, addressing, and changing behaviors that interfere with learning. It is important that everyone on the behavior support team, and everyone who works with the behavior support team, function collaboratively to help the student become a more effective learner in his or her classroom.

The Team

The members of the team will vary depending on who works with the student and the student's unique needs. Generally speaking, the team should include the classroom teacher, other related service providers, a behavior analyst or school psychologist who is trained in completing functional behavior assessments and behavioral intervention plans, an administrator, and the parent or parents if possible. There are usually between three and five people on a team.

Members of the team are there to support the student, the teacher, and possibly the student's parents to make changes in the classroom environment and maybe in the home environment. It is not productive to blame the teacher for not yet having the skills to assist a particular student. It is the team's responsibility to help the teacher gain the required skills. It is also not productive to blame the child's troublesome behavior on lack of parent involvement, communication, or follow-through. Parents do not want their child to be unsuccessful in school. Parents do the best they can with the resources they have. It is the team's responsibility to work with parents to ensure that changes that need to be made at home are reasonable for parents to carry out.

Crisis Plan

If the behaviors of concern are dangerous or extremely disruptive, a crisis plan may be required. Dangerous and disruptive behaviors include behaviors such as severe self-injuring behavior requiring medical attention, aggression to staff or students, and property destruction that could cause injury to the student or staff. A crisis plan is not a teaching tool; it indicates what to do to keep everyone safe until a behavior support plan is in place. It is not advisable to use a crisis plan over a long period of time or at a high frequency. What the crisis plan looks like will depend on the student, the behaviors, and the resources available. Some common crisis plan interventions include adding extra staff in the classroom, excluding the student from the classroom for a period of time, having the student temporarily work in a separate room, using a protective hold, sending the student home, or using a suspension.

Defining the Behavior

Several team meetings may be required to discuss the interfering behaviors. The teacher's role in this discussion is critical. Only the teacher knows the structure of the class, how the challenging behaviors interfere with learning, and what is possible or not possible in the classroom. Teachers should be prepared to describe the challenging behavior, discuss interventions they have already tried, and document the results of those interventions. Providing data on the frequency and duration of troublesome behaviors is very important. The behavior analyst or school psychologist may spend some time observing the student and more carefully defining the behavior of interest. They may ask the teacher to take some more specific data or complete

one of the standard functional behavior assessment question forms.

Creating the Plan

After the observation, data collection, or both, the team will come together to discuss their findings and come to a consensus on the function of the interfering behavior. Based on these findings, a set of interventions will be discussed. The interventions can include any of the interventions discussed in this chapter, along with possible changes in the classroom environment. Ongoing data collection will be required. If extra resources are required, the administrator on the team is most likely responsible for finding them. It is important to write down the plan, even if it's just a series of bullet points. It is ideal to assign specific people to carry out specific aspects of the plan.

Implementing the Plan

The classroom teacher may require some training in implementing the interventions. It is critical that the behavior analyst or school psychologist carefully reviews the interventions with the teacher and is available to observe and coach the teacher when he or she begins to implement the plan. On some occasions, the behavior analyst or school psychologist may participate in the initial implementation of the interventions to serve as a model for the teacher and to troubleshoot any problematic issues related to the intervention. Classroom aides and related service providers may also require training before implementing the interventions.

Follow-up support should be frequent and certain for all members of the team who implement the intervention. It is best to arrange a schedule of follow-up visits so that the teacher and others know support is available when necessary. In addition, the behavior support team should meet periodically to review progress and make any required adjustments to the interventions. This review should be based on data collected in the intervening time period. The team will want to make decisions about and adjustments to the plan based on hard data, not on feelings and guesses. This can be a time-consuming and difficult process, but assisting students and teachers to have a more productive learning experience is well worth the effort.

SUMMARY

There are a variety of solutions for preventing and changing challenging behaviors in students with visual impairments and multiple disabilities. An excellent functional behavior assessment is the foundation for deciding which interventions are appropriate for a given student. An individualized plan must be developed for each student who exhibits troublesome behavior in the classroom. The function of the behavior is the most important variable in determining what behavioral support is most likely to effect behavior change. Providing the most appropriate behavioral intervention can be difficult and time-consuming and require some professional expertise above and beyond a teacher's usual skill set. There are many resources available online and through behavioral literature that can be helpful to teachers and administrators who are struggling with behavioral issues.

(See the Resources section at the end of this chapter.)

There are many interventions that teachers can implement if they have a solid foundation in behavioral interventions. Teachers come to their work with a variety of skills. Some teachers are adept at implementing behavior supports and some teachers struggle with these concepts. School administration and behavior support teams can assist teachers in developing the required skills and support them in teaching acceptable and appropriate social and learning behaviors to their students.

REFERENCES

Alberto, P. A., & Troutman, A. C. (2009). *Applied behavior analysis for teachers* (8th ed.). Upper Saddle River, NJ: Pearson Education.

Bosch, J., Van Dyke, D. C., Smith, S. M., & Poulton, S. (1997). Role of medical conditions in the exacerbation of self-injurious behavior: An exploratory study. *Mental Retardation, 35*(2), 124–130.

Cooper, J. O., Heron, T. E., & Heward, W. L. (2007). *Applied behavior analysis* (2nd ed.). Upper Saddle River, NJ: Pearson Education.

Doggett, R. A., Mueller, M. M., & Moore, J. W. (2002). Functional assessment informant record: Creation, evaluation, and future research. *Proven Practice: Prevention and Remediation Strategies for Schools, 4*, 25–30.

Durand, V. M. (1990). *Severe behavior problems: A functional communication training approach.* New York: Guilford Press.

Durand, V. M., & Crimmins, D. (1992). *The Motivational Assessment Scale (MAS).* Topeka, KS: Monaco & Associates.

Ghezzi, P. M. (2007). Discrete trials teaching. *Psychology in the Schools, 44*(7), 667–679.

Green, G. (2001). Behavior analytic instruction for learners with autism: Advances in stimulus control technology. *Focus on Autism and Other Developmental Disabilities, 16*(2), 72–85.

Gunsett, R. P., Mulick, J. A., Fernald, W. B., & Martin, J. L. (1989). Indications for medical screening prior to behavioral programming for severely and profoundly retarded clients. *Journal of Autism and Developmental Disorders, 19*(1), 167–172.

Individuals with Disabilities Education Improvement Act (IDEA), 20 U.S.C § 1400 (2004).

Iwata, B. A., & DeLeon, I. (1996). *The Functional Analysis Screening Tool (FAST)*. Gainesville: University of Florida, Florida Center on Self-Injury.

Iwata, B. A., Dorsey, M. F., Slifer, K. J., Bauman, K. E., & Richman, G. S. (1982). Toward a functional analysis of self-injury. *Analysis and Intervention in Developmental Disabilities, 2,* 3–20.

Iwata, B. A., Dorsey, M. F., Slifer, K. J., Bauman, K. E., & Richman, G. S. (1994). Toward a functional analysis of self-injury. *Journal of Applied Behavior Analysis, 27*(2), 197–209.

Lewis, T. J., Scott, T. M., & Sugai, G. (1994). The problem behavior questionnaire: A teacher-based instrument to develop functional hypotheses of problem behavior in general education classrooms. *Assessment for Effective Instruction, 19*(2–3), 103–115.

Lewis, T. J., Sugai, G., & Colvin, G. (1998). Reducing problem behavior through a school-wide system of effective behavioral support: Investigation of a school-wide social skills training program and contextual interventions. *School Psychology Review, 27*(3), 446–459.

McCartney, L. L. A., & LeBlanc, J. M. (1997). Errorless learning in educational environments: Using criterion-related cues to reduce errors. In D. M. Baer & E. M. Pinkton (Eds.), *Environment and behavior* (pp. 80–96). Boulder, CO: Westview Press.

McCurdy, B. L., Kunsch, C., & Reibstein, S. (2007). Secondary prevention in the urban school: Implementing the behavior education program. *Preventing School Failure, 51*(3), 12–19.

McCurdy, B. L., Mannella, M. C., & Eldridge, N. (2003). Positive behavior support in urban schools: Can we prevent the escalation of antisocial behavior? *Journal of Positive Behavior Interventions, 5*(3), 158–170.

O'Reilly, M. F. (1997). Functional analysis of episodic self-injury correlated with recurrent otitis media. *Journal of Applied Behavior Analysis, 30*(1), 165–167.

Paclawskyj, T. R., Matson, J. L., Rush, K. S., Smalls, Y., & Vollmer, T. R. (2000). Questions about behavioral function (QABF): A behavioral checklist for functional assessment of aberrant behavior. *Research in Developmental Disabilities, 21*(3), 223–229.

Premack, D. (1959). Toward empirical behavioral laws: I. Positive reinforcement. *Psychological Review, 66*(4), 219–233.

Roy, A., & Simon, G. B. (1987). Intestinal obstruction as a cause of death in the mentally handicapped. *Journal of Intellectual Disability Research, 31*(2), 193–197.

Smith, T. (2001). Discrete trial training in the treatment of autism. *Focus on Autism and Other Developmental Disabilities, 16*(2), 86–92.

Sugai, G., & Horner, R. (2002). The evolution of discipline practices: School-wide positive behavior supports. *Child & Family Behavior Therapy, 24*(1–2), 23–50.

Sugai, G., Sprague, J. R., Horner, R. H., & Walker, H. M. (2000). Preventing school violence: The use of office discipline referrals to assess and monitor school-wide discipline interventions. *Journal of Emotional and Behavioral Disorders, 8*(2), 94–101.

Touchette, P. E., MacDonald, R. F., & Langer, S. N. (1985). A scatter plot for identifying stimulus control of problem behavior. *Journal of Applied Behavior Analysis, 18*(4), 343–351.

Wieseler, N. A., Hanson, R. H., Chamberlain, T. P., & Thompson, T. (1985). Functional taxonomy of stereotypic and self-injurious behavior. *Mental Retardation, 23*(5), 230–234.

RESOURCES

For additional resources, see the General Resources section at the back of this book.

Assessments

Functional Analysis Screening Tool (FAST)
Source: Iwata, B. A., & DeLeon, I. (1996). *The Functional Analysis Screening Tool (FAST).* Gainesville: University of Florida, Florida Center on Self-Injury.

This 16-question survey relies on "yes," "no," and "NA" responses and includes information on the student's schedule, possible replacement behaviors, communication skills, preferences, and previous interventions that have been implemented.

Functional Assessment Informant Record for Teachers (FAIR-T)
Source: Doggett, R. A., Mueller, M. M., & Moore, J. W. (2002). Functional assessment informant record: Creation, evaluation, and future research. *Proven Practice: Prevention and Remediation Strategies for Schools, 4,* 25–30.

This 16-question profile of "yes" and "no" questions about when and where the behavior of concern occurs includes information on academic achievement, health status, the student's schedule, and problem behaviors in relation to frequency, intensity, length of time, and maintaining consequences.

Motivational Analysis Rating Scale (MARS)
Source: Wieseler, N. A., Hanson, R. H., Chamberlain, T. P., & Thompson, T. (1985). Functional taxonomy of stereotypic and self-injurious behavior. *Mental Retardation, 23*(5), 230–234.

This quick and easy six-question (two questions for each of the three functions) rating scale includes sensory, escape, and attention functions rated on a four-point rating scale. Does not include a category for the get-tangible-items function.

Motivational Assessment Scale (MAS)
Source: Durand, V. M., & Crimmins, D. (1992). *The Motivational Assessment Scale (MAS).* Topeka, KS: Monaco & Associates.

This 16-question survey relies on a 66-point rating scale that divides functions into four categories: sensory, escape, attention, and tangibles. Reliability closely relates to objective observations.

Problem Behavior Questionnaire (PBQ)
Source: Lewis, T. J., Scott, T. M., & Sugai, G. (1994). The problem behavior questionnaire: A teacher-based instrument to develop functional hypotheses of problem behavior in general education classrooms. *Assessment for Effective Instruction, 19*(2–3), 103–115.

This easy-to-fill-out 15-question questionnaire measures peer attention, teacher attention, escape/avoidance from peer attention, and escape/avoidance from teacher attention with a seven-point rating scale. Provides an analysis of setting events (environmental variables that may influence behavior) and is designed for use in the general education classroom. Does not include categories for get-tangible-items or sensory functions.

Questions about Behavioral Function (QABF)

Source: Paclawskyj, T. R., Matson, J. L., Rush, K. S., Smalls, Y., & Vollmer, T. R. (2000). Questions about behavioral function (QABF): A behavioral checklist for functional assessment of aberrant behavior. *Research in Developmental Disabilities, 21*(3), 223–229.

This 25-question survey relies on a three-point rating scale and divides functions of behavior into five categories: attention, escape, non-social, physical, and tangible. Inclusion of physical variables that may affect behavior is a valuable component.

Websites

Listed below are several websites that can be helpful in designing positive behavioral interventions and finding direct instruction materials.

Direct Instruction—Verbal Behavior—Precision Teaching

www.directinstruction.org

Offers resources for direct instruction, verbal behavior, and precision teaching curriculum, development, and training.

KidTools Support System (KTSS)

http://kidtools.org

Offers a variety of colorful pre-made materials, charts, and behavior programs that address self-management of academic and social behavior, organizational skills, and learning strategies for children ages 7 to 14 and can be downloaded for immediate use in the classroom. Included are tools for earning points for appropriate behaviors, making behavior contracts, developing behavior plans, and self-monitoring.

Positive Behavioral Interventions and Supports (PBIS)

U.S. Office of Special Education Programs Technical Assistance Center

www.pbis.org

Defines, develops, implements, and evaluates a multitiered approach to technical assistance that improves the capacity of states, districts, and schools to establish, scale up, and sustain the PBIS framework. Contains philosophy papers and training materials for administrators and teachers.

Organizations

Behavior Analyst Certification Board (BACB)

8051 Shaffer Parkway
Littleton, CO 80127
(720) 438-4321
Fax: (720) 468-4145
info@bacb.com
www.bacb.com

An international nonprofit, standard-setting organization established to meet professional credentialing needs identified by behavior analysts, governments, and consumers of behavior analysis services. The website has a locator function that allows users to search for behavior analysts by name or zip code.

National Institute for Direct Instruction (NIFDI)

P.O. Box 11248
Eugene, OR 97440
(541) 485-1973; (877) 485-1973
Fax: (541) 683-7543
info@nifdi.org
www.nifdi.org

A nonprofit organization that provides information and resources for administrators, teachers, and parents to help maximize student achievement through the direct instruction approach to logical instructional design. Offers curricula for math, reading, many of the sciences, social studies, spelling, and writing. The website contains information on the extensive and broad research base, including a searchable database of more than 200 article summaries.

Additional Readings

The following are a number of books that can be helpful in learning more about positive behavior interventions and behavioral psychology in schools.

Alberto, P. A., & Troutman, A. C. (2013). *Applied behavior analysis for teachers* (9th ed.). Upper Saddle River, NJ: Pearson Education.

Bambara, L. M., & Knoster, T. P. (2009). *Designing positive behavior support plans* (2nd ed.). Washington, DC: American Association on Intellectual and Developmental Disabilities.

Crone, D. A., Hawken, L. S., & Horner, R. H. (2010). *Responding to problem behavior in schools: The behavior education program* (2nd ed.). New York: Guilford Press.

Crone, D. A., & Horner, R. H. (2003). *Building positive behavior support systems in schools:*

Functional behavioral assessment. New York: Guilford Press.

Gardner III, R., Sainato, D. M., Cooper, J. O., Heron, T. E., Heward, W. L., Eshleman, J., & Grossi, T. A. (1994). *Behavior analysis in education: Focus on measurably superior instruction.* Pacific Grove, CA: Brooks/Cole Publishing.

Heward W. L., Heron, T. E., Neef, N. A., Peterson, S. M., Sainato, D. M., Cartledge, G. Y., . . . Dardig, J. C. (Eds.). (2005). *Focus on behavior analysis in education: Achievements, challenges, and opportunities.* Upper Saddle River, NJ: Pearson Education.

Hieneman, M., Childs, K., & Sergay, J. (2006). *Parenting with positive behavior support: A practical guide to resolving your child's difficult behavior.* Baltimore: Paul H. Brookes Publishing Co.

Luiselli, J. K., & Diament, C. (Eds.). (2002). *Behavior psychology in the schools: Innovations in evaluation, support, and consultation.* New York: Haworth Press.

Meyer, L. H., & Evans, I. M. (1989). *Nonaversive intervention for behavior problems: A manual for home and community.* Baltimore: Paul H. Brookes Publishing Co.

Part 5
Preparing for Life Before and After School

Chapter 14

The Early Childhood Years

· ·

Tanni L. Anthony

Key Points

- 🔑 Causes of visual impairment among young children with visual impairments and multiple disabilities

- 🔑 Elements of comprehensive sensory assessments and their importance in providing services to young children with visual impairments who have multiple disabilities

- 🔑 Developing strategies for promoting functional communication for young children with visual impairments and multiple disabilities by performing assessments and initiating activities based on hands-on experiential learning

- 🔑 Cognitive and play development of young children with visual impairments and multiple disabilities

- 🔑 Strategies within natural settings to enhance the development of cognitive and play skills for young children with visual impairments and multiple disabilities

- 🔑 Strategies to create developmentally appropriate preschool programs for young children with visual impairments and multiple disabilities

- 🔑 Strategies for preschool programs that support children with visual impairments and multiple disabilities using a multitiered system of supports to enhance learning and development

---

Wanda Jean is a 4-year-old with places to go and people to see! She uses an adapted mobility device to move within her classroom, school building, and in the community with her family. She recognizes some letters and knows that W is the first letter of her first name. She likes the letter W so much that her parents suggested she name her new pet bunny Wonderful Wabbit and helped her make a sign with two brailled Ws on his cage. Her parents have read to her since birth, and one of her favorite things to do is listen to stories that go along with the props in each story box at home and at school.

All three of the children in Wanda Jean's family have one or two daily chores posted on a list on the family's refrigerator. Glued next to Wanda Jean's brailled name are two alfalfa pellets to remind her that it is her job after dinner to go to the pantry where the bunny's food is stored on the lower shelf, put two scoops of the pellets into a plastic bucket, and walk to the nearby sunroom to fill Wonderful Wabbit's bowl of food. This is a new chore, and Wanda Jean's older sister often helps her with each of the steps, but Wanda Jean takes great delight in feeling her rabbit eat his pellets as they fall from her hand into his bowl.

Wanda Jean was born at 28 weeks' gestation and has significant visual impairment due to retinopathy of prematurity. She has mild cerebral palsy and fragile health that can keep her out of school for weeks at a time. She has a calendar system of tangible symbol cards with braille words for her daily school schedule and uses a combination of vocalizations, objects, increasingly more intelligible words, and core and topical vocabulary tactile symbols to make choices, answer questions, and express herself.

A teacher of students with visual impairments and a certified orientation and mobility (O&M) specialist are key members of Wanda's educational team, as are her parents, the preschool special education teacher, a speech-language pathologist, and physical and occupational therapists. The teacher of students with visual impairments works closely with the family and early childhood team to provide specially designed instruction to Wanda Jean in braille, self-help skills, socialization, and concept development specific to the early childhood curriculum. The O&M specialist and physical therapist worked together to devise an optimal adapted mobility device that

serves as a long cane and an orthopedic support tool. The O&M specialist works directly with Wanda Jean on new travel routes, including the recent addition of the home chore routine to feed the pet rabbit. An assistive technology specialist is available as a consultant to the team to ensure that Wanda Jean has access to both low- and high-tech tools and devices for her learning and emergent literacy needs. It takes a team to ensure Wanda Jean's daily routines are accessible and engaging to her. Everyone agrees: Wanda Jean does have people to meet, places to go, books to learn to read, and many, many things to learn.

Children with visual impairments and multiple disabilities are more similar to children without disabilities than they are different. All young children thrive with social-emotional support and meaningful relationships with their caregivers, other family members, and peers; opportunities to communicate preferences, needs, choices, and ideas and to be physically active; and ongoing occasions for age-appropriate learning experiences. What will be different for the young child with a visual impairment and multiple disabilities is the path and supports needed to achieve these same goals.

Professionals working with infants, toddlers, and preschool-age children should recognize these early years as a profoundly unique time period of human development. As such, the strategies utilized with young children will be unique in distinct ways from those used with older learners. Young children learn best through hands-on opportunities, play experiences, and the modeling of higher-level concepts and skills and with social support from others.

Members of the educational team must work closely with the child's family to identify and prioritize the child's needs. Family-centered and culturally responsive practices are critical to the effective provision of early intervention services (birth to 3 years), a smooth transition of the child to a preschool program, and a continued family-school partnership as the child enters a public school program. The characteristics of family-centered practices include (Anthony et al., 2003):

- focusing on each family's strengths, priorities, and concerns while respecting and honoring their diversity
- empowering families to make their own decisions about services and resources
- viewing the family holistically
- collaborating with families and other members of the early intervention team

The team will also want to address in the early years of a child's life the expanded core curriculum (ECC) for children and youths who are blind or visually impaired, the body of knowledge and skills that are needed by all learners with visual impairments due to their unique disability-specific needs. (See Chapters 1 and 5 for more on the ECC.) Like other general education curriculum components such as literacy, numeracy, and science, all ECC concepts and skills have their developmental origins in the early years. A key role of the teacher of students with visual impairments will be to teach and work with others to embed developmentally appropriate ECC activities into daily home and early childhood routines of the young child. It will be essential for the O&M specialist to address each child's spatial concepts and motor development skills and need to build self-initiated and purposeful movement and developmentally appropriate independent travel skills.

This chapter will address the need for well-designed, authentic assessment, early intervention, and preschool instructional practices, as well as broad strategies for individualized sensory, communication, cognitive, and emergent literacy supports for young children from birth through five years of age with visual impairments and multiple disabilities. Assessment, intervention, and instructional activities noted in this chapter are in alignment with the most current early childhood Recommended Practices from the Division for Early Childhood (DEC) of the Council for Exceptional Children, which were developed "to provide guidance to practitioners and families about the most effective ways to improve the learning outcomes and promote the development of young children, birth through five years of age, who have or are at-risk for developmental delays and disabilities" (Division for Early Childhood, 2014, p. 2). The DEC guidelines provide a blueprint for general research-supported early childhood practices with families and young children; they are an important resource for all professionals involved in the early education of all young children. Other supplemental and key discipline-specific professional standards and competencies that are needed for children who experience a specific disability or disabilities need to be followed in tandem with the DEC guidelines. Personnel working with this age group are encouraged to seek more comprehensive training on early childhood development and evidence-based practices for this young population of learners.

VISUAL IMPAIRMENT IN EARLY CHILDHOOD

It is helpful to begin with an understanding of the common causes of visual impairment in the early years, which often result in a young child with visual impairment having multiple disabilities and developmental challenges. This section provides an overview of prevalent etiologies and the associated disability characteristics of the youngest children with visual impairments. (See Appendix 1A in Chapter 1 for a detailed list of eye conditions and their effects and educational implications.)

Early-onset visual impairment, including blindness, is considered a low-incidence disability, estimated to occur at a rate of 12.2 per 1,000 school-age students (Odle, 2009). The majority of children within this population have multiple disabilities (Hatton, Ivy, & Boyer, 2013). A sample of one longitudinal study of 202 children between the ages of birth to five with blindness or visual impairment revealed approximately 60 percent had multiple disabilities (Ferrell, 1998).

To understand the complexity of this young population of children, it is important to review the three leading causes of pediatric blindness and visual impairment in the United States, each of which has a high association with concomitant disabilities. Both the longitudinal Project PRISM study (Ferrell, 1998) and the national Babies Count database, which was operated most recently by the American Printing House for the Blind (Hatton, 2001; Hatton et al., 2013), have corroborated the same three leading causes of early-onset significant visual impairment in the United States. As noted in Chapter 1, these causes, in order of prevalence, are cortical visual impairment, retinopathy of prematurity, and optic nerve hypoplasia.

Cortical Visual Impairment

Cortical visual impairment, also known as cerebral visual impairment (CVI), is seen throughout the world and is the leading cause of pediatric visual impairment in children who live in high-income countries where there is medical care to support premature and medically compromised infants (Gogate & Gilbert, 2007). CVI is a neurological visual disorder resulting from damage to the visual pathways or the visual processing areas of the brain, and it affects how a child responds to visual information (Dutton, McKillop, & Saidkasimova, 2006). Of the three leading causes of early-onset visual impairment, children with CVI are often diagnosed the latest (average 7.6 months) according to one national database of 2,150 children with pediatric visual impairments (Hatton et al., 2013).

Common causes of CVI include oxygen deprivation, intraventricular hemorrhage, head trauma, encephalopathy, hydrocephalus, structural brain anomalies, and central nervous system infections (Good et al., 1994; Teplin, 1995). Since CVI involves a history of neurological compromise, the child may also be diagnosed with a seizure disorder, other health impairments including feeding and sleeping challenges, cerebral palsy, intellectual disability, or some combination of these challenges.

Retinopathy of Prematurity

The second, or possibly the third, leading cause of pediatric visual impairment in the United States is retinopathy of prematurity, a disease that affects the retinal functioning of an infant born prematurely or, in rare cases, an infant born at full term. Infants with retinopathy of prematurity are often diagnosed early, at 3.4 months of age on average (Hatton et al., 2013).

The prevalence of retinopathy of prematurity appears to be decreasing in recent years, although the incidence of multiple disabilities in these infants has increased (Hatton et al., 2013). Babies diagnosed with retinopathy of prematurity are often the smallest, most health-compromised of infants born prematurely. Infants with low birth weights, fewer than 1,000 grams (just over 2.2 pounds), are at significant risk for vision concerns, including poor eye alignment (strabismus), mild to severe refractive error, and retinal compromise leading to permanent and serious visual impairment including blindness (Geddie, Bina, & Miller, 2007; Teplin, Greeley, & Anthony, 2009). If the premature infant also experienced an intracranial hemorrhage or another health condition resulting in a period of anoxia (lack of oxygen), there may be an additional diagnosis of cortical visual impairment. Children with retinopathy of prematurity may have multiple disabilities or developmental challenges (Hatton et al., 2013), including seizure disorder, other health impairments that include feeding and sleeping challenges, learning or intellectual disabil-

ities, cerebral palsy, or some combination of these challenges. Premature infants, especially those born before 28–32 weeks gestation, with a birth weight of fewer than 1,500 grams represent almost half of all children with cerebral palsy (Marlow, Wolke, Bracewell, & Samara, 2005).

Optic Nerve Hypoplasia

The incidence of optic nerve hypoplasia, a congenital condition characterized by the underdevelopment of the optic nerve in one or both eyes, is growing in more economically developed countries (Hatton, Schwietz, Boyer, & Rychwalski, 2007; Patel, McNally, Harrison, Lloyd, & Clayton, 2006). It may, in fact, now be the second leading cause of early-onset visual impairment and the first cause of ocular-based visual impairment according to some estimates (Borchert & Garcia-Filion, 2008; Patel et al., 2006). The mean age of diagnosis of optic nerve hypoplasia in one database study was 4.2 months of age (Hatton et al., 2013), though other health and educational diagnoses associated with optic nerve hypoplasia are likely to occur later.

Optic nerve hypoplasia may occur in isolation or in combination with other functional and anatomic central nervous system anomalies, including possible growth hormone deficiency (Borchert & Garcia-Filion, 2008). Children with optic nerve hypoplasia should be followed closely for endocrine problems, seizure disorder, gastrointestinal disturbances, sleep problems, and educational needs specific to developmental delays and a possible additional diagnosis of autism spectrum disorder (Fink & Borchert, 2011).

Infections

In addition to the three aforementioned leading pediatric visual impairment conditions, a number of other factors, such as infections, exposure to toxins, and genetic conditions, may contribute to a young child having an early-onset visual impairment associated with other disabilities. Prenatal infections account for 2 to 3 percent of all birth impairments (Kuhlmann & Autry, 2001). The STORCH infections, which include _s_yphilis, _t_oxoplasmosis, _o_ther infections, _r_ubella, _c_ytomegalovirus, and _h_erpes, involve the most common prenatal infections associated with congenital visual impairment. Both rubella and cytomegalovirus also have an associated incidence of a congenital or progressive sensorineural hearing loss (see Chapter 1). Rubella is not the serious concern it was in the United States in the 1960s, but cases continue to exist in immigrant populations coming to the United States or even within the United States when the mother has not been immunized against German measles. The Zika virus is a concern for today's population that will warrant close monitoring for its effects on vision, hearing, and general development. Postnatal infections, such as meningitis, may also cause neurological damage in the developing child, resulting in visual impairment, hearing impairment, intellectual disability, seizure disorder, cerebral palsy, or a combination of these challenges.

Exposure to Toxins

Prenatal exposure to toxins or noxious substances may also result in a myriad of congenital disabilities, including visual impairment. Infants exposed prenatally to alcohol and subsequently diagnosed with fetal alcohol spectrum disorder may experience a specific learning disability, intellectual disability, vision impairment, or other health impairments, including attention deficit hyperactivity disorder (ADHD). Prenatal exposure to some prescription or illegal narcotics may affect the developing fetus, trigger a premature birth, or both.

Syndromes

Children with diagnoses of Down, Goldenhar, Treacher Collins, and other syndromes often have a multitude of disability conditions affecting vision, hearing, general health, motor, and cognitive function. (See Appendix 1B in Chapter 1 for a list of syndromes that affect vision.) Concurrent vision and hearing loss are associated with many syndromes. The two leading pediatric causes of combined vision and hearing loss (deafblindness) include CHARGE and Usher syndromes. CHARGE syndrome presents with unilateral or bilateral colobomas, which involve the incomplete embryonic development of one or more of the choroid, iris, lens, optic nerve, or retina, and a constellation of effects including health (in particular, cardiac, respiratory, and growth problems), hearing, vestibular (balance), and intellectual abilities challenges. Children with Usher syndrome do not typically have disabilities beyond vision impairment and varying degrees of hearing loss, although Usher Type 1 (congenital deafness and early-onset retinitis pigmentosa) has a strong association with poor balance skills, which may affect the young child's quality of movement skills (Lieberman, Ponchillia, & Ponchillia, 2013).

It is likely that many children with early-onset visual impairment will also experience multiple disabilities. Each child is unique in his or her sensory, physical, cognitive, social, and communication abilities and needs. It is critical for the early childhood team to understand the singular and interactive contribution of each disability to the child's abilities and needs. It is imperative, therefore, that young children with visual impairments and multiple disabilities have careful and comprehensive clinical and educational assessments to determine their medical and early intervention and specialized instruction support needs. The next section will address sensory assessments designed to identify the child's sensory avenues of learning and need for sensory-based accommodations.

SENSORY ASSESSMENT

Each available sense serves as an important avenue of learning. Sensory-based learning begins at birth and continues throughout our lives. The early years should provide countless learning opportunities for very young children to coordinate sensory experiences with motor responses, building a progressively deeper and more expansive understanding of their bodies and surrounding environments. When one or more of a child's senses is impaired or absent, it is critical to gather information about the child's sensory abilities, preferences, and need for supports to enhance sensory-based learning.

Both clinical and educational professionals complete sensory assessments such as hearing and vision screenings. Clinical professionals include eye care specialists, such as ophthalmologists or optometrists, and hearing specialists, such as otolaryngologists (ear, nose, and throat doctors) or audiologists. Early intervention or school-based preschool education personnel involved in functional sensory assessment will include teachers of students with visual impairments, certified O&M specialists, teachers of children who are deaf, school audiologists, and occupational therapists. Both medically or clinically based examinations or evaluations and functional sensory assessments are needed to complete a full picture of the child's sensory abilities and needs.

Educationally based functional sensory assessments should be completed through a combination of reviewing available medical and educational records, interviewing the people who know the child best, observing the child across daily settings, and completing specific assessment tasks. Some assessments will be unique to children with visual impairments, and others should be completed universally on all young children.

Sensory assessment should be completed ahead of other developmental assessments or evaluations in order to inform the selection of appropriate next-step assessment materials and presentation strategies to accommodate the child's sensory needs. Sensory assessment serves as a key starting point for young children with visual impairments or deafblindness.

Vision and hearing screenings take place as a part of the multidisciplinary evaluation process to establish eligibility for early intervention services for infants and toddlers (Part C of the Individuals with Disabilities Education Improvement Act of 2004 [IDEA]); screenings should also take place for school-aged children (including preschoolers), when needed, to fulfill the IDEA Child Find requirement to identify children with disabilities and determine the nature and extent of the education and related services each child needs (Bartlett, Etscheidt, & Weisenstein, 2007). In addition to conducting vision or hearing screenings as a part of the special education evaluation, many school districts provide vision and hearing screenings on a periodic basis for all students.

Hearing Screening and Evaluation

All young children should be screened for potential hearing concerns. Hearing screening is especially important for children with visual impairments and multiple disabilities, as it will be essential to determine if hearing is and will continue to be a viable listening, communication, and learning avenue for them. (See Chapter 1 for a brief discussion of types of hearing loss.) Hearing has important ties to phonological awareness skills associated with reading. Hearing screening for very young children may be completed in clinical or educational settings, or both, with measures that may or may not require the child's volitional response and active participation. Advancements in hearing screening technology have helped to assure that all very young children can be screened for the general integrity of their hearing system. (For more information about the developmental impact of and evaluating early-onset hearing loss, see Abdala & Winter, 2014; Chen, 2014).

Most major hospitals throughout the United States now have universal newborn hearing screening programs that screen all infants for possible hearing concerns prior to their hospital discharge. Most children with congenital hearing loss are identified through universal newborn hearing screening and subsequent diagnostics (Anthony, Wiggin, Yoshinaga-Itano, & Raver, 2015). Newborn hearing screenings are usually conducted while the baby is sleeping. The two most common tools, otoacoustic emission testing and automated auditory brainstem response, are used to measure the general integrity of the infant's hearing system. If the infant fails this screening, the family is asked to bring the child back for a second screening to address the possible presence of a hearing loss. In some instances, an identified hearing concern may be treatable for infants who are born with or have acquired an early-onset unilateral or bilateral ear infection. For other infants, there may be a need to schedule further diagnostic evaluation to rule out or confirm the presence of a mild to profound sensorineural hearing loss (nerve deafness).

The mean age at which an early-onset sensorineural loss is identified has decreased dramatically with the advent of universal newborn hearing screening. The majority of children with congenital deafness and hearing loss are now identified by 3 months of age (Anthony et al., 2015). Early identification of a pediatric hearing loss has changed intervention practices and communication and language outcomes for those young children diagnosed with congenital hearing loss, including infants with a coinciding visual impairment. Since hearing loss can be progressive or manifest well after birth, all children, and especially those with visual impairments, should continue to have routine hearing screening checks to ensure that hearing remains a viable communication and learning sense.

Early hearing screening that may occur as a part of a Child Find process or regular school district screening program usually involves:

- a case history of the child's general health and development (such as diagnoses associated with pediatric or progressive hearing loss, history of ear infections, family history of hearing loss)
- a visual inspection of the child's ears
- measures to screen the child's general response to sounds

When a child has multiple disabilities, including visual impairment, it is vital for the Child Find or other educational team involved with the screening to consult with a teacher of students with visual impairments and other professionals, as needed, to address how best to conduct the hearing screening or school-based audiological evaluation, if this latter examination is needed to substantiate and quantify the presence of a unilateral or bilateral hearing loss. The team needs to discuss the positioning of the child for optimal listening and response to sounds, how to interpret the child's biophysical responses to sounds (changes in coloring or respiration, head turning or tilting, increase or decrease of body movement), and the wait time needed for the child to organize a response to the sounds presented.

A functional hearing assessment may be used to further quantify the child's response to sounds in the everyday environment. Additional functional hearing assessment may be especially important if the hearing screening or more advanced clinical measures are difficult to administer and interpret due to the complexity of the child's needs. The audiologist and the teacher trained in deafness or deafblindness may have recommended tools for functional hearing assessment that are appropriate for the young child with multiple disabilities. Sidebar 14.1 addresses four broad areas of data specific to a child's functional hearing that can be gathered by the team.

If the child is found to have hearing loss in addition to a visual impairment, the educational team should include professionals trained in deafness or hearing impairment (such as an educational audiologist, a teacher trained in deafness or deafblindness, and a speech-language pathologist) to address the unique communication, learning, and mobility needs of the child. When a child is deafblind, it is essential that the educational team understand the unique disability characteristics and educational needs associated with the dual sensory loss, as it is not as simple as hearing impairment plus visual impairment. Because of its deep and inherent complexity, deafblindness is a self-standing eligibility category for education services. The child who is deafblind, his or her family, and service providers are eligible to receive free technical assistance services from their state's federally funded Deaf-Blind Project (see the Resources section at the end of this chapter for information on the National Center on Deaf-Blindness).

✏ Sidebar 14.1

Broad Components of Functional Hearing Assessment

General Functioning

- Does the child show an awareness of visual, tactile, and auditory functioning?
- What motor behaviors indicate that the child is responding to different types of sensory information?

Responses to Auditory Information

- What observable behaviors indicate that the child is responding specifically to auditory information?
- Does the child still his or her body to a new sound in the environment or tilt his or her head to the side of a presented sound source?
- Does the child startle to loud sounds or become agitated in response to loud or unexpected sounds?

Patterns of Responses to Auditory Information

- Does the child demonstrate different or similar responses based on types and locations of presented sounds?
- Which sounds, and under what conditions of presentation, provide the most consistent responses from the child? For example, are there different responses to low pitch versus high pitch sounds, loud versus soft sounds, short versus long sound durations?
- Does the child react to rhythms or have a preference for a particular person's voice or a type of music?

Meaning of Auditory Information

- For what specific purposes does the child use auditory information?
- Can sounds be used to soothe the child or increase the child's alertness?
- Does the child show anticipation or actual recognition of a person or upcoming activity based on auditory information?
- Does the child recognize familiar words, such as his or her name?

Source: Adapted with permission from Durkel, J. (2005). Formal versus informal hearing tests: What is functional hearing? *See/Hear, 10*(3). Retrieved from http://www.tsbvi.edu/seehear/summer05/functional.htm

---

Vision Screening and Functional Vision Assessment

Children with multiple disabilities are at increased risk for both visual problems and visual impairments. Visual problems, which usually respond to medical interventions, may include refractive errors, strabismus, and am-blyopia (see Chapter 1). Visual problems may coexist with ocular and neurological conditions that cause permanent and significant visual impairment. Medical professionals involved with the child's birth and subsequent pediatric care may alert the family to the need for the child to have an eye care evaluation or the child may be referred to an eye care specialist based on a Child Find or other vision screening. Referral to an eye care specialist will be critical to ascertain the diagnosis and prognosis of a pediatric visual impairment. In the event that the child has CVI, an eye care specialist, neurologist, pediatrician, or another medical professional trained in the characteristics of CVI may give the diagnosis.

Once a student is identified as having a visual impairment, a teacher of students with visual impairments will be a critical team member to evaluate the child's functional vision. The vast majority of children identified with visual impairment, including learners with multiple disabilities, have low vision or signs of usable vision (Lueck & Heinze, 2004) and will benefit from a functional vision assessment (FVA) to ascertain the young child's visual preferences, abilities, and accommodative support needs to optimize visual learning. (See Chapter 3 for additional discussion of functional vision assessment.)

Before completing an FVA, the teacher of students with visual impairments will want to talk with the child's caregivers to determine if any prescription or over-the-counter medications are given to the child for a chronic medical condition. Children with visual impairment and multiple disabilities are likely to have health conditions that require medications. Medications may produce side effects such as drowsiness, dizziness, fatigue, or confusion, and may directly impact visual performance. Some anticonvulsant medications may cause nystagmus (involuntary rhythmic movement of the eyes), diplopia (double vision), photophobia (light sensitivity), compromised fixation and oculomotor movements,

and, in rare situations, even visual hallucinations. In addition to visual side effects, some medications are ototoxic, meaning they may have a temporary or permanent adverse impact on a child's hearing abilities.

An FVA protocol should be selected based on whether the child's visual impairment is ocular or neurological in origin. Few FVA tools have been designed for young children with visual impairments and multiple disabilities. Two companion tools designed specifically for children with CVI include the CVI Range and CVI Resolution Chart (Roman-Lantzy, 2007). Lueck and Dutton (2015) also provide information about the assessment of children with CVI.

An FVA for a young child with a visual impairment and multiple disabilities will include the following broad components (Anthony, 2000, 2008):

- Observation at different time periods across multiple days in order to address variables that may affect the child's visual performance, such as fatigue, side effects from medications, and medical circumstances such as seizures, poor digestion, or other health-related concerns.

- Observation in both familiar and unfamiliar settings that can be controlled, as much as possible, for auditory distractions, and analyzed for the impact of color, contrast, visual complexity, lighting, and glare.

- Attention to the child's positioning needs for optimal viewing response to visual targets. The child should be in a secure, supported posture, so that his or her energy can be directed toward the presented visual targets and not diverted toward maintaining a stable position.

- Close scrutiny of the types of visual targets the child responds to (such as familiar or unfamiliar [novel], shiny or reflective, illuminated, high contrast, particular colors, simple or complex, still or moving) and how the child reacts to visual information, such as cessation or increase of vocalizations, body stilling, increase of movements, changes in respiration, head tilting or turning toward the target, eye blinking or squinting, visual orienting, direct fixation and following, or directed visual reach.

- Analysis of the child's ability to respond to visual targets based on how they are presented (such as focal distance, angle of viewing, and visual array). Some children will be less responsive to a visual target that is "competing" with other visual information. Under those circumstances it will be necessary to take care to present one item at a time and without the visual clutter of a busy or congested background. Further careful documentation should be made about the child's ability to visually respond to objects in all visual quadrants, as it is common for children with eye conditions involving retinal damage or neurological compromise, such as CVI and cerebral palsy, to have visual field loss. Knowledge of a child's visual field abilities and deficits are critical for determining how visual information is best presented to the child, including how symbols or objects are placed on a communication display.

- Provision of needed (sometimes considerable) wait time for the child to organize a response to the presented visual targets.

Information about the child's functional vision abilities and needs will provide the team with insights about how best to present visual information to the child, including designing a visually based display of communication symbols. With the guidance of the teacher of students with visual impairments, the educational team should address the presentation distance, size, color, complexity, visual spacing, field location, and need for high background contrast of visual objects and symbols. Visual displays in books, on communication boards, and across learning tasks should be reviewed for the need for visual simplicity (lack of visual complexity or internal busyness). Environmental or task-specific illumination needs and strategies to reduce glare will also be vital factors to consider.

Based on the needs of the child, it may be wise to consult with a low vision specialist to determine whether there is an age-appropriate magnification tool for the child to use in the preschool classroom. For example, the child may benefit from a stand magnifier or video magnification when looking at picture details or small objects. (For more information about clinical vision evaluation and functional vision assessment of young children, see Orel-Bixler, 2014; Topor, 2014.)

In addition to hearing and vision screening, functional vision assessment, and possibly additional audiological evaluation and functional hearing assessment, the child may require additional sensory assessment to ensure that all avenues of learning have been analyzed and addressed for intervention and instructional purposes. The next section offers examples of additional assessments for a broader array of sensory domains.

Other Sensory Assessment Tools

The teacher of students with visual impairments needs to work closely with other team members to determine what other sensory assessment information would be beneficial for the educational programming needs of the young student with a visual impairment and multiple disabilities. Such assessments may be completed primarily by the teacher of students with visual impairments, and other professionals on the team may complete other assessment tools with the input of the teacher of students with visual impairments. Input should be gathered from caregivers with each of these assessments to ensure that an accurate, full-bodied picture is developed about the child's sensory skills and needs. A selection of broad sensory-based assessments that can be used to collect data about the sensory preferences and aversions of the young child with a visual impairment and multiple disabilities can be found in the Resources section at the end of this chapter.

It is important to note that the FVA may be completed in tandem with a learning media assessment (LMA) (Burnett & Sanford, 2008; Koenig & Holbrook, 1995) when the child can benefit from both assessments. The LMA is used to assess how a student with a visual impairment uses his or her vision, touch, and hearing, and, to a lesser extent, other senses, either singularly or in combination, to gain access to information (see Chapter 3). When a child is blind and there is no need to complete an FVA, the LMA may be completed independently.

It is important to note that there is no commercially available functional vision learning media assessment designed specifically for young children with visual impairments and multiple disabilities. For this population, it will be helpful to supplement the standard LMA forms designed for older learners with other sensory assessment tools such as those found in the Resources section at the end of this chapter. The goal in doing so is to combine and cross-check data results across these tools to define the sensory abilities, preferences, and needs of the child. Such an analysis will include the child's needs for learning and emergent literacy materials, equipment, and environmental supports.

As the FVA and more global sensory assessment tools are used to assess a child, careful attention should be given to the child's responses both to externally presented sensory information and to those periods of time when the child appears to be focused more on internal body sensations. Children with visual impairments and multiple disabilities may demonstrate repetitive, stereotypic, or what may be called self-stimulatory behaviors. Such behaviors are actual evidence of the child's sensory abilities or intrinsic sensory system regulation needs. The behaviors may consist of repetitive body movements or vocalizations (McHugh & Pyfer, 1999; Moss & Blaha, 1993; Roley, 1995) and may include:

- eye rubbing or eye poking
- head rubbing, shaking, or banging
- bouncing
- rocking
- spinning
- hand or arm flapping
- licking, chewing, flipping, or banging on objects
- vocalizing or making loud sounds

Such repetitive behaviors should be recognized as the child's active means of seeking needed sensory stimulation, modulating sensory regulation, or establishing or maintaining arousal and attention to the environment (Brambring & Tröster, 1992). These behaviors have an important function for the child, but they may interfere with socialization or learning opportunities. The team should discuss the purpose of each behavior (what need is it meeting or trying to meet) and identify an alternative, more acceptable way to provide the child with other more appropriate sensory input that may help to reduce behaviors that interfere with learning (Moss & Blaha, 1993; Roley, 1995). (See Chapter 13 for additional discussion of the function of and intervention with repetitive or self-stimulatory behaviors.) Teachers of students with visual impairments can assist the educational team in selecting tools to capture and then to interpret behaviors that are tied to sensory regulation, seeking, or aversion needs. This discussion should begin with an effort to understand the communication message behind the behaviors; one should always ask and investigate, "What is the child telling us about his or her state of alertness, medical status, experience with expecting something meaningful to do, sensory needs and preferences, and ability to use his or her body to regulate his or her senses?"

All of the gathered sensory information will, in fact, provide an important bridge to a comprehensive understanding of the child's communication abilities and needs. The team's ability to ultimately implement viable communication strategies to increase the child's interactions with peers and adults and to support true participation in learning activities is a fundamental component of an effective early intervention or preschool program for the child.

THE IMPORTANCE OF FUNCTIONAL COMMUNICATION

Every child is capable of communication, although not every young child will become a verbal or sign language communicator. *Communication* involves sending or receiving a message that is expressed and understood through a variety of modes that might include one or more of the following: facial expressions, body movements, sounds or speech, touch cues, objects, pictures, visual or tactile symbols, and oral or sign language. *Language* involves words that are written, spoken, or signed.

Regardless of the manner of communication, every child should be supported to have a communication system that is functional for both receptive (ability to receive and comprehend a communication message) and expressive (ability to send a communication message) skills. Competency in communication allows the child to both obtain and demonstrate knowledge, which is critical as the child advances through the educational system. Communication begins at birth and, based on ongoing interaction with others, continues to be supported and scaffolded for expanding modes of communication, increased vocabulary, and new topics of communication throughout one's lifetime. The ability to communicate to and with other people is a cornerstone of social-emotional development. (See

Chapter 7 for additional discussion of communication.)

For young children whose disabilities affect communication or language abilities, it is essential that their early intervention and preschool programs emphasize building a functional communication system. All early intervention and preschool team members should be involved in developing and implementing the communication program for the child. One can never start too early (and it is never too late) to address a child's need for a viable and functional communication system.

Communication is such an important need for people with disabilities that representatives from eight stakeholder organizations worked together in 1992 to create a document entitled A Communication Bill of Rights (presented in Sidebar 7.4 in Chapter 7; National Joint Committee for the Communication Needs of Persons with Severe Disabilities, 1992). This document asserts that everyone with a disability of any extent or severity has a fundamental right to affect, through communication, the conditions of their lives. The Communication Bill of Rights is a foundational charge to all parties of a child's educational team, starting in the early years and setting the stage for the child's ongoing communication needs across the preschool years, through all school years, and into adult life.

Communication and Language Assessment

The expressive and receptive communication abilities of each young child with visual impairment and multiple disabilities should be addressed through a team approach to ensure that the abilities and needs of the whole child are considered. One suggestion for collecting communication assessment data specific to a child with severe disabilities is to conduct a head-to-toe inventory of the child's behaviors that can then be analyzed by the team for their communication functions (Rowland, 2009, p. 15). For a child with more obvious communication and language abilities, caregivers can offer critical information by completing informal or formal questionnaire tools such as the *MacArthur-Bates Communicative Development Inventory (CDI): Words and Gestures* (Fenson et al., 2007) to document the child's understanding and use of early words or phrases. A speech-language pathologist can provide appropriate assessment protocols to decipher the expressive and receptive communication abilities of the child.

The teacher of students with visual impairments can assist with the team's understanding of how a visual impairment may affect a child's general communication development and, as needed, how best to design the visual access and tactile features of a selected communication symbol system. Listening skills should also be a focus on the child's communication program (Barclay, 2012). If the learner has combined vision and hearing loss, a professional trained in deafness or deafblindness will work with the team to review the child's need for tactile communication strategies, which may include manual sign language.

One tool that provides an important overview of a child's early communication skills is the Communication Matrix (Rowland, 2004, 2013). The Communication Matrix was designed for children and youths who are functioning at the earliest stages of communication development due to sensory, physical, or intellectual disabilities. The tool covers the communication skills found in children with typical communication development between birth and 24 months (Rowland, 2013). The Communication Matrix is not appropriate for children who are currently using formal language (verbal, sign, or through the successful and fluent use of a communication device). It is highly likely that most young children with visual impairments and multiple disabilities will benefit greatly from use of the Communication Matrix.

The Communication Matrix addresses four early basic reasons for communication across seven levels of expressive communicative competency (Rowland, 2004). The tool targets the following communication functions and messages:

- to refuse something not wanted
- to obtain something wanted
- to engage in social interactions
- to seek or provide information

The seven levels of communication competence (see Sidebar 14.2) are differentiated by the behaviors used to communicate, which become increasingly more intentional and symbolic in nature as the child understands that he or she can use sounds, facial expressions, and body movements to communicate a message to another person. In addition to the seven levels of communication, the team should collect data on the frequency and activity-specific details of the child's communicative behaviors.

Communication Strategies

The results of the Communication Matrix and other early expressive and receptive communication assessment tools should provide a comprehensive summary of all of the child's communication behaviors. This information will assist the team to determine the most appropriate intervention strategies to support the child's evolution to more intentional and symbolic communication. (See Chapter 7 for more information about communication strategies.) It is important to carefully analyze the results of communication assessments based on the combined sensory, cognitive, and physical impacts of the child's visual and multiple disabilities upon his or her communication. Examples include the following:

- Visual impairment may reduce a child's options for communicative behavior (such as eye gazing or eye pointing and imitation of conventional gestures).
- Hearing loss may affect speech and oral language abilities, as well as the ability for receptive communication with verbal information.
- Orthopedic challenges may limit the child's capacity for multiple modes of communication that involve vocalizations and body movements.

The modes of communication should be contrasted with the level of communication messages demonstrated by the child. A child with significant vision loss and cerebral palsy may have fewer communication modes, but may actually demonstrate a higher level of communicative intent and symbolic under-

Communication Matrix: Seven Levels of Communicative Competency

Level 1: Preintentional

Communication behaviors are reflexive, reactive, and not purposeful and are in response to behavioral states of the child. Caregivers respond to these body movements, sounds, and facial expressions to provide comfort, food, and care.

Level 2: Intentional

Communication behaviors become more volitional (under the control of the child), but are not expressed intentionally for the purpose of drawing attention or action from another person. Caregivers continue to respond to these behaviors, which now may include eye gaze, to provide comfort, food, general care, and items of interest.

Level 3: Unconventional

Body actions and vocalizations are used to communicate intentionally with another person. Simple gestures (such as tugging at a person to go somewhere) are now also used as specific communication behaviors. The child is still at a presymbolic level of communication.

Level 4: Conventional

The child uses presymbolic communication formats that are considered more socially acceptable and recognizable to more people. Communication expands to more formal and culturally recognized gestures (such as pointing, nodding, shaking head for yes and no, and waving good-bye) and vocalization in a conventional format. These behaviors are used concurrently toward another person and about a topic of conversation.

Level 5: Concrete Symbols

The child can now understand, use, and respond to symbolic referents for communication purposes. A concrete symbol physically resembles what it represents (for example, an empty cup=drink, a picture of a flower=a real flower, chain link=swing on playground). Concrete symbols can include an object, a picture, an iconic gesture, and sounds such as the buzz of a bee. Concrete symbols are used in conjunction with gestures and the beginning of sign or oral language. Some children may skip this level, progressing directly from Level 4 to Level 6, while others will need Level 5 to function as a bridge to more symbolic abilities or may find a meaningful and long-term means of communication using this level of representation.

Level 6: Abstract Symbols

The child uses a higher level of symbols, those that do not physically resemble what they are meant to represent. Abstract symbols include speech, manual signs, print or braille letters or words, and three-dimensional abstract symbols (a texture means a specific thing). At this stage, one abstract symbol is used at a time.

(continued)

(Sidebar 14.2 continued)

Level 7: Language
The child can now use combinations of two to three concrete or abstract symbols (or both) according to grammatical rules, as appropriate. The child may use oral language, sign language, print or braille words, or a combination of visual or tactile symbols to communicate.

Sources: Adapted from Rowland, C. (2004). *Communication matrix*. Portland: Oregon Health and Science University; Rowland, C. (2013). *Handbook: Online communication matrix*. Portland: Oregon Health and Science University. Retrieved from http://www.communicationmatrix.org/uploads/pdfs/handbook.pdf

standing than another child who has a larger repertoire of communication behaviors but functions at a lower level of communication.

The following three strategies promote the communication of a young child who is functioning at very early communication levels:

1. Being attentive and responsive to preintentional communication behaviors.
2. Setting up an interaction scenario that can be activated, paused, and continued based on the child's responses.
3. Following the child's lead or interests as conversational topics.

Being Attentive and Responsive to Preintentional Communication Behaviors

All children require and benefit from a responsive caregiving environment for both communication purposes and the foundation of social-emotional development. Children demonstrating the Level 1 and 2 communication behaviors identified in the Communication Matrix (Rowland, 2004) depend on others to interpret and respond consistently to their needs for attention and care. As the adult interprets and responds to the child's states and needs (the child is hungry, thirsty, cold, hot, uncomfortable, alert, and so on), the child learns that his or her vocalizations and body movements can be used to call upon the adult. This in turn reinforces intentionality of the child's vocalizations and body movements.

Setting Up a Communication Interaction Scenario

Every interaction with a child with a visual impairment and multiple disabilities or deafblindness should be designed to be a conversation (D. Brown, personal communication, September 17, 2015). This sets up an opportunity for give-and-take between the adult and the child. One method for reinforcing conversational opportunities is to apply information about the child's sensory preferences to set up a play interaction scenario between the child and an adult. The goal is to set up an interaction in which an action, sound, or visual spectacle that is under the control of the adult can be initiated to the enjoyment of the child. For example, a child may like the feel of being swung in a swing or bounced on a lap or the sound or sight of an activated wind-up toy. When the swinging or bouncing or the hum or visual movement of the wind-up toy is paused, the adult can wait for a response from the child to continue the activity. In the beginning of this type of exchange, the child may smile, fuss, vocalize, or move his or her body in response. This type of response can be credited as a signal to continue the activity. Over time the goal will be for the child to direct the communication behavior *to* the adult as a way to show true communicative intentionality ("I am telling you in this way that I would like the activity to continue"). The child may accomplish this by gazing from the object of interest to the communication partner (joint attention using vision), reaching out to touch the partner's body, taking the partner's hand, or another means that shows the child understands that he or she can tell the partner to continue the activity.

Following the Child's Lead in Conversation Topics

Another fundamental strategy to facilitate communication is to follow the child's lead or demonstrated interest in an object, person, or activity. A child's subject of interest can be viewed as a communication topic that can be used to capitalize on the child's motivation to participate in a communication turn-taking experience. Some children will be more obvious with their area of interest, as seen by what or whom they look at or directly interact with, while other children with more significant impairments may be less obvious with their interests.

To initiate a conversation of mutual interest, the adult can join the child's actions on an object or a person. As the child physically explores the object, so does the adult in a nonintrusive manner—the adult does not take or guide the child's hands, but "plays" next to the child's hands or uses a hand-under-hand approach in which the adult places his or her hands under the child's hands. For example, if the child strums his or her fingers over the edges of corrugated paper, the adult can take a turn making the same action. The adult can work to initiate a new action on the object as a way to invite the child to take a turn with the new action. This turn taking can be reinforced with verbal commentary about the object and its functions and characteristics. Care should be taken not to bombard the child with verbal commentary that may pull him or her away from exploring the object. The adult should comment after the child has taken his or her turn so the child can focus his or her attention on the words the adult is saying and not the object.

As a child shows true communicative intentionality, the programmatic focus moves toward assisting the child to expand his or her understanding and use of more symbolic and formalized communication, with the ultimate goal being use of language (verbal, sign, visual or tactile symbols, or some combination). The goal is to build an environment throughout the child's day that encourages, expects, and reinforces multiple communication exchanges between the child and others. The team should continue to capitalize on the child's preferences and interests. Strategies to advance the child's communication and receptive and expressive language abilities include these:

- embedding communication opportunities across the daily routine
- using communication cues
- using turn-taking exchanges
- providing opportunities for choice making
- using augmentative and alternative communication systems
- reading aloud

Embedding Communication Opportunities across Daily Routines

The early intervention team should analyze the child's daily schedule to ensure that ongoing and meaningful receptive and expressive communication activities are embedded in all of the classroom routines. It may be helpful to draft a shared schedule that details the sequence of the typical activities and routines, professionals involved, and specific strategies for the child to participate in communication interactions.

Using Communication Cues

Communication opportunities can include a variety of cues to alert the child of an upcoming task or event and embedded opportunities that allow for deliberate turn taking, choice making, commenting, and conversational dialogue. Communication cues may include specific touch actions on the child's body (tapping on the child's hip means time for a diaper change; a gentle tug under the arm means time to stand up) or the use of objects, tangible symbols, pictures, and verbal or sign language to announce the next activity. For some children, these cues will be offered by the adult just ahead of the next activity (for instance, handing the child a tambourine to signal that it's music time) or can be built into a calendar system where the child has a series of meaningful and portable symbols (selected from the child's personal experience and perspective) that define the sequence of his or her daily routine. (See Chapter 7 for more on calendar systems.) These tactile, visual, and auditory cues are part of the child's receptive communication experience. Tactile and visual symbols may also be used as tools for expressive communication by the child to indicate choices throughout daily routines.

Using Turn-Taking Exchanges

Expressive communication opportunities may include turn-taking exchanges. For example, playing on a teeter-totter, on a swing, in a rocking boat, or in a similar activity that the child enjoys offers opportunities for the child to communicate to ask for the activity to continue when it is momentarily paused.

Providing Opportunities for Choice Making

Choice making can occur during morning circle time, snack, and classroom center activities. Commenting or question-answering opportunities can be infused into activities, such as a reading a storybook together, where each child is asked for a response. The communication responses for these activities may be supported through objects, tangible symbols, pictures with word cards, and voice-output devices.

Using Augmentative and Alternative Communication Systems

The team should take care to build a communication system that is appropriate for the child's abilities. For example, the child who is demonstrating Levels 1–3 behaviors on the Communication Matrix (Rowland, 2004) should not be expected to use pictures or other types of iconic communication functionally in receptive or expressive communication tasks. Augmentative and alternative communication (AAC) systems, however, can be helpful for a young child at these earlier levels to learn communication roles and behaviors. A speech-language pathologist can provide guidance on how best to use AAC systems with children who are not yet at a symbolic level (Cress & Marvin, 2003).

When a communication display of symbols is designed for the child, the team will want to implement the concept of core vocabulary. *Core vocabulary* involves a small set of simple and familiar words (almost always no more than six letters) that are used frequently and across contexts (Cross, Baker, Klotz, & Badman, 1997). Most work on core vocabulary has linked vocabulary to particular age ranges with a focus on social and needs-based communication (Dennis, Erickson, & Hatch, 2013). For example, Sidebar 14.3 details a list of 26 words that constituted 96.3 percent of the total vocabulary used by toddlers in one study (Banajee, DiCarlo, & Stricklin, 2003). Preschoolers' high-frequency vocabulary constituted a list of 333 words (Marvin, Beukelman, & Bilyeu, 1994).

Sidebar 14.3

Twenty-six Core Vocabulary Words of Toddlers and Preschoolers

a	my
all	no
done	off
finished	on
go	out
help	some
here	that
I	the
in	want
is	what
it	yeah
mine	yes
more	you

Source: Banajee, M., DiCarlo, C., & Stricklin, S. B. (2003). Core vocabulary determination for toddlers. *Augmentative and Alternative Communication, 19*(2), 67–73.

Such lists provide a helpful place to begin with the development of a core vocabulary for a communication system display for very young children. Characteristics of core vocabulary for communication displays include the following (Hatch, Erickson, Dennis, & Cummings, 2013):

- a limited set of highly useful words
- a selection of words that apply across settings
- vocabulary that is made up mostly of pronouns, verbs, descriptors, and propositions (with very few nouns)
- consistent location of vocabulary on the communication display

The team will need to discuss how to display the selected vocabulary (as pictures or iconic symbols with the printed or brailled word) and how many item choices to give the child at one time. The teacher of students with visual impairments can provide guidance on the best size, spacing, font style, color, and contrast for the child's needs. In addition to core vocabulary, the team may develop communication displays with topic-specific or "fringe" words that may be used in targeted settings in the preschool classroom, such as in the different learning centers. For example, topic-specific words such as "food," "buy," "money," and "store" may be on a communication display in the preschool's pretend grocery store.

Reading Aloud

One of the best methods to build vocabulary is to read aloud to the child on a daily basis. There is no prerequisite age or language ability to begin to read to a child. Families of children with visual impairments and multiple disabilities may need encouragement and assistance with adapted books to read to their child on a daily basis. The teacher of students with visual impairments can assist the family and preschool staff with finding books with simple, clear pictures and, as appropriate, with adding braille and tactile illustrations to the text. Story boxes (see Chapter 8) can be made that contain one or more relevant objects from the story that can be offered to the child to hold and explore, and as the story is read, to bring more meaning to the words in the story. Another strategy is to select one or two objects from the

child's daily routine to create a story basket. As the child takes an item from the basket, the adult can tell a story about the name of the object, its characteristics, and how the child used the object that day. Later, such objects can be put into a tactile book. The child's system for both expressive and receptive communication can be built into reading the activities, so that there are meaningful opportunities for the child to engage in interaction about the book's content and respond to comprehension questions. (See Chapter 8 for more about literacy activities.)

As the educational team addresses the system of communication supports provided to the child throughout the day, it is important to periodically cross-check with the Communication Bill of Rights (see Sidebar 7.4 in Chapter 7) to ensure that each of its tenets are fully addressed across the child's learning environments and daily schedule. In addition, the team should rate the implementation of the child's expressive and receptive communication program against the programmatic quality indicators published by the Colorado Department of Education (2010; see Sidebar 14.4).

Communication and language skills go hand in hand with a child's cognitive development as the child moves toward or demonstrates the understanding of auditory (voice or environmental sounds), visual, and/or tactile symbols. As the team addresses a young child's communication needs, it should focus concurrently on building concept and emergent literacy development as a means to expand vocabulary, provide background knowledge for listening and responding

Communication Program Quality Indicators

Expressive Communication Program Quality Indicators

- Does the child have a meaningful communication system (verbal, AAC, sign language) that is efficient, effective, and understandable across a variety of environments and when communicating with a variety of people?
- Is the communication system child centered, age appropriate, and in a format that meets the child's sensory needs (for example, attention to visual array; use of color, contrast, optical enhancement; use of objects; sign language)?
- Is the communication system taught systematically and practiced across all of the child's settings (home and school) to build skills in requesting, rejecting, greeting, directing and gaining attention, social interactions, and gaining information?
- Is the communication meaningful, linguistically appropriate, and congruent with the child's personal interests, desires, and needs?
- Do the child and his or her communication partners use the communication system consistently throughout his or her day and settings? Are there opportunities for family, community members, and staff to be trained on the use of the child's communication system?
- Is there ongoing progress monitoring the child's communication to identify the need for vocabulary expansion, the need for an increase in form and function to a higher level of symbolic communication, or the child's ability to use new technologies?

Receptive Communication Program Quality Indicators

- Communication with the child is adapted to his or her receptive modality and language ability so the child can respond to questions, meet his or her needs, participate in daily routines, and participate in preschool classroom activities.
- Educational team members present directions to a student in a consistent modality matched to his or her age, modality, and language ability.
- Educational opportunities are embedded throughout the student's day to increase his or her receptive vocabulary and are evidenced by the child making meaningful choices in a variety of environments.

Source: Adapted with permission from Colorado Department of Education, Exceptional Student Leadership Unit. (2010). *Quality indicators for assessing individualized services for students (K–12) with significant support needs* (pp. 7–8). Denver, CO: Author.

to stories, and building memory. When a functional communication system is put into place, the child can be a true participant in the learning activities in his or her home and preschool environment.

COGNITIVE AND PLAY DEVELOPMENT

Professionals working with very young children will benefit from understanding early childhood development with a special focus on cognitive development theory (such as the work of Piaget [1952] and Vygotsky [1978]) so that learning activities can be designed to support the evolution of the construction of knowledge or concepts.

The first five years of life—from infancy to toddlerhood to the preschool years—involve very distinct stages of learning. A primary focus in the early years is on the importance of play and interaction with objects as a vehicle for the child's self-initiated learning discoveries. A principal role of adults is to *scaffold*, or provide temporary support for extending, the child's current level of knowledge (called the *zone of proximal development*) so that the child can progress to the next level through social guidance, modeling, and support (Vygotsky, 1978). The role of an adult partner or more knowledgeable peer in play and social interaction scenarios is paramount to building a bridge to the next developmental level.

The first two years, known as the *sensorimotor stage*, the child builds an understanding of the world through sensory exploration of objects (Piaget, 1952). During this time pe-

riod, children learn about their bodies, other people, and objects in their immediate world through multiple and direct object interactions. Hallmark features of the sensorimotor stage include a growing understanding of cause-and-effect and means-and-ends behaviors that allow the child to understand that his or her actions using his or her body and objects as tools can produce desired results.

The second phase of cognitive development, from 2 to 7 years of age, is the *preoperational stage* of development (Piaget, 1952). During this stage, learning moves from explicit sensory and hands-on motor experience to more internalized learning and thinking. The child now understands early representational or symbolic thought. The child participates in pretend play (for example, using a block to represent a cell phone), may recognize the familiar logos of fast-food restaurants, and recognizes a favorite cereal box visually by its packaging or by a tactile symbol placed on the box.

Important gradual steps of concept development include:

- recognizing the key features or salient properties of objects, actions, or events
- observing and noting similarities and differences
- developing early classification categories for common properties and groupings of objects, people, and activities

Through experience and the ability to first match and then sort by feature, young children learn to classify items by their physical properties of basic color, shape, texture, size, weight, temperature, and function; where items belong (what objects can be found in the kitchen versus the bathroom, for example); and whom the objects belong to (such as mom's shoes versus brother's shoes) (Linder, 2008a). Such categorization ultimately serves as a means of organizing information for everyday use.

Young children with visual impairments and multiple disabilities are at risk for delays in developing concepts, for developing fragmented concepts, or for failure to develop concepts at all. This is the result of several factors, including the following:

- The visual lure of reaching out in space to interact with an object may be absent or diminished, and the child may be unable to observe the effect of the body's actions on objects due to the child's visual (and possibly hearing) impairment.
- The child's ability to learn incidentally, by observing surrounding people, objects, and activities, may be compromised by limited hands-on experiences with items in a meaningful contextual setting or activity; lack of deliberate exposure to the function and use of objects; and reduced practice opportunities with play interactions.
- Low expectations of the child's abilities, and people in the child's life who reinforce learned helplessness by always doing things to and for the child, can also diminish the child's ability to advance his or her knowledge or skills. A child continually reinforced to be a passive learner will not learn the task at hand, but in fact, will learn to wait for others to complete tasks on his or her behalf.
- Orthopedic challenges may restrict the child's ability to maintain a stable posture

for interacting with objects or may limit the range and accuracy of body movements needed to act on nearby objects.

- A child may or may not have an intellectual disability. Delays in cognitive development may be difficult to tease out from the impact of sensory and possible physical challenges the child experiences. The team will want to "presume competence" (United Nations Educational, Scientific and Cultural Organization, 2012), as explained in Sidebar 14.5.

All these barriers to development of concepts and knowledge can be addressed by high expectations, deliberate guidance and teaching, and opportunities for meaningful participation.

Knowledge of early cognitive development and the impacts that visual impairment and multiple disabilities have on learning can help to guide the educational team's appropriate and meaningful assessment of the child. The goal is not to determine an age-range score (for example, that the child is functioning at the level of a 3-month-old), but to understand what the child knows under specific conditions (with attention to sensory, positioning, and communication response needs, for example) and what the appropriate next-step learning targets are for the child.

Cognitive and Play Assessment

The teacher of students with visual impairments needs to take on a number of roles when working with the early educational team: first, to help identify authentic and appropriate cognitive assessment tools for the young child with a visual impairment and

---

🗝 Sidebar 14.5

Explanation of "Presuming Competence"

Following is an excerpt of an interview with Professor Douglas Biklen, winner of the UNESCO/Emir Jaber al-Ahmad al-Jaber al-Sabah Prize to promote Quality Education for Persons with Intellectual Disabilities, posted on the United Nations Educational, Scientific, and Cultural Organization (UNESCO) website.

Can you explain the concept of "presuming competence" and how it relates to inclusive education?

When Anne Sullivan first worked with Helen Keller, she approached her with the presumption that she was competent, that Helen's problem emanated from her not having an effective means of communication. Even before Anne began to work with Helen, there was evidence of her desire to communicate—she used pantomime to show her interest in making ice cream or wanting toast with butter. But it was Anne's introduction of spelling and words that proved liberating for Helen.

The principle of "presuming competence," is simply to act as Anne Sullivan did. Assume that a child has intellectual ability, provide opportunities [for the child] to be exposed to learning, assume the child wants to learn and assert him or herself in the world. To not presume competence is to assume that some individuals cannot learn, develop, or participate in the world. Presuming competence is nothing less than a Hippocratic oath for educators. It is a framework that says, approach each child as wanting to be fully included, wanting acceptance and appreciation, wanting to learn, wanting to be heard, wanting to contribute. By presuming competence, educators place the burden on themselves to come up with ever more creative, innovative ways for individuals to learn. The question is no longer who can be included or who can learn, but how can we achieve inclusive education. We begin by presuming competence.

Source: Reprinted with permission from United Nations Educational, Scientific, and Cultural Organization. (2012). Douglas Biklen: "Begin by presuming competence." Retrieved from http://www.unesco.org/new/en /media-services/single-view/news/douglas_biklen_winner_of_unesco_kuwait_prize_begin_by_presuming _competence/#.VtCKbtJwWM8

---

multiple disabilities; second, to assist with assessment administration based on the sensory needs of the child; and third, to help interpret the results of the assessment and plan for next-step interventions. A helpful guide for the team is an assessment overview by Rowland (2009), which details appropriate assessment considerations and practices for children with deafblindness and multiple disabilities.

Data from the sensory assessments will help to inform the selection of one or more cognitive assessment tools that allow for adaptations of testing materials as well as procedures to best accommodate the sensory, physical, and cognitive access needs of the child during assessment. If a commercial assessment tool is selected, the educational team should determine if the test items or constructs belong to one of these three categories (Friedman & Calvello, 1989):

1. Do not require any adaptation since vision is not required to complete the task.
2. Require adaptation to ensure accessibility for the child, such as replacing an unfamiliar object with a familiar one; changing color, contrast, or complexity of objects and their background; altering an object to make it easier to grasp (for example, putting a foam curler on a crayon); or providing time for part-to-whole exploration.
3. Are not adaptable as they involve purely visual tasks (such as identification of self in mirror or naming of a color).

It is not equivalent, nor is it advisable, to substitute a tactile task for those that are based solely on the visual sense and assume that the original test item construct has been maintained.

Assessment tools with a hierarchical list of cognitive tasks that are given this level of analysis with regard to the child's needs and adaptation of the items will provide insight into the child's attainment of cognitive milestones, but may not provide sufficient detail of the cognitive status of the child with complex developmental needs. For some children, the steps between test items are too great and do not reflect the child's true knowledge and skills. In such instances it may be more practical to find tools that provide assessment specific to the child's interaction with everyday materials and routines.

Two assessment designs may provide more comprehensive information about a child's overall developmental status, including a focus on cognitive skills. Both can readily accommodate the results of the sensory assessments for material selection and task presentation. The Routines-Based Assessment (McWilliam & Freund, 2006) is designed to gather information from interviews (focused conversations) first with the child's caregivers about home routines and then with preschool staff about classroom routines. The goal is to understand what routines the child experiences on a regular basis, what the child can do in the identified routines, and what skills the child needs to be more successful in each routine with regard to engagement, independence, and social relationships. The teacher of students with visual impairments is essential in the analysis of the sensory supports needed by the child to be a full benefactor and participant in the daily routines of his or her home or preschool environment.

The second popular assessment design for children from birth through 6 years of age is the *Transdisciplinary Play-Based Assessment (TPBA)* (Linder, 2008b), which provides an assessment framework for all developmental domains, including cognition, through observation of the child's play. The TPBA assessment involves the child's caregivers, a designated play facilitator (who represents his or her professional discipline on the assessment team), and additional team members representing other disciplines such as early childhood special education; occupational, physical, and speech therapy; O&M; and developmental psychology.

If a child is suspected of or identified as having a visual impairment, a teacher of students with visual impairments needs to be a member of the TPBA team and may be best suited as the play facilitator. In this role, the teacher of students with visual impairments can work with the team to gather the materials that will be used during the assessment and be in control of how objects are displayed or presented to the child based on his or her sensory needs during the assessment. The play facilitator engages the child in both unstructured play (following the child's lead of self-initiated body actions or self-selected objects) and structured or more directed play activities that can provide scaffolding so that the child can show a next level of knowledge or skill set.

During these play interactions, the other professionals observe the child and complete their discipline- or domain-specific TPBA protocols. For example, a physical therapist will likely complete the protocol specific to the child's gross motor milestones, postural tone, and ability to sustain positions, grade movement, motor plan, and demonstrate other sensorimotor attributes. If an O&M specialist participates in the TBPA, he or she will also take assessment notes specific to the child's motor (mobility) skills, as well as cognitive (orientation) concepts and skills to add to the team's understanding of the child's developmental status and needs. Other roles for the teacher of students with visual impairments

will be to complete a vision screening assessment, a functional vision assessment, or both during the TBPA; provide insight as to how all early developmental domains may be affected by the child's visual impairment; and assist the team with interpreting the assessment results based on an understanding of how early-onset visual impairment affects all developmental domains. (More information about social play is discussed in the context of social skills in Chapter 10.)

Cognitive and Play Strategies

The educational team needs to work together to identify how best to support active learning for the child. *Active learning* involves the child initiating actions him- or herself to act on objects in daily routines. For all young children, these actions start as random movements that become more intentional as the child learns that moving his or her body in a certain way (cause) results in something the child enjoys (effect). A random swat may activate the movement of a dangling Slinky or sound the chimes of a nearby musical toy. As the child has multiple opportunities to practice and refine these movements, he or she becomes more proficient with batting, reaching, kicking, and shaking objects for a desired effect. By using a play-based model of interaction, the adult can also model or guide the child to a higher level of play as the child learns to control his or her body movements for a desired response and understands other aspects of an object's function and use. Such movements later become more deliberate actions, as the young child learns to reach for a drink at snack time, use an alternative pencil (any tool that can be used to make a mark or indicate a letter choice for a written response when a traditional writing tool such as a pencil cannot be used by the child) to scribble or draw on a page, or select a particular item on a communication display to answer a question about a character in the story read in preschool class.

When a young child has a visual impairment and multiple disabilities affecting motor control, it is important to set up learning scenarios where even the most minimal of body movements can result in rewarded response. This may involve setting up a play environment in which objects are situated on or very close to the child's body, so that a simple arm movement may result in the jingle of a bell, rustle of Mylar paper, or the activation of a recorded message by pressing on a pressure switch. Just as the young child learns to use his or her vocalizations and body movements for intentional communication, children in the early stages of play discovery learn to be intentional with their body actions to make something happen with an object. Sidebar 14.6 details how to set up an active learning play environment that includes the three broad strategies of attending to the child's preferences, ensuring proximity to play materials, and providing opportunities for practice.

A child's posture provides a base for his or her movement and function. Young children who have low postural tone (a common characteristic of pediatric visual impairment) or an orthopedic impairment such as cerebral palsy may require support in maintaining a stable posture. A physical or occupational therapist can be consulted on how best to support a child's positioning needs for different learning tasks. Simple low-technology tools such as

---

🔑 Sidebar 14.6

Setting Up an Active Learning Play Environment

Preferences

Select items that reflect the child's sensory abilities and preferences based on the results of a sensory assessment. For example, pay attention to visual characteristics such as light, reflection, color, contrast, movement, complexity, novelty, and familiarity need. Address auditory preferences with sound-producing toys or objects and by creating a play environment with limited auditory distractions. Attend to tactile preferences that invite active exploration (such as vibration, tactual ridges) versus resistance to touch (such as cold, wet, sticky). The goal is to engage the child in a highly motivating activity.

Proximity

Attend to the child's position for optimal interaction with the involved play items. Special materials or equipment may be needed to support the child in his or her optimal position. The play items should be positioned to accommodate the focal distance, visual field, visual array, and range of movement needs of the child.

Practice

Ensure that the play environment is designed so that the child can practice the motor actions needed to produce a desired response from an object. This may include using materials to keep play items stable or prevent them from rolling or falling out of the child's reach.

foam or cushion supports, rolled towels, boppies (a C-shaped pillow), rolls, bolsters, and wedges can be used to position and stabilize a child with low postural tone. Adapted chairs, sidelyers, vertical standers, adjustable-height benches, or other specially designed equipment may be recommended for children with orthopedic impairment who require more support to maintain a specific position. A variety of adaptation materials and equipment may be needed to maintain the different positions a child needs across his or her daily activities.

Attention should also be given to the position of play and learning materials. Early play areas can be designed to accommodate the child's range of body movements and sensory abilities and preferences. For example, some children with visual impairments and multiple disabilities or deafblindness may be more likely to explore with their heads or feet before using their hands to investigate new things (Greeley & Anthony, 1995). With this in mind, play areas may focus initially on placing objects with interesting sound production qualities (such as pom-poms, Mylar paper, and sounding, vibrating, or switch-activated objects) near a child's feet for exploration. Types of individualized defined play spaces can be designed in the home setting, such as a play mat with surrounding rolled-towel borders that keep toys in close proximity or a plastic laundry basket that can hold the sitting child and his or her playthings during bath time. The play space can be designed to accommodate prone (on tummy), supine (on back), side lying, or sitting positions, with or without support, as needed.

Other ways to keep play items in close proximity include using trays with side rims or shallow bins. These trays or bins can be held secure in one place with Dycem or another type of nonslip material or with the use of a C-clamp. Play items can be tethered safely with elastic or tie cords to body vests or a pegboard. A child may also benefit from the Little Room (Nielsen, 1992), which is a space that can be constructed from plexiglass wall modules from which play objects are suspended. A Little Room is another example of a responsive play scenario that can be immensely rewarding for the child to interact with objects in close proximity while an adult observes in order to learn more about the object preferences and range of motion abilities of the child.

Careful attention is needed to ensure that any elastic cords or ties securing the objects cannot harm the child. As with any play situation involving young children, adult supervision is necessary at all times. While they are supervising the child, the adults can observe which items seem to be of the most interest to the child, along with their characteristics and location in relation to the child's body. These data will inform the team about the child's sensory abilities and preferences, as well as his or her physical abilities. It is important to realize that an item a child seems to be interested in may simply be what the child can see and physically reach, as opposed to evidence of his or her true interest in the object as a play item.

The National Association for the Education of Young Children (NAEYC; n.d.) offers guidance on the safest and most appropriate play materials for young children, recommending toys that are well-constructed, free from toxic substances, use lead-free paint, are shatterproof, and are easily cleaned. In addition to or instead of commercial toys, play items can be cardboard boxes, Mylar paper, metal or plastic cups and bowls, and other everyday home objects. For young children with visual impairments and multiple disabilities, the educational team can work together to identify and provide play materials appropriate for the child's age and development. Toys with large knobs or buttons may be easier to activate for a child with motor challenges.

Assistive technology (see Chapter 12) should be addressed to assist the child with sensory and physical access to play materials. Adaptive switch devices may be beneficial to activate battery-operated toys, tape recorders, or other devices. One teacher of students with visual impairments described a young child with a visual impairment and multiple disabilities who used a button switch to activate a spinner for games with peers (N. Cozart, personal communication, June 12, 2015). Her participation in games was to start the spinner for each player. She looked to each player and approximated his or her name upon their turn. It was motivating and social learning for the child. Tablet apps also can be used for a variety of early play, learning, and emergent literacy concepts.

Care should be taken not to provide preschool children with baby toys such as rattles or infant mouthing items. If a child remains at a lower developmental level of cognitive play, the team needs to work to identify more age-appropriate toys or playthings that can serve as simple cause-and-effect practice tools. If the child has an orthopedic impairment that restricts voluntary body movements, the team needs to identify developmentally appropriate play items and learning materials that can be operated with simple body movements. For example, an adaptive switch can be used to take a turn racing battery-operated cars in the school gym. A dramatic play center may include an alternative pencil for a child to use to "take orders" at a pretend restaurant.

Preference, proximity, and practice are important strategies to use throughout a child's early years to ensure that he or she has sensory and physical access to learning materials. The preschool team will need to be proactive to ensure that cognitive access is also always addressed, for a final "P" strategy of true participation. The preschool-age child should always be a participant in the daily learning routines of his or her early childhood program. The next section will address general tenets of early childhood special education classrooms for preschoolers with disabilities, including those with visual impairments and multiple disabilities.

THE PRESCHOOL CLASSROOM

Ideally, a child with a visual impairment and multiple disabilities will attend a preschool classroom that includes peers without disabilities, but he or she may also attend separate classrooms of preschoolers with disabilities based on determination of the child's least restrictive environment (see Chapters 1 and 2). The preschool setting design and curriculum may be highly individualized across school district settings. The following general programmatic components are recommended by national early childhood experts (Division for Early Childhood, 2014; McWilliam & Scott, 2001; NAEYC, 2003):

- a developmentally appropriate curriculum with a focus on child-engagement, play, and hands-on learning strategies
- a physical classroom environment and learning activities designed using universal and tiers design principles for learning to optimize cognitive, socialization, communication, and movement outcomes
- embedded instruction
- integrated therapies

Developmentally Appropriate Curriculum

A well-planned, engaging, linguistically and developmentally appropriate, and culturally responsive curriculum implemented by qualified teachers who promote learning in appropriate ways can contribute significantly to positive outcomes for all children (NAEYC, 2003). NAEYC and the National Association of Early Childhood Specialists in State Departments of Education crafted a position statement that details the following eight key tenets of a viable curriculum for preschoolers, including those with disabilities:

1. Children are socially, cognitively, physically, and artistically active and engaged.
2. Curriculum goals are clearly defined and shared by all. Teaching strategies and related activities are designed to be in support of curriculum goals.
3. The curriculum is centered on evidenced-based practices and interventions that are developmentally, culturally, and linguistically relevant for children in the classroom.
4. Teaching strategies are customized to the children's ages, developmental capacities, cultures, languages, abilities, preferences, and impact from disabilities.
5. The curriculum's content and implementation builds on the children's prior learning, and is inclusive of all children.
6. The content of the curriculum is comprehensive and addresses all developmental domains and foundational concepts of literacy (reading and writing), math, science, and social studies.
7. Professional standards validate the curriculum's subject matter content.
8. There is evidence that the curriculum, if implemented appropriately, will offer benefits to all children.

In addition to the established preschool curriculum, young children with visual impairments and multiple disabilities should be offered developmentally appropriate strategies tied to the ECC. The teacher of students with visual impairments and O&M specialist can work with the educational team to address the child's early learning needs tied to compensatory skills, O&M, social interaction, independent living, recreation and leisure, sensory efficiency, assistive technology, career education, and self-determination.

Multitiered System of Supports and Universal Design for Learning

Many preschool programs in public schools utilize a multitiered system of supports

(MTSS) framework. MTSS is a whole-school, data-driven, prevention-based framework for improving learning and behavioral outcomes for every student through a layered continuum of evidence-based practices (Colorado Department of Education, n.d.). This layered continuum of supports includes universal, targeted, and intensive levels of interventions based on the needs of the individual child. It allows preschoolers with a disability to learn the skills they need in the context of the classroom, during play, when they are involved in natural routines. Interventions are customized to the child's learning, social-emotional, and mobility needs, and data is taken to confirm that the child is making progress. For the child with a visual impairment and multiple disabilities, the MTSS framework provides an ongoing opportunity for team problem solving. With the use of the collective expertise of both early childhood and special education experts, specifically including teachers of students with visual impairments and O&M specialists, the focus is not on the child's disabilities but on his or her needs as a full participant and active learner in the preschool classroom and the curriculum.

Universally designed preschool classrooms offer all children a variety of tools and activities to increase their access to and participation in the curriculum (see Chapter 6). Preschool educators focus on engaging and motivating children by using multisensory and multimodal strategies, including the use of assistive technology tools, to build on each child's unique interests. The physical environment of a universally designed preschool classroom should also be designed to optimize access and social-emotional, communi-cation, cognitive, play, and motor engagement. There should be space for needed assistive technology, such as communication devices, braillewriters, adaptive seating equipment, wheelchairs, and other tools used to ensure each child's access to and active participation in classroom activities. The layout should allow for various play centers (such as for dramatic play) and learning centers (such as for math and literacy).

Embedded Instruction

A child's educational goals, as defined by the Individualized Education Program (IEP), should be developed and written around his or her daily routines. Instruction to meet the goals should be embedded throughout the child's day. This allows the child to learn and practice a concept or a skill within the naturally occurring activities of an established classroom routine, such as recognizing and using certain symbols during a circle time activity or learning to use a spoon during snack time. Such routine-based interventions can also be incorporated into the family's routines at home to reinforce a new concept or skill. Experts in preschool content, special education, and visual impairment or deafblindness need to work together to determine how best to modify preschool instructional content for a given child. The teacher of students with visual impairments needs to work closely with the family and preschool staff on how to ensure full sensory accessibility to the learning tasks, and on developing specific activities to achieve goals that are unique to a child with visual impairment, such as early tactile discrimination and emergent braille tasks.

Integrated Therapy and Instruction

National policymakers strongly discourage pullout therapies where the child is removed from the classroom routine for a specialized therapy. Pullout services are typically provided in short sessions, with the therapist working directly with the child outside the preschool classroom. Integrated therapy services are offered in the classroom context, with a focus on classroom routines and content, and may involve the child's peers. When a therapy is provided in the context of the child's classroom, teachers and specialists consult with one another four times more often that they do when the therapy is completed in a separate setting (McWilliam & Scott, 2001). Sidebar 14.7 presents 10 reasons for integrated therapies that apply to teacher of students with visual impairments and O&M specialist service time with a child.

Related service providers such as occupational therapists, physical therapists, and speech-language pathologists can work closely with the preschool teacher to determine how best to provide integrated instruction and therapy. The teacher of students with visual impairments also needs to consider how best to work directly with the child within the classroom routines. The teacher of students with visual impairments has an ongoing role to address the visual and tactile accessibility of routine-based activities and to provide specially designed instruction to the child within the context of the preschool. For example, one preschooler with low vision and multiple disabilities worked on visual engagement and attentiveness with a cause-and-effect app on

---

✒ Sidebar 14.7

Ten Really Good Reasons Why Therapies Should Be Integrated

1. Children learn the skills needed in the places they will use them.
2. Children have increased opportunities to practice the skill.
3. Children's social relationships are fostered.
4. Children do not miss out on any classroom activities.
5. Teachers see what therapists do to help children and expand their skills.
6. Therapists can see whether or not the strategies they develop are feasible.
7. Teachers and therapists focus on skills that will be immediately useful for a child.
8. Therapists can work directly with teachers as problems arise.
9. Assessments can be done across a variety of classroom routines.
10. It is the right thing to do!

Source: Reprinted with permission from McWilliam, R. A., & Scott, S. (2001). *Integrating therapy into the classroom* (p. 1). Chapel Hill: University of North Carolina–Chapel Hill, Frank Porter Graham Child Development Center. Retrieved from http://csd.wp.uncg.edu/wp-content/uploads/sites/6/2012/12/Integrating-Therapy-Into-Classrooms1.pdf

---

the iPad (N. Cozart, personal correspondence, June 12, 2015). The child sustained visual attention for longer periods of time when presented with the app on the iPad, and leaned in when the iPad was pulled a few inches away. The teacher of students with visual impairments worked with the physical therapist during their time together in the preschool classroom, so they could each give perspective on the physical and learning support needs of the child and how best to position the iPad for the best visual access. Over time, with the help of the physical therapist and speech-language pathologist, the child started making choices with the use of two iPads.

The O&M specialist is instrumental in working with children with visual impairments and multiple disabilities to advance motor skills, orientation concepts, and purposeful movement routes that can be taught within the classroom setting. In addition, the O&M specialist may need to work with a child outside the classroom based on identified O&M goals, which may include the natural routines of getting to and from the classroom at the beginning and end of the preschool day or excursions to other sites within the school building.

SUMMARY

Infants, toddlers, and preschoolers represent a very unique period of human development that needs to be well understood by the professionals who work with children with visual impairments and multiple disabilities and their families. The young child with a visual impairment and multiple disabilities will benefit from a family-centered, team approach to authentic and developmentally appropriate assessments across all early learning domains, with a strong early focus on sensory-based assessments. Such assessments will support the team in determining how best to address the child's needs within his or her daily routines. It is essential that each child has a functional communication system for interacting with others and sensory, physical, and cognitive access to play and learning activities in order to be a meaningful participant and active learner. The teacher of students with visual impairments is a key professional on the educational team, and is essential to the appropriate assessment of a child with a visual impairment and multiple disabilities, along with the identification of the access, intervention, and needs of the child. The teacher of students with visual impairments will need to work closely with the family and other professionals to build an effective program for the child.

REFERENCES

Abdala, C., & Winter, M. (2014). Pediatric audiology: Evaluating and managing hearing loss in young children. In D. Chen (Ed.), *Essential elements in early intervention: Visual impairment and multiple disabilities* (2nd ed., pp. 341–391). New York: AFB Press.

Anthony, T., Bishop, V., Gleason, D., Greeley, J. C., Hatton, D., Miller, T., . . . Tompkins, C. (2003). *Family-centered practices for infants and young children with visual impairments.* Position paper of the Division on Visual Impairments. Arlington, VA: Council for Exceptional Children.

Anthony, T. L. (2000). Performing a functional low vision assessment. In F. M. D'Andrea & C. Farrenkopf (Eds.), *Looking to learn: Promoting literacy for students with low vision* (pp. 32–83). New York: AFB Press.

Anthony, T. L. (2003). *Individual Sensory Learning Profile Interview (ISLPI).* Chapel Hill: University of North Carolina–Chapel Hill, FPG Child Development Institute, Early Intervention Training Center for Infants and Toddlers with Visual Impairments.

Anthony, T. L. (2008). Vision development. In T. Linder (Ed.), *Transdisciplinary play-based assessment* (2nd ed., pp. 65–93). Baltimore: Paul H. Brookes Publishing Co.

Anthony, T. L., Wiggin, M. P., Yoshinaga-Itano, C., & Raver, S. A. (2015). Infants and toddlers with sensory disabilities. In S. A. Raver & D. C. Childress (Eds.), *Family-centered early intervention: Supporting infants and toddlers in natural environments.* (pp. 216–254). Baltimore: Paul H. Brookes Publishing Co.

Banajee, M., DiCarlo, C., & Stricklin, S. B. (2003). Core vocabulary determination for toddlers. *Augmentative and Alternative Communication, 19*(2), 67–73.

Barclay, L. A. (2012). Appendix A: The listening skills continuum. In L. A. Barclay (Ed.), *Learning to listen/Listening to learn: Teaching listening skills to students with visual impairments* (pp. 483–510). New York: AFB Press.

Bartlett, L. D., Etscheidt, S., & Weisenstein, G. R. (2007). Inclusion basics. In *Special education law and practice in public schools* (2nd ed., pp. 2–18). Upper Saddle River, NJ: Pearson Education.

Borchert, M., & Garcia-Filion, P. (2008). The syndrome of optic nerve hypoplasia. *Current Neurology and Neuroscience Reports, 8*(5), 395–403.

Brambring, M., & Tröster, H. (1992). On the stability of stereotyped behaviors in blind infants and preschoolers. *Journal of Visual Impairment & Blindness, 86*(2), 105–110.

Burnett, R., & Sanford, L. (2008). *FVLMA for students who are pre-academic or academic and visually impaired in grades K–12: Practi-tioner's guidebook.* Louisville, KY: American Printing House for the Blind.

Chen, D. (2014). Understanding hearing loss: Implications for early intervention. In D. Chen (Ed.), *Essential elements in early intervention: Visual impairment and multiple disabilities* (2nd ed., pp. 294–340). New York: AFB Press.

Colorado Department of Education. (n.d.). Multi-tiered system of supports. Denver, CO: Author. Retrieved from http://www.cde.state.co.us/mtss

Colorado Department of Education, Exceptional Student Leadership Unit. (2010). *Quality indicators for assessing individualized services for students (K–12) with significant support needs.* Denver, CO: Author.

Cress, C. J., & Marvin, C. A. (2003). Common questions about AAC services in early intervention. *Augmentative and Alternative Communication 19*(4), 254–272.

Cross, R. T., Baker, B. R., Klotz, L. S., & Badman, A. L. (1997). Static and dynamic keyboards: Semantic compaction in both worlds. *Proceedings of the 18th Annual Southeast Augmentative Communication Conference,* 9–17.

Dennis, A., Erickson, K., & Hatch, P. (2013). *The Dynamic Learning Maps core vocabulary: Overview* [Technical Review]. Chapel Hill: University of North Carolina–Chapel Hill. Retrieved from http://www.med.unc.edu/ahs/clds/files/vocabulary-overview

Division for Early Childhood. (2014). *DEC recommended practices in early intervention/early childhood special education 2014.* Los Angeles, CA: Author. Retrieved from http://www.dec-sped.org/recommendedpractices

Durkel, J. (2005). Formal versus informal hearing tests: What is functional hearing? *See/Hear, 10*(3). Retrieved from http://www.tsbvi.edu/seehear/summer05/functional.htm

Dutton, G. N., McKillop, E. C. A., & Saidka-simova, S. (2006). Visual problems as a result of brain damage in children. *British Journal of Ophthalmology, 90*(8), 932–933.

Fenson, L., Marchman, V. A., Thal, D. J., Dale, P. S., Reznick, J. S., & Bates, E. (2007). *MacArthur-Bates Communicative Development Inventory (CDI): Words and gestures.* Baltimore: Paul H. Brookes Publishing Co.

Ferrell, K. A. (with Shaw, A. R., & Deitz, S. J.) (1998). *Project PRISM: A longitudinal study of developmental patterns of children who are visually impaired. Final Report* (CFDA 84.023C—Field-initiated research H023C10188). Greeley: University of Northern Colorado.

Fink, C., & Borchert, M. (2011). Optic nerve hypoplasia and autism: Common features of spectrum diseases. *Journal of Visual Impairment & Blindness, 105*(6), 334–338.

Friedman, C. T., & Calvello, G. (1989). Developmental assessment. In D. Chen, C. T. Friedman, & G. Cavello (Eds.), *Parents and visually impaired infants.* Louisville, KY: American Printing House for the Blind.

Geddie, B. E., Bina, M. J., & Miller, M. M. (2007). Vision and visual impairments. In M. L. Batshaw, L. Pellegrino, & N. J. Roizen (Eds.), *Children with disabilities* (6th ed., pp. 169–188). Baltimore: Paul H. Brookes Publishing Co.

Gogate, P., & Gilbert, C. (2007). Blindness in children: A worldwide perspective. *Community Eye Health, 20*(62), 32–33.

Good, W. V., Jan, J. E., DeSa, L., Barkovich, A. J., Groenveld, M., & Hoyt, C. S. (1994). Cortical visual impairment in children. *Survey of Ophthalmology, 38*(4), 351–364.

Greeley, J., & Anthony, T. L. (1995). Play interaction with infants and toddlers who are deafblind: Setting the stage. *Seminars in Hearing 16*(2), 185–191.

Hatch, P., Erickson, K., Dennis, A., & Cummings, M. (2013, November). *Journey to the core: Developing a core vocabulary for the common core.* Presented at the American Speech-Language-Hearing Association Annual Convention, Philadelphia, PA.

Hatton, D. D. (2001). Model registry of early childhood visual impairment: First-year results. *Journal of Visual Impairment & Blindness, 95*(7), 418–433.

Hatton, D. D., Ivy, S. E., & Boyer, C. (2013). Severe visual impairments in infants and toddlers in the United States. *Journal of Visual Impairment & Blindness, 107*(5), 325–337.

Hatton D. D., Schwietz, E., Boyer, B., & Rychwalski, P. (2007). Babies Count: The national registry for children with visual impairments, birth to 3 years. *Journal of the American Association for Pediatric Ophthalmology and Strabismus, 11*(4), 351–355.

Individuals with Disabilities Education Improvement Act (IDEA), 20 U.S.C. § 1400 (2004).

Koenig, A. J., & Holbrook, M. C. (1995). *Learning media assessment of students with visual impairments: A resource guide for teachers* (2nd ed.). Austin: Texas School for the Blind and Visually Impaired.

Korsten, J. E., Foss, T. V., & Berry, L. M. (2007). *Every move counts clicks and chats: Sensory-based approach: Communication and assistive technology.* Kansas City, KS: EMC, Inc.

Kuhlmann, R. S., & Autry, A. M. (2001). An approach to nonbacterial infections in pregnancy. *Clinical Family Practice, 3*, 267–286.

Lieberman, L. J., Ponchillia, P. E., & Ponchillia, S. V. (2013). Visual impairment and deafblindness: An overview. In *Physical education and sports for people with visual impairments and deafblindness: Foundations of instruction* (pp. 27–51). New York: AFB Press.

Linder, T. (2008a). Cognitive development domain. In T. Linder (Ed.), *Transdisciplinary Play-Based Assessment (TPBA2)* (2nd ed., pp. 313–397). Baltimore: Paul H. Brookes Publishing Co.

Linder, T. (2008b). *Transdisciplinary Play-Based Assessment (TPBA2)* (2nd ed.). Baltimore: Paul H. Brookes Publishing Co.

Lueck, A. H., & Dutton, G. N. (Eds.). (2015). *Vision and the brain: Understanding cerebral visual impairment in children.* New York: AFB Press.

Lueck, A. H., & Heinze, T. (2004). Interventions for young children with visual impairments and students with visual and multiple disabilities. In A. H. Lueck (Ed.), *Functional vision: A practitioner's guide to evaluation and intervention* (pp. 277–351). New York: AFB Press.

Marlow, N., Wolke, D., Bracewell, M. A., & Samara, M. (2005). Neurologic and developmental disability at six years of age after extremely premature birth. *The New England Journal of Medicine, 352*(1), 9–19.

Marvin, C. A., Beukelman, D. R., & Bilyeu, D. (1994). Vocabulary-use patterns in preschool children: Effects of context and time sampling. *Augmentative and Alternative Communication, 10*(4), 224–236.

McHugh, E., & Pyfer, J. (1999). The development of rocking among children who are blind. *Journal of Visual Impairment & Blindness, 93*(2), 82–95.

McWilliam, R., & Freund, P. (2006). *National individualizing preschool inclusion project: Implementation manual* (2nd ed.). Nashville, TN: Vanderbilt University Medical Center, Center for Child Development.

McWilliam, R. A., & Scott, S. (2001). *Integrating therapy into the classroom.* Chapel Hill: University of North Carolina–Chapel Hill, Frank Porter Graham Child Development Center. Retrieved from http://csd.wp.uncg.edu/wp-content/uploads/sites/6/2012/12/Integrating-Therapy-Into-Classrooms1.pdf

Moss, K., & Blaha, R. (1993). Looking at self-stimulation in the pursuit of leisure or I'm okay, you have a mannerism, *See/Hear, 5*(3). Retrieved from http://www.tsbvi.edu/seehear/archive/mannerism.html

National Association for the Education of Young Children. (2003). *Early childhood curriculum, assessment, and program evaluation: Building an effective, accountable system in programs for children birth through age 8.* Joint position statement with the National Association of Early Childhood Specialists in State Departments of Education. Washington, DC: Author. Retrieved from https://www.naeyc.org/files/naeyc/file/positions/CAPEexpand.pdf

National Association for the Education of Young Children. (n.d.). Good toys for young children. Washington, DC: Author. Retrieved from http://www.naeyc.org/ecp/resources/goodtoys

National Joint Committee for the Communication Needs of Persons with Severe Disabilities. (1992). Guidelines for meeting the communication needs of persons with severe disabilities. *ASHA, 34*(Suppl. 7), 1–8.

Nielsen, L. (1992). *Space and self: Active learning by means of the Little Room.* Copenhagen, Denmark: Sikon.

Odle, T. (2009). Visual impairments. Retrieved from http://www.education.com/reference/article/visual-impairments1/

Orel-Bixler, D. (2014). Clinical vision assessments for young children. In D. Chen (Ed.), *Essential elements in early intervention: Visual impairment and multiple disabilities* (2nd ed., pp. 135–213). New York: AFB Press.

Patel, L., McNally, R. J., Harrison, E., Lloyd, I. C., & Clayton, P. E. (2006). Geographical distribution of optic nerve hypoplasia and septo-optic dysplasia in northwest England. *Journal of Pediatrics, 148*(1), 85–88.

Piaget, J. (1952). *The origins of intelligence in children*. New York: International Universities Press.

Roley, S. S. (1995). Roles and responsibilities of selected disciplines: Occupational therapy for young children with multiple disabilities. In D. Chen & J. Dote-Kwan (Eds.), *Starting points: Instructional practices for young children whose multiple disabilities include visual impairment* (pp. 98–106). Los Angeles, CA: Blind Children's Center.

Roman-Lantzy, C. (2007). *Cortical visual impairment: An approach to assessment and intervention*. New York: AFB Press.

Rowland, C. (2004). *Communication matrix*. Portland: Oregon Health and Science University.

Rowland, C. (2013). *Handbook: Online communication matrix*. Portland: Oregon Health and Science University. Retrieved from http://www.communicationmatrix.org/uploads/pdfs/handbook.pdf

Rowland, C. (Ed.). (2009). *Assessing communication and learning in young children who are deafblind or who have multiple disabilities*. Portland: Oregon Health and Science University.

Scoggin, K. (2012). *Likes and dislikes form*. Wenatchee: Washington Sensory Disabilities Services. Retrieved from http://www.wsdsonline.org/deaf-blind/db-downloadable-documents/

Smith, M. (2005). *The Sensory Learning Kit (SLK)*. Louisville, KY: American Printing House for the Blind.

Teplin, S. W. (1995). Visual impairment in infants and young children. *Infants and Young Children, 8*(1), 18–51.

Teplin, S. W., Greeley, J., and Anthony, T. L. (2009). Blindness and visual impairment. In W. B. Carey, A. C. Crocker, W. L. Coleman, E. R., Elias, & H. M. Feldman (Eds.), *Developmental-behavioral pediatrics* (4th ed., pp. 698–716). Philadelphia: Saunders Elsevier.

Topor, I. (2014). Functional vision assessment and early intervention practices. In D. Chen (Ed.), *Essential elements in early intervention: Visual impairment and multiple disabilities* (2nd ed. pp. 214–293). New York: AFB Press.

United Nations Educational, Scientific and Cultural Organization. (2012). Douglas Biklen: "Begin by presuming competence." Paris, France: Author. Retrieved from http://www.unesco.org/new/en/media-services/single-view/news/douglas_biklen_winner_of_unesco_kuwait_prize_begin_by_presuming_competence/#.VtCKbtJwWM8

Vygotsky, L. S. (1978). *Mind in society: The development of higher psychological processes* (M. Cole, V. John-Steiner, S. Scribner, & E. Souberman, Eds.). Cambridge, MA: Harvard University Press.

RESOURCES

For additional resources, see the General Resources section at the back of this book.

Assessments
Broad Sensory Assessments
Every Move Counts, Clicks, and Chats (EMC3)
Source: Korsten, J. E., Foss, T. V., & Berry, L. M. (2007). *Every move counts clicks and chats:*

Sensory-based approach: Communication and assistive technology. Kansas City, KS: EMC, Inc.

A sensory-based approach to communication and assistive technology for individuals with significant sensory motor differences, developmental differences, and autism. Compiles information about a child's sensory responsiveness to a variety of assessment activities. Teachers of students with visual impairments should be consulted to ensure activities are adapted and results interpreted appropriately for a child who is blind or visually impaired with additional disabilities, including deaf-blindness.

Individual Sensory Learning Profile Interview (ISLPI)
Source: Anthony, T. L. (2003). *Individual Sensory Learning Profile Interview (ISLPI)*. Chapel Hill: University of North Carolina–Chapel Hill, FPG Child Development Institute, Early Intervention Training Center for Infants and Toddlers with Visual Impairments.

A profile that collects information on preferences, abilities, and needs specific to visual, auditory, tactile, vestibular, olfactory, and taste stimuli. Interview and observation are used to determine what specific types of sensory information may arouse a child's interest and serve as a motivator for listening, learning, communicating, moving, and exploring. Designed for teachers of students with visual impairments or O&M specialists, along with input of other team members.

Learning Media Assessment (LMA)
Source: Koenig, A. J., & Holbrook, M. C. (1995). *Learning media assessment of students with visual impairments: A resource guide for teachers* (2nd ed.). Austin: Texas School for the Blind and Visually Impaired.

An assessment (in particular, the Sensory Channel form) that provides information about a child's sensory learning style and how vision, hearing, and touch are used either singularly or in unison (as primary or secondary sensory modes) for learning, movement, and emergent literacy tasks. Observation data are used to support the selection of appropriate learning and (emergent) literacy materials, equipment, and need for specially designed instruction. To be completed by the teacher of students with visual impairments, with the assistance of others who know the child well.

Likes and Dislikes Form
Source: Scoggin, K. (2012). *Likes and dislikes form*. Wenatchee: Washington Sensory Disabilities Services. Retrieved from http://www.wsdsonline.org/deaf-blind/db-downloadable-documents/

A form that records a child's preferences (likes) and aversions (dislikes) related to food, smells, touch, movement, vibration, sights, sounds, muscles, people, places, activities, toys, self-stimulation behaviors, and "other." Provides information on which items and/or activities are motivating or disruptive to the child. To be completed by caregivers and intervention or school personnel who know the child well.

Sensory Learning Kit (SLK)
Source: Smith, M. (2005). *The Sensory Learning Kit (SLK)*. Louisville, KY: American Printing House for the Blind.

A kit composed of sensory items and written materials to gather information about the most significantly challenged learners and their responses and interests to a variety of defined sensory-based experience activities. Under direction of a teacher of students with visual impairments, can be used to development skills and to help create daily schedules, lesson plans, and alternative assessments for play or functional routines.

Other Assessments

Communication Matrix
Sources: Rowland, C. (2004). *Communication matrix*. Portland: Oregon Health and Science University; Rowland, C. (2013). *Handbook: Online communication matrix*. Portland: Oregon Health and Science University. Retrieved from http://www.communicationmatrix.org/uploads/pdfs/handbook.pdf

An assessment tool designed to pinpoint exactly how an individual is communicating and to provide a framework for determining logical communication goals. Designed primarily for speech-language pathologists and educators to document expressive communication skills of children who have severe or multiple disabilities, including children with sensory, motor, and cognitive impairments. The online version is currently available free of charge in a variety of languages. A print copy designed specifically for parents can also be purchased in English or Spanish.

CVI Range and **CVI Resolution Chart**
Source: Roman-Lantzy, C. (2007). *Cortical visual impairment: An approach to assessment and intervention*. New York: AFB Press.

An assessment instrument designed specifically for children with cortical visual impairment to determine a child's level of visual functioning and the effect of the various characteristics of CVI. Can be used by a teacher of students with visual impairments to determine whether a child requires educational vision intervention in living and learning settings.

MacArthur-Bates Communicative Development Inventory (CDI)
Source: Fenson, L., Marchman, V. A., Thal, D. J., Dale, P. S., Reznick, J. S., & Bates, E. (2007). *MacArthur-Bates Communicative Development Inventory (CDI): Words and gestures*. Baltimore: Paul H. Brookes Publishing Co.

A questionnaire that captures parents' knowledge of their child's emerging language skills and documents a child's understanding and use of early words or phrases. Enables professionals to tap into parents' knowledge about their children's communicative development for use in screening and developing a prognosis for children with language delays.

Routines-Based Assessment for Functional Intervention Planning
Source: McWilliam, R., & Freund, P. (2006). *National individualizing preschool inclusion project: Implementation manual* (2nd ed.). Nashville, TN: Vanderbilt University Medical Center, Center for Child Development.

An assessment designed to gather information first from interviews (focused conversations) with a child's caregivers about home routines and then with preschool staff about classroom routines. The goal is to understand what routines the child experiences on a regular basis, what the child can do in the identified routines, and what skills the child needs to be more successful in each routine in regard to engagement, independence, and social relationships.

Transdisciplinary Play-Based Assessment (TPBA)
Source: Linder, T. (2008). *Transdisciplinary Play-Based Assessment (TPBA2)* (2nd ed.). Baltimore: Paul H. Brookes Publishing Co.

An assessment framework for children from birth through 6 years of age for all developmental domains, including cognition, through observation of the child's play. Involves the child's caregiver(s), a designated play facilitator, and additional team members representing other disciplines.

Organizations

National Association for the Education of Young Children (NAEYC)
1313 L Street, NW, Suite 500
Washington, DC 20005
(202) 232-8777; (800) 424-2460
Fax: (202) 328-1846
www.naeyc.org

A professional membership organization that works to promote high-quality early learning for all young children, birth through age 8, by connecting early childhood practice, policy, and research and supporting all who care for, educate, and work on behalf of young children. Also offers guidance on the safest and most appropriate toys for young children.

National Center on Deaf-Blindness (NCDB)
345 N. Monmouth Avenue
Monmouth, OR 97361
(503) 838-8754
Fax: (503) 838-8150
info@nationaldb.org
https://nationaldb.org/

A national technical assistance center funded by the federal Department of Education that works to improve the quality of life for children who are deafblind and their families. Runs the Deaf-Blind Project, a federally funded program that provides free technical assistance services to children who are deafblind, their families, and service providers in their state.

Additional Readings

Division for Early Childhood. (2014). *DEC recommended practices in early intervention/ early childhood special education 2014*. Los Angeles, CA: Author. Retrieved from http://www.dec-sped.org/recommendedpractices

A set of guidelines developed to provide guidance to families and practitioners about the most effective ways to improve the learning outcomes and promote the development of young children birth through 5 years of age who have, or are at risk for, developmental delays and disabilities.

Rowland, C. (Ed.). (2009). *Assessing communication and learning in young children who are deafblind or who have multiple disabilities*. Portland: Oregon Health and Science University.

An assessment overview that details appropriate assessment considerations and practices for children with deafblindness and multiple disabilities. This three-phase assessment effort involves professionals and family members working together as a team.

Chapter 15

Planning an Effective Transition
• •

Betsy L. McGinnity

Key Points

🔑 The legal requirements and implications for transition from school to adult life and the specific implications for students with visual impairments who have multiple disabilities

🔑 Assessment, planning, and instructional strategies to support an effective transition

🔑 The important role that families have in planning for transition and strategies to empower families to fulfill this role

🔑 The importance of collaboration with adult services agencies and the school's role in fostering collaboration

---

Madeline turns 16 in a few months. She was born prematurely and has significant vision loss and cerebral palsy. She is able to walk but has significant motor impairment. Madeline communicates well, although her speech may be difficult for those unfamiliar with her to understand. She requires support and adaptation to access the general education curriculum.

Her counselor meets with Madeline and her family a few weeks before the Individualized Education Program (IEP) meeting at which they will discuss transition planning to help them prepare. Madeline and her family also did some planning at home. At first it is hard for them to describe their vision for life after school. While her parents imagine further education, Madeline thinks she might like to work after high school. However, because she has no real work experience, Madeline is not sure what kind of job she wants.

Transportation is also a significant barrier. Madeline rides on a special bus to and from school. For any other activity, she depends on her parents to drive her. Madeline's social life mostly revolves around her family; she does very little on her own.

The more they talk, the clearer a vision for life after school becomes. At the transition planning IEP meeting, Madeline is able to say that she wants to work after high school and maybe take some adult education classes. She wants to live in her own apartment and travel by herself to meet friends at the mall. She also wants to be thin and fit. Madeline's family supports her vision.

The vision for life after school helps the IEP team to identify several areas where Madeline needs focused instruction. Training in orientation and mobility (O&M) becomes a high priority so that Madeline can develop the skills necessary to use public transportation. Supporting Madeline's desire to learn more about jobs she might want is also identified as an area for exploration. Madeline's family agree to help her become more independent at home so she can begin to develop the skills she will need to live on her own. Finally, Madeline enrolls in an exercise class at the local YMCA.

During Thomas's sophomore year in high school his counselor starts talking to him about his goals for the future. Thomas has Norrie syndrome and is experiencing increasing hearing loss in addition to blindness. He has some good academic skills, particularly in braille and reading. However, his math skills are very weak and many of his other academic skills are well below grade level. Thomas and his family always planned for him to attend college like his siblings, but Thomas's grades might not allow that to happen.

The previous summer, Thomas attended an outreach program that helped him try out several different kinds of jobs. He worked in a factory, an office, and in the Braille and Talking Book Library. He hated the factory because the ambient noise made it almost impossible for him to hear. The office provided a pleasant work environment, but the work required too many repetitive tasks that Thomas found boring. *His favorite placement was in the library, where the quiet environment allowed him to utilize his skills in braille and offered him opportunities to have conversations with co-workers.*

The counselor decides that it might be helpful to form a person-centered planning team for Thomas. The team includes Thomas, his parents, his brother and sister, his teacher, and a counselor from the Commission for the Blind. A neighbor who has always liked Thomas and who shares his interest in birds also joined the team. Over time, the team grows and changes. Thomas is able to be an active member as long as people pay attention to his need for an assistive listening device and only one person speaks at a time.

The team develops a vision for Thomas's future based on his strengths, interests, and preferences. The vision includes continuing education at a community college, volunteer work at the Audubon Society, part-time work in a quiet office, and continuing to live with his family. Thomas thinks that he might like to live on his own at some time in the future, but not immediately after high school. The team develops a series of post-school goals for Thomas.

Each team member contributes to a successful outcome. Thomas's mother works at the local community college and is able to help Thomas find support to audit classes and get help from the student services center to travel back and forth to classroom buildings. In addition, Thomas receives intensive O&M training from the state Commission for the Blind.

Thomas's neighbor, a volunteer at the Audubon Society, is able to introduce Thomas to his contacts there and help him secure a volunteer position. He also offers to give Thomas a ride back and forth since their work schedules coincided.

Thomas's vocational rehabilitation counselor helps him locate part-time work in an office. Although some of the tasks are repetitive, Thomas is gaining skills and work experiences that will help him in the future.

Deidre is legally blind and has health issues, including a seizure disorder. She had a number of work experiences as part of her high school work-study program. During that time, Deidre learned that having a repetitive and predictable job was less stressful for her. She also liked having control of her work space. Deidre has to convince members of her transition team that these characteristics are more important to her than a higher salary or more intellectually challenging work.

After graduation, Deirdre gets a job in a hotel laundry managing the linens area. Although the job is not glamorous, it offers Deidre exactly what she wanted, predictability and control of her environment. Advocating for herself was a critical factor in allowing Deidre to have an outcome that supported her preferences.

For the past 25 years, as students with disabilities who benefited from federal legislation granting them the right to free appropriate public education and received special education services have graduated or aged out of school, transition has been an area of concern for them. Achieving good outcomes for students after they leave high school requires careful planning that begins early, while students are in elementary grades. The Individuals with Disabilities Education Improvement Act of 2004 (IDEA) has very specific requirements related to transition planning.

Planning for life after school is critical for students with visual impairments and multiple disabilities. Making decisions about post-secondary school housing, education, and career choices is important for every student. For students with disabilities, these decisions may be challenging and may require more structured and thoughtful planning than for typical students. Students with visual impairments and multiple disabilities face further barriers and require even more careful, strategic planning in order to achieve successful post-school outcomes. This planning needs to begin early and should be an integral part of every student's IEP.

This chapter will describe a process for developing a transition plan and will detail the areas that must be included, such as instructional education and training, career and employment, community experience and participation, and post-school adult living. It will review the importance of including the transition goals and objectives in the IEP to ensure that it is a major focus of the educational program. The chapter will also describe the important role of the teacher of students with visual impairments in the process of transition planning—a role critical to ensuring that the student with visual impairments and multiple disabilities is prepared for graduation day.

REQUIREMENTS FOR TRANSITION FROM SCHOOL TO ADULT LIFE

Students with visual impairments and multiple disabilities have a legal right to free appropriate public education, as described in earlier chapters. IDEA guarantees that these students have access to the services they need to achieve that education. However, those guarantees end when a student graduates from high school or ages out of special education services, at age 21 or 22 in most states. Beyond high school, very few services are mandated. Students and their families exit the familiar world of comprehensive educational services to enter a fragmented world of adult services that may be dependent on funding, eligibility criteria, and time-limited services. The move into postsecondary services can be challenging and confusing for students and their families. Therefore it is critical that planning for this profound change is comprehensive and begins early.

Although students go through other transitions during their educational careers, for the purposes of this chapter, *transition* can be defined as the movement from the relatively sheltered environment of school to adult life beyond this environment. The world of disability services outside of the school system is typically not well understood by students, families, and other members of the educational team. From early childhood through age 21, services are mandated and delivered in a comprehensive package. It is often difficult for families and teachers to understand how substantially different the world is beyond the classroom. The student who ages out of special education services does not change significantly on his or her 22nd birthday, but although the student's needs may be the same, the system is very different. Adult services are not mandated. Usually, the only guarantee is that the student may apply for services and receive an assessment. Eligibility requirements may also be different. A student who is considered visually impaired by his or her school may not meet the criteria established for adult services. Even if the student is deemed eligible, services are often dependent on funding. Waiting lists are not uncommon.

In the most recent reauthorization of IDEA in 2004, the language around transition was strengthened. IEP teams are required to talk to families and students about their desired post-school outcomes. Goals to support these desired outcomes must be included in the IEP. The initial legislation for special education, the Education for All Handicapped Children Act of 1975, called for *access* to services for all children; IDEA 1997 described an *outcome-oriented process*; IDEA 2004 focuses on a *results-oriented process*. As a result of this shift in focus, school districts are being held accountable for effective transition planning and, in turn, are seeking assistance from teachers of students with visual impairments to define and develop effective transition plans for students with visual impairments including those with multiple disabilities.

IDEA Regulations on Secondary Transition

IDEA 2004 includes a range of transition services and requirements (34 C.F.R § 300.320[b] and 300.321[b]).

Transition Planning Start Date

Planning for transition must begin no later than the school year in which the student turns 16. In many states, planning may begin as early as age 14, particularly when students have multiple or complex disabilities.

Student Participation

Students must be invited to participate in the IEP meeting if transition planning will be discussed. Not all students with visual impairments and multiple disabilities will be comfortable or have the skills required to participate in formal IEP meetings. It is very important that the IEP team develop a strategy to have the student's opinions included in these discussions. One strategy that has proven successful includes having a smaller pre-meeting with the student, the student's family, and a few key IEP team members. At this meeting, language and vocabulary can be controlled and the student can be encouraged to ask questions. If the student's ability to communicate and attend precludes direct participation, some teams have included the student symbolically by having a large portrait of him or her in the meeting room. In some instances, the student's family and close friends will need to speak on the student's behalf at the IEP meeting.

Age of Majority

When a student turns 15, the IEP team must inform parents that the student will be considered an adult and a decision maker when he or she reaches the age of majority. Most states have determined that 18 is the age of majority but, since this is determined by state law, this is not true for all states (see Sidebar 15.1). The idea that their child may be considered competent to make the decisions that come with the age of majority is a difficult concept for families, who are used to protecting their children. In some cases, the family may want to explore maintaining guardianship (see Sidebar 15.2). Families may need to seek advice from a lawyer who specializes in this area of the law. There are many options, including limited guardianship, that can be considered. Financial planning is another issue with which a specialist can assist. In other instances, this reminder can spur the family and the whole IEP team to explore ways to help prepare the student for this upcoming responsibility.

Assessment Requirements

When a student is in this transition phase, beginning no later than age 16, the IEP must include assessments to help identify the skills the student needs to achieve his or her desired post-school outcomes. These may include formal vocational assessments, interest inventories, or independent living assessments, along with informal assessments such as interviews, observations, and portfolios. The assessments needed to inform the transition planning process should be included in

Age of Majority

Maureen P. Reardon

Generally, each state has the right to establish the rights and responsibilities of adulthood. In most states, that means the implementation of certain civil rights (such as the right to vote and the necessity to register for the military draft), the ability to contract (to enter into agreements for the purchase of items of value, such as a home or automobile, to apply for and receive credit cards, to enter into marriage, and the like), to make the decisions accorded to adults (to make medical decisions, to enter into personal relationships—including the decision to be or not to be sexually active—to make educational decisions, and so on) and, of course, the right to implement the decisions made following these examples.

Assessing the needs of an individual in the context of his or her plan for adult living is a highly individualized process. State laws vary on what constitutes legal capacity and incapacity, and most states have processes to ensure that people with disabilities are permitted to exercise their civil and personal rights. It is important to acknowledge that parents know their children (whether they have disabilities or don't) and that different parents or guardians have different dreams and hopes for their children. Those dreams and hopes are deeply affected by the specials needs of a given child or young adult. IEP teams and families need to be well aware of the needs of a given student before the student reaches the age of majority, or the age at which he or she is legally considered an adult.

The IEP team should also discuss issues of legal capacity, asking questions such as:

- Will this student make wise financial decisions, or does he or she need the guidance of another adult?
- Will this student live on his or her own, or will he or she need a group home setting?
- Is the student going to college, to some kind of vocational training, or will he or she fill his or her life with volunteer work and community-based experiences?
- Is this student capable of traveling in the community?
- Does the student have the intellectual capacity to understand medical information and make informed medical choices?
- Can this student manage prescribed medications?
- What kind of assistance does this student need?
- Does the student understand that issues of his or her personal safety and financial security may require someone else's aid?
- What does the student understand about human sexuality, and what is the likelihood that the student will make good decisions about his or her own behavior?

- What can a parent, guardian, or responsible adult do if it appears that a young adult is vulnerable, or is incapable of understanding at a level that gives him or her the opportunity to make good decisions?

For many young people, making good decisions is a process of trial and error—and a young adult with a disability is no more or less able to engage in that trial and error process successfully than a typical young adult. If a young adult has a severe cognitive disability, the court should be informed that the individual is not, or may not be, capable of understanding and signing a power of attorney (see Sidebar 15.2).

Sidebar 15.2

Protections for Students with Disabilities: Powers of Attorney, Conservatorships, and Guardianships

Maureen P. Reardon

There are several options for protections for students with disabilities who may need assistance with decision making. Typically, these options include powers of attorney, conservatorships, or guardianships.

Powers of Attorney

In considering what to do for students with disabilities who will need assistance and support in decision making as adults, a straightforward method is for a young adult to select a person to act for him or her by signing a document appointing an "agent" or "attorney in fact." There are limitations to this avenue, as discussed below, although it is a primary avenue for consideration. Any competent individual can sign a power of attorney, appointing someone to act as his or her "attorney in fact." That is, a student can appoint someone he or she trusts to manage certain tasks for him or her. For example, a student might sign a financial power of attorney allowing someone to manage his or her finances, a personal care power of attorney directing someone to manage his or her personal care, or a health care power of attorney, allowing someone to make medical decisions on his or her behalf.

Health care powers of attorney have particular importance. These documents appoint someone (a health care agent) to make medical decisions when a person is incapable of making such decisions, instructing the health care agent about the ill person's wishes, and even give instructions on end-of-life decisions.

Details about a person's health care and medical records are among the most private information that exists about an individual. For students with disabilities, signing

(continued)

a health care power of attorney may mean their health care agent is entitled to the student's health care information, diagnosis, treatment, disclosures, and the like. This allows medical professionals to share the student's health care information and decisions with the health care agent, who is then able to support the student in understanding his or her condition and treatment options and exercising various options with better information and the support of a trusted individual. If the person selected as the health care agent is not related to the student, it is unlikely that medical staff will share any information unless permitted to do so in writing.

Limitations of Powers of Attorney

Note that it is stated above that any *competent* individual can sign such a power of attorney. One question, then, is whether a student with an intellectual disability is competent to sign a power of attorney. In some states, an application for managing the affairs of another (discussed in the next section) includes questions about why signing a power of attorney instead would be insufficient (for example, California Probate Code § 1821[a][3], alternatives to conservatorship). It is important to find out the extent to which powers of attorney are available avenues for a student with disabilities in a particular state or locale. For example, what are the requirements for understanding the power of attorney being granted? People with what kinds of disabilities may utilize such a power? Parents will need to determine whether powers of attorney will suffice in the state in which they reside.

If powers of attorney are not available or will not be effective because of an individual student's lack of competency to exercise his or her own rights, parents, relatives, friends, and concerned adults can consider guardianships or conservatorships.

Guardianships or Conservatorships

Each state sets its own process for obtaining a guardianship or conservatorship (that is, a proceeding in a court to appoint a person to act on behalf of a person with a disability). It can be a "paper intensive" process, requiring notice to interested persons, a full statement of the need for the appointment, and a formal request for the orders the guardian or conservator is seeking. Some states will automatically appoint an attorney for the student with disabilities, who can and will object to certain orders unless there is a strong showing for the need for those orders. It can also be an expensive process. Each state determines its own requirements for appointment of a guardian or conservator, and it is wise for families to consult a local attorney familiar with the process and requirements.

The driving force in any decision to seek a guardianship or conservatorship of a student with a disability is the protection of the student, and like all decisions involving students with exceptional needs, it is a highly individualized process. For some families, having a child who is blind triggers all sorts of protective instincts, and yet helping a student achieve their highest level of personal independence is a primary function of individualized educational planning. Helping students to make their own decisions is a vital learning process. Parents, educators, IEP teams, and the visually impaired students all have a voice in this process, and IEP team meetings are excellent forums for discussion and decision making at this critical stage in development. It is particularly important that educators and families discuss these issues openly, and in time to make and implement good decisions.

The information presented here does not constitute legal advice and is for informational purposes only. The law varies widely from state to state, and consultation with a local, licensed attorney is recommended.

the transition plan. Along with indicating what assessments are needed, the team will need to identify when each assessment is needed in order to best inform the transition planning process. The teacher of students with visual impairments plays an important role in identifying what assessments are appropriate for a student with a visual impairment including those with multiple disabilities.

Consultations

In addition, the IEP team must determine whether consultation with adult service agencies is needed and how such consultation will be obtained. For students with visual impairments and multiple disabilities, often more than one adult service agency will need to become involved. The school may need to develop interagency agreements in order to meet the transition needs of students with visual impairments and multiple disabilities. Here again is a place in which the teacher of students with visual impairments has a significant role. The teacher of students with visual impairments will want to develop relationships with the agencies that serve adults with visual impairments and share the information he or she obtains through these relationships with the rest of the educational team.

CHALLENGES FOR STUDENTS WITH VISUAL AND MULTIPLE DISABILITIES

As students with visual impairments and multiple disabilities begin the transition process, they face a number of special challenges, which may include some or all of the following:

- limited understanding of what it means to be an adult
- lack of role models
- splinter skills and knowledge gaps
- lack of job-readiness experiences
- limited understanding of social expectations and behavioral norms
- limited opportunities to be self-sufficient

Transition planning is especially critical for students with visual impairments and multiple disabilities. As has been mentioned numerous times in this text, students with visual impairments do not have access to the same level of incidental learning that their sighted peers do. Having multiple disabilities can compound this problem. Other students learn a great deal about what it means to be an adult and what adults do by observing their parents, neighbors, and teachers. Students who do not have access to this information may not have a clear understanding of what it means to be an adult in our society. Students with visual impairments and multiple disabilities are also much less likely to find role models in the adult community in whom they can see themselves. Because many things must be taught directly to these students in order for them to learn skills, they may have significant gaps in knowledge and splinter skills. *Splinter skills* refer to the ability to do a specific task without being able to generalize to other tasks. For example, a student may be able to put on a jacket with buttons but cannot generalize the buttoning skill to other clothing items. Careful planning and assessment needs to occur to help identify these gaps in skills.

It is likely that students with visual impairments and multiple disabilities have not had access to some of the typical job-readiness experiences that their sighted peers may have had, such as having a paper route, running a lemonade stand, or babysitting a neighbor's child. Experiences such as these help students imagine themselves as workers and responsible young adults.

These students may also lack access to feedback about social expectations and behavioral norms. Sighted teens learn a great deal about their own behavior through nonverbal feedback from others. A disparaging look from a peer goes a long way toward re-

shaping behavior. Students with visual impairments and multiple disabilities need to develop strategies to get feedback about their social behaviors. They also need honest, direct feedback from trusted friends, teachers, and family members. (See Chapter 10 for further information on social skills.)

Finally, because of the impacts of vision loss and other disabilities, it is likely that these students have had fewer opportunities to learn to be independent and self-sufficient. Providing opportunities to practice these skills should be a major focus of the transition goals in the IEP.

PLANNING FOR TRANSITION

Although developing a good, comprehensive transition plan may not address all the issues in the adult service system, such as lack of sufficient funding or limited service options, it can help prepare the student and his or her family for the changes ahead. The transition plan should address the student in a holistic way, looking at all aspects of his or her future post-school life. Areas to be addressed include:

- further training (academic, vocational, or both)
- employment
- housing or independent living arrangements
- transportation
- recreation and social life

Although the primary decision makers in this process are the student and his or her family, the teacher of students with visual impairments can play a significant role in helping to shape a transition plan that addresses the student's unique needs and strengths. The teacher of students with visual impairment's knowledge of strategies to enhance a student's ability to be as independent as possible in self-care, to travel safely within environments, and to utilize technology to access job tasks are just a few of the ways in which he or she can contribute.

A major obstacle that students and their families may face relates to limited expectations. For many years, the unemployment rate for individuals with disabilities has been extremely high. That rate is even higher for individuals with visual impairments. It is significantly higher still for those with multiple disabilities (Carter, Austin, & Trainor, 2012; Cavenaugh & Giesen, 2012; Connors, Curtis, Wall Emerson, & Dormitorio, 2014; McDonnall, 2011; McDonnall & O'Mally, 2012). Many people in education and adult services know and are affected by these statistics, with the result being lowered expectations for employment for transition-age youth. It is important for students and their families to have a clear vision of the future and to maintain focus on their vision while acknowledging the realities of the current employment situation.

Research has demonstrated that there are identifiable factors that affect successful employment outcomes for youth with visual impairment or blindness, including those with multiple disabilities. In an analysis of research, McDonnall and Crudden (2009) identified several critical factors that contribute to a successful employment outcome, including work experience, academic competence, self-

determination, use of assistive technology, and whether or not the student feels empowered to determine his or her future. To the extent possible, transition teams should address these factors in their planning. While a student's complex needs may place limits on areas like academic competence or empowerment, there are still many ways for teachers and families to help the student develop skills.

Specific instructional areas that must be included in the student's transitional IEP include:

- work experience
- academic competence (supplementary skills)
- self-determination
- assistive technology
- empowerment

See Sidebar 15.3 for suggestions for instructional strategies in these areas.

Self-determination empowers each of us to participate and succeed in daily life.

Being empowered provides an individual with the skills to determine his or her needs and wishes. For many students with visual impairments and multiple disabilities, self-determination is challenging. Because these students have multiple challenges, they often have fewer opportunities to make decisions. While a typical fifth grader may make hundreds of little decisions throughout the day, such as what to wear, whether or not to join in a game of tag, or what part of his or her lunch to trade, students with visual impairments and multiple disabilities often have these choices made for them. It is imperative

Instructional Strategies for Teaching Employment Transition Skills

The following are some suggestions for experiences that can help students attain skills in specific instructional areas throughout their school career:

Work Experience

- Elementary school: performing school jobs such as collecting attendance and delivering mail; feeding a pet at home.
- Middle school: volunteering at a food pantry, participating in a community service project.
- High school: having a part-time job, assuming responsibility for a household task (such as doing laundry or making lunches).

Academic Competence (Supplementary Skills)

- Elementary school: learning to follow a schedule, successfully managing transitions.
- Middle school: getting ready for school as independently as possible, gathering materials needed for class, learning to use assistive technology and accommodations.
- High school: preparing for classes as independently as possible, requesting necessary accommodations.

Self-Determination

- Elementary school: developing communication skills, making choices with consequences.
- Middle school: learning to negotiate, having opportunities to make personal decisions.
- High school: communicating needs and preferences, learning to be persuasive.

Assistive Technology

- Elementary school: learning to use assistive devices, understanding cause and effect, using mobility aids.
- Middle school: understanding when to use which device, expanding repertoire of technology.
- High school: managing and fully utilizing assistive technology.

Engendering Empowerment

- Elementary school: teachers, family, and peers honoring student's choices and communication.
- Middle school: teachers, family, and peers giving responsibilities to the student that are similar to peers; honoring student's choices and decisions.
- High school: teachers, family, and peers having age-appropriate expectations and fostering as much independence as possible.

that meaningful choice making, decision making, and goal setting are included in a student's life at school and at home. In addition, learning the consequences of choices and decisions is also an important part of becoming self-determined. These students need opportunities to take risks and make mistakes.

ASSESSMENT FOR TRANSITION

Planning for transition includes assessment of the student's abilities. The assessment process can include both formal and informal assessments. The teacher of students with visual impairments should ensure that appropriate assessments are included to address the needs of students with visual impairments, including the following:

- functional vision assessment (see Chapter 3)
- learning media assessment (see Chapter 3)
- orientation and mobility assessment (see Chapter 9)
- independent living skills assessment (see Chapter 11)
- assessment of compensatory skills (see Chapter 3)
- assistive technology assessment (see Chapter 12)
- social skills assessment (see Chapter 10)
- vocational skills assessment (discussed in this chapter)
- self-determination skills assessment (see Chapter 10)
- sensory skills assessment (see Chapter 3)

Sitlington and Clark (2001) suggest that transition assessment should answer these three basic questions:

1. What skills and abilities does the student have currently?
2. What does the student want to accomplish?
3. How can the student reach these goals?

Formal Assessment

The typical areas for assessment for transition planning include academic assessment as well as vocational and independent living assessments. These assessments can be conducted via formal and informal assessment tools. Formal measures are often less effective for students with visual impairments and multiple disabilities (Rowland, 2009) and require students to have greater academic ability than students with visual impairments and multiple disabilities possess. Informal assessments can include checklists, interest inventories, portfolios, person-centered planning, observation, rating scales, and data collection.

Informal Assessment

Today the two most common approaches to informal assessment are portfolio assessment and person-centered planning, which are quite effective and appropriate for students with visual impairments and multiple disabilities.

Portfolio Assessment

A portfolio assessment is a systematic collection of a student's work and related material that depicts his or her activities, accomplishments, and achievements in one or more school subjects. The goal is to help students assemble portfolios that illustrate their talents, represent their capabilities, and tell their stories of school achievement (Venn, 2000, pp. 530–531).

Portfolio assessments offer a good alternative to more standardized measures for seeking answers for this student population to the three questions a transition assessment needs to answer. Portfolios can be used as a way to demonstrate a student's progress toward IEP goals and objectives.

There are many different styles of portfolio assessments, and they can easily be customized to match a particular student's characteristics. Regardless of the style of portfolio used, a portfolio should capture in some way the student's current functioning. This may be done with a short biographical description that includes the student's interests and skills as well as the areas in which the student needs to enhance skills. The portfolio should also include some future goals for the student and some paths the student could pursue to achieve those goals. Portfolios can be "living" documents that demonstrate achievement over time. This assessment needs to begin early in the transition process in order to have an impact on instruction.

One very effective use of portfolios is to demonstrate the skills a student has acquired in a series of work-study placements. The portfolio can include photographs and descriptions demonstrating how work tasks were completed, the student's reflections of what skills he or she developed, and the student's assessment of the strengths and benefits of the job as well as the difficulties and barriers encountered.

Portfolio assessments and portfolio records of students' experiences can also enhance students' empowerment. Particularly for students with limited communication ability, the portfolio can serve as a record of their experiences and their reaction to them. Portfolios can also make clear what kinds of supports and accommodations enable a student to be successful. Students with visual impairments and multiple disabilities often use story boxes and experience stories as part of literacy instruction. These stories describe the student's experiences in pictures, objects, words, or a combination, as a way to help the student recall an activity and share it with others (see Chapter 8 for more on story boxes and experience stories). In much the same way, portfolios can be set up to offer students a way to talk about their skills, preferences, and experiences. Items to incorporate in a portfolio include (Bridgeo, Gicklhorn, & Zatta, 2007):

- personal information
- preferences, strengths, skills, likes, and dislikes
- photographs of work experiences showing environments, adaptations, and modifications
- descriptions about how the student interacts with coworkers and how the student travels in the work environment

Person-Centered Planning

Person-centered planning is another type of informal assessment. Person-centered planning calls for a collaborative approach that puts the student with a disability at the center of the planning process and in control as much as is feasible. "Person-centered transition assessment focuses on assisting youths with disabilities in discovering their unique preferences, experiences, skills, and support needs" (Kochhar-Bryant & Greene, 2009, p. 243). A hallmark of person-centered planning is the involvement of the student in making decisions about his or her future. In most instances, this happens in partnership with her family. "Family involvement has emerged as one of the few consistent indicators leading to successful adult outcomes" (Bakken & Obiakor, 2008, p. 23).

A critical feature of person-centered planning is the involvement of a skilled facilitator. The person-centered planning team usually includes the student; his or her family, friends, and extended family; school personnel; community members; and a skilled facilitator. (Sidebar 15.4 explains more about the person-centered planning team and how it differs from the IEP team.) The group is charged with developing a positive description of the student, focusing on his or her strengths, interests, and preferences. Together, the person-centered planning team develops a vision for the future and an action plan for realizing that vision. Often, the facilitator will help the group develop these items using charts with images rather than lists. Making the information accessible and engaging for all team members is critical. The success of the method relies on group support and involvement. Sidebar 15.5 provides an example of information that was compiled by the person-centered planning team for Thomas, one of the students introduced at the beginning of this chapter.

✎ Sidebar 15.4

The Difference between an IEP Team and a Person-Centered Planning Team

While a number of the same people may participate in a student's IEP and person-centered planning teams, the roles and focuses of these teams are different—they are often complementary, but they are not the same.

The IEP team focuses on the Individualized Education Program, its implementation, and the student's progress on goals. Meetings of the IEP team are somewhat formal and are governed by laws and procedures. Certain members are required (a parent or guardian, a general education teacher, a special education teacher, a representative of the local education agency, an individual who can interpret evaluation results, and, when appropriate, the student). Ultimately, the IEP team is responsible for ensuring that the student receives a free appropriate public education.

The person-centered planning team usually comprises a group of individuals who have volunteered to participate. With the exception of the facilitator and the focus person (the student), there aren't any strict rules for membership or limits on participation. The group comes together to help the student attain the goals and dreams that he or she identifies. Membership is often fluid; people join and leave the team as the individual's dreams and goals develop and change.

🔑 Sidebar 15.5

Information Compiled by the Person-Centered Planning Team for Thomas

Strengths/Likes
- reading/braille
- quiet environments
- tasks that require thinking/problem solving
- talking with friends and coworkers
- birds
- people who take the time to use his FM system

Challenges/Dislikes
- math
- noisy environments
- repetitive tasks
- feeling isolated
- feeling insecure about travelling

Vision for the Future (Short-term, Post-school)
- part-time work
- taking one or two classes
- developing confidence in O&M skills
- spending time with friends
- perusing hobbies and interests

IMMEDIATE PLAN

What	Lead Person	Supports
Audit classes at community college	Mom	Student support services
Travel to classes	O&M instructor	Student volunteers
Office job	Vocational rehabilitation counselor	Coworkers
Volunteer at Audubon	Neighbor or friend	Other volunteers

Person-centered planning is much more successful when the student is actively involved. Figuring out the best strategies for involving the student is the responsibility of the whole team. Often, students need training, support, and practice to learn to advocate for themselves. It can be more challenging when the student is nonverbal, has significant cognitive limitations, or both.

Additional Areas to Include in Transition Assessment

Another important area to include in transition assessment is the student's need for assistive technology (see Chapter 12). This should include domains where assistive technology could enhance the student's independent functioning as well as a plan to provide training and instruction for the student to develop skills to use these technologies. Because technology changes so rapidly, this part of the assessment should be revisited throughout the transition period.

Assessments of adaptive behavior (such as the Vineland Adaptive Behavior Scales, Sparrow, Cicchetti, & Saulnier, 2016; see Chapter 3) and independent living skills, although not required for all students, are especially important for students with visual impairments and multiple disabilities. Adaptive behavior refers to an individual's typical performance of the day-to-day activities required for personal and social self-sufficiency. Adaptive strategies to accomplish tasks are vital for these students to possess. Specific training in O&M and independent living skills is also very important (see Chapters 9 and 11). While many students who are visually impaired and have additional physical or cognitive limitations may not use traditional O&M techniques, they can use adapted strategies that can greatly improve their ability to travel within certain environments.

DEVELOPING THE TRANSITION PLAN

The transition plan leads to the provision of transition services. IDEA (2004, 34 C.F.R § 300.43[a]) defines transition services as:

> A coordinated set of activities for a child with a disability that:
>
> - Is designed to be within a results-oriented process, that is focused on improving the academic and functional achievement of the child with a disabil-

ity to facilitate the child's movement from school to post-school activities, including postsecondary education, vocational education, integrated employment (including supported employment), continuing and adult education, adult services, independent living, or community participation;

- Is based on the individual child's needs, taking into account the child's strengths, preferences, and interests; and
- Includes
  - ○ Instruction;
  - ○ Related services;
  - ○ Community experiences;
  - ○ The development of employment and other post-school adult living objectives; and,
  - ○ If appropriate, acquisition of daily living skills and functional vocational evaluation.

Each state has developed its own transition planning form which requires the team to gather the information listed. A transition planning form provides the IEP team and others with a way to document the team's transition discussion. Sidebar 15.6 provides an example of the information that is important to include in the transition plan.

Components of the Transition Plan

There are three sections to the transition plan:

1. postsecondary vision
2. disability needs
3. action plan

Resource Material to Be Gathered for the Transition Planning Form

This list of resource material is meant to be a reference tool to be used by the student, family, and other transition team members when filling out the transition planning form and creating the transition plan. Each state will have its own form to be completed, but the discussion should focus on the areas listed here. The plan consists of three parts: Postsecondary Vision, Disability-Related Needs, and Action Plan.

Postsecondary Vision

This section should correspond with the vision statement on the IEP. In collaboration with the student and family, consider the student's preferences and interests, and the desired outcomes for postsecondary education or training, employment, and adult living. The following options are examples of what may be included.

Education
- college
- community college
- technical training programs
- apprentice programs
- military
- job training programs
- job corps programs
- adult education

Employment/Day Program
- full-time employment
- part-time employment
- supported employment
- volunteer work
- work-study programs
- internships
- sheltered work
- day habilitation

Housing
- independent living/own apartment
- apartment living with part-time supports
- subsidized housing
- apartment/group home living with full-time supports
- adult foster care
- home with family

Other
- transportation
- leisure and recreation
- community participation

Disability-Related Needs

This section should correspond with the goals and objectives section of the IEP. Identify the skills (disability related) that require IEP goals and/or related services. Consider all skills (disability related) necessary for the student to achieve his or her postsecondary vision. *Use the Disability-Related Needs Checklist (Figure 15.1) when developing this section.*

Identify needs for access to expertise in the specialized areas of disability-specific skills (the expanded core curriculum), which ensure access and participation within the general educational curriculum for students with blindness and visual impairments, and deaf-blindness, including those with multiple disabilities. These disability-specific skills of the expanded core curriculum include areas of assessment mandated in IDEA 2004 that address the unique needs of students with blindness, visual impairment, and deafblindness. Areas include:

- *Functional vision assessment*—to determine how the student's visual impairment affects his or her functioning
- *Learning media assessment*—to determine most appropriate media (regular print, large print, braille, auditory, or some combination) for students to access the curriculum
- *Orientation and mobility assessment*—to determine age-appropriate movement, safety skills, and independent travel in familiar and unfamiliar settings in school and community settings
- *Activities of daily living*—to determine age-appropriate abilities and independence in functional life skills
- *Compensatory skills*—skills needed to compensate for vision loss
- *Assistive technology*
- *Social skills*
- *Self-advocacy*
- *Vocational skills*
- *Sensory skills*—efficient use of visual, auditory, and tactile senses

Action Plan

Outline how the student can develop self-determination skills and be prepared both academically and functionally to transition to post-school activities in order to achieve his or her postsecondary vision. Indicate how special educators, family members, adult service providers, or others in the community will help the student develop the necessary skills.

Instruction

Is there a course of study or specific skill development needed that will help the student reach his or her postsecondary vision?

- self-advocacy skills
- disability awareness
- communication skills
- self-disclosure
- organizational skills
- study and time management
- test-taking and note-taking skills
- college exploration or research
- rights and responsibilities after high school
- identification of learning styles, strengths, and needs
- academic courses (such as math, science, English language arts, foreign language, social studies)

Employment

Are there employment opportunities and/or specific skills that will help the student reach his or her postsecondary vision?

- instruction on how to find a job/job-finding strategies
- completing a job application
- interviewing skills
- learning about employer expectations

(continued)

(Sidebar 15.6 continued)

- learning employability skills (such as punctuality, appropriate attire, cleanliness, hygiene)
- connection to vocational rehabilitation
- participating in job shadowing
- locating and attending job fairs

Community Experiences

Are there certain types of community experiences that will help the student achieve his or her postsecondary vision?

- registering to vote and/or selective service
- participation in clubs or organizations in the community based around interests
- obtaining a driver's license or ID
- accessing public or community transportation

Post-school Adult Living

Are there certain types of adult living experiences that will help the student achieve his or her postsecondary vision?

Acquisition of Daily Living Skills

Does the student need additional instruction in daily living skills to achieve his or her postsecondary vision?

- money management (balancing check book, budgeting)
- self-care and hygiene
- personal safety
- telephone skills
- emergency preparedness
- computer skills
- meal preparation
- housekeeping skills

Postsecondary Vision for the Student

This statement should correspond with the vision statement on the IEP. In collaboration with the student and family, the statement should consider the student's preferences and interests and include the desired outcomes for postsecondary education and training, employment, and adult living. It is important that sufficient time be spent formulating the vision, as this will drive the transition process.

Description of Disability-Related Needs

This section should include the transition assessment findings and correspond with the goals on the IEP. The disability-related skills that require IEP goals and related services should be identified in this section. Careful attention should be paid to including skill areas that fall under the expanded core curriculum (ECC). The Disability-Related Needs Checklist (see Figure 15.1) includes each of the nine areas of the ECC. Members of the transition planning team should complete the checklist by indicating the student's instructional needs and ensuring that those needs are addressed in the IEP.

Action Plan

The action plan should outline how the student can develop self-determination skills and be prepared both academically and functionally to transition to post-school activities in

Figure 15.1
Disability-Related Needs Checklist

DISABILITY-RELATED NEEDS CHECKLIST

This checklist has been designed for transition teams to use as they are developing a transition plan. Using this checklist, the team identifies the priority areas of needs to be addressed in the IEP. The team must consider the disability-related skills that require IEP goals or related services for the student to achieve his or her post-school vision.

Compensatory or Functional Academic (Including Communication)
☐ Community-based, real-life instruction
☐ Literacy
☐ Numeracy
☐ Time awareness
☐ Communication system

Career Education
☐ Job searching
☐ Career exploration
　☐ Direct work experience
　☐ Knowledge of jobs
　☐ Job preferences, aptitudes, and strengths
☐ Work skills
☐ Behavior
☐ Compensation
☐ Volunteerism and community service
☐ Concept development

Orientation and Mobility
☐ Indoor travel
☐ Outdoor travel
☐ Transportation
☐ Accessing community resources

☐ Using technology for travel
☐ Self-advocacy and communication within the community
☐ Ability to train others regarding assistance needed
☐ Safety in public, interacting with public
☐ Ability to evacuate
☐ Use of travel devices

Independent Living
☐ Self-care (personal grooming, including clothing management)
☐ Home management
☐ Finances
☐ Meal prep
☐ Awareness of living options
☐ Management of support providers
☐ Medical and health management
☐ Mealtime
☐ Organization
☐ Ability to prioritize
☐ Ability to make choices

Social Interaction
☐ Expressing wants and needs
☐ Functional communication
☐ Recognizing other's needs
☐ Emotional regulation
☐ Negotiating conflict
☐ Appropriate body language and comportment
☐ Discriminating behavior for the situation
☐ Boundary issues
☐ Conversational skills

(continued)

549

(Figure 15.1 continued)

☐ Following guidelines and rules
☐ Developing friendships

Recreation and Leisure

☐ Developing interests
☐ Independent leisure skills
☐ Awareness of community resources
☐ Transportation skills and resources
☐ Social networking opportunities
☐ Cooperative leisure skills
☐ Fitness
☐ Time management

Assistive Technology

☐ Computer
  ☐ Communication (Internet, e-mail, word processing, specific software, hardware, adaptive software)
☐ Adaptive equipment
  ☐ Wheelchairs
  ☐ Speech devices
  ☐ Switches
☐ Print and picture media
☐ Use of computer software and voice-output devices
☐ Low vision devices
☐ Braille and written communication

☐ Devices for reading access and download
☐ Devices for independent living
☐ Maintaining assistive technology
☐ Vendor access

Sensory Efficiency

☐ O&M aids
☐ Auditory devices
☐ Low vision devices
☐ Sensory processing, sensory integration, management
☐ Communication modes and devices
☐ Environmental access and adaptations
☐ Figuring out community resources—awareness and access
☐ Auditory description

Self-Determination

☐ Self-advocacy
☐ Accessing community supports
☐ Awareness of political issues and their impacts on the individual
☐ Identifying needs and the support available to meet those needs
☐ Behavior regulation
☐ Choice making

order to achieve his or her postsecondary vision. The plan should indicate how the educational team, family members, and adult service providers or others in the community will help the student develop the necessary skills. (See Figure 15.2 for a sample action plan form.)

The action plan should address the following areas:

- **Instruction:** Is there a course of study or specific courses needed that will help the student reach his or her postsecondary vision?

- **Employment:** Are there employment opportunities or specific skills that will help the student reach his or her postsecondary vision?

Figure 15.2
Action Plan Form

ACTION PLAN				
Transition Service	Goals	Actions	By Whom and By When	Time Frame
Instruction/ education and training				
Career/ employment/ further education				
Community experiences/ participation				
Post-school adult living				

- **Community experiences:** Are there certain types of community experiences that will help the student reach his or her postsecondary vision?
- **Post-school adult living:** Are there certain independent living skills that will help the student reach his or her postsecondary vision?

The action plan should also include the following information:

- the goals assigned to each area
- the actions needed to meet the instructional goals
- the agency or person responsible
- the time frame

See Figure 15.3 for an example of Madeline's action plan.

Each state is responsible for incorporating these transition mandates into the IEP process, and each state has developed a set of guidelines and forms to meet this requirement. The forms and checklists included in this chapter are simply models and supplementary materials to assist with developing a good transition plan.

Figure 15.3
Madeline's Action Plan

	ACTION PLAN			
Transition Service	**Goals**	**Actions**	**By Whom and by When**	**Time Frame**
Instruction/ education and training	*Madeline would like to explore the possibility of eventually going to community college.*	*Madeline will:* • *identify community colleges that are nearby* • *visit community colleges* • *identify entrance requirements for community colleges* • *take required entrance tests*	*Madeline, parents, teacher of students with visual impairments, general education teacher, guidance counselor*	*Junior and senior years of high school*
Career/ employment/ further education	*Madeline would like to be employed after she finishes high school.*	*Madeline will:* • *have the opportunity to participate in a variety of job exploration activities to identify her strengths and preferences for work* • *complete an interest inventory to assist with identifying types of work that might be most suitable for her interests* • *pursue part-time employment (weekends, summer) in her local community* • *develop a vocational portfolio which will include a resume as well as photos and other items that will support her job search* • *participate in practice interviews to prepare for job interviews*	*Madeline, parents, teacher of students with visual impairments, general education teacher, vocational department, guidance counselor*	*Junior and senior years of high school*

Community experiences/ participation	Madeline would like to take some adult education classes after she graduates from high school.	Madeline will identify the adult education classes available in her community	Madeline, parents, teacher of students with visual impairments, general education teacher, guidance counselor	Junior and senior years of high school
Post-school adult living	Madeline would like to live in her own apartment with staff support. She would like to have a roommate. She would like to develop her independent living skills.	Madeline will continue to develop her: • self-care skills • social skills and self-advocacy skills • money skills including budgeting • household management skills • cooking skills	Madeline, parents, teacher of students with visual impairments, general education teacher, guidance counselor	Junior and senior years of high school

THE ROLE OF THE FAMILY IN PLANNING FOR TRANSITION

It is important for students and their families to know that they alone can define what success means when it comes to a student's life after high school. A student's learning characteristics and skills are only some of the components that go into determining how to define success. The values, hopes, and dreams of the individual family members and the family unit as a whole are all critical elements in determining what a successful post-school outcome is for a particular student. These may be very different for each individual. Employment may

be an important goal for some students, while attaining a high quality of life may be a better goal for others. Supported employment, customized employment, and volunteer work are all possible outcomes. Sidebar 15.7 shows different ways in which "employment" can be interpreted for different students.

Every family needs to be empowered to take a critical role in planning for the transition of a son or daughter. Families, particularly the parents, are often the only consistent members of the IEP team throughout the student's time in school. Families know their family member better than anyone else on the team, and they will be the only team members who travel with the student into life

---

Sidebar 15.7

Success in Life after High School

For some students with visual impairments and multiple disabilities, success means employment after they leave high school. But employment can be defined in a variety of ways:

- Competitive employment: individual works like anyone else in a company and may or may not use adaptive technology; receives competitive wages.
- Supported employment: individual may use a job coach or other adaptation to perform a job.
- Customized employment: individual and employer carve out a job that utilizes the individual's strengths and skills.

- Volunteer work: individual contributes to a community or organization with or without support and accommodations.
- Community-based day activity centers: individual participates in a variety of activities, (creative, recreational, functional) in a group with other adults who have disabilities.

However, successful post-school outcomes include much more than "employment," no matter how it is defined. Being a successful adult includes having meaningful relationships and a comfortable place to live, taking part in recreational activities, and pursuing adult education.

---

beyond school. It is very important to make families feel comfortable expressing their views in planning meetings. Team members need to appreciate the unique and valuable perspective family members bring to the discussion.

Utilizing strategies such as person-centered planning can help families feel empowered. Avoiding jargon and recognizing that titles, roles, and official status have no place in a person-centered meeting can also help. Most important, though, team members need to understand that in the person-centered planning process everyone has something to contribute.

COLLABORATION WITH ADULT SERVICES AGENCIES

One of the biggest adjustments students and their families have to make in the process of transition is to look beyond the IEP team and the school for resources. Students with visual impairments and multiple disabilities often spend at least two decades receiving special education services. Beginning with early intervention, through high school, and often up to age 21, they and their parents have relied on one system to address most of their needs.

Learning to trust other agencies can be difficult and stressful.

Including adult service agencies in transition planning can be significant in helping students and their families make this transition. Schools that have developed collaborative relationships with state vocational rehabilitation agencies, commissions for the blind, and departments of developmental services can greatly assist their students and their students' families in adjusting to life beyond school. An IEP team that understands and can describe the role of these agencies and how they can assist the student, can be the bridge that helps students and their families learn to work with community agencies. Students and their families might find it helpful to begin working with community-based agencies while the student is still in school. Sidebar 15.8 describes some of the agencies and services that individuals may be dealing with after high school.

Although interagency collaboration is specifically called for in IDEA and there are many individual examples of successful interagency collaboration, there is no clearly defined, evidence-based formula for successful interagency collaboration (National Secondary Transition Technical Assistance Center, 2009). Because students with visual impairment and multiple disabilities often have complex needs, as adults they may be served and supported by more than one adult service agency. Involving those agencies in planning for transition can be very beneficial. No individual professional can know everything about services. Sometimes educators know very little about the adult service system and the adult service system may not know much about special education. Involving representatives from a variety of service agencies to be part of the discussion can help dispel misinformation and bring clarity to the planning discussion. If representatives are unable to attend, it should be the responsibility of a transition team member to learn about the offerings and eligibility requirements for the range of possible adult services from which the student may benefit.

SUMMARY

Achieving good post-school outcomes for students with visual impairments and multiple disabilities requires careful planning that begins in elementary school. IDEA has very specific requirements related to transition planning that must be followed.

Students with visual impairments and multiple disabilities face special challenges in preparing for life beyond school. These students may have gaps in knowledge and experience because they lack access to incidental learning. Specific teaching and remediation may be necessary to help fill in the gaps, including access to adult role models, opportunities to develop job-readiness skills and to try out work experiences, and opportunities to practice self-sufficiency and self-advocacy.

Person-centered planning is an effective tool that can be used to assist families and educational teams in planning for life after school. Person-centered planning can augment the transition plan required by IDEA and offers opportunities for involvement and engagement with a wider circle of people dedicated to the student's success.

Services for Young Adults with Visual Impairments and Multiple Disabilities

Maureen P. Reardon

The array of services available to young adults with disabilities has grown and changed over time.

Financial Support and Insurance

There are three important federal programs that offer financial support, medical insurance, and services to young adults with visual impairments and multiple disabilities.

1. **Supplemental Security Income (SSI).**
   SSI is a federal income-supplement program funded by general tax revenues (not Social Security taxes). SSI is designed to help people who are elderly, blind, or disabled, and who have little or no income. SSI provides cash to meet basic needs for food, clothing, and shelter. (For more information, see the Resources section at the end of this chapter.)
2. **Medicaid.** Medicaid is the major source of public funding for long-term services and supports provided in home and community settings. Medicaid is implemented by each state and may provide medical support for those who are unable to pay for or obtain services through private insurance. Although Medicaid originally funded hospitals and institutions, more recently it has funded community-based services. Many states utilize a waiver from certain Medicare regulations to provide services that help people avoid being placed in a facility like a nursing home.
3. **Vocational Rehabilitation.** Each state has one or more vocational rehabilitation agencies funded primarily with federal dollars. Vocational rehabilitation provides services related to employment, technology, assessment, training, and independent living as well as other services. Some states have specific vocational rehabilitation agencies for individuals who are blind or deaf, and some vocational rehabilitation agencies have counselors with specific training or expertise in deafblindness. Some vocational rehabilitation agencies serve all disability groups. The American Foundation for the Blind's (AFB) online Directory of Services (see the Resources section at the end of this chapter) lists the vocational rehabilitation agencies in each state.

Other Agencies

Many students with visual impairments and multiple disabilities may also receive services from state agencies designed to offer training and support to individuals with developmental disabilities. These services may include case management, training, day programs, recreational services, residential services, and other kinds of community support.

There are also a variety of organizations for individuals with specific disabilities as well as independent living centers that may provide support and social connections for students as they transition from school to adult living. The AFB Directory of Services lists many of these other agencies. See also the General Resources section at the back of this book for other organizations that provide information and referral services.

Families are vital partners in planning for a successful transition. This time period can be extremely stressful for families, but their student's ultimate success depends on family involvement. Long after teachers and therapists have left a student's life, the family remains as a consistent force. The more the IEP team empowers the student and his or her family, the greater the chances of success.

Partnerships between schools and adult service agencies also foster successful outcomes. It is important for school personnel to work to include adult service agencies in planning and to help families begin to establish positive work relationships with adult service agencies.

Many students who have visual impairments and multiple disabilities make the transition to life beyond school quite successfully. What that adult life looks like depends on the needs, dreams, and preferences of the student. Quality of life is dependent on having meaningful relationships, engaging in activities that are fulfilling, and feeling like a valued and contributing member of the community.

REFERENCES

Bakken, J. P., & Obiakor, F. E. (2008). *Transition planning for students with disabilities: What educators and service providers can do.* Springfield, IL: Charles C Thomas.

Bridgeo, W., Gicklhorn, C., & Zatta, M. (2007). *School-to-work: Developing transition portfolios for students with significant disabilities.* Watertown, MA: Perkins School for the Blind.

Carter, E. W., Austin, D., & Trainor, A. A. (2012). Predictors of postschool employment outcomes for young adults with severe disabilities. *Journal of Disability Policy Studies, 23*(1), 50–63.

Cavenaugh, B., & Giesen J. M. (2012). A systematic review of transition interventions affecting the employability of youths with visual impairments. *Journal of Visual Impairment & Blindness, 106*(7), 400–413.

Connors, E., Curtis, A., Wall Emerson, R., & Dormitorio, B. (2014). Longitudinal analysis of factors associated with successful outcomes for transition-age youths with visual impairments. *Journal of Visual Impairment & Blindness, 108*(2), 95–106.

Education for All Handicapped Children Act, Pub. L. No. 94–142 (1975).

Individuals with Disabilities Education Act Amendments of 1997, Pub. L. No. 105–17 (1997).

Individuals with Disabilities Education Improvement Act (IDEA), 20 U.S.C. § 1400 (2004).

Kochhar-Bryant, C. A., & Greene, G. (2009). *Pathways to successful transition for youth with disabilities: A developmental process* (2nd ed.). Upper Saddle River, NJ: Pearson Education.

McDonnall, M. C. (2011). Predictors of employment for youths with visual impairments: Findings from the second National Longitudinal Transition Study. *Journal of Visual Impairment & Blindness, 105*(8), 453–466.

McDonnall, M. C., & Crudden, A. (2009). Factors affecting the successful employment of transition-age youths with visual impairments. *Journal of Visual Impairment & Blindness, 103*(6), 329–341.

McDonnall, M. C., & O'Mally, J. (2012). Characteristics of early work experiences and their association with future employment. *Journal of Visual Impairment & Blindness, 106*(3), 133–144.

National Secondary Transition Technical Assistance Center. (2009). Interagency collaboration annotated bibliography. Charlotte, NC: Author.

Rowland, C. (Ed.). (2009). *Assessing communication and learning in young children who are deaf-blind or who have multiple disabilities.* Portland: Oregon Health and Science University.

Sitlington, P. L., & Clark, G. M. (2001). Career/vocational assessment: A critical component of transition planning. *Assessment for Effective Intervention, 26*(4), 5–22.

Sparrow, S. S., Cicchetti, D. V., & Saulnier, C. A. (2016). *Vineland adaptive behavior scales (Vineland-3)* (3rd ed.). San Antonio, TX: Pearson.

Venn, J. J. (2000). *Assessing students with special needs* (2nd ed.). Upper Saddle River, NJ: Merrill.

RESOURCES

For additional resources, see the General Resources section at the back of this book.

Websites
CareerConnect
American Foundation for the Blind
www.afb.org/careerconnect

An employment information resource for job seekers who are blind or visually impaired. Presents employment information, career exploration tools, and extensive job seeking guidance for students and adults with vision loss and the professionals who work with them.

Directory of Services for Blind and Visually Impaired Persons
American Foundation for the Blind
www.afb.org/directory.aspx

A fully accessible and searchable online database providing useful, comprehensive information that helps persons who are visually impaired and their families find the assistance they need and to help professionals identify, coordinate, and deliver services effectively. Contains information on more than 2,000 organizations and agencies that serve people who are blind or visually impaired in the United States and Canada.

Organizations
National Center on Secondary Education and Transition
Institute on Community Integration
University of Minnesota

6 Pattee Hall
150 Pillsbury Drive SE
Minneapolis, MN 55455
(612) 624-5659
Fax: (612) 624-9344
ncset@umn.edu
www.ncset.org

Coordinates national resources, offers technical assistance, and disseminates information related to secondary education and transition for youth with disabilities in order to create opportunities for youth to achieve successful futures.

Social Security Administration
(800) 772-1213
TTY: (800) 325-0778
www.ssa.gov/ssi

Administers SSI, a federal income-supplement program designed to help people who are elderly, blind, or disabled, who have little or no income, by providing cash to meet basic needs for food, clothing, and shelter. Delivers a broad range of services online and through its network of over 1,400 offices.

General Resources

In addition to the resources listed at the end of each chapter in this book, this section provides information about professional organizations in the fields that collaborate to work with students who are visually impaired and have multiple disabilities, sources of information and referral, sources of books for young children and students, and sources of products mentioned in this book. For more detailed listings of organizations and sources of products and services, see the American Foundation for the Blind's Directory of Services online at www.afb.org/directory.

PROFESSIONAL AND NATIONAL ORGANIZATIONS AND SOURCES OF INFORMATION

American Foundation for the Blind (AFB)
2 Penn Plaza, Suite 1102
New York, NY 10121
(212) 502-7600; (800) 232-5463
Fax: (888) 545-8331
info@afb.org
www.afb.org

Serves as an information clearinghouse for people who are visually impaired, their families, professionals, schools, organizations, corporations, and the public. Operates a toll-free information hotline; conducts research and mounts program initiatives to promote the inclusion of people with visual impairments, especially in the areas of literacy, technology, aging, and employment; and advocates for services and legislation. AFB Press, its publishing arm, publishes books, pamphlets, DVDs, and electronic and online products, including the *Directory of Services for Blind and Visually Impaired Persons in the United States and Canada* (www.afb.org /directory), the *Journal of Visual Impairment & Blindness* (www.jvib.org), and *AccessWorld* (www.afb.org/aw). AFB maintains a number of web-based initiatives, including FamilyConnect (www.FamilyConnect.org), an online, multimedia community for parents and families of visually impaired children; Career-Connect (www.afb.org/careerconnect), a resource for learning about the range and diversity of jobs performed by adults who are blind or visually impaired throughout the United States and Canada; and VisionAware (www.VisionAware.org), an informational website for adults with vision loss, their families, caregivers, health care providers, and social service professionals.

American Occupational Therapy Association (AOTA)
4720 Montgomery Lane, Suite 200
Bethesda, MD 20814-3449
(800) 729-2682 (member); (301) 652-6611 (nonmember)
TDD: (800) 377-8555
Fax: (301) 652-7711
www.aota.org

Advances the quality, availability, use, and support of occupational therapy through standard-setting, advocacy, education, and research on behalf of its members and the public. Assures the quality of occupational therapy services, improves consumer access to health care services, and promotes the professional development of members.

American Physical Therapy Association (APTA)
1111 North Fairfax Street
Alexandria, VA 22314-1488
(703) 684-2782; (800) 999-2782
TDD: (703) 683-6748
Fax: (703) 684-7343
www.apta.org

Seeks to improve the health and quality of life of individuals in society by advancing physical therapist practice, education, and research, and by increasing the awareness and understanding of physical therapy's role in the nation's health care system.

American Printing House for the Blind (APH)
1839 Frankfort Avenue
P.O. Box 6085
Louisville, KY 40206-0085
(502) 895-2405; (800) 223-1839
Fax: (502) 899-2284
info@aph.org
www.aph.org

Offers educational, workplace, and independent living products and services for people with visual impairments. Administers the Federal Quota Program to provide funds for purchase of educational materials for students with visual impairments; conducts educational research and development; and maintains the AFB M. C. Migel Library. Maintains an informational website and reference-catalog databases providing information about textbooks and other materials produced in accessible media, and houses the National Instructional Materials Access Center. (See also listing under Sources of Books for Children and Sources of Products.)

American Psychological Association (APA)
750 First Street, NE
Washington, DC 20002-4242
(202) 336-5500; (800) 374-2721
TDD/TTY: (202) 336-6123
www.apa.org

Advances the creation, communication, and application of psychological knowledge to benefit society and improve people's lives by encouraging the development and application of psychology in the broadest manner; promoting research in psychology; improving the qualifications of psychologists by establishing high standards of ethics, conduct, education, and achievement; and increasing and disseminating psychological knowledge.

American Speech-Language-Hearing Association (ASHA)
2200 Research Boulevard
Rockville, MD 20850-3289
(800) 498-2071 (member); (800) 638-8255 (nonmember)
TTY: (301) 296-5650
Fax: (301) 296-8580
www.asha.org

Works to make effective communication accessible and achievable for all by empowering and supporting audiologists, speech-language pathologists, and speech, language, and hearing scientists through advancing science, setting standards, fostering excellence in professional practice, and advocating for members and those they serve.

Association for Education and Rehabilitation of the Blind and Visually Impaired (AER)
1703 N. Beauregard Street, Suite 440
Alexandria, VA 22311
(703) 671-4500; (877) 492-2708
Fax: (703) 671-6391
aer@aerbvi.org
http://aerbvi.org

Serves as the primary professional organization for teachers, counselors, orientation and mobility specialists, and other professionals in the field of blindness and low vision. Organized into a variety of special divisions, AER promotes all phases of education and work for people of all ages who are blind or visually impaired, strives to expand their opportunities to take a contributory place in society, and disseminates information.

Council for Exceptional Children (CEC) Division on Visual Impairment and Deafblindness (DVIB)
2900 Crystal Drive, Suite 1000
Arlington, VA 22202-3557
(888) 232-7733
TTY: (866) 915-5000
Fax: (703) 264-9494
service@cec.sped.org
www.cec.sped.org
http://community.cec.sped.org/DVI/Home

Serves educators and other individuals serving children with disabilities and children who are gifted. Is organized into a variety of specialized divisions. The Division on Visual Impairment and Deafblindness works to advance the education of individuals with visual impairments and deafblindness and to promote related educational, scientific, and charitable purposes. It publishes the *Visual Impairment and Deafblind Education Quarterly.*

Hadley Institute for the Blind and Visually Impaired
700 Elm Street
Winnetka, IL 60093-2554
(847) 446-8111; (800) 323-4238
Fax: (847) 446-9820
TTY: (847) 441-8111
info@hadley.edu
www.hadley.edu

Allows students to study at home with free correspondence courses and online materials through its accredited distance education program. Courses are offered to families, professionals working with people who are blind or who have low vision, high school students preparing for college, and adults who have become blind.

National Association of Parents of Children with Visual Impairments (NAPVI)
15 West 65th Street
New York, NY 10023
(212) 769-7819; (800) 562-6265
napvi@Lighthouseguild.org
www.napvi.org

Provides leadership, support, and training to assist parents in helping their children reach their full potential. Enables parents to find information and resources for their children who are blind or visually impaired, including those with additional disabilities. Dedicated to parent education, giving emotional support, initiating outreach programs, networking, and advocating for the educational needs and welfare of children who are blind or visually impaired.

National Center on Deaf-Blindness (NCDB)
345 N. Monmouth Avenue
Monmouth, OR 97361
(503) 838-8754
Fax: (503) 838-8150
info@nationaldb.org
https://nationaldb.org/

Is a national technical assistance center funded by the federal Department of Education that works to improve the quality of life for children who are deafblind and their families. Runs the Deaf-Blind Project, a federally funded program that provides free technical assistance services to children who are deafblind, their families, and service providers in their state.

National Coalition on Deafblindness

175 North Beacon Street
Watertown, MA 02472
(617) 972-7768
Fax: (617) 923-8076
www.thedbcoalition.org

Provides information and advocacy in a collaborative way to policy makers, fiscal agents, educational professionals, and community leaders on behalf of children and youth who are deafblind, in conjunction and partnership with adults who are deafblind, families, and stakeholders.

National Federation of the Blind (NFB)

200 East Wells Street at Jernigan Place
Baltimore, MD 21230
(410) 659-9314
Fax: (410) 685-5653
nfb@nfb.org
www.nfb.org

Strives to improve social and economic conditions of people who are blind and to integrate people who are blind or who have low vision as equal members of society. Evaluates and assists in establishing programs and provides public education and scholarships. Interest groups include the National Organization of Parents of Blind Children and the Committee on the Concerns of the Deaf-Blind. Publishes *The Braille Monitor* and *Future Reflections*, a magazine for families.

Perkins School for the Blind

175 North Beacon Street
Watertown, MA 02472
(617) 924-3434
info@Perkins.org
www.Perkins.org
www.perkinselearning.org

Operates as a school for the blind that also publishes books, sells products for students with visual impairments, and offers an informational website that includes teaching resources and instructional strategies, professional development, and family support. Perkins eLearning, an online portal designed to provide resources and professional development opportunities to professionals working with students with visual impairments including those with additional disabilities and deafblindness, offers webcasts and webinars on a variety of topics. (See also additional listing under Sources of Products).

TASH

2013 H Street NW, Suite 404
Washington, DC 20006
(202) 540-9020
Fax: (202) 540-9019
info@tash.org
www.tash.org

Serves as an advocacy organization for professionals who work with infants, children, and youths with severe disabilities and their families. Promotes full inclusion and participation of people with disabilities in all aspects of life through local chapters. Publishes a monthly newsletter, quarterly journal, and other publications.

Texas School for the Blind and Visually Impaired (TSBVI)

1100 West 45th Street
Austin, TX 78756-3494
(512) 454-8631; (800) 872-5273
TTY: (512) 206-9451
Fax: (512) 206-9453
www.tsbvi.edu

Serves as a specialized school and learning center for students with visual impairments, publishes books, and offers online information and resources about visual impairment, instruction, technology, assessment, and a wide range of other topics related to the education of students who are blind or visually impaired. Is also a statewide resource for parents of these children and the professionals who serve them, from birth through transition from school.

SOURCES OF BOOKS FOR CHILDREN

The companies listed in this section provide books in alternate formats for young children and students.

American Printing House for the Blind (APH)
1839 Frankfort Avenue
P.O. Box 6085
Louisville, KY 40206-0085
(502) 895-2405; (800) 223-1839
Fax: (502) 899-2284
info@aph.org
www.aph.org

Publishes a wide variety of print/braille books with tactile pictures for preschoolers; the Early Braille Trade Books (sets of leveled print/braille books); the *Building on Patterns* reading series; and many other braille reading materials for students of all ages. Distributes a wide variety of products and instructional materials for teaching braille.

Bookshare
480 California Avenue, Suite 201
Palo Alto, CA 94306
(650) 644-3400
Fax: (650) 475-1066
info@bookshare.org
www.bookshare.org

Administers the world's largest accessible digital library for persons with print disabilities. Memberships are free for U.S. students with qualifying print disabilities. Members can download books from the website in any of a variety of text or audio formats.

Learning Ally
20 Roszel Road
Princeton, NJ 08540
(800) 221-4792
www.learningally.org

Distributes digitally recorded textbooks and literature titles to empower students with reading-related learning disabilities and visual impairments reach their full potential.

National Braille Press (NBP)
88 St. Stephen Street
Boston, MA 02115
(617) 266-6160; (888) 965-8965
(800) 548-7323 ext. 520 (Bookstore)
Fax: (617) 437-0456
contact@nbp.org
www.nbp.org

Promotes braille literacy for children and adults through publishing and outreach programs. Publishes multiple books in braille for children, including *A Braille Spelling Dictionary for Beginning Writers* (updated in 2015 to reflect UEB changes); print/braille and braille-only books at all levels, including some with tactile graphics; and raised-line coloring books. Also sponsors a Children's Braille Book Club; the Read Books! Program, which offers free materials to introduce children from birth to age 7 and their families to braille literacy; and the Great Expectations program, which provides resources and tips for creating a multisensory reading and listening experience with featured books.

National Library Service for the Blind and Physically Handicapped (NLS)
Library of Congress
1291 Taylor Street, NW
Washington, DC 20542-4962
(202) 707-5100; (800) 424-8567
TDD/TTY: (202) 707-0744
Fax: (202) 707-0712
nls@loc.gov
www.loc.gov/nls

Administers the Braille and Talking Book Library Service, a free program that loans recorded and braille books and magazines as well as specially designed playback equipment to residents of the United States who are unable to read or use standard print materials. Talking Books are delivered to eligible borrowers through local cooperating libraries throughout the United States. It also offers audio, braille, and print/braille books for preschool through grade 8 and periodicals for children who are blind or have physical disabilities.

Seedlings Braille Books for Children
P.O. Box 51924
Livonia, MI 48151-5924
(734) 427-8552; (800) 777-8552
Fax: (734) 427-8552
info@seedlings.org
www.seedlings.org

Publishes and distributes high-quality braille books for children of all ages, including print and braille preschool picture board books and beginning reader print and braille books, including a variety in uncontracted braille. Its Book Angel program provides braille readers with three free books a year from the Seedlings catalog.

SOURCES OF PRODUCTS

The companies listed in this section sell a wide variety of assistive devices and specialized products that help people with visual impairments and other disabilities carry out educational and everyday activities, including adapted clocks and watches; adapted games; braille and large-print products, books, and supplies; braillers; computer software and access products; diabetes management products; educational and teaching materials and adapted products; kitchen and housekeeping items; labeling and marking products; lighting; low vision devices; mobility devices; money identifiers; personal care products; recreation and leisure products; talking products; telephones and accessories; and writing and reading devices.

AbleNet, Inc.
2625 Patton Road
Roseville, MN 55113-1308
(651) 294-2200; (800) 322-0956
Fax: (651) 294-2259
customerservice@ablenetinc.com
www.ablenetinc.com

Ai Squared
130 Taconic Business Park Road
Manchester Center, VT 05255
(802) 362-3612
Fax: (802) 362-1670
www.aisquared.com

American Printing House for the Blind (APH)
1839 Frankfort Avenue
P.O. Box 6085
Louisville, KY 40206-0085
(502) 895-2405; (800) 223-1839
Fax: (502) 899-2284
info@aph.org
www.aph.org

Enabling Devices
50 Broadway
Hawthorne, NY 10532
(914) 747-3070; (800) 832-8697
Fax: (914) 747-3480
www.enablingdevices.com

Freedom Scientific
11800 31st Court North
St. Petersburg, FL 33716
(727) 803-8000; (800) 444-4443
Fax: (727) 803-8001
www.freedomscientific.com

HIMS Inc.
4616 West Howard Lane, Suite 960
Austin, TX 78728
(888) 520-4467
Fax: (512) 837-2011
sales@hims-inc.com
https://hims-inc.com/

HumanWare
1 UPS Way
P.O. Box 800
Champlain, NY 12919
(800) 722-3393
Fax: (888) 871-4828
info@humanware.com
www.humanware.com

Independent Living Aids
137 Rano Road
Buffalo, NY 14207
(855) 746-7452; (800) 537-2118
Fax: (516) 937-3906
www.independentliving.com

LS&S
145 River Rock Drive
Buffalo, NY 14207
(716) 348-3500; (800) 468-4789
TTY: (866) 317-8533
Fax: (877) 498-1482
LSSinfo@lssproducts.com
www.lssproducts.com

Maddak
661 Route 23 South
Wayne, NJ 07470
(973) 628-7600; (800) 443-4926
Fax: (973) 305-0841
custservice@maddak.com
www.maddak.com

Maxi-Aids
42 Executive Boulevard
Farmingdale, NY 11735
(631) 752-0521 (Information); (800) 522-6294
(Orders)
TTY: (631) 752-0738
Fax: (631) 752-0689
www.maxiaids.com

Perkins Solutions
175 North Beacon Street
Watertown, MA 02472
(617) 972-7308; (855) 206-8353
Fax: (617) 926-2027
solutions@perkins.org
www.perkinsproducts.org

Sendero Group
Davis, CA 95616
(888) 757-6810
Fax: (888) 757-6807
orders@senderogroup.com
www.senderogroup.com

Index

• •

Note: The letters *f, s,* and *t* following page numbers refer to forms or figures, sidebars, and tables, respectively.

CPSIA information can be obtained
at www.ICGtesting.com
Printed in the USA
BVHW01s0931180818
524346BV00009B/1/P